Illustrator:
Ken Tunell

Editors:
Barbara M. Wally, M.S.
Dona Herweck Rice

Editorial Project Manager:
Ina Massler Levin, M.A.

Editor in Chief:
Sharon Coan, M.S. Ed.

Art Director:
Elayne Roberts

Associate Designer:
Denise Bauer

Cover Artist:
Larry Bauer

Product Manager:
Phil Garcia

Imaging:
Ralph Olmedo, Jr.

Researcher:
Christine Johnson

Publishers:
Rachelle Cracchiolo, M.S. Ed.
Mary Dupuy Smith, M.S. Ed.

The 20th CENTURY

D1710285

Authors:

Mary Ellen Sterling, M.Ed.
Dona Herweck Rice

Teacher Created Materials, Inc.
P.O. Box 1040
Huntington Beach, CA 92647
ISBN-1-57690-100-9

©1997 Teacher Created Materials, Inc.   Made in U.S.A.

Table of Contents

Table of Contents *(cont.)*

Introduction

The 20th Century is a book which examines the political, economic, social, cultural, scientific, and technological advances of the twentieth century and introduces students to the individuals who made history in each decade. While other books in this series focus on individual decades, this volume features the century as a whole. Highlighting significant people and events, the book clearly shows the ebb and flow of all aspects of the human experience throughout one of the most eventful centuries of all time.

In order to tie together the events over the course of the century, refer to the topical categories per decade throughout the book. For example, if you wish to focus on women in the century, look to the Social Issues section in each decade for a good overview. The book also allows you to focus easily on separate decades since it is organized accordingly.

One can look with wonder over the dynamic twentieth century to see the many changes, advances, struggles, and successes it has offered. From horse-drawn carriages to Concorde jets, from local newspapers to the Internet, from industrial revolution to high-tech wonders, the century has brought about enormous transformations and exponential growth.

This book includes the following:

- ❑ planning guides—summaries and suggested activities for introducing the key issues and events of the century

- ❑ personality profiles—brief biographies of important individuals of the century

- ❑ event synopses—brief summaries of the significant events of the century

- ❑ language experience ideas—suggestions for writing and vocabulary building

- ❑ group activities— suggestions for activities to foster cooperative learning

- ❑ topics for further research—suggestions for extending the unit

- ❑ literature connections—summaries of related books and suggested activities for expanding them

- ❑ curriculum connections—activities and projects for math, art, language arts, social studies, and music

- ❑ culminating activities—student projects that involve knowledge of the entire century

- ❑ computer applications—suggestions for selecting and using software to supplement this unit

- ❑ bibliography—suggestions for additional resources on the century

- ❑ index—topics and personalities can be found quickly

To keep this valuable resource intact so that it can be used year after year, you may wish to punch holes in the pages and store them in a three-ring binder.

Time Line

Use the time line form on page six to create a time line for any decade of the century. Pages can be strung together to create a time line for the entire century. You may wish to enlarge the time lines. To add color, use a different colored highlighter for each category on the time line. Following are some suggested uses for a time line.

Time Line

	1940	1941	1945	1946	1947	1948	1949	
Politics and Economics	The Office of Production Management is created to coordinate defense output. The Land-Lease Act is signed. FDR declares a state of emergency. FDR is elected to a third term. On June 28 the Alien Registration Act passes. The first U.S. peacetime draft is instituted.	The Fair Employment Practices Commission is formed to carry out a presidential order banning discrimination on defense industries. The U.S. Freezes all Japanese assets in America. The Army Air Forces (AAF) are combined under General "Hap" Arnold. Pearl Harbor, Hawaii, is bombed on December 7, 1941. December 8: the U.S. declares war on Japan. The Purple Heart medal is awarded to a woman for the first time. Price controls begin in the U.S.	President Roosevelt is inaugurated for a fourth term. FDR dies on April 12. Vice President Harry S. Truman becomes President. On May 7 the Germans surrender unconditionally to General Eisenhower in Rheims, France. Truman, Churchill and Stalin meet at Potsdam to plan the invocation of Germany. A nationwide demand is ordered to save fuel. The Nuremberg Trials of Nazis for war crimes begin with the indictment of 24 former Nazi leaders on October 18.	The U.S. Supreme Court rules that segregation on buses is illegal. The Atomic Energy Commission is established. Workers around the nation go on strike; 200,000 in Chicago at a meat-packing plant; 800,000 steel workers in Pittsburgh.	Truman sets up a loyalty-security program for government employees. The Truman Doctrine is passed on March 12. On June 23 the Taft-Hartley Act, which limits labor unions, passes over Truman's veto. On July 26 the National Security Act passes, unifying the armed forces under the Defense Department and creating the CIA. Witnesses and refuse to answer questions from the House Un-American Activities Committee about suspected Communist infiltration of Hollywood are blacklisted by the industry.	Newspaper headlines read: "Dewey Defeats Truman," but Truman wins the election. Truman orders an end to racial segregation in the armed services. Congress votes to fund the Voice of America radio network. U.S. and Britain pilots begin airlifting food and supplies to residents of West Berlin. Russians, who control East Berlin, blockade West Berlin. Truman proposes his Point Four program of technical assistance to underdeveloped nations.	Beginning January 2, the Great Blizzard of '49 blankets the central plains and Rocky Mountain regions, reaching as far south as New Mexico and Arizona. The series of storms lasts 48 days, and temperatures drop as low as 50 degrees below 0. On April 4, NATO, the North Atlantic Treaty Organization, is created. The U.S. Canada and ten western European countries agree to treat an attack on one as an attack on all.	Politics and Economics
Social and Cultural	Superman has his own radio show; kryptonite is introduced. Benjamin O. Davis becomes the first African American general. M&M candies are developed by the Mars Company. Walt Disney's Fantasia debuts. Ernest Hemingway's novel of the Spanish Civil War, For Whom the Bell Tolls, is published. Native Son by Richard Wright is published.	Mt. Rushmore is completed. Rubber rationing begins. Joe DiMaggio has the longest hitting streak in major league baseball history. Curious George books debut. Orson Welles writes, directs, produces, and stars in Citizen Kane.	Elizabeth Taylor makes her film debut in National Velvet. Most rationing ends with the war.	Walt Disney pairs live action with animation in the biggest movie of the year, Song of the South. The first CARE (Cooperative American Relief Everywhere) package is sent to France.	Jackie Robinson becomes the first African American baseball player in the major leagues. The Common Sense Book of Baby and Child Care by Dr. Benjamin Spock is published. The advice revolutionized the way that children were raised. The Diary of Anne Frank is published. The World Series baseball game is televised for the first time. Howdy Doody airs, featuring the first great puppet of the television age.	Congress declares June 14 Flag Day. Leo Fender begins marketing the Broadcaster, the first mass-produced solid-body electric guitar. The Huntom-Globetrotters defeat the Minneapolis Lakers in "The Pro Basketball Game of the Year."	Bikini bathing suits first appear in the U.S. George Orwell publishes 1984, a novel about a future society in which individual freedom is lost to a powerful government. Disposable diapers are introduced.	Social and Cultural
Science and Technology	The first successful helicopter flight takes place. Germany tests its first jet fighter, the He 280.	The Manhattan Project begins. Penicillin is produced by American drug companies. The first disposable aerosol cans are invented.	On July 16, the first atomic bomb is tested at Alamogordo, New Mexico. On August 6 the U.S. drops a uranium bomb on Hiroshima, Japan. Three days later, a plutonium bomb is dropped on Nagasaki. The Japanese surrender on August 15. The first railroad car with observation dome is in use. ENIAC, the first electronic computer, is built.	Trans World Airlines inaugurates its first transatlantic passenger flight. The U.S. Navy explodes an underwater atomic bomb at Bikini Island. The first electric blanket is made. Admiral Byrd lands with his expedition in Antarctica.	Boulder Dam is renamed Hoover Dam in honor of former President Herbert Hoover. Buckminster Fuller builds the first geodesic dome. Reynolds Wrap aluminum foil is marketed. The Tommy is first patented and sold. Chuck Yeager breaks the sound barrier, flying at 670 mph. Radioisotopes testing is perfected.	The transistor is invented. Long-playing records are invented. The first rocket missiles are tested. The Polaroid Land Camera is introduced by Edwin Land. The big bang theory of the creation of the universe is proposed.	The Russians test their first atomic weapon. The first jet airliner, the Comet, is developed. Cortisone, used to treat arthritis, is discovered. The first rocket to reach outer space is fired in New Mexico.	Science and Technology

Suggested Activities

1. Use the time line to assess students' initial knowledge of a decade. Using the information from the decade that you have selected, fill in a time line for the period. Construct a web to find out what the students know about the important events and individuals. Find out what they would like to know. Plan your lessons accordingly.

2. Assign each group of students a specific year within a decade. As they research the year, let them add pictures, names, and events to the appropriate area of a time line.

3. Assign students to find out what events were happening around the world during a decade you have chosen. Tell them to add that information to the time line.

4. After adding names, places, and events to the time line, use the information gathered as a guide for assessment. Base your quizzes and exams on those people, places, and events that you have studied.

5. Have students research further some of the events and people you have listed on the time line. Reports can be presented orally or in writing format.

6. Use the time line as a springboard for class discussion—for example: Who was the most famous or influential person of the 1920s? When and how did flight in heavier-than-air machinery come to be? How was life in the sixties similar to today?

7. Divide the students into three groups and assign each group a different area: politics and economics, society and culture, and science and technology. Have each group brainstorm important related people, places, and events that occurred during the period you are studying. Create a group mural depicting these important happenings. Get permission to decorate a hallway wall or tape several sheets of butcher paper together to make a giant canvas.

8. As a class, create a time line for the entire century. You will need to clear space on the walls around the classroom so that the entire time line can be displayed.

9. Create personal time lines. Each student can incorporate significant events from his or her life with national and world events occurring at the same time.

See page 509 for information about time lines via the computer.

Time Line *(cont.)*

	Politics and Economics	Society and Culture	Science and Technology
year: _____			
year: _____			
year: _____			

Introducing the Decade

Here are a number of interesting ways to introduce a particular decade of the century. Try as many as you like. Modify them to suit your own classroom needs and teaching style.

1. Conduct discussion sessions as outlined on page 10, focussing on the selected decade.

2. Set up a special table with toys and games from the period you are studying. Schedule times for groups of students to go to the center to experiment with the toys.

3. Fill a jar with popular candies or a snack from the time. Have the students estimate how many treats there are in the jar. Award prizes for correct answers.

4. In each decade, people have found something popular to collect. For example, in the nineties, children collected POGs. In the twenties, they collected bottle caps. With the class, brainstorm a list of everyday things you might collect. Let each student choose one to collect throughout your unit. On a specified day, have the students take turns sharing their collections.

5. Listen to music from the era. If possible, enlist the help of a music teacher to help the students sing the songs. For arrangements and music, see *The Decade Series* (Hal Leonard Publishing Corporation).

6. Provide groups of students with magazines and scissors. Direct them to cut out pictures of things and conveniences that would not have been found during the period you will be studying. Discuss and review all the choices in whole group before creating a class collage. The alternative is to cut out things that would have existed during the period. You decide.

7. Lay out a display table with samples of things (or pictures/models of them) that came into being in the decade you are studying. Allow the students time to explore. You might also have them bring in some of the items for display.

8. Have the students create advertisements for modern products in the style of the advertising of the time. Back issues of *Life* magazine are an excellent source for period advertising. Many libraries have *Life* on microfiche.

9. Using the doll patterns on page 18, have the students draw and color clothing in the style of the period you are studying. A good reference for period styles can be found in the bibliography on page 510. Several samples are also found throughout these pages.

10. Construct time capsules. Divide the students into small groups and use the methods on page nine. Watch a film or read a book from the era you are going to study.

11. Write a note to the students, using some "buzzwords" from the era. Buzzwords can be found at the end of each section.

12. Bring in black and white photos of celebrities and leaders from the time. Display them all in a collage on the bulletin board. As you study the period, challenge the students to identify the people.

13. Conduct "interviews" of individuals from the period you will be studying. Use the form on page eight.

14. Designate a decade day and encourage students to dress in the style of the decade you are studying. Costumes may be brought from home, or the students can make life-size clothing from paper in the style of the day to wear over their clothes in class.

Period Interview

Here is a guide for you to use when "interviewing" a figure from the period you are studying. Add any other questions you may have for this person. Remember to respond to the questions as the person you are interviewing.

Name _____

Date of Birth _____

Place of Birth _____

Occupation _____

1. Tell some things about your early childhood memories. _____
   _____
   _____

2. Explain what events in your childhood influenced your choice of career. _____
   _____
   _____

3. Who were some people who influenced your career? _____
   _____
   _____

4. What were some of the obstacles and struggles you encountered throughout your career? Explain how you overcame them. _____
   _____
   _____

5. What do you think you will be most remembered for after you are gone? _____
   _____
   _____
   _____
   _____

6. What would you like written as your epitaph? (Write this epitaph on the tombstone at the right.)

   _____

   _____

   _____

   _____

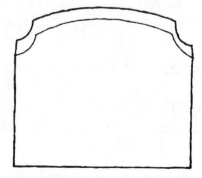

Decade Time Capsule

Imagine that you and your friends are living in the time period you are going to study. As people during this time, you want to preserve the things you know for future generations. Read and answer the following questions and determine what information to include in your time capsule. Cut pictures and articles from magazines and newspapers to represent things from the period, collect artifacts, and write stories and articles. Once you have your collection, use the suggestions below to decide how to freeze your memories.

What to Collect

1. What books do you like to read?

2. Who are some of your favorite movie actors?

3. What are some brand new products on the market? How much do they cost?

4. What are some chores you have to do at home?

5. How much allowance do you receive? How do you spend your money?

6. What does your mother or father typically serve for dinner?

7. What types of snacks are available? How much do they cost?

8. What games do you like to play? What types of toys are available?

9. Who are some important people in the news these days? What has made them famous?

10. What does your mother or father do for a living?

Ways to Freeze Memories

A. Paste the stories onto the pages of a notebook or photo album or store your mementos in a decorated and labeled shoe box.

B. Create a period time capsule on disk, using a computer program like *The Amazing Writing Machine* (Broderbund) or *The Writing Center* (The Learning Company). Make some hard copies for your classroom library.

C. Create a giant collage. Cut the side from a large appliance box and paint it with gesso or tempera paint. Attach artifacts, articles, etc. to the dried surface with a glue gun.

Note to the Teacher: Provide reference materials for the period. See the bibliography on page 510 for many excellent ideas.

Discussing the Decade

Create interest with a lively discussion. Suggested topics and methods follow.

Boys vs. Girls

Describe clothing worn by men and women during the period you will study. Have the boys and girls respond to their respective questions.

Girls: If you lived in the time described, would you have worn those clothes? Defend your answer. Do you think your parents would approve if you decided to dress that way? What might be some of their objections?

Boys: If you were a boy during this time, would you have worn the clothes described? Defend your answer. How do you think others might react to you? Would you care what they thought?

With the whole class, discuss the girls' response and then the boys'. Extend the discussion by asking students to compare the clothing from that period to the clothing today. Brainstorm a list of similarities between the two styles and possible reactions to them both.

Modern Technology

Many appliances we take for granted today may not have existed during the period you are going to study. Ask the students to brainstorm some technologies that are available now and list them on the board or overhead projector. Discuss which of these technologies existed during the time you are studying and circle them. Leave the list on display.

Write this statement and question on the board or overhead projector and give students time to think about them before proceeding with a discussion. *During the (fill in decade)s, the American lifestyle changed dramatically due to the advent of new technology. What were some of these technologies?* Add to your list any technologies not mentioned in the first part of the activity. Extend the lesson with this question: *Can the same statement be applied to the current decade?*

Famous People

Ask the class to brainstorm a list of famous people from the period or assign pairs to research a list of ten popular figures, along with their occupations. List all the names and occupations on the board or overhead projector. Then challenge the students to determine what they would like to ask these people about life in their times and record their responses on the board. When doing the interviews (page eight), have the students add questions from the board. When the interviews are complete, have the students share them with one another. Ask them to pay careful attention to any interviews of the same individual, pointing out the similarities and differences.

         10

Presidential Knowledge

Select any or all of the following ideas for studying the presidents presented throughout this book. Adapt the activities as needed.

Additions Divide the students into teams. Give each team a different presidential profile from this book. Assign them to do further research and to add more facts to the pages.

Mapping I Assign students to label a flag pin with the name of each president. Have them place each pin in the correct location of each president's birth on a large display map.

Mapping II Give each group of students a copy of page 12. Have them complete the page. They will need to use almanacs or other reference books to find all the necessary information.

Vice Presidents Have each student research a different Vice President (very few facts are given in this book about the Vice Presidents). Put the information together in a class book.

First Ladies Divide the students into groups or pairs. Assign each team a First Lady to research. Have them find at least ten facts about her, including her birthdate, place of birth, date of death (if applicable), and education. Make a chart from a large sheet of butcher paper and place it on a table or other flat surface. Ask the groups to write their facts and draw a portrait of their First Lady in the appropriate sections of the chart. Display the chart on a classroom wall.

Descriptions With the class, brainstorm a list of words or phrases that aptly describe each president (do not try to do all at once; simply focus on the decade you are studying). For example, President Hoover might be described as a self-made millionaire, orphan, and humanitarian. Ask the students to cite examples from the president's life story to explain their descriptions.

Comparisons Pair the students to work on this project. Direct the pairs to fold a large sheet of drawing paper into fourths. At the top of each fourth, write the name of a different president and then list each president's greatest achievements during his term in office. Ask the students to rate each president on a scale of one to five. One is the lowest; five is highest. Have them write defenses for their choices on separate pieces of paper.

Campaign Buttons Have the students create a campaign button for each president. Cut buttons from construction paper or cardboard. Include an original slogan and/or a picture or drawing of the presidential candidate.

Requirements Review the requirements for candidates for the office of president of the United States (page 13) and the electoral process. For more on these topics, see Teacher Created Materials #582 *Thematic Unit: U.S. Constitution.*

Elections

Use an almanac or other reference book to help with the necessary information for this page.

1. Graph the electoral votes from an election here.

Electoral Votes for 19____ Election

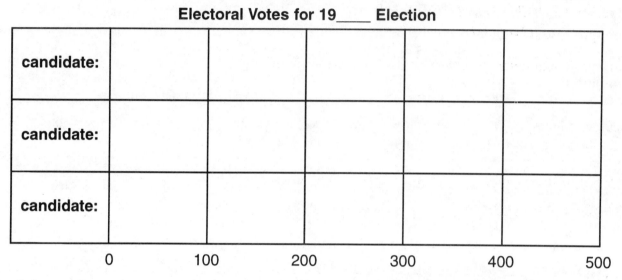

candidate:					
candidate:					
candidate:					

0   100   200   300   400   500

2. Color red the states won by the Democratic candidate. Color blue the states won by the Republican candidate.

Could You Be President?

Article II, Section I, of the Constitution establishes certain requirements for the presidency.

No Person except a natural born Citizen, or a Citizen of the United States, at the time of the Adoption of this Constitution, shall be eligible to the Office of the President; neither shall any person be eligible to that Office who shall not have attained the Age of thirty five Years, and been fourteen Years a Resident within the United States.

List the basic requirements for the office of the president of the United States:

1. _____

2. _____

3. _____

Based on this information, discuss and answer the following questions.

1. Do you think these are fair requirements for the office of president? Why or why not?

   _____

   _____

2. What additional requirements do you think should be added to this list? For example, should there be an educational requirement—college graduates only—or should anyone of any educational level be allowed to run?

   _____

   _____

   _____

3. What personal and social qualities should a person who is running for the presidency possess? Explain each of your choices.

   _____

   _____

4. In retrospect, which of the four presidents during the twenties did the best job while in office? What were the qualities that gave him this edge?

   _____

   _____

   _____

5. Would you want to be president? Why or why not? What do you think you could take to the presidency that is currently missing?

   _____

   _____

   _____

Then and Now

Complete the information below for the period you are studying and for today. You will need to research for answers.

	Then_____	Now_____
Population		
Minimum wage		
Price of 1 loaf of bread		
Price of 1 dozen eggs		
Price of 1 gallon of milk		
Price of average home		
Typical transportation		
Common names		
Favorite books		
Favorite entertainers		
World leaders		
Trends		
Innovations		

Famous Firsts

Find out about three things first used in the decade you are studying. Write them on the blanks next to the numbers. In the other boxes, write a description of those items at that time and then the state of those items today. Note all the changes carefully.

Selections	In 19____	Today
1. _____		
2. _____		
3. _____		

15

Popular Songs

In the column on the left, list at least six popular songs from the period you are studying. You will have to do some research to find them. In the column on the right, list a modern day song that is about the same subject.

Decade_____

Song of Then	Song of Now
_____	_____
_____	_____
_____	_____
_____	_____
_____	_____
_____	_____
_____	_____
_____	_____
_____	_____
_____	_____
_____	_____

World Leaders

Fill in the chart for leaders from different nations, one each for the period you are studying and one from today.

In 19_____	Today
Nation	
Name	
Title	
Type of government	
Years in power	
Greatest achievements	
Greatest failures	
Nation	
Name	
Title	
Type of government	
Years in power	
Greatest achievements	
Greatest failures	

Paper Dolls

Find out about a popular clothing style during the time you are studying. Draw and color that style on one paper doll. Draw and color clothes that person would wear today on the second doll. (Alternative: Color both as yourself, the first in clothing from the past and the second as you are.)

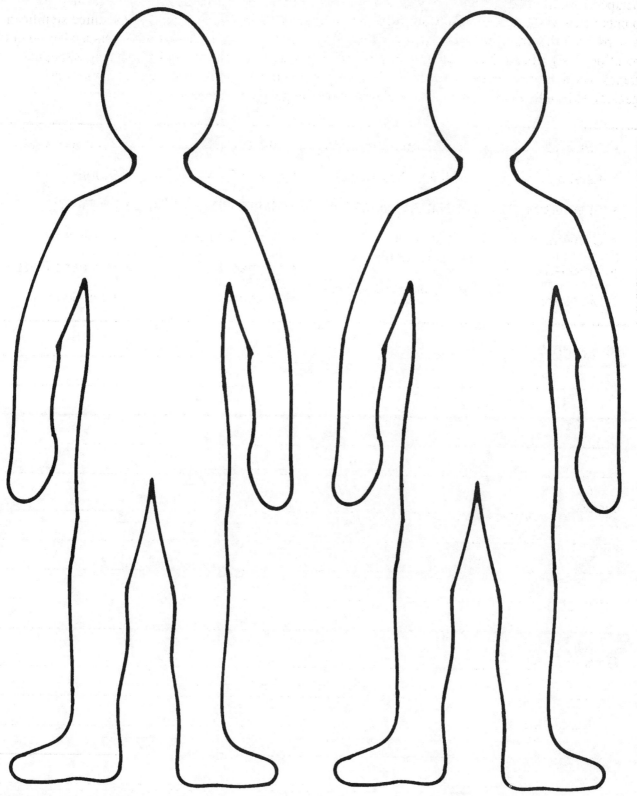

Their Point of View

Memory is always subjective, and therefore history is frequently subjective as well. In addition to facts, history books may contain interpretations, or present the facts from an individual's or group's perspective. In order to complete your study of a specific time or decade, consider it from a variety of points of view. In the box below are listed a number of sociological groups. Choose three significant groups from the time you are studying and tell about the period from each group's perspective. Include mention of significant facts of the time, such as economic developments, political changes, popular trends, and important events. While writing, keep in mind that the perspectives you present are generalized; individuals within groups always have unique points of view.

• Africans	• African Americans	• Upper Class	• Teenagers
• Asians	• Asian Americans	• Lower Class	• Elderly
• Australians	• Native Americans	• Middle Class	• Farmers
• Canadians	• Hispanic Americans	• South Americans	• Politicians
• Europeans		• Women	• Business People
• Mexicans	• Immigrants	• Children	• Homeless

Group: _____

_____

_____

_____

_____

Group: _____

_____

_____

_____

_____

Group: _____

_____

_____

_____

_____

Nineteen Hundreds Overview

- The dawn of the Golden Age came in 1900. People around the world looked for growth and opportunity in the new century, and many believed that their opportunities would come in America. Throughout the decade, millions of immigrants flocked to the United States in search of the "American Dream." Some found it while others lived their lives in pursuit of it, but always there remained the hope that hard work and determination would lead to a golden future.

- Queen Victoria died in 1901, marking the end of the Victorian Age. For 63 years she had been the symbol of the British Empire, of which the British said with pride, "The sun never sets on the Empire."

- Colonies and territories came with a price. Sometimes the citizens did not wish to be ruled by a country overseas, and turmoil ensued. The rush for power throughout Europe and Africa served, in part, as a catalyst for the great war of the next decade. The Boxer Rebellion, the Boer War, the Russo-Japanese War, and revolution in Russia added to the growing world turmoil, as did riots and rebellions in Spain, France, Turkey, the Gold Coast, and Tanganyika.

- As a result of the Spanish-American War, the United States gained control of the former Spanish colonies of Guam, Cuba, and Puerto Rico. A treaty with France and Great Britain created American Samoa in the South Pacific, and Hawaii was annexed.

- Oklahoma became a state in 1907, bringing the number to 46.

- Natural disasters struck around the globe. Mt. Pelee in the Caribbean and Mt. Vesuvius in Italy both erupted with tragic results. Italy, South America, and the United States all saw earthquakes that cost millions in damages and destroyed thousands of lives.

- President McKinley was assassinated near the beginning of the decade. Theodore Roosevelt, the former Rough Rider and Vice President, took the helm for most of the decade. Roosevelt fought hard to keep big business in check. He is perhaps most popularly remembered today for his namesake, the Teddy bear.

- In 1907, Roosevelt sent "the Great White Fleet" of American naval ships around the world to demonstrate American strength.

- The International Ladies Garment Workers Union began in 1900. The Industrial Workers of the World, a militant labor union sometimes called "Wobblies," was founded in 1905.

- Industry and invention revolutionized the world. Earlier inventions such as the telephone and the electric light came into widespread use. Automobiles began to replace bicycles and horse-drawn vehicles, and wireless communications connected the world in new ways.

- Lyman Frank Baum published *The Wonderful Wizard of Oz* in 1900. The first of 14 books about Oz, it has become a children's classic.

- Cinema moved from vaudeville houses to small theaters, called nickelodeons. *The Great Train Robbery* set the pace for melodramas, and Georges Melies of France experimented with special effects in *A Trip to the Moon*. Film censorship began in 1909.

- The Wright brothers brought flight to the world with their successful ride at Kittyhawk, North Carolina.

- The age of the automobile came under full swing as Henry Ford introduced the mass-produced Model T Ford.

- At the close of the decade, Peary and Henson became the first people to reach the North Pole, decreasing the amount of unexplored land on the planet. Little did the average person think that the close of the new century would bring exploration beyond the planet and throughout the galaxy.

Assassination

The first president of the new decade was William McKinley, a Civil War veteran who was instrumental in bringing the United States into position as a world power. He is also noted for his efforts to minimize big business.

McKinley believed that government needed to deal with the problem of industrial consolidation in which businesses in the same industry joined together to create large, monopolizing businesses. On September 5, 1901, President McKinley spoke at the Pan American Exposition in Buffalo, New York, on this issue as well as the issue of tariffs. He had modified his earlier views in support of protective tariffs for businesses to support, instead, free commerce through reciprocal trade agreements. These are agreements between countries to reduce each other's tariffs mutually. McKinley believed that these agreements would help to increase "the outlets for our increasing production." He declared that "The period of exclusiveness is past."

Certainly not everyone was in support of McKinley's new ideas. Many did not want government restrictions and regulations on business. One such man, Leon F. Czolgosz, an anarchist, was among the crowd at the Pan American Exposition. On September 6, the day after McKinley spoke, Czolgosz and others attended a reception held by the president at the exhibition's Temple of Music. Czolgosz carried a revolver covered with a handkerchief wrapped about his hand like a bandage. As President McKinley approached him and reached out to shake his hand, Czolgosz reached out his left hand as if to shake and fired twice with the gun held in his right. The first bullet ricocheted off McKinley's jacket button, but the second pierced his stomach.

President McKinley was rushed to the hospital for surgery. He continued to live for eight days; however, his wound became infected and gangrene set in. Though at first it was thought that he would recover, on September 14, 1901, President McKinley died.

At the time of the shooting, Vice President Theodore Roosevelt was hiking in the Adirondack Mountains of New York. He was told that the president would probably recover. However, later word was sent that McKinley was near death. Roosevelt rushed back, but by the time he reached Buffalo on the fourteenth, the president was dead. Roosevelt was sworn into office on the same day.

Leon Czolgosz was tried for murder and eventually executed by electrocution.

Suggested Activities

Research and Compare Find out about other assassinations and assassination attempts in the history of the presidency. Compare them, particularly the motives.

Modern Medicine Early in the twentieth century, death through infection was much more common than it is today. Research to determine what medical advances have come about to help reduce the risks.

Assassin Find out more about the life of Leon Czolgosz and his motive for killing President McKinley.

Modern Travel Compare the time it took Roosevelt to get from the Adirondacks to Buffalo to the time it would take the vice president to make that trip today. What accounts for the time difference?

Suffragettes

Throughout the nineteenth century, groups of women organized and demonstrated to reform education, establish rights to property, and provide opportunities for certain previously unattainable professions (such as medicine) for women. By the time the twentieth century dawned, they had begun to focus their goals on the right to vote, also known as *suffrage*. These women reformers became known as suffragettes.

There was strong resistance to the movement throughout the country and, in fact, the Western world. Women everywhere were fighting for the right to vote, but tradition, prejudice, and even a sense in some of moral righteousness proved difficult to combat. However, the suffragettes persisted. They themselves sometimes disagreed on tactics; however, they strongly believed that all methods of reform should be strictly legal so as to combat any suggestion that women are emotionally volatile and therefore incompetent to vote.

The National American Woman Suffrage Association (NAWSA) was highly active at this time. It held conventions, waged state-by-state campaigns, and distributed literature to bring about change. Suffragettes followed the example of women in Britain who were fighting for the vote and held parades and outdoor speeches on a regular basis. Eventually, the cause realized that it needed to appeal to two factions of women, both the social reformers and those seeking equal rights. The social reformers realized that they needed the vote to bring about change, and college-educated, working, and career-minded women were natural supporters for equal rights. The union of the two groups proved successful. Little by little, individual states began to give the vote to women, though it would not be until the close of another decade that the United States Constitution was amended to give women the vote.

Suggested Activities

Research Research their lives and influences on the suffrage movement: Alice Paul, Lady Astor, Lucy Stone, Henry Blackwell, Susan B. Anthony, Elizabeth Cady Stanton.

Voting and the Sexes Examine the differences in voting results when only males vote, when only females vote, and when both sexes vote. Conduct class votes on various subjects. Have all voters mark their ballots M for male or F for female, or provide differently colored ballots to each sex. Discuss the results and differences, if any. Consider a wide variety of topics for voting.

NAWSA The NAWSA was formed from the combination of the National Woman Suffrage Association (NWSA) and the American Woman Suffrage Association (AWSA). Research to find out more about these organizations and their dynamic founders. How did the two differ from one another, and why did they decide to join forces?

Hawaii

Throughout the nineteenth century, Hawaii's sugar cane industry grew into large money-making ventures. Businesses founded by descendants of American missionaries and whalers increasingly wished to dismantle the Hawaiian monarchy and to make Hawaii a territory of the United States, thereby increasing profits. However, King David Kalakaua and his sister, Queen Liliuokalani (*Lē-lē´-ŏ̆o-ō-kă-lă´-nē*) who ruled Hawaii at the end of the nineteenth century hoped to retain Hawaii for native Hawaiians, and preserve their own culture.

Queen Liliuokalani

In 1893 a handful of American and European residents with the help of American marines and sailors overthrew the last monarch, Queen Liliuokalani. These individuals formed the Republic of Hawaii in 1894 and elected Sanford B. Dole, the U.S Consul, as its first and only president. The American business executives continued to push for United States rule (under which they would be exempt from paying the high McKinley tariff imposed on foreign products shipped to the continental United States). In 1898 Hawaii was annexed as a possession of the United States, and finally, despite some Hawaiian opposition, on June 14, 1900, Hawaii became a United States territory. As such, all residents became U.S. citizens. Dole was appointed by President McKinley as the first governor of the new territory.

Suggested Activities

Statehood Hawaii became a state in 1959, making it the youngest of all states in the union. Find out the facts about how statehood came to be.

Dole Company Find out about the Dole Company and its origins and operations in Hawaii.

Pineapple Pineapple joined sugar as an important Hawaiian crop at the beginning of the twentieth century. Research this plant and its place in the history and economy of Hawaii.

Hula Traditional hula dances tell the stories of Hawaiian history, and its important people. The dance was banned by early missionaries. King Kalakaua worked to preserve and restore the hula dance as part of Hawaiian culture. Learn a simple traditional hula or create one to tell a story.

Music Queen Liliuokalani, the sister of King Kalakaua, composed a number of songs, including "Aloha Oe," which means "farewell to you." If possible, listen to this song in Hawaiian and English.

William McKinley

25th President, 1897–1901

Vice Presidents: Garret A. Hobart (1897–1899); Theodore Roosevelt (1901)

Born: January 29, 1843, in Niles, Ohio

Died: September 14, 1901

Party: Republican

Parents: William and Nancy McKinley

First Lady: Ida Saxton

Children: Katherine; a second daughter died in infancy

Education: Allegheny College (did not graduate); law school in Albany, NY

Famous Firsts:

- McKinley was the first president of the new century.

Achievements:

- McKinley and his secretary, George Cortelyou, developed new procedures for interacting with the press, including the distribution of press releases and the provision of space in the White House where reporters could work. McKinley made himself accessible to the press on a regular basis.

- McKinley is credited with strengthening the power of the presidency. He is also noted for bringing the United States into position as a world power.

- While under intense enemy assault during the battle of Antietam, nineteen-year-old McKinley took food to his regiment, earning him honors for bravery under fire.

- McKinley oversaw the Gold Standard Act of 1900, making only gold, not silver, exchangeable for money in the U.S.

- Under his leadership, the U.S. took possession of Guam, Puerto Rico, the Philippines, Hawaii, and part of American Samoa.

Interesting Facts:

- McKinley was devoted to his wife and very protective of her because she was an invalid and an epileptic. He was never far from her or away from her for more than a few hours. He often left meetings just to check on her. His devotion to her was such that when he was shot, he called out to his secretary, "My wife—be careful, Cortelyou, how you tell her!"

- Those who knew McKinley considered him a very kind and gentle man. For example, when he thought that he would need to declare war on Spain, it is reported that he broke into sobs. Also, after he was shot, he asked the bystanders in attendance not to harm Czolgosz, the man who attacked him.

- McKinley was the first man in his town of Poland, Ohio, to volunteer to fight in the Civil War.

- The 23rd Ohio Infantry to which McKinley belonged during the War was commanded by future President Rutherford B. Hayes.

- Through the 1870s and 1880s, McKinley served seven terms in Congress. He then served as governor in Ohio.

- The president was noted as a gifted public speaker and was generally popular and well liked.

Theodore Roosevelt

26th President, 1901–1909

Vice President: Charles W. Fairbanks (1905–1909)

Born: October 27, 1858, in New York City

Died: January 6, 1919

Party: Republican

Parents: Theodore Roosevelt and Martha Bulloch

First Lady: Edith Kermit Carow (first wife, Alice Hathaway Lee, died in 1884)

Children: Alice; Theodore, Jr.; Kermit; Ethel Carow; Archibald Bulloch; Quentin

Nickname: Teddy or T.R. (Teedie as a child)

Education: Harvard University

Famous Firsts:

- Roosevelt was the youngest man (age 42) ever to become president.
- He was the first American to receive the Nobel peace prize.
- He was the first president to ride in an automobile and to fly in an airplane.
- Roosevelt was the first president to travel to a foreign country (Panama) while in office.
- Roosevelt coined the term "muckraker," signifying writers who portrayed social ills.

Achievements:

- Roosevelt began construction of the Panama Canal.
- He helped bring an end to the Russo-Japanese War.
- Roosevelt was known as a "trust buster," breaking up the power of large corporations.
- Roosevelt established five national parks and added about 150 million acres to the national forests. He also established the United States Forest Service, set aside eighteen sites as national monuments, and created the first bird and game preserves.
- In 1902, the White House was remodelled and enlarged.

Interesting Facts:

- After a cartoonist drew Roosevelt with a bear cub, the "Teddy bear" became popular.
- The Rough Riders, commanded by Roosevelt during the Spanish-American War, were comprised primarily of former college athletes and Western cowboys.
- He was a distant relation of future President Franklin Delano Roosevelt.
- Frequent illnesses, including asthma, were catalysts for young Theodore to build his strength and lead an extremely active and strenuous life. He regularly worked out in a gymnasium, rode horses, swam, hunted, hiked, and boxed.
- Roosevelt's foreign policy, "Speak softly and carry a big stick," was a West African proverb.
- His first wife and his mother died on the same day, February 14, 1884.
- Roosevelt frequently swam across the icy Potomac in the wintertime.
- Roosevelt's is one of four faces carved on Mt. Rushmore.

Election Facts and Figures

	Election of 1896	Election of 1900	Election of 1904
Democrats	William Jennings Bryan of Nebraska, a prominent orator, was the democratic nominee along with Arthur Sewall, a wealthy Maine shipbuilder, as his running mate.	William Jennings Bryan was once again the democratic nominee; Adlai E. Stevenson, Vice President under Grover Cleveland, was his running mate.	Judge Alton B. Parker of the New York Supreme Court was the Democratic nominee with Henry G. Davis of West Virginia as his running mate.
Republicans	William McKinley, the 1892 candidate, ran with Garret A. Hobart of New Jersey.	President McKinley ran for a second term, this time with Theodore Roosevelt, a war hero and New York governor, as his running mate.	President Roosevelt (President since 1901 when McKinley died) was unanimously nominated by his party, and Senator Charles W. Fairbanks of Indiana became his running mate.
Issues	The primary issue was whether or not silver should be allowed to back American currency. McKinley supported free silver while in Congress but as a candidate supported the gold standard.	Free silver was again an issue as well as big business and illegal monopolies (trusts).	Parker argued that the office of the president was usurping authority. Roosevelt called for support of his "square deal" policies which involved social reform.
Slogans	"Free silver" and "gold standard" were the words most often heard in this election.	"A Full Dinner Bucket" was the successful slogan used by the McKinley/Roosevelt ticket.	Roosevelt's campaign centered around the phrase "A square deal for all."
Results	McKinley took 271 electoral votes to Bryan's 176. McKinley had more than 7 million popular votes and Bryan had more than 6.5 million.	McKinley's electoral vote was 292 against Bryan's 155; the popular vote was similar to the previous election, with slightly more for McKinley and slightly fewer for Bryan.	Roosevelt won by a larger popular vote margin than any previous president. He took more than 7.5 million votes (336 electoral) and Parker took just over 5 million (140 electoral). (For the election of 1908, see page 81.)

The Golden Age

People of the nineteenth century generally looked to the twentieth century to make their dreams come true. The turn of the century was seen as an opportunity for fulfillment of bright promises made through the growth and industrialization of the 1800s. It was hoped that the year 1900 and beyond would bring the realization of possibilities. For many, it was looked to as the dawning of a Golden Age.

The majority of the previous century had been lived in the Victorian Era (page 63), but now was the time for change. The new century would complete the millennium, and many felt that anything was possible. Progress and prosperity were around the corner, and more than anything, people of the Western world were certain that peace was here to stay.

However, as the next decade proved, peace was not permanent and many more changes were to come. Even so, the new century did bring amazing advances in technology, medicine, international relations, and more. Here are a few that came in the years 1900–1909.

Planck and Einstein The decade opened in 1900 with Max Planck's proposition of a quantum theory which revolutionized the field of physics. In 1905, Albert Einstein made a name for himself with his publication of *Relativity, The Special and General Theory*. The work of both men would eventually earn them Nobel prizes in the coming years.

Photography In 1900, the Kodak Brownie Box camera was introduced, making home photography accessible and simple.

Radio The first transatlantic radio transmission came in 1901. The first voice and music radio broadcast in the United States came about in 1906.

Flight In December of 1903, Wilbur and Orville Wright's first plane flew for the first time. By 1908, they had closed a contract with the U.S. Department of War for the first military airplane. The first commercial airline followed in 1909.

Automobiles The Ford Motor Company was founded in 1903. In the next decade, cars would become commonplace.

Curie Marie Curie discovered radium and polonium in 1904.

Subways The incredible New York subway opened its first section in 1904. New York's subway system is still world-renowned. New York also awed the world with the Williamsburg Bridge in 1903 and the Manhattan Bridge in 1909.

North Pole The impossible happened: two men, Robert E. Peary and Matthew Henson, reached the North Pole in 1909. It seemed there was nowhere in the world where man could not go.

Suggested Activity

Research Find out more about any of the advances listed above. What led to their development? What improvements or changes have been made to them since?

Gandhi

Mohandas Gandhi is considered by many to be the greatest spiritual and political leader of the early twentieth century. He is also considered by the people of India to be the father of their nation. There he is called the Mahatma, Great Soul.

Gandhi lived his life in a search for truth, and he believed that truth could only be found through compassion and tolerance of others. Further, he believed that truthful solutions to problems could always be found if one persevered.

Gandhi was born on October 2, 1869, in Porbandar, India. Shy and serious, he married his wife, Kasturba, at the age of thirteen through an arranged marriage. The couple had four children. Gandhi studied law in London and returned to India in 1891 to practice. Two years later, he went to South Africa to do legal work, but he met with great discrimination, as did most Indians although they were British subjects and South Africa was under British rule. Although he was assigned to South Africa for only one year, he remained for twenty–one years to fight discrimination. He developed a method of using passive resistance and noncooperation to effect social change. This method, which he called *Satyagraha* (truth and firmness) was based in part on the teachings of Christ and the works of Leo Tolstoy and Henry David Thoreau. He stressed the need for honor; the way people behaved was of the utmost importance.

After his years in South Africa, Gandhi returned to India where he quickly became the leader of the Indian nationalist movement. He led the people in a fight of nonviolent resistance and protest to British rule. Often he fasted in protest, and he was jailed several times, but no matter what, he persevered.

Eventually, after many years, India did gain its independence. However, the nation split in two and Hindus, Muslims, and other groups fought against one another. Gandhi turned his nonviolent protests to the cause of uniting all groups in harmony. Ironically, while on the way to a prayer meeting, an assassin's bullet killed this man of peace just twelve days after religious leaders agreed to stop fighting.

About Gandhi, Albert Einstein is quoted as having said, "Generations to come will scarcely believe that such a one as this walked the earth in flesh and blood."

Suggested Activities

British Empire In the early twentieth century, the British Empire held lands around the world, among them India and South Africa. Find out more about this period of time and what eventually happened to the vast empire.

Animal Rights Gandhi believed that it was morally wrong to kill animals for food or clothing. Discuss your views on this subject.

Marriage In Gandhi's culture and among his caste (socio-economic level in India), arranged marriage was common and the age of thirteen for marriage was not considered young. Research to learn about marriage in other parts of the world at this time as well as the practices of marriage around the world today. Chart the comparisons.

Social Leaders Compare Gandhi to other leaders who have urged nonviolent protest, most notably Martin Luther King, Jr.

Booker T. Washington

Booker T. Washington, born a slave, became arguably the most influential black leader of his time. He urged education, primarily through the Tuskegee Normal and Industrial Institute which he founded in 1881 (now Tuskegee University), as well as economic advancement for blacks. Perhaps most significantly, he became a trusted advisor to Presidents Roosevelt and Taft and influenced the appointments of several blacks to positions in the federal government.

Born in 1856, Booker Taliaferro Washington lived as a slave in Hales Ford, Virginia, until emancipation in 1865. His family moved to West Virginia where Washington labored in the mines and salt furnaces while studying at the Hampton Institute, an industrial school for blacks. Eventually, Washington became a teacher at the school and then took many of its theories and practices and put them into the framework of the new school he developed in Tuskegee. Specific trades were taught at the school, such as carpentry, mechanics, and teaching. In order to support the school, Washington became an expert fund-raiser. The school began to draw attention and became a model of industrial education.

Washington had very specific reasons why his school would teach trades as opposed to a traditional college education. He believed that the way out of poverty for blacks was hard work through trades so that they could purchase property, and then, once they were economically secure landowners, political and civil rights would follow. Washington urged blacks to focus on education and economic growth and to stop focussing their demands on equal rights. At the same time, he urged whites to give blacks better jobs.

Washington spoke publicly on many occasions. Perhaps his most famous speech was the "Atlanta Compromise." In it, Washington accepted inequality for blacks in exchange for economic growth. However, this does not mean that Washington did not support equal rights. He carefully avoided publicly supporting issues that would displease prominent Southern whites, but at the same time he secretly financed lawsuits that fought to maintain black rights and oppose segregation. He also funded and ran a number of black newspapers.

Despite Washington's prominence, there were backlashes and some opposition, particularly through W.E.B. Du Bois (page 30), who felt that Washington was surrendering rights for economic gain and that higher education was vital for black advancement. Du Bois also objected to Washington's control of so many newspapers, believing that such control allowed only Washington's opinions to be heard. By 1910, Washington's influence was on the decline.

Suggested Activities

Read Read *Up From Slavery: An Autobiography* (Corner House, 1971). It was first published in 1901, and in it Washington explains his life as well as his theories.

Tuskegee Research the Tuskegee Institute and its history. Find out about the curriculum and attendance today.

Washington v. Du Bois Discuss the view of these two black leaders. Do you agree with Washington's or Du Bois' point of view?

Advisor Washington was one of the first black advisors to a President, paving the way for future blacks not only to advise but to hold the office of president, as well. Investigate the roles that advisors have made to the presidency over time. How influential can they be? How influential was Washington? Should advisors have influence in the first place?

W.E.B. Du Bois and the NAACP

Like Booker T. Washington, William Edward Burghardt Du Bois was a prominent black leader early in the twentieth century. However, his beliefs and perspectives differed radically from Washington's.

Du Bois was born in Massachusetts in 1868, and he lived for nearly one hundred years. He graduated from Fisk University in 1888, and in 1895 he became the first black to earn a Ph.D. from Harvard University. He then became a professor at Atlanta University as well as a renowned author, particularly for *The Souls of Black Folk* (Fawcett, 1961), a collection of essays and sketches published in 1903.

Booker T. Washington and W.E.B. Du Bois shared the same goal—advancement and equality for blacks; however, while Washington urged hard work in place of demands for equality, Du Bois believed that blacks must be relentless in speaking against discrimination and fighting prejudice. Du Bois supported college education while Washington put his power behind trade.

In order to fight racial discrimination, Du Bois founded the Niagara Movement in 1905. The next step came in 1909, as he and approximately sixty other blacks and whites founded the National Association for the Advancement of Colored People (NAACP). The NAACP works tirelessly to end discrimination through legal action and legislation, and it attempts to reduce hunger and poverty for people of color as well. In its first thirty years, it also worked to halt violence against blacks, particularly through the passage and enforcement of antilynching laws. Just after its inception, the NAACP began to produce *Crisis*, a magazine filled with stories of blacks who have achieved success. For twenty-four years, Du Bois was its editor.

Today, the NAACP is headquartered in Baltimore with a legislative bureau in Washington, D.C. Out of the NAACP has grown the NAACP Legal Defense and Educational Fund in New York City. The Fund has been independent since 1957.

After many years of working with the NAACP, Du Bois grew dissatisfied and frustrated by the slow progress toward racial equality in society and the law. In the two years just prior to his death, Du Bois joined the Communist party and moved to Ghana where he died in 1963.

Suggested Activities

Find Out More To learn more about the NAACP, read *History and Achievement of the NAACP* by Jacqueline L. Harris (Watts, 1992). You can also write directly to the NAACP at 485 Mt. Hope Drive, Baltimore, Maryland 21215.

Read If your library has access to them, locate and read old copies of *Crisis*. As a class, write your own modern issue of the magazine.

Communism Discuss why you think Communism held appeal for Du Bois.

Carry Nation

There are not many who have come to represent a righteous and strident call for morality in quite the way Carry Nation has. Her name has become synonymous with moral action, although certainly not everyone of her time agreed with her idea of morality.

Carry Nation was born Carry Amelia Moore in Kentucky (1846). At twenty, she married a drunkard, Dr. Charles Gloyd, who died shortly after they were married. After ten years of supporting herself by teaching and renting out rooms, she married a lawyer and minister named David Nation. She became devoutly religious at this time and professed that she saw visions. Nation was convinced that she was divinely protected and divinely chosen. A fire in 1889 that burned much of her town but left her property untouched increased her belief. So did her name—Carry A. Nation. She felt quite certain it was a message to her from Providence.

In 1889, Mr. and Mrs. Nation moved to Kansas. There was a law in Kansas at this time banning the sale of liquor, but it was not enforced. Carry Nation took it upon herself to enforce it. In 1890, she began to pray outside saloons, and later, through the first decade of the twentieth century, she began to smash them. When she is pictured today, she is still seen carrying her Bible and wielding her hatchet, her tools of destruction.

One might not think that one woman could make much difference; however, the nearly six-foot (183 cm) Carry Nation and her hatchet did extensive damage and closed the saloons in her town as well as many others throughout Kansas. Although she was often arrested for disturbing the peace, she continued to fight in her personal crusade.

Nation was also opposed to other things she found morally corrupt, such as the use of tobacco and immodest dress in women. Many felt her sense of righteousness was justified, so she developed quite a following of imitators and fans who admired her courage. However, many others were angered by her intolerant actions and dismissed her for her inappropriate and outrageous behavior. In 1901, Nation's husband divorced her on the grounds of desertion.

━━━━━ Suggested Activities ━━━━━

Discussion Discuss the following questions:

- Are there any causes you feel so passionately about that you would feel justified in taking matters into your own hands?

- What social activists today might you compare to Carry Nation? How do you feel about their work?

Write Have the students write on the following topic: Carry Nation felt called upon to lead her crusade. What do you feel called upon to do in life?

Prohibition The crusade of Carry Nation was, in part, instrumental in bringing about Prohibition in 1919. Research Prohibition in the United States and what happened to the amendment banning the sale of alcohol throughout the country.

Earthquake!

San Francisco was a booming and prosperous port town in 1906, but at 5:13 a.m. on April 18, all that changed. A massive earthquake struck the city and surrounding area. Fires broke out throughout the city due to severed electric lines, overturned lamps, and the explosion of gas mains. Even worse, the city's water mains were also damaged, retarding the firefighters' ability to fight the raging flames. For three days the flames spread, largely unchecked. Finally, firefighters began dynamiting blocks of buildings just to stop the fire from spreading. When the damage was assessed, 3,000 lives had been lost, 250,000 people were homeless, and more than 28,000 buildings were destroyed. Damage to property was in excess of 500 million dollars.

A strong earthquake struck the city again in 1989; however, this time only twelve lives were lost. The difference was largely due to architectural and technological advances that have made newer buildings better able to withstand powerful earthquakes.

To learn more about some kinds of earthquakes, try the experiments below.

Materials: cardboard box, metal pan, uncooked beans or rice, deck of cards, dominoes, building blocks

Procedure:

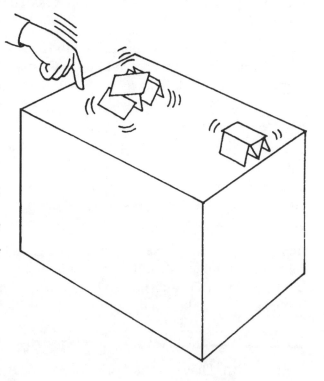

1. Begin with the cardboard box. Turn it upside down. Build two small houses of cards, one near the edge of the box and one further away.

2. Tap your fingers gently eight to ten times on the box in front of the closest house. Watch the movement of both houses. You should see that the house closest to the tapping receives the most damage, although the walls of both houses will shift position. The different effects are caused by waves of energy sent by the tapping (earthquake). The vibrating energy weakens as it travels.

3. Repeat the experiment, this time with two houses of dominoes. Watch the results.

4. Repeat it once more, this time with block houses. Again, watch the results. The three kinds of structures will show the ability of structures to withstand earthquakes.

5. If desired, the three different housing materials can be built on different surfaces and the experiment repeated. This will show how the various surfaces alter the effects of the quake's energy waves. After the cardboard box, try an overturned metal pan. Next, invert the pan and fill it with dry rice or beans, and then build the structures on them. What happens in each scenario?

The Nobel Prize

Alfred Bernhard Nobel (1833–1896) was a Swedish chemist and industrialist who invented dynamite. The sale of dynamite and other explosives made Nobel a very wealthy man. In his will, he set aside nine million dollars. The interest earned by this money was to be used to present cash awards each year in each of five categories that benefitted humanity: physics, chemistry, physiology or medicine, literature of an idealistic nature, and the most effective work toward international peace. The prizes were first presented in 1901. In 1969, a sixth prize for economic science was added by the Bank of Sweden. By the late twentieth century, the value of each of the prizes had reached approximately $900,000.

Use encyclopedias and other reference materials to match the names of the Nobel prize winners below with their achievements.

1. _____ Mother Teresa

    a. work on the physiology of digestion

2. _____ Marie Curie

    b. stories, novels, and poems

3. _____ Ivan Pavlov

    c. stating the quantum theory of light

4. _____ Martin Luther King, Jr.

    d. work with Women's International League for Peace and Freedom

5. _____ George Bernard Shaw

    e. discovery of radioactivity and studies of uranium

6. _____ Rudyard Kipling

    f. humanitarian work in Africa

7. _____ Toni Morrison

    g. novels

8. _____ Max Planck

    h. plays

9. _____ Jane Addams

    i. aiding India's poor

10. _____ Albert Schweitzer

    j. leading nonviolent civil rights demonstrations in the U.S.

Teacher: Fold under these answers before duplicating.

1.i 2.e 3.a 4.j 5.h 6.b 7.g 8.c 9.d 10.f

The Graduate

Helen Keller

Helen Adams Keller was born in 1880 normal and healthy, but at age one and one-half she suffered what the doctor called "acute congestion of the stomach and brain." The illness destroyed her sight and hearing. For nearly five years afterwards, Keller was almost completely cut off from the rest of the world, unable to speak and communicating only through giggles and choked screams.

At the advice of Alexander Graham Bell, Keller's father wrote to the Perkins Institution for the Blind in Boston. Just before Keller was seven, Anne Mansfield Sullivan arrived to undertake her teaching. Together they developed a way to communicate, Sullivan spelling into the hand of Keller manually. Once the girl understood the method, her learning was rapid. Within three years, Keller was a fluent reader and writer of Braille, the alphabet of the blind.

At age ten, Keller took lessons from a teacher of the deaf to learn how to speak. At sixteen, she went to preparatory school and continued her studies at Radcliffe College. Anne Sullivan attended classes with her as her interpreter. In 1904, the impossible happened. The blind and deaf young woman, once entirely unable to communicate, graduated from college—with honors.

Helen Keller went on to be a noted author (her books have been translated into over fifty languages) and lecturer. Communication became her gift to the world. She worked for the remainder of her life to help the blind and deaf, doing such things as starting the Helen Keller Endowment Fund and working with soldiers in World War II who had been blinded in battle.

Some of Keller's books include *The Story of My Life* (1902), *Optimism* (1903), *The World I Live In* (1908), and *Teacher* (1955) which is the story of Anne Sullivan. Helen Keller's early life has been immortalized in the award-winning play *The Miracle Worker* (1959) and the motion picture of the same name.

Suggested Activities

Braille Below you will find the Braille alphabet as it appears visually, along with four words made with their own dot code. In reality, the dots are raised indentations on paper. Use the system of dots as you see it to write a message. Have a classmate translate your work.

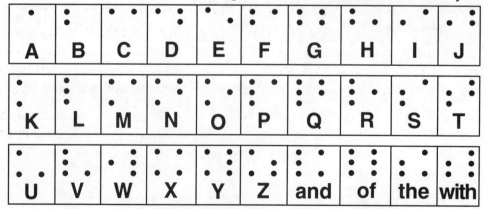

College Helen Keller was able to attend and graduate from college, but it is unlikely that she would have been able to do so without the help of Anne Sullivan. Do some investigating to find out what help is available in colleges today for people with special needs.

Boy Scouts

In 1907, Robert Baden-Powell of Britain began the Boy Scouts movement by organizing a camp for boys. The following year, he published the first Boy Scout manual. One year later, an American businessman, William D. Boyce, was traveling in England when he became lost in a London fog. A British Boy Scout helped him find his way. Boyce, impressed by the Scout's actions, brought the organization to the United States. It has grown by leaps and bounds ever since, spreading to more than 130 countries with over 24 million members.

The Boy Scouts is an organization that was founded to teach young people leadership and good citizenship. Service to God, country, and others is intrinsic to the Boy Scout way of life. The Scouting organization teaches its members to learn by doing, and therefore they are given hands-on, cooperative experiences in the areas of camping, first aid, outdoor cooking, swimming, woodworking, and more.

Boy Scouts take an oath in which they promise to do their duty. They also pledge to follow the Scout Law, which has twelve points. The law states that a Scout is

- trustworthy
- loyal
- helpful
- friendly

- courteous
- kind
- obedient
- cheerful

- thrifty
- brave
- clean
- reverent

Scouts earn badges and promotions in their troops as they grow and accomplish the work set before them to learn and do. Today, any boy from six to twenty years of age may be a Scout member; girls from fourteen to twenty may join the Explorers, a division of the Boy Scouts.

Suggested Activities

Scout Oath Each Boy Scout swears the Boy Scout Oath. It states, "On my honor, I will do my best:/ To do my duty to God and my country, and to obey the Scout Law./ To help other people at all times./ To keep myself physically strong, mentally awake, and morally straight." Write your own oath that states the way in which you believe you should live your life.

Scout Law The twelve points of the Scout Law are listed above. Write each of the points on a sheet of paper. Next to each, write how well you honor that part of the Law in your own life. Also write what points you would include in a law you wrote for yourself.

World Series

At the turn of the century, baseball was capturing the hearts and spirits of the American people. To capitalize on this growing passion, the first post-season baseball series, called the World Series, was played in 1903 between the leader of the American League (Boston) and the leader of the National League (Pittsburgh). Boston took the series five games to three. The World Series has been played every year since except 1904 (due to an internal dispute) and 1994 (due to a player strike). Eventually, the series was won by the best out of seven games; therefore, to take the championship a team needed four victories.

Baseball and its heroes have been imortalized in poetry, plays, and more than 400 songs. "Take Me Out to the Ball Game," written in 1908, is perhaps the most enduring and well-known of these baseball songs. American children throughout the nation generally grow up with a familiarity with baseball. Even young children can usually recognize the equipment of the game.

How well do you really know baseball? Complete the activity below to find out.

Suggested Activity

Using the diagram, write the names of the positions played next to their corresponding letters.

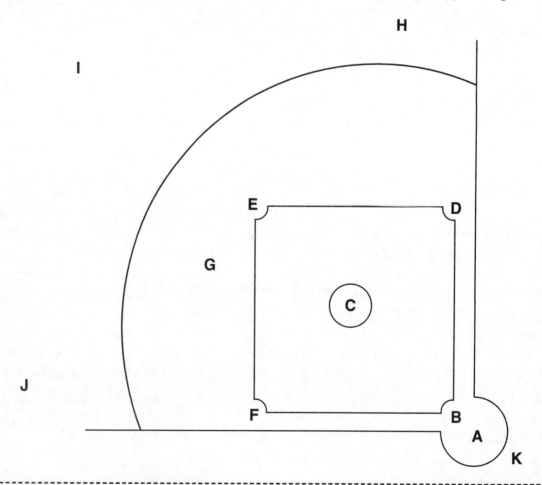

Teacher: Fold under these answers before duplicating.

A.catcher B.batter C.pitcher D.first base E.second base F.third base G.shortstop H.right fielder I.center fielder J.left fielder K.umpire

Davis Cup

In the world of international men's tennis, the Davis Cup is the most prized team trophy. It began with an intercollegiate and doubles tennis champion named Dwight Filley Davis, who, in 1900, donated the silver cup. Competition in his name began that year. Each year since, excepting 1901, 1910, and the years of the two world wars, the Davis Cup has been in continuous competition.

To earn the Davis Cup, the top sixteen qualifying nations compete in a single elimination tournament. A separate tournament is played among the nonqualifying nations divided into four zones. The leader of each zone advances to Davis Cup competition in the following year, replacing the losing teams of the previous Cup competition.

When play for the Cup began, the competitors were teams from America and the British Isles. By World War I, six more nations joined, and by 1984, there were a total of sixty-two nations in competition. Up until 1927, only America, Great Britain, and Australasia (a combined team of Australia and New Zealand) had won the trophy, but France won in 1927 as well as in the next six tournaments. However, France has not won since, and Great Britain has not won since 1937. From then until 1974, the cup went to either America or Australia (now in solitary competition). South Africa became the victor in 1974 but only through default. At the time, many nations objected to South African politics. In the final round of competition, South Africa and India were set to play for the championship, but India refused, despite the fact that its win would mean the first win for an Asian nation. India's default led to South Africa's victory.

Today, the sport of tennis is filled with professionals, but in earlier years, it was not. In fact, professionals were barred from Davis Cup play until 1968.

Suggested Activities

Winners Research to find the winners of each of the Davis Cup competitions. Make mathematical graphs comparing the leading nations, runners-up, scores, and more.

War Disruptions War and conflicts have often put a halt to international athletic competitions. Have a class discussion considering why this is so, if such disruptions are necessary, and what might be done about them if they should happen in the future.

Playing Tennis Allow the class to study the basic rules of tennis and to play the game. Take some physical education time learning to serve, return the ball, volley, and more.

Default In 1974, South Africa topped India in the Davis Cup competition by default. Research to find the facts behind this unusual result.

Politics Dwight Davis went on to become a successful lawyer, lieutenant colonel in the army, secretary of war under President Calvin Coolidge, and governor general of the Philippines. What other prominent political figures can you name with distinguished careers in collegiate and/or professional athletics? It may require research to find out. As a class, determine how many names you can find, their political accomplishments, and their athletic successes.

Flight

At the turn of the century, very few believed that flight
was possible in a heavier-than-air machine. Two of the
few who did believe were Wilbur and Orville Wright.
Wilbur Wright was born in 1867 in Indiana, and
Orville was born four years later in Ohio. As children
the two were fascinated by mechanics and even earned
small amounts of money by selling homemade
mechanical toys. Both went to school, but neither
received a high school diploma. When they grew up,
Orville built a printing press and started a printing
business, developing a weekly newspaper which
Wilbur edited. Next, they tried their hands at renting
and selling bicycles, and finally they began to
manufacture the bikes themselves.

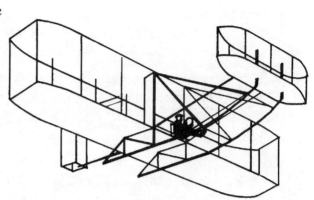

In 1896 the brothers read about the death of a pioneer
glider named Otto Lilienthal, and his work sparked their interest. They started to read everything
available on aeronautics and soon became as expert on the subject as any pioneer could be. The
Wrights then contacted the National Weather Bureau to determine the best place to carry out their
experiments with flight. The Bureau advised them to try a narrow strip of sandy land called Kill Devil
Hill near Kittyhawk, North Carolina. In 1900, they tested a glider that could hold a person, and in 1901
they tried again with a larger glider. Neither glider could lift as they had hoped, although they did
achieve some success in controlling balance.

The Wright brothers felt confident that flight was possible; therefore, they theorized that previous data
concerning air pressure on curved surfaces must be inaccurate. They built their own wind tunnel and
over 200 model wings in order to make their own pressure tables. Their tables became the first reliable
ones ever made.

In 1902 they tried a third glider, using their new information. It vastly exceeded the success of all
previous gliders, with some glides exceeding 600 feet (180 meters). This led the brothers to plan and
build a power airplane. In 1903, at a cost just under one thousand dollars, the plane was complete. Its
wings measured 40.5 feet (12 meters), and it weighed 750 pounds (340 kilograms) with the pilot. In
September of 1903, they arrived in Kittyhawk, but a series of bad storms and defects delayed them.
However, on December 17, 1903, they achieved flight.

Over the next few years, their experiments produced even longer and better flights. On October 5,
1905, their plane flew for 24.2 miles (38.9 kilometers) in just over 38 minutes. In 1908, they closed a
contract with the United States Department of War for the first military airplane ever made.

The brothers went on to exhibit flight in France and the United States as well as to teach others to be
pilots. Eventually, the inevitable happened: on September 17, 1908, Orville and his passenger,
Lieutenant Thomas E. Selfridge, crashed due to a malfunction. Orville recovered but Selfridge died.
However, the work of the brothers continued until Wilbur died of typhoid fever in 1912. Orville carried
on alone until his death in 1948. Today they are remembered as the fathers of modern flight.

Suggested Activity

Models Construct model airplanes from paper, testing their aerodynamic qualities. Conduct
experiments and use your data to build the best possible plane. An excellent resource is
Teacher Created Materials #281 *Thematic Unit: Flight.*

Zeppelins

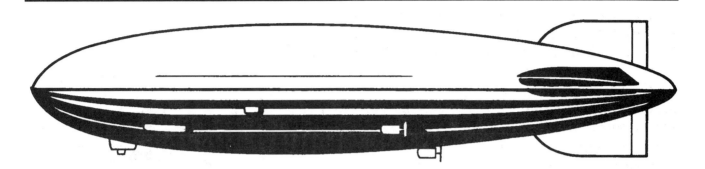

Airships, also called dirigibles, are lighter-than-air flying vehicles with engines to move them through the air and steering that allows them to be controlled. Hot air ballons and blimps were the primary method of human flight throughout the 1800s, but it was in the early 1900s that the best remembered type of airship, the *zeppelin*, was developed and ruled supreme.

Henri Giffard, a French engineer, developed the first powered and manned airship in the mid-nineteenth century. It used a nonrigid cigar-shaped gas bag with a three-horsepower (2.2-kilowatt) steam engine and a rudder supported below it in a gondola. In 1884, two French inventors named Charles Renard and Arthur Krebs completed the airship *La France* with a battery-powered electric motor (about 9-horsepower/7-kilowatt), rudder, and elevator. Brazilian inventor Alberto Santos-Dumont flew around the Eiffel Tower in an airship in 1901, earning him great popularity around the world.

In the midst of this, Count Ferdinand von Zeppelin was developing his own airship. His design featured a rigid frame which held individual gas cells. In 1900, he flew his first, called the LZ-1. It could reach a top speed of approximately 17 miles (27 kilometers) per hour. He followed this airship with the LZ-2 in 1905 and the LZ-3 in 1906. It was the LZ-3 that the German army procured, and it became the first military zeppelin. It was of supreme use to them in the next decade during World War I.

Another first for flight came in the first decade. In 1909, Count von Zeppelin developed the first commercial airline, DELAG. Commercial flights in zeppelins remained popular for several years. However, their use came to an abrupt halt with the explosion of the *Hindenburg* in 1937. From that time on, the airplane has set the exclusive standard for commercial flight.

Suggested Activities

World War I Research to determine the ways in which the Germans used zeppelins during World War I. Compare their success with the airplanes developed in the United States.

Hindenburg Find out why the *Hindenburg* exploded and what happened to the passengers.

David Schwarz Schwarz is another important name in the development of airships; however, while his ideas were sound, his airship crashed. Determine what contributions he made to the development of airships.

Hot Air Balloons If you live in an area where hot air balloons are commonly flown, take a field trip to explore them up close. Compare such balloons with the zeppelin, making a chart that shows their similarities and differences.

Goodyear Probably the most famous airships in use today are the Goodyear blimps. Find out how they operate and why they are used.

Pavlov's Dogs

For Ivan Petrovich Pavlov, dogs certainly were man's best friend.

Pavlov was a Russian physiologist who, in the early 1900s, experimented with dogs and other animals to prove that certain reflex responses can become conditioned responses to new, unrelated stimuli. The best known experiments conducted by Pavlov involved a dog, a bell, and meat. Pavlov knew that the dog's natural reflex at the smell of meat was to salivate. He began to ring a bell every time a dog was presented with meat. Eventually, Pavlov had only to ring the bell, and even though no meat was present, the dog began to salivate anyway. The animal's response had become conditioned, transferred to the new stimulus of the bell.

In 1904, Ivan Pavlov won the Nobel prize for physiology and medicine. The award was granted for his research concerning digestion. He found that the vagus nerve controls the flow of the stomach's and pancreas' digestive juices.

Suggested Activities

Experiment The best way to learn about Pavlov's work is clearly to conduct experiments such as his on your own. If space and time allow, conduct similar experiments with a mouse or other small animal that you can easily care for in your classroom. Do not be concerned for the animal's safety since such learned responses do the animal no harm whatsoever.

The students are probably already familiar with how their pets become excited at the sound of a can opener, believing it to be the animal's food. However, Pavlov showed something a little more: the animal's physiological response actually transferred due to the stimulus of the bell. It was not merely that he became excited with the sound of the bell.

To begin, brainstorm and discuss with the class other ways in which they may have witnessed the results that Pavlov got during his research. Also brainstorm for ways in which the class can conduct similar experiments. Remind them that the point is to transfer a physiological response from a natural stimuli to an artificial stimuli. Be sure to carefully follow and log your progress and results.

Scientific Research Pavlov won the Nobel prize for his research. If you do not wish to recreate experiments and research like Pavlov's, be sure to allow the students to conduct their own research on other scientific topics, carefully keeping records of all they hypothesize and do, as well as the results.

The Mad Scientists

Every now and then the world meets an individual who, early in his career, may have been ridiculed or scorned for his "crazy" ideas—ideas that are later shown to be nothing less than genius. Two such men are Max Planck and Albert Einstein.

In 1900, a German theoretical physicist, Max Karl Ernst Ludwig Planck, proposed a law of radiation, including a quantum theory. The field of physics was completely revolutionized by the theory. Up until this time, scientists believed that energy flowed continuously; however, this belief did not explain the absorption and emission of energy by matter. Planck's theory did.

The quantum theory shows that an object that completely absorbs radiant energy (a black body) can only absorb and emit the energy in tiny pieces called *quanta*. To measure the energy of each quantum, one must multiply the frequency of the radiant energy (v) by a universal constant (h), also known as Planck's constant. Therefore, energy (E) equals the constant multiplied by the frequency (hv), or $E = hv$. This is demonstrated in the example of a red and a blue flame. Less energy (heat) is emitted from a red flame than a blue flame because the frequency of red light is less than blue; thus, the heat from a red flame is cooler than the heat from a blue flame.

Another German physicist, Albert Einstein, wrote several revolutionizing papers in the early part of the century. In 1905, these papers were published in a physics journal. The papers showed the nature of light, that it was both a particle (quanta) and a wave. This led to a greater understanding of atoms. In fact, Einstein was the first to show that atoms existed, and he demonstrated how the size of atoms could be calculated. Another paper in 1905 presented Einstein's special theory, which was the beginning of his theory of relativity, perhaps the best known and significant theory in the history of physics. The special theory states that time, matter, and motion are related, and the formula $E = mc^2$ comes of this. E represents energy, m is mass, and c is the speed of light. The speed of light is extremely high, so the formula shows that even a small mass can become a great deal of energy. Additionally, the theory explains that the direction in which a mass is moving and the speed at which it is traveling may depend on the position from which it is measured.

The theory of relativity has a component part which Einstein published ten years later. This general theory involved gravity, improving upon the theory of Sir Isaac Newton. Einstein's completed theory of relativity and his work with atoms meant a great deal to the world of science. It was his dream that atomic energy would help the world tremendously. He was greatly disturbed by the fact that his work led to the atomic bomb.

Einstein continued to provide incredible information throughout the remainder of his life, attempting to solve problems that others did not even know existed. Since his death in 1955, other physicists have been trying to solve the problems first raised by Einstein.

In 1918, Planck won a Nobel prize for his work. Einstein won a Nobel prize in 1921.

Suggested Activity

Relativity First, discuss with the class the meaning of relativity. Then, to determine the relative nature of direction, have the students consider the following. A bus is moving north. A rider on the bus is walking toward the back of the bus. A pedestrian is standing on the sidewalk as the bus comes toward her. A car on the other side of the road is going past the bus. If you are on the bus, in which direction is the bus passenger moving? If you are on the ground, in which direction is the bus passenger moving? If you are in the car, in which direction is the bus passenger moving? (Consider other relative motions as well.)

New York Underground

Subways have been in existence since London opened its first underground passenger line in 1863. It was built to expedite travel in the heavily populated city. People could go from one part of the city to another in just minutes, whereas the time on foot or by horse-drawn carriage would take much longer, particularly as it involved combatting the many others above ground trying to do the same.

Immigration in the nineteenth century added vastly to the population of New York by the turn of the century. New York officials felt the best solution to traffic problems was to build a subway of their own. First opened in 1904, New York's subway is now one of the most extensive and famous in the world. The first line, the Interborough Rapid Transit (IRT) operates in Manhattan and a large section of the Bronx, with branches in Brooklyn and Queens. The Independent Subway (IND) has lines in all boroughs but Staten Island. The Brooklyn-Manhattan Transit Company (BMT) has lines in Brooklyn, Manhattan, and Queens.

Today, New York's subways are enclosed. However, when the trains were first constructed, they were open air. This means that there were no roofs but merely benches attached to a flat base that rolled along the tracks. Ladies in tall and feathered hats, a popular style of the time, certainly needed to take care in those fast moving cars.

The New York subway is primarily an open cut subway. This is made by tearing out the streets and building the subway in big ditches. When two lines are going to cross, one roadbed is dug at a deeper level than the other. A cover is often placed above such open cut subways, and it is then called a cut and cover. Open cut subways such as New York's are usually rectangular in shape, as opposed to tube subways (bored through the earth without displacing the surface) which are usually circular or semicircular.

The original subways were run by steam locomotives. Since 1890, all have been run by electricity. New York's subway, of course, has always used electricity.

Suggested Activities

Mass Transit Subways were formed in order to move many people in a short amount of time. Discuss the pros and cons of such a venture. How is it helpful to society? How is it harmful? Consider also the other forms of mass transit commonly in use today. Which are the most effective?

Effectiveness Although subways have proved beneficial in many parts of the world, other places resist them for a variety of reasons, including safety and cost. Research to determine which major cities use them and why, as well as the major cities that do not.

Crime Research and consider the crime rates on subways and discuss what precautions and preventative steps can be taken in the future. Ask the class what would they do if their commission was to make subways crime free.

The Father of Psychoanalysis

Sigmund Freud

Born Sigismund Solomon Freud on May 6, 1856, Sigmund Freud grew to be one of the greatest researchers and theorists in the field of psychology. The eldest of eight children (two older brothers from his father's first marriage were adults when Sigmund was born), Freud lived in poverty throughout his early years. A Jewish philanthropic society paid for his medical education, and Freud became quite skilled and effective, particularly in the field of histology, the study of the structure of tissues. Freud then became a neurologist, married, and had children, all the while investigating new theories and ideas. Eventually, his focus shifted from the physiological to the psychological, or from the brain to the mind. It is for this work that Freud is most greatly remembered.

In 1900, Freud published the work for which he is most noted, *The Interpretation of Dreams*. This book deals with dreams, the mechanics behind them, and the unconscious mind through which they are formed. From this work developed Freud's Wednesday Psychological Group, which later became the Vienna Psycho-Analytical Society, a group of colleagues and students who met to study Freud's investigations. Then in 1904, Freud published his very popular *The Psychopathology of Everyday Life*. This book studied imperfect mental functions, such as forgetting and slips of the tongue. The theories Freud presented in this book are more widely accepted today than any theories presented in his other works.

Freud led a very happy personal life with his wife and six children, but his professional life was not always so. Often, he was ridiculed and dismissed, as many great pioneers are. However, he had a well developed sense of humor, and his philosophy was to continue to present new evidence no matter what. He never stopped to argue with his critics.

As time went on, other analysts grew to accept, expand upon, and alter the work of Freud, most notably Carl Jung. Freud continued his investigations throughout it all. When Naziism sprang up in his homeland, Freud began to focus on the nature and origin of Judaism. This was the work he pursued throughout the remainder of his life.

Today, the entire field of psychoanalysis is said to have its roots in the work of Sigmund Freud.

Suggested Activities

Dream Journal Over a period of one week, keep a journal of your dreams. Most analysts today believe that only the individual doing the dreaming can know for certain what the dreams mean, since individuals have their own symbologies. After a week, look over your dreams and determine what you think they mean.

Research There are many dream dictionaries on the market which suggest ideas for what symbols in dreams mean. At your discretion, provide some of those meanings to the students and allow them to discuss their merits.

Anna Freud The daughter of Sigmund Freud, Anna Freud grew up to be a psychoanalyst. Research to find out more about the life and work of Anna Freud.

Beatrix Potter and Peter Rabbit

Beatrix Helen Potter was born on July 6, 1866, in London, England. She lived there with her wealthy parents throughout most of the year, but the family spent their holidays in the country. It was there that Potter developed a familiarity with, and a love for, wild animals. Although she had difficulties in her life that made her unhappy, the animals and her imagination always gave her joy.

At age 27, Potter became an author of children's literature in an unusual way. She sent illustrated stories to a sick child. The stories were collected and printed privately in 1900. They were called *The Tale of Peter Rabbit*. In the following year, a publisher's edition that included her now famous watercolor drawings was printed. The delightful book is still in print today and continues to sell very well.

Potter wrote other children's books over the next several years, including *Squirrel Nutkin*, *Mrs. Tittlemouse*, and *Mr. Jeremy Fisher*. Although the animals are given personalities and voices, their natures remain constant with that of real animals. Therefore, although the books are fanciful, they are also realistic, just as are Potter's illustrations.

When she was nearly fifty years old, Potter married a lawyer named William Heelis. The two lived on a farm called Hill Top in Sawrey, Lancashire. There, Potter raised sheep and lived in the natural setting she loved. When she died in 1943, her farm was bequeathed to the National Trust. It remains open to the public.

Suggested Activity

Drawing Beatrix Potter took care to make her illustrations both realistic and fanciful. Have the students attempt their own realistic drawings. If possible, let them view some real animals and draw them. You can also have them attempt to duplicate other realistic drawings or photographs. They can begin by drawing them in the boxes below.

| rabbit | rabbit |
| squirrel | squirrel |

Just So

Rudyard Kipling is one of the most popular and prolific authors the world has known. He was the first author of his native England to win a Nobel prize for literature (1907).

Kipling was born in India to British parents. His parents, like other English parents, sent him to school in England when he was five. He boarded there with foster parents for five years, and then later attended a school for sons of army officers, also in England. The unhappy tale of his early years in England became the subject of one of his first stories (1888), and the friendships, pranks, and adolescent brutalities of English public schools became the subject of another.

In all, Kipling received an adequate education, but since the family could not afford to send him to college, he returned to India. He had been active in journalism while in school, so he pursued the career and became a newspaperman. The papers he worked for printed some of his stories and poems in addition to his articles.

Rudyard Kipling

Throughout the later years of the nineteenth century, Kipling published many books, including *The Jungle Book* and *Captains Courageous*. Arguably his finest novel came in 1900. It was called *Kim*, and his excellent knowledge of Indian culture and people helped to make it such an engaging and rich novel. It is considered a classic of British fiction. The book was followed by another favorite, Kipling's *Just So Stories*, which tell humorous stories of how some natural things came to be (such as how the elephant got its trunk). In all, Kipling wrote more than 300 short stories, numerous novels, and many poems. It was for his complete work that the Nobel committee honored him in 1907.

Kipling died in 1937 while writing his autobiography.

Suggested Activities

Tell Me Why Kipling used his imagination to explain how things came to be in his *Just So Stories*. Have the students write stories of their own. Preface their writing with the reading of some of Kipling's work as well as myths from various cultures. Then let them write their own and share them with the class. They can choose their own topics, or you can provide them with the following ideas.

- why the snow is white
- why the snake slithers
- how the Andes Mountains were formed
- how the eagle got its wings
- how the cheetah got its spots
- why the lion has a roar
- why the ant is strong
- why the monkey has a tail
- how the orange got its peel

Comparison Read *The Jungle Book* by Kipling. Then watch the Disney cartoon version as well as the live action version. Compare the three and discuss their merits.

The Funny Papers

People around the world read the funny pages in their newspapers each day, and they cannot imagine their papers without them. But before 1907, there were no funny pages. There was not even a comic strip. That all changed with a man named Bud Fisher.

Bud Fisher had an idea, and with the help of the *San Francisco Chronicle*, he made it a reality. Cartoonists had been drawing individual cartoons for quite awhile, but Fisher wanted to print a strip that would appear in the paper each day. *The Chronicle* liked the idea. Fisher's strip was called *Mr. Mutt*. Later he changed the name, and it became one of the most endearing strips of all time: *Mutt and Jeff*.

Suggested Activity

See You in the Funny Papers Comic strips all share the same basic format. The problem, or setup, is presented in the first one to several panels, with the solution and punchline coming in the last panel. Write a comic strip of your own. You will need to create a set of characters that can repeat in the strip each day. The strip will need to tell or show a joke or something humorous. Use the panels below.

Picasso and Cubism

It is said by many that no artist of the 1900s was more significant to the world of art than Pablo Picasso. He certainly was the dominant artist of the time.

Picasso created art in many forms: paintings, sculptures, prints, drawings, and ceramics. He also developed the style of collage, incorporating things such as wallpaper and newsprint in the work of art. Yet, perhaps he is best known for a brand new style which he pioneered. The style is called *cubism*.

At the turn of the century, impressionism, pointillism, and symbolism were the three prominent styles of art. Picasso experimented with them, but always he was reaching for something new—a new way to express himself artistically. In 1907, he fully captured his new style with jagged and distorted images. The painting that did this is called *Les Demoiselles d'Avignon*. Inspired by primitive art and Picasso's interest in African and Iberian sculptures, the painting revolutionized the art world in the 1900s. It should be said that at the same time, an artist named George Braque was independently creating a similar style. It is Picasso, however, whose name is indelibly linked with cubism.

Cubism is an entirely new way of seeing nature and art. From the time of the Renaissance, artists had been painting in a way that incorporated atmospheric and linear perspective. In the nineteenth century, a group of artists experimented with perspective, creating a balance between the three-dimensional illusion created by the painting and the two-dimensional nature of the canvas itself. However, with all the experimentation, there was really no distortion of objects and the space around them.

In 1907, Picasso and Braque demonstrated that a figure could be distorted and transformed from the traditional planes. From there, it was an easy step to see that a painting could consist of an abstract arrangement of lines, shapes, and colors. Cubism, it seems, was the beginning of nonobjective art. Just as Albert Einstein, a contemporary in the world of science, was beginning to show, perspective is relative.

Suggested Activities

Cubist Art Your local library should have a variety of art texts that include prints of major works of art. Look through them to find Picasso's *Guernica* and *Three Musicians*, as well as *Les Demoiselles d'Avignon*. Also look for work by Braque and later cubists such as Juan Gris and Willem de Kooning. Compare and discuss the styles. Ask the students how cubism is different from realistic paintings. Also ask their opinions of the style.

Artists Allow the students to attempt cubist works of their own. Provide them with an object, such as a vase of flowers or bowl of fruit, and ask them to draw or paint it in Picasso's style. Have the class choose and discuss the most successful attempts.

An American in Paris

Mary Cassatt was born in America in 1844, but she spent most of her life in France. Much of her art belongs to the great French impressionist movement. In the early part of the nineteenth century, she was a preeminent and respected artist.

Mary Cassatt

Cassatt always considered herself an American (she is quoted as saying, "I am an American, definitely and frankly American"), but she believed that Europe, and particularly France, was the place to be for an artist. At first, her father, a prominent Philadelphia banker, disapproved of her going. He suggested she attend the Academy of Fine Arts in Philadelphia instead. She did, from 1861–1865, but it never satisfied her. She decided to stay with family friends in France, and her father made no objection to a visit. But for Cassatt, it became a lifetime.

Mary Cassatt was privileged not only with a great talent but also with the means to follow the career of her choice, though that was greatly uncommon for women of the time. Cassatt was independently wealthy, so she was able early in life to do things that women normally did not do. She did, in fact, become an important artist and, though alone, she lived far away from her home and family. This was unusual for women of her era, who usually married and raised families. Certainly, Cassatt never had any financial struggles, and her place in society was always secure due to the prominence of her family, so she did not have issues of money and consequence to hinder her, but even so, her choices for the time were rare, and she had her share of struggle making her mark.

Cassatt studied in Italy before making her home in Paris. There she continued to explore impressionism, a style of painting that seeks to show the effects of light on objects. She became very good friends with the noteworthy French Impressionist, Edgar Degas. Like Degas, she began to show the influence of Japanese wood cuts in her art from 1882 onward.

Cassatt is best known for her typical subject matter, mothers and their young children. These subjects were not posed but were shown performing everyday activities, such as in her famous work *The Bath*. The mood of much of her work is serene and quiet. She captures the moments in typical expressionistic style—bright, light colors and sketchy brushstrokes, cleverly depicting what the eye may capture in a glance.

A proponent of the Impressionist movement, Cassat urged American collectors to purchase impressionistic art. She succeeded in her attempts, and she is generally noted as having had influence on the spread and notoriety of the movement.

In 1904 Mary Cassatt was awarded the French Legion of Honor for her work.

Suggested Activities

Career Choices While Cassatt was a single woman, painting with the impressionists, most women of the time married, raised children, and ran their homes. Cassatt's work was not traditional. Ask the students if, today, they could choose their life's career and family circumstances, what they would be. Have them either discuss or write about these hopes and dreams.

Artists Ask the students to create a work of art in honor of both Mary Cassatt and their own families. Each student can draw, color, or paint a picture of himself or herself as a young child with a special person who took care of him or her perhaps him or her mother, father, or grandparent.

Ziegfeld Follies

The year was 1907, and a Chicago-born theater producer developed one of the most enduring pieces of musical theater history. His name was Florenz Ziegfeld, and the show was the *Ziegfeld Follies*.

Ziegfeld was the son of the founder of the Chicago Musical College, so music surrounded him from the time of his birth. He met his wife in 1896 while producing a play, *A Parlor Match*, in which she was featured. The producer later developed several shows that featured his wife, Anna Held. These shows included songs, fine settings, and fancy costumes. They became the forerunner for the soon-to-be *Ziegfeld Follies*.

The Follies ran annually from 1907 through 1927, and Ziegfeld billed them "An American Institution," which indeed they became. They featured a chorus of beautiful women, elaborately costumed in lavish and imaginative settings. The shows were always extravagant and lush, beautiful to behold. Ziegfeld withheld nothing in his productions, spending money freely. In fact, it is said that he was known to discard a set on which he had spent a great deal of money after it had been used in only one performance.

The shows were a treat for the ears as well as the eyes, for Ziegfeld hired such luminary composers as Irving Berlin and Jerome Kern to provide songs. He also hired a number of talented future stars such as W.C. Fields, Will Rogers, Fanny Brice, Eddie Cantor, Paulette Goddard, Marion Davies, and Irene Dunne.

The Ziegfeld Follies began with an elaborate production that celebrated the Gibson Girl (page 54). The producer was always interested in bringing forward lovely women and glorifying in (and capitalizing on) their beauty. Ziegfeld often used the slogan "Glorifying the American Girl." The Ziegfeld girls were slender and graceful, and they became a model for feminine beauty.

There are a number of Hollywood movies from the early years of filmmaking that capture the spirit of *The Follies*, and some like *Funny Girl* (the story of Fanny Brice) tell actual accounts of the Follies and the people who performed in them. (Use your discretion in viewing *Funny Girl* or excerpted scenes as a class.)

Ziegfeld went on to produce other musicals such as *Rio Rita* and *Show Boat*. His marriage ended in divorce, but he married again in 1914 to the actress Billie Burke, best known as Glinda in *The Wizard of Oz*. He died in 1932.

Suggested Activities

History Trace the history of musical theater in the United States and how the *Ziegfeld Follies* have influenced later productions. Also learn about the lives and careers of famous *Follies* performers.

Performance As a class, produce and stage a one-song musical production in the style of the *Ziegfeld Follies*. Design and make elaborate sets and costumes. Include both boys and girls in a dance production. View some old Hollywood films to help give you ideas. The film *Easter Parade* includes a good sequence, and it is acceptable for all age groups.

Ford and the Tin Lizzie

The nineteenth century went out in a horse-drawn carriage; the twentieth century came in on wheels. This was due in large part to the world-renowned automotive tycoon, Henry Ford.

Henry Ford was born in 1863 on a farm in what later became Dearborn, Michigan. In his early years, he was a machinist and an engineer with a growing interest in a new invention called the automobile. In 1893, he built his first successful gasoline engine, and he built his first automobile in 1896. Finally, in 1903, he began the Ford Motor Company.

In the first years of the century, automobiles were made one at a time, with no standard parts. This process made them very expensive. Henry Ford wanted to bring cars to the masses. He decided that "The way to make automobiles is to make them all alike." So he designed a simple and reliable car that many people could afford—the Model T. They were even all the same color, black, and the car's slogan was "Any color you like as long as it's black."

The Model T, or Tin Lizzie as it affectionately came to be known, made its debut in 1908. The following year, Ford turned over his entire business to the production of Model T's.

When Model T's debuted, they cost $825, a reasonable price compared to other automobiles of the time but too high for the average citizen. Ford and his team of executive officers developed a plan by which to lower the cost of production. They determined that if employees in their factories worked on an assembly line, each employee responsible for the same task on each car, they could reduce the time it took to build one car from 12.5 hours to 1.5 hours, multiplying production considerably. This was an incredible savings. Ford passed on the savings to his customers and the increased profits to his employees. The cost of the Model T dropped to $550, $440, $345, and finally, $290 by 1924. This was a price that the average family could afford. Henry Ford also lowered his employees' work day from nine to eight hours and raised their pay to five dollars a day, about double that of workers in other plants. His employees also received part of the company's profits in Ford's profit-sharing plan.

For twenty years, the Model T outsold all other cars. In 1927, the last Model T, number 15,007,003 rolled off the line. The next several decades saw the rise of the General Motors Company, but Ford came back strong in the fifties and sixties under the leadership of Henry Ford's grandson.

In his later years, Henry Ford ran for public office and became involved in several charitable and peace-keeping ventures. Beside the incredible legacy of the Ford Motor Company, he left behind him the restored historical buildings of Greenfield Village and the Henry Ford Museum, which includes exhibits in science, industry, and art. Both sites are in Dearborn.

Suggested Activity

Assembly Lines Choose a project that requires several steps, perhaps an arts and crafts project that involves tracing, coloring, cutting, and gluing. Have each student complete the project. Keep track of the time it takes each one. Then, divide the students into teams, each team having as many members as there are steps in the project. Have them complete the project in assembly line fashion (doing it several times for familiarity), timing them as they go. Compare the time for individual completion as opposed to teamwork. Also compare quality.

Wireless

Guglielmo is a rather unusual name, but Marconi certainly is not when it comes to the world of radio. Guglielmo Marconi was an Italian inventor who sent the first radio signals through the air, and early in the twentieth century, sent those signals all the way across the Atlantic Ocean.

Marconi was born in 1874. He was greatly interested in sound waves, and by the time he was twenty-one years of age, he had sent radio signals through the air instead of through the electric wires previously used in the telegraph system. The inventor used electromagnetic (radio) waves to send the signals, and his system of radio became known as wireless telegraphy.

A great day came in 1901. After effort, trial, and error, Marconi succeeded in sending waves across the

Guglielmo Marconi

Atlantic from Cornwall, England, to Newfoundland, Canada, a distance of more than 2,000 miles (3,300 kilometers). Though faint, the sound Marconi received was audible. This led the way for huge advancements, particularly concerning ships which used his technology to send distress signals when they were sinking or in trouble. Such radio communications also led to the capture and arrest of Dr. Crippen, a murderer, who was escaping aboard a cruise liner. He was the first murderer to be caught via radio while in flight.

Marconi sent his messages in Morse code. In 1906, American physicist Reginald Aubrey Fessenden made the first wireless broadcast of speech and music, paving the way for radio as we know it. Later in the same year, Fessenden pioneered two-way transatlantic wireless telegraphy.

Suggested Activities

Research Research to learn more about the history of radio. If available, bring in samples of radios from previous decades. Learn about the type of transmissions they used and what technological advancements make today's radios so clear and strong.

Listen As a class, listen to a limited number of radio minutes on each of various stations. (Use your own discretion.) Have the students write comparisons of the broadcasts, particularly comparing their worth and cultural, social, and informative value.

Brainstorm Throughout the century, the radio has had many uses. Brainstorm and research as many as the class can name.

Carnegie's Philanthropy

Born in Scotland in 1835, Andrew Carnegie moved with his family to the United States when he was twelve. He taught himself to send telegraph messages, and this led to a position with the Pennsylvania Railroad. Carnegie advanced quickly through the company and with his earnings began to invest in iron.

In his mid-thirties, Carnegie traveled to Europe. It was there he took an interest in steel, and this became the root of his great fortune. Over the years, he built a huge steel company that withstood hard times and competition to be the industry leader. His talents as a salesman and his business savvy grew his company by leaps and bounds. When he decided to sell his company in 1901 to businessman J. P. Morgan for $480 million dollars, he was heralded as the richest man in the world.

After his retirement from the steel industry, Carnegie chose to spend his remaining years working for the common good. Although he did not believe in charity, he did believe that it was essential for wealthy people to help others help

Andrew Carnegie

themselves. He began many such helping organizations and funds for those who worked in education or who worked to help others. It is estimated that he donated approximately $350 million dollars to various causes. Carnegie built the world famous Carnegie Hall in New York City, and perhaps most notably, he was instrumental in the development of more than 2,500 public libraries around the world.

When Carnegie died in 1919, he left behind him a legacy of philanthropy that is seldom matched. He was truly one of the great businessmen and philanthropists of the century.

Suggested Activities

$350 Million Have each student make a list of the ways in which they would spend $350 million dollars on philanthropic causes.

Helping Others Take on a class project that involves helping others to help themselves. This might be tutoring, teaching a skill, or helping a small business get up and running by handling some appropriate tasks.

Carnegie Hall Many performers look to Carnegie Hall as being the ultimate place to perform. Trace its history and the entertainers who have performed there. Ask the students why they think it has come to be so famous.

Mother's Day

At the urging of Anna Jarvis of Grafton, West Virginia, Mother's Day was first celebrated on a large scale on May 10, 1908. Here is its history.

A day called Mothering Sunday originated in England many years ago. It took place in the middle of the Lenten (pre-Easter) season each year. Julia Ward-Lowe, the author of "The Battle Hymn of the Republic" and suffragette, first suggested a Mother's Day in the United States in 1872. She thought the day should be dedicated to the observance of peace. For several years, she held annual observances of the day in Boston, but it did not gain national support. In 1887, a Kentucky teacher named Mary Towles Sasseen began annual Mother's Day celebrations, and in 1904, Frank E. Hering of Indiana did the same. But it was not until three years later that the interest was ignited in Anna Jarvis, and she began a campaign for the

Anna Jarvis

national observance of the holiday. She selected the second Sunday in May for the celebration. In May of 1908, churches in Grafton and Philadelphia began the tradition. A Grafton church devoted its service to the memory of Jarvis' mother, Anna Reeves Jarvis.

The Methodist Episcopalian Church to which Anna Jarvis belonged designated her as the founder of Mother's Day at a conference in 1912, and the conference also adopted her chosen date of the second Sunday in May for the observance. In May of 1914, President Woodrow Wilson signed a resolution recommending that government recognize and observe Mother's Day, and in 1915, it was declared a national holiday.

Anna Jarvis began one more Mother's Day tradition. On the first Mother's Day, she wore a carnation in memory of her mother. Traditionally, people wear colored carnations if their mothers are living and white if they are not.

Suggested Activities

Mothers Have the students write poems, make cards, or create other pieces of art to honor their mothers. Also discuss what it is that makes a good mother. Let the students share all their views.

Children Some students wonder why there is a Mother's Day and a Father's Day but no Children's Day (although some cultures, such as the Japanese, do have such a day). Ask the students to discuss why they think this is. Also have them plan a Children's Day celebration or suggest some possible Children's Day traditions.

Holidays Research to determine the origination of several national holidays. Have the students brainstorm for additional holidays they feel would be worthwhile.

Charles Gibson and His Girls

The pinnacle of feminine style at the turn of the century was the creation of Charles Dana Gibson, and she was called the Gibson Girl. A Gibson Girl is poised, athletic, attractive, and intelligent, and she represents the best of society. Many women of the early twentieth century strove to imitate the Gibson Girl; others merely idolized her.

Gibson himself was an illustrator, born in Roxbury, Massachusetts, who achieved quite an extensive fame through his creation. It is interesting to note that in his early years, this famed illustrator never cared to draw. Scissors were his tool of choice. He would cut silhouettes freehand of every subject from farm animals, to the circus, to the people he knew. Amazingly, he did most of the cutting purely from memory, making entire scenes in one sheet of paper. As a child, Gibson is recorded as having told his mother, "They read such a nice story in the class today. See, I will make you a picture of it."

Charles Gibson is also noteworthy for his hand in the evolution of the bathing suit for women. A popular song of the time, which originated in the Ziegfeld Follies, has the beautiful Gibson Girl singing out,

> *So one day we rose*
>
> *In revolt of long clothes,*
>
> *And presented this tearful petition:*
>
> *Mister Gibson, Mister Gibson!*
>
> *Why can't we take a swim?*
>
> *Gibson complied.*

Suggested Activity

Silhouettes You can cut your own silhouette images, even without the memory and skilled hand of Charles Dana Gibson.

Materials

magazines and newspapers, scissors, black paper, brightly colored or white paper, glue stick

Directions

Look through the magazines and newspapers to find an image that appeals to you with a striking silhouette (outline). Cut around the image. Glue it to the black paper, being sure that the entire surface is fastened down. Cut around the outline of the image. Turn it over. Glue the picture side to a circle or square of the colored or white paper. You now have a silhouette image.

Boer War

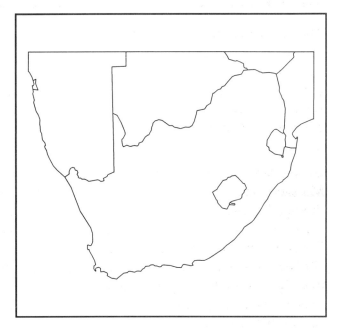

The new century dawned under the cloud of war. Through the latter portion of the nineteenth century, the British had been enlarging their empire, including regions of Africa. However, the Boers (now Afrikaners), primarily farmers of Dutch heritage, of the northern South African regions of the Orange Free State and the South African Republic (later Transvaal), did not want to be under British rule. They also objected to the Uitlanders (foreigners), who were mainly British subjects. The South African Republic had been annexed by Britain in 1877. In 1880 and 1881, the Boers fought for and won independence. This battle is sometimes referred to as the First Boer War.

The turmoil continued a few years later. In 1886, gold was discovered in the Witwatersrand field, and *Uitlanders* rushed to garner some of the wealth. Although the Boers fought politically to keep them out, the Uitlanders continued to battle against them. Peaceful attempts to settle failed, and so the Orange Free State and the South African Republic declared war on Britain in 1899. Interestingly, many Europeans, including some British, opposed British policy in South Africa prior to and during the war.

The beginning of the war was successful for the Boers and they won many battles; however, the war heroes, Lord Roberts and Lord Kitchener, arrived with a number of British troops in 1900 and turned the tide of the war. The Boer Army, under the leadership of General Botha, finally had to surrender in September of 1900. Guerrillas, however, continued to fight, but they, too, surrendered in May of 1902. The Orange Free State and the South African Republic became British colonies, and the Boers swore allegiance to King Edward VII.

The British agreed not to retaliate against or punish the Boers for their actions in the war. The Treaty of Vereeniging was signed on May 31, 1902.

Suggested Activities

Geography Locate the pertinent regions (including Holland) on a current world map. Use atlases and other reference books to document the political changes in the regions from the start of the century to its close.

War Heroes Lord Roberts, Lord Kitchener, and General Louis Botha were all heroes of the Boer War. Learn more about them and discuss their achievements. Hold a class discussion on the question: Who was the greatest soldier?

Empire Determine all the colonies and holdings of the British Empire at the turn of the century. Discuss the justifications (or lack thereof) for the British nation to hold and govern so many countries around the world.

Peary, Henson, and the North Pole

At the start of the twentieth century, the Arctic Circle was largely uncharted, and no known person had travelled to the icy North Pole. Robert Edwin Peary set out to change all that.

In the late 1800s, Peary explored the interior and north of Greenland, proving that Greenland was an island and also making a variety of scientific discoveries about polar areas. These ventures ignited his interest in the Arctic region.

In 1898, Peary attempted to reach the North Pole. He set out in a ship called the *Windward*, and though he was gone for four years, he never reached the pole. Instead, he reached a latitude of 84° 17' 27", which is approximately 390 miles (630 kilometers) south of the North Pole. Although this was a record (no one had ever traveled so far), he had not reached his goal.

A few years later, in 1905, Peary tried once more, this time on the *Roosevelt*. This special ship was designed to sail among floes, which are masses of moving ice. The ship was able to travel as far north as Ellesmere Island. Peary and his crew continued northward on sledges over the icy Arctic Ocean. He and his group reached latitude 87° 6', a distance 200 miles (320 kilometers) south of the pole. Again, he had set a record but missed his goal.

Throughout his expeditions, Peary traveled with another explorer named Matthew Alexander Henson. Henson was part of Peary's team for more than twenty years, acting as chief assistant and dog driver, a vital job in ice and snow-covered areas. Henson was also noteworthy as an African American in an occupation usually reserved for white Americans. He told of his experiences in his 1912 book, *A Black Explorer at the North Pole*.

A third attempt to reach the North Pole began in 1908, and Peary and his party (a group consisting of four Eskimos and Henson) traveled on sledges from Ellesmere Island once more. They were able to reach latitude 89° 57', 3 miles (5 kilometers) from the pole. The group became too tired to continue. They slept for a few hours, and then Peary and two Eskimos (Henson and the other two Eskimos stayed behind) decided to push onward. They crisscrossed the area to be sure they actually stepped foot on the location of the pole. The date was April 6, and Peary had reached the North Pole.

While at the pole, Peary took soundings which proved the Arctic at the pole was not shallow as had been previously believed. He also took photographs. When Peary and his crew returned, others were skeptical. One man, Frederick A. Cook, claimed to have already reached the pole. However, Cook's claims proved false, and the U.S. Congress gave credit to Peary. In 1988, the *National Geographic*, which had helped to support Peary's expedition, had Peary's claims investigated by a British explorer named Wally Herbert. Herbert's investigation raised questions about the validity of Peary's expedition. However, in 1989 a new study was made, concluding that Peary's camp was no further than 5 miles (8 kilometers) from the pole, and that Peary did indeed reach it. Photographs showing the sun's position at the time as well as Peary's ocean soundings helped to support his claim.

Peary was finally vindicated. He died in 1920. Henson lived until 1955.

Suggested Activity

Geography Draw maps of the Arctic area, including latitude lines that show the location of the North Pole.

Boxer Rebellion

Throughout the late 1800s, a movement in China was spreading to destroy Western and Japanese influence in the country. Out of this movement sprang the Boxer Rebellion.

A secret organization called *Yihequan* (Righteous and Harmonious Fists), a group that stemmed from the White Lotus sect, began the movement in opposition to the Manchus, the rulers of China. The organization's members were nicknamed Boxers by the Westerners because of their practice of gymnastics and other calisthenics. By the 1890s, the Boxers had begun to oppose all foreign influence in their homeland. Many Chinese supported these anti-foreign sentiments, and even the Manchus did in secret.

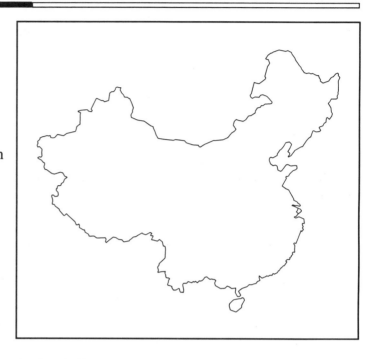

In 1900, the Boxers banned together to wipe out foreign influence in any way they could. They murdered foreigners, missionaries, Chinese Christians, and supporters of foreign ideas, and they burned countless homes, schools, and churches. Foreign diplomats became alarmed at their actions and called for troops to combat the Boxers. At this, the Manchus declared war against all foreign powers. From June 21 to August 14, 1900, Boxers and military troops attacked the residences of foreign diplomats in Beijing. The diplomats, Chinese Christians, and foreign civilians resisted their attacks until a force from eight foreign nations arrived and squelched the uprising.

In the following year, the Manchus and eleven other nations signed a pact called The Boxer Protocol. China agreed to punish and execute several leaders of the uprising as well as to pay approximately $330 million in damages. Some of this money was returned by the United States in 1908 under the condition it would be used for education in China. In later years, Japan and Britain followed America's lead and did the same.

Suggested Activities

Geography Locate China, Japan, Britain, and the United States on a map.

Research Read about the Manchus and their government. Determine what facets of their government troubled the Boxers. Also research to learn about Western influence in China today. A great deal has changed over the course of the twentieth century, and western influence can be seen in many ways around the world.

Discuss The Boxers were greatly opposed to Western influence. Ask the students to discuss why this was so and to share their own feelings and ideas about foreign influence on a nation. Ask them to put themselves in place of the Boxers and others around the world who are angered by foreign influence.

Revolution of 1905

At the turn of the century, Russia was a place of unrest and mounting revolutionary ideas. Marxism was on the rise, and from it sprang a revolutionary leader, Vladimir Ulyanov. Today, the world remembers Ulyanov by the name he took in 1901 to confuse the police: Lenin.

Lenin was a leader in the Russian Social Democratic Party, formed in 1898. The party split in 1903 over membership disputes. The minority, *Mensheviks*, wanted few restrictions on party membership and favored democratic practices. The majority, of which Lenin was the leader, became known as the *Bolsheviks*. They urged limited party membership and rule of the proletariat (workers) by trained professionals.

Lenin

At the time, Tsar Nicholas II was in power in Russia, but there was a growing lack of support for his rule. People wanted more freedom, higher wages, and better representation. On Sunday, January 22, 1905, Father George Gapon, a Russian Orthodox priest, organized a group of 200,000 to make a peaceful march on the Winter Palace in St. Petersburg (later Leningrad, after Lenin). The marchers were unarmed, but government troops were ordered to fire on the crowd. Hundreds were killed or wounded. The conflict became known as Bloody Sunday, and it added fuel to the mounting revolutionary fire.

At the same time, conflict between Russia and Japan was mounting. They both had interest in the same land, particularly Korea and Manchuria. In 1902, England made an alliance with Japan in protest of the Russians. In 1904, Japan attacked a Russian fleet, unprovoked and without warning. They followed this with a declaration of war on Russia. The Japanese led the war, but with the help of American President Theodore Roosevelt, the fighting ceased after a little more than a year. A peace treaty was signed in 1905. The treaty gave the Liaodong Peninsula, Korea, the southern half of Sakhalin Island, and railway rights in Manchuria to Japan. This territory established Japan as a world power.

In Russia, the unrest grew, partly as a result of the Russo-Japanese war. Strikes broke out and military and peasant groups revolted. Nicholas agreed to establish a fully elected lawmaking body, grant the right to vote, establish freedom of speech, and pardon all political exiles, including Lenin, but the protests continued. Lenin returned to Russia in November of 1905 and called for a full revolt. Russia seemed on a course that could not be halted or altered. A mass strike began in December, and soon it developed into full revolution. By the end of the month, the revolution had been crushed, but time would show that the revolution of 1905 was, as Lenin declared, merely a "general rehearsal (for) the victory" of the revolution that was to come.

Suggested Activities

History Follow the path began by the Revolution of 1905, tracing it through the full revolution that brought communism to Russia through most of the twentieth century. Also learn about Lenin's role in the later revolution and what finally became of the Bolshevik leader.

Application and Projection Have the students write about the American Revolution of 1776, altering history to show an American loss. How might that have changed history? What do they think might have happened?

Empress in China

The year 1908 saw the death of one of the most manipulative and cruelest leaders of all time. It is believed by many that she was murdered for her treachery. Her name was Empress Dowager T'zu-hsi (Cixi).

Empress T'zu-hsi

Born in 1835, T'zu-hsi was Emperor Hsien Feng's concubine. She bore him a son, and from this time became his favorite of all the concubines. It is said that as early as 1851, she had effective control of the imperial court. At the Emperor's death in 1862, she stole his royal seal. The seal was required for all documents so that they could be officially signed. Without the seal, members of the court could not take over the monarchy. With the aid of the seal, T'zu-hsi was able to steal the Emperor's royal seat and become Empress herself.

While her son was young, the Empress ruled alone. In 1875, her child died of the smallpox. The Empress appointed her nephew, Kuang Hsu, as the heir, but she continued to rule. When Kuang Hsu was twenty-one and able to rule on his own, she used her influence in court to have him taken prisoner when he tried to make reforms.

At the turn of the century, the Empress was in full support of the Boxer Rebellion (page 57) because she wanted to return China to the days before there was any European influence. Personal control was always her goal. She managed to defeat all attempts at modernization and change throughout her very long rule.

During her time, the Empress was known for her love of the theater. She greatly enjoyed acting in plays, and it was said that she always looked as though she were ready for the stage. Photographs of her show her heavily made up.

When she was an old woman, it became clear that she was going to die. She wished to control China until the very end, and therefore she had Kuang Hsu executed so that he would die before her. She then appointed Pu Yi, who was two years old, as her successor. Pu Yi was the final emperor in China.

Suggested Activities

History Read about the rule of Pu Yi and how the succession of emperors in China came to an end.

Women Although cruel, Empress T'zu-hsi is notable as a woman who ruled in a world largely run by men. Learn about other world leaders who are/were women and the variety of ways in which they have governed.

Writing The Empress' treachery, although heinous, makes for an interesting story. Have the students write short stories or plays that tell of the life of T'zu-hsi.

Pogroms and the Pale of Settlement

When the new century began, anti-Jewish sentiment was well in place. As early as 1871, Russian soldiers, called *Cossacks,* carried out mob attacks in which Jewish homes and businesses were burned and people killed. These attacks were called *pogroms.* It is said that they lasted until 1906, although certainly anti-Jewish behavior did not end with them. The horrors of the coming Holocaust would prove that.

Violence against and oppression of Jews goes back in history for thousands of years. In Europe in the eighteenth century, Jews were not allowed to live in Russia, and, in fact, a Pale of Settlement was drawn, restricting Jews from many other countries as well. The Pale continued to remain in place for many years (laws finally removed it in 1917), and there were even towns within the Pale that did not allow Jews to reside or work there. Often, they were only allowed to hold certain jobs in the places where they did reside. Jews frequently lived in a state of poverty. Violence against them was commonplace. Despite the violence against them, Jewish males were often forced to defend Russia in the service of the Russian army for twenty-five years.

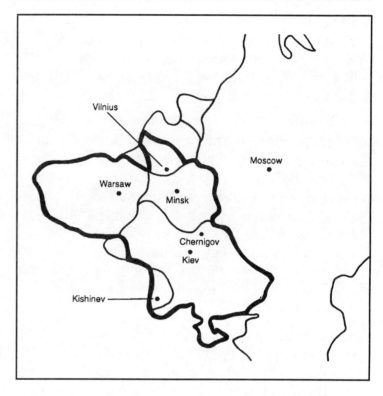

In June of 1906, peasant mobs attacked a Jewish settlement, killing hundreds. The peasants claimed to the police that the Jews had fired on a religious service, killing several children and a priest. The police, without any true investigation, took the side of the peasants. They distributed fliers throughout Russia, declaring that all Jews should be destroyed.

Although there was talk in the Russian legislature of attempting to stop violence against Jews, little was done. Persecution continued almost unchecked. This was perhaps the greatest catalyst for the mass migration of Jews to America in the nineteenth and early twentieth centuries.

Suggested Activities

History Read about and discuss the Holocaust. Use your discretion. There are countless excellent resources available, but some may be too disturbing for your students' age group.

Film The animated movie *An American Tail* illustrates the random and violent action of the Cossacks, although, of course, the film uses cats and mice to depict the Jews and their persecutors. Nonetheless, the film may prove a good resource for discussing and writing about the persecution of the Jews late in the nineteenth century and early in the twentieth. *Schindler's List* is perhaps the finest film on the subject of the Holocaust, but it should only be viewed by mature students and adults. This film is R-rated. Be sure to get school district approval and written parent permission before showing it to students.

Evans and Knossos

British archeologist and numismatist (student of coins and medals) Sir Arthur John Evans was born in Hertfordshire, England, in July of 1851. He received an extensive education and later spent many years in the Balkans studying archeological sites.

In the ensuing years, Evans developed a great interest in the Mycenean culture of ancient Greece. He was convinced that he would find the origins of the civilization on Crete, Greece's largest island. He also believed that the Myceneans had a system of writing that was previously unknown.

Evans began excavations at the site of the Palace of King Minos at Knossos, Crete, in 1908. He uncovered the 3,000 year old palace, believed to be the Labyrinth found in the myth of Theseus. Over the next twenty-five years, he also discovered many beautiful artifacts of the Bronze Age as well as evidence of two pictographic systems of writing. The archeologist's work shed much light on the cultures of the time and place. Evans called this culture Minoan after King Minos. His work demonstrated that Minoan Crete was the center of a sea empire, connected with Tiryns and Mycenae. He also learned that the culture was in regular contact with Egypt and Europe for almost one thousand years. About 1400 B.C. the civilization came to an abrupt end. It is unclear what became of it, although it is known that Romans invaded the island around 66 B.C. and made Crete a province.

The Minoan culture is one of the first European civilizations. It began nearly 5,000 years ago, and Crete was, indeed, its birthplace. The first people came from Asia Minor (now Turkey), and over the course of 3,000 years developed an advanced culture. The Minoan culture made exemplary advances in engineering, architecture, and art.

In 1911, Evans was knighted for the archeological work he had done. He died in 1941.

Suggested Activities

Archeology The science of archeology is painstaking. The work must be done carefully and over a period of time. In order to learn about archeology firsthand, develop a site on which your students can dig. Within the sand or dirt, bury a variety of objects that the students can later uncover. Chart your work carefully! Provide the students with information that will lead them to the site. Allow them to dig just as an archeologist might. If possible, invite an archeologist to be a part of your excavation and to share with the students some archaeologic information.

Cricketeer

If you ask U.S. citizens to name some legendary athletes, they may name Mantle or Aaron, Jordan or Johnson, or countless others, but it would be a rare individual to name Grace. Yet William Gilbert (W.G.) Grace was perhaps the most phenomenal athlete of his time and arguably the most famous man of Victorian England. Due to his excellence, thousands of people flocked to the cricket fields to see the game, just as long as they could see Grace as well.

W.G. Grace was an amateur English cricketeer whose playing career lasted from 1865 to 1908. When he retired in 1908, he had earned nearly 55,000 runs and taken almost 3,000 wickets in first-class cricket. He was still opening batsman for England when he was fifty years old.

Grace was born in Downend, Gloucestershire, England, on July 18, 1848. He always had a love for cricket, so it is no surprise that he spent a lifetime playing it, beginning when he was seventeen and playing until he was sixty. Always an excellent player, Grace's two best seasons came in 1871 and 1876. In 1871, he totaled more than 2,700 runs in 39 innings, becoming the first player to score more than 2,000 in one season. In 1876, he scored 344 runs for Marylebone Cricket Club against Kent, 177 runs for Gloucestershire against Nottinghamshire, and 318 "not out" against Yorkshire, all in consecutive innings. Grace also captained the first English Test Match against Australia in 1880. It was a bittersweet day when this giant of the cricket field retired from the game he had dominated for four decades.

Part of the reason Grace's fame spread, as well as the popularity of cricket, was the fact that railroad travel made it possible for cricket teams to travel easily around the country, allowing many to see them play in person.

Cricket became highly respectable. It came to represent part of the code of honor and respectability cherished by English gentlemen. Not only was it manly, but it was "decent" as well.

W.G. Grace died in 1915 at the age of sixty-seven.

Suggested Activities

Cricket Learn to play the game! Your local library is sure to have one of many books available on the basic tenets of the sport. Learn them as part of your physical education exercises.

Statistics Follow the play of some popular cricketeers today. Keep track of their statistics and use them for mathematical exercises.

Long Live the Queen

It was a long life, indeed, for Queen Victoria who ruled from 1837 until her death on January 22, 1901. Born in 1819, her reign began at the death of William IV. Three years after she was crowned, she married Albert, prince of Saxe-Coburg-Gotha. He lived until 1861. Victoria's name is used to describe the period of time during which she reigned, its characteristics and its attitudes. All of it died with her at the dawning of the twentieth century.

Queen Victoria

At birth, Victoria's arrival was not particularly noteworthy. It was merely a series of deaths and changes that brought her to reign. Yet her reign became one of the longest and most influential in Britain's history. Crowned Queen of England, Ireland, and Empress of India, Victoria dominated the middle and latter nineteenth century. Her reign can be seen roughly in two parts, each approximately thirty years. The first was characterized by a rapid growth in industry, a swelling of the population, the rising of a strong, industrial middle class, and only moderate political reforms. There was prosperity and stability. The nation was complacent, happy in its good fortune. The masses strongly supported national virtues which became linked indelibly with the Victorian Age: industriousness, piety, charity, and moral righteousness. Victorians saw themselves as dramatically improved over their ancestors in intelligence and morality.

The second half of Victoria's reign is characterized by a decline in the birth rate, the threat of mass unemployment, economic crisis, and developments in science that threatened longstanding religious beliefs. Poverty, the plight of the working class, child labor, conflict among the classes—these became the themes of the later years. The literature of Charles Dickens deals extensively with these themes.

Part of the shift in focus during the Victorian Age was due to the publication of Darwin's *Origin of Species*. Religious views were shaken and conflicts arose. Darwin, as well as others, were hurrying the destruction of traditional Victorian values. In addition, the rise in the middle class created even greater tensions and disparity within the working class.

At the death of Victoria in 1901, traditional values were already at a very low ebb. The woman and the age came to a close. A new era was dawning, and rigid morality would have no part in it.

Victoria was succeeded by her son, Edward VII, who ruled throughout the rest of the decade.

Suggested Activities

Reading Lytton Strachey's *Queen Victoria* (Harcourt Brace Jovanovich) was a ground-breaking biography when it was published in 1921. Read excerpts of it to the class.

Also read any number of works that come from the Victorian Age. Dickens' novels are considered by many to be the classic works of Victorian England.

Discussion Lead the class in a discussion of the Victorian Age versus the Golden Age of the twentieth century.

The Commonwealth of Australia

Australia is the only country that is also a continent. Aborigines have been living in Australia for at least 40,000 years, but whites, who comprise most of the population today, first arrived there in 1788 as prisoners exiled to the new colonies owned by Great Britain. Most of these prisoners were debtors and petty criminals.

In the mid-nineteenth century, Australia was explored, and in 1851, gold was discovered. In ten years, the population of 400,000 grew to 1,100,000, the bulk of the rise due to goldseekers who did not find enough gold to earn their passage home. Meanwhile, convicts were still shipped to the colonies until 1868. More than 160,000 convicts were sent in all.

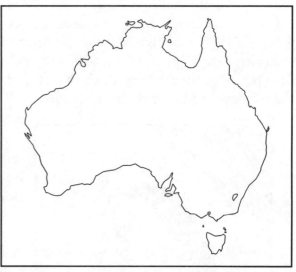

As the population grew, inevitably so did the call for self-government. Britain granted self-government to most colonies but maintained the management of defense and foreign relations. All the colonies were self-governed by 1890.

In the next decade, there was growing support for a union of the colonies. The people felt that they would be better off as a single nation with a unified government so that they could deal with their common problems and help one another. A constitution was drawn up in 1897 and 1898, and in 1898 and 1899 the people approved it. Britain gave its approval in 1900. The colonies became the six states of a new nation on January 1, 1901. The Commonwealth of Australia was born.

Today, Australia is a farming and mining nation with a strong support for the arts. There is a high standard of living for most Australians. Although Australia is the sixth largest country in terms of landmass, it is sparsely populated with an average of six people per square mile (two per square kilometer) and a population of about twenty million. Its climate is dry and sunny with large, open spaces. Much of the population lives along the southeastern coast. Sydney and Melbourne, its two largest cities, can be found there. Canberra, its capital, is slightly inland.

The official language of Australia is English, and its government is a constitutional monarchy. The monarch of England is the head of state.

One of the most famous landmarks of Australia is the Sydney Opera House. One of its most famous personalities is Olivia Newton John, a popular singer of the 1970s and 1980s.

Australia's flag is comprised of the British Union flag, one large star representing the nation's states and territories and five stars depicting the Southern Cross constellation.

Suggested Activities

Cartography Have the students make maps of Australia, showing its states and territories as well as its major geological features.

Favorite Australians Research to find the names and histories of some of Australia's most famous citizens.

Debate Hold a debate on the topic of international relocation for prisoners. Is it justified and humane?

Passages

Births

1900
- Thomas Wolfe, American writer
- Kurt Weill, German composer
- Aaron Copeland, American composer

1901
- Walt Disney, film producer and theme park creator
- Enrico Fermi, Nobel Prize winning physicist

1902
- William Walton, English composer
- John Steinbeck, American novelist

1903
- Evelyn Waugh, English novelist

1904
- Graham Greene, English novelist
- Marlene Dietrich, German-born actress
- Salvador Dali, Spanish painter
- George M. Balanchine, choreographer

1905
- C. P. Snow, English writer

1906
- Samuel Beckett, Irish dramatist
- Greta Garbo, Swedish-born actress

1907
- W. H. Auden, English poet

1908
- Ian Fleming, English author, creator of the character, James Bond

1909
- Robert Helpmann, British-Australia ballet dancer and choreographer

Deaths

1900
- Oscar Wilde, Irish poet, dramatist, and novelist
- Friedrich Nietzsche, German philosopher
- Stephen Crane, American author

1901
- Queen Victoria, British monarch
- Henri Toulouse-Lautrec, artist
- Giuseppe Verdi, Italian composer

1902
- Cecil Rhodes, British financier and originator of the Rhodes scholarship
- Elizabeth Cady Stanton, American suffragette
- Samuel Butler, English author
- Emile Zola, French writer and critic

1903
- King Alexander I and Queen Draga of Serbia
- Pope Leo XIII
- Herbert Spencer, English philosopher
- James Whistler, America painter
- Paul Gauguin, French painter

1904
- Anton Chekhov, Russian playwright and short story writer

1905
- Jules Verne, French author

1906
- P. L. Dunbar, African American poet
- Henrik Ibsen, Norwegian dramatist
- Paul Cezanne, French artist
- Pierre Curie, Nobel prize winning French physicist

1907
- Oscar II, King of Sweden
- Shah of Persia

1908
- King Carlos I, Portuguese monarch
- T'zu-Hsi, Chinese Empress
- Grover Cleveland, former United States President

1909
- Frederick Remington, American artist
- King Leopold II of the Belgians

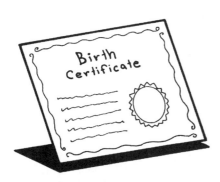

Famous Firsts

In the 1900s, the United States saw the first

. . . American Bowling Club tournament held in Chicago.

. . . coast-to-coast crossing of America by car (65 days).

. . . baseball World Series and home run in a World Series.

. . . subway in New York.

. . . American Olympics at St. Louis.

. . . Davis Cup in tennis.

. . . woman arrested for smoking a cigarette in public.

. . . neon light signs.

. . . Rotary Club organization.

. . . Mother's Day.

. . . daily comic strip.

. . . black world heavyweight boxing champion, Jack Johnson.

. . . baseball season where spitballs were illegal.

. . . manned flight in a heavier-than-air plane.

. . . Model T Ford and vehicle from the newly created General Motors.

. . . American to play cricket for the Gentlemen of England.

. . . permanent waves.

. . . air-conditioned factory.

. . . auto advertisement in a magazine.

. . . postage stamps issued in book form.

. . . car to be driven faster than one mile per minute.

. . . person to go over the Niagara Falls in a barrel.

. . . Tournament of Roses football game in Pasadena, California.

. . . black woman, M.L. Walker, to serve as a bank president.

. . . radio distress signal.

. . . ice cream cones.

. . . forest fire lookout tower and watchman service.

. . . Jewish member of the President's Cabinet, Oscar S. Straus.

. . . black to win a Rhodes scholarship, A.L.R. Locke.

. . . Bibles placed in hotel rooms.

. . . coin with a picture of a president.

. . . movie made in Los Angeles.

. . . electric washing machine marketed.

. . . steam-operated pressing machine.

. . . international woman suffrage association.

Buzzwords

New inventions, habits, lifestyles, and occupations cause people to invent new words. The first decade of the new century was no exception. Listed below are some of the words and phrases that came into popular use throughout the decade.

Airspeed This is the speed of an aircraft determined by its relationship with the air instead of the ground.

Bonehead This expression meant a stupid or ignorant person, someone who has only bone and no brains in his or her head

Borderline This word for boundary or dividing line can also mean a person or thing on the edge.

Boy Scout This name in used for a young individual belonging to a group begun by Robert Baden-Powell, the purpose of which was to teach self-reliance, good citizenship, and outdoor skills.

Buffer Zone This refers to an independent and neutral place, person, or circumstance located between two antagonistic places, people, or circumstances.

Garage This is a shelter or storage facility for an automobile.

Grandfather Clause The Constitutions of some southern states contained a provision intended to prevent blacks from voting. It read "No person shall vote in this state if he is unable to read and write, unless his father or grandfather was a voter before 1867."

Recessive This word means anything that tends to go backward, or recede.

Right Wing This usually refers to extremely conservative political views.

Rip Cord This is a rope fastened to the gas bag of a balloon or dirigible so that pulling it will open the bag, release the gas, and cause descent. It is also a rope used for opening a parachute during descent.

Rocky Mountain Spotted Fever This acute, infectious disease is caused by *Rickettsia* (a microorganism) from ticks found in the area around the Rocky Mountains; it causes pain, fever, and spotty red skin blemishes.

Scrimmage Line This is an imaginary line in football on which the ball sits at the beginning of each play and along which players on both teams line up.

Septic Tank This refers to a tank in which waste matter decomposes through the action of bacteria.

Turtleneck This is a high collar that folds over and fits snugly around the neck.

Wireless This is a telegraph system that sends sound signals by radio waves.

World Power This refers to any nation or organization with enough power to have influence around the world.

World War This term means war among several countries of the world.

Worthwhile This refers to anything valuable or important enough to repay the time, effort, or money spent in obtaining it.

Writing Prompts and Literature Ideas

Writing Prompts Use these suggestions for journal writing or as daily writing exercises. Some research or discussion may be appropriate before assigning a particular topic.

- Write a firsthand narrative as though you are witness to the shooting of President McKinley.
- You are a member of the suffragette movement. Write a speech in support of your cause.
- Queen Liliuokalani of Hawaii saw the end of Hawaii's monarchy. She is also noteworthy as a writer of songs. Write the lyrics to a song in tribute of her or her beautiful land.
- The Teddy bear is named for President Theodore Roosevelt. Invent a toy named after the current president. Describe your toy and create a slogan to sell it.
- Imagine you are your age at the turn of the century, January 1, 1900. Write a diary entry for that day.
- You are playing with your friends in the streets of your Kansas town when you see a tall woman dressed in black and carrying a hatchet march angrily into a local saloon. You hear crashes, bangs, and the sound of glass breaking. You walk to the door to peek inside, and you see that the woman is Carry Nation. Write what you observe.
- You and your family have survived the earthquake and fires in San Francisco in 1906. Tell about your experiences.
- You are a student at Radcliffe College, taking classes with a young blind and deaf woman named Helen Keller. How do you imagine that she is able to study and learn?
- Beatrix Potter gave animals some human characteristics. Write an original tale of an animal that has some human qualities.

Literature Ideas The following books can be used to supplement and enhance the study of the 1900s.

- *The Call of the Wild* by Jack London (1903)

  This is Jack London's timeless novel of Buck, the dog, who is stolen from his comfortable home and finds himself as a sledge dog in the Klondike. Buck must adapt to survive. He does, triumphantly. This novel should be read by students no earlier than upper elementary.

- *The Hound of the Baskervilles* by Sir Arthur Conan Doyle (1902)

  A classic Sherlock Holmes novel, this story will paint a clear and detailed picture of the turn of the century in London. See also other Holmes novels. Please note that the vocabulary is elevated.

- *Peter Pan* by James Barrie (1904)

  One of the first novels for students, this classic book, although fantasy, will provide a sense of time and place at the turn of the century.

- *The Wind in the Willows* by Kenneth Grahame (1908)

  This book of Mr. Toad and his cronies is pure fantasy, but it can be read with an eye for the time since the animal characters have human characteristics and dwell in human-like settings.

- *Anne of Green Gables* by Lucy Maud Montgomery (1908)

  This and the following novels in the Anne series depict the early years of the twentieth century with great skill and clarity. They are "must reads," not only for the time but the endearing character of Anne Shirley. Mark Twain referred to her as the most endearing child character of all time.

- *On the Other Side of the Hill* by Roger Lea MacBride (1995)

  This is the story of Laura Ingalls Wilder's daughter Rose at around the turn of the century while she was a young girl growing up with her parents in the Ozark Mountains.

'Teens Overview

- World War I began as a local war between Austria-Hungary and Serbia. As a result of conflicts in the Balkan states, the rise of nationalism, and a series of international alliances, it rapidly became a general European struggle. Eventually it was a global war involving 32 nations. The 28 nations known as the *Allies and Associated Powers* included Great Britain, France, Russia, Italy, and, eventually, the United States. The Central Powers consisted of Germany, Austria-Hungary, Turkey, and Bulgaria. Acts of heroism and tragedy filled the newspapers daily, and people on the home fronts focussed their energies to "helping the cause" in whatever ways they could.

- Heroes and villains came to the forefront throughout the war and in its aftermath. Frequently mentioned names included Lenin, Rasputin, Mussolini, Lloyd George, Kitchener, Von Hindenburg, Mata Hari, the Kaiser, Tsar Nicholas II, Trotsky, Stalin, the Red Baron, General John J. Pershing, Bernard Baruch, and Herbert Hoover.

- Trenches, tanks, submarines, zeppelins, poison gas, long-range bombers, and fighter planes were used for the first time.

- Power in Europe and Russia shifted dramatically both during the Great War and as a result of its effects. New leaders offered hope to the impoverished and battle-scarred masses.

- Labor disputes continued. A tragic fire at the Triangle Shirtwaist Company killed 146 employees. That and other tragedies built momentum for enhanced labor laws.

- The call for women's rights, especially the vote, grew as the economy at home depended more and more on the work of women while the men were away fighting the war. The end of the decade brought victory to the suffragists.

- President Woodrow Wilson's Fourteen Point plan for peace included the formation of a League of Nations.

- Mexico faced a revolution in an effort to oust its dictator, Porfirio Diaz.

- Inventor Thomas Edison developed talking pictures, which would soon revolutionize the entertainment industry. In Hollywood, California, a film mecca was begun by Cecil B. De Mille. A small group of actors began a new company, United Artists, in order to produce films.

- The Indianapolis Motor Speedway held its first five hundred mile race. The first winner, Ray Harroun, drove at the speed of seventy-five miles per hour.

- In 1913 the Sixteenth Amendment to the U.S. Constitution made income taxes legal. Three months later the Seventeenth Amendment was ratified. It provided for the election of United States senators by direct, popular vote. Prior to this, they had been elected by their state legislatures.

- The Selective Service began its draft of young men for military duty.

- China saw its last emperor and closed the 260-year reign of the Manchu dynasty.

- The new luxury liner, the *Titanic*, struck an iceberg on its maiden voyage and sunk. Nearly 1,600 people drowned due to a shortage of lifeboats on board.

- New Mexico and Arizona joined the United States in 1912.

- Jim Thorpe, a Native American, amazed audiences at the 1912 Olympics. Many considered him the greatest athlete ever. However, he was later stripped of his medals for having played professional baseball for a short period of time.

- The Panama Canal, once considered an impossible venture, was opened in 1913.

- Kindergartens became popular in the United States, and several states added them to their school programs.

- Daylight savings time began in an effort to save electricity to help the war effort.

The Great War

Fought on three continents, the war that lasted from 1914 through 1918 was known simply as the Great War. When a second such war began, its name was then changed to World War I. Below are listed some of the major events of the war that tore nations—and the world—apart.

1911   Germany is growing in power, and the French and the British are alarmed. The Germans send a gunboat to Agadir, Morocco, which is under French protection, resulting in the Agadir Crisis in which France and Germany narrowly avoid a war. France and Great Britain feel certain that Germany is a threat to world peace. Austria-Hungary and Britain increase their respective navies.

Turkish rule over the Balkan states is showing breakdown. Revolt seems certain.

1912   The Balkan states revolt against Turkey.

1913   Having defeated the Turks, the Balkan states begin to fight among themselves. Other nations take sides in their war.

1914   Archduke Francis Ferdinand, heir to the throne of Austria-Hungary, and his wife, Sophie, are assassinated on June 28 while visiting Sarajevo, Bosnia, part of the Austro-Hungarian Empire. The assassin, Gavrilo Princip, is a Serbian. Austria-Hungary blames the Serbians and declares war on them and on Russia, which is fighting in defense of Serbia. Germany joins forces with Austria-Hungary, as does Turkey. The three are the Central Powers. Germans march through Belgium and attempt to take Paris. Belgium joins forces with Serbia, as does Britain which has a treaty with Belgium. Russia, Serbia, France, Belgium, and Britain become the Allies. Germany's Kaiser calls for victory by autumn. The Allies are confident the war will end by Christmas.

Trench warfare is used for the first time in Belgium and France. The Allies halt the Germans at the bloody Battle of the Marne, protecting Paris for the time being. The Russian General Samsonov shoots himself after failing to invade Germany and losing 120,000 men to Germany as prisoners.

On Christmas Day in Ypres, Belgium, soldiers from both sides gather together peacefully talking and sharing cigarettes. By the end of the year, there are hundreds of thousands of casualties.

1915   Germany uses chlorine gas in Ypres, the first time poison gas has been used in war. The Germans wear face masks to protect themselves.

Russia attempts to keep Germany out of Poland. Bulgaria aids Germany, and they overtake Poland, capturing Serbia. The Allies fight to protect the Dardanelles Channel, which is a crucial passageway for the Russians. It is blocked by Turkey. They make several attempts from the Gallipoli Peninsula, but they repeatedly fail and finally withdraw. The Anzacs (Australian and New Zealand Army Corps), who have just joined the war, are particularly noted for their bravery at Gallipoli.

The Great War *(cont.)*

1915 *(cont.)*

A British nurse named Edith Cavell, head of the Brussels School of Nursing, is executed by the Germans for helping British soldiers to escape.

The British liner, the *Lusitania*, the largest passenger ship in the world, is torpedoed by a German U-boat (submarine) off the Irish coast. The ship is unarmed and carries nearly 2,000 passengers and crew members, many of whom die, including nearly 130 Americans. The Germans have orders to stop all supplies from reaching Britain; every ship is suspect. The United States is outraged, and many believe that President Wilson will not be able to keep the United States out of the war, although Germany apologizes for its error.

Italy joins the Allies.

1916

The Battle of Jutland, the only major navy battle of the war, is fought and hundreds die. There is no victor.

France experiences massive casualties at Verdun where Germans use flame throwers and gas shells. Meanwhile, the Allies attack at the Somme, attempting to relieve the soldiers at Verdun. However, nearly two million die.

Lord Kitchener, the British secretary of war, is drowned when his ship hits a mine. Kitchener is famous for his recruiting poster. David Lloyd George replaces Kitchener.

In September, the Allies introduce their new weapon, the tank.

Russia attacks Austria, gaining sixty miles (100 kilometers) and 400,000 prisoners.

President Wilson is reelected under the slogan "He kept us out of the war."

1917

The Russian people, tired of the war, begin to revolt. They blame the tsar for their two million casualties and impoverished conditions at home. V. I. Lenin and the Bolsheviks overtake the government and sign an armistice with Germany. Russia is out of the war.

In April, after three years of attempting to stay out of the war and bring peace to the world, President Wilson and the United States Congress declare war on the Germans. Public opinion is almost completely won over due to an intercepted telegram from the German foreign minister to his ambassador in Mexico. In it, the Germans offer to aid Mexico in recovering its previous holdings, now a part of the United States (Texas, New Mexico, and Arizona). Millions of Americans enlist in the U.S. Army and travel "Over There" to the Western front.

The Italians experience total defeat at Caporetto, where the Germans and Austria-Hungary gain huge areas of land. The surviving Italian soldiers retreat, leaving their weapons behind on the battlefield.

China declares war on Germany and Austria.

Germany creates the Hindenburg Line, a 31-mile (50 kilometer) system of trenches with concrete dugouts, barbed wire, and access to railroads for supplies.

Passchendaele, France, becomes the scene of one of the bloodiest battles in the war. It is fought in constant rain and mud, and the shooting is relentless.

The Red Cross receives the Nobel peace prize for its volunteer work on the battlefields of the world.

The Great War (cont.)

1918   President Wilson outlines Fourteen Points for peace, including the formation of a League of Nations to protect independence for all nations.

In the Spring, the Germans leave the Hindenburg Line to make two offensives. The first is at the Marne, where the Allies once again defend themselves with heavy casualties. At the same time, they battle the other offensive at the Lys River in Belgium. The German general Erich von Ludendorff asks the Kaiser to make peace. Ludendorff is dismissed from his duties.

Thousands of American troops arrive in France. A series of Allied counterattacks result in victories. An Allied war victory seems imminent.

The ace German pilot, the Red Baron, is killed. Allies pay tribute to him and his skill, although he was an enemy.

Hundreds of Germans surrender in the face of intense attacks by Allied planes and tanks.

Turkey is defeated by the British, led by General Edmund Allenby. Lt. Col. T. E. Lawrence has been highly effective in the war against the Turks.

Austria-Hungary becomes a republic and is out of the war.

An epidemic of influenza strikes around the world, causing millions of deaths.

Nicholas, the former tsar of Russia, and his family are executed by the Bolsheviks.

At 11 A.M. on the eleventh day of the eleventh month, an armistice is signed by the Allies and Germany. The four-year war is over. France and Belgium have been nearly destroyed.

The United States comes out of the war with its land intact and its economy strong. It is in a favorable position to become a major world leader. Many European nations are devastated and impoverished.

1919   Terms for peace are agreed upon by the victorious nations at the Palace of Versailles in Paris, France. President Wilson urges the creation of a League of Nations. The German chancellor resigns, refusing to sign the treaty. It calls for Germany to pay 33 million dollars to the Allies in reparations and to reduce its army and arsenal of weapons. On June 28, two German representatives silently enter the Palace and sign the treaty, and still silent, they leave. Germany feels it has been forced to accept unreasonable terms. Poland, a part of Russia for fifty years, is made an independent country by the treaty.

German prisoners of war sink seventy German ships docked at Scapa Flow, Scotland. They say they are under orders never to surrender their warships.

There is a Communist revolt in Germany, but it is squelched.

The Fascist Party is formed by Benito Mussolini in Italy and grows rapidly.

Suggested Activities

Research Have each student research one major event of World War I and present the information he or she finds to the class.

Cartography Draw maps showing European boundaries before World War I and after. Also draw a map of modern-day Europe.

Read and Write Collect firsthand accounts of the war and share them in the class as a reader's theater. Then have the students write their own accounts as though they are soldiers fighting the war or civilians caught in the middle of it.

The Lusitania

On Saturday, May 1, 1915, the British passenger liner, *Lusitania*, set sail from Pier 54 in New York, headed for Liverpool, England. On board were 702 crew members, 1,257 passengers, and the captain, William Thomas Turner. Of the passengers, 159 were Americans and 168 were infants and children.

On board the *Lusitania* was the typical cargo carried on an ocean liner. Since the *Lusitania* was the largest passenger ship in the world, it could carry a great deal. Perhaps that is why it also carried something extra: 4,200 cases of small-caliber cartridges and other munitions.

The trip across the Atlantic was uneventful, despite the fact that New York reporters had called this the "Last Voyage of the *Lusitania*." War had begun nine months ago among Britain, Germany, and many other nations. There were rumors that the Germans, in their new submarines called U-boats (short for *Unterseeboot*), were likely to torpedo any enemy ship. This was, in fact, quite true. German officers had orders to sink all ships because any ship might be carrying supplies to Britain. Even passenger ships might hold food for the soldiers, and the Germans wished to stop any advantage. In the recent weeks, they had torpedoed hundreds of merchant ships in these waters.

On Friday, May 7, the *Lusitania* neared the Irish coast, and everyone was relieved to think they had sailed the ocean without incident. However, it was troubling to discover that the waters were empty. Irish ships were scheduled to escort the *Lusitania* into shore, but they were nowhere to be found. Instead, a torpedo came hurtling through the water, fired from below the surface by a German U-boat. It tore a hole in the *Lusitania*, causing it to list drastically. Many people were killed instantly. Others tried to board and release the lifeboats. The listing ship tipped back and forth, causing the lifeboats to crash against its sides. Hundreds of evacuees were thrown into the water. In eighteen minutes, the *Lusitania*–which was supposed to be unsinkable–had sunk. The captain stayed until the end, eventually clinging to a floating chair for safety. The survivors of the attack held pieces of wood and other buoyant objects to keep themselves afloat. Six of the original forty-eight lifeboats made it safely to the water.

In all, more than 1,200 people died. Children and infants comprised about ten percent of that number, and Americans accounted for 128 of the dead.

President Wilson made a formal protest to the German government, which issued an apology for the error. However, many Americans were outraged, as were nations around the world. The sinking of the *Lusitania* became a rallying cry for troops everywhere, and eventually it became one of the catalysts for America's entry into the Great War.

Suggested Activities

Writing Write a diary account as though you are a passenger on the *Lusitania*. Write another from the perspective of a German crewman on the attacking U-boat.

Liners Learn about the history of passenger ships and the changes made in them from the time of the *Lusitania* to the present.

Discussion Ask the class to discuss the roles of the British and the Germans in the *Lusitania* disaster. Were the Germans, the British, or both in the wrong?

The Last Tsar and the Red Scare

In 1900, the Russian Empire was vast and sprawling, but the empire was a relatively ineffective one. Revolution broke out in 1905 when workers marched to the palace of the tsar in St. Petersburg to ask for reforms. Government troops fired on the unarmed citizens, killing and wounding hundreds. Bloody Sunday, as it was known, became a catalyst for liberal leaders who were gaining in strength. Tsar Nicholas II was forced to create a *Duma*, a fully elected group of lawmakers whose purpose was to advise the tsar. However, civil unrest continued due to such disasters as the Russo-Japanese War of 1905 and a general strike in the same year. Revolutionaries formed a Soviet (council) called the Soviet of Workers' Duties. In response, the tsar gave the Duma power to accept or reject all laws, and this appeased some; however, revolutionary rumblings grew. The Dumas proved ineffective because the tsar would not release much power to them.

Tsar Nicholas II

War was declared on Russia in 1914 by Germany. Russia joined wholly in the battles; however, the war took a grave toll not only on lives but on food, fuel, and housing. Much of the Russian army was untrained, and they questioned the efficacy of the war. Soldiers in the rear did not wish to move to the front, where they would almost certainly be killed. They did not believe in or support the government of the tsar, so they had little motivation as many of the other Allied nations did.

Nicholas was rapidly losing support. At the time, he made a variety of unwise decisions in terms of placements in top positions. Many believe that his ill-judged actions were the result of his association with Grigori Efimovich Rasputin, a "holy man" who, while saving the tsar's son from the effects of hemophilia, grew to have tremendous influence on the tsar and his wife. Rasputin was murdered by a group of nobles in 1916, but the leaders he had influenced the tsar to appoint remained in position. So did national distrust in the tsar.

By 1917, the Russian people had grown sick of the war and the tsar's ineffectiveness. Massive revolution broke out in March. Nicholas ordered the dismantling of the Duma, but it refused and took over temporary control of the government. The tsar abdicated the throne on March 15, and he, his wife, and his entire family of five children, including the *tsarevich* (heir apparent to the throne), were imprisoned.

Revolutionaries continued their battle; however, the effects of World War I had weakened them. A smaller group of revolutionaries became stronger in the face of the national chaos and confusion. In October (November by today's calendar in Russia) 1917, this group, the Bolsheviks, stormed the Winter Palace, headquarters for the temporary government, and they took control. They were directed by V. I. Lenin, who became Russia's new leader. Lenin completely withdrew Russia from World War I, took over Russia's industries, seized most of the nation's farm products, and changed the name of the Labor Party to the Russian Communist Party.

Tsar Nicholas and his family disappeared in Siberia in 1918. It was believed that Bolshevik revolutionaries killed the tsar and his family and secretly buried the bodies.

The Last Tsar and the Red Scare (cont.)

Meanwhile, in the United States in 1919, the "Red Scare" stormed across the nation. On April 28, a package containing a bomb was delivered to the home of Senator Thomas Hartwick, badly injuring his maid. In June, another bomb was sent to Attorney General A. Mitchell Palmer. Panic swept throughout the nation, and 6,000 people (primarily foreigners) were arrested for attempting to overthrow the government. Almost none were convicted. However, suspicion of immigrants who did not speak English–or whose ancestors did not speak English—continued to grow. Individuals with political opinions that differed from the norm were suspected of being Russian spies. They were called "radicals," and they were ostracized.

Civil War continued in Russia from 1918 through 1920 between the Communists and the anti-Communists. The Communists won, and in 1922 they created a new nation, the Union of Soviet Socialist Republics (U.S.S.R.). The U.S.S.R. would remain intact for seventy years until revolution once again brought great change to the area.

Suggested Activities

Research Find out more about the leadership of Tsar Nicholas II and the influence of Rasputin.

Cartography Draw a map of the Russian Empire circa 1900 and another circa 1922. How do they differ? Also draw a modern map of Russia. How is it different still?

Politics and History Report on the political history between the United States and Russia from 1900 to the present. How have diplomatic ties been strained and how have they strengthened?

Prominent People Research the lives of some prominent people involved in the Russian Revolution. Names include V. I. Lenin, Alexander Kerensky, Grigori Rasputin, Tsar Nicholas II, Joseph Stalin, Karl Marx, and others.

A Mystery Anna Anderson, who died in Charlottesville, Virginia, in 1984, claimed for 40 years that she was Nicholas II's youngest daughter, the Grand Duchess Anastasia. In the 1950s, a film, *Anastasia*, starring Ingrid Bergman, told a fictionalized version of this story. In 1989, scientific tests done on remains found in a mass grave in Siberia in 1979 proved them to be those of the tsar, the tsarina, three daughters and four followers. Alexis, heir to the throne, and one daughter, both known to have been in the royal party, were missing. Research Anna Anderson's claims, the reaction of related royalty, and the role of modern science in establishing the truth. Was she really a Romanov? What do you think happened to the children missing from the grave?

Rasputin Rasputin proved hard for the Russians to kill. Three attempts were made until they were finally successful. Find out what they tried and how they eventually did away with the "holy man" whom they believed to be an influence of evil.

Bolsheviks Learn about what the Bolsheviks stood for and the kind of government they were interested in developing.

Revolutions Have the students compare and contrast, either in writing or orally, the American Revolution and the Russian Revolution.

Women Legislators

Nellie Letitia McClung was born in Chatsworth, Ontario, Canada, in 1873. Seven years later, Jeannette Rankin was born near Missoula, Montana. Neither woman knew the other during her lifetime; however, they were separately fighting similar battles in their neighboring nations.

Nellie McClung was a leading political reformer in Canada in the early twentieth century. In 1912, she helped to form the Winnipeg Political Equality League, founded to help win suffrage for women. In 1916, the League proved successful, and the right to vote was granted to the women of Manitoba (the province in which Winnipeg is located). Two years later, all of Canada's women had the right to vote.

McClung also served on the legislature of the province of Alberta from 1921 to 1926. In 1927, she and four other women fought a groundbreaking battle in court over whether or not women were considered "persons" under the British North America Act, Canada's Constitution of the time. They won their case in 1929, allowing women in Canada to serve on the nation's Senate. McClung was truly a legislative reformer.

Nellie Letitia McClung

Jeannette Rankin

Another such reformer was Jeannette Rankin who, at the same time as McClung, was fighting a legislative battle in America. Also like McClung, Rankin won. In 1914, Rankin led a campaign in her home state of Montana to give women the vote. She was victorious. Her campaign included riding back and forth across her state on horseback, talking to as many people as she could. In 1916, she was elected by the people of Montana to serve in the United States House of Representatives as a congresswoman at large. As such, she became the first woman elected to the United States Congress. In 1940, Rankin was again elected to the House of Representatives for a single term. While in Congress, she voted against United States participation in World War I, and she was the only member of the House to vote against U.S. participation in World War II. In her later years, Rankin opposed U.S. participation in the Korean War and the Vietnam War.

Nellie McClung died in 1951, and Jeannette Rankin died in 1973. However, the memorable legacies of the two women live on.

Suggested Activities

Women in Politics Learn about other notable women in U.S. and Canadian politics. What have been their contributions? Pay particular attention to the women serving today.

Suffrage Trace the histories of suffrage for women around the world. How have the battles differed and how have they been the same? What people—men and women—helped to bring the right to vote for women?

William Howard Taft

27th President, 1909–1913

Vice President: James S. Sherman
Born: September 15, 1857, in Cincinnati, Ohio
Died: March 8, 1930
Party: Republican
Parents: Alphonso Taft, Louise Maria Torrey
First Lady: Helen Herron
Children: Robert, Helen, Charles
Nickname: Big Bill
Education: Yale College and Cincinnati Law School
Famous Firsts:

- Taft was the first president to serve on the Supreme Court.
- He was the first to protect federal lands on which oil had been found.
- He bought the first cars used at the White House, and he built the first garage for their storage.
- Taft was the first president to throw out the first ball on the opening day of the baseball season.
- Always large, Taft was the heaviest president ever, weighing 332 pounds at his inauguration.
- Under President McKinley's appointment, he became the first commissioner of the Philippines, a holding the United States won from Spain in 1900.
- He was the first president to be buried at Arlington National Cemetery. The only other president buried there is John F. Kennedy.

Achievements:

- He took steps toward establishing a federal budget by having his cabinet members submit reports of their needs. It was estimated that he saved the nation $42 million in 1910.
- Taft actualized many of Roosevelt's programs by working them into law during his presidency.
- He was very successful in protecting federal lands set aside for conservation. In fact, he was even more successful than Teddy Roosevelt, whose name is usually linked with conservation.
- Taft oversaw twice as many prosecutions under the Sherman Anti-Trust Act as did Roosevelt. Most impressively, Taft succeeded in breaking up the Standard Oil Company monopoly.
- The Sixteenth and Seventeenth Amendments were passed while Taft was in office.
- New Mexico and Arizona became states during his presidency.
- After the presidency, Taft became a law professor at Yale, the president of the American Bar Association, chairman of the National War Labor Board, and Chief Justice of the United States.

Interesting Facts:

- Taft never really wanted to be president. His desire was to serve on the Supreme Court.
- Due to Taft's size, a new bathtub had to be placed in the White House. It could hold four adults.
- Taft was often criticized for playing golf, a rich man's game. However, he played while conducting business with important leaders, a fact that the newspapers never reported.
- The president was most criticized because of his differences with Teddy Roosevelt. Although Roosevelt had handpicked Taft as his successor, he later changed his mind when he saw that Taft was more conservative than he liked. Taft had also changed members of Roosevelt's old cabinet, although Roosevelt had promised them they could keep their positions. Taft was deeply hurt by Roosevelt's rejection. Roosevelt had been his mentor. The strife between the two split the Republican party, and made the way easier for a Democratic president in the next election.

Woodrow Wilson

28th President, 1913–1921

Vice President: Thomas R. Marshall

Born: December 29, 1856, in Stanton, Virginia

Died: February 23, 1924

Party: Democrat

Parents: Joseph Ruggles, Jessie Janet Woodrow

First Ladies: Ellen Louise Axson, Edith Bolling Galt

Children: Margaret, Jessie, Eleanor

Nickname: Professor

Education: Ph.D.

Famous Firsts:

- Wilson was the first president to hold a press conference.
- He was the most educated president and the first with a Ph.D.
- Wilson was the first president to travel to Europe.
- He was the first to be widowed and to marry while in office.

Achievements:

- With the ratification of the Sixteenth Amendment, income tax became legal. The Federal Reserve Act was instituted; this agency controlled the money supply.
- In 1917, he was forced to declare war against Germany. For three years, he had been able to maintain U.S. neutrality in the Great War.
- On January 8, 1918, Wilson presented his Fourteen Points for Peace.
- He negotiated the Treaty of Versailles, which also established the League of Nations.
- For his work in ending World War I, Wilson was awarded the Nobel peace prize.

Interesting Facts:

- After suffering a stroke, Wilson allowed his wife to handle lesser government details. She decided which matters were important enough to bring to his attention.
- Wilson typed his own letters on a typewriter that could type in either English or Greek.
- He did not have an inaugural ball because he considered them to be frivolous.
- Wilson's second wife, Edith, was a descendent of Pocahontas.
- Two of Wilson's three daughters were married at the White House.
- The Wilsons kept a flock of sheep on the White House lawn to keep the grass trimmed. After the lambs' wool was sheared, it was sold, and the money was donated to the Red Cross.
- Edith Wilson spent a great deal of time sewing for the Red Cross during the time that the United States fought in World War I.

Fourteen Points

On January 8, 1918, President Woodrow Wilson made a speech to Congress. In it, he outlined fourteen points for peace and prosperity in the world after the war. The son of a Presbyterian minister, Wilson often took a moral stance in his politics, believing the role of the president was to lead the moral direction of the nation. Wilson's plan, which was called the *Fourteen Points*, was part of his overall plan to do just that.

Wilson also wished to build the morale of the Allies, weary and embittered from the long war. The Central Powers likewise needed to be appeased and assured of just treatment despite their losses. In presenting his ideas, Wilson said, "We demand that the world be made fit and safe to live in . . . against force and selfish aggression. The program of the world's peace is our only program." He also declared that the *Fourteen Points* were "the moral climax of the final war for liberty."

The *Fourteen Points* that Wilson outlined are as follows:

1. No secret diplomacy
2. Freedom of the seas in both peace and war
3. Removal of international barriers to trade; international establishment of equal trade conditions
4. Arms reductions around the world
5. Impartial adjustment of all colonial claims
6. No foreign interference in Russian affairs
7. Complete Belgian sovereignty
8. Alsace-Lorraine returned to France
9. Equitable redrawing of Italian boundaries for all internal nationalities
10. Autonomous development in Austro-Hungary of all internal nationalities (self-determination)
11. Serbian access to the sea; restoration of the Balkan nations
12. Sovereignty for the Turkish parts of the Ottoman Empire
13. Independence for Poland and access to the sea
14. Formation of an independent body of arbitration or League of Nations (see page 80)

On the night of October 3, 1918, after their massive offensive had failed, the Germans sent a note to President Wilson. In it, they called for a truce and negotiations based on Wilson's *Fourteen Points*.

When he made his proposal to Congress, Wilson did not offer any details about how to make the plan work; nonetheless, he received enormous public support for his ideas. However, the council at the Paris Peace Conference of 1919 did present a great deal of opposition. Wilson was forced to modify his ideas and to make compromises while negotiating the peace treaties.

The League of Nations

The final point of President Wilson's fourteen point plan was the formation of a League of Nations. In Paris, Wilson outlined a plan for the League. He said that it would be an international organization, the purpose of which was to preserve peace throughout the world. Every nation in the world would be a member, and each nation would have an equal vote. Any controversy within the League would be turned over to the Central Council. The Council would consist of France, Britain, Italy, Japan, the United States, and five small nations. It would serve as arbiter to these controversies, and it would propose peaceful and fair solutions. Any nations which refused to accept the decision of the Council would suffer economic sanctions and, perhaps, joint military action. Wilson told the Allies that peace depended "upon one great force . . . the moral force of the public opinion of the world."

After great debate, the diplomats agreed to the tenets of the treaty, accepting the League of Nations. Wilson returned to the United States after negotiating the treaty in Europe for six months. Meanwhile, his health had begin to fail him, and his control over the United States government had diminished during his long absence. Upon his return, he discovered that Congressional response to the tenets of the treaty was not altogether favorable. A group of thirty-nine Republican senators led by Henry Cabot Lodge opposed the League of Nations, citing several flaws in its structure. These flaws included the lack of procedures for members to withdraw from the League, the failure of the League to recognize the Monroe Doctrine, and the ability of the Central Council to disregard the internal affairs of a nation when it makes a decision regarding it.

Wilson and the Republicans were at odds. For the president, the League of Nations was the most important component of the treaty. However, the Senators in opposition believed that the United States should remain "isolationist," staying out of international affairs. They wanted the League of Nations dropped from the treaty.

Wilson went on a national campaign to garner support for the League. However, after three weeks of exhaustive traveling and speaking, he physically broke down. Upon his return to Washington, he suffered a stroke as well. While he was recuperating, he refused to renegotiate the treaty. The Senate defeated it in March of 1920.

Of course, the Allies had already agreed to the treaty, and the League went on without the United States, although not so soundly. The terms of the treaty, however, were never acceptable to the Germans, and the vast economic burdens placed on the nation gave way for the rise of another revolutionary, Adolf Hitler, just a short time later. The ineffective League of Nations would be powerless to stop the growing crisis, and Wilson's Fourteen Points were all but wasted.

Suggested Activities

History Find out what happened to the League of Nations in the years following the Treaty of Versailles. Also, research the United Nations and its relationship to the League.

The First Lady During the end of his presidency, Wilson's wife, Edith, managed a number of his affairs, deciding for herself which matters needed to be brought before the president. Find out more about her role during this critical period in U.S. history.

Election Facts and Figures

	Election of 1908	Election of 1912	Election of 1916
Democrats	William Jennings Bryan of Nebraska made his third attempt at the presidency under the Democratic ticket. John W. Kern, a Democratic leader from Indiana, was his running mate.	Governor Woodrow Wilson of New Jersey was the nominee and Governor Thomas R. Marshall of Indiana was his running mate.	Wilson was easily renominated with Marshall at his side.
Republicans	William Howard Taft was Theodore Roosevelt's choice for his successor. James S. Sherman, a Congressman from New York, was his running mate.	Former President Roosevelt, decided to run again. His opposition to Taft split the party, but Taft got the nomination.	Justice Charles Evans Hughes of the Supreme Court became the nominee.
Other		Roosevelt ran under the Progressive "Bullmoose" Party with Senator Hiram W. Johnson of California.	
Issues	Government corruption and unfair business practices were major issues. Bryan was a supporter of income tax, prohibition, and women's suffrage. All his causes eventually became law.	Checks on big business, honest government, conservation, and social justice were the issues.	The Great War, child labor, laws for workers, and women's suffrage were the issues.
Slogans	Taft campaigned as "Bill."	"New Nationalism" was a phrase coined by Roosevelt to represent the issues. He also talked about giving everyone a "Square Deal." Wilson's platform was called the "New Freedom."	Wilson's campaign slogan was "He kept us out of war."
Results	Taft took 321 electoral votes to Bryan's 162.	The split in the Republican party helped to bring about a Democratic win, Wilson took 435 electoral votes, Roosevelt took 88, and the incumbent president, Taft, took only 8.	Wilson won, but narrowly. Had California voted Republican, Hughes would have been elected. The final electoral vote was Wilson 277, Hughes 254.

Triangle Shirtwaist Company

Immigration reached its peak in the first twenty years of the century. In that time, countless immigrants took low paying jobs with poor working conditions simply to make money to survive. They had no other choice. However, workers were becoming increasingly vocal about the work environment and low wages, and strikes were commonplace—although controversial—occurrences.

In February of 1910, the employees of 13 firms in New York City held a strike for better conditions. The strike proved unsuccessful, and the demands were denied. One of these firms was the Triangle Shirtwaist Company on Greene Street.

March 25, 1911, was payday at Triangle, and it was almost quitting time. On the tenth floor, paychecks had been distributed to the many workers, most of whom were Jewish and Italian immigrant girls. Suddenly and without warning, a raging fire broke out and swept through the floor. The one available escape route could not possibly let all the employees pass. Very few escaped. The others either burned or leapt to their deaths out the tenth-floor window, still clutching their paychecks. In all, 146 young girls and women died.

Although the building was proclaimed to be fireproof by the city fire inspectors, it had no sprinkler system and only one exit. A second exit was bolted shut. According to the surviving workers, the second door was fastened to keep employees from stealing spools of thread. However, due to the recent strikes and labor unrest, it was believed by many that the door was bolted to keep outside labor agitators from getting inside to incite the workers.

The tragedy at Triangle drew the attention of the nation, horrified at the needless deaths. News of the fire also brought to light much of the poor conditions under which the girls had worked. Therefore, the lives of the girls were not lost in vain, because their tragedy helped the momentum for improved labor laws and working conditions.

Suggested Activities

Sweat Shops The Triangle Shirtwaist Company was one of many sweat shops in big cities such as New York. Find out more about sweat shops and the working conditions there.

Immigration New York was a center for immigration throughout the late nineteenth and early twentieth centuries. Learn more about the patterns of immigration at the time, where people came from, and why them came to America. This research should lead to an understanding of why many were willing to tolerate the poor working conditions of sweat shops and other businesses.

Labor Reform

The 1910s were important times for laborers who were fighting for improved labor practices, including working conditions, wages, workday length, and the limiting of child labor. A number of unions and labor leaders came to the forefront, and labor was an important issue during every presidential campaign. Here are some of the major labor-related events of the 1910s.

1910   Frederick W. Taylor, the self-proclaimed "father of scientific management," put forth a scientific approach to work. Taylor observed workers everywhere and outlined for businesses precise ways to curb "excess" time. Businesses hailed the engineer; laborers condemned him.

1912   Fifty thousand workers in the textile mill industry of Lawrence, Massachusetts, began to strike in January. The strikers, who represented twenty-eight nationalities, were seeking increased wages. When legislation reduced the work week to 54 hours from 56 for women and children, the woolen and cotton mill workers saw their paychecks cut. During the strike, which sometimes turned violent, two workers were killed. Business leaders blamed the strike on civil unrest in foreign nations. The strikers were backed by the Industrial Workers of the World, a powerful labor union.

1913   A New Jersey strike was lost by the Industrial Workers of the World after the arrest of many strikers, which broke the workers' morale.
Striking mine workers in Ludlow, Colorado, were killed by National Guardsmen who said they were simply trying to restore order in the face of near anarchy. The dead included three men, two women, and thirteen children.
A battle over labor in Butte, Montana, ended with the complete dismantling of the thirty-six year old union, the Western Federation of Miners local. The Union lost support when it failed to protect hundreds of fired workers. The state militia was required to keep the peace in Butte.

1914   With the new Clayton Antitrust Act, Congress gave organized labor the right to strike, to boycott, and to picket peacefully. Prior to this time, unions could be prosecuted for striking. The act also outlawed a number of corrupt business practices.

1916   In 1916, there were 1.8 million child laborers in the United States. The Keating-Owen Act, a federal child labor law, was passed in that year, banning interstate commerce of products made by children under fourteen years of age. Also, children under age sixteen were banned from working in mines, working at night, and working more than eight hours per day. Southerners in the cotton-producing states were the most opposed to this new legislation.

1918   One million women were working in factories due to the war overseas in which millions of men were fighting. However, many labor unions would not accept the women or help them to receive fair treatment. The women were universally paid less than the men had been.

1919   Three hundred fifty thousand steel workers held a strike for three months. The strike was often violent and resulted in twenty deaths. The workers demanded union recognition, an eight-hour work day, and the end of 24-hour shifts. Though their efforts failed, their solidarity helped to strengthen organized labor everywhere.
An International Labor Conference in Washington endorsed an eight-hour work day.

—— Suggested Activities ——

People Mary Harris "Mother" Jones, William "Big Bill" Haywood, William Z. Foster, Blackie Ford, and Joseph Ettor were just some of the important labor leaders of the time. Eugene Debs was also noteworthy as a socialist and supporter of the working class individual. Find out about these labor leaders, what they did, and why labor laws were so important to them.
Today Follow a current strike or boycott. Report to the class on the details and results.

Selective Service

When war in Europe broke out, the people in the United States strongly supported the Allies (although many immigrants of German descent stood in favor of the Central Powers). The U.S. government felt secure that, should they join the war, millions of young men would voluntarily enlist. There was a common belief at the time that dying for one's country was a noble and valiant thing.

The United States managed to retain a neutral position in the war for three years, but growing hostilities and antagonism drove the United States to declare war in 1917. Immediately, millions of men enlisted. Patriotism, the threat of German victory, and Uncle Sam all persuaded them to fight. As President Wilson said, "The world must be made safe for democracy," and the young men agreed.

Around the nation, recruiting posters could be seen, bearing the now famous image of Uncle Sam calling for American support. An artist named James Montgomery Flagg painted the image. The Army added the words "I Want You for (the) U.S. Army." Millions answered the call.

The president and the secretary of war, Newton D. Baker, felt confident that these recruitment tactics would be enough to build a strong army. Others believed that the numbers of enlisted men would need to be supplemented with draftees. The draft is a process of selecting individuals for military service. Certain individuals are excluded for health and other reasons. Those that are acceptable are chosen in random fashion. They must then join the armed services, regardless of their desire to do so.

Throughout the length of the Great War, Americans debated the value of the draft. Many believed that it was the best way to strengthen the military. Others felt that individual free choice should never be taken away, and they opposed it for humanitarian reasons. Their critics said that racism was really the only reason the opponents of the draft did not want it since they would have to fight alongside members of races whom they did not like.

In February of 1917, President Wilson and Mr. Baker reversed their positions on the draft. They authorized the Selective Service Act, a bill mandating draft registration for every young man of suitable age. Congress then approved the act and made it law. The Selective Service System, headed by Provost Marshal General Enoch H. Crowder, was now in effect.

Suggested Activities

Drawing Have the students design and draw recruiting posters.

Discussion As a class, discuss the draft and students opinions of it.

The Unsinkable Titanic

In April of 1912, approximately 2,200 passengers and crew members boarded the *Titanic*, a new luxury liner ready for its maiden voyage. The *Titanic* had the best of everything, and only the elite could afford passage. Some even paid more than $4,000 for the trip, while many of the crew did not even earn $1,000 in a year. The ship's promoters claimed that their vessel was unsinkable, primarily because its hull had sixteen watertight compartments. Even if two compartments flooded, the ship would still float. Everyone had complete confidence in the boat.

A number of famous people were on board, including millionaire John Jacob Astor and his wife, as well as Isidor and Ida Straus, the wealthy department store owners. In general, the passengers had complete confidence in the ship because the best design and latest technology was at their fingertips.

Late on the night of April 14, the *Titanic* was sailing in the North Atlantic Ocean on its trip from Southampton, England, to New York City. The ship was traveling at a speed of twenty-one knots (nautical miles per hour), which was nearly top speed. Since there was danger of icebergs in the area, the ship's speed was far too fast. At 11:40 P.M., the *Titanic* rubbed alongside an iceberg for approximately ten seconds. That was enough. The hull of the ship was made of a type of steel that became brittle in the icy waters of the North Atlantic. Several small cracks appeared instantly, and seams unriveted. Water started to pour inside, weakening the hull still further.

Six distress signals were sent out immediately. Another passenger ship, the *California*, was just twenty minutes away at the time; however, its radio operator was not on duty, so no one there heard the *Titanic's* signal. Another ship, the *Carpathia*, was approximately four hours away, and it responded to the signal. However, when the *Carpathia* arrived at 4:00 A.M., it was too late for many of the passengers. The *Titanic* had long since sunk. Just after 2:00 A.M., water had flooded through the hull to the ship's bow, causing the entire vessel to split in two.

At first, the passengers aboard the ship were calm, expecting to reach lifeboats with ease and then be rescued by other ships. They did not know that the *Titanic's* lifeboats only had room for approximately 1,200 people, far less than the number of people on board. When the passengers and crew saw how dire the situation was, many stepped aside for younger passengers to board lifeboats safely. Among these heroes were the Astors and Strauses. Captain Edward J. Smith went down with his ship. In all, 705 people survived the wreck, most of them women and children. The remaining 1,517 died in the icy waters of the North Atlantic Ocean.

When the ship was first endangered, the band on board began to play a ragtime melody to encourage the passengers. As time passed and the situation grew grim, they continued to play, but this time it was an old English hymn calling for mercy and compassion from God.

In 1985, a team of scientists found the wreckage of the *Titanic* 12,500 feet (3,800 meters) beneath the sea. Although people had previously thought that a large gash was immediately ripped in the boat because of the iceberg, the scientists were able to prove that the steel composition of the hull was truly the fatal flaw as was the speed at which the boat was traveling.

Suggested Activities

Read Find reports of the studies made from the 1985 expedition. What did they reveal about the ship and its passengers? What did the scientists do to find the wreck?

Writing Imagine you are a *Titanic* survivor, floating away on a lifeboat while hundreds of others are struggling in the freezing water. Write what you think and experience.

Kindergartens

Kindergarten means "children's garden" in German. Friedrich Frobel established the first kindergarten in Blankenburg, Germany in 1837. His purpose was to support young children in developing freely, and he wanted to teach them about the nature of God. One of Frobel's pupils, Margaretha Meyer Schurz, began the first American kindergarten. Word of mouth spread the popularity of her school. Public kindergartens began to appear in the United States and Canada in the 1870s, and their purpose was primarily educational. Slowly the movement grew.

By the turn of the century, kindergartens could be found in most large cities. However, it was not until the second decade of the new century that they spread like wildfire. Suddenly, kindergartens were everywhere, and they were extremely popular. Had their popularity diminished, they would today be called a fad of the 1910s.

Suggested Activity

Investigation Arrange to visit a modern kindergarten. While there, observe what you see and answer the questions below. Then, research to find answers to the same questions for a kindergarten circa 1915. How do the modern and earlier kindergartens compare?

	Modern	**Earlier**
How many children are in the class?		
How many teachers are there?		
What are the main activities the children do?		
Using your best reasoning, what is the purpose of this kindergarten?		

Hooray for Hollywood

Today Hollywood is renowned as the movie-making capital of the world, but that was not always the case. It had to begin somewhere-or with someone. That someone was Cecil B. De Mille.

The Nestor Company built the first film studio in Hollywood in 1911, but it was De Mille who brought the area notoriety and made it the film center. When sent to produce *The Squaw Man* in Flagstaff, Arizona, De Mille promptly turned away from the flatlands of Arizona and headed for sunny California. Hollywood was a prime location with its mild climate and close proximity to a variety of natural settings. It was small and quiet, a country town surrounded by lemon groves. De Mille rented a barn in Hollywood and began his project.

The director's experiences while making the film could have made a film themselves. Someone sabotaged his first negative, he was shot at twice, and he had to sleep in the barn–with the owner's horses–in order to protect himself and his remaining negative. De Mille also went overboard on his budget, tripling the scheduled cost. When the film was finally shown, it was wrongly perforated and needed to be redone. However, after all the trouble and turmoil of creating that one, simple movie, De Mille found himself with a hit on his hands–the first hit that Hollywood had ever made.

Other producers and directors flocked to Hollywood to take advantage of the location. So many came, in fact, that by 1914, some boarding houses hung signs that read: "No dogs, no actors." Nonetheless, the number of movie people coming to Hollywood grew so rapidly that soon it became the movie capital that we know today.

A small group of actors and a director were also influential in beginning Hollywood's movie fame. They called themselves the United Artists. The United Artists was a movie-making organization begun in 1919 by the actors Charlie Chaplin, Douglas Fairbanks, Sr., and Mary Pickford, as well as the director D.W. Griffith. They started the company in order to have greater creative control in the movies they made. Chaplin was known as the Little Tramp, and he was a Hollywood favorite by this time (page 137). Fairbanks made his film debut in 1915, but became a Hollywood staple in the 1920s. Mary Pickford and Fairbanks married in 1920, and she was already a star known as "America's Sweetheart" (page 97). Griffith was highly influential in turning filmmaking into an art form. The film production strategies he developed from 1908 to 1912 became the basis for moviemaking. From 1913 on, he was an influential Hollywood director.

By 1916, fifty-two companies were headquartered in Hollywood. In just six years, the once little country town became the movie mecca of the world.

Suggested Activities

Movies Trace the history of the movies. Have the students report on famous movie stars, influential business leaders, moviemaking awards, and the technical aspects of film production.

People Learn more about the lives of De Mille, Chaplin, Fairbanks, Pickford, and Griffith.

Industry The city of Hollywood—which is actually a district of Los Angeles—became the center of the moviemaking industry. Have the class brainstorm and research to find other towns that are central to other industries.

The Black Sox

It was a dark time for baseball in 1919. The greatest team in the nation, the Chicago White Sox, was involved in a scandal from which it would take the team and the sport years to recover.

The White Sox team of 1919 was one of the best ever. Eddie Cicotte and Claude "Lefty" Williams were extraordinary pitchers who threw like lighting. Joseph Jefferson Jackson, nicknamed "Shoeless Joe" because he once played without shoes rather than wear a new pair which had given him blisters, had a lifetime batting average of .356, the third highest in baseball history. The team easily took the American League pennant, and they were shoo-ins to win the World Series. Instead, they lost, and one year later, eight players on the team were permanently barred from baseball. Here is what happened.

The White Sox and the Cincinnati Reds faced off in game one of the Series. Just as play began, rumors started to spread that the White Sox were planning to throw the series, meaning they were intentionally going to lose. Cicotte did, in fact, lose the opening game with a score of 9–1. During the second game, he committed two errors in one inning, which was unheard of for the always skilled and precise player. Again, the Reds won, 2-0. The next three games were lost under the pitching of Williams. (At that time, the World Series was won with five victories instead of today's four.) The fans were stunned. They could not believe the series had actually been lost. The White Sox pitchers were the best in the game.

For the next several months, there were many rumors that the players on the team had accepted bribes from gamblers in exchange for losing the Series. If the gamblers could be certain of the White Sox's loss, they could clean up by betting for the underdogs, the Cincinnati Reds.

One year later, eight team members were arrested: Cicotte, Williams, Gandil, Jackson, Happy Felsch, Swede Risberg, Fred McMullin, and Buck Weaver. According to the indictment, first baseman Chick Gandil took money from gamblers and passed it among the other players on the team. Reporters started referring to the team as the Black Sox. Fans were heartbroken, and they did not want to believe it was true. A story was circulated at the time that as Joe Jackson left the Chicago Courthouse he was stopped by a young boy who tugged on Jackson's sleeve, looked up with tears in his eyes and said, "Say it ain't so, Joe."

Although a jury in the civil trial aquitted the eight players, baseball commissioner Kenesaw Mountain Landis permanently barred them from professional baseball. The White Sox would not win another pennant for forty years. Perhaps it took that long to live down the legacy of the scandal.

Suggested Activities

Skits In small groups, have the students write skits enacting different scenes from the White Sox scandal. They can perform their skits for one another.

Play Ball During physical education time, learn the basics of baseball and play a game.

Debate When Shoeless Joe died in 1951, his dying words were: "I don't deserve this thing that's happened to me. I'm going to meet the greatest umpire of all—and he knows I'm innocent. . . . Goodbye, good buddy." Jackson never asked to be reinstated in baseball. There are those who believe that because of his lifetime batting record, he should be entered in Baseball's Hall of Fame. Form sides to debate the question. Research to learn what needs to be done to clear the name of Shoeless Joe.

Jack Johnson and the Great White Hope

Teacher Note: The subject matter of this story in history is controversial and likely to spark some heated discussion. Use your own discretion.

One of the great athletes of the early twentieth century was the champion boxer, Jack Johnson. Johnson is also noteworthy as a groundbreaker in the sport, and, indeed, in American society.

On December 26, 1908, a fight took place in Sydney, Australia, between the current world heavyweight boxing champion, Tommy Burns, a white man, and an up-and-coming boxer, Jack Johnson, who was black. White fans were stunned when Johnson won the match. Racism was strong at the time, and many whites believed they belonged to a superior race. After Johnson won, they called for "the great white hope," a white boxer to beat the black man. Whites were further angered by Johnson because they felt he was overly confident and even arrogant in his attitude. He knew he was talented, and he was not afraid to say so. Matters were complicated when Johnson married two times, each time to a white woman. For racist whites, this was unacceptable and Johnson needed to be "put down."

Johnson's most famous fight came on Independence Day 1910. The public's cry for a white fighter to beat the black champion, and a healthy cash reward, encouraged thirty-five-year-old former champion Jim Jeffries to come out of retirement after five years. The public was sure he would put the "upstart" in his place. In a grueling fifteen round match in Reno, Nevada, Jeffries fought relentlessly, despite the beating he received, and Johnson fought with full power, despite the deep cut he sustained over his right eye in the sixth round. Johnson, ever confident, was heard to say during the match, "I thought this fellow could hit." Johnson beat Jeffries, winning by a knockout, to maintain his title.

After the match, racist sentiment caused a series of riots across the country. In all, eight black people were killed in the rioting. One man was simply riding a trolley car in New Orleans, proclaiming Johnson's victory, when a white man fatally stabbed him.

The rioting and racism of 1910 surrounding Johnson's victory was merely a symptom of the larger race problem that would continue in the nation throughout the twentieth century. However, Johnson's victory did help to carve the way for future black athletes to gain success, receiving fame and fortune instead of hatred and outrage.

Suggested Activities

Black Athletes Learn about the accomplishments of other black athletes in the first portion of the twentieth century and how they broke ground for black athletes to come.

Boxing Learn about the sport of boxing, how it is played, and who the significant boxers of history have been.

Discussion Boxing has become a controversial sport. Some think it is a true test of physical skill while others say it is ruthlessly brutal and that it should be outlawed. Have the class discuss the issue.

The Georgia Peach

Ty Cobb

Tyrus Raymond Cobb was born in Banks County, Georgia, in 1886. Little did his proud parents know that their baby boy would become a baseball legend known as "The Georgia Peach."

Ty Cobb had an amazing twenty-four year life as a professional baseball player. He was with the Detroit Tigers from 1905 until 1926, and he was their manager from 1921 until he left the team. In 1927 and 1928, he played with the Philadelphia Athletics.

During his long career, Cobb made and held a number of baseball records. He is the all-time leading hitter in the major leagues, with a lifetime batting average of .367. His record career total of 4,191 hits was not broken until Pete Rose did so in 1985. Cobb won twelve American League batting titles, nine of them in a row from 1907 to 1915. During his long career, he also stole 892 bases, and in 1915, he had the record for most bases stolen in a season with 96 in all. He was certainly a crucial part of his team's three pennants in a row from 1907–1909.

Besides his excellent batting, Cobb was known for his ability to steal bases. He had a reputation as a fierce player who used rough play to intimidate the other team. This, coupled with his aggressive playing nature, enabled him to be a stolen-base leader. Cobb frequently turned a base hit into a double or triple by stealing bases. Once he gained two bases on a bunt.

Cobb used whatever legal methods he could to intimidate his rivals, but it was also rumored that he sharpened the spikes of his cleats. If true, this would certainly have gotten the attention of the opposing teams.

Of course, although Cobb's stealing of bases might be chalked up to aggression, his outstanding hitting was pure talent. In his first year, he hit only .240, but in each year after that he hit no less than .300. This feat is still unrivaled.

As a final triumph, Ty Cobb was one of the first five players elected to the newly established National Baseball Hall of Fame in 1936. This is a record that can never be broken.

Suggested Activities

Stealing Bases: During physical education time, practice stealing bases. See who can rival Ty Cobb—not for his rough playing but for his success.

Classroom Baseball: Hold a mock baseball game in class. Prepare a number of questions or problems in the subject areas you are studying. Divide the class into two teams, and designate them as "home" and "visitors" or allow them to select team names. Draw a scoreboard on the chalkboard. The "pitcher" reads a question for a "batter" of the opposing team. Score a base hit for a correctly answered question or a strike for a wrong answer. You may choose to adjust the scoring so that an answer with several parts is a double or triple or a single incorrect answer is a strikeout. Recycle any questions that receive incorrect answers. Three outs and the other team is up to bat. Play nine innings in all, if you like.

Jim Thorpe

Jim Thorpe is widely considered one of the greatest athletes of all time. His talents ranged from football to baseball to track and field, and he was successful in all those areas. Born in Oklahoma in 1887, Thorpe, a Native American, began to show his athletic skill at the Carlisle Indian Industrial School in Pennsylvania. Because of him, the small school achieved national recognition.

In the 1912 Olympics in Stockholm, Sweden, Thorpe became the first athlete to win both the pentathlon and decathlon. He also came in first in the 200-meter dash and the 1,500-meter run. Russia's Tsar Nicholas II sent Thorpe a silver model of a Viking ship as a tribute to his skill, and the King of Sweden called him "the greatest athlete in the world." Thorpe had earned a small salary as a baseball player in 1909 and 1910 and because this gave him professional status, not the amateur status required to compete in Olympic games, his medals were taken away about a month after he received them. In 1982, twenty-nine years after Thorpe's death, the International Olympic Committee reconsidered and restored the medals.

A multitalented athlete, Jim Thorpe played professional baseball for three major league teams (1913–1919) and football for seven teams (1915–1930). He became the first president of the American Professional Football Association (now the National Football League) and one of the first men admitted into the National Football Foundation's Hall of Fame (1951). Today, though athletes show masterful skill in their fields, it is quite rare for a single athlete to compete so successfully in several different sports.

Suggested Activities

Pentathlon As a tribute to Thorpe, and as a means to show your own athletic skill, hold your own classroom pentathlon. The traditional events are the long jump, javelin throw, 200-meter run, discus throw, and 1,500-meter run. These are not conducive to classes. Choose five activities to hold in your pentathlon. They can be fun like banana tossing or hopscotch. Most importantly, have fun!

Olympics The Olympic Games of 1912 were also notable for two other reasons. First, they were the first Olympics that allowed women to compete, although they only did so in swimming and diving. Find out more about these groundbreaking women athletes of the 1912 games. The second reason is that the Americans won thirteen out of the twenty-eight possible golds. Who were the gold medal winners of the 1912 Olympics?

Multitalented Athletes Some athletes have played professionally in more than one sport, including Bo Jackson and Michael Jordan. Name any other athletes you can who have done this and tell the sports in which they have played. Have any of them been as successful in two or more sports as Jim Thorpe was?

Tanks

Existing wheeled armored vehicles used to transport artillery did not maneuver well in mud or over trenches. As a result, the British developed the *tank*, a kind of armored landship that moves on a caterpillar tread system, enabling it to cover almost any terrain. Because the new vehicles were shipped in crates marked "water tank" to conceal their purpose from the enemy, they became known simply as tanks. The first tanks were used against the Germans in the Battle of the Somme in 1916. During this battle, they were slow and difficult to operate. An eight-man crew was required for the first tanks, including four men to steer. Improvements followed quickly, and tanks were used successfully in the Battle of Cambrai in 1917. By the end of the war Britain had built 2,350 tanks of 13 different types, and one man could drive the vehicle. France built some 4,000 light-weight tanks. The war ended before America could manufacture any tanks.

Tanks have continued to play major roles in wars since then. In World War II, every fighting nation used tanks. The German armored divisions, called panzers, were especially successful during the war. In 1944, tanks helped the Allies sweep across Germany, setting the way for victory in the war.

As tanks became an important part of the arsenal, weapons were developed specifically to stop them. In the Arab-Israeli War of 1973, over 6,000 tanks were used, but almost half of them were destroyed just eighteen days into the war by precision-guided missiles that easily wiped out the tanks. In the Persian Gulf War of 1991, the United States used more than 2,000 tanks, but few were lost. However, Iraq lost in excess of 3,500 tanks. This statistic showed that tanks were still useful, but weaponry and experience were even more important.

A model of a U.S. Army M1A1 battle tank can be seen below. The tank is covered in armor, and particularly heavy armor covers the front end behind which the driver sits. The engine and transmission are in the back, and a continuous track rolls underneath. The gunner sits behind the driver, and the commander sits behind him or her, also acting as a gunner. The loader sits behind but in front of the ammunition. Above the crew is the machine gun, and to the front of the tank is the 120-mm gun.

Suggested Activity

Label the elements of the tank diagram.

machine gun	ammunition	continuous track	driver	commander
120-mm gun	frontal armor	engine and transmission	gunner	loader

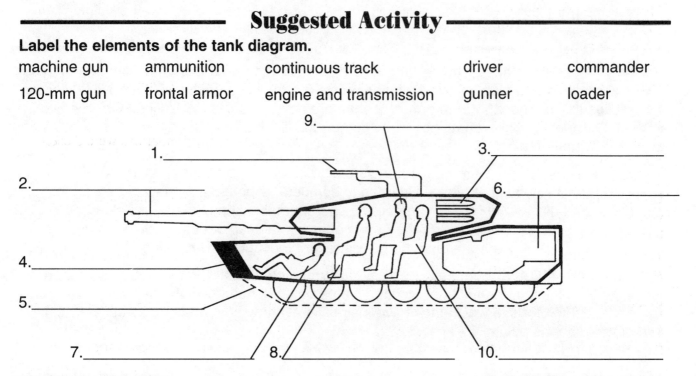

Submarines

Submarines are ships that travel under the water. Most are designed for use during war. They are made of material that will not crush under the pressure of the sea. A submarines generally has a propeller, rudders, and diving planes in the back and a periscope, diving planes, a hatch, and a radar system above. It also has tubes for shooting torpedoes.
(See the diagram.)

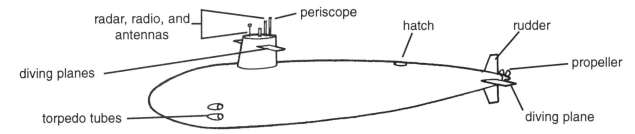

Submarines were used successfully as warships for the first time during World War I. Here is a history of their development prior to the Great War and their usage during it.

1620 The first useable submarine was invented by Cornelius van Drebbel, a Dutch scientist. It was a wooden rowboat covered with waterproof hides.

1776 The *Turtle* was used in the Revolutionary War. It was a one-man submarine, created by Yale student David Bushnell. It was operated by a hand-cranked propeller. It attempted to sink a British warship in New York harbor, but it failed. However, this was the first time a submarine was used to attack another boat.

1800 The *Nautilus* was invented by Robert Fulton, an American. During demonstrations, it sank a number of ships. However, neither Britain nor France, to whom Fulton tried to sell his copper-covered vessel, was interested in purchasing it.

1864 *The Hunley*, a Confederate submarine, became the first underwater ship to sink another ship in wartime. It used an explosive attached to a long pole. It rammed the *Housatonic*, a Union ship, in Charleston Harbor; however, it sank with its target. *The Hunley* was found by a team of explorers in 1995.

1898 The *U.S.S. Holland* was sold to the United States Navy by American John P. Holland. It was the first U.S. submarine, and it was powered by gasoline engine and electric batteries.

1902 The periscope was invented by Simon Lake, an American. It used magnifying lenses so the submarine operators could see targets at a distance. Lake also invented wheels on submarines so they could drive along the ocean floor.

1908 The first diesel-powered submarines were used by the British. Most submarines were diesel-powered until the 1950s when nuclear power was developed.

1914–1918 Germany used the submarine as a lethal warship. A German submarine was known as a U-boat, short for *Unterseeboote*. U-boats sank many enemy ships, including merchant and passenger vessels. The sinking of U.S. ships by Germany's submarines was influential in the U.S.'s eventual entry into the war.

The most infamous attack by a U-boat during World War I was the torpedoing of the *Lusitania* in 1915. Approximately 1,200 passengers were killed, including 128 Americans. (See page 73)

——— Suggested Activity ———

Types Submarines come in two main types: attack and ballistic. Find out about the differences between the two, how they are powered, and how the crews live on them.

Carl Jung

Teacher Note: The content of Jung's theories is sensitive. Discussion of it will require discretion.

Carl Gustav Jung was born in Basel, Switzerland, to a minister. When he was young, he was very interested in superstition and mythology. Jung entered the University of Basel in 1895 and studied archeology; however, his interests changed. In 1902, he graduated from the University of Zurich as a physician, and he began a psychiatric practice in Zurich.

At first, Jung followed the practices of Freud (page 43), and in 1907 the two became close friends. However, they split in 1913, partly because Jung believed that Freud emphasized the importance of sexual instincts too strongly but also because Jung saw broader applications for the field of psychology than did Freud. From that time forward, Jung developed his own theories of the unconscious and human relationships. He also spent a long period of time analyzing himself.

In 1917, Jung published his great work, *Psychology* of the *Unconscious*. In it, the reader can learn much of what Jung theorized. Like Freud, Jung believed that everyone is driven by his or her unconscious mind, the place where personal drives and desires reside. However, Jung did not believe that sexuality was really important to a person until puberty. Jung asserted that the personalities of a child's parents have great influence on that child. He also believed that people share a *collective unconscious*, through which they are all connected, regardless of race, time, and experience. In the collective unconscious there are archetypes, thought patterns that everyone has over different ways of being. These archetypes allow people to think and react just as their ancestors did. Jung felt that great wisdom could be found in the collective unconscious and that therapy could be used to help people uncover it.

Perhaps most significantly, Jung developed the concepts of *introvert* and *extrovert*. He said that an introvert is a person who depends primarily on himself or herself to get his or her needs met. An extrovert relies on the company of his or others for fulfillment of needs. Jung felt therapy could be useful to people in helping them balance themselves as both introverts and extroverts.

Throughout his career, Jung went back to the concepts in superstition and mythology that he enjoyed so much when he was a child. He believed that they were linked to the archetypes that existed in the collective unconscious. Religion, in particular, helped people express their unconscious need for this collective fulfillment.

Suggested Activities

Venn Diagram Study both Jung and Freud, two important theorists of the early twentieth century, using a Venn diagram. Discuss what you find.

Introvert and Extrovert Devise a test to determine if a person is a stronger introvert or extrovert. This test should be a series of questions that provide people with two choices for answers. For example, at a party, do you usually talk a lot with one or two people or visit briefly with many people? An introvert would tend to do the former and an extrovert would do the latter.

Vitamins

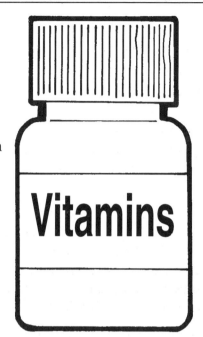

Vitamins are essential parts of the diet of living things; however, it was not until 1912 that vitamins were actually identified as such. Here is their history.

While carbohydrates, fat, and protein make up 98% of the dry weight consumed by people, the other 2% comes in vitamins and nutrients. The importance of these nutrients was recognized for the first time in the Middle Ages. At that time, some fortressed cities were cut off from fresh supplies while they were under siege. The deterioration of health and sometimes death resulted from this lack of fresh provisions. Then, in the early 1500s, when prolonged voyages became a possibility, deficiency diseases aboard ships were common. For example, during Queen Elizabeth's reign at the end of the sixteenth century, approximately 10,000 men in her navy died of scurvy. The men were amply provided for with approximately 4,000 calories a day, including hardbread biscuits, salt meat or dried fish, butter, cheese, dried peas, and beer, and these rations contained everything the people thought was necessary for a healthful life. Instead, the men developed rotten gums, loose teeth, bad breath, swollen cheeks, bruises, and aches and pains, all the signs of scurvy. Physicians at the time determined that certain medicines made of plants cured the scurvy.

Across the seas in Japan, the Japanese navy was experiencing something similar, this time with a disease called beri-beri. Sometimes as much as two-thirds of a Japanese crew became afflicted with the disease. Through these experiences, it was learned that fresh plants were vital to a healthy life.

In 1906, Sir Frederick Galen Hopkins wrote an article stating that "accessory nutrients" were needed to maintain good health. In 1912, a substance was isolated from rice polish. It was an "accessory nutrient" that could prevent *beri-beri*. Vital for the preservation of life, it was also an *amine* (amino acid-like substance). These two words were combined, and the nutrient was called a "vitamine."

Many experiments were conducted on animals, testing the power of vitamines—now vitamins. The first such experiment to isolate and name a particular vitamin was also in 1912. Hopkins found that rats died on a diet of sugar, starch, fat, protein, and inorganic salts, but when they were also given a teaspoon of milk each day, they began to thrive. He believed that an "accessory food factor" was in the milk. He and others began to search for this accessory. Within a year, a fat-soluble substance was extracted from egg yolks, butter, and fish livers, and when it was removed from the rats' diets, their eyes became diseased. In 1914, researchers separated a water solution from rice bran, and this solution cured beri-beri. The extract from egg yolks and other foods was called "fat-soluble A," and the water solution was called "water-soluble B." In 1919, the first became known as vitamin A. Later it was called *retinol* because it was shown to be important to eyes and the retina. Over time, other vitamins were isolated and named, and today it is known that these vitamins are essential to good health.

Suggested Activities

Chart Make a chart of the major vitamins and some of their sources.

Agriculture As a class, choose several common vitamins and then find plants that contain them. Plant those seeds and care for them as they grow. When the vegetables are ready, eat them.

The Pen Is Mightier Than the Sword

The 1910s were filled with quality literature by some of the world's finest writers. Here are three such writers who were popular at the time.

Jack London John Griffith London was born in 1876 in San Francisco, California. He was raised in poverty by his mother, Flora Wellman, and her husband, John London. By the age of ten, the young boy was already working selling newspapers, and at fourteen he worked in a cannery. A series of other jobs followed in his teens, and by eighteen he was traveling the United States as a hobo. At about this time, he made a decision to live by his intellect and become a writer. London educated himself, reading and writing up to twenty hours per day. Just before the turn of the century, he sold his first story. By 1905, London had become the most widely read and highest paid author in America. Some of his novels include *The Call of the Wild*, *The Sea Wolf*, *White Fang*, and *John Barleycorn*, which is somewhat autobiographical.

London's books remained popular into the 1910s, although his publications of that decade did not match the success of the first. In 1916 at the age of forty, London died of a drug overdose.

Upton Sinclair A muckraker* of the early twentieth century, Upton Beall Sinclair's work exposed social and political corruption. Many of his novels were based on actual events.

Born in 1878, Sinclair was a popular and influential author by 1906 when his best-known book, *The Jungle* was published. Information in the book shocked President Roosevelt and influenced the passage of the Pure Food and Drug Act of the same year. In the 1910s and forward, Sinclair tuned to politics and social causes as well as his career as a writer. He was once a candidate for governor in California, but was narrowly defeated. He also helped to form the American Civil Liberties Union and the League for Industrial Democracy. In 1943, he won the Pulitzer prize for fiction. Sinclair died in 1968 after a long and successful career.

A muckraker was a writer whose goal was to expose social and political problems.

Edith Wharton Edith Wharton wrote of the middle class and aristocracy of New York society in the late nineteenth and early twentieth centuries. She herself was born into a prominent New York family in 1862, and she first achieved success in 1902 with *The Valley of Decision*. During World War I, her novels were greatly influenced by her experience; she received the Cross of the Legion Honor for her relief work in Paris during the war.

Wharton's books deal primarily with psychological characterizations of people faced with moral and social dilemmas. Some of her most famous works are *The Age of Innocence* (for which she won the Pulitzer prize) and *Ethan Frome*. The works question the boundaries and mores of society, as Wharton herself did, supporting her husband throughout their marriage. When the two divorced in 1913, she moved to France. Wharton died in 1937 after many years of success.

Suggested Activities

Reading Read excerpts from any of the above named authors' works, carefully selecting passages appropriate for your class. London's *White Fang* and *The Call of the Wild* are probably the most accessible for young readers.

Writers Each of these prominent writers of the 1910s exposed social, political, and/or cultural problems, although they did so in different ways. Write short stories with the same goals. Share them as a class and discuss the different ways in which the students meet the goals.

America's Sweetheart

Born Gladys Marie Smith in 1893, Mary Pickford became the most popular actress of the early days of moviemaking. She was known as America's Sweetheart because of her huge popularity. In all, she appeared in 194 films.

Mary Pickford

Pickford's debut came in 1909. She grew to enormous popularity in the following years. Most notably, *The Poor Little Rich Girl* of 1917 made her one of the biggest stars of the time. *Rebecca of Sunnybrook Farm* of the same year was also a noteworthy film in her extensive career. Pickford's heroines were generally innocent and determined, fostering her image as America's Sweetheart—the ideal girl.

The actress won the Academy Award in the category of best actress for her performance in *Coquette*, a 1928 film. She also received an honorary Academy Award in 1976 for lifetime achievement.

In 1919, Pickford was one of the founders of United Artists, one of the first filmmaking companies in the new movie town, Hollywood. Her co-founders were actor Charlie Chaplin, director D. W. Griffith, and fellow actor and future husband, Douglas Fairbanks, Sr. At this time, she was earning a million dollars each year, an enormous sum. Pickford and Fairbanks were married in 1920.

When Pickford retired from moviemaking in 1933, she had made nearly 200 films in just twenty-four years. Mary Pickford, America's Sweetheart, died in 1979.

Suggested Activities

Silent Movies Pickford's early days were in silent films. Have small groups each write and produce a short silent film. Play for them a silent film or two (some can be found on video), asking them to take note of the exaggerated expressions, text cards, and musical overlay. Their silent films can either be videotaped and played for the class or enacted in silent-film style.

In order to prepare their films, the students will need to do the following:

- Brainstorm for a story idea. Classic tales of good v. evil are best.
- Outline the events of the story. Remember, they should be quite visual with little dialogue.
- Plan the text that will go on the cards.
- Prepare costumes and props.
- Rehearse.
- Dress in costume, ready the props, and roll film!

Viewing If available in your area, rent a video copy of *The Poor Little Rich Girl* or *Rebecca of Sunnybrook Farm*. Both are acceptable for students.

Music Music has always played an important part in moviemaking, adding to the emotional content of the story. Give the students a list of emotions (happy, sad, angry, fearful, etc.) and ask them to find instrumental music that conveys each of those emotions. You may wish to do this as a class exercise, collecting samples of music the students bring in and determining as a class what they signify. It would be interesting to have the students write down an emotion while they listen to the music. Make a class chart showing what each person has written and compare responses.

The Song-and-Dance Man

In 1878, in Providence, Rhode Island, George Michael Cohan was born. He would became one of the most famous men of World War I. More precisely, he became famous for the most famous song, "Over There."

George M. Cohan

As a child, Cohan and his talented family performed in vaudeville as "The Four Cohans." When he was a teenager, he began to write vaudeville skits and songs himself. By the early 1900s, Cohan was one of the most popular people in the American theater. Throughout his long career, he wrote more than forty plays and musicals, producing, directing, and starring in most of them himself.

Cohan's work was particularly noteworthy for its high-spirited music and enthusiastic show quality. Generally, there was a patriotic flair and fervor to the music as well. It is no surprise then that his song entitled "Over There" became the most popular patriotic song—and perhaps the most popular song–during World War I. Everyone was singing it, and it was influential in encouraging many enlistees to sign up for military service overseas.

The plays of Cohan include *Broadway Jones*, *Seven Keys to Baldpate*, and *The Song-and-Dance Man*. However, his plays are not particularly remembered. It is the music of George M. Cohan that lives on in American culture. Songs such as "I'm a Yankee Doodle Dandy," "You're a Grand Old Flag," and "Give My Regards to Broadway," are classics of American popular music.

Cohan lived his life in the world of the theater. He died in 1942, a successful and prominent man.

Suggested Activities

Listen and Sing Locate recordings of Cohan's music, being sure to include "Over There." (Cohan's music is easy to find, and there are many sources.) Play the music for the class. Learn the songs and sing them yourselves.

Vaudeville Early in the century, vaudeville enjoyed great popularity. However, the movies finally put an end to vaudeville. Research vaudeville and some of its famous acts. If desired, have the class put on its own vaudeville show. Many old movies recreate vaudeville. Look to titles starring such celebrities as Judy Garland, Gene Kelly, Fred Astaire, and Donald O'Connor, and you will find many examples.

Stars When vaudeville died out, many performers found new careers in the movies and on radio. Some later moved to television. Will Rogers, Burns and Allen, Bob Hope, Harry Houdini, Jack Benny, W.C. Fields, Milton Berle, and Edgar Bergen all began their career in vaudeville. Choose one of these famous performers and trace his on her career after vaudeville.

Ragtime

Scott Joplin, the son of a former slave, loved music all his life. Born in Texarkana, Texas, in 1868, he left home at fourteen and traveled about the Mississippi Valley playing piano in saloons. He wound up at the Maple Leaf Club in Sedalia, Missouri. In Sedalia several of his compositions were published, including his famous, "Maple Leaf Rag." During his lifetime, Scott Joplin wrote or collaborated on over sixty pieces of music and became a leading composer of what is known as *ragtime*, or simply rag.

Ragtime was very popular in the United States around the turn of the century and for the next several years. The term ragtime is short for "ragged time," and it refers to a type of music that is sometimes irregularly accented (or syncopated) and then regularly accented. The music is very energetic. Ragtime started as improvisational music, but composers like Joplin gave it a written form.

Scott Joplin

Ragtime was also the perfect music for some popular dances of the 1900s and 1910s, including the Turkey Trot, the Cakewalk, and the Grizzly Bear. These were dances designed to make children laugh, but they were also intended to be as different from traditional dance (such as the waltz) as possible. However, their strange and unprecedented movements had some people calling the dances indecent, immoral, and disgusting. These people said the same thing about the ragtime music itself.

Though Joplin's life ended sadly and too soon (he died in 1917 in a mental hospital), he left a legacy of music that continues to delight and entertain. Joplin even received a special citation from the Advisory Board on the Pulitzer Prizes in the 1970s for his contribution to music. In fact, the seventies saw a revival of interest in his music due to a popular movie of the time called *The Sting*.

Suggested Activities

Listen In the classroom, listen to a recording of Scott Joplin's ragtime music. While listening, close your eyes and see what pictures come into your head as you listen. When the music is finished, quickly write down all the things the music made you think and feel. In small groups of three or four, share one of those things. Were your thoughts and feelings similar or very different?

Musical Match-up Music often accompanies scenes and events in movies, plays, and other productions. It is selected as a complement to a particular experience. What experience do you think ragtime would represent well? As a class, brainstorm some appropriate places and situations to play Joplin's music.

Dancing A number of books on the history of dance will tell you about such popular dances as the ones listed above. Learn to do them as a class. Dance them while listening to some ragtime music.

Nijinsky

The 1910s saw the rise and fall of one of the most legendary ballet dancers ever known and the most popular male dancer of his time. His name was Vaslav Nijinsky.

Vaslav Nijinsky

Nijinsky was born in Kiev, Ukraine, in 1889. He began to study dance in 1898 at the St. Petersburg Imperial School of Ballet. He gained attention quickly, and he was asked to join Sergei Diaghilev's ballet company. In 1909, the company went to Paris to perform in Diaghilev's Ballet Russes. These were elaborate productions that featured stage designs by such artistic masters as Matisse and Picasso and musical compositions by the world-renowned Ravel and Debussy. Nijinsky and the company were an enormous success. Crowds gathered for more of this amazing young star. The company traveled around the world, and everywhere they went, Nijinsky brought down the house. Although he was short with especially thick thigh muscles and a slope to his shoulders, his body seemed to lengthen and alter itself, depending on the roles he played. He became known for the incredible way in which he could master his body and his movements.

In 1913, Nijinsky married a fellow dancer, a ballet student with his company. This angered Diaghilev, and he dismissed his star male dancer. However, in 1916, Nijinsky once again joined with his old company, this time in the United States. His career flourished, and his dancing was up to the same quality it had been in years past.

Through the course of his career, Nijinsky created and choreographed a number of important roles, including Petrouchka and the faun in *The Afternoon of the Faun*. Many of his roles are still danced today, although it is a rare dancer who can attain Nijinsky's mastery. There is a famous story told of his skill. During the exit scene in *Le Spectre de la Rose*, Nijinsky is said to have risen slowly, leapt dramatically across a window ledge, and then stopped in midair—or so it seemed. The audience said that just as he stopped at the peak of his jump, he disappeared. Whether this story is true or not, it demonstrates the impact that Nijinsky's dancing and body control had on his audiences.

Sadly, by 1919, Nijinsky's career had come to an end. He suffered from mental illness, and in that year, he became completely mad. Though he continued to live for thirty-one years, he would never perform again.

Suggested Activities

Video View videotape of some modern ballet dancers, such as Barishnikov. Barishnikov's *Nutcracker* is wonderfully done and easy to find on video.

Ballet Learn the five basic ballet positions. They can be found in any reference book on ballet.

Artists and Composers Find out about Matisse, Picasso, Ravel, and Debussy. Look at or listen to some of their work.

Isadora Duncan

Isadora Duncan was the dance sensation of Europe from 1899 until her death in 1927. She almost single-handedly revolutionized classical dance, and she helped to bring about a new wave of modern dance.

Duncan was born in San Francisco in 1877. As a child, she loved to dance, but she refused to take ballet lessons. She found ballet too regimented and restrictive. She liked to dance naturally, in line with her own internal sense of rhythm and movement. Duncan believed that dance was an individual expression.

Her first dances were based on works of poetry that inspired her. She then became intrigued by literature, classical music, and figures from paintings and sculptures. She is perhaps best known for dancing that is based on forms from ancient Greek vases and mythology. Duncan also used nature as her inspiration, mimicking waves and other natural phenomena.

Her style met with disapproval in the United States, so she moved to Europe at the age of twenty-one and performed there. Since she did not have much money, she sailed across the sea on a cattle boat. Once in Europe, she became a renowned innovator and dance sensation.

Isadora Duncan regularly danced barefoot in flowing, loose tunics. Her clothing was sometimes revealing, even see-through, and many people were shocked. On one occasion in Berlin, her performance was banned because the police said it was obscene. Duncan's private life was also shocking to many people, particularly Americans. She had many male companions, and her two children were born illegitimately. In 1913, a tragic and strange accident occurred. Her children were traveling in a car with their governess and a chauffeur. When the car broke down on a hill, the chauffeur got out. However, the car rolled back down the incline and into a river. The children, aged seven and five, and the governess were drowned.

Duncan's dancing brought her world fame, and in 1921, the new ruler of Russia, V. I. Lenin, invited her to live in Moscow. He even provided her with a house. While there, she taught dancing, and she established dancing schools for children in Russia, Germany, and France. She also married a Russian poet.

More tragedy came Duncan's way in 1925 when her husband hanged himself. Two years later, she herself died in a freak accident. While traveling in a car, her long scarf became wrapped in a spoked wheel of the vehicle. It immediately strangled her as the car sped forward.

Suggested Activities

Movement Imitating Duncan's style, have the students move as things from nature might, such as waves, clouds, wind, and other phenomena.

Classical Art Share pictures of some pieces of classical art with the students. Be sure to choose images that have figures on them. Ask then students to mirror the images and to attempt to move like they might.

End of the Wild West

In 1917, an era came to an end with the death of Buffalo Bill, a legend of the old West. Today, Buffalo Bill's exploits are controversial, but at the time he was a celebrity of great stature.

Born William Frederick Cody in 1846, Buffalo Bill spent his lifetime in a number of occupations throughout the Western frontier, and in the last several decades prior to his death, he was a national showman. Here is the story of his life.

Buffalo Bill Cody

When Cody was eight years old, his family moved from his birthplace of Le Claire, Iowa, to Kansas. His father died when he was eleven years old, and Cody began to work. First, he was a messenger for a freight firm. He took a year off to attend school, and then he traveled with wagon trains going west, first as a caretaker of livestock and then as a horse driver. In 1860, he was a rider for the legendary, but short-lived, pony express.

The Civil War followed, and Cody joined the Union Kansas militias and the Ninth Kansas Volunteers. He was also a teamster in the Seventh Kansas Volunteer Cavalry. When the war ended in 1865, Cody became a hotel operator and a freighter; however, he lost his wagon and horses to Indians. He tried land speculation and railroad construction as well, but he became famous as a hunter of buffalo. After killing the animals, he would provide their meat to the railroad in order to feed the men building the rails across Kansas. Cody proved to be an excellent shot with his rifle, and so the workmen on the railroad lines nicknamed him "Buffalo Bill." In fact, it is said that he killed 4,000 buffalo in just eighteen months.

In 1868, Cody became a scout for the military while they battled with the Indians in the West. He also served as a guide for buffalo hunters. In 1872, he took part in a battle between Indians and the military on the Platte River, for which Congress awarded him the Medal of Honor (which they later rescinded because Cody was not then a member of the military).

It was in 1872 that Cody began his career on the stage. Theaters across the nation hosted the "Wild West" show, starring Buffalo Bill Cody. It was a big success. Cody followed it in 1883 with "Buffalo Bill's Wild West," which ran for thirty years. It included demonstrations by Cody and by other Western figures, such as the sure-fire shot Annie Oakley. Oakley was noteworthy at the time for having shot the ash from a cigarette in the mouth of Germany's Kaiser. Buffalo Bill's show traveled throughout the United States and in parts of Europe. He performed until shortly before he died.

In 1894, Cody moved to a home in the Bighorn Basin of Wyoming. He died in 1917 and was buried on Lookout Mountain near Denver, Colorado. His passing served as a reminder that the old West had truly died.

Suggested Activities

Out with the Old The Western frontier was no longer wild by the turn of the century, but fragments of the old West remained for a number of years. Find out about some of the other final figures from the old West.

Buffalo Cody took part in the mass killing of buffalo that nearly made the species extinct. Research to find out about this practice and its effect on the native people of the land.

Show Time Prepare a show depicting a certain time and place, such as Buffalo Bill's show did about the Wild West. Have the students prepare different skits under a central theme. Preferably, choose a time from the twentieth century. In this way, the students will learn about history as they prepare their skits.

Father's Day

When Sonora Louise Smart Dodd of Spokane, Washington, heard a sermon at her church concerning Mother's Day, she got the idea for a day to honor fathers in the same way. Dodd wished especially to honor her own father, William Jackson Smart, who had raised his six children alone after his wife died in 1898.

The young woman began a petition recommending that Spokane adopt an annual Father's Day celebration. She also got the support of the Spokane Ministerial Association and the Young Men's Christian Association (YMCA). Dodd's efforts were finally successful, and on June 19, 1910, the first Father's Day was celebrated in Spokane.

After that time, many people and groups tried to make the day a national holiday; it was not until 1972 that President Richard Nixon signed the day into law.

Today, Father's Day is celebrated around the world. In the United States and Canada, it falls on the third Sunday in June. On that day, people honor their fathers with gifts, cards, and special tributes.

Suggested Activities

Fathers Have the students write poems, make cards, or create other pieces of art to honor their fathers. Also discuss what it is that makes a good father. Let the students share all their views.

Holidays Research to determine the origination of several national holidays. Have the students brainstorm for additional holidays they feel would be worthwhile. Have them focus particularly on the people they think should be so honored.

My Dad Is In the space below, let the students freewrite the continuation of the words "My Dad is . . ." Instruct them to write without stopping to think but merely putting down whatever comes to mind. These freewrites may make nice Father's Day gifts.

My Dad is . . . _____

What's New?

Like every decade, the 1910s were filled with new and popular ideas, inventions, and styles. Here are some of them.

Raggedy Ann The popular doll was created by political cartoonist John Gruelle at the request of his terminally ill daughter. Eight-year-old Marcella Gruelle found an old rag doll in the family attic in 1915. The doll was faceless, so she took it to her father. He drew a face on the doll and asked his wife to restuff it. She did, and she added the now-trademark heart to its chest. The heart read "I love you." The redheaded rag doll quickly became famous nationally, and soon every little girl wanted her own Raggedy Ann.

Life Savers A candy maker from Cleveland in 1912 developed a peppermint candy with a hole in the middle. He called it a Life Saver since it resembled a life preserver.

Oreos A new cookie was developed in 1912. It was made of two chocolate wafers sandwiching a cream filling. It was named the Oreo Biscuit, and it was developed by the National Biscuit Company (now Nabisco).

Cranberry Sauce Today's Thanksgiving dinner would not have been complete were it not for the Ocean Spray Cranberry Company in 1912. In that year they first produced cranberry sauce, a sweetened jelly made from cranberries.

Jazz In 1917, it was spelled *jass*, but it was still the exciting music known today by its free-flowing, syncopated sound. It was said to have been developed in New Orleans by black musicians, who had extended it from ragtime, blues, and other musical forms. The Original Dixieland Jass Band was the first to use the word officially.

Lincoln Logs John Wright, the son of famous architect and designer Frank Lloyd Wright, developed Lincoln Logs in 1916 so that children could build their own structures. He got the idea while watching the construction of a hotel in Tokyo.

Hobble Skirts Women in 1910 were seen to hobble around due to their new fashion. Hobble skirts were made very tight at the ankle so that women could not move freely. The style caused such an uproar that the pope condemned it publicly.

Tango Also in 1910 a new dance craze shocked the clergy. It was called the tango, and it was a romantic dance that alternated short, quick steps with long, low ones.

Kinetophone Thomas Edison's latest invention of 1910 combined sound and picture recording. "Talking pictures" were just around the corner.

Suggested Activities

Research Choose any one of the items listed above and research to find more details about its development. Also attempt to find early advertising of the products or depictions of the dances or styles.

Brainstorm As a class, brainstorm for the new items that you think will still be popular in the next century.

End of an Empire

At the onset of World War I, the Ottoman Empire was a sprawling one, spreading throughout the continents of Africa and Europe. It was ruled by an elite group of Turks, although Turks were a minority. By the end of the war, the more than six-hundred-year reign of the Ottoman Empire would end.

In 1908, a small group of young Turks became frustrated with the Ottoman Empire. Once, briefly, a democracy had existed there with a democratic constitution. The new ruler, Abd al-Hamid II, had accepted the constitution when he came to power in 1876, but by 1878 he had suspended it and ruled with complete authority. The sultan modernized the Ottoman Army in order to fortify his authority; however, the new army would eventually lead to his own destruction. Abd al-Hamid's rule came to an end in 1909 when the rebels forced his abdication and deposed him. The new Turkish army remained strong, and to this day it plays an important part in the politics of the nation.

About this time, segments of the Empire were being taken over by other nations. Britain had gained control of Egypt and Cyprus, joining them to its growing British Empire. The British also encouraged dissension among the Arab tribes in the Arabian peninsula, part of the Ottoman Empire. France took the tiny nation of Morocco, and Libya went to Italy.

The new leaders of the Empire chose to become allies with the rising powers of Germany. This helped them for awhile, but eventually it proved to be the downfall of their world. The battles of World War I became more than the new leadership could handle, and British soldiers and guerrillas bested them in the end.

The last European segments of the Ottoman Empire were the Balkan states. In 1912 and 1913, there was an internal power struggle in the Balkans. This struggle would eventually spark the greatest war the world had ever known. When Archduke Franz Ferdinand of Austria-Hungary was assassinated, the fallout between Serbia and Bosnia caused nations around the world to take sides and to battle for the Balkans as well as each other's territory.

During the course of the rebellion and war, a holocaust occurred in Armenia to rival the later Holocaust of Jews in Europe. Tragically, millions of Armenians were murdered by leaders struggling for power in the shaky Empire. The Armenians were wiped out in a battle for control and autonomy with prejudice and hatred at its base. This massacre foreshadowed the infamous one that was already brewing in Germany and its surrounding nations.

The Turks lost the war in 1918 to British troops under the leadership of British General Edmund Allenby and the legendary British officer known as Lawrence of Arabia (page 106). When Germany was finally defeated and the peace terms were agreed upon, the Ottoman Empire was completely disbanded. Only death and destruction remained in its place.

Suggested Activities

Cartography Draw maps of the Ottoman Empire, coloring in and labeling the significant nations.

Holocaust Learn more about the Armenian massacres of the early 1900s. Also find out about the status of Armenia today.

Lawrence of Arabia

Victory came to the British in Turkey in 1918 under the leadership of General Edmund Allenby and an archeologist named T. E. Lawrence. Although Allenby was the true hero of the war in Turkey, it was Lawrence who gained legendary status. He became known as Lawrence of Arabia.

Thomas Edward Lawrence was born in Tremadoc, Wales. In his early adulthood, he studied archeology, the Near East, and the Arabic language at Oxford University in England. He then took employment with the British government as an archeologist.

When World War I began, T. E. Lawrence was sent to head the military intelligence department in Egypt. He was eventually made a colonel in the British Army. As such, he worked with the Arabs to lead a revolt against the ancient Ottoman Empire (page 105). It was during this time that he

Thomas Edward Lawrence

developed a deep affinity with the Arab cause and took it as his own. Lawrence became an expert at guerrilla warfare, and he was instrumental in the Arab arrival in Damascus, the capital of Syria, which became the final turning point in the war for the Turks. Allenby also arrived in Damascus at the same time.

After the war, Lawrence refused all honors the military and the Arabs wished to bestow upon him. However, he was hailed as a hero by the British and Arabs alike. The Arabs called him "the uncrowned king of Arabia."

When the peace treaty negotiations began in Versailles, Lawrence went to plead the cause of the Arabs. They wished to be an independent nation. However, he failed to convince the other negotiators.

After the war, Lawrence was made an adviser to Arab affairs by the British Colonial Office, but he resigned a year later, displeased with the fame and notoriety he had achieved. In 1922, he joined the Royal Air Force (R.A.F.) under the pseudonym, J. H. Ross, but his true identity was discovered. He then joined the tank corps under the assumed name, T. E. Shaw, and in 1925 he returned to the R.A.F. as Shaw, legally changing his name.

It is strange that after surviving so many years of adventures and dangerous, guerrilla exploits, the legendary Lawrence of Arabia finally died in a motorcycle accident in England. The year was 1935.

Suggested Activities

Movie View the film *Lawrence of Arabia*, a classic of American cinema. Determine if and how the movie differs from the true story of T. E. Lawrence. As with any film, view it first before sharing it with your class and be sure to get approval from your administration and students' parents.

Cartography Draw maps of the principle nations involved in Lawrence's World War I adventures. They include Judea, Palestine, Syria, and Turkey.

Read Lawrence published a book in 1926 called *The Seven Pillars of Wisdom*. A shortened version called *Revolt in the Desert* was published in 1927. In them, the author tells of his exploits in Arabia. Try to locate copies or excerpts from the books and share them with the class.

Trotsky

Leon Trotsky might have been the leader of the Union of Soviet Socialist Republics, but it was not to be. Instead, he was second in command to Lenin, and he later lost power to Joseph Stalin. Nonetheless, he was an important and influential leader in the politics of Russia and the new U.S.S.R.

Born Lev Davidovich Bronstein in the Ukraine, 1879, Trotsky was the son of wealthy parents. By his teens, he had become part of a revolutionary movement in Russia, and he spent two years as a Social Democrat. In 1898, he was arrested and sent to Siberian exile. However, he escaped to London in 1902, and it was there that he met V.I. Lenin. Trotsky followed Lenin's lead and changed his name, so as to be undetected by the Russian government.

In 1905, Trotsky returned to Russia and took part in the revolution there. Due to his leadership of the St. Petersburg Soviet in 1905, he was once again arrested. He escaped in 1907 and spent the next ten years in western Europe as a revolutionary writer and editor. When World War I began, France and Spain expelled Trotsky, and he was sent to New York.

In 1917, while in New York, Trotsky heard of the fall of the Tsar (pages 74 and 75). He returned to Russia and, once again, joined Lenin. Together, they plotted and achieved the Bolshevik takeover in October (November by today's calendar) of 1917. Trotsky was appointed by Lenin as the first Soviet commissar of foreign affairs. Next, he became the first Soviet commissar of war.

Civil war followed in Russia in 1918–1920, and Trotsky organized the powerful Red Army. He became a prominent leader in the newly formed U.S.S.R., second only to Lenin. When Lenin died, most people believed that Trotsky would step into his place. However, another leader, Joseph Stalin, outwitted Trotsky and usurped his place.

In 1927, Trotsky was expelled from the Communist Party. In 1928, he was exiled to Soviet Central Asia, and he was deported to Turkey in 1929. From there, he moved to Norway and finally to Mexico. In 1930, while in Mexico, he published his life story, entitled *My Life: An Attempt at an Autobiography*.

In 1940, Stalin decided that he had been too lenient on Trotsky, who had continued to battle the U.S.S.R. leader from overseas. Stalin sent an agent of his secret police to Mexico to assassinate the former leader. On August 21, 1940, Trotsky was murdered.

Suggested Activities

Read A book entitled *Leon Trotsky* by Hedda Garza (Chelsea House, 1986) is suitable for students. In it, they can learn more about the life of this influential leader. Older students will enjoy George Orwell's *Animal Farm*, an allegory of the Russian Revolution with animals depicting the various Bolshevik leaders, including Trotsky, Stalin, and Lenin.

Autobiography Trotsky made "an attempt at an autobiography." Have the students do the same, writing their own life stories and publishing them in self-made books.

German Leaders

Kaiser Wilhelm II and Paul von Hindenburg were two prominent German leaders who came to international recognition and infamy throughout the course of World War I.

Kaiser Wilhelm II The last emperor of Germany, Kaiser Wilhelm II was also the nephew of Britain's monarch, King Edward VII, and the cousin of Tsar Nicholas II of Russia. King Edward and the Kaiser did not get along, and both took part in an arms race during the 1900s and into the 1910s. This arms race eventually contributed to the outbreak of World War I. The Kaiser received most of the blame for the war, although today it is believed that the Russians and Austrians were equal partners in its inception.

Although he was paralyzed in his left arm, the Kaiser hid his infirmity and ruled with tremendous authority. Under his leadership, Germany gained in prosperity and boosted its trade and manufacturing. His empire also grew with the addition of colonies in Africa and on islands in the Pacific Ocean. The Kaiser built an army and navy that were virtually unrivalled. It was these achievements that brought Germany into conflict with the British Empire.

Under the Kaiser's reign, Germany broke an alliance with Russia, which eventually forced the nation to fight World War I on two fronts, against both the British and the Russians as well as their allies.

The Kaiser was noted around the world for his brutality and ruthlessness in war. Even people in his own nation were known to oppose his hardline tactics. In 1918, the German navy mutinied and internal revolution broke out. On November 7 of that year, the prime minister of Germany demanded the abdication of the Kaiser, and two days later, Wilhelm II gave up his throne. He fled to the Netherlands, a neutral country in world politics, where he lived in comfortable exile until his death in 1941.

Paul von Hindenburg Von Hindenburg was Germany's military leader during World War I, and from 1925 until his death in 1934, he was the nation's president. It was Hindenburg who appointed Adolf Hitler as chancellor in 1933.

Hindenburg was a military hero who became a general in 1896 and retired in 1911. When World War I began, he came out of retirement to command the German Eighth Army. General Erich von Ludendorff became his second in command, and the two went on to win many victories for the powerful German Army. In 1916, Hindenburg was named supreme commander of all German forces.

In 1917, Hindenburg created the Siegfried Line to shorten the western front and to ease the burden of Germany's soldiers. The line—called the Hindenburg Line by the Allies—held fast for more than a year. The Allies eventually broke it in September 1918, and that brought about the end of the war.

As president, Hindenburg lost ground to the growing Nazi party, but he used his power to keep Hitler out of control. However, by 1932, the Nazis had the strongest control, and Hindenburg was forced to give Hitler the position of chancellor on January 30, 1933. When Hindenburg died in 1934, Hitler dismantled the presidency and became the supreme authority.

Suggested Activity

History Trace the line of Germany's political leadership throughout the twentieth century.

"You Are the Man I Want"

Horatio Herbert Kitchener, first Earl of Khartoum and of Broome, was born in County Kerry, Ireland, in 1850. He was educated at the Royal Military Academy at Woolwich. His military skills were sharpened over the years in Palestine, Cyprus, Egypt, and South Africa. It was during World War I, however, that he gained international fame. As the British secretary of war, Kitchener's face was immortalized on thousands of recruiting posters with such captions as "You Are the Man I Want," "Your Country Needs You," and "(Kitchener's face) Wants You: Join Your Country's Army." Kitchener's recruitment program developed an extensive British army, highly significant to the eventual victory by the Allies. In all, three million men enlisted for duty at the western front.

Horatio Herbert Kitchener

Kitchener is considered to be the last great military hero of Britain. Highly trained as an army engineer, Kitchener demonstrated exceptional talent for detail, planning and organizing attacks, and defense. However, he was at heart a soldier, and he thrilled in the battle.

In 1871, France and Germany were at odds, and Britain was neutral. A young army officer at the time, Kitchener secretly went off to take part in the conflict, almost creating an international incident. Another time, while on sick leave, he went to Egypt, where growing tensions were heading for war. Notoriety came to him at the end of the nineteenth century for his actions as second in command during the Boer War of South Africa. His efforts played a major part in victory there. He then became commander of the South African army, and brought victory despite long battles against guerilla warfare.

Kitchener served as governor general of the Sudan and commander of the Egyptian Army. His leadership toppled the Dervishes, an aggressive religious group fighting for power at the time. Kitchener also reoccupied Khartoum for the British army, an area they had previously gained but lost. He served as commander in chief to the British army in India, and he was influential in Australia and New Zealand in bringing about reforms to their armies. After serving as head of the British administration in Egypt, Kitchener was made Earl of Khartoum and Broome in 1914. It was at that point that he was made secretary of war for the British.

A brave and strong leader for the first two years of the war, Kitchener made a voyage to Russia in 1916 to meet with the Tsar about new battle tactics. However, his ship struck a mine in unswept waters, and Kitchener was drowned. His death was an untimely shock to the struggling British who looked to him for leadership and victory. He was replaced as secretary of war by David Lloyd George.

Suggested Activities

History Learn more about the history of the British army.

Recruiting Design modern-day recruitment posters. What figures and images do you think would prove successful in encouraging young people to enlist for active war duty?

Spies and Aces

Several figures came to prominence during the Great War, not for their leadership but for their legendary qualities. Three such figures were Mata Hari, the Red Baron, and Eddie Rickenbacker.

Mata Hari Margaretha Geertruida Zelle was born in Leeuwarden, Netherlands, in 1876. She grew to become the popular exotic dancer, Mata Hari. Mata Hari began dancing in France after her marriage failed. Her style was exotic, and she pretended to be Javanese. Quickly, her fame spread throughout Europe, and she became noted for her strange and sensual dances.

Mata Hari's dancing began to lose popularity after awhile. At that time, she apparently became involved with a network of German spies with whom she is said to have worked during World War I. The French discovered her treachery, and in 1917 they executed her on charges of spying for the Germans.

The Red Baron On April 21, 1918, the World War II flying ace known as the Red Baron finally met his end. Baron Manfred von Richthofen was considered by his native Germany to be a modern-day knight of the sky. During World War I, he gunned down eighty enemy planes. The world came to know him as the Red Knight or, more popularly, the Red Baron because of his red airplane.

The Red Baron was noted for his exceptional flying skill and the bravery with which he maneuvered. Upon his death, Allied soldiers gathered souvenirs from his plane. Although he fought for the enemy, the Allies also formed an honor guard at the Red Baron's funeral.

Eddie Rickenbacker Captain Eddie Rickenbacker was the top American flying ace during World War I. In 1918, he was recognized for having shot down 22 planes and four observation balloons in just six month's time. Fourteen of his victories (downed planes) came in just one month. Rickenbacker did not begin to fly until he was 26 years old, one year before he joined the United States Army Air Service.

As a child, Rickenbacker was poor. He had to drop out of school when his father died. It was very unusual for a fighter pilot in World War I to be poor and uneducated. However, Rickenbacker had ambition. He became an expert auto mechanic and race car driver. In fact, he suggested to the United States military that they employ race car drivers as their fighter pilots. The military ignored him, and they thought it was ridiculous for him to think he could learn to fly at such a relatively late age. But he did, and the rest was history.

Suggested Activities

Spies and Aces Every modern war has known a number of spies and flying aces. As a class, find out about some of the most famous and what they did. Put their stories together in a book of war heroes and villains.

Java Mata Hari pretended to be a dancer from Java. Locate the nation on a map. Find out about its government, culture, and customs.

Barons A baron is a level of aristocracy in some European nations. Find out what this classification means as well as other titles of distinction, such as earl, duke, viscount, and so forth.

Aces The term "ace" originated in World War I. Research to determine what it means and how a person qualifies as an ace. (There *are* official guidelines.)

Fascism

The Fascist Party that saw its glory days in the mid-twentieth century had its beginnings in the 1900s and 1910s with a man who came to be known as Il Duce (the leader), Benito Mussolini.

Mussolini was born in Dovia, Italy, in 1883. For a short time, he was an elementary school teacher. In 1902, he developed an interest in socialism. He then served in the Italian military from 1905 to 1906, and afterwards he became a socialist leader, working for a socialist newspaper in Austria. However, the Austrians expelled him from their country because of his revolutionary tendencies.

In 1912, Mussolini became the editor of the official socialist newspaper in Italy. He used the paper to encourage Italian involvement in World War I; however, many in the Socialist Party disagreed with him. Mussolini decided to resign from that paper and to found

Benito Mussolini

his own. In 1914, he began Il Popolo d'Italia, again using the paper to encourage Italian participation in a war against Germany and Austria. Mussolini was expelled once more, this time from the Socialist Party.

Italy did enter the war in 1915. Mussolini served in the Italian Army from 1915 until 1917, when he was wounded. He spent the next two years building upon his ideas and developing a new way of thinking. Out of this came Fasci di Combattimento (Combat Groups), the foundation of Mussolini's new party. It would come to be known as the National Fascist Party in 1921. Mussolini's movement encouraged Italian interests and patriotism as well as government ownership of all resources. It also supported warlike policies and the persecution of minorities. In the 1920s, the fascists used violence to combat opposing parties.

Mussolini's goal was to make Italy a major power in the world, rivaling the greatest empires. Fortunately for the world, his plans did not prove successful. After World War II, the people of his own country executed him.

Suggested Activities

Cartography Draw maps of Italy before World War I and in the modern day. How do they differ?

Fascism Research to find out more about the Fascist party and its rise and fall in Europe. Compare it to Naziism.

History Find out about the Italian government since the era of Mussolini.

Dictators Research to learn out about other dictators in history, as Mussolini became in his later years. You can also hold a class experiment. Investigate what government is like under dictatorial leadership. Appoint a student or group of students to be the class dictators. Establish a period of time for their rule. Then switch and have the dictators be the governed and vice versa. Afterwards, have the class discuss their experiences.

Mexican Revolution

The 1910s were filled with revolution in Mexico. The nation saw several leaders during that time and a great deal of bloodshed.

Porfirio Díaz was the Mexican dictator in 1910, but opposition to him had been growing for the past decade. In the 1910 election, Francisco I. Madero chose to run in opposition to the dictator. Díaz had his opponent jailed until after the election. Díaz won, and Madero fled to the United States.

Madero had always opposed violence, but he saw no other way to rid the nation of the dictator than through revolution. In November of 1910, Madero called for revolution in Mexico. Several bands of revolutionaries sprang up throughout the nation. In May of 1911, Díaz' own government officials forced him from office in order to halt further revolutionary bloodshed. Madero, the Father of the Mexican Revolution, became president that year.

However, Mexico was split into many factions by this time, and Madero could not bring them together. In February of 1913, Madero was murdered by the forces of General Victoriano Huerta, who then seized power. Mexico was once again split in its loyalties. Many people, hoping for an end to the violence, supported Huerta. Others put their support behind Venustiano Carranza, a state governor. The United States also stood in support of Carranza, openly opposing the murder of Madero and halting economic aid to Mexico.

At this time, seamen on an American ship docked in a Mexican port were arrested for no reason. Although they were released and an apology was issued, the United States demanded a twenty-one-gun salute to the American flag. Huerta refused. American marines and sailors swarmed on Vera Cruz and captured the city. Nineteen Americans were killed and 126 Mexicans lost their lives. In July 1914, the United States and Carranza succeeded in overthrowing Huerta, who was forced to leave the country.

Carranza's government soon split in its own battle for power. Out of the revolution came two rebel leaders, Francisco "Pancho" Villa and Emiliano Zapata. They each led rebel forces in Mexico, vying for control and fighting Carranza's rule. In 1915, the United States stopped the export of guns to Carranza's opposers. In revenge, Pancho Villa raided the small American town of Columbus, New Mexico, killing eighteen Americans and burning the town. President Woodrow Wilson sent General John J. Pershing across the border to capture Villa. The army trailed Villa for three hundred miles, angering the Mexican government by their interference. However, Villa eluded capture.

In 1916, Carranza's government was recognized by most of Mexico, and in 1917, a new constitution was adopted. However, Carranza did not follow through on the laws of the constitution, and revolution broke out once more. In 1920, Carranza was killed by General Alvaro Obregon's rebellion. Obregon later became president of Mexico.

The United States abruptly withdrew from involvement in Mexico in 1917, just when it seemed full-scale war between the two nations could not be avoided. America's full attention was on Europe where it was about to enter the first World War.

Suggested Activities

Cartography Draw a map of Mexico and the United States.

History Trace the intertwined history of Mexico and the United States, focussing on where the two nations stand in relationship to one another today.

Panama Canal

For many years, sailors had wished for a shortened way to navigate their ships from the Pacific Ocean to the Atlantic. At the turn of the century, the journey took seven thousand miles (11,270 kilometers). However, beginning on August 15, 1914, it became a trip of forty miles (64.4 kilometers).

Panama is a small nation lying at the base of Central America and at the northwest corner of Columbia, South America. Its area is relatively narrow. In the 1880s, the French attempted to build a canal across the nation, but their plans were ineffective. They also had to deal with rampant jungle diseases such as malaria and yellow fever. France gave up its efforts.

In 1904, the United States, under the leadership of President Theodore Roosevelt, gained the rights to build a canal through Panama. The project began with a vengeance. Americans arrived in Central America by the thousands, hoping to capitalize on high wages. However, the problems of disease and climate were the same for the Americans as they had been for the French. In order to succeed, different tactics had to be taken.

President Roosevelt hired a chief engineer, General George W. Goethals, to head the project. Goethals and his team developed a system of locks that would raise and lower the water level for the passage of ships. General William Gorgas was brought on board to curb the effects of malaria and yellow fever. Although he was not able to stop the diseases, he did reduce the death toll from thirty-nine per thousand workers in 1906 to seven per thousand workers by 1914. However, throughout the project, nearly six thousand workers died.

The entire project required the removal of 240 million cubic yards of earth. The number of workers employed reached, at its peak, 40,000, and the cost for the project, which took ten years to complete, was more than $350 million.

Finally complete in summer 1914, the Panama Canal let pass its first ship, the *Alcon*, on August 15 with a shipload of officials on board. As they sailed the meager miles from ocean to ocean, no one seemed to mind the toll the canal had taken, and they rejoiced in the fifteen or so hours it took to sail completely through the passage. Although the canal could never repay the lives lost, it has more than repaid the financial costs. Today, approximately seventy ships pass through the canal each day at a cost of approximately $7,000 in tolls.

Suggested Activities

Cartography Draw Panama and the location of the canal on a map. Also draw a map showing the route that needed to be taken by ships prior to the canal's completion in 1914.

Disease Find out about malaria and yellow fever and how they were treated in the years of the Panama Canal's construction. Also find out how they are treated today.

Research and Discussion Find out the importance to the United States of the Panama Canal. Determine why it was considered worth spending lives and money in order to construct the canal. Discuss what you find.

History Trace the history of the canal from the time it was built until the present. Does the United States still maintain rights to the canal?

Passages

Births

1910
- Sy Oliver, American jazz composer

1911
- Phil Silvers, American comedian
- Lucille Ball, American actress

1912
- Charles Addams, American cartoonist

1913
- Richard Nixon, United States president
- Albert Camus, French author
- John Mitchell, U.S. Attorney General
- Danny Kaye, American actor

1914
- Tennessee Williams, American dramatist
- Pierre Balmain, Parisian fashion designer

1915
- Saul Bellow, American novelist
- Arthur Miller, American dramatist
- Orson Welles, American filmmaker

1916
- Keenan Wynn, American actor
- Jackie Gleason, American actor and comedian

1917
- John Fitzgerald Kennedy, United States president
- Ferdinand Marcos, Philippine president
- Buddy Rich, American jazz drummer

1918
- Billy Graham, American evangelist
- Leonard Bernstein, American composer and conductor
- Rita Hayworth, American actress

1919
- Sir Edmund Percival Hillary, New Zealand explorer
- An Wang, American founder of Wang laboratories
- Malcolm Forbes, American publisher and businessman

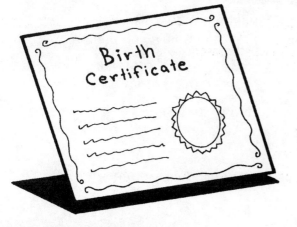

Deaths

1910
- King Edward VII, king of England
- Mark Twain, American author and humorist
- Count Leo Tolstoy, Russian novelist and philosopher
- Mary Baker Eddy, founder of Christian Science
- Julia Ward Howe, American writer and suffragist
- Henri Rousseau, French painter
- Florence Nightingale, noted American Civil War nurse

1911
- W. S. Gilbert, librettist

1912
- August Strindberg, Swedish dramatist

1913
- Harriet Tubman, American abolitionist and freedom fighter
- King George I, Greek monarch
- J.P. Morgan, American financier

1914
- Archduke Francis Ferdinand, heir to Austrian throne
- Pope Pius X, Roman Catholic leader

1915
- Rupert Brooke, English poet
- Booker T. Washington, American educator
- W. G. Grace, English cricketeer

1916
- Henry James, American novelist
- Rasputin, Russian monk
- Thomas Eakins, American artist

1917
- Edgar Degas, French artist
- Auguste Rodin, French sculptor
- Count Ferdinand von Zeppelin of Germany
- "Buffalo Bill" Cody, American hunter and showman

1918
- Claude Debussy, French composer

1919
- Theodore Roosevelt, United States president
- Sir Wilfred Laurier, first French-Canadian prime minister of Canada
- Louis Botha, South African general and statesman
- W. W. Campbell, Canadian poet
- A. D. Juilliard, founder of Juilliard School of Music in New York
- Andrew Carnegie, American industrialist and philanthropist
- Frank W. Woolworth, founder of the American five-and-ten-cent stores

Famous Firsts

In the 1910s, the United States saw the first

. . . celebration of Father's Day.

. . . electric self-starter for cars from General Motors.

. . . Indianapolis 500 automobile race.

. . . identification of vitamins.

. . . aircraft takeoff from the deck of a ship.

. . . senators elected by popular vote.

. . . income tax.

. . . wireless telegraph message sent across the Atlantic Ocean.

. . . legalized celebration of Mother's Day.

. . . establishment of the U.S. Coast Guard.

. . . skyscrapers of unlimited height built in New York.

. . . National Park Service.

. . . transcontinental telephone call.

. . . Tournament of Roses football game.

. . . Pulitzer Prize.

. . . airmail stamps and airmail service.

. . . municipal airport.

. . . jazz music.

. . . Oreo cookies, Life Savers, and cranberry sauce.

. . . neon signs.

. . . Hollywood movie studios.

. . . black world heavyweight boxing champion.

. . . woman elected to the U.S. House of Representatives.

. . . ship sail through the Panama Canal.

. . . talking movies with Edison's kinetophone.

. . . President to throw out the first ball in the baseball season.

. . . female licensed pilot.

. . . birth control clinic.

. . . constitutional right to vote for women.

. . . constitutional prohibition of the sale of alcohol.

. . . mechanical air conditioner, designed by W.H. Carrier.

Buzzwords

New inventions, habits, lifestyles, and occupations cause people to invent new words. The second decade of the new century was no exception. Listed below are some of the words and phrases that came into popular use throughout the decade.

Ace This term, which originated in France during World War I, denotes aviators who shoot down at least five enemy aircraft during war. The downing must be confirmed by an eyewitness or be recorded on film in order to qualify.

Airplane Originally *aeroplane*, this is an aircraft kept aloft by aerodynamic force.

Allergy This refers to a condition of unusual sensitivity to a substance, often characterized by systemic disturbances.

Backpack This word for a type of knapsack, usually attached to a frame and worn on the back of a hiker, originated during World War I.

Big shot This is a slang expression denoting someone who is influential.

Camouflage First used during World War I, this word came from the French *camoufler*; it means to disguise or to change the appearance of people or things to protect them from being sighted by the enemy.

Cellophane This is a thin, transparent product made from cellulose.

Collage This is a type of art in which bits of flat materials are pasted together onto a surface for their symbolic or metaphoric significance.

Cutting remark This slang expression suggests a comment made to emotionally injure an individual.

Dog tag This is a term for a military identification tag worn by a soldier around the neck. It comes from the tag's resemblance to an identification tag on a dog's collar.

Intelligence test This refers to a standardized series of questions or problems meant to test an individual's intellect.

It's a cinch. This slang expression means that something is done with ease.

Jazz This type of syncopated, heavily accented music originated with New Orleans black musicians and was originally improvisational.

Joyride This is slang for a trip by motor car taken just for the joy of riding.

Lousy This slang term means bad, foul, or inferior.

Lowbrow In slang, this term of contempt designates an individual lacking a high degree of cultural knowledge or intellectual prowess.

Lunatic fringe This term originally was slang for hair bangs; now it means an extremist or irrational member of a group.

Movie A shortened form of moving picture, this word refers to films.

Peachy This is slang for fine or excellent.

Pinch hit This term comes from baseball and means to bat in the place of the regular player when a hit is especially needed.

Radio station This is a building with equipment for broadcasting radio waves.

Spill the beans. This slang expression means to tell a secret, especially accidentally.

String along This slang expression means to hold someone's interest without satisfying his desire.

Sure When used as slang, this word means certainly.

Writing Prompts and Literature Ideas

Writing Prompts Use these suggestions for journal writing or as daily writing exercises. Some research or discussion may be appropriate before assigning a particular topic.

- You are a soldier on the western front during World War I. Write a page from your diary.

- You are in your home town in 1917, waiting for your older brother to return from war. Write a page from your diary.

- As a child laborer in a large New York factory in 1912, you suffer low wages, long hours, and poor working conditions. Write a conversation you have with the children working near you.

- You are in the room while the Treaty of Versailles is being negotiated. Describe what happens.

- Pancho Villa is the leader of your gang of rebels. One evening, you are all sitting around a campfire in the Mexican desert. Write the conversation you share.

- Write a speech from the perspective of a suffragette demanding the vote.

- Write a speech that President Wilson might have given Congress to convince them to join the League of Nations.

- You are part of the crew on the *Titanic*, and you survive the wreck. Tell your account to a newspaper reporter.

- You are ringside as Jack Johnson defeats Jim Jeffries. Describe the scene as well as the crowd.

Literature Ideas The following books can be used to supplement and enhance the study of the 1910s.

- ***All Quiet on the Western Front*** by Erique Maria Remarque (Little, Brown and Company, 1929)

  Originally published in German, this novel tells of a group of young German soldiers fighting the last days of World War I. The novel is especially realistic and poignant because the author was, in fact, a drafted soldier for the German Army. As the author writes in the preface of the book, "I will try simply to tell of a generation of men who, even though they may have escaped its shells, were destroyed by the war." Remarque left Nazi Germany in 1932 and settled in the United States.

- ***Rilla of Ingleside*** by Lucy Maud Montgomery (J.B. Lippincott Company, 1921)

  Eighth in the series of books beginning with *Anne of Green Gables*, *Rilla of Ingleside* tells the story of Anne's youngest daughter, Rilla Blythe. Rilla is fifteen years old when World War I breaks out in Canada's mother country of England. Her brothers and friends enlist to fight as British citizens. The story tells of the war experience from the perspective of the people back on the home front. A great deal of detail about the people and events of the war is included, but it is all interwoven with the feelings and efforts of the families and friends waiting for the war to be over and for their young men to return home. The story includes its share of tragedy, but as in all the Anne novels, there is always a stronger human spirit that rises above adversity.

- ***War Games*** by Michael Foreman (Arcade, 1994)

  Set in France in 1914, this book tells the story of four English friends who enlist in the army. The boys are sent to the western front and posted as sentries very close to the German trenches. Barbed wire, dead bodies, and devastation surround them, but on Christmas Eve an impromptu truce is observed. The armies take turns serenading one another with Christmas carols. On Christmas Day the peace is continued as the men shake hands, bury the dead, and then engage in a soccer game. Days later, however, the fighting resumes. This book is somewhat based on actual events.

Twenties Overview

When Warren Harding campaigned for the presidency in 1920, he promised a "return to normalcy." For most Americans, this meant a return to life as it had been before World War I, but the war had changed America and the world too much. Harding's brief administration is remembered for its corruption, especially the Teapot Dome scandal. After Harding's untimely death in 1923, Calvin Coolidge was sworn into office. Believing that "The chief business of America is business," Coolidge shepherded tax laws through Congress that were mostly favorable to businesses. In 1928 Herbert Hoover, who promised "four years of prosperity," won the presidency by a landslide. After the stock market crash of 1929, Hoover was largely blamed for the disaster.

Prohibition became the law of the land in 1920. No one is certain whether drinking increased during Prohibition or not, but it did spread among women and youth and became a symbol of defiance. It also gave rise to organized crime and increased violence. Bootlegging was a big business.

By the end of the twenties many families had automobiles—a novelty at the beginning of the decade. Radios brought nightly comedy shows and news to families throughout the country and changed political campaigns. People flocked to the movies, and in 1927 they even had sound.

Musicians George Gershwin and Aaron Copland, writers Ernest Hemingway and F. Scott Fitzgerald, and artists Mary Cassatt and Grant Wood became prominent. In the predominantly black-populated section of Harlem in New York City, the Harlem Renaissance produced a host of great African American writers, artists, and musicians.

Fostered by presidents who favored business, the stock market reached new heights before the crash on October 29, 1929. At first President Hoover believed that the situation was temporary and refused to allow government aid for homeless and out-of-work people. His seeming insensitivity to the plight of the American people cost him the election of 1930.

For Discussion

1. What innovations were making their way into the everyday lives of the American people during the 1920s? How did these innovations change the lifestyles of the typical American?

2. Can you imagine your life now with only radio and no television? How would your life be different if that were the case?

3. Was it fair for the American public to blame Hoover for the effects of the stock market crash? How could this disaster possibly have been avoided?

4. What safety improvements have been made in the automobile since its invention? What problems has the automobile brought to our lives? How would your life be different without the automobile?

1920s Politics and Economics

On this page you will find a summary of some of the most significant political and economic events of the twenties decade. Further discussions of the topics can be found on the indicated pages.

Prohibition Called the "noble experiment," the Eighteenth Amendment, which made the manufacture, sale, and transportation of liquor illegal, became the law of the land on January 20, 1920. Read more about Prohibition and its consequences on page 129 of this book.

Women's Rights In August of 1920, women's long fight for the vote ended with ratification of the Nineteenth Amendment to the Constitution. For further information about women and the vote, see page 131 of this book.

The Red Scare Attorney General A. Mitchell Palmer, who hoped to be president, took advantage of the public's alarm over labor riots at home and Communist rebellions overseas. The result was a Red Scare that ruined many lives. Read page 120 for more information about the Red Scare.

Teapot Dome Scandal Warren G. Harding appointed friends to positions of power. They used their public offices for personal gain, accepting bribes from business interests and giving away priceless oil reserves. This scandal is one of the most blatant acts of government corruption ever seen. See page 121 for more details about the Teapot Dome Scandal.

Scopes Trial John Scopes was indicted for teaching the theory of evolution. The trial was intended to test the Tennessee law against teaching such theories and the First Amendment separation of church and state. For more details about the Scopes trial see page 135.

Immigration America's "open door" policy toward immigration ended with the institution of quota laws in 1921. Many Americans feared that they would lose their jobs to newcomers who were willing to work for less pay. Others were suspicious of newcomers with their different customs and languages.

Stock Market Crash After the stock market fell on October 29, 1929, people lost their jobs, companies went out of business, and belt tightening became a way of life for everyone. A number of factors contributed to the fall of the stock market in 1929, including buying on margin and the ensuing selling panic. Read more about the stock market crash on page 122.

The Red Scare

Communism is a system of government in which most property and goods belong to the state. Its citizens are expected to share the proceeds, and there is a noticeable absence of classes. Anarchy is the absence of government authority or law, and its followers believe that all forms of government are oppressive and should be abolished. Both of these radical ideas were viewed as threats to America during the twenties.

In 1917 Russian communists revolted and took control of their government. Two years later, there were reports of similar revolutions throughout Europe. Some people feared that the communists wanted to take over the United States' government. When thousands of coal miners and steelworkers went out on strike in 1919, rumors led many Americans to conclude that such strikes were the result of communist infiltration.

In April postal workers discovered bombs addressed to government leaders, including A. Mitchell Palmer, President Wilson's attorney general. Palmer, who wanted to become president, inflamed public opinion and began a campaign against the communists. Government agents invaded private homes, raided union offices, and deported 249 immigrants. Early in 1920, seven thousand people were arrested in an attempt to find the people responsible for sending the bombs. Palmer predicted a communist attack in May of 1920, but it did not materialize, and Palmer was discredited. In September of 1920 a bomb exploded on Wall Street, killing thirty-eight people and injuring a number of others. Although it apparently was an anarchist plot, Americans took it in stride.

The Sacco-Vanzetti Case

Nicola Sacco and Bartolomeo Vanzetti were anarchists and Italian immigrants who were arrested and tried for the holdup murder of a paymaster and his guard at a shoe factory in South Braintree, Massachusetts. Convicted in spite of strong evidence of their innocence, they were electrocuted. The debate over their guilt or innocence continues to this day.

Suggested Activities

Communism Have the students pool their pens and pencils in a central location, a large coffee can, for example. Whenever they need a pen or pencil they can take one from the container, but it cannot be one of their own. After experimenting with this system for a day or two, discuss with the class how they felt about sharing their utensils with others.

The Sacco-Vanzetti Trial Discuss the effects of public sentiment on criminal trials. Ask students if they believe the pair received a fair trial. Why or why not? Would the outcome be the same today?

Reference

The Sacco-Vanzetti Trial by Doreen Rappaport (HarperCollins, 1992).

The Teapot Dome Scandal

When the facts about the Teapot Dome Scandal emerged, the American people were shocked and outraged.

Who: President Harding appointed some of his friends to cabinet positions, delegating important responsibilities to men who were not qualified. Albert B. Fall was his Secretary of the Interior.

What: Congress designated land in California and Wyoming to ensure that enough oil would be available for the U.S. Navy in case of emergencies, i.e., war. Interior Secretary Fall secretly plotted to have these oil reserves turned over to his department. He then sold the drilling leases to private developers in return for bribes and kickbacks. A Senate investigation uncovered the scheme.

Where: This controversy centered on the oil reserves in Teapot Dome near Casper, Wyoming, and in Elk Hills, California.

When: Fall leased the oil reserves to oil companies in 1922. The scandal broke on October 23, 1923, two months after President Harding's death.

Why: Fall received over three hundred thousand dollars in cash, stock, and cattle in return for the lands. He was convicted for accepting a bribe and achieved the dubious distinction of becoming the first cabinet member in American history to go to jail.

Afterward: President Harding suffered a fatal heart attack before the Senate finished its report about the scandal. People were angry when they heard the news. It certainly changed their opinions of Harding. In Harding's defense, it is thought that he never personally profitted from these corrupt dealings.

Suggested Activities

Speculation Ask students how they think the public would have reacted if President Harding had been alive when the Senate completed its investigation of this scandal. Have them write a paragraph telling whether he should or should not have been impeached by Congress.

Corruption Interior Secretary Fall was the first cabinet member to serve jail time for his crimes. He was not the only crooked politician in Harding's administration. Assign groups to research other members of the "Poker Cabinet."

Crooks Harding may not have realized that the friends he appointed to office were ill qualified for their jobs or that some were crooks who would end up stealing money from the government. Brainstorm a list of ways a president can make sure that only qualified, honest people are given important government offices.

Black Tuesday

On Tuesday, October 29, 1929, the stock market collapsed. Ten billion dollars in stock were lost in very heavy trading in only a few hours that day. Stocks that had sold for twenty to forty dollars a share just a few weeks ago now sold for pennies. High rollers who had been speculating in the market were immediately bankrupted. President Hoover's claim that the country's business was "on a sound and prosperous basis" proved to be tragically incorrect. In the weeks and months that followed, the effects were even more profound. Five thousand banks failed and closed their doors, causing over nine million people to lose their savings accounts. For the first three years following the stock market crash, an average of 100,000 jobs were lost each week. Since so many people were out of work or in danger of losing their jobs, people began to economize and avoided unnecessary purchases. As demand for goods decreased, businesses were forced to lay off workers, adding to unemployment. Soon, people's money ran out, and they were unable to pay their mortgages and other debts. They lost their homes, cars, and other valuables. Hardship became a way of life. Some families were forced to live in shacks made of discarded lumber and cardboard. These shanty towns became known as "Hoovervilles," and the newspapers they used for blankets were called "Hoover blankets."

Suggested Activities

Cause and Effect Briefly review with the class the relationship between cause and effect. Establish that cause is the reason something happens and effect is the action that takes place in response to the cause. Discuss with the class some of the following causes and effects from the paragraphs about Black Tuesday.

a. People economized and avoided unnecessary purchases (cause); demand for goods decreased and businesses laid off additional workers (effects).

b. The stock market crashed (cause); high rollers were bankrupted, banks failed, and nine million people lost their savings (effects).

c. Millions of people were out of work (cause); they began to economize (effect).

Priorities Group the students and have them make a list of at least 15 ways they think families during the depression began to economize. In whole-group compare the different lists. Extend the activity with a discussion of how they would economize today if their family support member suddenly lost his or her job. Compare these methods with the lists for depression families.

Simulated Crash To help students understand how and why the stock market crashed, engage them in a simulation activity. Complete directions and game cards can be found on pages 85 to 88 in Teacher Created Materials #480—*American History Simulations.*

Understanding the Stock Market

In order to fully comprehend the implications and importance of the stock market crash, it is necessary to understand how the stock market works. Use the background information on this page and the flow chart on page 124 to help students learn the terms and ways of the stock market world. Follow this lesson with the activities on page 125.

As a pre-test, write each term on the chalkboard or overhead projector. Ask the students to number a sheet of paper from one to ten. Read a definition aloud (see answer key) and have students write the correct answer, choosing from the list.

Make a copy of the What Is the Stock Market? section for each pair or small group. Instruct the pairs or groups to find definitions for each of the 10 words within the text of the story and compare the answers to their pre-test responses.

What Is the Stock Market?

The business of buying and selling stocks is known as the stock market. Stocks, or shares in a company, are bought and sold in a place called the stock exchange. The most important stock exchange is on Wall Street in New York City. Usually the stock market reflects the business world. If business is good, the value of stocks, or shares in a business, go up, and it is called a bull market. If business is poor, however, stocks go down, and the market is called a bear market.

During the twenties the prevailing market was a bull market. By 1927 more and more people were getting rich from their investments in the stock market. This led others to use all their savings to invest in the market for a handsome profit or dividend. After all, they wanted to cash in on an easy way to make money. Some people began buying on margin, which means they would pay a percentage of the purchase price and then borrow the rest of the money from the stockbroker who sold them the stocks. When a panic of wild selling caused the prices of stocks to plummet in mid-1929, a devastating crash followed. Stockbrokers had to sell as the stock prices fell, leaving people with worthless stock holdings. Worse yet, stockholders still owed money on their stocks because they had purchased them on margin. People had to sell their homes or cars to repay their loans. Businesses began losing money and were forced to lay off masses of workers. Banks that loaned the money in the first place had to close their doors when the loans went unpaid. Today the Securities and Exchange Commission, or the SEC as it is commonly called, regulates the stocks and bonds, or securities, market. An independent government agency, the SEC was formed in 1934 with Joseph P. Kennedy as its first chairman.

1. bear market _____

2. stockbroker _____

3. dividend _____

4. stock exchange _____

5. SEC _____

6. bull market _____

7. panic _____

8. stock _____

9. margin _____

10. stock market _____

Stock Market Flow Chart

Make a transparency of this page for use on the overhead projector. Read and discuss the steps together.

To create a hands-on activity, make enough copies of this page for each group of students (cover up the numbers before copying). Cut apart the rectangles from one page and place them in an envelope labeled Stock Market Flow Chart. Continue in the same manner for all copies. Give each group an envelope and direct them to put the flow chart in correct sequence. To make this activity self-correcting, write a code on the back of each section. For example, step 1 could be labeled ab, step 2 cd, step 3 ef, etc.

1. The XYZ Games Company manufactures board games, and it wants to expand its operation. Since money is needed to buy a new plant and more sophisticated equipment, the company looks for people who will invest money in the company.

2. XYZ Games Company decides to go public and sells shares, called stocks, in its company. Ten thousand shares are offered at $100 each. Everyone who buys a share in the company becomes a part owner, or shareholder, of the XYZ Games Company.

3. The new games are a huge success and earn large profits for the company. Stockholders are given a percentage of the profits; this percentage is called a dividend.

4. XYZ continues to do well and demand for stock in the company increases. However, there are only 10,000 shares. People are willing to pay more than the $100 asking price for the shares. Soon, XYZ stock sells for $200 per share.

5. As more and more people try to enter the booming stock market, a new purchasing tactic becomes common—buying stocks on margin. That is, a small amount is paid down, and the rest of the money is borrowed from the stockbroker, the person who sells stocks. People are using their entire savings just trying to cash in on these windfall profits.

6. In October of 1929 a panic ensues when everyone begins to sell and no one wants to buy. What this means to the stockholder is that when the stock price drops, the stockbroker sells it. The stockholder not only loses his down payment, but he still owes the stockbroker the remaining purchase price borrowed to buy the stock. The stockbroker, in turn, owes money to the bank from which the money was borrowed.

7. In order to repay these loans, some people sell their houses and cars. No one has enough money to buy games from XYZ Company, so it closes its doors. Hundreds of workers lose their jobs. Banks close due to unpaid loans—they have no money.

8. A depression sweeps the country. Twenty-five percent of the work force is unemployed. All kinds of people, both rich and poor, are affected. Business activity declines, prices fall, and unemployment remains high for the next ten years.

Reading the Stock Pages

Have you ever looked at the stock quotations in your daily newspaper? At first glance, it may seem like a jumble of numbers. But there is an easy way to make sense of it all. A sample from a stock page is shown below. This entry is from the New York Stock Exchange. Following the entry is an explanation of all the letters and numbers.

Stock	Div.	PE	Sales	Close	Chg.
Albertsn	.52	18	3126	29 $7/8$	$3/8$
AmExp	.90	14	10170	39 $5/8$	$1/8$
BankAm	1.84	9	13144	54 $1/2$	$1/4$

Stock Stock refers to the name of the company, usually abbreviated, i.e., Albertsn stands for Albertsons (a grocery chain); AmExp for American Express (credit card company); BankAm for Bank of America.

Div. Div. is the abbreviation for dividend. The dividend is expressed in dollars and cents. For Albertsons, the dividend is 52 cents; for American Express it is 90 cents; for Bank of America it is one dollar and 84 cents.

PE. The price-earnings ratio (PE) is the ratio of the current market price of a share of stock to the corporation's annual earnings per share. The PE of Alberstons is 18.

Sales This figure shows in thousands the number of shares sold that day. 3,126,000 shares of Albertsons were sold; 10,170,000 shares of American Express were sold; 13,144,000 shares of Bank of America were sold.

Close Close refers to the price of the last share sold. Albertsons closing price was $29 $7/8$; American Express' closing price was $39 $5/8$; Bank of America's closing price was $54 $1/2$.

Chg. Chg. is the abbreviation for change. This figure shows the difference between the closing price today and the closing price the day before. Note that the closing price for the day before is not shown on the chart. The plus (+) sign before the change means that the price is up; a minus sign (-) indicates the price is down. The change for Albertsons is up $3/8$ and American Express is up $1/8$. Bank of America is down $1/4$.

Note: Some stock pages contain more than one list of stocks. The New York Stock Exchange, the American Stock Exchange, and NASDAQ each list diffrent stocks.

Think and Discuss

With a partner solve the following problems based on the stock market sample at the top of this page. Check your answers with another pair.

1. Figure out the closing price of Albertsons for the day before.
2. What was Bank of America's closing price for the day before?
3. Which stock sold the most shares that day?
4. What is the difference between the number of shares sold in the two highest sellers?
5. What is the average amount of dividends paid by the three companies?
6. What is the difference between the two lowest closing prices?

Warren Gamaliel Harding

29th President, 1921–1923

Vice President: Calvin Coolidge

Born: November 2, 1865, in Corsica, Ohio

Died: August 2, 1923

Party: Republican

Parents: George Tyron Harding, Phoebe Elizabeth Dickerson

First Lady: Florence Kling De Wolfe

Children: None

Nickname: Wobbly Warren

Education: B.S. from Ohio Central College in Iberia, Ohio

Warren Gamaliel Harding

Famous Firsts:

- Harding was the first president to ride to his inauguration in an automobile and to speak over the radio.
- He was the first president to be born after the Civil War.
- Harding was the first president since the Civil War to speak in the South on behalf of equal rights for African Americans.

Achievements:

- With his promise of a "return to normalcy," Harding won the 1920 presidential election by a landslide.
- A new government office called the Bureau of the Budget was proposed; its job was to make a formal, unified budget for government spending.
- He signed the Immigration Restriction Act of 1921, establishing the first quotas on immigration in the nation's history.
- From November 1921 to February 1922, Harding convened the Washington Conference for the Limitation of Armament. The United States, Great Britain, Japan, France, and Italy all agreed to limit the size of their armies.

Interesting Facts:

- Despite the fact that he had voted for prohibition when he was a senator, Harding secretly stocked the White House with illegal bootleg liquor.
- Harding held numerous poker games which often ran late into the night. Many of his cabinet members were among the regular players. During one game, the president gambled away a complete set of White House china.
- Warren Harding was the first president for whom women could vote.
- Harding's Airedale, Laddie Boy, delivered the president's newspaper to him every day. Laddie Boy even had his own valet.

Calvin Coolidge

30th President, 1923–1929

Calvin Coolidge

Vice President: Charles G. Dawes

Born: July 4, 1872, in Plymouth, Vermont

Died: January 5, 1933

Party: Republican

Parents: John Calvin Coolidge, Victoria Josephine Moor

First Lady: Grace Anna Goodhue

Children: John; Calvin, Jr.

Nickname: Silent Cal

Education: Cum laude graduate of Amherst College; admitted to the bar in 1897

Famous Firsts:

- His first cabinet meeting lasted only 15 minutes.

Achievements:

- Coolidge often said "The chief business of America is business" and encouraged the speculative "Bull Market" of 1928. He also felt that the business of government was to keep out of business. In keeping with his policy, tax laws favorable to business were passed.

- Twice Coolidge vetoed the McNaury-Haugen farm bill, which provided that the government would purchase surplus crops from U.S. farmers at a fixed price and resell them abroad.

- Coolidge promoted commercial aviation, and in 1926 Congress passed the Air Commerce Act, which placed commercial aviation under federal regulation.

- In 1928 the Kellogg-Briand Pact was ratified. Countries who signed the agreement promised not to use war as a tool of national policy.

Interesting Facts:

- While Coolidge was governor of Massachusetts, the police force in Boston went on strike. He sent in the state troops and upheld the decision to fire the strikers. In a terse reply to the AFL leader, Samuel Gompers, Coolidge said, "There is no right to strike against the public safety by anybody, anywhere, any time."

- Coolidge was known for his thriftiness. In order to economize at the White House, guests were served plain ice water in paper cups.

- Nicknamed "Silent Cal" because he never wasted words, his reply to a woman who bet that she could get him to say at least three words was, "You lose."

Election Facts and Figures

	Election of 1920	Election of 1924	Election of 1928
Democrats	James M. Cox of Ohio ran for president with Franklin Roos as his running mate.	West Virginia lawyer John W. Davis was nominated on the 103rd ballot.	New York Governor Alfred E. Smith, was the first Roman Catholic nominated by a major political party.
Republicans	Senator Warren G. Harding of Ohio ran for president; his running mate was Governor Calvin Coolidge of Massachusetts.	Calvin Coolidge was unanimously nominated. Charles G. Davis was Coolidge's running mate.	Secretary of Commerce Herbert Hoover ran a low-key campaign, hinting at an early end to poverty.
Issues	Democrat Cox urged Americans to work hard for a lasting peace while the Republicans attacked Wilson's record, claiming he had been unprepared for war, and discredited Wilson's League of Nations.	Republicans feared voters might hold the scandals of the previous office against them, but Coolidge's direct manner following Harding's death seemed to steady the country.	While Smith was campaigning for religious tolerance, Republicans printed pamphlets claiming Smith would be the pope's servant if elected.
Slogans	Harding promised a "return to normalcy."	Keep cool with Coolidge.	Hoover coins said, "Good for 4 years of prosperity."
Results	Harding-Coolidge received 404 electoral votes to Cox-Roos 127.	Coolidge won with 382 electoral votes versus 136 for Davis. Robert M. LaFollette of the Progressive Party received 13 electoral votes.	Hoover carried 40 of the 48 states with a 444 to 87 electoral vote.

Prohibition

What is Prohibition? Prohibition, or the outlawing of the consumption of all alcoholic beverages, may seem like an unmanageable task on a national level. At the beginning of the twentieth century, there were those who thought otherwise. At the outset, the majority of Americans supported the Eighteenth Amendment, believing that a world without liquor would be a better place. After a few years, it became apparent that its drawbacks outweighed any possible benefits.

Alcohol-Related Problems Alcoholism was a prevalent problem in nineteenth century America. Men would drink away whole paychecks, leaving no money to support their families. Some women's groups, religious groups, and reformers fought for prohibition. Many states became dry; that is, they passed laws which made it illegal to buy or to sell liquor. The fight did not stop there, however, because some people wanted to make the entire nation dry. This would take a constitutional amendment.

Why Prohibition Was Supported Prohibition was supported by religious groups that believed drinking was sinful. Business leaders also favored prohibition, thinking it would reduce absenteeism at work. Other groups blamed poverty, disease, and crime on alcoholism. Physicians spoke out about the dangers of alcohol consumption to unborn babies and noted that in large families where the parents drank, the children were often mentally retarded. When the United States entered World War I, a strong argument for personal sacrifice and the need for grain to aid in the war effort led Congress to pass the Eighteenth Amendment. It read: "After one year from the ratification of this article the manufacture, sale, or transportation of intoxicating liquors within, the importation thereof into, or the exportation thereof from the United States and all territory subject to the jurisdiction thereof for beverage purposes is hereby prohibited." Ratified by 36 states in January of 1919, the Prohibition Amendment took effect in January 1920.

Why Prohibition Did Not Work Prohibition made drinking more attractive to many people. Consumption of alcohol by women and young people increased. Gangsters like Al Capone of Chicago took over the illegal activity of selling liquor. Speakeasies popped up all over the country — by 1933 there were more than 200,000 speakeasies throughout the United States. Prohibition laws became the most disliked and disobeyed laws in U.S. history. Congress did not foresee problems with enforcement of the law and did not provide enough money for agents.

Effects of Prohibition The restrictions of Prohibition probably caused the outrageous behaviors of the 1920s. Speakeasies, nightclubs, and blind pigs had abundant business. Making "bathtub gin" and brewing beer became popular pastimes. Disregard for Prohibition created contempt for other laws and made crime a big business.

Suggested Activities

Class Debate Have two groups of students prepare for and debate this question: Could the lessons of Prohibition be applied to the current drug problem in the United States?

Response Ask students to respond in writing to this question: Should Prohibition be reinstated? Why or why not? Discuss their written responses in whole group.

Words Have the students define these and other Prohibition-era terms: *dry, bootleggers, rumrunners, temperance, speakeasies, teetotaler, jake leg, blind pig.*

Campaign Many communities and large corporations have created campaign slogans, signs, and materials against drinking and driving. Assign individuals or pairs to create a poster that might help convince people not to drink and drive. Display all the posters on the classroom walls.

Coming to America

Immigration was not new to the 1920s, but the complexion for the situation changed dramatically in the early part of the twentieth century. From its earliest years the United States of America had an open door policy toward immigrants, placing few restrictions on the number of people entering this country. It was not until 1882 that the first law was passed banning people from a specific country. The Chinese Exclusion Act forbade Chinese laborers because it was feared that they would work for lower pay. In 1907 a "gentleman's agreement" between the United States and Japan barred Japanese immigrants.

In the early 1900s there were two groups who sought to have the doors closed to certain ethnic members. American laborers feared that they would lose their jobs to new immigrants, who were willing to work for lower wages. A second group believed that the newcomers were inferior. Still, it was not until 1917 that restrictions were in place, preventing thirty-three different categories of people from obtaining entry to the United States.

Immigration in the 1920s changed in another important way. Prior to 1880 newcomers originated mostly from countries in northern and western Europe. When the immigrant population shifted to southern and eastern European countries, some Americans became alarmed at the customs and languages. World War I placed a temporary halt to the problem as very few people came to America during that period. Once the war ended, the wave of immigrants rose steadily, with over 600,000 people arriving in 1921. With the passage of a new law that same year, immigration was limited by a quota system. The National Origins Act of 1924 established severe quotas for southern and eastern European countries. For example, 100,000 Italians had arrived in one year in the early 1900s, but the new quota limited Italy to 5,082 people per year; Greece was allowed only 307 people per year, while Russia was permitted 2,784 per year. Not until the 1960s, when Lyndon Johnson became president, did those quota laws change.

Suggested Activities

Respond Have the students respond to this question: Are quota laws for immigration fair or necessary? With the class, discuss some possible solutions for this dilemma.

Charts Divide the students into groups and have them make charts comparing 1920s immigration with current immigration. Include topics such as length of travel, mode of travel, cities of entry, and countries of origin.

References

Do People Grow on Family Trees? by Ira Wolfman (Workman Publishing, 1991).
Teacher Created Materials #234 *Thematic Unit—Immigration*.

The Nineteenth Amendment

The framers of the Constitution of the United States gave little, if any, thought to the rights of women. Women could not own property in most states, and very few worked outside the home. Education for women was considered unnecessary and frivolous. As essential as women were to the family structure, they did not have equal status with men on any front.

For years women lobbied for their right to vote. Susan B. Anthony was a major force in organizing women in the mid-nineteenth century. Her fight for the right to vote was carried on by the suffragists in the early 1900s. Marches and motorcades were staged; banners were displayed with the women's pleas. Police arrested and jailed some of these women, but that did not deter them.

Finally, in June of 1919, Congress passed the Nineteenth Amendment. The necessary states quickly ratified the amendment, and it became law on August 26, 1920. With just 28 words, women were granted full rights to vote.

Suggested Activities

Response Have students respond in writing to the following questions. Why was the Nineteenth Amendment necessary in the first place? Did the Constitution imply that women could vote? Did it ever state in the Constitution that women could not vote?

Banners Pair or group the students. Have them create posters or banners, complete with slogans for the suffragists to use, and stage a mock demonstration. Role play with male students giving the female students reasons why women should not be able to vote; females can respond appropriately.

Note: Design posters or banners, using a computer program like *Print Shop Deluxe* (Broderbund, 800-521-6263) or *Super Print* (Scholastic, 800-541-5513). Tape the printed panels together and glue them to sheets of tagboard for more durability. Attach cardboard strip handles to posters for individuals. Let groups of students help carry the long banners.

Research Give students a choice of these three suffragists to research: Elizabeth Cady Stanton, Susan B. Anthony, or Carrie Chapman Catt. Make a group chart divided into three sections, each headed with the name of a different suffragist. Let students write at least one interesting fact in the appropriate section.

Writing Assign students to write one page about the Nineteenth Amendment, using either of the following titles: What the Nineteenth Amendment Means to Me or How the Nineteenth Amendment Changed the Course of History.

References

For a prepared teaching unit on women's suffrage, write to National Women's History Project, 7738 Bell Rd., Windsor, CA 95492 or call (707) 838-6000 for more information.

You Want Women to Vote, Lizzie Stanton? by Jean Fritz (G. P. Putnam's Sons, 1995).

The Fight for Birth Control

Teacher's Note: *The information on this page may not be suitable for all students. Please review it carefully before presenting it to your class.*

As a child Margaret Sanger witnessed her own mother's struggle with numerous pregnancies. In thirty years the woman conceived eighteen times and gave birth to only eleven living children. Weakened and exhausted by the many pregnancies, Sanger's mother died at the age of fifty. This living example inspired Sanger to pursue her mission in life—to deliver information about birth control to all women.

In the year 1910, very little in the way of contraception was available. The Comstock law, which declared it obscene to provide information about birth control, had been passed. Poor, uneducated women had nowhere to turn. It was, indeed, a frightening situation. As a public-health nurse in New York's lower east side in 1912, Sanger was appalled by the conditions endured by the women she saw. Poverty, disease, and death rates were high; yet, the women continued to bear children. Determined to provide relief for these women, Sanger wrote a series of articles about reproduction for a socialist newspaper. When one was declared obscene under the Comstock law, Sanger fought back and founded a newspaper called *Woman Rebel*. Before she could be tried for her crime, Sanger left for Europe, where she studied what other countries were doing about family planning.

Margaret Sanger

On her return to the United States, the case was dismissed, but Sanger was not through. In 1916 in Brooklyn, New York, she and her sister, Ethel Byrne, opened America's first birth control clinic. Arrested for keeping a public nuisance, the pair was jailed for thirty days. The resulting publicity served to help Sanger's cause, and New York state revised its laws.

In the meantime, Sanger's personal life was disintegrating. Her five-year-old daughter died of pneumonia, and Sanger and her husband divorced. Later, she married a wealthy businessman who wholeheartedly supported her efforts. Through it all she continued her fight for birth control and in 1921 organized the American Birth Control League, now known as Planned Parenthood. Six years later she helped plan the first world population conference which was held in Geneva, Switzerland.

In 1966, six years after the first birth control pills for women were marketed, Margaret Sanger died. Thanks to the efforts of this indomitable woman, information about effective birth control is now widely available.

Suggested Activity

Discussion With the class discuss this question: How did Margaret Sanger contribute to the quality of life for women in the early part of the twentieth century?

Uncovering the KKK

There are those who maintain that certain races, religions, and nationalities are superior to others. The Ku Klux Klan, commonly called the KKK, is one such group. To learn more about their activities, particularly in the 1920s, read the information below.

What It Is The Ku Klux Klan is an organization of people who hate other groups of people, particularly those who are not native-born, Protestant, and white. Members of the KKK especially oppose the advancement of blacks, Jews, and other minorities.

Origins In 1865 or 1866 a group of Confederate Army veterans in Pulaski, Tennessee, formed a social club. The name Ku Klux Klan is taken from the Greek word *kyklos* which means circle and the English word *clan*. Members of this group believed in the superiority of whites and began terrorizing African Americans to prevent them from voting. Klan members wore robes and white hoods to hide their identities and even draped sheets over their horses. They burned crosses to frighten blacks, Jews, and other minorities, and threatened, beat, and lynched their victims. The Ku Klux Klan spread rapidly throughout the southern United States. Following a Congressional investigation in 1871, the Klan activities diminished.

A Return After World War I, agricultural depression, migration, and other social and economic factors caused social unrest. The Klan philosophy was broadened to include anti-foreign, anti-Catholic, anti-Semitic and anti-urban principles. At its height in the mid-twenties, the revived KKK had between 4 ½ and 6 million members and heavily influenced the government of at least seven states. Some called it "The Invisible Empire."

Election of 1928 During the 1928 presidential election, the group played a pivotal role. Al Smith, the Democratic presidential candidate, was an Irish Catholic. The KKK maintained that if Smith were elected, the Catholic pope would rule America from Rome. Many believed their propaganda, and Smith was easily defeated.

Suggested Activities

Terms Write the words *hate, bigotry,* and *racism* on the chalkboard. With the class define and discuss what they mean. Discuss why people hate and what role fear plays in discrimination.

Threats In 1924 African American actor Paul Robeson was threatened by the KKK for playing the role of a black man married to a white woman in *All God's Children Got Wings.* Discuss with the students the acceptance of mixed-race couples today. What are the concerns about these relationships? How does society view such relationships?

Quote One Grand Wizard, a KKK leader, once said, "Negroes, Catholics, and Jews are the undesirable elements in America." Ask students to respond to that statement.

The Harlem Renaissance

Terms *Harlem* is an area of New York City which became a black community during the twenties. *Renaissance* means a rebirth or revival of intellectual and/or artistic achievement. Michaelangelo was a product of the Italian Renaissance, which marked the transition from medieval to modern times.

Purposes This literary movement gave black men and women a chance to create their own images and express their unique experiences as black Americans in the United States. College-educated African American men and women flocked to Harlem to share their ideas, write poetry and novels, paint pictures, and produce movies. Their written and artistic works celebrated the vitality of life and reflected the black cultural heritage.

Harlem became a great center of African American culture as the community found a new sense of independence and developed pride in its own traditions.

Problems The rapid growth of the area brought its own set of problems, including overcrowding and high rents. The death rate for African Americans was almost twice that for whites. Unable to support themselves with their art, African Americans often took menial jobs. White people flocked to Harlem, which they thought of as an alien and exotic place, for the fresh nightlife, but they regarded blacks as primitive and one-dimensional. Blacks were not accepted as equals and could not be served in many of the Harlem theaters and clubs where they performed. Writers and artists alike worked hard to dispel these myths, and the resulting art and culture are testimonies to their diverse abilities.

Suggested Activities

Poets Read some selections from the poetry of both Langston Hughes and Countee Cullen. Who employed a more traditional style? Which style do the students prefer? Why?

Musicians Duke Ellington and Louis Armstrong played jazz music. What instrument did each play? How did they get a start in their careers? How were their styles alike and different?

Novelist Zora Neale Hurston used her skills as an anthropologist to explore the culture of her Florida hometown. She listened to and collected folk tales such as "Why the Porpoise Has His Tail on Crossways" and "How the Woodpecker Nearly Drowned the Whole World." Have students choose one of these titles and write a creative tale.

Discussion Have students discuss how African Americans' experience of life in the twenties differed from that of their white counterparts.

Back to Africa During the early twenties Marcus Garvey, who owned a fleet of steamships, urged African Americans to be proud of their African roots and suggested that they return to Africa to establish a free black nation. With the class discuss whether the Back to Africa movement would have helped or hurt the African American's position in America had it been carried out.

The Monkey Trial

The Scopes Trial, sometimes called the Monkey Trial, was the best-known trial of the decade. Its main issue was the public school's right to teach the science of evolution.

Background Information Evolution is the theory which traces life on earth through millions of years of development from simple one-celled creatures through increasingly complex plants and animals to humans. Fundamentalist Christians, among others, believe in the creation story that is told in the Bible. The Bible states that the world was created in six days. In 1925 the Tennessee legislature passed a law prohibiting the teaching of any theory that denies the creation story of the Bible. It also prohibited teaching that man evolved from lower animals.

When and Where The trial took place in Dayton, Tennessee, in the summer of 1925.

How the Trial Came About In 1920 the ACLU (American Civil Liberties Union) offered to pay the legal expenses of anyone interested in testing the Tennessee law. The ACLU believed that the law was unconstitutional since the First Amendment provides for the separation of church and state. This amendment guarantees that the government cannot pick your beliefs, force you to attend church, or make you pay taxes to support a particular church, for example.

The Players The defendant is John Scopes, a 24-year-old school teacher.

Clarence Darrow, an attorney and an agnostic (someone who is unsure whether there is a God or not), represents Scopes.

William Jennings Bryan heads up the prosecution for the state of Tennessee. Well known and well liked, Bryan has run for president three times and is a fundamentalist.

Arguments Darrow attempted to prove that church doctrine is being imposed on public schools because the 1925 Tennessee state law tells citizens what they should believe. Bryan accused Darrow of wanting to slur the Bible.

Settlement Scopes was convicted and fined $100, but the conviction was later reversed because of a small legal error.

Present Day In the 1980s Arkansas and Louisiana passed laws requiring public schools that teach evolution to devote equal time to the teaching of creationism. In 1987 the Supreme Court found that these laws are in conflict with the First Amendment.

Suggested Activities

Opinion Ask the students their opinions about the following question: Would the outcome of the case be the same if it were tried today? Why or why not?

First Amendment. Assign the students to find and copy the text of the First Amendment. With the class discuss what it means.

Public Opinion Most people at the time did not take the trial seriously and called it the Monkey Trial. What part do monkeys play in the trial?

The Walt Disney Story

Although his own childhood was not happy, Walt Disney brought joy to children worldwide with his cartoon characters and theme parks. His best known creation is Mickey Mouse, described by Disney as "a nice fellow who never does anybody any harm." Walter Elias Disney debuted on December 5, 1901, the fourth of five children born to Elias and Flora Disney. Disney's early years were spent on a farm in Marceline, Missouri, where he developed an interest in drawing. The family moved to Kansas City in 1910. Disney continued his art and at 14 enrolled in classes at the Kansas City Art Institute. World War I provided the opportunity to leave his abusive father. He quit school after ninth grade and, too young for combat, served as a Red Cross ambulance driver in France. In 1919, Disney and a friend formed an art company and made some animated cartoons.

Walt Disney

Four years later he moved to California, where he and his brother, Roy, began Walt Disney Productions. Disney created a character he called Mortimer the Mouse. His wife, Lillian, suggested a name that was less stuffy, and Mickey was born. In 1928, with Disney providing his voice, Mickey Mouse starred in *Steamboat Willie,* the first cartoon to use *synchronized* sound (sound that matched the movements and actions in the film).

The success of Mickey Mouse was only the beginning. In the thirties Mickey acquired a number of cartoon pals, including Donald Duck, Pluto, Minnie Mouse, and Goofy. Disney continued to explore and innovate, developing better technologies to tell his stories. The thirties brought the world's first feature-length animated film, *Snow White and the Seven Dwarfs,* and in 1941 animation and live action were combined for the first time in *The Reluctant Dragon.* In the 1950s, Disney added live action features, nature films, and feature films for television. His cast of characters was featured on weekly television programs and on the daily *Mickey Mouse Club.* Disney earned more than 30 Academy Awards for his work.

Walt Disney died in 1966, but the studio he founded continues the Disney tradition, bringing new technology to films. Disney's spirit lives on in his memorable characters and theme parks.

Suggested Activities

Mickey Designs Mickey Mouse has been merchandised in numerous forms: on clothing, eating utensils, jewelry, etc. Group the students and have them design a new product featuring Mickey Mouse.

Catalog Brainstorm a list of Disney films. Categorize them by technique (live, animated, etc.) or by subject "lands," like fantasy land, tomorrow land, etc.

Reference

The Man Behind the Magic by Katherine and Richard Greene (Viking, 1990).

The Master Clown of Silent Movies

He was an actor, director, and a music composer. A man of extremes, his life went from utter poverty to wealth, from being adored to being hated to being honored around the world. His name was Charlie Chaplin, the best and most-loved pantomime artist who ever lived. Chaplin was born Charles Spencer Chaplin in London on April 16, 1889, to Charles Chaplin, Sr. and Hannah, popular music hall entertainers. At the age of five, Chaplin made his debut, and his singing and dancing delighted the audience. When he was 17, Chaplin and his brother Sydney found work with England's most popular pantomime artist. Chaplin learned quickly to use his body instead of words to create laughter. Four years later, Chaplin and the troupe were off to America.

Although the show was not a particular success, Chaplin was, and he landed a contract with the movies. At first, Chaplin was uneasy with the acting style of the day, which consisted mostly of exaggerated facial gestures and body movements coupled with a lot of slapstick. Sound was not recorded, and there were no scripts. Sets were close to one another and noisy; in a word, the scene was chaotic. Chaplin determined to make the best of the situation and transformed himself with baggy old pants, a tight jacket and tie, a derby, huge shoes, and a skinny bamboo cane. The Little Tramp was born. Audiences loved him, and after only three years he was a world-famous star and a millionaire.

Charlie Chaplin

During the depression of the thirties, the tide turned against him. Some people accused Chaplin of being un-American because he had never become a U.S. citizen. Others called him a communist and claimed he had not paid taxes. Amid this and other criticisms, Chaplin traveled to Europe in 1952 and did not return. The U.S. government would not allow it unless hearings were held on both his political and personal lives. He lived in Switzerland with his wife and children. Not until April 1972, when he was to receive a special Academy Award for his lifetime achievement, did he return to visit the U.S. New audiences had discovered his work, and he was once again the beloved master clown of the movies.

Suggested Activities

Pantomimes In the movie *The Gold Rush*, Chaplin eats his boot and makes it appear that he is enjoying a special treat. Let students take turns pantomiming this scene or another from any of his films.

Charades Write the names of some of Chaplin's films on separate index cards. Ask for volunteers to pantomomine the titles for the rest of the class: *The Kid, The Gold Rush, City Lights, The Tramp, Modern Times.*

Skits Group the students and have them write and act skits with no words. Let the groups take turns performing for the rest of the class.

Satchel Paige and the Negro League

During the 1920s, organized baseball was separated into all-white and all-black leagues. Players on teams in the Negro leagues, as they were called, received low wages, and equipment was shabby. Because many businesses would not accommodate African Americans, the players sometimes had to sleep on the bus or in the dugout at the ball park. Despite these hardships, the players remained dedicated to their work.

Leroy "Satchel" Paige, regarded as one of the greatest pitchers in the history of baseball, started his career in the Negro leagues.

Leroy Robert Paige was born to John and Lula Paige of Mobile, Alabama, in 1906. His nickname, Satchel, originated either from his satchel-sized feet or from

Satchel Paige

the baggage (satchels) that he carried on his job at Union Station. From playing sandlot baseball, Satchel Paige progressed to teams in the All-Negro Southern Association. While playing for the Mobile Tigers in 1924, he was paid according to how collections went among the spectators. If enough money had been collected, he received $1 for the game. If not, he was given a keg of lemonade. From this humble beginning, Paige went on to command one of the highest salaries in baseball in his day. Often booked as a solo star, he guaranteed nine strikeouts in three innings to any team that agreed to his asking price ($500 to $2,000 per game).

Professional baseball leagues became integrated in 1947, and African American players were accepted as members of major league teams. The following year, Paige was hired by the Cleveland Indians. He was the oldest "rookie" ever and the first African American pitcher in the American League. When Paige retired from the St. Louis Browns five years later, he had been named most valuable pitcher. Satchel Paige was inducted into the National Baseball Hall of Fame in 1971.

Suggested Activities

Discussion Discuss with students: How many professional baseball players today do they think would still play the game if their pay depended on how much was collected from the spectators?

Math Problems During his lifetime Satchel Paige played about 2,500 games and won 2,000 of them. What percentage did he lose? Share some other statistics about Paige and let students write their own word problems. For example, of 2,500 games, 300 were shutouts and 55 were no-hitters. In 1933 Paige pitched 31 games and lost only 4.

Others Some other Negro League players include Josh Gibson, Cool Papa Bell, Oscar Charleston, and Judy Johnson. Challenge students to find out more about these players.

References

Take a Walk in Their Shoes by Glennette Tilley Turner (Puffin Books, 1989).

Satchel Paige by David Shirley (Chelsea House, 1993).

The Story of Negro League Baseball by William Brashler (Ticknor & Fields, 1994).

The Sultan of Swat

Babe Ruth

George Herman Ruth was one of the most famous baseball players of all time. A flamboyant figure, he brought excitement to an otherwise tranquil sport. A southpaw in a game where most of the players were right-handed, and with a barrel-shaped body and spindly legs, he did not fit the image of a world-class athlete.

Born in 1895, Ruth grew up on the streets of Baltimore, fending for himself, and by the age of eight had gotten into trouble. Young George was sent to a Catholic boys' home, where he played baseball. An invaluable team member, he could play just about any position.

In 1914 Ruth began his career as a Baltimore Oriole rookie. After only five weeks Ruth was sold to Boston when the team's owner needed money. There, he served as a pitcher and showed his prowess as a hitter. Because he could hit the ball harder and farther than any other team member, he held two positions—in some games he pitched and in other games he played first base. By 1918, Babe Ruth was recognized as the best left-handed pitcher in baseball. He also led the American League in home runs. In 1920 the Red Sox sold him to the New York Yankees, where he would set records and bring baseball to a new level.

Formerly, baseball had been a pitcher's game, but Ruth changed all that; now it was a hitter's game. Ruth set many records that stood unchanged for years. In 1920 he broke the 1884 record of 24 home runs in one season by hitting 54. The next year he hit 59 homers and scored a total of 177 runs. In 1927 Ruth hit 60 home runs, a record that stood for 34 years. Attendance at games increased so much that the Yankees built Yankee Stadium, sometimes known as "the house that Ruth built." At forty, fat from eating and drinking too much, Ruth hit three home runs in his last professional baseball game. It was an amazing feat by an amazing athlete.

Suggested Activities

Records Ruth's 1927 record of 60 home runs stood unbroken until 1961. Have students research to find the following information: What player broke Ruth's record? Who currently holds the home run record? What is this record?

Candy Bars People mistakenly think that Baby Ruth candy bars were named after Babe Ruth. Assign students to research the true story behind the name of the candy bar.

Salary In 1930 Babe Ruth signed a contract for an unprecedented $80,000 per year, more money than the president of the U.S. earned. Compare Ruth's salary to today's presidential salary and to baseball players' earnings.

Another Babe Babe Didrikson Zaharias was another famous athlete of this period. An outstanding golfer, softball star, tennis player, swimmer, and diver, this Babe won Olympic medals in three track and field events in 1932. Compare her achievements with those of some contemporary female athletes.

Transatlantic Flight

After World War I, the availability of surplus equipment and trained pilots led to the growth of commercial aviation. Barnstormers presented air shows and provided short rides for the public, and airplanes carried mail across the country. Soon attention focused on the possibility of transatlantic flight. In 1919 a wealthy hotel man offered a $25,000 prize to anyone who could fly nonstop from New York to Paris.

Such a flight was extremely hazardous. The pilot would have to fly thousands of miles over a stormy ocean and would face rain clouds, dense fog, and even icebergs. Over the next eight years several pilots, including explorer Richard Evelyn Byrd, tried and failed. Then, in May of 1927, an unknown airmail pilot named Charles Lindbergh accepted the challenge.

Charles Lindbergh

His plane, the *Spirit of St. Louis*, was ill equipped for such a dangerous undertaking. It had no radio, and the pilot's seat was a wicker chair. Because the plane carried as much fuel as possible, there was no room left for any excess weight. All that Lindbergh carried on board with him was a quart of water, a paper sack full of sandwiches, a map, letters of introduction, and a rubber raft. Staying awake and alert throughout the 33½ hour flight proved to be a major challenge for Lindbergh.

A raucous, cheering crowd greeted Lindbergh when he landed in Paris. After meeting European kings and princes, Lindbergh and the *Spirit of St. Louis* returned home, where he was showered with parades and celebrations. A world hero at the age of 25, Lindbergh's feat inspired a popular song, a dance, and popular fashions.

Lindbergh refused numerous offers for moneymaking opportunities following his historic flight. He continued to be a strong advocate of aviation and flew 50 combat missions in World War II. In 1953 he earned a Pulitzer prize for *The Spirit of St. Louis*, which chronicled his historic flight.

Suggested Activities

Aviation History Teach students about the history of flight. Read aloud the book *The Wright Brothers: How They Invented the Airplane* by Russell Freedman (Holiday House, 1991). Discuss the adversities Lindbergh faced.

Female Pilot In 1922 Bessie Coleman became the first licensed African American pilot in America. Because of the existing prejudice against blacks, Coleman had to travel to France, where she learned how to fly. Coleman was honored in 1995 by the U.S. Post Office with a 32-cent stamp. Have students research this woman's background and accomplishments.

Earhart Amelia Earhart became as famous as Lindbergh when she flew solo across the Atlantic in 1932. In 1937 she attempted to fly around the world. Her plane disappeared somewhere in the South Pacific six weeks into the journey. Assign students to research what happened to Earhart and her co-pilot.

Mapping Assign students to create a map of Lindbergh's flight across the Atlantic.

References

Lindbergh by Chris L. Demarest (Crown Publishers, Inc., 1993).

Barnstormers & Daredevils by K. C. Tessendorf (Macmillan, 1988).

A Space Pioneer

Robert Goddard's dreams of space and interplanetary travel were influenced by two books—*The War of the Worlds* by H. G. Wells and *From the Earth to the Moon* by Jules Verne. After reading and rereading both novels, he was convinced that space travel was indeed a possibility. A Massachusetts physicist, Goddard first conducted research on improving solid fuel rockets.

In 1923 Goddard began testing a rocket with liquid fuel, gasoline, and liquid oxygen, and three years later he launched the world's first successful liquid-fueled rocket. It flew 184 feet (56 m), reached an altitude of 41 feet (12.5 m), and traveled at 60 miles (100 k) per hour.

From 1930 to 1935 Robert Goddard continued to launch rockets, attaining higher and higher speeds and heights. He developed ways to guide rockets and even devised parachutes which allowed the rockets to return safely to earth. Sadly, the U.S. government took little note of these accomplishments during Goddard's lifetime. Not until 24 years after his death in 1945 would the dream of landing on the moon become a reality.

Suggested Activities

Bottle Rockets Make outdoor bottle rocket launchers. For each rocket you will need 1 brightly colored ribbon bow, 1 thumbtack, 1 1-quart (1 L) soda bottle with a cork to fit, ½ cup (125 mL) of vinegar, ½ cup (125 mL) of water, 1 teaspoon (5 mL) of baking soda, and a 4" (10 cm) square piece of paper towel. With the thumbtack attach the bow to the cork. Pour the water and vinegar into the bottle. Place the teaspoon of baking soda in the center of the paper towel square, roll it up, and twist the ends. Go outside and drop the paper towel packet into the bottle. Fit the cork tightly into the mouth of the bottle and set it on a flat surface. Stand back and watch the cork fly into the air.

The Isaac Newton Connection Newton's three laws of motion explain how rockets work and why they can fly in outer space. Read about the life of Newton. See pages 95 and 96 in Teacher Created Materials #493 *Focus on Scientists* for hands-on experiments.

Discussion With the class discuss the importance of Goddard's work and how his early experiments paved the way for space exploration. Ask students for their opinions about why the U.S. government did not pay much attention to his work at that time.

References

Robert H. Goddard by Karin Clafford Farley (Silver Burdett Press, 1991).

The War of the Worlds by H. G. Wells. (Various editions)

From the Earth to the Moon by Jules Verne. (Various editions)

Star Light, Star Bright

Annie Jump Cannon was an extraordinary woman, particularly for her time. In the late 1800s very few women progressed in their educations beyond grade school or high school. Few careers were open to women, and it was expected that they marry and raise families. Cannon was born on December 18, 1863. Her father was a shipbuilder, and her mother was a typical homemaker, except for an interesting hobby—stargazing. When Cannon was very young, she and her mother would climb to the rooftop of their home and spend hours observing the stars through a telescope. As a schoolgirl, Cannon excelled in her studies, and her teachers convinced her parents to provide her with a higher education.

Annie Jump Cannon

At 16 Cannon began studies at Wellsley College. After graduation, she worked in the Harvard Observatory where she assisted in cataloging stars. Star pictures were taken by combining photographs with telescopes that were specially equipped with prisms. The resulting photograph showed the different bands of light produced by each star. Using the information from the photographic plates, Cannon classified the stars.

Astronomers had been using an A, B, C classification system, but Cannon found a better arrangement that is standard for astronomers even today. Between 1915 and 1924 Cannon produced nine volumes of the *Henry Draper Catalog,* a guidebook for astrophysicists. This achievement made her famous. During her lifetime Cannon cataloged over 350,000 stars and also discovered five *novae* (stars that suddenly become brighter and then fade). In recognition of her pioneering work, Annie Jump Cannon was the first woman awarded an honorary doctorate from Oxford.

Suggested Activities

Hobbies Cannon's mother's hobby was stargazing, and she included Cannon in this fascinating activity. Discuss with the class how they think this early experience with the stars influenced Cannon's future work. Ask them about any hobbies they may have and how they became interested in those particular areas.

Numbering Through the course of her career Annie Jump Cannon catalogued over 350,000 stars. As a class project, draw 350,000 stars. Attach a large sheet of butcher paper to a classroom wall. When students have spare time (or use a rotating schedule), they can add stars to the sheet. Let students draw the stars or use a star-shaped stamp.

Prisms When she was a child, Cannon spent many hours enjoying the dancing rainbows produced by the prisms from her mother's candelabra. Hang some prisms in front of a classroom window and observe the light displays. For some information on making your own prisms see Teacher Created Materials #493 *Focus on Scientists.*

Homework Assign the class to observe the stars each evening for a week. In class each morning discuss their observations and any pictures they have drawn of the star formations they have seen.

Coming of Age

Margaret Mead

Margaret Mead was part of a revolution that changed the roles of men and women in society. In her work she sought to show people the need to live full, rich lives, unrestricted by society's limitations of male or female roles. Her goals were to bring about world peace, to promote multicultural understanding, and to help children everywhere.

Mead's story began on December 16, 1901, when she was the first born into a busy and unconventional household in Philadelphia, Pennsylvania. Both her mother, Emily Fogg, and her paternal grandmother, Martha Mead, had careers of their own at a time when it was highly unusual for women to work outside the home. As a sociologist Emily often spoke out about the living conditions of poor women. Martha Mead was an educator and school principal who directed her granddaughter's education. Because her parents' jobs required frequent moves, Mead had lived in 60 different homes by the time she was in junior high school. For Mead the moves were an adventure, and she adapted easily to each new environment. Of special interest to her was what made families so alike and yet so different.

After her 1923 graduation from Barnard College, she received a grant to do field work among the Polynesian people of Samoa. By her own admission, Mead knew little about what she was getting into or how to proceed, but she eventually developed a system for recording her experiences. Based on observations of 68 Manu'a village girls over a six-month period, she concluded that Samoan female adolescents experienced an easier transition to adulthood than did their American counterparts. The information Mead had so meticulously documented formed the basis of her dissertation at Columbia University and was published as *Coming of Age in Samoa: A Psychological Study of Primitive Youth for Western Civilization* (William Morrow, 1928). On later field studies in New Guinea and Bali, Mead employed the techniques of note-taking, interviewing, observing, and photographing that continue to be used by cultural anthropologists.

Margaret Mead did not slow down until 1978, when a serious illness caught up with her. On November 15, 1978, she died from pancreatic cancer. Nine national memorial services were held in memory of this great pioneering anthropologist.

Suggested Activities

Modern Anthropologists Ask students to imagine that they have received a grant to study the culture on a new planet. Direct them to make a booklet of notes, interviews, observations, and pictures of the adolescent boys and girls that they observe there.

Alike Yet Different Mead was curious about how families were alike yet different. Pair the students and have them take turns interviewing one another to find out how their families are alike yet different. Discuss the results with the whole group.

References

The Importance of Margaret Mead by Rafael Tilton (Lucent Books, 1994).

Teacher Created Materials #493 Focus on Scientists.

Revolutionizing the Auto Industry

Henry Ford

Some people mistakenly think that Henry Ford invented the automobile. His name is synonymous with the auto industry because he improved the manufacturing process, making an existing invention affordable. In doing so, he changed American life.

Ford was born on July 30, 1863, on a farm near Dearborn, Michigan. From his childhood he showed an interest in engines, and at the age of sixteen he became a machinist. In 1888 he married Clara Bryant, who actively encouraged Ford to build and experiment with engines. By 1896 he had built his first automobile.

Seven years later Ford organized the Ford Motor Company. Because they were built individually by hand, cars were very expensive, and only a few Americans could afford them. Ford revolutionized the automobile industry by using an assembly-line method of production. This system of mass production saved money, and Ford was able to sell cars for less. In 1908 the Model T, sometimes known as the "tin Lizzie," debuted. The initial price was $850. In addition to the assembly-line technique, the Ford Company produced its own parts, glass, and steel. By eliminating the independent suppliers' high prices, the company saved even more money. These savings were passed on to the consumer, and Model T prices dropped to $290 in 1924. Between 1908 and 1927, over half the cars sold in the nation were Fords. Finally, automobiles were affordable for most families.

Ford also implemented some other changes in the work force. He reduced the work day from the standard nine hours to eight hours and increased the minimum wage to $5 per day. A profit-sharing plan for employees was instituted. With all of these incentives, workers flocked to the Ford plant. Despite these innovations, Ford products declined in popularity during the latter part of the twenties as General Motors began offering a wider variety of luxuries, such as different colors for exteriors, heaters, and yearly designs. In 1919 Henry Ford stepped down as president of his own company and named his son Edsel to take his place. Henry Ford died on April 7, 1947.

Suggested Activities

Imagine Affordable automobiles revolutionized living in the twenties. With the whole group, discuss the impact the automobile has made on present-day living. Ask students how life today might be different without cars.

Assembly Line Let individual students take turns putting together a snap-together model or a puzzle; have them record their time. Then group the students and direct them to assemble the model or puzzle by assigning each member a specific task. Have them compare their individual time with the group time of assembling the project. Ask them what they can conclude about assembly-line production.

A Treatment for Diabetes

Diabetes mellitus, more commonly known as sugar diabetes, is a disease affecting millions of people worldwide. A person who has this disease is unable to metabolize sugar properly and cannot turn it into energy. Normally, a body derives most of its energy from carbohydrates. Once inside the body carbohydrates are broken down into a simple sugar called *glucose*, which is converted into energy. Diabetics are unable to complete this process, however, and the result is a buildup of glucose in the bloodstream and urine. Unchecked, diabetes can cause blindness, kidney failure, and heart disease.

Before this century doctors could do little but watch helplessly as their diabetic patients slowly died. Relief was finally provided in 1922 when Frederick Banting, a Canadian orthopedic surgeon, first tested insulin on a human being. Banting grew up in Ontario, Canada, where he was born in 1891. Although his father wanted him to be a minister, Frederick had other plans. After graduation from medical school and serving in the Canadian Army Medical Corps, he set up a practice. To supplement his income he took on a teaching job. While preparing for a lecture on the pancreas, Banting decided he needed more information on the organ. When he realized the connection between the islets of Langerhans in the pancreas and diabetes, he began his experiments with dogs. Using fluids extracted from dogs' pancreatic ducts, Banting and his research partner, Charles Best, were able to create an injection for diabetic dogs. Results were immediate and dramatic. After further testing, insulin was formulated for human beings. In 1923 Frederick Banting was awarded the Nobel prize in medicine and physiology for this important contribution to mankind.

Suggested Activity

Circle the names of all the foods that are primary sources of carbohydrates.

• cheese	• yogurt	• bread	• candy bars
• butter	• pasta	• green beans	• steak
• cookies	• pancakes	• eggs	• crackers
• pears	• corn	• rice	• cantaloupe
• doughnuts	• zucchini	• oranges	• bagels
• broccoli	• lettuce	• milk	

Langston Hughes, an Everyday Poet

African American Langston Hughes is widely regarded as one
of America's greatest poets. From the time he was in grade
school he knew that he wanted to be a writer. Despite the
adversities of a broken home and racial prejudice, Hughes was
able to overcome these obstacles to fulfill his dreams.

Langston Hughes was born on February 1, 1902, in Joplin,
Missouri, to Carrie and James Hughes. James Hughes had been
studying law, but at that time in Missouri, African Americans
were not allowed to become lawyers. Disillusioned, he moved
to Toluca, Mexico.

Mrs. Hughes refused to go. She worked to support herself and
Hughes. It was not always easy, but somehow they managed to
get by. One important thing Carrie Hughes did was to pass on
her love of reading to her son. By the time he had completed
grammar school, Hughes had written his first poem, one in
honor of his graduation.

Langston Hughes

Because his mother could not afford to pay for his college education, Hughes worked at various jobs,
including deckhand, laundry worker, and dishwasher. One summer, he even earned money by working
on his father's ranch in Mexico. During the long train ride there, Hughes composed a poem, "The
Negro Speaks of Rivers," and sent it to a New York City magazine. James Hughes agreed to pay for his
son's education, but only on the condition that he study engineering. When his son's poem was
published later that summer, the elder Hughes relented. Hughes' long and successful career was off to
a great start.

Altogether, Langston Hughes amassed a body of work that included poetry, plays, short stories, articles,
and a series of books based on the character Simple. In addition, he founded theater companies
throughout the United States for young people to learn playwriting and performing skills. Langston
Hughes died on May 22, 1967.

Suggested Activities

Unpublished Poetry A children's book editor at Oxford University Press discovered Langston
Hughes' unpublished manuscript, *The Sweet and Sour Animal Book* (Oxford University Press,
1994). Share these alphabet poems with the class. Direct the students to write some of their
own alphabet poems in the style of Langston Hughes.

Biography Read aloud selections from a biography of Langston Hughes. Ask students to
explain why Hughes deserves the title Poet Laureate of Harlem.

References

Extraordinary Black Americans: From Colonial to Contemporary Times by Susan Altman
(Children's Press, 1989).

Instructor January/February 1995 ("Put on a Play About Langston Hughes" by Helen H.
Moore, pages 66–70; "Kids' Art Brings Poems to Life" by Wendy Murray, pages 74–76).

Lives of the Writers by Kathleen Krull (Harcourt Brace & Co., 1994).

Essence of the Twenties

F. Scott Fitzgerald

F. Scott Fitzgerald coined the phrase "The Jazz Age," and his short stories and novels captured the essence of the Roaring Twenties. His work reflected the indulgences and excesses of the times, as well as his personal struggles.

Fitzgerald was born September 24, 1896, in St. Paul, Minnesota, to Mary and Edward Fitzgerald and named for a distant relative, Francis Scott Key. Because of Edward Fitzgerald's sporadic employment, the family was forced to move frequently. In order to cope, young Scott invented an inner world of his own. He read passionately and told imaginative tales. His mother encouraged him to excel and made no attempts to discipline him.

School bored young Fitzgerald. While his teachers lectured, he busied himself writing stories in the back of his geography or Latin book. His family sent him east to a small Catholic boarding school. There he quickly became one of the most unpopular students. He talked so much that he was considered a show-off, and he irritated his fellow students by endlessly analyzing them.

Although he failed the entrance exams for Princeton, he convinced the appeals committee that he would, indeed, make a good Princeton student and was admitted in 1913. In 1917 Fitzgerald left Princeton without a degree and joined the army.

While he was stationed in Alabama in 1918, he met Zelda Sayre, and the two married after the publication of his first novel, *This Side of Paradise,* in 1920. Like the characters in his second novel, *The Beautiful and the Damned,* the Fitzgeralds led lives of partying, drinking, and endless talking. *The Great Gatsby,* written in Paris and published in 1925, is considered by most readers to be Fitzgerald's best book.

Fitzgerald's drinking led to alcoholism, and Zelda suffered from mental illness. Their life together became increasingly unhappy. With the stock market crash of 1929, Fitzgerald's lucrative career came to an end. In the mid-thirties he left for Hollywood to work as a scriptwriter. At the time of his death in 1941 he was working on a novel, *The Last Tycoon.* Although it was unfinished, the manuscript was published as a series of unrevised chapters and notes.

Suggested Activity

Another Title *This Side of Paradise* was originally named *The Romantic Egotist.* Find out about other popular books that were written with other original titles in mind. For example, author Peter Benchley toyed with such titles as *Leviathan Rising* and *Great White* before he and his editor settled for *Jaws.* Read more fascinating stories behind book titles in *Now All We Need Is a Title: Famous Book Titles and How They Got That Way* by Andre Bernard (W. W. Norton & Company, 1994).

The Mount Rushmore Story

Gutzon Borglum

On March 25, 1867, John Gutzon de la Mothe Borglum was born in the Idaho Territory. His parents had immigrated to the U.S. from Denmark in 1864 and then traveled to the Territory by wagon train. Borglum's childhood was filled with Danish legends, the art of the old masters, and the culture of the Crow and Sioux. At 17 Borglum decided to devote his life to art.

Borglum studied under the famous French sculptor Auguste Rodin. His career flourished, and he received numerous commissions, both in the United States and Europe. Doane Robinson, secretary of the South Dakota Historical Society, asked Borglum to carve a sculpture in the Black Hills as a tourist attraction. A fanatic patriot, Borglum had no trouble saying "yes" to the plan. The site was Mount Rushmore, which rises 6,040 feet (1,804 m) above sea level. Towering 500 feet (152 m) above its nearest neighboring mountains, its granite face is approximately 1,000 feet (304 m) long and 400 feet (122 m) high. Borglum selected four presidents: George Washington to represent America's independence and the Constitution, Thomas Jefferson for his concern for westward expansion, Abraham Lincoln for his ability to hold the country together during the Civil War, and Theodore Roosevelt for his strong ties to South Dakota. Construction on Mount Rushmore did not began until late 1927. In 1929 Congress authorized it as a national memorial.

Borglum died before the completion of the monument in 1941, and his son Lincoln took on the remainder of the project. Today, the memorial grounds boast a visitor's center, an amphitheater, walks and trails, night lighting, and a museum of what was once Borglum's studio. The National Park Service regularly inspects and makes necessary repairs to the sculpture.

Suggested Activities

Controversy Direct students to research the concerns of Native Americans who inhabit the area. Find out about their own Crazy Horse memorial not far from Mount Rushmore.

Geology The Black Hills are one of the oldest geological formations on Earth. Over the years a number of rock types built up over one another to form them. Mountains in the center of the hills are composed of igneous granite and metamorphic mica schist with fingers of granite squeezed in between the mica. Have students research igneous, metamorphic, and sedimentary rocks and create a chart which shows their characteristics and how they are formed.

Reference

The Mount Rushmore Story by Judith St.George (G. P. Putnam's Sons, 1985).

Jacob Lawrence and the Great Migration Series

One of the biggest population shifts in the history of the United States occurred during the period around World War I as hundreds of African Americans left their homes and farms in the South and migrated north to industrial cities in search of employment. Jacob Lawrence grew up knowing people on the move. Indeed, his own family was part of the first big wave of migration between 1916 and 1919. His parents met while they were en route to New York. His mother was from Virginia, while his father was born in South Carolina.

Jacob Lawrence

Lawrence was born in 1917 in Atlantic City, New Jersey. When he was 13, the family moved to Harlem in New York City. There Lawrence went to school and attended an after-school arts-and-crafts program. It was during this period that he decided to become an artist. At first, he just made designs but later progressed to painting street scenes. Inspiration was not far away. Friends and teachers helped him understand how his own experiences fit into the history of all African Americans in the United States. He also spent countless hours at the Schomburg Library, reading books about the great migration.

In 1940, at the age of 22, he began his Migration series. One year later it was completed. The series consisted of 60 numbered panels that told the story of the people who made the choice to move away from their homes. In his own words, ". . . I wanted to show what made the people get on those northbound trains. I also wanted to show what it cost to ride them." Each panel measured a mere 18" x 12" (45 cm x 30 cm), but altogether they made a powerful and moving statement.

Suggested Activities

Response Ask students to respond to this question: What sacrifices did people make in migrating North? If students have a hard time answering this, start by asking them what sacrifices they would have to make if they were to move to a different geographical location.

Creative Writing Direct the students to write a creative story about the family members who got left behind. Before beginning writing, brainstorm with the class and come up with some reasons that families or family members may have been left.

Art Series Create a class mural to chronicle an event at school. After the class has determined an event and planned panels that tell the story, divide the students into groups. Let each group work on a separate 18" x 12" (45 cm x 30 cm) panel. Display the finished panels on a classroom wall. Have the groups take turns telling the story.

Comparisons Compare the art of Jacob Lawrence with that of Romare Bearden, another artist who captured African American life in the 1920s.

Reference
The Great Migration by Jacob Lawrence (HarperCollins Publishers, 1993).

Empress of the Blues

One of the first great blues performers in the United States was African American Bessie Smith. Born in Chattanooga, Tennessee, in 1894, Smith lived the blues. Her family was poor, and to earn money she began singing on street corners when she was just a little girl. Smith made her professional debut at the age of nine at the Ivory Theater in her hometown. Later, she began traveling the Southern circuit of segregated black theaters and tent shows. Sometimes they would perform special shows for white audiences. Everyone who heard Bessie Smith sing was mesmerized by her voice. After landing a recording contract with Columbia Records, her first release, "Down-Hearted Blues," sold over one million copies. Her many subsequent hits helped save the company from bankruptcy. At the peak of her career, she earned $2,000 per week, but, as was customary in those days with African American performers, she received no royalties. Altogether, Smith recorded 160 songs, many of

Bessie Smith

which she wrote herself. Her trademark costumes—satin gown, headdress, and a long strand of pearls—earned her the title Empress of the Blues. A problem with alcohol coupled with the Depression led to the decline of Bessie Smith's meteoric career. In 1937 she was killed in a car accident and buried in an unmarked grave. Her family was unable to afford a headstone. In 1970 singer Janis Joplin and some other musicians decided to pay tribute to this long-forgotten talent. They purchased a headstone and had it engraved with the following epitaph: "The greatest blues singer in the world will never stop singing."

Suggested Activities

An Epitaph Discuss the meaning of the epitaph on Bessie Smith's headstone. Direct the students to design and draw an appropriate headstone for Bessie Smith's grave. Compose a new epitaph for the headstone.

Influence Bessie Smith's singing style influenced many later stars, including Mahalia Jackson, Billie Holiday, and Janis Joplin. Assign students to research these three singers, when they lived and how they sang. If possible, listen to some of their musical recordings.

Sing the Blues Divide the students into small groups. Have them write and perform a blues song that Smith might have sung.

References

Herstory: Women Who Changed the World edited by Ruth Ashby and Deborah Gore Ohrn (Viking, 1995).

Black American History Makers by George L. Lee (Ballantine Books, 1989).

From Ballots to Breadlines: American Women 1920–1940 by Sarah Jane Deutsch (Oxford University Press, 1994).

Kids Make Music by Avery Hart and Paul Mantell (Williamson Publishing, 1993).

Music Is My Language

Louis Armstrong

He grew up to be one of the greatest and best-loved jazz musicians the world has ever known. It was an amazing accomplishment, considering his youth. Louis Armstrong was born in the New Orleans ghetto on August 4, 1901. His family lived in a wooden shanty that had no electricity or plumbing. Nearby streets were lined with honky-tonks where drinks were cheap and fights were frequent. When he was just an infant, his father abandoned the family, and Armstrong was raised by his paternal grandmother. He attended school until the fifth grade, when he had to leave to help earn money by peddling newspapers and delivering coal.

An incident that occurred when he was 13 changed the course of his life. Trying to show off to a group of friends, Armstrong fired a pistol belonging to his stepfather. The prank sent him to the Colored Waifs' Home, a reform school for African American boys. As luck would have it, the school had a marching band, and Armstrong learned to play the cornet. After his release he went back to his former day jobs and spent nights combing the honky-tonks for a chance to sit in with the bands.

In 1922 Joe Oliver, the king of jazz trumpeters, asked Armstrong to join his band. It was during this time that Armstrong met and married Lillian Hardin, the band's young piano player. With her encouragement, Armstrong was eventually able to strike out on his own. By the mid-twenties he had organized the Hot Five, the Hot Seven, and the Savoy Ballroom Five. Throughout his career Louis Armstrong performed in Europe, South America, the Far East, Canada, and all over the United States. Music was his language, and he had no trouble communicating wherever he went. He is best-known for the new style that he created, giving his horn a voice-like quality, and for his distinctive singing voice. Nicknamed "Satchmo," a shortened form of satchel mouth due to his wide smile, Louis Armstrong died in 1971.

Suggested Activities

Collage Armstrong was also an artist. He enjoyed making collages and often carried scissors so he could cut out magazine and newspaper articles. After arranging them on a scrapbook page, he would tape his cutouts together. Assign students to collect movie ticket stubs, schoolwork, candy wrappers, and other items for one week. Have students arrange the items on a cardboard background and glue them to the surface to make a biographical collage which documents a week in their lives. (This idea was taken from the October 1994 issue of *Cobblestone:* "Louis Armstrong and the Art of Jazz.")

Definition Jazz, a mix of ragtime, blues, and black spirituals, was invented by African Americans in the twenties. Listen to one or more recordings of Louis Armstrong's music, like *Louis Armstrong: The Hot Fives Volume I,* or Ella Fitzgerald and Louis Armstrong: *Ella and Louis.* Have the students draw abstract pictures using lines, marks, and shapes, while they listen to this music.

A Rhapsody in Blue

Although his life span was brief, George Gershwin achieved fame in his own time. Today he continues to be regarded as one of the great musicians of the twentieth century. A popular composer, he was the first musician to take jazz music into concert halls. His *Rhapsody in Blue* remains as a testament to his ability to combine a distinctive jazzy feeling with the sounds and techniques of classical pianists.

Gershwin was born in Brooklyn, New York, in 1898 to poor Jewish immigrants. By the time he was twelve years old, Gershwin could play the piano. A few years later he dropped out of high school to work for a music publisher as a song plugger. Gershwin promoted songs by playing them for interested performers. In 1917 he became a rehearsal pianist for a musical play, and by the

George Gershwin

next year he had a steady job working for a music company. The company paid him $35 a week; that included all rights to publish any songs he wrote.

Gershwin's first hit song was "Swanee," sung by Al Jolson in 1920. One year later Gershwin wrote the score for a Broadway musical. Three years later he teamed up with his brother, Ira, to write the hit *Lady, Be Good!* which starred Fred Astaire on Broadway. Gershwin composed the music while Ira provided the lyrics for such popular songs as "I Got Rhythm" and "Embraceable You." By the beginning of the thirties, Gershwin had also written scores for films, including *Damsel in Distress* and *Goldwyn Follies.*

Gershwin also wanted to compose serious music, and in 1924, *Rhapsody in Blue* debuted, followed by *An American in Paris* in 1928. In 1929 he made his debut as a conductor for the New York Philharmonic Orchestra. In spite of his busy career composing for stage and films, Gershwin was able to make time to tour American cities and perform with major orchestras. Perhaps his most ambitious undertaking was the full-length opera *Porgy and Bess.* Based on a novel by DuBose Heyward, the story tells about the life of rural Blacks living in South Carolina.

Unfortunately, Gershwin's life ended all too soon; he died of a brain tumor at the age of 38, while at the height of his creativity. He left a legacy of beautiful and moving music. Generation after generation has rediscovered this national treasure, ensuring that Gershwin's music will never die.

Suggested Activities

Concerto Explain that *Rhapsody in Blue* is a concerto, a composition written for an orchestra and one or more instruments. If possible, listen to a recording of *Rhapsody in Blue.* Have the students identify the leading instrument. Listen to some concertos by some classical composers and compare them to Gershwin's concerto.

Contributions Discuss with the class Gershwin's contributions to the jazz movement. Compare how his jazz differed from that of Louis Armstrong or Duke Ellington.

Everyday Dress in the 1920s

The 1920s brought revolution in styles of dress, especially for women and children. Read about the changes for each group and then do one or more of the activities.

Children Traditionally, children were dressed as miniature adults. In the twenties, one-piece rompers for infants and playsuits for older boys and girls were introduced.

Teenagers Fashion had overlooked the teen years, taking young people straight from childhood to adulthood. When teens went to fight in World War I, a new market developed, and fashions just for teenagers were created. Magazines like *Seventeen* emerged for this new teenage market.

Women Hemlines rose for the first time in history and exposed women's legs. The thick, cotton stockings available at the time were quickly replaced with rayon. Head-hugging cloche hats fit over the short, bobbed haircuts sported by most women. Flesh-colored, all-in-one undergarments replaced restrictive, tight-laced corsets and camisoles. Women plucked their eyebrows and wore rouge and lipstick.

Men Styles became more relaxed and lighter, thanks to the sporting influence. Tennis sweaters and polo shirts were allowed for casual, as well as sporting, attire. Lindbergh's transatlantic flight spawned a cult following and a new look: leather jackets and helmets worn with goggles. Raccoon coats were popular.

Suggested Activities

It Girl — Actress Clara Bow epitomized the 1920s look. With her cupid-bow lips and kohl-rimmed eyes she became known as the "It Girl". Find a picture of Clara Bow (an excellent resource is *Fashions of a Decade: The 1920s* by Jacqueline Herald). Compare her look with today's fashionable look. Have students search through magazines to find their idea of today's "It Girl"; make a class collage of all the pictures.

Fashion — Swimwear was quite modest in the 1920s. Bathing suits were less restrictive but still required short-sleeved or sleeveless tunics over thigh-covering bottoms. In women's tennis, the knee-length tennis dress was introduced, but it had to be worn with white stockings. Designer Rene Lacoste introduced his soft collared, short-sleeved polo shirt with an alligator motif (still seen today) for men. Coco Chanel designed golfing outfits of jersey which made movement much easier and more comfortable. Ask students to find other 1920s influences that are still around today. Have students draw some sports fashions from the 1920s.

Bobbed Hair — Bobs were worn by over 90% of the American women during the twenties. Read F. Scott Fitzgerald's short story "Bernice Bobs Her Hair." Assign the students to write their own stories about a traumatic haircutting experience.

Sewing Machine — Electric sewing machines were first introduced in the twenties. Discuss what impact this invention had on the fashion world.

Elsewhere . . .

This chronology gives a few of the important events around the globe during the 1920s. Have students research further any people and events that interest them.

1920
- Mohandas Gandhi reorganizes the Indian National Congress Party. Through peaceful protests he strives to free India from British rule.
- Civil War flares up in Ireland.
- Austrian Sigmund Freud publishes a book about his theory of psychoanalysis.
- Adolph Hitler forms the Nazi Party.
- Palestine becomes a British mandate.

1921
- New Zealand becomes a member of the League of Nations.
- In China, Mao Tse Tung helps form the Chinese Communist Party.
- Ireland is divided. Its south becomes a separate country called the Irish Free State.

1922
- Benito Mussolini becomes the Italian prime minister. Having set up the Fascist Party, he now becomes the country's dictator.
- Egypt becomes an independent country under British influence.
- The tomb of Egyptian Pharaoh Tutankhamen is discoverd by archaeologists Howard Carter and Lord Carnarvon.
- The USSR is formed.
- King Faud I becomes sultan of Egypt.

1923
- Turkey becomes a republic. General Mustafa Kemal, its first president, introduces the Western alphabet to replace Arabic writing.
- An earthquake in Tokyo kills over 130,000 people.
- Two Swedish scientists, von Platen and Munters, design the first electric refrigerator.
- The dictatorship of Primo de Rivera begins in Spain.
- On the art scene, an exhibition of Bauhaus is held.

1924
- The first winter Olympics are held in France.
- Stalin takes control of the USSR and kills millions who oppose his ideas to modernize farming and industry.
- The Ford Motor Company manufactures its ten millionth automobile.

1925
- Hitler's Mein Kampf is published.
- Art deco is exhibited in Paris.
- Dr. Howard Carter uncovers the mummified body of Tutankhamen.

1926
- A Norwegian, Rotheim, invents aerosol, which allows liquids to be sprayed in fine mists.
- All union members in England are on strike.
- Panama and the U.S. agree to protect the Panama Canal during wartime.
- In Great Britain, John Logie Baird develops the television.
- A. A. Milne writes Winnie-the-Pooh.

1927
- Canberra becomes the federal capital of Australia.
- Chiang Kai-shek takes Shanghai.

1928
- Stalin launches his Five-Year Plan.
- Trotsky is sent into exile.
- Japanese massacre Chinese civilians.
- Mt. Etna erupts in Italy.

1929
- The Serb-Croat-Slovene kingdom becomes known as Yugoslavia.
- The Graf Zeppelin makes an around-the-world flight.
- There is Arab-Jewish rioting in Palestine.

Gabriela Mistral

Educator, poet, and diplomat are three titles that aptly describe Gabriela Mistral, for she was each of these at different times in her life. An educator first, Gabriela sought solace in writing poetry after an old boyfriend committed suicide. As she became serious about her writing she took a pen name: Gabriela was for the Archangel Gabriel. Mistral was from the cold winds that blow down from the Alps and across the plains of France. While she was able to combine careers in both teaching and poetry writing, Mistral took some thirteen years off from the two to become a diplomat for her country. In all three fields she was an excellent role model for South America.

Gabriela Mistral

Born Lucila Godoy Alcayaga in 1889 in northern Chile, Mistral was raised by her mother and home-educated by her sister, a teacher. Encouraged by her sister, Gabriela went on to become a teacher, too, and taught in rural secondary schools. In 1918 she was appointed director of a secondary school for girls. Before the appointment, though, her first book of poetry had been published to rave reviews. Gabriela continued with her educational career and in 1922 was invited by the Mexican minister of education to help him start educational programs for the poor in his country. That same year her poetry collection titled *Desolación* made its debut.

In 1925 Gabriela began her diplomatic career when she was named the Chilean delegate to the United Nations. From 1926 to 1939 she served as head of the Cultural Committee in Paris. Following this post she worked as the Chilean Consul in Madrid. After being diagnosed with diabetes in 1944, Mistral moved to the United States, where she taught at Barnard college and acted as a cultural attache. There she returned to her writing. Gabriela began to write more poems and also some novels about Chilean life. In 1944 Gabriela Mistral became the first South American writer to win the Nobel prize for literature.

Suggested Activities

Pen Name Gabriela Mistral was a pen name. With the class, brainstorm a list of other writers who have used pen names. Discuss the purpose of pen names.

Chile Let the students locate Chile on a map. Briefly discuss the culture there.

Research Find out more about this writer's life. Some sources to use include *Herstory* edited by Ruth Ashby and Deborah Gore Ohrn (Viking, 1995), and *100 Women Who Shaped World History* by Gail Meyer Rolka (Bluewood Books, 1994). Compare the accounts of Mistral's life in the two sources. Which facts are different? What might account for these discrepancies?

The Tomb of Tutankhamen

The Egyptians may have been the first archaeologists. They investigated and recorded evidence of their past, including inscriptions hundreds of years old. It would be centuries before some of their own evidences were discovered by others, however. In 1922, after years of searching, British explorer Howard Carter found the burial tomb of Tutankhamen. Nearly 4,000 years old, the tomb was crammed with treasures. It took close to six years to record and preserve the thousands of valuable artifacts that were found there. One room alone contained 171 objects and pieces of furniture.

Suggested Activities

Puzzle In the box that follows is a list of some objects found in King Tutankhamen's tomb. Make a word-search puzzle with the words. Exchange it with a classmate.

alabaster	food	mummy	shabti
amulets	funerary bed	perfume	statues
Anubis	games	sarcophagus	throne
canopic jars	gold jewelry	scarab	vanity boxes
chariots	hieroglyphics	scrolls	vases
couches	incense	Senet	

Research Research to find the purpose of each of the items listed above. Also find other items stored in the tomb as well as the reasons why they were buried with Tutankhamen.

Fashion Tutmania was the rage in 1922 after King Tut's tomb was discovered. Draw and design a bracelet and necklace with an Egyptian theme.

Catalog Make a list of all the items found in one room of your house or school. Briefly describe each item and its purpose. How does your list compare to a room in King Tut's tomb?

An Australian Quiz

When you think of Australia, you probably associate it with Crocodile Dundee, Mad Max, and *The Thorn Birds* because these characters and stories come from Australia. In 1927 when Canberra became the federal capital of Australia, those names were not the household words that they are today. Test your knowledge of Australia with the following quiz.

Read each statement and decide if it is true or false. In the space provided, write **T** if the statement is true or **F** if it is false.

1._____ Australia is the world's smallest continent.

2._____ The platypus is a native Australian animal.

3._____ Spain is larger than the continent of Australia.

4._____ Australia is smaller than India.

5._____ The first Europeans to reach Australia were the French.

6._____ When it was first explored, it was called New South Wales.

7._____ Captain Cook claimed Australia for England.

8._____ The British established a penal colony called Botany Bay.

9._____ Aborigines were the first to settle in Australia.

10._____ Gold was discovered in Australia in 1851.

11._____ Eight colonies form the Commonwealth of Australia.

12._____ The Great Barrier Reef is the world's largest coral reef.

Suggested Activities

Language Write some typical Australian words and phrases on the board, e.g., *sheila* (woman), *tucker* (food), *dinkim* (honest), *bonzer* (great). Discuss them with the class. Assign students to write a creative story, using as many of the words as they can.

Native Animals Australia is home to a number of unique animals, including the cassowary, emu, kangaroo, koala, wombat, bandicoot, echidna, and platypus. Divide the students into groups and assign each a different animal to research. Tell them to find and copy a picture of their animal, along with five interesting facts. Share the completed reports in whole group.

A. A. Milne, Children's Author

A. A. Milne

Alan Alexander Milne, better known as A. A. Milne, is the author of *Winnie-the-Pooh* stories for children. He was born on January 18, 1882, in London, England, and was the youngest of three boys. An unambitious student, he discovered writing when his brother bet him he couldn't compose a verse as well as he could. But Milne surprised his brother with a well-written poem, and the two collaborated on verse for a couple of years.

After graduating from Trinity College in Cambridge in 1903, Milne became a free-lance journalist. By 1906 he was working at *Punch* magazine as an assistant editor. Seven years later he married Dorothy Daphne de Selincourt. The two had met at her coming-out party and over the years continued to be good friends. During World War I Milne joined the Royal Warwickshire Regiment, a reserve battalion, and served in France. In his spare time he was able to write his first children's book and a play to entertain the troops. When he returned to civilian life he continued with his writing career. On August 21, 1920, his only son, Christopher Robin, was born. Milne wrote poems regularly for *Punch*, and in 1924 a collection of poems, *When We Were Very Young*, was published. It received good reviews both in Britain and in the United States. A second collection of verses, *Now We Are Six*, was published in 1927, but the book that established him as a major children's author was the 1926 story *Winnie-the-Pooh*.

Winnie and Eeyore and Christopher Robin have become some of children's favorite storybook characters. In recent years they were immortalized on screen by the Walt Disney company, which made its first motion picture about Winnie-the-Pooh in 1965. Other animated adventures and some filmstrips have followed, including *Winnie-the-Pooh and the Honey Tree*.

After Milne's death in 1956, his book *The World of Pooh* received the Lewis Carroll Shelf Award. Six years later the same award was presented for his book *The World of Christopher Robin*. Probably Milne's greatest reward was his readers' undying affection for the characters at Pooh Corner.

Suggested Activities

Poetry Read aloud some verse from Milne's *When We Were Very Young* or *Now We Are Six*. Tell the students to think back in time to when they were six years old. Direct them to write a poem about their favorite activity then or an adventure that they remember.

Update With the class brainstorm some adventures that Christopher Robin and Winnie-the-Pooh might have if the story were set in ancient Egypt or in medieval times, for example. Pair the students and have them write a new adventure in a new setting for the two characters.

The Discovery of Penicillin

One of the world's most important medical breakthroughs was the discovery of penicillin during the 1920s. Since the 1870s scientists had thought it would be possible to use some microorganisms to kill disease-causing microorganisms, but until Alexander Fleming came along, no one had been able to make the idea work.

Born in 1881 on a farm in Lochfield, Ayrshire, Scotland, Alexander Fleming entered medical school when he was twenty years old. After graduating in 1908, he joined a research group. World War I interrupted his career, yet it influenced his future research. Appalled by the primitive methods of treating war wounds, Fleming determined that once he was back in a lab setting, he would experiment with ways to clean wounds of infectious microorganisms. One method he employed was to grow cultures of a bacteria that caused painful boils. As he later examined one of the containers, he noticed that it was covered with colonies of fuzzy green mold. A second look showed that the mold seemed to be dissolving some of the bacteria. The green fuzzy mold, called *penicillium*, led to the development of penicillin.

Through a series of controlled experiments, Fleming demonstrated that bacteria could be destroyed by injecting it with fluid filtered from the mold. Because it was so difficult to extract pure antibiotic substance, Fleming's 1928 penicillin research was shelved. Ten years later research was revived by two chemists, Howard Florey and Ernst Chain, at Oxford University in England. The team successfully tested the drug on humans, and by 1943 at least 500,000 people a month were being treated with the antibacterial. In 1945 Florey, Chain, and Fleming received the Nobel Prize for physiology or medicine. Thanks to their careful observations and painstaking work, diseases such as pneumonia and blood poisoning are no longer automatic death sentences for humans. In addition, other diseases, such as strep throat, sexually transmitted diseases, and urinary tract infections can now be easily cured with penicillin derivatives.

Suggested Activity

Grow Mold

Materials: (You will need one of each item listed for each student or group of students.) self-sealing plastic bag, black marking pen, slice of white bread, ½ teaspoon (2.5 mL) of water

Procedure:
- Tell students to label their bags with their names.
- Place the bread inside the bag.
- Pour the water into the bag and seal.
- Place the bag in a warm, dark place.
- Make written observations every day for five days.

Extensions: Experiment with the variables. For example, have some students use wheat bread or place some bags in a refrigerator to see what happens. For more experiments on growing mold, see *Janice Van Cleeve's Biology for Every Kid* by Janice Van Cleeve (John Wiley & Sons, Inc., 1990).

Stalin's Five-Year Plan

Read the following paragraphs about Stalin's economic plans for Russia. Use the lines provided and the back of this paper, if necessary, to answer the questions that follow.

After Lenin died in 1924, a power struggle developed between Leon Trotsky and Joseph Stalin, two high officials of the Communist Party. The two factions fought bitterly for four years. In the end, Stalin emerged victorious, and Trotsky went into exile. Stalin soon announced the end of Lenin's economic plan and instituted a master plan of economic growth. Called the Five-Year Plan, it established industrial, agricultural, and social goals for the next five years. (In all, there were three five-year plans, but only the first one, instituted during the twenties, will be discussed here.)

Targets were set for industry to achieve. Factories were required to meet huge production quotas, or else the workers and those in charge were punished. This led some factory managers to exaggerate their production figures. The rapid industrialization also brought about some problems for Soviet citizens. Many people were forced to move to new cities where living conditions were appalling. Although the output of capital goods rose by almost thirteen times its starting point, the production of consumer goods increased by only four times.

As for agriculture, the Five-Year Plan changed the organization of Soviet farming to collective farms (*kolkhozy*) or state farms (*sovkhozy*). On a collective farm, the peasants turned over all their land and resources to a collective in return for a share of the profits. On a state farm, all land and goods were owned by the state and laborers worked for wages. At first the Soviet government had to force the peasants into collective farms—some were shot, some starved to death, and others were deported to remote labor camps in the USSR. Overall, the policy was an economic failure and disastrous in human terms.

QUESTIONS

1. You are a farmer in 1928 Russia. If you were given the choice between a *kolkhozy* and a *sovkhozy,* which would you choose? Explain your answer. _____

   _____

   _____

   _____

2. Why do you think the Five-Year Plan was a failure in human terms? _____

   _____

   _____

   _____

Modern Art

On this page you will meet two influential artists of the first half of the twentieth century. Both developed innovative methods of artistic expression and are still popular today. Try your hand at their methods with the suggested art projects.

Pablo Picasso (1881–1973, Spain)

The son of a mediocre painter, Pablo Picasso could draw before he could talk. By the time he was sixteen he had mastered the art of drawing. He shocked the world with his unorthodox styles, especially Cubism. This major artistic breakthrough shattered all former rules of artistic convention. Vital until his death at age 91, Picasso produced an estimated 50,000 pieces of art.

Picasso Portraits

Materials: black and colored crayons, white construction paper

Directions:

- With the black crayon draw an oval which fills up most of the space on the paper.

- Draw a right or left profile down the middle of the face (see diagram).

- On one side draw a front view of an eye, on the other draw a side view of an eye.

- Draw a mouth, hair, and other facial features.

- Color in the facial features, using different colors on each side.

Piet Mondrian (1872–1944, Holland)

Mondrian is most famous for the patterns he created from lines, rectangles, and squares. After studying art in Paris, he stopped painting recognizable figures and landscapes and tried new ways to express his thoughts. During the 1920s he employed three basic units in his work: the straight line, the right angle, and the use of the three primary colors (red, yellow, blue) and three noncolors (white, black, gray). Although he died in 1944, Mondrian's style can be seen in furniture and architecture today.

Mondrian Moods

Materials: ruler; black marking pen; red, blue and yellow colored pencils; white drawing paper

Directions: Use the ruler and black marking pen to draw a series of horizontal and vertical lines on the paper. Vary the thickness of the lines for a more interesting piece.

Fill in some of the resulting rectangles with red, blue, and yellow colored pencils.

Writing History

Transport yourself back in time and imagine the sights, feelings, and sounds of the events below. Choose one situation to write about.

1. After years of fruitless searching, Howard Carter and his men have just entered the first room of King Tutankhamen's tomb. It contains over 150 objects and pieces of furniture. Write a conversation Carter might have had with the head member of his crew as they surveyed the room for the first time.

2. You are Richard Byrd flying over Antarctica for the first time in history. You see the *aurora australis*, or southerns lights. Write a diary entry to explain your feelings as you viewed this magnificent phenomenon or write a poem about the experience.

3. While you are climbing the mountains of Tibet, you spy a half-man, half-beast running in the distance. You're sure it's Big Foot a creature first "discovered" in 1921. Write a postcard to a friend back home, describing Big Foot and explaining the sight.

4. It is 1928 and you are living near Mt. Etna in Sicily. Suddenly, the volcano begins to erupt! Make a list of 20 things you hear people say as they try to escape the deadly force.

5. John Logie Baird of Britain has just invented the television and you are one of the first persons to see it demonstrated. You represent an investment group. Write a letter convincing the group that television will be the next important medium. Explain how it will affect communication and education.

6. It is 1924, and you are a newspaper correspondent in France attending the first-ever winter Olympics. Ski jumping and figure skating are two of the events. Write a news article about the events during one of those competitions.

7. When Lucila Godoy Alcayaga began writing poetry, she chose Gabriela Mistral as her pen name, Gabriela for the Archangel Gabriel and Mistral for the winds across southern France. Choose a pen name for yourself and explain your sources.

8. As dictator, Joseph Stalin initiated a Five-Year Plan to bring his country's economy in line with the advanced countries. You are Stalin's speech writer. Write a speech he will deliver to his countrymen to convince them that such drastic measures are necessary. Include explanations of the consequences of not cooperating.

9. You are Christopher Robin, A. A. Milne's only son, and the basis for the character of the same name in the *Winnie-the-Pooh* books. Write a letter to your father, telling him why you like or dislike being the subject of his books. Tell him if it has been mostly a positive or a negative experience.

10. It is a Sunday at the Olympics, and you are scheduled to compete. You are favored to win, but your religion forbids you to do anything except worship on the Sabbath. What do you do? Write a plan of action you have that would satisfy all those involved.

Passages

Births

1920

- Author Isaac Asimov was born on January 2. A prolific writer, he was known for his science-fiction books.

- Eugenie Clark was born on May 4. She spent her life studying sharks and was known as the Shark Lady.

1924

- Shirley Chisholm, the first African American woman elected to Congress, was born on November 30.

1925

- Maria Tallchief, the first internationally recognized Native American ballerina, was born on January 25.

- The first female prime minister of Great Britain, Margaret Thatcher, was born on October 13. Elected in 1979, Ms. Thatcher remained in office until 1990, when she resigned.

1929

- Civil rights leader Martin Luther King, Jr. was born on January 15. A minister and charismatic public speaker, he advocated nonviolent protest.

- Anne Frank was born on June 12. Her diary account of her life spent hiding from the Nazis made her famous posthumously.

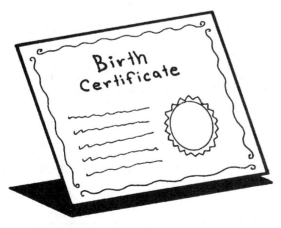

Deaths

1921

- Enrico Caruso was a famous Italian operatic tenor. His recordings brought him worldwide fame.

1922

- Newspaper reporter Nellie Bly was famous for traveling around the world in 72 days.

1923

- Wilhelm Roentgen was the German scientist who received a Nobel prize for physics for his discovery of x-rays.

- President Harding died while on a cross-country tour.

1924

- Ex-President Woodrow Wilson died after a lengthy illness. In 1920 he was awarded the Nobel peace prize.

- Vladimir Lenin, Russia's leader, led the successful revolution that brought the Communist government to power.

1925

- William Jennings Bryan was an unsuccessful candidate for president in three elections and prosecutor at the Scopes Trial in 1925.

1926

- Rudolph Valentino was a romantic star of the silent screen. One of his most famous and popular roles was in *The Sheik*.

- Famed magician and escapologist Harry Houdini died of a burst appendix.

- American impressionist painter Mary Cassatt had studied and painted mostly in France.

1928

- On December 14, 1911, Norwegian explorer Roald Amundsen was the first man to reach the South Pole.

Twenties Facts and Figures

The United States in 1920

Population	121,767,000 (in 1929)
Price of one gallon of milk	$.58
Average annual income	$1,574
Books	*A Farewell to Arms*, Ernest Hemingway; *The Bridge of San Luis Rey*, Thornton Wilder; *The Great Gatsby*, F. Scott Fitzgerald
Children's books	*Tom Swift* series; *Ruth Fielding* series; *The Velveteen Rabbit*, Margery Williams; *Winnie-the-Pooh*, A. A. Milne; *Bambi*, Felix Salten; *The Story of Dr. Doolittle*, Hugh Lofting
Toys	baby dolls that say mama, paper dolls, teddy bears, scooters, wagons, metal trucks, Tinker Toys, Erector sets
Movies	*Treasure Island* (1920), *Ben Hur* (1926), *The Broadway Melody* (1929)
Movie Stars	Mary Pickford, Greta Garbo, Lillian Gish, Gloria Swanson, Al Jolson, Jackie Coogan, Douglas Fairbanks, Lon Chaney, Rudolph Valentino, Rin Tin Tin, Laurel and Hardy
Fashions	bobs, short hemlines, cloche hats, knickers, Lindbergh leather jackets and caps, raccoon coats
Favorite sports	tennis, golf
Sports heroes	Dizzy Dean, Lou Gehrig, Babe Didrikson, Jack Dempsey, Gene Tunney, Sonja Henie, Johnny Weissmuller, Bobby Jones, Helen Wills, Bill Tilden
Famous women	Amelia Earhart, Jeanette Rankin, Carrie Chapman Catt, Gertrude Stein, Zora Neale Hurston, Gertrude Ederle, Annie Oakley, Dr. Florence Sabin, Bessie Smith, Bessie Coleman
Notorious crime figures	Al Capone, Bugs Moran, Leopold and Loeb
Crazes	Mah-jongg, marathon dances, the Charleston, flagpole sitting, King Tut, ouija boards, crossword puzzles
Comic and cartoon characters	Felix the Cat, Mickey Mouse, Little Orphan Annie, the Katzenjammer Kids
Popular sayings	*You're the cat's meow* (you look great). *He's a flat tire* (he's boring).
Games	marbles, the statue game, jump rope, roller skating
Songs	"Yes Sir, That's My Baby"; "Five Foot Two, Eyes of Blue"; "Sweet Georgia Brown"; "Ain't We Got Fun"; "Does the Spearmint Lose Its Flavor on the Bedpost Overnight?"
New foods	Welch's grape jelly; Eskimo Pie; Wrigley's chewing gum
Other innovations	TV tube, model A Ford, moving pictures with sound, cartoon features, zippers, Band-Aids, Kleenex

Famous Firsts

The box below lists a number of famous firsts in the 1920s. Choose any five and write one on each line below. In the first space after each item, explain how it improved the quality of life in the 1920s. Use the second space to tell how your life today would be different without that item.

- first electric pop-up toaster
- first permanent wave for hair
- Scotch tape
- first contact lens for eyes

- first radio broadcast
- electric razor patented
- dry ice invented
- transatlantic radio telephone

- antitoxin for scarlet fever
- first motion picture
- first successful liquid-fueled rocket
- hair dryer

- potato chips manufactured
- frozen vegetables introduced

Choice ...... **1920s Quality of Life** ...... **Life Today**

1. _____

2. _____

3. _____

4. _____

5. _____

Writing Prompts and Literature Ideas

Writing Prompts Use these suggestions for journal writing or as daily writing exercises. Some research or discussion may be appropriate before assigning a particular topic.

- The stock market crash of 1929 brought an abrupt end to the boom times of the twenties. Describe your life before and after the crash. In diary accounts tell how it affected your family and standard of living.

- You are a teenage girl in the 1920s and all your girlfriends are getting their hair bobbed and wearing short skirts. Your mother forbids you to indulge in these new trends. Write a conversation you might have with your mother, explaining why you should be allowed to participate in these new fashions.

- During Lindbergh's flight across the Atlantic, he sometimes flew along just above the waves. When he spotted a small fishing fleet, he circled one boat and shouted out, "Which way to Ireland?" The stunned fisherman offered no reply. If you were that fisherman, what would be your reaction and response?

- Your father is a moonshiner, and he expects you to follow in his footsteps. At first, you are willing to go along with his wishes, but then something changes your mind. Write a conversation with your dad in which you explain what happened to change your mind.

- In *Giants of Jazz* by Studs Terkel (HarperCollins, 1975), the author states that each jazz singer has his or her own definition of the blues: for example, *"Blues ain't nothin' but a good man feelin' bad." "Blues is the landlord knockin' at the gate." "Blues is a cryin' woman whose man's gone off an' left her."* Write your own definition of the blues.

- Walt Disney wants to create a new cartoon to highlight Mickey Mouse. Write and illustrate a storyboard (cartoon strip) for Mickey's new movie.

Literature Ideas The following books can be used to supplement and enhance the study of the 1920s.

- *Ticket to the Twenties* by Mary Blocksma (Little, Brown and Company, 1993)
  Clothing, entertainment, fads, women, sports, and family life are just a few of the topics presented in this fascinating look at daily life in the 1920s. Pictures, time lines, and firsts add greatly to the interest factor.

- *Jump at de Sun: The Story of Zora Neale Hurston* by A.P. Porter (Carolrhoda Books, 1992)
  The life of the vibrant writer is told in this book. It can be supplemented with the reading of some of Hurston's own works.

- *Moonshiner's Son* by Carolyn Reeder (Macmillan Publishing Company, 1993)
  The lead character is training to be a moonshiner, just like his rather, in this believable and well-written story that eloquently represents both sides of the prohibition issue.

- *Bill* by Chap Reaver (Delacorte Press, 1994)
  This is the story of Jessica Gates whose bootlegging father is arrested by revenue agents during prohibition.

Thirties Overview

The stock market crash of 1929 brought an abrupt end to the good times that had preceded it. As the days wore on, it became evident that the economy was not going to be able to mend itself. President Hoover firmly believed that the government should stay out of business and refused to offer any help until 1932. Billions of dollars were lent to failing businesses under the Reconstruction Finance Corporation bill. It was too little and far too late to help end the epidemic of bank failures. As for the unemployed, Hoover felt that any type of assistance would produce even more out-of-work people. His advice to the needy was to seek help from charitable organizations, but they, too, were overburdened and lacked sufficient donations. Most people felt that their president had forsaken them and was indifferent to their plight.

In the election of 1932, Herbert Hoover was soundly defeated by Franklin Delano Roosevelt, who promised the nation a New Deal. One of the first things the new president did was to close all banks so that federal auditors could examine their records. Only then were financially sound banks reopened. Next on his list was getting people back to work. On March 31, 1933, the Civilian Conservation Corps provided jobs for nearly three million young men. More helpful legislation quickly followed. In fact, Roosevelt's first one hundred days in office produced a flurry of legislation that would help the economy recover.

Recovery was a long, slow process, however, and millions suffered from homelessness and unemployment. In the Midwest, erosion problems and drought caused a dust storm that wiped out farms from Oklahoma to Texas. Thousands of "Okies" migrated to California's fertile land in search of work. What they faced was not enough jobs and prejudice from the Californians. Throughout the country, factory and mill workers began to stage strikes for better pay and working conditions. Tactics such as sit-in strikes enabled workers to gain decent benefits and safe conditions.

Radio dominated American life, much like television would decades later. Through his fireside chats, President Roosevelt explained his policies and reassured America. Programs such as *The Lone Ranger* and *Amos' 'n' Andy* helped people forget their troubles. At the movies, Bugs Bunny and Porky Pig debuted and kept everyone laughing. Double features, two movies for the price of one, helped people economize on entertainment. Child star Shirley Temple charmed audiences with her singing and dancing. Even President Roosevelt acknowledged the tiny actor's contributions.

At the end of the 1930s, focus shifted overseas with the rise of fascism in Germany, Italy, and Japan. At first, Roosevelt did not challenge the isolationists, but after war began in 1939, the nation rallied firmly behind Great Britain and its allies. America was quickly swept into a world war and a new era in history.

Important Thirties Legislation

In addition to the New Deal, Congress passed a great deal of other legislation in the thirties. Here is a look at some of these acts and explanations of their provisions.

Smoot-Hawley Tariff Act The purpose of this 1930 bill was to increase sales of U.S. products by raising the cost of imported goods with a tariff. Instead, an international trade war developed as other nations raised their tariffs in response. The result was that the sale of U.S. goods overseas was drastically reduced, worsening the worldwide depression.

Reconstruction Finance Corporation Hoover refused to allow government aid to the unemployed and homeless. In 1932, however, he created the RFC, which loaned two billion dollars to businesses, banks, and state governments. It was not nearly enough and did very little for the economy.

Twentieth Amendment This amendment, passed in 1933, fixed the beginning of the presidential and vice-presidential terms at noon on January 20 rather than March 4, as it had been. It also fixed the beginning of terms of senators and representatives at noon on January 3.

Twenty-first Amendment In 1933 a second Constitutional amendment, the twenty-first, was passed. This one abolished Prohibition and allowed the sale of alcoholic beverages to be controlled by the states.

Good Neighbor Policy In Roosevelt's first inaugural address in 1933, he said he wanted to dedicate this nation to the policy of the good neighbor. The U.S. adopted a friendlier attitude toward Latin America.

Emergency Banking Act On March 6, 1933, President Roosevelt closed all banks that had remained open. Three days later Congress passed this act to keep the banks closed until auditors could determine which banks were financially sound enough to reopen.

Neutrality Act While European countries and Japan and China were becoming increasingly aggressive, the U.S. embraced isolationism and ignored these events. Beginning in August, 1935, Congress passed a series of neutrality acts that prevented America from selling arms to nations at war. It was thought that banning arms would prohibit fighting.

National Labor Relations Act Also known as the Wagner Act, this law was passed on July 5, 1935. It reinstated protections granted labor unions under the NIRA and set up the National Labor Relations Board to investigate and punish unfair practices.

Suggested Activities

Isolationism With the class, discuss why the U.S. adopted an isolationist attitude. Debate whether this was a good idea or not.

Prohibition The Twenty-first Amendment allowed states to determine policies concerning the sale of alcoholic beverages. Have the students find out their state's policy.

New Deal Quiz

Use the questions on this page to assess students' knowledge about the New Deal programs. After studying the New Deal at length, use this page again as a post-test. Make a transparency of this page for use on the overhead projector or copy the names in the box below onto the chalkboard for all to see. After you have read each clue, tell students to choose and write the answer from the names in the box.

❑ National Recovery Administration	❑ Securities and Exchange Commission
❑ Federal Emergency Relief Administration	❑ National Industry Recovery Act
❑ Civilian Conservation Corps	❑ Social Security Act
❑ National Labor Relations Board	❑ Agricultural Adjustment Act
❑ Tennessee Valley Authority	❑ Fair Labor Standards Act
❑ Federal Deposit Insurance Corporation	❑ Farm Security Administration
	❑ Works Progress Administration

1. _____ raised the minimum wage to 40 cents per hour

2. _____ established a federal pension for the elderly

3. _____ paid farmers to limit the crops they grew

4. _____ gave jobs to young men in environmental improvement projects

5. _____ guaranteed workers the right to join labor unions and call strikes

6. _____ insured bank deposits up to $5,000

7. _____ provided funding for the development of the Tennessee River Valley

8. _____ gave money to local and state relief organizations

9. _____ created work codes and industry safety regulations

10. _____ reorganized all New Deal programs under this federal agency

11. _____ loaned money to sharecroppers to buy their own land

12. _____ encouraged business owners and labor unions to cooperate in regulating prices

13. _____ regulated and reformed financial practices, particularly buying stocks

Answers

(Cover before using this page.) 1. Fair Labor Standards Act 2. Social Security Act 3. Agricultural Adjustment Act 4. Civilian Conservation Corps 5. National Labor Relations Board 6. Federal Deposit Insurance Corporation 7. Tennessee Valley Authority 8. Federal Emergency Relief Administration 9. National Industry Recovery Act 10. Works Progress Administration 11. Farm Security Administration 12. National Recovery Administration 13. Securities and Exchange Commission

The New Deal

Immediately after his inauguration, FDR mapped out a number of proposals to aid economic recovery. Farmers, young people, and needy people were the target groups whom the president especially wanted to help. From FDR's historic First Hundred Days (March 9 to June 16, 1933) to 1938, Congress passed the legislative acts listed in the chart below. Because they were referred to by initials, they became known as Roosevelt's alphabet soup.

Initials	Program	Provisions
AAA	Agricultural Adjustment Act	set a new national farm policy, by providing that farmers be paid to limit the production of crops and livestock
CCC	Civilian Conservation Corps	gave jobs to more than two million young men in environmental improvement projects, especially the National Park System
FERA	Federal Emergency Relief Act	gave money to local and state relief organizations
FDIC	Federal Deposit Insurance Corporation	insured bank deposits up to $5,000 and eliminated the fear of bank failures
FLSA	Fair Labor Standards Act	raised minimum wage to 40 cents per hour and shortened the work week to forty hours; last major piece of New Deal legislation
FSA	Farm Security Administration	loaned money to sharecroppers and tenant farmers so they could purchase their own land
HOLC	Home Owners Loan Corporation	reduced interest on loans and provided for postponement of payments
NIRC	National Industry Recovery Act	created work codes and industry safety regulations
NLRB	National Labor Relations Board	guaranteed workers the right to join labor unions and call strikes
NRA	National Recovery Administration	encouraged business owners and labor unions to cooperate in regulating prices, production, and wages
PWA	Public Works Administration	provided four billion dollars for the construction of highways and public buildings
SEC	Securities and Exchange Commission	created to regulate and reform financial practices, particularly buying stocks on credit
SS	Social Security	established a federal pension system for elderly Americans by using money from payroll deductions and matching employer contributions
TVA	Tennessee Valley Authority	provided funding for the development of the Tennessee River Valley; taught farmers better farming techniques
WPA	Works Progress Administration	reorganized all New Deal relief programs under this single federal agency in 1935; employed workers on large construction projects and gave jobs to writers and artists

In-Depth

This page provides an in-depth look at three of the New Deal programs enacted by Congress during the Hundred Days. After reading the provisions, respond to the statement following each summary.

Civilian Conservation Corps

- It was based on the idea of getting people away from the cities and back to the countryside.

- More than 250,000 men between the ages of 18 and 25 were hired. Free room and board were provided in work camps.

- Workers did construction and conservation work from morning until midnight for $30 per month, $25 of which was sent home to their families.

Respond: Some critics felt that the **CCC** was too militaristic because workers had to wear uniforms and live in military barracks.

Agricultural Adjustment Act

- There were huge surpluses of grain and farm commodities which drove prices down.

- **AAA** agents talked to farmers and offered them payment for not growing crops.

- In 1933 the **AAA** ordered the slaughter of six million pigs and the burning of millions of oranges.

Respond: Secretary of Agriculture Harry Wallace did not particularly like these reduction measures, but he called the times desperate and said that desperate measures were necessary.

National Recovery Administration

The most famous piece of New Deal legislation, the **NRA** allowed businesses to fix fair prices for their products, thereby preventing one company from undercutting another one's prices. Industries were encouraged to establish limits for amounts they would produce.

- The **NRA** established a minimum wage, child labor rules, and set a maximum number of hours employees worked.

- Businessmen who voluntarily complied with the **NRA** received signs which read "We do our part" to display in their windows.

- The Supreme Court ruled in 1935 that the **NIRA**, which established the **NRA**, was unconstitutional.

Respond: The **NRA** was the most important piece of legislation passed by Congress during the first Roosevelt administration.

Labor Unions

The status of labor unions changed for the better during the thirties. New tactics were employed to help workers achieve safe working conditions and appropriate benefits. Read about these innovations below.

History of Unions The second half of the nineteenth century brought some major changes in the way people worked. Machines made mass production possible and relied less on an individual's skill. No job was secure, and employers took advantage of the situation. Some workers banded together to form unions and were able to negotiate their terms of employment with management. When Samuel Gompers helped found the American Federation of Labor in 1886, he had hopes that it would be a union for all workers. However, minorities, women, immigrants, and the unskilled were often left out.

Unions of the Thirties During the 1930s the situation escalated as workers demanded pay raises and job security. When employers rejected these demands, a wave of strikes swept the country. Some strikes resulted in violence. On Memorial Day in 1937, several thousand workers demonstrated in front of the Republic Steel Plant in South Chicago. Angry words were exchanged, followed by a thrown pop bottle. Shots were fired and tear gas grenades were thrown into the crowd. Ten strikers died, and 90 others were wounded in the melee.

Sit-Down Strikes A new type of strike was organized during the thirties, the sit-down strike. These were different from previous strikes because workers sat at their machines and refused to work or to leave. A sit-down strike at one General Motors plant kept the company shut down for six weeks. Sit-down tactics were declared illegal by the U.S. Supreme Court in 1934.

Union Leaders Auto assembly and steel production workers wanted the same benefits afforded to skilled craftsmen. John L. Lewis was the leader of the United Mine Workers. In 1935 he and seven others broke with the American Federation of Labor (AFL) to form the Committee for Industrial Organization, commonly called the CIO, Lewis served as the group's president until 1940. On December 5, 1955, the AFL (American Federation of Labor) merged with the CIO to form the AFL-CIO.

David Dubinsky immigrated to the U.S. in 1911 after being banished from Russia for organizing labor unions. After taking a job as a garment cutter in New York City, he soon began fighting for workers' rights. By 1932 he had become the International Ladies Garment Workers Union president. Under his leadership, the group conducted a series of strikes which subsequently brought the workers improved conditions and shorter hours. Dubinsky also saw to it that the union established a pension fund, health centers, and educational programs for its members.

Suggested Activity

Read For an in-depth look at labor unions in America, read the October 1992 issue of *Cobblestone*, "The History of Labor," or the book *The Great Depression* by R. Conrad Stein (Children's Press, 1993).

Crime in America

Prohibition was still in effect at the beginning of the 1930s, and bootlegging was a big business for the mobs. The economic climate of the Depression encouraged more criminal activity. Here are the stories of some of the most notorious criminals of the times.

Al Capone One of the most infamous gang leaders of the time was Al Capone. Also known as "Scarface," he built his empire in Chicago and controlled the city's large-scale criminal activities. He traveled in a $20,000, seven-ton armored car and wore a $50,000 diamond ring. Capone was never found guilty of any killings, but he was imprisoned for income tax evasion in 1931. After his release, he retired to Florida where he died in 1947.

Al Capone

John Herbert Dillinger After his gang pulled off a series of midwestern bank robberies, Dillinger gained national attention. His group consisted of some prison inmates he had helped to escape. When he crossed state lines, he became a fugitive and was the first criminal named Public Enemy #1 by FBI director J. Edgar Hoover. Federal agents finally shot and killed Dillinger as he exited a movie theater in Chicago on July 22, 1934.

Bonnie and Clyde On the morning of May 23, 1934, crime partners Bonnie Parker and Clyde Barrow were ambushed and killed near Arcadia, Louisiana, as officers pumped 167 bullets into their car. The two, better known as Bonnie and Clyde, began their vicious, cruel crime spree in Texas in February 1932. Together they murdered 12 people, including eight policemen or guards. Frank Hamer trailed the couple through six states and over 15,000 miles before catching up with them. After the attack the bodies, still in the car, were moved to Arcadia, where they were displayed until relatives claimed them. Today, the original Bonnie and Clyde death car can be seen at the Imperial Palace Hotel in Las Vegas, Nevada. During the sixties, Warren Beatty and Faye Dunaway starred in a movie about this famous pair.

Pretty Boy Floyd Charles "Pretty Boy" Floyd was a notorious Oklahoma outlaw. Inspired by Jesse James, he pulled off a number of bank robberies. Many people supported him because, they reasoned, he was just stealing from the banks who had robbed them of their money and land. FBI agent Melvin Purvis, who had led the Dillinger manhunt, focused on Floyd, who was shot and killed in Ohio on October 22, 1934. Family, friends and 20,000 others attended his funeral in Oklahoma.

Suggested Activities

Research Assign the students to research the life of Melvin Purvis.

Ages Bonnie Parker was only 19 when she was killed by agents. Have the students find out the ages of the other criminals at the time of their deaths.

Reference

Outlaws, Mobsters, and Murderers by Diana Claitor (1991).

About the Great Depression

This overview will help students understand more about the causes and effects of the Great Depression. Use it as a study guide and a springboard for discussions.

Definition The Great Depression was a period of severe decline in business activity accompanied by falling prices and high unemployment. During the Depression nearly 13 million people were out of work, banks closed, savings were wiped out, and the stock market collapsed.

Causes A number of factors worked together to cause the Great Depression. Six of them are listed here.

1. Businesses during the twenties had kept prices and profits high while keeping wages low. This meant that labor could not afford to buy what it produced.

2. After World War I farmers kept up their high levels of production, and surpluses piled up. Supply became greater than demand, thus driving prices down.

3. Industry had built more and larger plants, allowing them to produce more goods than they could sell.

4. The introduction of labor-saving machinery put men out of jobs in a number of industries.

5. World War I left the worldwide economy shaky.

6. Installment buying allowed people to purchase on credit, and people piled up debts. They used their money to buy stocks on margin, hoping that prices would rise and they would make a profit.

Effects The effects of the Great Depression were many and included the obvious—hunger, poverty, and homelessness. Another effect was psychological in nature. Men were expected to work, and joblessness was considered a result of laziness. When millions could not find jobs during the Depression, they felt ashamed, even though the situation was not their fault. Some put up a brave, false front, while others kept to themselves to avoid revealing their situation and true feelings.

How People Coped People were forced to change their lives during the Depression. There was no unemployment insurance to fall back on or Social Security benefits, either. People found ways to cope the best they could. Belt tightening became a way of life. Some people had to turn to charity, friends, or family for help. Two or more families often crowded into one apartment, splitting the rent. Meat became a luxury, as did eating out at a restaurant. When electric bills were too high for some to pay, they resorted to kerosene lamps.

Government Intervention As the Depression raged on, it was obvious that some government help would be necessary to get the economy back on its feet. President Hoover did not believe in either government intervention in business or direct assistance for the people. When Franklin Roosevelt was elected president, he quickly took action. In a flurry of legislative activity during a period known as the First Hundred Days, Congress passed a number of innovative laws, some of which are still in effect today. Read more about them on pages 170 and 171.

Unemployment Math

Learn the facts and figures of unemployment during the Great Depression. Read the statements in each section below. Solve the problems, based on the facts and figures. Show your work in the space provided or on the back of the page.

1 *Fact*: In the U.S. in 1930, over 60,000 workers were losing their jobs every week.

Problem: At that rate, how many workers would lose their jobs in 24 weeks?

2 *Fact*: The Dust Bowl migration was the largest migration of people in U.S. history. Between 1935 and 1940 over one million people from Oklahoma, Texas, Arkansas, and Missouri moved to California. (Use one million to find the answer.)

Problem: If an equal number of people from each state migrated to California, how many people came from each state?

3 *Fact*: Okies were paid 25 cents an hour to pick cotton. The average field hand worked 16 hours per day, 7 days a week.

Problem: How much would a field hand worker earn in one week?

4 *Fact*: In 1933 in Illinois one 56-pound bushel of corn sold for 10 cents.

Problem: How much was each pound of corn worth?

5 *Fact*: By 1932 at least one out of four, or approximately 12 million people, was unemployed. (Use 12 million to find the answer.)

Problem: How many people were employed?

6 *Fact*: In 1930 the Willys automobile plant's work force shrank from 28,000 in March to 4,000 in November.

Problem: What percent of the work force was left in November?

7 *Fact*: By 1931 the nation's unemployment figure was a staggering 13.6 million—this represented $\frac{1}{3}$ of the labor force.

Problem: What was the total number of the employment force?

8 *Fact*: Fourteen thousand hoboes used the Missouri Pacific Railroad in the summer of 1929. By 1931 the figure had jumped to 185,000.

Problem: What was the difference between the number of hoboes using the railroad in 1929 and 1931?

Herbert Clark Hoover

31st President, 1929–1933

Herbert Hoover

Vice President: Charles Curtis

Born: August 10, 1874, in West Branch, Iowa

Died: October 20, 1964

Party: Republican

Parents: Jesse Clark Hoover, Hulda Randall Minthorn

First Lady: Lou Henry

Children: Herbert, Jr.; Allan

Nickname: Chief

Education: Degree in engineering from Stanford University

Famous Firsts:

- Hoover was the first president born west of the Mississippi River and the first to have an asteroid named after him.
- He was the first president to have a telephone on his desk.

Achievements:

- He established the Veterans' Administration.
- Not until 1932 did he create the Reconstruction Finance Corporation, which loaned billions of dollars to businesses and banks to help them out of the Depression.
- In 1930 Congress passed the Smoot-Hawley Tariff, which raised tariff rates to record high levels. Hoover hoped that the tariff would increase sales of U.S. products by raising the prices of imported goods. Unfortunately, this led to an international trade war when other nations also raised their tariffs.

Interesting Facts:

- Herbert Hoover spent his own money on entertainment while serving as president. Furthermore, he never accepted his salary for the presidency.
- During his term in office, Hoover never attended the theater.
- Herbert Hoover held honorary degrees from over 50 American universities.
- First Lady Lou Henry spoke four languages fluently, including Chinese. Hoover himself spoke Chinese, and the couple often used the language to protect themselves from eavesdroppers.
- Hoover's son Allan had two pet alligators, which could sometimes be found wandering around the White House.
- Hoover was a dedicated and excellent fly fisherman.
- A self-made millionaire, Hoover managed the distribution of 18 million tons of food to starving people in Europe during World War I. The term *hooverize* was coined in honor of him; it meant to conserve food for the war effort.
- In a 1962 survey conducted by the School of Engineering and Applied Science at Columbia University, Thomas Edison and Herbert Hoover were named the two greatest engineers in U.S. history.

Franklin Delano Roosevelt

32nd President, 1933–1945

Vice Presidents: John N. Garner; Harry A. Wallace; Harry S. Truman

Born: January 30, 1882 at Hyde Park, New York

Died: April 12, 1945

Party: Democrat

Parents: James Roosevelt, Sara Delano

First Lady: Anna Eleanor Roosevelt

Children: Anna, James, Franklin, Elliot, Franklin Delano, John

Nickname: FDR

Education: Graduate of Harvard University, attended Columbia Law School

Franklin Delano Roosevelt

Famous Firsts:

- FDR was the first defeated vice-presidential nominee to be elected president. He was the first president to appoint a woman to his cabinet.

- He was the first president to appear on television.

- His wife was the first wife of a president to make public statements on current issues.

- He was the first and only person elected to four terms as president.

Achievements:

- His New Deal initiated new programs which put people to work.

- FDR began a series of informal radio talks called fireside chats to inform the nation about conditions and what the government was doing about them.

- Before his election as president, FDR served in the New York State Senate, was assistant secretary of the Navy under Woodrow Wilson, was nominated for vice-president in the 1920 election, and served as governor of New York State for two terms.

- Although he was partially paralyzed by poliomyelitis in 1921, he continued his political career.

- He attended conferences with world leaders to map out peace strategies.

Interesting Facts:

- Former president Theodore Roosevelt was Franklin's fifth cousin and Eleanor Roosevelt's uncle.

- It was Teddy Roosevelt who gave his niece Eleanor in marriage to Franklin.

- As a young boy FDR was taken to the White House to meet President Grover Cleveland, who told the boy he hoped he never had the misfortune of becoming president.

- In his first term FDR held 337 press conferences. Hoover had held only 66.

- FDR's portrait appears on one side of the dime.

The Depression's First Lady

Lou Henry Hoover was born in Waterloo, Iowa, in 1874, but she grew up in California. She led an athletic life, hunting, camping, and horseback riding with her father. At Stanford University, she was the only female in the geology department and the first woman in America to earn a college degree in the subject. It was at Stanford that Lou Henry met her future husband, Herbert Hoover. Devoted to the Girl Scouts, she first became a girl scout leader in 1917 and in 1922 was elected the group's national president. Her work with the Girl Scouts continued even during her term as first lady.

Lou Henry Hoover

After their marriage, the Hoovers sailed for China, where Hoover had taken a job as a mining engineer. They spent the next three decades living in China, England, Australia, New Zealand, Burma, and Russia. Lou Hoover mastered the Chinese language, as did her husband. While they were in the White House, they communicated in Chinese when they did not want others to know what they were discussing. During their time abroad, the Hoovers coordinated relief efforts for refugees in Belgium and won international prominence for their humanitarian work. *Hooverize*, the act of economizing, became a commonly used term and was meant to compliment the doer. Throughout their travels, Lou Hoover remained a devoted mother to her two sons.

After the Hoovers returned to the United States, Lou Hoover became active in women's issues. She founded the National Women's Athletic Association to support and encourage physical exercise. She held the unusual view for the times that women should be afforded an equal opportunity to become involved in competitive sports. In addition, she was active in the League of Women Voters and the National Geographic Society. She often spoke to groups of young women about careers.

When she moved into the White House, Lou Hoover was a 55-year-old grandmother. Uncertain of her role as first lady, she chose a conservative path and no longer remained active in her many causes. As the Depression progressed, she retreated even more from the public eye. By the time the Hoovers left the presidency, public opinion was no longer on their side. Lou Hoover died in 1944.

Suggested Activities

Comparisions Compare Mrs. Hoover's views about women's roles in society with those of Eleanor Roosevelt. How are they alike? How are they different?

Public Opinion At one time the Hoovers were considered great humanitarians. Discuss what turned public opinion against the Hoovers.

Response Ask students to respond to this question: If you were Mrs. Hoover, what would you have done to gather support from the American public?

"First Lady of the World"

She was a person of action, a friend of the poor and oppressed, and a champion of human rights. Her actions helped change the role of first lady, and she became one of the most beloved figures in U.S. history. Her name was Anna Eleanor Roosevelt.

Born to Anna and Elliott Roosevelt on October 11, 1884, she lived a privileged life, complete with servants, governesses, and maids to attend her and her two brothers. Despite the family's wealth, however, Roosevelt's childhood was an unhappy one. Her mother, a beauty and a member of New York's wealthy society, cruelly nicknamed her daughter "granny," which made Roosevelt feel that she was ugly and awkward. Before she was ten years old, her parents and a brother died. She lived with her grandmother and, at fifteen, was sent to boarding school in England.

Eleanor Roosevelt

Here she was introduced to new ideas which helped draw her out of her shell. After returning to the U.S. in 1902, she caught the eye of her handsome, distant cousin, Franklin Delano Roosevelt, and the two married on March 17, 1905.

The young couple quickly became a family. They had four children in their first five years together, and two more children followed. Like other wealthy young wives, Eleanor Roosevelt served on charity boards and attended classes in literature, art, and music. When Roosevelt's political career took off, she became a politician's wife, speaking on behalf of her husband, doing volunteer work, and visiting the troops during World War I. In 1918, she discovered some love notes from Lucy Mercer to Roosevelt. Devastated, she poured herself into social causes—world peace, civil rights, and women's issues. The marriage remained intact, but it was never the same for the deeply wounded Eleanor Roosevelt.

In the summer of 1921, Franklin Roosevelt contracted poliomyeltis. Seven years later, with his wife's support, he reentered politics. His legs were paralyzed but not his mind. She became his eyes and legs, visiting places that he could not. Unlike other presidents' wives, she did not stay in the background but began campaigning for a variety of social issues. Even after Franklin Roosevelt's death, Eleanor Roosevelt continued her work as a spokesperson for human decency.

Suggested Activities

The United Nations Find out about Eleanor Roosevelt's role in the United Nations. Explain what the Universal Declaration of Human Rights is and how it is enforced.

Women's Rights Eleanor Roosevelt began a series of regular press conferences for women only, and she supported the idea that women had a right to work. Make a list of some of her other views about women's rights.

Civil Rights Mrs. Roosevelt invited African American singer Marian Anderson to perform at the Washington Monument. Find out what events led to this performance and Roosevelt's role in them.

Election Facts and Figures

	Election of 1932	Election of 1936
Democrats	Franklin Delano Roosevelt was the innovative governor of New York. Crippled since 1921 from polio, the energetic politician flew to Chicago after his nomination to become the first presidential candidate to deliver an acceptance speech in person. John Nance Garner was Roosevelt's running mate.	Franklin Roosevelt, whose programs seemed to be working, was unanimously renominated for a second term. He had farmers, workers, the unemployed, and African Americans firmly on his side.
Republicans	President Herbert Hoover was renominated by his party in spite of the blame that was placed on the Republican administration for the economic crisis.	Alfred M. Landon, the governor of Kansas, was the Republican nominee. The Republican Party was viewed by many as the party of wealthy conservatives.
Other	Norman Thomas, a Socialist, also ran in this election. Although he gathered over 880,000 popular votes, he failed to get any electoral votes.	A third party candidate ran in this election, William Lemke of the Union Party. He gathered over 880,000 popular votes but no electoral votes.
Slogans	Kick out depression with a Democratic vote.	Campaign buttons for FDR read "We want F.D.R. again."
Issues	The Great Depression remained the focus of this election. Roosevelt proposed public works programs and government aid to farmers to help the economy recover. Hoover, however, continued to warn against government aid.	Landon said the New Deal undermined American traditions of individualism and self-sufficiency. He wanted the federal government to stay out of business affairs. Roosevelt reminded the American public that the Great Depression had started during a Republican administration. He believed that it was the government's responsibility to protect workers and regulate the economy.
Winner	Roosevelt won by a resounding majority. He carried forty-two of the forty-eight states with 472 to 59 electoral votes.	Franklin Delano Roosevelt won with 523 to 8 electoral votes.

Farmers and the Dust Bowl

Farmers did not share in the prosperity of World War I, and things were worse after the recession of 1921. Federal support for agriculture ended, and many farmers, who had expanded their production to meet wartime needs, lost their land and stock. For those who survived, low crop prices meant low income. In the thirties wheat prices dropped to below what it cost to grow the crop. Rather than sell at such prices, some farmers destroyed their own crops. A series of natural disasters made matters even worse and led to the greatest westward migration that the United States has ever seen.

Americans had long disregarded the warnings of conservationists. Farmers had misused the land, depleting fertile soil and then moving on to farm new land. In the Great Plains, farmers plowed up natural grasses to plant wheat. Agriculturalists, who advised the use of contour plowing to prevent erosion and planting trees as windbreaks, were ignored. When a seven-year drought struck, beginning in 1931, winds blew the topsoil into thick, dark clouds of dust that sometimes lasted for several days. To protect themselves from the dust storms, farmers hung damp sheets over the windows of their homes. Still, dust poured through the cracks of the farmhouse walls, leaving dust in their food, hair, eyes, mouths, and pockets. For many, there was nothing left to do but leave their farms and head west.

Over three million people eventually migrated from the Great Plains region to California, where there was the promise of jobs. In most cases, that was all it was—a promise. Conditions in California proved little better than the farms they had left. While there was not much dust to contend with, there were not nearly enough jobs. Californians resented these new people and labeled them "Okies," a synonym for dumb and lazy. Hatred against them was so great that some farmers destroyed their surplus food rather than share it with the starving Okie families.

Finally, the government stepped in and created some labor camps in the San Joaquin Valley, which provided relief and education for the migrants. Much was written about these people and their struggles. John Steinbeck's novel *The Grapes of Wrath* described conditions among the Okies in California. Dorothea Lange photographed and documented their misery, while Woody Guthrie sang songs about their predicament. It was a dark time in American history in more ways than one.

——— Suggested Activities ———

Documentation Read more about the people who called attention to the sufferings of the Okies. See page 182 for information about Dorothea Lange, page 198 for the story of Woody Guthrie, and page 194 for a study of John Steinbeck.

In Depth For an in-depth look at the Dust Bowl, read the book *Children of the Dust Bowl: The True Story of the School at Weedpatch Camp* by Jerry Stanley (Crown Publishers, Inc., 1992).

FSA Photographer

Dortohea Lange

Dorothea Margaretta Nutzhorn was born on May 25, 1895, in Hoboken, New Jersey. Her father, Henry Martin Nutzhorn, was a lawyer and her mother, Joan Lange, sang in recitals. When Dorothea was just seven years old she contracted polio, which left her with a limp and one foot smaller than the other. Five years later, Mr. Nutzhorn abandoned the family. After school Dorothea Nutzhorn would visit her mother at the library where she worked and read the art books. Bored with high school, Nutzhorn often skipped classes and went to museums and art exhibitions. To please her mother, she enrolled in a training school for teachers after graduation, but her dream was photography. She studied photography under Clarence White, a well-known member of a group called the Photo-Secession. Early in her career, she changed her last name from Nutzhorn to Lange, her mother's maiden name.

At 20 Lange set out to travel around the world, supporting herself by selling photographs. Her money ran out in San Francisco, where she settled and opened a studio specializing in portraits. Lange was accepted by San Francisco's painters, writers, and photographers. On March 21, 1920, she married painter Maynard Dixon. Together they had two sons.

Lange was moved by the sight of the homeless men wandering the streets of San Francisco and began to photograph them. Her pictures won immediate recognition from fellow photographers and led to her work for the FSA. She teamed up with writer Paul Taylor to document the lives and struggles of the migrant workers in California. In 1935 Lange divorced her husband and married Paul Taylor.

A collection of Lange's photographs, called *An American Exodus: A Record of Human Erosion*, was published in 1939. Two years later she gave up a Guggenheim Fellowship in order to record the evacuation and internment of Japanese Americans following the attack on Pearl Harbor. After the war, several photo essays by Lange were featued in *Life* magazine. Dorothea Lange continued to document American life through her photography until her death on October 11, 1965.

Suggested Activities

Trademark Lange's trademark photo, *Migrant Mother*, showed the despair of a migrant woman and her children in their lean-to shelter. Display a copy of this photo to the class. Discuss what the woman in the picture might be thinking.

Documentary Lange's photographs are done in a documentary style. Discuss this style with the class. Let them create a documentary of your classroom lifestyle, using inexpensive disposable cameras. Arrange the pictures in a large montage.

Learn More Dorothea Lange's works are housed in the Library of Congress, the National Archives in Washington, D.C., and at the Oakland Museum in Oakland, California. If you have access to any of these facilities, arrange a class visit.

Reference

Dorothea Lange by Robyn Montana Turner (Little, Brown and Company, 1994). It contains a number of her photographs.

Hull House

Hull House was one of America's first community centers. Anyone who arrived there could count on welcome assistance. In addition, it offered cultural activities, educational classes, and hope to the struggling families who used its facilities. The founder of this institution was Jane Addams, one of the most important social reformers in U.S. history.

Jane Addams was born on September 6, 1860, in Cedarville, Illinois. The youngest of eight children, she was only two years old when her mother died. Addams's father was a respected state senator who encouraged her to read by giving her five cents for every book she read and discussed with him. He also encouraged her to attend medical school, but recurring back problems and an operation changed her plans. After traveling to Europe and witnessing abject poverty, she decided to do something to help other people. In London she visited Toynbee Hall, an experimental project in a poverty-ridden area. She returned to the States with the intention of building a similar project.

Jane Addams

In the industrial slums of Chicago, Addams found a brick mansion formerly owned by Charles Hull. After leasing it, she and her friend, Ellen Gates Starr, refurbished the newly-named Hull House. Child care for working mothers and after-school activities for children were offered first. Gradually, evening classes and social clubs were organized for the adults. Addams campaigned successfully for state laws to regulate child labor. She championed the eight-hour day for working women and was also able to obtain much-needed housing reform. To call attention to these causes, Addams lectured on college campuses and spoke to civic organizations. She campaigned for women's right to vote and was able to talk civic leaders into financial support of her programs. Somehow, she found time to write books about her experiences.

Public opinion turned against Jane Addams when she spoke out against World War I. Afterwards, many thought she had done the right thing, and in 1931 she was awarded the Nobel Peace Prize, a first for women. Addams donated her $16,480 prize money to the Women's International League for Peace and Freedom. By the time of Addams' death on May 21, 1935, Hull House had expanded to a whole city block of buildings and grounds.

Suggested Activities

Necessity Have the students research why a settlement house was necessary in Chicago in the early 1900s.

Labor Laws With the class, discuss child labor conditions in the 1900s. Find out how Jane Addams and others helped change these laws. What child labor laws are in effect today?

Reference

Peace and Bread, the Story of Jane Addams by Stephanie Sammartino McPherson (Carolrhoda Books, Inc., 1993).

The Great Educator

Mary McLeod Bethune was born on July 10, 1875, in Mayesville, North Carolina, the second to last of seventeen children in a deeply religious Methodist family. Her parents were former slaves who had become sharecroppers. To earn extra income Mrs. McLeod continued to cook meals for her former owner.

As a child McLeod desperately wanted to learn to read and write, but there were no schools open to African Americans. When she was eleven, a missionary school for blacks opened up in town and she walked five miles each way to attend the school, which was only open three months out of the year — the rest of the year children were expected to help work in the fields. Every evening when she returned home, McLeod taught her eager siblings the lessons she had learned in school.

Mary McLeod Bethune

After receiving a scholarship and attending Scotia Seminary, McLeod became head of a mission school in Florida. In 1899 she married Albert Bethune, a teacher. When Bethune learned that the Florida East Coast Railroad was being built, she became concerned about the African Americans who were moving there. No schools would be available to them, so on October 3, 1903, she opened her own school. At first there were only five female students in addition to her own son, but within two years there were 250 students in attendance. In addition to the school, Bethune organized a hospital for blacks and started the Better Boys Club to provide youngsters with a better place to go than poolrooms and bars. Eventually, her school merged with Cookman Institute for Boys to become Bethune-Cookman College.

A tireless worker, Bethune campaigned for black freedom rights and for all women's rights. She organized the National Council of Negro Women, and for ten years during the Roosevelt administration, she served as head of the National Youth Administration. A close friend of Eleanor Roosevelt, Bethune promoted Roosevelt's New Deal to the black population and organized the "Black Cabinet." This group of professionals and advisors promoted black issues in Washington. When the Office of Minority Affairs was instituted, Bethune was appointed as administrator. In addition, she served as vice-president of the Urban League and president of the Association of Colored Women.

After her retirement, Bethune continued to work for equality for all people until her death on May 18, 1955, just before her 80th birthday.

Suggested Activities

Motto The motto for Bethune's original school was, "Enter to learn, depart to serve." Ask students to explain what they think the motto means.

Play Let groups of students perform a short skit about Mary McLeod Bethune. Groups can write their own or use the prepared dialogue from *Take a Walk in Their Shoes* by Glennette Tilley Turner (Puffin Books, 1989).

A Great Contralto

One of the most famous contralto singers the United States has ever known was African American Marian Anderson. Born in Philadelphia, Pennsylvania, on February 29, 1897, Anderson sang in church choirs from the age of six. The oldest of three children, she was performing at parties by the time she was fourteen. Impressed by her natural talent, the church members set up a trust fund to help pay for her musical training. At nineteen Anderson began formal voice lessons and sang at churches, theaters, and small colleges. After placing first in a major competition in 1925, she performed with the New York Philharmonic. A Rosenwald Fellowship followed in 1930. It was a promising start, but racial prejudice posed a number of obstacles. Although she received a standing ovation at New York's Town Hall and all of her concerts met with rave reviews, racial segregation prevented her from performing with an opera company. Since European audiences were more accepting of persons of color, Anderson began a European tour which met with acclaim wherever she performed.

Marian Anderson

After five years abroad Anderson returned to the States. In 1939 she was scheduled to perform at Constitution Hall in Washington, D.C., but the Daughters of the American Revolution denied her use of the building because of her race. First Lady Eleanor Roosevelt was a member of the DAR, but when she heard about Anderson's treatment, she resigned in protest. Instead, Roosevelt arranged for Anderson to sing at the Lincoln Memorial. Anyone who wished to hear Anderson could attend this free concert. Seventy-five thousand people attended, far more than would have fit into Constitution Hall.

Throughout her singing career, Marian Anderson worked for equal rights for African Americans. In 1942 the Marian Anderson Award for young, talented singers was established. Then Anderson became the first African American to sing in a leading role at the Metropolitan Opera in New York City. In 1958 she was appointed as a delegate to the United Nations by President Eisenhower. She also performed at the inaugurations of Presidents Eisenhower and Kennedy. Marian Anderson died at age 96 in Portland, Oregon, after a stroke. She will long be remembered as the woman who first gained entry to the formerly all-white American opera world.

Suggested Activities

Voices Marian Anderson was a contralto. Tell the students to research and find out the differences among the following terms: contralto, soprano, and baritone.

Opera Listen to a recording of Marian Anderson singing opera.

Memorable Stars

Many memorable moments were provided by the Depression-time stars outlined below. After reading about them, do some research and answer the questions that follow each selection.

Shirley Temple Child star Shirley Temple first charmed audiences in 1934 with a brief song and dance routine. Starring roles soon followed. Her films did so well that they kept several studios out of bankruptcy. Hollywood's curly-haired Dimpled Darling bolstered sagging Depression spirits. Shirley Temple merchandise also became a big hit with young children, who clamored for Shirley Temple clothing, books, and dolls.

Shirley Temple

Question: Shirley Temple later married and entered politics. Find out her married name and what roles she served in government.

King Kong The original *King Kong* was produced in 1933, just two years after the Empire State Building was completed. Actress Fay Wray played the heroine opposite the ferocious primate. In reality, King Kong was an 18-inch model. Thanks to 1930s advances in filmmaking technology, Willis O'Brien was able to create the special effects that made the gorilla appear gigantic.

Question: What special effects were used in the most current production of *King Kong*? Who starred in that version?

Bugs Bunny Walt Disney's Mickey Mouse had been around for almost ten years when the wisecracking Bugs Bunny came on the celluloid scene. His first appearance was in the Warner Brothers cartoon *Porky's Hare Hunt.* "What's up, Doc?" became the phrase most often associated with the rascally and lovable rabbit.

Question: Voices for Porky, Bugs Bunny, and other characters were provided by one man. Who was he?

The Marx Brothers Originally there were five Marx Brothers, but Gummo left the vaudeville act before the group ever made a movie. In the late 1920s and on into the 1930s, the Marx Brothers brought their comic talents to the silver screen. Groucho, Harpo, and Chico were the main characters in a series of films that poked fun at stuffy, rich people. Zeppo played romantic roles until the mid-1930's when he left the team.

Question: How would you compare the antics of the Marx Brothers to those of other comedy troupes such as the Three Stooges or Laurel and Hardy?

Clark Gable

Clark Gable For thirty years he reigned as the undisputed King of Hollywood and even today he remains a true Hollywood legend. His first role was in a silent film, but his reputation grew after several supporting roles in talkies. In 1934 Clark Gable won an Academy Award for best actor in the film *It Happened One Night.* Probably his most memorable role, though, was as Rhett Butler in the 1939 *Gone with the Wind.* After the death of his wife, actress Carole Lombard, Gable was never quite the same. He died of a heart attack shortly after filming *The Misfits* in 1961.

Question: The Clark Gable and Carole Lombard romance is legendary. What was Lombard doing at the time of her death?

Olympic Star

The tenth child born to Henry and Emma Owens was sickly as a child. His lungs were weak and remained that way even into adulthood, but James Cleveland "Jesse" Owens was a fighter, and someday he would make a name for himself.

Jesse Owens

J. C., as he was commonly known, was born on September 12, 1913. His parents were sharecroppers, and his mother did other people's laundry to earn extra money. There was little time for school for J. C. and his siblings because they had to work in the cotton fields. In 1921 Henry Owens sold his mule and moved his family to Cleveland, Ohio, in search of a better life. Although he could not find steady employment, the children could attend school. When a teacher asked the shy J. C. his name, she heard him say "Jesse" rather than J.C. From then on he was Jesse Owens.

When he was only 14 Coach Charles Riley took an interest in Owens and helped him train. Owens began breaking national records while he was still in high school. When Ohio State University recruited Owens for their track team, he did not think he could afford it. Coach Riley found Owens work operating a freight elevator and also got a job for Henry Owens as a janitor. During a meet on May 25, 1935, Owens broke five world records and tied another. The following year he went to the Olympics in Berlin, Germany. Of the 66 participants on the American track and field team, 10, including Owens, were blacks. At that time, Adolf Hitler was in command of Germany. He and his followers believed that the Germans were superior to all other races. Hitler was in attendance at the games as Jesse Owens proved him wrong. First Owens won the 100 meter dash, then the 200 meter dash. After a shaky start in the broad jump he went on to set a record that would stand until 1960. Owens's fourth gold medal at the Olympics came as a member of the relay team.

In 1935 Owens married his high school sweetheart, Ruth, and they had three daughters. At first after the Olympics, Owens was treated like a star. Some people made him business offers, while others tried to take advantage of him. He started his own business with mixed success. Later, he worked with children in a recreation department. On March 31, 1980, Jesse Owens died of lung cancer at the age of 66. He had been greatly honored during his lifetime. President Ford gave him the Medal of Freedom, and President Carter awarded him with the Living Legends Award. Today, Owens' name is synonymous with track and field.

Suggested Activities

Explanations Ask students how experts explain the faster times and longer distances achieved by today's track-and-field stars.

Three D's Owens claimed that the three D's helped make him an Olympic champion: discipline, dedication, and determination. With the students discuss how these three attributes might help a person achieve his/her athletic goals.

Joe Louis

During World War II, many were called upon to help their country. Joe Louis was just one of the many. While serving in the Army, he continued to defend the heavyweight boxing title that he had held since 1937. He donated much of his prize money to the Navy Relief Society, which helped the war effort. Louis was soon regarded as a national hero, and songs and posters celebrated his patriotism. His life story is an inspiring one. From the depths of poverty, he literally fought his way to stardom.

Joe Louis

On May 13, 1914, Joe Louis Barrow was born just outside Lafayette, Alabama. He was the seventh of eight children born to Lillie and Munroe Barrow. The family was poor and lived in a shack that had no windows and no electricity. Kerosene lamps lit the home. As a child Barrow helped his family by doing chores around the house and working in the fields. During the late twenties the family moved to Detroit in search of a better life. Barrow first took an interest in boxing with the boys in the neighborhood. Serious training in the sport came later at the Brewster Recreation Center. Barrow quit school, began full-time work at a factory, and continued to box on weekends. It was during this time that Barrow dropped his last name. He was afraid that his mother would not approve of his choice of career. After losing a fight with a former Olympic fighter, Louis stayed out of the ring for several months. When he re-entered the ring, a leading businessman offered financial support to this promising new boxer. A professional coach, Jack Blackburn, trained and conditioned Louis and discussed strategy with him. As a result, Louis won his first 22 fights in the heavyweight division. In 1935 he won the Associated Press Male Athlete of the Year award. The time came, though, when Louis lost a fight. After German fighter Max Schmeling defeated Louis in 1936, he trained again with Blackburn and was able to regain the heavyweight championship in 1937. The following year Louis had another fight with Schmeling. This time he defeated the German in the first round.

Between the years of 1937 and 1948 Joe Louis defended his title 25 times without a loss. His skill in the ring earned him the respect of many, and his conduct outside the arena brought back dignity to the sport. Generous with friends and charities, he donated heavily to educational causes. After retiring Louis enjoyed golfing and working as a goodwill ambassador for Caesar's Palace in Las Vegas, Nevada. Joe Louis died on April 12, 1981.

Suggested Activities

Last Fight Louis' last fight was against Rocky Marciano on October 26, 1951. Find out where it was fought. Learn more about Marciano.

Record Find out if Joe Louis' record of 25 title fights without a loss still stands.

Innovations in Flight

Two important innovations in flight took place near the end of the thirties. One was the construction of the first functional helicopter. The second was the introduction of the jet engine.

The Helicopter

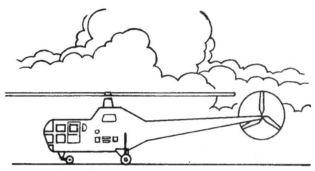

The first helicopter design was drawn by Leonardo da Vinci in 1499. It was never built, and scientists today say that it never would have been able to fly. Through the ages men toyed with the idea, but not until Paul Cornu did a working helicopter emerge. He was able to fly his design one foot in altitude before crashing the twin-rotor machine. The first truly successful helicopter was not invented until the late 1930s. Russian-American designer Igor Sikorsky pioneered a new design for helicopters which is the basis for many types used today. His 1938 VS-300 used a tail rotor to counteract the tendency of the helicopter body to spin around the main motor, which lifts the craft off the ground. Probably the most versatile of the flying machines, the helicopter's whirling blades enable it to shoot straight up in the air and hover in one spot for long periods of time. In addition, a helicopter can take off and land in a relatively small area.

The Jet Engine

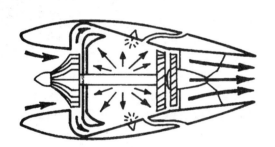

The jet engine was born in the late 1930s. A revolution in aviation, it remains the standard propulsion system for all high-performance aircraft. Plans for the jet engine were invented and patented by Sir Frank Whittle a British Royal Air Force officer and test pilot. The first long distance flight by a jet aircraft was made by the German Heinkel HE-178 on August 27, 1939. Almost five years later, during World War II, the German ME 262 was the first jet to engage the enemy.

Suggested Activities

Model Have the students draw helicopters and label these parts: instrument panel, pitch controls, rotor blades, tail rotor, drag hinges, and jet engine.

Venn Diagram Let pairs of students construct Venn diagrams to compare a helicopter and an airplane.

History Direct the students to create a time line tracing the history of aircraft from WW I through WW II.

Chart Group the students. Direct the groups to construct a chart that shows how the turbojet engine works.

References

Timelines: Flight by David Jeffris (Franklin Watts, 1991).

Eyewitness Books: Flying Machines by Andrew Nahum (Alfred A. Knopf, 1990).

First Lady of the Air

Amelia Earhart was born on July 24, 1897, in Atchison, Kansas, to Amy Otis and Edwin Earhart. As a child she loved to read adventure stories, explore, and learn. Encouraged by her parents, Earhart collected spiders and lizards, explored caves, and went sledding. Athletic as well, Earhart played baseball and football.

An exhibit of stunt flying caught her attention in 1920. Soon Earhart had her first flying lesson, and immediately she knew that this was what she wanted to do with her life. By working at a variety of jobs, she was able to pay for lessons from pioneer female pilot Neta Snook. For her twenty-fifth birthday, Earhart bought herself an airplane. By 1929 she had founded the 99s, a group of women fliers who were devoted to making sure that women had the same flight opportunities as men.

Amelia Earhart

In 1931 she married George Palmer Putnam. He had to ask her six times before she accepted his proposal. Earhart kept her own last name, and the two called each other by their initials. Putnam helped her organize the details of her flights and handled business details, including the use of Earhart's name to endorse flight luggage and a line of sports clothing. Earhart kept a log of her flights and wrote two books based upon her data. Later, she became aviation director of *Cosmopolitan* magazine and also took up lecturing. On May 21, 1932, she set out to become the first woman to fly solo across the Atlantic. For her feat she received the cross of the French Legion of Honor and the gold medal of the National Geographic Society.

Five years later, Earhart began planning a flight for research. Her "flying lab" would be used to study how high altitudes, long distances, and extreme temperatures affected the airplanes and the people who flew in them. With navigator Fred Noonan as her only crew, she set out on a flight from New Guinea to Howland Island in the mid-Pacific, but she never reached her destination. No trace of the plane was ever found, despite privately funded searches. Later, rumors surfaced which suggested that she had been on a secret spy mission. Just 40 years old when she disappeared, Amelia Earhart inspired male and female pilots for generations to come.

Suggested Activity

Records Amelia Earhart set a number of women's air records, including speed, altitude, and fastest transcontinental flight. Direct the students to research and find figures for these flights.

References

Cobblestone Magazine (July, 1990).

Amelia Earhart by Richard Tames (Franklin Watts, 1989).

Wizard of Tuskegee

George Washingon Carver began raising peanuts at Tuskegee Institute's experimental station around 1903. Over the years he developed more than 300 products from this simple legume, 100 products from the sweet potato, and found 60 uses for the pecan. By the early 1920s he had gained increasing attention, but it was not until the thirties that he received the recognition due him.

Carver had been born into slavery on a farm near Diamond, Missouri. He never knew his mother, who had been abducted by slave raiders when he was an infant. His father had been killed in a farming accident about the time that George was born. For most of his youth he was raised by a white couple, Susan and Moses Carter. When he was just twelve years old Carver left home in search of an education. His quest took him to Missouri, Kansas, and Iowa, where he graduated from Iowa State College in 1894. Two years later Carver accepted a position at Tuskegee Institute at the request of its founder, Booker T. Washington. There Carver had teaching duties, as well as an experiment station where he conducted his work. In 1889 he began to issue periodicals which explained his experiments and provided practical applications. For example, one pamphlet was titled *How to Build Up Worn Out Soils*.

George Washington Carver

Carver's continued work drew attention from several sources. England elected him a fellow of the Royal Society for the Encouragement of the Arts in 1916. One year later, the U.S. government called on Carver to discuss his bread-making process, which used sweet potato as a partial substitute for wheat. Inventor Thomas Edison offered Carver a job at his lab, complete with an enormous salary, but George did not want to leave the South. His reputation continued to grow throughout the twenties and thirties. He was a popular speaker and often in demand. His peanut oil massages as a therapy for polio victims aroused a great deal of public interest.

In 1938 a film, *The Story of Dr. Carver*, was made of the scientist's life. George even had a small part in the film, portraying himself as an older man. After his death on January 5, 1943, George Washington Carver was buried on the campus of Tuskegee Institute where he had worked for so many years. In 1948 the U.S. honored Carver with a commemorative stamp featuring his portrait.

Suggested Activities

Research Direct the students to research a list of twenty products that can be made from peanuts. Compile the lists.

More For prepared lessons about Carver, see Teacher Created Materials #493—*Focus on Scientists*.

Reference

George Washington Carver by Gene Adair (Chelsea House Publishers, 1988).

Farthest from the Sun

The planet Pluto was discovered on February 18, 1930, by astonomer
Clyde Tombaugh at an observatory near Flagstaff, Arizona. The
farthest planet from the sun, Pluto is the smallest at 1,416 miles (2,284
km) in diameter. It is also the slowest, moving at 10,600 miles
(17,066 km) per hour, and coldest of the planets. Its average distance
from the sun is 3.7 billion miles (5.9 billion km), and it takes 248.4
years for Pluto to make one full revolution around the sun. Rotation
on its axis takes six days, nine hours, and 17 minutes. Pluto also has
one moon and a strangely shaped orbit.

To learn more about Pluto's orbit, find the square root of each number
in the chart below. Every time you find that answer in the message,
write its corresponding letter in the space provided.

m	$\sqrt{49}$	___	r	$\sqrt{25}$	___	s	$\sqrt{4}$	___
f	$\sqrt{196}$	___	n	$\sqrt{144}$	___	l	$\sqrt{100}$	___
y	$\sqrt{16}$	___	h	$\sqrt{36}$	___	p	$\sqrt{64}$	___
c	$\sqrt{9}$	___	v	$\sqrt{1}$	___	w	$\sqrt{81}$	___
d	$\sqrt{169}$	___	b	$\sqrt{225}$	___	t	$\sqrt{121}$	___

___ i ___ ___ e 1979, ___ ___ u ___ o ___ a ___ ___ e e ___ ___ ___ o ___ e ___
 2   12   3   8 10 11   6   2   15   12   3 10   2   5

___ o ___ ___ e ___ u ___ ___ ___ a ___ ___ e ___ ___ u ___ e. U ___ ___ i ___
 11   11 6   2   12 11 6   12   12   8 11   12   12 11 10

___ a ___ ___ ___ o ___ 1999, ___ ___ e ___ ___ ___ u ___ o ___ o ___ e ___
 7   5 3 6   14   9   6   12 8 10   11   7   1   2

___ e ___ o ___ ___ ___ ___ e ___ ___ u ___ e, i ___ ___ i ___ ___ ___ e ___ ___ e
 15   4   12 13   12   8 11 12   11   9   10 10 15   11 6

e i g ___ ___ ___ ___ ___ ___ a ___ e ___ ___ ___ o ___ ___ ___ e ___ u ___.
     11 6 11 6 8 10   12   11 14 5   7   11 6   2   12

Thirties Literature

Literature of the thirties reflected the attitudes and feelings of the Great Depression. Writers told about the sufferings faced by all families of the era. Some novels were metaphors of what was happening in American society. Read the information below about some of the most famous thirties authors and their works.

Pearl S. Buck Born in 1893 in Hillsboro, West Virginia, Buck grew up in China, where parents were missionaries. Her first book of fiction, *East Wind: West Wind,* was published in 1930 when she was 38. Her best-known book, *The Good Earth*, won the 1932 Pulitzer Prize. She was the first American woman to earn this coveted award. Buck wrote more than 65 books and hundreds of short stories throughout her career.

Sinclair Lewis Lewis's writings attacked the weaknesses he saw in American society and won him international fame. In 1926, *Arrowsmith* earned him a Pulitzer Prize. Four years later he won the Nobel Prize for literature. He was the first American author to win this prestigious award. His 1927 book, *Elmer Gantry*, was later made into a movie starring Burt Lancaster.

Margaret Mitchell During her brief life (1900 to 1949) Margaret Mitchell wrote only one novel, but it was a blockbuster. *Gone with the Wind* won the 1937 Pulitzer Prize and two years later was made into a phenomenally successful film. The film starred Clark Gable and Vivien Leigh and met with equal success when it was re-released in the late sixties.

Gertrude Stein While living in Paris, Stein wrote her famous novel *The Autobiography of Alice B. Toklas,* which was actually a chronicle of her own life. It tells of her friendships with the likes of writer Ernest Hemingway and artists Pablo Picasso and Henri Matisse. Stein served as a literary critic and is credited with the phrase "lost generation" as it applied to writers of the thirties.

━━━ Suggested Activities ━━━

Research Direct the students to research and find out more about any of these writers. As they do so, have them find out what problems these writers had to overcome before becoming successful.

Charts Group the students and have them make group charts comparing the styles and subject matter of the four authors named on this page.

Novels Assign the students to make a list of the best-known works by each author. Let them choose one of the books to read. Students can share favorite parts of the books with partners.

John Steinbeck

John Steinbeck began his writing career during the Great Depression when poverty, homelessness, and unemployment were sweeping the nation. Angered by the poverty that so many were forced to endure, he tried to raise public consciousness and urged social reform. He often wrote about the dark side of the American dream and probably succeeded best in his novel *The Grapes of Wrath*. As he observed the Okie families who migrated to the fertile valleys of California, he witnessed their courage and faith. Inspired by their actions, he wrote what was to become one of his greatest novels.

When *The Grapes of Wrath* became the number one best-selling book in America in 1939, the public was forced to look at the treatment that the migrants were undergoing at the hands of Californians. Outraged by their characterization, California farmers condemned his book. Others wanted it banned for the use of profanity. Despite these and other criticisms, the book won a Pulitzer Prize in 1940.

John Steinbeck was born on February 27, 1902, in Salinas, California, to accountant John Ernst and Olive Hamilton Steinbeck. He was the third child and only son of the couple. As a child he was encouraged to read aloud, and in school he excelled at English. After graduation from Salinas High School, he enrolled at Stanford University, mostly to please his parents. A shy student, he preferred to spend his time writing in solitude. In the spring of 1925 Steinbeck left Stanford without a degree and headed to Lake Tahoe, Nevada, where a job as a maintenance man awaited him. During his two-year stay he was able to complete his first novel, *Cup of Gold*. Its modest sales bolstered his self-confidence and, in 1929, he returned to California. Tragedy struck in 1933 when Steinbeck's mother died; two years later his father died. Intermingled with his sadness was his joy in publishing *Tortilla Flats*. It was a success and gained him national attention. *Of Mice and Men* followed in 1937 and became an immediate best seller.

John Steinbeck continued to write well into the 1960s. In 1962 he was awarded the prestigious Nobel prize for literature, a fitting tribute for a remarkable career. Steinbeck died on December 20, 1968.

Suggested Activity

Biography Have the students write a brief biography or create a time line of events of Steinbeck's life. A good resource for this activity is the book *John Steinbeck* by Tom Ito (Lucent Books, 1994). It also contains an annotated bibliography of some of his other books.

Art Forms of the Thirties

A variety of art forms surfaced during the thirties. You can read about two of of them below. Try your hand at each one with the art projects provided.

Mobiles

Traditional sculpture is heavy and massive, and it stands still, but American artist Alexander Calder saw it differently. On a visit to Piet Mondrian's studio, Calder admired the colored rectangles covering the walls. Afterwards, he decided to make moving Mondrians. Calder's mobiles featured discs of sheet metal painted black, white, and primary colors, which were suspended from wires and rods. The slightest wind caused the shapes to move and dance. Make your own mobile with this easy project.

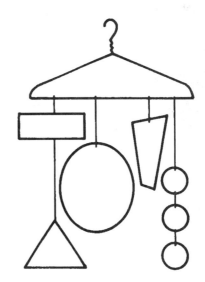

Materials: wire coat hanger, invisible thread (available at sewing supply stores) or fishing line, scissors, one-hole punch, aluminum foil or pie plates

Directions: With scissors cut geometric shapes from the aluminum. Punch a hole at the top of each shape. Cut a different length of thread for each shape. Thread one piece of string through the hole of each shape and knot it. Tie the loose end of each string to the bottom of the coat hanger. Suspend the hanger from the ceiling and watch the shapes move.

American Scene

As part of the New Deal program, the Works Progress Administration put a number of people to work, including artists like Thomas Hart Benton. A government subsidy of $23.86 per week allowed Benton and other artists to experiment with new styles. Benton, the leader of the American Scene School of Art, depicted idealized versions of Americans at work and play. Workers, for example, were shown as muscular and powerful. Other artists of the American Scene adopted a more realistic approach. Grant Wood was one of these realists, but he added another twist— primitivism. His most famous painting is *American Gothic*, which shows simple country folk in realistic style. Follow the directions below to draw your own American Scene picture.

Materials: photocopies of *American Gothic*, scissors, glue, white construction paper, pencil, colored pencils

Directions: Use scissors to cut out the two faces from the photocopy of *American Gothic*. Glue the picture to a sheet of construction paper. With pencil draw new portraits in the cut-out spaces. Color with the colored pencils.

Grandma Moses

Mrs. Anna Mary Moses

Louis Caldor was an amateur collector especially interested in primitive art. He was on his way home from a vacation when he stopped at a drugstore in Hoosik Falls, New York. Sitting in the window was a group of small, dusty paintings. Caldor was amazed to learn that the pictures had been there for a year and was even more amazed to learn that their creator was an elderly woman, Mrs. Anna Mary Moses. Caldor purchased the whole collection and then went to Mrs. Moses' farmhouse to meet her.

Grandma Moses, as her family and friends called her, was born on September 7, 1860, near Greenwich, New York. She was the third oldest child and first daughter of Margaret Shanahan and Russell King Robertson. During her growing up years, Robertson spent a lot of time outdoors. By her twelfth birthday she was ready to leave home and obtained employment as a hired girl. Her chores included cleaning, cooking, sewing, and gardening for a childless couple. Robertson continued to work for other families until she met and married Thomas Salmon Moses.

Altogether, the couple had ten children, five of whom died in infancy. The usual family responsibilities kept Moses busy during the ensuing years. When her husband died in 1927, Anna Mary Moses was 66 years old, and she knew she had to keep busy. She supplemented the housework, cooking, and sewing with needlepoint. As her arthritis grew worse, needlepoint became increasingly difficult for her. One day her sister Celestia suggested that it might be easier to paint pictures rather than stitch them.

Using materials she had at home and housepaint from a local hardware store, Grandma Moses launched a new career for herself. Currier and Ives prints provided her inspiration as she painted vivid scenes from memory. Her first painting was done on canvas, but later ones were done on a background of Masonite, a type of board used in construction.

Her son, Hugh, first took Moses' artwork to the drugstore for display. No one had paid much attention to them until Caldor came along. After a year of lobbying, Caldor arranged exhibits for Grandma Moses' work. In the years that followed, Grandma Moses wrote a book of anecdotes about her life, made appearances on television, and gave radio interviews. She continued to paint until her death on December 13, 1961.

Suggested Activities

Exhibit Display pictures of Grandma Moses' art work. Some color samples can be found in the book *Grandma Moses* by Tom Biracree (Chelsea House Publishers, 1989). Instruct the students to use as many words and phrases as they can think of to describe her work.

More For an art lesson and a follow-up page about Grandma Moses, see Teacher Created Materials #494—*Focus on Artists*.

Swing Was the Thing

Swing was the musical choice of the 1930s. This popular dance music was played by the big bands led by Benny Goodman, Count Basie, Glenn Miller, and a host of others. Read the following information about some of these talented musicians.

Benny Goodman

Count Basie

Glenn Miller

Benny Goodman

Known as the King of Swing, Benny Goodman was the eighth of ten children born to David and Dora Goodman. His father greatly encouraged him to study his music. A small boy with owlish glasses, Goodman had been assigned the clarinet by Hull House Boys' Band director Jimmy Silvestri. It was the lightest instrument, just right for Goodman's size. When Silvestri told David Goodman that his son had talent, Mr. Goodman sought out the best teacher available. Under the direction of Franz Schoepp, young Goodman learned to play the music of the masters, but he dreamed of playing jazz. He played with a variety of groups until 1934, when the Benny Goodman band was founded. As the members experimented, they invented a new form of music, swing, that got American youth on its feet and onto the dance floor.

Count Basie

Basie, an African American, was born in New Jersey in 1904, but was raised in the Midwest. His mother taught him to play piano, although he was more interested in the drums. At thirteen he formed his own group. One day when his pianist failed to show up, he filled in while a friend took his place at the drums. From then on, the piano was his instrument. In 1935 Count Basie formed a big band. Like many big bands of the era, his was large, with as many as 17 musicians. In time his energetic dance music earned him the honor of being the leader of Kansas City-style swing.

Glenn Miller

Born in 1904 in Clarinda, Iowa, Miller was raised in Nebraska and Missouri. At twelve he took up the trombone so he could play in the town band. Miller, who never finished high school, played in a number of bands in the twenties. By the mid-thirties he was an arranger and a musician with the Dorsey Brothers. In 1937 he formed his own band. "Little Brown Jug," recorded in 1939, was their first instrumental hit. When Miller joined the army in 1942, his assignment was as the leader of the Army Air Corps Band. Two years later he was killed in an airplane crash while touring.

———— Suggested Activities ————

Breaking Barriers Benny Goodman broke the color barrier by hiring and performing with African American musicians. He nurtured the talents of guitarist Charley Christian and vibraharpist Lionel Hampton. Have students find out more about either of these musicians.

Others Trumpeter Harry James and drummer Gene Krupa were also former Goodman band members. Learn more about them and their musical accomplishments.

References

Giants of Jazz by Studs Terkel (HarperCollins, revised 1975).

Jazz by Richard Carlin (Facts on File, 1991).

A Rambling Man

Woodrow "Woody" Wilson Guthrie was born in Oklahoma on July 14, 1912, to Charley and Nora Guthrie. Because he was small for his age and had curly hair, his schoolmates found it easy to make fun of him. To fend off the bullies, Guthrie played harmonica and danced for them. He left school at 13 and went on the road.

For a while he worked at a drugstore where the boss had a guitar. Between customers Guthrie taught himself how to play. He wrote his own songs while recalling his mother's mournful ballads. Further inspiration for writing these songs was provided by the people he encountered and the books and newspapers that he read. Guthrie was a prolific songwriter who composed his tunes on anything available — napkins, paper bags, and typing paper. His powerful and original lyrics were set to traditional folk melodies. Some were delivered in a distinctive "talking blues" style. One month, while working in Oregon on a documentary film, he wrote 26 songs. His topics were mostly America and the American people. After he heard Irving Berlin's song, "God Bless America," Guthrie decided that it was not realistic and did not represent our country properly. Soon he responded

Woody Guthrie

with his own creation, "This Land Is Your Land." As he toured the country, he sang on radio shows, at parties, and at political rallies. In California he even sang for the Dust Bowl migrants.

An average guitar player with a flat, dry voice, Woody Guthrie was funny and had a graceful Oklahoma drawl. He wore blue jeans and shaved only when he felt like it. On the road he bathed only when he felt like it, also. He smoked one cigarette right after the other and was described as a walking suitcase because he sometimes wore as many as five shirts at a time. He married three times and had eight children. He gave most of his money away because he felt that it corrupted people. For most of the last 15 years of his life, he was hospitalized with a progressive nerve disease. Woody Guthrie died at the age of 55, but his legacy lives on in his son, Arlo, who sings the same talking blues that made his father famous.

Suggested Activities

"Alice's Restaurant" Listen to a recording of "Alice's Restaurant" made by Arlo Guthrie or to Woody Guthrie's *Dust Bowl Ballads* (reissued by Rounder, Cambridge Massachusetts, 1988). Pay special attention to parts that are examples of the talking blues.

Influences Bob Dylan began his career by learning hundreds of Woody Guthrie songs. He even held his guitar like Guthrie. Research and compare Guthrie with Bob Dylan.

Song Fest Sing "God Bless America" and "This Land Is Your Land." Compare the messages of each song.

Thirties' Inventions

The thirties gave life to a number of advances in technology which altered and improved the American lifestyle. Read about some of these devices below. Research more about any inventors or inventions that interest you.

1930
- ❑ A synthetic rubber, called *neoprene* was developed by DuPont Laboratories.
- ❑ The photo flash bulb was invented, making it easier to take photographs.
- ❑ Ruth Wakefield wanted to alter her specialty, a cookie called Butter Drop Dos, by adding bits of semi-sweet chocolate. The chocolate did not melt as anticipated. Instead, a new cookie was invented—the Toll House cookie.

1931
- ❑ This year saw the manufacture of the first electric dry shaver.
- ❑ In this same year Alka Seltzer was first introduced. A combination of aspirin and baking soda, it helped combat colds.

1932
- ❑ Before 1932 whipped cream was not used much in soda fountains because it was difficult to make. A fresh batch had to be whipped up by hand every day. Chemistry major Charles Goetz changed all that when he discovered that adding nitrous oxide to a canister of whipped cream allowed it to be sprayed.

1933
- ❑ The Dy Dee Doll came on the market. It could drink a bottle of water and then wet itself.

1934
- ❑ Cat's Eye road studs were first developed. A definite road improvement, they helped drivers to identify and stay in their proper lanes.

1935
- ❑ Carlton Magee had invented parking meters in 1933, but they did not go into use until 1935.
- ❑ Charles Richter, a seismologist, developed the Richter Scale to measure ground movement during an earthquake.

1937
- ❑ Jet engines were invented.
- ❑ Wallace H. Carothers of DuPont Laboratories patented nylon. Its first applications were toothbrushes and stockings.

1938
- ❑ Chester Carlson invented the electrophotography machine which is more commonly known as the photocopier. Carlson wanted to find an easier way to prepare duplicate copies of detailed drawings and elaborate charts for patent law. It was not until 1955 that the Xerox copier attracted many buyers.

1939
- ❑ FM radio transmission was developed.
- ❑ The electric guitar debuted.
- ❑ The first air-conditioned automobile was demonstrated.
- ❑ Books were now available in paperback.
- ❑ The pest control spray DDT (later banned by the United States due to its toxicity to animals and humans) was developed.
- ❑ Igor Sikorsky constructed the first successful helicopter.

Fashions of the Thirties

Thirties fashions were influenced by the economic climate, increased popularity of sports, the movies, and royalty. Read how each of these factors helped shape the clothing of the 1930s.

Economic Climate As unemployment rose and incomes fell, the fashion industry had to respond to the economic and social changes. New machinery allowed clothes to be mass-produced at a cheaper rate than ever before. More practical clothes were being turned out, too, in the form of economical and washable fabrics. Synthetic silks, mainly rayon, were used in dress designs and even stockings. The new rayon was stronger and more elastic than previous artificial silks. Women's shapes in the thirties returned to a more normal state. A curvy figure, definite waist, and broadened shoulders replaced the flat-chested, boyish look of the 20s. Hemlines fell, and it was acceptable for women to wear slacks for the first time.

Popularity of Sports Physical activity and sun worshiping reached cult proportions in the thirties. Clothing designs reflected the new interest in sports. Even those who were content to watch could wear spectator sports clothes, like navy blue jackets and white skirts, while watching tennis or polo matches. For those participating in tennis, there was a wonderful innovation— elastic waistbands for tennis pants and shorts. On the beach, men wore trunks, a change from the one-piece swimsuits of the twenties, which covered their chests. Women bathers adopted a one-piece or two-piece swimsuit, pared down from the overskirts of earlier swimwear styles.

Movies and Royalty Movies influenced what people wore or did not wear. For example, in one movie scene Clark Gable took off his shirt to reveal a bare chest. Afterward, sales of undershirts plummeted 40%. When a popular movie star wore a particular type of hat in a film, women would immediately copy the look. Stars' hair styles were also copied. Claudette Colbert's bangs became popular, as did Greta Garbo's bobbed hairdo. For men, the Prince of Wales, who later became King Edward VIII, set the fashion tone of the late 1930s. His wide-legged pants, which fit snugly around the hips, were copied by many. In evening wear the fashion of wearing a white vest under a dinner jacket was revived.

Suggested Activities

Influence With the class, discuss how movies influence fashions today.

Opinions Ask the students their opinions on these fashion influences: MTV, teen magazines, rock and other musical groups, and sports heroes. Ask each student to choose which factor influences his/her clothes the most and explain why.

Elsewhere . . .

The Great Depression affected people throughout the world and helped set the stage for World War II. Some of the important events of the thirties are listed below. Instruct the students to find out more about the events that interest them.

1930 • Gandhi leads a civil disobedience campaign in India.
- The economic crisis is worldwide, as 30 million people are without work in the world's industrial countries.
- The first World Cup soccer game is played in Montevideo, Uruguay.

1931 • A huge earthquake strikes in New Zealand.
- Revolution erupts in Spain; the king is deposed.
- The National Government comes to power in Great Britain.
- The German dirigible *Graf Zeppelin* flies around the world.

1932 • The French president is assassinated.
- The *Normandie*, the world's largest liner, is launched by France.
- British author Aldous Huxley's *Brave New World* is the most talked about novel.

1933 • Hitler becomes Chancellor of Germany.
- Japan and Germany withdraw from the League of Nations.
- Quintuplets are born in Canada—all girls.

1934 • Austrian Chancellor Dollfuss is assassinated.
- King Alexander of Yugoslavia is assassinated.
- The Soviet Union joins the League of Nations.
- German President von Hindenburg dies and Adolf Hitler declares himself *der Fuhrer*.
- Civil war erupts in China.

1935 • Persia changes its name to Iran.
- Italy invades Abyssinia Ethiopia.
- The League of Nations bans the sale of arms to Italy.
- Mao-Tse-tung leads 100,000 soldiers in The Long March; only 30,000 survive the ordeal.
- The Nazis ban jazz music.
- Canada pioneers the first broadcast quiz show.

1936 • Sergei Prokofiev writes *Peter and the Wolf*. It remains one of the most popular children's instrumental compositions of all time.
- The Volkswagen debuts in Germany.
- Edward VIII becomes King of England and abdicates in favor of his brother, the Duke of York.
- The Olympics are held in Berlin, Germany.
- Civil war breaks out in Spain.
- Sixteen-year-old Prince Farouk succeeds to the throne of Egypt.
- Italy and Germany form the Rome-Berlin Axis.

1937 • The German airship *Hindenburg* explodes, killing 34.
- The Germans destroy the Spanish town of Guernica.
- Japanese planes sink the U.S. gunboat *Panay* in Chinese waters.

1938 • Germany annexes Austria.
- The ballpoint pen is invented by Laszlo Biro, a Hungarian journalist.

1939 • World War II begins when Germany invades Poland.
- Russia invades Finland.
- Britain and France declare war on Germany.
- Italy invades Albania.
- Swiss chemist Paul Miller develops DDT.

The Dionne Quintuplets

On May 28, 1934, a most remarkable event took place when five baby girls were born in a single birth to the Dionne family of Callendar, Ontario, Canada. The Dionne quints were the first medically and genetically documented set of quintuplets who had ever survived. This may not seem like such an amazing feat, but at the time there were no fertility drugs nor were there advanced medical facilities available to help premature newborns, such as the Dionne quints, survive.

Emilie, Yvonne, Cecile, Marie, and Annette became international celebrities during their early years. In addition to attracting tourists to northern Ontario, the girls made three feature films and endorsed a number of products, from cod liver oil to automobiles. For a while, the girls were kept as wards of the state, but in 1941 they were returned to their natural family. Today, the birth of five living infants is still newsworthy, but it is not as uncommon an event as it was in the 1930s.

All of the following words are based on the prefix *quin*, which means five. Write each word from the box next to its proper definition, below.

• quint	• quintessence
• quinquennial	• quintuplets
• quintet	• quintal
• quintillion	• quintus
• quintuplicate	• quintuple

1. musical composition for 5 musicians _____
2. to multiply by 5 _____
3. shortened name for quintuplet _____
4. one of a group of 5 _____
5. happening once every 5 years _____
6. five offspring born in a single birth _____
7. the most perfect essence _____
8. the cardinal number equal to 10 to the 18th power _____
9. Latin word for fifth _____
10. a unit of mass equal to 100 kilograms _____

T. S. Eliot

Thomas Stearns Eliot, later known simply as T. S. Eliot, was born in 1888 in St. Louis, Missouri. After attending private schools there, he studied literature at Harvard University, the Sorbonne in Paris, and Oxford University in England. In 1914 he settled in London and 13 years later, in 1927, he became a British subject.

T. S. Eliot

During his years in England, Eliot wrote poetry. His first major poem, "The Love Song of J. Alfred Prufrock," revealed an original style filled with rhetorical language and clichés mixed with humor and pessimism. It was his 1922 poem "The Waste Land" which created the biggest stir in the literary community. A long, complex piece, it contained many obscure literary references, some of which were in different languages. Not everyone liked it, but some viewed it as a masterpiece.

In addition to poetry, T. S. Eliot wrote several dramas. Throughout all of his works, he employed symbols and themes, such as images of nature and childhood, and the writing techniques of irony and precise language. Later in this century, Eliot's poetry collection, *Old Possum's Book of Practical Cats*, became the basis for the popular Broadway musical *Cats*. Eliot, who died in 1965, is credited with fostering the careers of many other emerging poets.

T. S. Eliot used clichés in some of his poems, including "The Love Song of J. Alfred Prufrock." A *cliché* is a familiar word or phrase which has been used so much that it is no longer an effective way of saying something. For example, *fresh as a daisy* is a cliché for alert and refreshed; *sharp as a tack* is a cliché for someone who is very witty.

Listed below are some other clichés you might know. Supply the missing word in each one.

1. The news about the contest winners sure took the wind out of my _____.

2. I'm tickled _____ over my new computer game.

3. Since her boyfriend left she's been feeling down in the _____.

4. After seeing the news about the homeless people, I should just count my _____.

5. That guy is just a big fish in a small _____.

6. Your new hairdo makes you look like a million _____.

7. Our family is careful not to wash its dirty laundry in _____.

8. Their teacher expects them to know the math backwards and _____.

9. I place all the blame for the experiment's failure on your _____.

10. You should be further along at this stage of the _____

11. _____ your words carefully before you speak.

12. My dream guy is someone who's tall, dark, and _____.

A Love Story

On January 20, 1936, Edward VIII succeeded his father, King George V, as the King of England, but he was unhappy in his role. He was in love with a twice-divorced American woman, Wallis Warfield Simpson, and he very much wanted to marry her. British law, however, prohibited a divorced woman from becoming the Queen of England. After only eleven months on the throne, Edward abdicated in favor of his younger brother, George VI. Soon afterwards, Edward left England in self-imposed exile. After his brother named him the Duke of Windsor, Edward married Mrs. Simpson in June 1937. The Duke and Duchess of Windsor lived in Paris, except during World War II, when Edward served as governor in the Bahamas. Their marriage lasted 35 years. Edward died in 1972, and Wallis died in 1986.

Many consider the Edward-Wallis affair the quintessential love story, but there are many other couples who are legendary for their romances. Here are 20 additional famous pairs—some fictional and some nonfictional. See if you can name the missing partner in each case below.

Duke and Duchess of Windsor

1. Napoleon and _____

2. Superman and _____

3. _____ and Cleopatra

4. John Alden and _____

5. Robin Hood and _____

6. Dagwood and _____

7. Romeo and _____

8. _____ and the Beast

9. _____ and Eva Perón

10. Adam and _____

11. _____ and Yoko Ono

12. Popeye and _____

13. Porky Pig and _____

14. Héloise and _____

15. George Burns and _____

16. _____ and Mickey

17. Robert Browning and _____

18. _____ and Penelope

19. Sleeping Beauty and _____

20. _____ and Psyche

Peter and the Wolf

Russian composer Sergei Prokofiev is most famous for his symphony *Peter and the Wolf*. Written especially for children, it tells the story of a little boy, Peter, who saves a bird. Characters are represented by various instruments as a narrator guides the listener through the musical story. A delightful story, it also serves as a wonderful introduction to classical music and the types of instruments in an orchestra.

Sergei Prokofiev was destined to become a symphony composer. Even before he was born in 1891, his mother played Chopin and Beethoven on the piano for hours every day. After seeing Tchaikovsky's classic *The Sleeping Beauty*, he wrote his first opera and titled it *The Giant*. He was only eight at the time. An offbeat personality, Prokofiev rarely smiled and made himself unpopular by saying exactly what he thought. At first, his music was also unpopular; critics even picked on his appearance. His unorthodox style of playing piano did not endear him to audiences, either, but he never gave up. A workaholic, he thought nothing of composing fourteen hours a day with no time off to eat. In addition to music Prokofiev loved to play chess. He was an excellent player and even kept notes on his chess games.

Prokofiev's last opera, *A Tale of a Real Man*, was banned for political reasons in his own country by leader Josef Stalin. Politics were also a factor in the delay of the announcement of Prokofiev's death. When he died of a stroke in 1953, his death was not revealed for one week because Stalin had died on the same day.

Listen to the narrated version of *Peter and the Wolf*. Identify the instruments, listed below, which represent each character from the symphony. Draw lines from the characters in Column A to the instruments in Column B. Find a book about symphonies or Prokofiev to help you find the right answers.

Column A	Column B
1. Peter	drums
2. bird	bassoon
3. duck	flute
4. cat	oboe
5. hunters	horns
6. wolf	string quartet
7. Peter's grandfather	bass clarinet

A Surprising Olympics

Adolf Hitler was the chancellor of Germany and had initiated his Aryan supremacy campaign when the Berlin Games opened in Germany in 1936. Hitler's anti-Semitic and anti-black policies alarmed some officials, who wanted to stage a boycott of the games. Avery Brundage, head of the Olympic Committee, urged participation, and, in the end, he won.

The American track and field team included Jesse Owens (see page 187) and nine other African American athletes. The blacks were treated derisively in the German press and were jeered and insulted as they filed past Hitler's box on opening day. Despite this hostile atmosphere, the ten blacks on the team won a total of eight gold medals, three silver medals, and two bronze medals. One member of the team, Jesse Owens, singlehandedly refuted Hitler's theory of racial superiority by winning gold medals in four events - the 100-meter dash, the 200-meter dash, the broad jump, and the 400-meter relay.

Although Hitler snubbed the winning black athletes by refusing to shake hands with them after they won their events, the athletes themselves were more forgiving. In the broad jump, for example, Owens was in a close competition with the German star athlete Lutz Long. Not only did Owens defeat Long but he also set a world record. To the astonishment of the crowd, Owens and Long walked arm in arm around the giant stadium.

The 1936 Summer Olympics did not hold all the surprises of the Olympics of the thirties decade. Listed below are some other Olympic firsts and interesting facts of the 1932 and 1936 Olympiads. Choose one topic that interests you and write a report, expanding on any aspect of the subject.

- ❑ The 1932 Winter Olympics were held in Lake Placid, New York, despite the growing Depression. American atheletes won all four speed skating medals and were victorious in both the two-man and four-man bobsledding events.

- ❑ In 1932 the Summer Olympics were also held in the United States, this time in Los Angeles, California. The concept of athletes living in an Olympic Village was introduced there, as was the victory stand. It also marked the first time photo-timing was used during events.

The star of the 1932 Summer Olympics was 18-year-old American track-and-field athlete Babe Didrikson. She set world records and took home gold medals in two of the three events in which she participated. Her unusual style in the high jump brought criticism from the judges and even some other jumpers. Although her innovation of going over the bar head first cost her a gold medal, the method was later adopted by nearly all high jumpers.

- ❑ The Winter Olympics of 1936 were held in Garmisch-Partenkirchan, Germany. A blizzard marked the opening ceremonies, but thousands braved the weather anyway.

- ❑ The 1936 Summer Olympiad was also hosted by Germany, this time in Berlin. Hitler again tried to use the games as a way to make a political statement, but his tactics backfired as black athletes won event after event.

A Cure for Yellow Fever

It is almost unthinkable that the bite of the tiny Aedes aegypti mosquito could cause terrible pain and suffering and even death, yet this insect is responsible for spreading one of the most dangerous diseases affecting mankind—yellow fever. Known by more than 150 names, yellow fever causes its victims' skin and the whites of their eyes to turn yellow. In addition, there is intense pain and fever before death.

During the 1930s Max Theiler, a South African expert on tropical diseases, observed that in areas where yellow fever had been present for many years, the native inhabitants seemed immune to the disease. He determined to set up a system to study its transmission. Theiler concentrated on infecting laboratory mice with the virus. He noticed that as the yellow fever was passed from one mouse to another, the virus changed and became weaker. When he injected some of this weakened virus into monkeys, they showed no signs of the disease. Theiler's pioneering work opened up the possibility of a vaccination for humans. Later research teams used Theiler's work as their basis for developing a new strain of the virus that could be used in creating vaccinations against yellow fever. In 1951 Max Theiler was awarded the Nobel Prize for physiology or medicine for his pioneering research.

Yellow fever played an interesting part in the early expansion of the United States of America. Supply the correct missing vowels in the words below to uncover this interesting story.

A l ___ rg ___ s ___ cti ___ n of N ___ rth Am ___ r ___ ca was ___ wned by

Fr ___ nce at the b ___ ginn ___ ng of the 19th c ___ nt ___ ry. In 1802

th ___ ir ___ mper ___ r, Nap ___ le ___ n, s___nt an ___ rmy to

Amer ___ ca to st ___ p a reb ___ ll ___ on in the C ___ ribbe ___ n. It

was n ___ t l ___ ng b ___ fore the tr ___ ps wer ___ dev ___ stat ___ d by

y ___ ll ___ w f ___ v ___ r. Only 4,000 of the 33,000 m ___ n s ___ nt to

___ mer ___ ca esc ___ p ___ d the ep ___ dem ___ c.

The Long Journey

On September 19, 1931, Chinese Nationalist leader Chiang Kai-shek signed a truce with Japan. One month later, he began the task of eliminating his Communist enemy, Mao-Tse-tung. As Chiang's toops closed in on Mao's forces, Mao broke out and led his 100,000 supporters on a march across China.

To find out more details about this long journey, write the letter of the alphabet that comes before the letter that appears below each space. For example if the letter below the space is an F, write an E on the line since E comes before F in the alphabet. When you are through, read the seven facts.

1. Mao led his s _ _ _ _ _ _ _ _ _ on a _ _ _ _ -long, 6,000-
             t v q q p s u f s t   z f b s
   _ _ _ _ walk across China.
   n j m f

2. This dangerous journey is known as the _ _ _ _ _ _ _ _ _.
                                              m p o h   n b s d i

3. _ _ _ _ _ and _ _ _ _ _ _ _ _ were included in the walk.
   x p n f o   d i j m e s f o

4. _ _ _ _ _ _ _ was carried by _ _ _ _ _ _.
   c b h h b h f   i p s t f t

5. In all, only _ _ _ _ _ thousand _ _ _ _ _ _ _ _.
            f j h i u   t v s w j w f e

6. At the end of the journey, the _ _ _ _ _ _ _ _ _ set up a _ _ _ _ _ _ _ _ _
                             g p m m p x f s t   d p n n v o j t u
   government in Yenan.

7. From Yenan, Mao _ _ _ _ _ _ _ to overtake all of _ _ _ _ _.
                     q m p u u f e   d i j o b

In the space below, write another fact about Mao. Use the same alphabet code as above for some of the words. Exchange papers with a partner, and see if you can figure out each other's facts.

_____

_____

_____

_____

_____

_____

The Beginnings of War

With so many problems on the home front, few people paid attention to the growing tensions in Europe and other foreign countries. However, events continued to unfold that would culminate in World War II. Here is a list of some of the happenings that precipitated world conflict in 1939.

September 1930
- More than six million Germans vote for Adolf Hilter's National Socialist Party, transforming the Nazis into Germany's second most powerful political party.

September 1931
- Japanese troops seize the province of Manchuria in northern China.

February 1933
- Adolf Hitler becomes Chancellor of Germany, beginning his twelve-year reign as dictator.

March 1933
- Germany establishes the first concentration camp in Dachau, outside of Munich.

October 1934
- Chinese leader Chiang Kai-shek begins to eliminate his enemies; Mao Tse-tung leads 100,000 followers on a year-long, six thousand mile march.

September 1935
- In Germany, the Nazi government enacts the Nuremberg Laws, which take away citizenship rights of German-Jews.

October 1935
- Italian dictator Benito Mussolini invades Ethiopia.

July 1936
- The Spanish Civil War begins.

October 1936
- Mussolini and Hitler form the Rome-Berlin Axis.

December 1937
- Japanese forces capture the city of Nanjing, China. A U.S. gunboat, the *Panay*, is bombed by the Japanese in the Yangtze River. War is averted when Japan apologizes and pays indemnity.

March 1938
- Nazi troops force the annexation of Austria to Germany.

September 1938
- Great Britain, France, and Italy agree to allow Hitler to take over the Czech Sudetenland.

November 1938
- After a Jew kills a Nazi official in Paris, Nazis retaliate by looting and burning 7,500 Jewish businesses, synogogues, and homes.

March 1939
- Hitler occupies Czechoslovakia and makes it part of Germany.

March 1939
- Madrid falls to Franco's troops; the Spanish Civil War ends.

April 1939
- Italy invades Albania and makes it part of Italy.

May 1939
- Hitler and Mussolini sign the Pact of Steel.

September 1, 1939
- World War II begins when Germany invades Poland.

September 3, 1939
- Britain and France declare war on Germany.

September 10, 1939
- Canada declares war on Germany.

November 30, 1939
- The Soviet Union invades Finland.

Suggested Activities

Terms Define these terms and identify which events they are related to: *anschluss, kristallnacht, appeasement, isolationism, concentration camp, annex, pact, neutrality.*

Discussion With the class, discuss why Roosevelt initially wanted to stay out of war and how he kept the U.S. from entering the war any earlier than it did.

World Leaders

On this page and the next, you will find information about the political leaders who shaped the events of the thirties and led the way into the forties. Students can use this information for study guides and as a springboard for class discussions.

Joseph Stalin 1875–1953

A communist dictator, Stalin succeeded Lenin as leader of the Soviet Union. He pushed the USSR to industrialize in order to compete with the rest of the world. His Five Year Plan outlined production goals to be reached by 1933. Stalin built *gulags*, or prison camps, where people who did not meet these goals or who disagreed with them were imprisoned. Millions died or were executed. Stalin joined Hitler in crushing Poland but later accepted aid from the Allies after Germany attacked Russia.

Benito Mussolini 1883–1945

Known as Il Duce, Mussolini became leader of the Fascist party. Promising to make Italy strong and powerful, he built up a dictatorship and used violence against his opponents. Fascists controlled all levels of society, from unions to politics. In 1935 Mussolini seized the country of Ethiopia (formerly Abyssinia) in Africa and later occupied Albania. He became Hitler's closest ally during World War II. The two formed the Rome-Berlin Axis in 1936.

Mao Tse-tung 1893–1976

In 1921 the Chinese Communist party was founded, and Mao Tse-tung served as one of its founders and its first leader. Ten years later he proclaimed a Chinese Soviet Republic but was subsequently driven away. Mao then led his 100,000 supporters on the Long March of 6,000 miles to a safe place in northern China. After World War II he defeated the Nationalists and made China into a Communist state.

Adolf Hitler 1889–1945

Hitler was an Austrian megalomaniac who founded the German Nazi Party. Believing that the Germans were superior to Jews and other races, his party's aim was to set up a race of pure Germans. From 1939 to 1941 Hitler's armies overran most of Europe, but the tide turned when he attempted to seize Russia. The combined forces of Russia, the U.S., and Great Britain defeated Hitler during World War II. In 1945 Hitler committed suicide as Allied forces moved in on his bunker.

World Leaders *(cont.)*

Francisco Franco 1892–1975

In 1931 King Alfonso XIII of Spain abdicated his throne due to the people's discontent with the monarchy. The democratic republic which followed was weak, and a civil war broke out in 1936. Francisco Franco led the attack. When his party won, Franco became the head of state, serving as dictator from 1937 until his death in 1975.

Mohandas Gandhi 1869–1948

By the late 1890s most of India was under British control. World War I had weakened Britain's economy, and it had become difficult to maintain the country. From 1920 on, Indian lawyer Mohandas Gandhi urged civil disobedience and nonviolent resistance against the regime. He often fasted for days to call attention to injustices. In 1948 India won its independence, but Gandhi was murdered a few months later. Today, Gandhi is called the Father of India.

Neville Chamberlain 1869–1940

This British Prime Minister began his political career in 1918 as a member of the British Parliament. In 1937 he became Prime Minister. Chamberlain supported a policy of appeasement and foolishly believed that by giving Hitler what he wanted a major war could be avoided. However, he was wrong to think that Hitler would stop when he invaded Czechoslovakia. Poland was next on Hitler's list, and Britain came to the country's defense in 1939. Chamberlain died shortly after resigning in 1940.

Winston Churchill 1874–1965

Churchill had held a number of government posts, but his war preparedness stance kept him from gaining power. It was not until after Chamberlain resigned in 1940 that Winston Churchill became Prime Minister of Great Britain. Early in the war Great Britain stood alone in its fight against Nazi Germany, but the British refused to give in. Churchill's great speeches and famous V for victory salute encouraged everyone. A brilliant statesman and orator, he is considered to be the architect for victory during World War II.

Passages

Births

1930
- astronaut Edwin E. (Buzz) Aldrin
- actor Clint Eastwood

1931
- novelist Toni Morrison
- baseball legend Mickey Mantle
- Desmond Tutu, elected the first Black bishop of Johannesburg, South Africa

1932
- children's author Judy Blume
- actress Elizabeth Taylor
- Edward M. Kennedy, politician and brother of assassinated President John F. Kennedy

1933
- Corazón Aquino, president of the Philippines
- Jocelyn Elders, the first African American U.S. surgeon general

1934
- baseball greats Roberto Clemente and Hank Aaron
- Italian actress Sophia Loren
- Gloria Steinem, feminist, writer, and founder of *Ms. Magazine*

1935
- Elvis Presley, the king of rock and roll
- Geraldine Ferraro, first woman to run for U.S. vice-president

1936
- basketball legend Wilt Chamberlain
- African American Congresswoman Barbara Jordan
- Winnie Mandela, who with husband Nelson fought against apartheid in South Africa

1937
- Colin Powell, first black chairman of the joint chiefs of staff
- comedian Bill Cosby
- actress Jane Fonda
- actor Dustin Hoffman

1938
- Janet Reno, first female Attorney General
- race car driver Janet Guthrie, first woman to compete at Indianapolis

1939
- Marian Wright Edelman, founder and president of the Children's Defense Fund

Deaths

1930
- English author D. H. Lawrence, most noted for *Lady Chatterly's Lover*
- Sir Arthur Conan Doyle, creator of detective Sherlock Holmes

1931
- Thomas Edison, the Wizard of Menlo Park, on October 18 at the age of 84; considered the greatest inventor America has ever known
- Knute Rockne, football coaching legend, in an airplane crash on March 31
- African American Daniel Hale Williams, who performed the first successful heart operation

1932
- George Eastman, inventor of the Kodak camera

1933
- President Calvin Coolidge, 30th U.S. president

1934
- Marie Curie, female scientist and winner of two Nobel prizes

1935
- U.S. humorist and satirist Will Rogers
- English writer T. E. Lawrence, author of *Lawrence of Arabia*
- Jane Addams, founder of Hull House

1936
- Children's author Rudyard Kipling; best known for his *Jungle Book* and *Just So Stories*

1937
- Bessie Smith, jazz singer known as Empress of the Blues
- Amelia Earhart, famed female aviator
- George Gershwin, songwriter of many successful shows and movies
- Actress Jean Harlow, noted for her comedic sense

1939
- Sigmund Freud, called the father of psychoanalysis

Thirties Facts and Figures

The United States in 1930

Population:	122,775,046
National Debt:	$16,185,309,831
Movies:	*Gone With the Wind, King Kong, The Wizard of Oz, Modern Times, It Happened One Night, Mutiny on the Bounty, You Can't Take It With You, Snow White and the Seven Dwarfs*
Movie Stars:	Clark Gable, Carole Lombard, Erroll Flynn, Fay Wray, Judy Garland, Humphrey Bogart, Shirley Temple, Jean Harlow, Marlene Dietrich, Groucho Marx, Greta Garbo, Claudette Colbert
Songs:	"Whistle While You Work," "Thanks for the Memories," "Brother Can You Spare a Dime?," "Pennies from Heaven," "Over the Rainbow," "God Bless America," "Winter Wonderland," "Jeepers Creepers," "Easter Parade"
Books:	*The Good Earth* by Pearl S. Buck, *Mourning Becomes Electra* by Eugene O'Neill, *The Thin Man* by Danshiell Hammett, *Ulysses* by James Joyce, *The Grapes of Wrath* by John Steinbeck, *Gone with the Wind* by Margaret Mitchell, *Tender Is the Night* by F. Scott Fitzgerald, *To Have and Have Not* by Ernest Hemingway, *Autobiography of Alice B. Toklas* by Gertrude Stein
Radio Shows:	*Burns and Allen, Amos 'n' Andy, FDR's Fireside Chats, The Kate Smith Show*
Men's Fashions:	muffler scarf; small, soft caps; straw boaters
Women's Fashions:	hats and gloves for social occasions; rayon stockings; tailored, loose-fitting clothing; extravagant night attire; nylons, $1.15 per pair; slacks
Comic and Cartoon Characters:	Superman, Snow White, Bugs Bunny
Automobiles:	1930 Deusenberg – $14,000, 1939 Ford V-8 – $800, 1939 LaSalle – $1,320
Crazes:	candid camera, swing music and dance, Big Apple dance in 1937
Games:	Monopoly, kick-the-can, potsy
Toys:	yo-yos, roller skates, jump ropes

Famous Firsts

As with every decade, the thirties ushered in a number of firsts. Some of these American firsts are listed below by year.

1930 The first frozen foods are sold. The first pinball game is manufactured. Wonder Bread® becomes the nation's first pre-sliced bread. The first stewardess, Ellen Church, flies for United Airlines. The first supermarket opens in Queens, New York.

1931 The first nonstop flight crosses the Pacific. The first electric dry shaver is manufactured. An American woman, Jane Addams, wins the Nobel Peace Prize. The game Scrabble® is invented. Harold C. Urey discovers deuterium (heavy water). The first Gallup Poll is conducted. Walt Disney produces the first color film, *Flowers and Trees*.

1932 Vitamin D is discovered. A yellow fever vaccine is developed. Amelia Earhart is the first woman to fly solo across the Atlantic. Edwin Land invents Polarized glass. The frozen waffle is invented, and Eggo® Food Products is founded.

1933 In Camden, New Jersey, the first drive-in movie theater opens. The first U.S. aircraft carrier is launched. The first singing telegram is introduced by the Postal Telegram Company in New York.

1934 In Fort Worth, Texas, the first washing machines are installed for public use. The outside of the Washington Monument is scrubbed for the first time. Cleaning takes five months at a cost of $100,000.

1935 The first parking meters are installed in Oklahoma City, Oklahoma. For the first time beer is sold in cans. Cincinnati's Crosley Field is the site of the first night baseball game. The first use of a lie detector is allowed in court in Portage, Wisconsin. Monopoly®, the board game, is distributed by Parker Brothers.

1936 The Baseball Hall of Fame opens in Cooperstown, New York. In Toledo, Ohio, the first all-glass building is erected.

1937 Nylon is used for stockings. Insulin is used to control diabetes. In Chicago, the first blood bank opens. The first transcontinental radio program is broadcast in the U.S. Connecticut issues the first permanent automobile license plates. The National Foundation for Infantile Paralysis is founded; it raises money through the March of Dimes. The canned luncheon meat Spam is invented.

1938 The first Xerox® graphic copy is made. Walt Disney releases the first feature length cartoon, *Snow White and the Seven Dwarfs*. Construction begins on the Jefferson Memorial. The first radar-equipped passenger ship goes into operation.

1939 The world's first FM radio station is constructed. In Stratford, Connecticut, the first successful helicopter is built. The first air-conditioned automobile is shown. America's first television program is broadcast.

Writing Prompts and Literature Ideas

Writing Prompts Use these suggestions for journal writing or as daily writing exercises. Some research or discussion may be appropriate before assigning a particular topic.

- You are Adolf Hitler and have just witnessed Jesse Owens' performance at the Berlin Olympics. Write a message you would give to the German athletes whom Owens defeated.

- The Empire State Building was built during the Great Depression and remains one of the tallest buildings in the world. Write a list of ten things you might have heard people say when they first viewed the structure.

- Woody Guthrie composed and sang songs about the people of the Depression. Write a song about a child of the Dust Bowl or a child whose parents were migrant workers.

- To calm the American people, FDR told them, " . . . the only thing we have to fear is fear itself." Write a radio speech you would have given if you were President Roosevelt.

- You have just met Clark Gable, star of the movie *Gone With the Wind*. Write a conversation you might have with him about his performance in that film.

- When outlaws Bonnie and Clyde were apprehended, police shot them 167 times. Write a news story that tells how the couple was finally caught and executed.

- In 1934, there were 250,000 teenage hoboes. Write a story about your worst adventure as a teenage hobo.

- The comic book character, Superman, was first introduced in 1938. Create a cartoon strip with Superman and write an early adventure that he might have had, one appropriate for Depression times.

Literature Ideas The following books can be used to supplement and enhance the study of the 1930s.

- ***Nothing to Fear*** by Jackie French Koller (Harcourt Brace Jovanovich, 1991)
  The close-knit, Irish Garvey family faces the same problems as countless other Americans during the Great depression—unemployment. The satisfying conclusion to the story shows that there is always hope, even in the bleakest of situations.

- ***A Jar of Dreams*** by Yoshiko Uchida (Aladdin Paperbacks, 1991)
  Eleven-year-old Rinko must deal with prejudice as well as the common struggles of the Depression. Rinko's aunt from Japan teaches Rinko to embrace her heritage and shows the entire family how to release their fears and follow their dreams. This heartwarming story makes an excellent read-aloud.

- ***Mississippi Bridge*** by Mildred D. Taylor (Bantam Skylark, 1991)
  A group of black passengers are forced to get off a bus to make room for the white passengers. The discharged passengers walk away, and the bus roars off to a tragic end. This powerful story offers a great deal for discussion.

- ***Children of the Dust Bowl: The True Story of the School at Weedpatch Camp*** by Jerry Stanley (Crown Publishers, Inc., 1992)
  This moving story of the Okie families from 1936 to 1940 provides background information, maps, and plenty of photographs which document the years of massive migration to California. The true story of how one man provided hope and education for the migrant workers is truly inspirational. This book is a must-have for studying the 1930s.

Forties Overview

Following World War I, Americans adopted a policy of isolationism. Attention was focused on the Great Depression and events at home, and few people concerned themselves with foreign affairs.

Throughout the twenties and thirties, political and economic unrest brought dictators to power. As the thirties progressed, America modified its previous Neutrality Act, which refused aid to warring nations. To help allies, a "cash and carry" policy allowed the sale of arms to Britain and France. It became apparent soon after Germany's invasion of Poland on September 1, 1939, that America would join the battle. On October 29, 1940, the first peacetime draft was initiated. When Roosevelt ran for his unprecedented third term, war was the major issue. The U.S. did not actively enter the war until the Japanese attack on Pearl Harbor on December 7, 1941. With amazing speed the country mobilized for war.

With the establishment of the WAACs (Women's Auxiliary Army Corps) and WAVES (Women Accepted for Voluntary Emergency Services) in 1942, women began to officially serve in the military. While they were not allowed in actual combat, some served as nurses and others as secretaries. One group of women pilots taught males how to fly and also ferried war planes. As more and more men went off to war, an increasing number of women joined the work force. They took jobs in munitions factories and learned how to build jeeps, tanks, and planes. The government actively recruited more women workers with posters featuring the character Rosie the Riveter. Women were able to earn more money than they ever had, and they found personal satisfaction in knowing they could perform as well as men.

On the home front, every citizen was asked to contribute to the war effort. Sugar, butter, coffee, meat and other foodstuffs were rationed. War ration books were issued in 1942 with coupons for various items. People were encouraged to plant "victory gardens" to help replace rations sent overseas. In addition, a number of other materials were controlled by the government, for example, tin, aluminum, and rubber. War bonds were established by the government to help pay for the war, and even school children were encouraged to buy them.

Roosevelt provided strong leadership for most of World War II. When he died, three months after beginning his fourth term, Vice President Harry Truman took on the role of Commander-in-Chief. On August 15, 1945, the war ended, and America demobilized. The munitions and supplies factories closed. Women in the work force quit or were sent home to make jobs available for the returning veterans. Eager to get on with their lives, the veterans began families. In fact, 63 million babies were born in the U.S. between 1946 and 1960. This increase from the previous birth rate came to be known as the "baby boom." The true impact of this phenomenon would not be felt until the 1960s.

Wartime Legislation

Much of the 1940s legislation reflected the unfolding events of World War II. Read about these acts and their main provisions below.

June 28, 1940 — **Alien Registration Act** *(Also known as the Smith Act)* All foreigners living in the U.S.A. are required to register with the government and be fingerprinted. It also makes encouraging the overthrow of the government illegal.

September 16, 1940 — **Selective Service** The first peacetime draft in U.S. history is enacted. All young men between ages 21 and 36 are required to register with the Selective Service. A lottery system determines who will serve.

March 11, 1941 — **Lend-Lease Act** It provides funds to U.S. overseas allies to purchase war supplies and weapons. Payments from Britain, China, and the Soviet Union will be delayed until after the war.

December 8, 1941 — **Declaration of War** In response to Japan's attack on Pearl Harbor on December 7, 1941, FDR asks Congress for a declaration of war against Japan.

February 20, 1942 — **Executive Order 9066** President Roosevelt orders the internment of people of Japanese ancestry. Most of those sent to the detention camps are American born.

May 14, 1942 — **WAACs** Congress establishes the Women's Auxiliary Army Corps.

July 30, 1942 — **WAVES** Congress establishes the Women Accepted for Voluntary Emergency Services.

June 22, 1944 — **Servicemen's Readjustment Act** *(commonly known as the G.I. Bill of Rights)* It provides low-interest housing loans and college scholarships for returning G.I.s.

June 1945 — **The United Nations Charter** The Senate debates for only six days before agreeing to U.S. participation in the newly-created organization.

March 12, 1947 — **Truman Doctrine** To aid countries threatened by Communism, President Truman asks for 400 million dollars in aide to Greece and Turkey.

June 23, 1947 — **Taft-Hartley Act** This leislation makes it more difficult for unions to organize. It bans the closed shop (a business which hires only union members) and is passed—over Truman's veto—in response to the many strikes in January 1946.

July 26, 1947 — **Marshall Plan** Fearing that Europe might fall to communism without some kind of aid, Secretary of State George Marshall proposes this plan which provides 14 billion dollars in aid to the rebuilding of Europe.

July 26 1948 — **End to Racial Discrimination** President Truman bans racial discrimination in federal hiring and ends segregation in the armed forces.

The FBI Story

Origins The Federal Bureau of Investigation is the investigative division of the U.S. Justice Department. Originally founded in 1908 during Teddy Roosevelt's administration, the Bureau of Investigation officially became known as the Federal Bureau of Investigation in 1935.

Early Powers The Bureau's responsibilities included enforcing federal laws. After World War I the agency helped break up the power of the Ku Klux Klan. During Harding's administration, the Teapot Dome Scandal was handled by the agency.

Directors Theodore Roosevelt had his attorney general, Charles J. Bonaparte, create an investigative service within the Department of Justice. During Harding's administration William J. Burns was appointed as director with J. Edgar Hoover as his assistant. When the Teapot Dome scandal hearings dragged on for four years, Burns resigned in disgust, and Hoover was named the new acting director. In December of 1924 he became the director of the FBI and remained in that position for 48 years until his death in 1972.

Accomplishments Hoover took swift action to clean up the agency and instituted strict codes of conduct for the agents. When Congress created the Bureau's identification division in 1924, fingerprints from all over the country were sent to a central location in Washington, D.C. Hoover established a training school for new recruits to teach modern criminology. He also created a criminal laboratory where evidence could be analyzed.

World War II During the war, the FBI worked to prevent Nazi spies and saboteurs from doing any damage to U.S. security. The primary role of the FBI after World War II was to investigate communist activity in America.

J. Edgar Hoover

About Hoover J. Edgar Hoover was born on January 1, 1895, to Dickerson Hoover, Sr., a worker for the government, and Annie, a homemaker and forceful woman. J. Edgar remained especially close to his mother and lived in his parents' house his first 43 years. Not until his mother died did he move out on his own. As a youth he sang in the church choir and concentrated on his schoolwork, preferring family to friends. He graduated from high school as class valedictorian and attended law school at George Washington University. After receiving his law degree, he worked as a clerk in the Justice Department where he earned numerous promotions.

References

The Story of the FBI by Jim Hargrove (Children's Press, 1988).

The True Story of J.Edgar Hoover and the FBI by Barry Denenberg (Scholastic Inc, 1993)

The United Nations

World War I and World War II proved that once major conflict broke out it was nearly impossible for the great powers to remain neutral. Clearly, some type of international organization was needed to maintain lasting peace. The United Nations was founded for this very purpose. Here is an inside look at the United Nations.

History Following World War I, people put their hopes for a lasting peace in the League of Nations, but it was unsuccessful at uniting the various governments of the world. Even the United States did not join the organization despite the fact that its own President Wilson had initiated the idea. Following World War II the Allies created a similar organization and named it the United Nations.

Purpose The main purpose of the United Nations (or UN, as it is called) is to maintain worldwide peace by helping countries resolve their conflicts before they resort to war. Its secondary purposes are to promote equal rights, to develop international cooperation, and to encourage respect for human rights and fundamental freedoms.

Accomplishments Some 350 treaties and conventions have been accepted by the UN members since its inception. World conferences based on special topics have been held. Programs have been established to give early warnings about disasters. Its peace-keeping forces help with disputes among member states.

Membership When it first began on June 6, 1945, fifty one nations signed the charter in San Francisco. Today the United Nations is headquartered in New York City and has grown to include 159 countries or about 98% of the earth's people.

Specialized Agencies Twelve specialized agencies were established by the UN from 1945 to 1959 to organize cooperative help where it is needed. For example, United Nations Children's Emergency Fund *(UNICEF)* provides money, food, and medical supplies in emergency situations. Other agencies include the World Health Organization *(WHO)*, and The United Nations Educational, Scientific and Cultural Organization *(UNESCO)*.

Suggested Activities

Human Rights The General Assembly of the UN drew up a list of rights that governments should grant to their citizens. Known as the Universal Declaration of Human Rights, it included freedom of speech and religion and the right to education and work. Some countries ignored these rights. Research and find out the role of Amnesty International in preserving these rights.

Debate Conduct a class debate in which students discuss the effectiveness of the UN as a peace-keeping agency.

Diagram Pair the students and have them draw and label a diagram of the United Nations and its governing bodies and related agencies.

UNICEF As a class, participate in the UNICEF fund-raising event at Halloween.

Reference

The United Nations 50th Anniversary Book by Barbara Brenner (Atheneum Books for Young Readers, 1995).

World War II and Its Origins

This list outlines the events which provided the origins of World War II. For an in-depth look at this topic, see the book *The Origins of World War II* by Peter Allen (The Bookwright Press, 1992).

1. At the Paris Peace talks following World War I, Germany was treated harshly. A festering resentment began.

2. President Wilson helped create the League of Nations to prevent future secret alliances among countries. However, the U.S. never joined the League, and both Germany and Japan left the organization.

3. Following the war, the U.S. embraced an isolationist attitude, Great Britain adopted a pacifist foreign policy, and the French pressed for a high level of reparation payments from Germany.

4. When Mussolini became dictator of Italy, he set up the Fascist Party and promoted an aggressive foreign policy. In the Soviet Union, Stalin gained control of the Communist Party and worked to reorganize agriculture and develop industry in his country.

5. At the end of the nineteenth century, Japan had emerged as a world power. In 1931 Japan began a campaign against Manchuria. By 1935 the Japanese had reached the Great Wall of China.

6. When Chiang Kai-shek became dictator of China, he remained on good terms with the U.S. As the leader of the Nationalist Government, he waged civil war against the Communists and initially appeased the Japanese.

7. Throughout the thirties, the Nazi party gained power in Germany, and eventually Hitler was appointed chancellor. After banning all political parties other than the Nazis, he began building his reign of terror and adopted an aggressive expansionist policy.

8. Italian troops invaded Abyssinia and occupied it in May 1936. That same year a small German force marched peacefully into the Rhineland. On July 18, 1936, civil war broke out in Spain.

9. In 1938 Hitler annexed Austria and demanded the Sudetenland, an area of Czechoslovakia with a German population. The Czechoslovakian government resisted but received no support from the Allies, Britain, and France. Britain's prime minister, Neville Chamberlain, chose to appease Hitler in order to avoid war.

10. Late in 1936, Chiang Kai-shek was forced to join the Communists in fighting Japan. By mid-1937 Japan's continued aggression against China caused an unofficial war that lasted throughout World War II. Japan ignored international disapproval and even attacked the U.S. gunboat, *Panay*. Japan apologized for the incident and paid compensation.

11. In 1939 the British policy of appeasement was reversed when German troops invaded Poland. Britain and France, bound by their alliance with Poland, declared war on Germany on September 3.

12. In September of 1940 Japan, Germany, and Italy signed a Tripartite Pact, pledging mutual support if the U.S. entered the war.

13. Japan negotiated a neutrality pact with Russia in the spring of 1941. At the time Russia was a passive partner to Germany.

14. In 1941 discussions with Japan, the U.S. told Japan to withdraw from China. The talks failed, and the U.S. imposed a ban on all trade with Japan. On December 7, 1941, Japan carried out a surprise attack against the U.S. Four days later Hitler declared war on the United States.

World Figures

Check students' knowledge of world figures during World War II with this oral quiz. Copy the list of names (in the box below) onto the chalkboard or overhead projector. Instruct the students to number a sheet of paper from 1 to 12. Read aloud the clues for each number below, giving students time to choose and write the name of the correct leader. After all twelve have been read, correct the answers together.

NOTE: For your easy reference, answers have been provided at the bottom of this page.

Harry S. Truman	Franklin D. Roosevelt	Neville Chamberlain
Josef Stalin	Hideki Tojo	Mao Tse-tung
Adolf Hitler	Chiang Kai-shek	Benito Mussolini
Winston Churchill	Francisco Franco	Charles de Gaulle

1. During Spain's civil war he led the Nationalist rebels against the Republican government. From 1939 to 1975 he served as Spain's leader.
2. In 1933 this former lawyer was elected president of the U.S.; he kept the country out of war until Pearl Harbor was bombed.
3. A soldier and journalist before establishing the Italian fascist party in 1919, he allied with Germany at the beginning of World War II.
4. After succeeding Lenin, he became the most powerful man in the Soviet Union by making himself dictator.
5. Britain's prime minister from 1937 to 1940, he pursued a policy of appeasement towards Hitler and Mussolini.
6. After serving as vice president for only four months, he became president of the United States. It was his decision to drop an atomic bomb on Japan in an effort to end the war.
7. This former war minister was Japan's prime minister from 1941 to 1944; he argued in favor of an aggressive expansionist policy.
8. The founder and leader of the Nazi party, he called himself *der Führer*. In 1945 he was finally defeated by the combined forces of the United States, Soviet Union, Great Britain, and other Allies.
9. This French general fled to England when France fell. He became the symbol of the French resistance during the War. After the Normandy invasion, he served as president of the provisional government (1944-1946).
10. He led 100,000 followers on the Long March. In 1949 he created the People's Republic of China.
11. After England's prime minister resigned in 1940, he succeeded to the position and led his country into war against Germany.
12. As dictator he resisted Japanese aggressors. Later, his troops were defeated by Mao Tse-tung Red Army.

Answers:

1.Francisco Franco 2. Franklin D. Roosevelt 3. Benito Mussolini 4. Josef Stalin 5. Neville Chamberlain 6. Harry S. Truman 7. Hideki Tojo 8. Adolf Hitler 9. Charles de Gaulle 10. Mao-Tse-tung 11. Winston Churchill 12. Chiang Kai-Shek

War Heroes

Several individual heroes emerged from the fighting on the various fronts during World War II. Read about these famous figures and their accomplishments.

General Dwight David Eisenhower Known as "Ike," he was a 1915 graduate of West Point Military Academy. In 1942 Eisenhower was appointed to lead the Allied invasion of North Africa. After his victories in Africa and Italy, Eisenhower became the supreme commander of the Allied Expeditionary Forces, planning and executing the D-Day invasion at Normandy in 1944 and the subsequent Battle of the Bulge. A popular hero, Eisenhower served as U.S. President from 1953 to 1961.

Nimitz

Patton

Bradley

Ernie Pyle Known as the voice of the G.I., Ernie Pyle was the infantryman's favorite reporter. As the war raged through Europe, Africa, and the Pacific, he would spend weeks on the front lines before returning to the rear, where he would write several columns. In 1943, he received the Pulitzer Prize for his reporting. Pyle was killed by a Japanese sniper on April 18, 1945.

General Douglas MacArthur A 1917 graduate of West Point, MacArthur had one of the highest academic records in the school's history and was a highly decorated soldier in WW I. In 1942, when the Japanese forced him out of the Philippines, he vowed "I shall return." MacArthur directed the Allied occupation of Japan from 1945 to 1951.

Chips Part husky and part German shepherd, the dog named Chips captured four Italian gunmen in Sicily and was credited for single-handedly eliminating a machine gun nest. Awarded the Army's Distinguished Service Cross for his efforts, it was withdrawn when the War Department ruled dogs ineligible for medals.

General George Patton A 1909 graduate of West Point, he was a controversial figure. He was major general in charge of the Third Army. Patton led the Allied drive through France into Germany.

General Omar Bradley A 1915 graduate of West Point, Bradley was the general in command of the American Forces in Europe. He planned the overall battle strategy during the drive into Germany. A popular officer, he eventually earned the rank of five-star general.

Lieutenant Colonel James H. Doolittle After the bombing of Pearl Harbor, Doolittle was assigned to mount a surprise attack against Japan. He organized B-25 land-based bombers to lift off the deck of a U.S. aircraft carrier. His bomber led the mission which stunned the Japanese. On the return flight every crew but one bailed out or crash-landed in China or the Soviet Union.

Admiral Chester Nimitz An outstanding student at Annapolis, he was one of the navy's best strategists. As commander in chief of the U.S. Pacific Fleet, Admiral Nimitz led the U.S. naval forces to victory in the battle of Coral Sea. He also masterminded the strategy for the battle at Midway.

WW II Aircraft

Although aircraft were used to fight World War I, new technology and new flight tactics were employed heavily during World War II. Some of the innovative types of aircraft used in World War II are shown below.

B-29 Superfortress

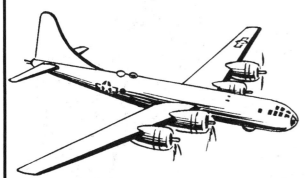

1. *American* This heavy-duty bomber of WW II, carried eight tons of bombs, and could fly 360 miles per hour.

Spitfire

2. *English* It could fire numerous rounds each minute and was known for its elegant design.

Zero Fighter

3. *Japanese* A model of efficiency, it was used in the kamikaze (suicide) attacks.

B-17

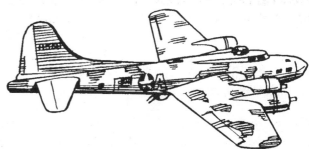

4. *American* The Boeing Flying Fortress was the world's first operational four-engine bomber and was the standard bomber used by the Army.

Stuka

5. *German* It was capable of dropping 1,100-pound bombs with deadly accuracy.

Messerschmitt

6. *German* It was the first jet plane to engage in battle.

Chronology of World War II

Some of the important events of World War II are listed in the chronology that follows. Use this page for your reference.

1939

September   Germany invades Poland. Great Britain and France declare war on Germany.

1940

April   German forces capture Norway and much of western Europe.

May   Churchill becomes Great Britain's prime minister.

June   Italy joins the war on the Axis' side. (Germany and Japan)

October   The Battle of Britain ends.

1941

June   Germany invades the USSR.

December   Japan attacks Pearl Harbor. The United States enters the war.

1942

February   Japan captures Singapore.

May   The Battle of the Coral Sea takes place.

June   The U.S. Navy is victorious in Battle at Midway. Allies invade Morocco and Algeria.

October   Allies defeat Germans and Italians at El Alamein in Egypt.

November   Russians defeat Germans at Stalingrad.

1943

July   Allies land in Sicily and southern Italy.

September   Italy surrenders.

1944

June   Allies invade western Europe on D-Day, June 6.

July   A plot to kill Hitler fails.

October   In the Battle of Leyte Gulf, the U.S. fleet defeats Japan.

1945

January   Russians invade Germany from the east.

March   Allies cross the Rhine River.

April   In the East, U.S. troops recapture the Philippines.

May   Hitler commits suicide. Fighting ends in Europe.

August   U.S. airplanes drop atomic bombs on Hiroshima and Nagasaki. Japan surrenders.

On the back of this paper, write a chronology of important events in the war on the Pacific front.

Mapping the War

World War II presents itself with a number of possible mapping activities. Some suggested projects are listed below. Use the maps on page 226 or have the students draw their own maps as specified. Pair or group the students and assign each a different mapping activity. When all projects have been completed let one group at a time share their assignments with the rest of the class. Compile all the maps into a classroom book about World War II.

1. Use a map of Europe. Title the map "German and Italian Aggression in Europe in 1939." Color all the German-invaded countries red; label each country with its correct name. Color the Italian-invaded countries green; label each country with its name.

2. On a map of the Pacific region, color red all the countries which were Japanese territories in 1941. Label each country with its name. Give the map an appropriate title.

3. Map the European theater war battles. Draw a symbol of your choice to show where battles took place, for example, Dunkirk, Nunzio, and Kursk. Label each city with its name. On the back of the map, list each city and tell who fought there and who won.

4. Use a map of Europe to show which countries were Allied forces, which were Axis powers, and which remained neutral. Color all Allied countries blue, color all Axis countries red and leave all neutral countries white. Label each country with its name.

5. Draw a map of the island of Oahu. Locate and label the following military installations: Hickam Field, Wheeler Field, Pearl Harbor, Bellows Field, Barbers Point Marine Base, Haleiwa Field, and Kaneohe Naval Air Station. Draw appropriate symbols, such as planes, to indicate the path taken by the Japanese forces and the damage done to U.S. forces. Make a list of all the U.S. Navy ships which were sunk or damaged in the attack on Pearl Harbor.

6. Make a map which reflects the changes in boundaries of European countries after World War II. Label each country. Make a list of those that were newly created and another list of those that were eliminated.

7. Map the Battle of the Bulge, the D-Day invasion, or the Battle of Britain. Draw different symbols for each set of forces. Label the cities in which the battles were fought. Use arrows to show the directions in which the various forces moved.

8. Draw a map of Germany; copy it. Label one map "Pre World War II." Label the other map "Post-World War II." Show the differences in internal boundaries between the two time periods.

References

Cobblestone Magazine (January 1993 issue) "World War II: Americans in Europe."

World War II by Tom McGowen (Franklin Watts, 1993).

Maps of European and Pacific Theaters

European Theater

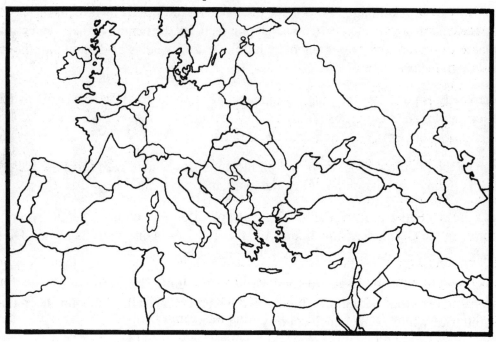

Pacific Theater

The Holocaust

Millions of lives were lost during World War II, but not all of them were due to combat. When the Nazis came to power in Germany, they began to persecute Jews. Adolf Hitler, in a desire to promote a "master race" of pure Aryans, was determined to wipe out the entire Jewish population. Because many German Jews were economically successful, had good jobs, and owned nice houses, Hitler's misguided reasoning held them responsible for inflation, the Depression, and other German problems. Hitler also believed that the Aryan race was superior and that Jews were polluting it. Many other people believed in this theory, too. In order to eliminate the "Jewish problem," Hitler built walled prisons called concentration camps in Germany, Poland, and Austria.

Some of these prisons were work camps, while others were nothing more than death factories. Prisoners at working camps like Bergen-Belsen and Dachau in Germany made supplies for the German army. On their arrival at a camp, prisoners' clothing and belongings were taken away. Their heads were shaved and numbers were tattooed on their arms for identification. Conditions at these camps were deplorable. Many inhabitants froze to death; others died from disease or lack of food. Some were killed when they were no longer able to work. At the death camps, such as Auschwitz and Treblinka in Poland, prisoners were taken to a shower, but the rooms were locked and pumped full of deadly gas through the shower heads. Later their bodies were burned in huge ovens. In addition, some prisoners were subjected to supposedly scientific testing, surgeries without anesthesia, and gruesome experiments. In all, over six million Jews were killed—that number represented 40% of the world's Jewish population. Additionally, five million disabled, homosexuals, Gypsies, and political opponents of the Nazis were eliminated. The Holocaust was a dark period in history, one that must not be repeated.

Suggested Activities

Research Research and discuss any of the following questions: When and how were the camps liberated? Why wasn't more done by other countries to alleviate the situation? What were the results of the Nuremberg Trials?

References

Never to Forget: The Jews of the Holocaust by Milton Meltzer (HarperCollins, 1976).

Smoke and Ashes: The Story of the Holocaust by Barbara Rogasky (Holiday, 1988).

Anne Frank by Richard Tames (Franklin Watts, 1989).

(Numerous books and articles exist on this topic.)

Teacher Note: The movie *Schindler's List* is also recommended. You will need to get school-district and parent permission in writing before showing this film as the movie is R-rated.

Facts of War

All of the math problems below are based on facts gathered from World War II. Make a transparency of this page. Call on a student to read aloud the first problem. Ask him/her to identify which operation should be used to solve the problem and what word clues were used to determine the correct operation. Have the students work a solution at their desks. Call on one student to go to the board to show all work. Discuss in whole group. Repeat the procedure for each problem.

Note: Answers have been provided at the bottom of this page for your easy reference. Cover them while using this page with the class.

1. It cost the United States $304 billion to wage World War II. One-sixth of this cost was covered by war bonds. How much money was covered by war bonds? Operation_____ Solution_____	2. At the Pearl Harbor naval base attack on December 7, 1941, 2,403 Americans died and 1,178 were wounded. How many persons were killed and wounded altogether? Operation_____ Solution_____
3. On July 29, 1945, the *USS Indianapolis* was ripped apart by Japanese torpedoes. Of the 1,199 crew members only 316 survived. How many died in the attack? Operation_____ Solution_____	4. Prisoners of war in German camps lost an average of 38 pounds. If a soldier weighed 176 pounds when he was captured, how much did he weigh when he was released? Operation_____ Solution_____
5. Throughout the entire World War II, 60 million people died, two-thirds of them were children. How many children died during the war? Operation_____ Solution_____	6. U.S. schoolchildren kept albums of 10 cent and 25 cent stamps which were used to buy war bonds. $331 in stamps paid for 1 machine gun, 1 telephone, 1 tent, 5 steel helmets, and 9 tools. On average, how much did each item cost? Operation_____ Solution_____
7. Prisoners of war in Japanese camps lost an average of 61 pounds. If a soldier weighed 150 pounds when he was captured, how much did he weigh when he was released? Operation_____ Solution_____	8. In one year school sales of war bonds bought 2,900 planes and 44,000 jeeps. How many more jeeps were purchased than planes? Operation_____ Solution_____

Answers

1. Division; $50.66 billion 2. Addition; 3,581 3. Subtraction; 883 4. Subtraction; 138 pounds 5. Multiply by $\frac{2}{3}$; 40,000,000 6. Divide by 17 items; $19.47 7. Subtraction; 89 pounds 8. Subtraction; 41,100 jeeps

Harry S. Truman

33rd President, 1945–1953

Vice President: Alben W. Barkley

Born: May 8, 1884, in Lamar, Missouri

Died: December 26, 1972

Party: Democrat

Parents: John Anderson Truman and Martha Ellen Young

First Lady: Elizabeth (Bess) Virginia Wallace

Child: Margaret

Nickname: Man from Independence

Famous Firsts:

- He was the first president to take office during wartime.
- He was the first president to travel underwater in a modern submarine and was the first and only president to use the atomic bomb on another country.

Achievements:

- He was elected to the U.S. Senate in 1934 and reelected in 1940.
- Truman represented the U.S. at the signing of the United Nations' charter in June 1945.
- He signed the NATO treaty for mutual defense among 12 nations.
- On March 13, 1947 Truman issued his policy for "containment" of Communism, later called the Truman Doctrine.
- When the Soviets blockaded West Berlin in 1948, Truman ordered an airlift to the city. Constant shuttles kept the West Berliners supplied with food, coal, and necessities.
- His Fair Deal increased Social Security benefits, raised the minimum wage from 40 cents to 75 cents per hour, and appropriated money for constructing low-income housing.
- He fired General MacArthur after MacArthur publicly voiced his unhappiness with Truman's refusal to allow a war with China.
- Truman began the fight to integrate schools.
- He appointed the first African American federal judge.
- He ended segregation in the army, navy, and marines.

Interesting Facts:

- Truman served as an artillery officer in WW I.
- Only five weeks into his vice presidency he became President.
- He kept a sign on his desk that read, "The buck stops here." Truman was known for his feisty character and occasional use of foul language.
- As a child he had to wear thick glasses. Because the glasses were expensive, he was not allowed to play contact sports and took piano lessons instead.
- After serving in WW I, he opened a men's clothing store in Kansas City.
- In the 1948 election, the *Chicago Tribune* ran a headline, "Dewey Defeats Truman." However, Truman won the election.
- He did not have a middle name. The S. was only an initial.

Note: For information on Franklin Delano Roosevelt, see page 177.

First Things First

Find out how well you know the events of Harry S. Truman's life. Cut apart the rectangles below and place them in correct chronological order. Check your answers with a partner.

a. was re-elected to the U.S. Senate
b. called an emergency meeting of the UN when North Korea invaded South Korea
c. served as an artillery officer in World War I
d. attended the Potsdam Conference, which sent an ultimatum to Japan
e. relieved General MacArthur of his command
f. chosen by FDR to be his running mate in the '44 election
g. opened a men's clothing store in Kansas City
h. presented his plan for "containment" of Communism (Truman Doctrine)
i. used an executive order to end racial segregation in the armed forces
j. ordered atomic bombs dropped on Hiroshima and Nagasaki
k. married Bess Wallace
l. became President of the United States upon FDR's death
m. won the presidential election against Thomas Dewey
n. ordered an airlift to West Berlin
o. was elected to the U.S. Senate

Two First Ladies

The chart on this page compares some facts about first ladies Eleanor Roosevelt and Bess Truman. Research to learn two more facts about each one and add the new facts to the chart on the back of the page.

Eleanor Roosevelt

She was born in 1884.

She first met her husband at a family gathering when she was 19.

She married in 1905.

The family consisted of four sons and one daughter (a fifth son died).

She became first lady at age 48.

She was known as a gracious and energetic hostess.

She gave White House visitors silver spoons as souvenirs.

She adopted many of her own causes, including rebuilding American confidence and supporting New Deal policies.

She was unafraid to voice her own opinion.

A controversial figure, some thought she contributed too much to her husband's presidency.

She was known as an energetic, active, and very visible first lady.

After her husband's death, she remained in the public eye; was later appointed to the UN.

She died in 1962.

Elizabeth "Bess" Truman

She was born in 1885.

She met her husband in Sunday School when they were children.

She married in 1919.

The Trumans had one daughter, Margaret.

She became first lady at age 60.

She was a gracious hostess.

For souvenirs she gave away store-bought buttons.

She adopted no causes as first lady.

She remained quiet and in the background.

She caused little controversy.

She put her daughter and husband first in her life.

She was happy to leave the White House.

She died in 1982 at age 97, the longest-lived first lady in American history.

War and Post-War Elections

Use the information in the chart below to answer the questions that follow. Circle the correct answer.

Year	Candidate	Party	Popular Votes	Electoral Votes
1940	Franklin Delano Roosevelt	Democrat	27,307,819	449
	Wendell Willkie	Republican	22,321,018	82
1944	Franklin Delano Roosevelt	Democrat	25,606,812	432
	Thomas E. Dewey	Republican	22,014,745	99
1948	Harry S. Truman	Democrat	24,105,812	303
	Thomas E. Dewey	Republican	21,970,065	189
	Strom Thurmond	State's Rights	1,169,063	39
	Henry A. Wallace	Progressive	1,157,172	0

1. In which election were the most total votes cast?

    1940   **1944**   **1948**

2. In which election were the least total votes cast?

    1940   **1944**   **1948**

3. In which election did a candidate earn the most electoral votes?

    1940   **1944**   **1948**

4. In which election did a candidate earn the least electoral votes?

    1940   **1944**   **1948**

5. In which election was there the least difference in electoral votes between the top two candidates?

    1940   **1944**   **1948**

6. In which election was there the most difference in electoral votes between the top two candidates?

    1940   **1944**   **1948**

7. In which election was the difference the greatest between the top two candidates popular votes?

    1940   **1944**   **1948**

8. In which election was the difference the least between the top two candidates popular votes?

    1940   **1944**   **1948**

232

Life on the Home Front

During World War II women faced new challenges. As more and more men were drafted, women were pressed into working outside the home. Some volunteered for duty in the armed services (see page 235). Even those who stayed at home were asked to make sacrifices for their country.

While women on the home front did not face the imminent dangers of war, they were faced with a number of obstacles. For one thing they had few household appliances. Clothes had to be washed by hand or with a hand-cranked machine. Meals were prepared from scratch as there were few convenience foods. Food preparation became even more difficult as popular foods were rationed. Women were encouraged to attend special classes that taught them how to use little-known foods (such as eggplant) in different dishes. Families were encouraged to grow "victory gardens"; more than 75% of American housewives preserved and canned the resulting produce.

As more and more men were drafted, women had to take on even more responsibilities. Twenty-five percent joined volunteer organizations. Some worked as aircraft spotters looking for enemy planes, while others learned to drive ambulances. Three million women joined the Red Cross where they organized blood banks, rolled bandages, and packed kits for soldiers. United Service Organizations (USOs) were established in 1941 on various U.S. military bases to support soldiers. Women served as hostesses and dance partners. Women, especially celebrities, helped sell war bonds.

As manufacturers faced a shortage of male workers, they, too, began recruiting women. Because Americans believed that a woman's place was at home, companies had to convince women that they were needed and capable of building ships, planes, and tanks. Patriotic ads appeared in magazines with Rosie the Riveter as the symbol of working women. In time, women worked alongside men and in many cases took over welding, riveting, and machinists' positions. These experiences helped women become more self-confident and provided the potential for futures very different from the ones they had faced only two or three years earlier.

Suggested Activities

African Americans Black American women wanted to serve their country, too, but it took a presidential order to fight discrimination. What was Executive Order 8802, and how did it come about?

Problems Women in the work force faced a number of problems: negative attitudes of male coworkers, lack of acceptance by unions, proper clothing for work. Assign students to research each of these problems. Discuss how each was resolved.

Rationing

Read the paragraph below about wartime rationing and complete one activity in each of the six categories that follow.

A popular motto during World War II was "Use it up, wear it out, make it do, or do without." It served as a reminder to everyone on the home front to do his/her part for the war effort. Soldiers' needs came before those of Americans at home. In order to ensure that our soldiers would not lack essential supplies, a system of rationing was instituted. Food rationing started gradually with items like sugar and coffee but soon progressed into a fairly complicated system of points and coupons. The Office of Price Controls, or the OPA, was created to set limits on items. It initiated the rationing of a wide variety of items including food, gasoline, and even shoes. Each American was given a set number of ration coupons per month. Coupons worth blue points were used to purchase processed foods, such as canned vegetables, jellies, and bottled tomato juice. Red point coupons were needed to buy meat, butter, cheese, and other fats. When a particular item was purchased, the correct number of coupons had to be turned in, along with the purchase price. Updated tables kept consumers informed of food point values. For example, a sirloin steak might cost 13 red stamps, while a can of fruit cocktail might cost ten blue stamps. These rationing schedules changed often due to supply and demand.

1. **Knowledge**

   a. Define the term rationing

   b. Make a chart listing some items that could be purchased with blue points and red points.

2. **Comprehension**

   a. Describe how items were rationed during World War II.

   b. Explain the purpose of rationing during World War II.

3. **Application**

   a. Tell how you would react if rationing were instituted in the U.S. today.

   b. Explain how rationing at home helped the soldiers at war.

4. **Analysis**

   a. Research the topic of rationing and make a list of ten things that were not rationed.

   b. Tell what conclusions you can draw about rationing and its effects on everyday life.

5. **Synthesis**

   a. Create a rationing plan for your classroom supplies.

   b. Compose a new motto to remind people to do their part for the war effort.

6. **Evaluation**

   a. Write an argument for reinstating the rationing of gasoline.

   b. Make a list and then compare the pros and cons of rationing.

WAACs, WAVES, and Nurses

History Traditionally, women had been regarded as physically and mentally unfit for the horrors of war. A few women participated in the American Revolution by accompanying their husbands to the battlefield, where they cooked and washed for the entire regiment. Some women, notably Deborah Sampson, donned men's clothing and participated as soldiers. Over the years the number of women wanting to serve in the military grew.

WAACs When a peacetime draft was initiated in 1940, women once again expressed their willingness to serve their country. In 1941, Edith Nourse Rogers, a Congressional representative from Massachusetts, submitted legislation to establish the Women's Army Auxiliary Corps, WAAC. Despite some opposition, the bill was passed on May 15, 1942. On July 20, 1947, the first trainees studied military customs, leadership training techniques, and even voice control. They lived in barracks which offered little privacy and were divided into living quarters for blacks and whites, reflecting conditions for black enlisted men.

WAVES The success of the WAAC program led to the formation of the Navy WAVES (Women Accepted for Voluntary Emergency Service) and the Coast Guard SPARS (taken from their motto *Semper Paratus*, Latin for "always prepared"). As the war progressed, women in the WAVES began to work in areas including clerical duties, supply operations, and even operated airport control towers.

Nurses Nurses were more readily accepted by the armed services. The ANC (Army Nurse Corp) had been established in 1901, and women nurses had served commendably in World War I. At the beginning of World War II there were only 700 women ANC members. Those accepted for the World War II ANC underwent a tough four-week training program in the California deserts. To build up strength, they hiked 20 miles a day with 30-pound backpacks. They also ran through an obstacle course to learn how to dodge flying bullets. Unfortunately, women nurses faced the greatest hardship and dangers of all women who served in the war. More than 200 nurses were killed in the line of duty.

Suggested Activities

POWs Some nurses were captured on Corregidor and taken to the Philippines where they were held for nearly three years. Find out about conditions at their POW camp.

Supplies As medical supplies were quickly exhausted, nurses had to make do with what they had on hand. Make a list of some of the substitutes they devised for bandages, stretchers, and blood supplies.

Inequalities Discuss what inequalities and prejudices women in the services had to endure. How did their pay compare to the men's? Were black women accepted as equals in the service?

War Photographer

Margaret Bourke-White became a well-known photojournalist in the 1930s. A pioneer of the photo news essay, she was the first foreign photographer allowed to take motion pictures inside the USSR. Her work was featured in magazines like *Fortune* and *Life,* and she published several books. Next she wanted to cover the war. With the help of the powerful publisher Henry R. Luce, Bourke-White was allowed to accompany the troops and take pictures.

Margaret Bourke-White

Born in New York City in 1906 to Joseph and Minnie Bourke-White, Margaret Bourke-White inherited a love of photography from her father, who was an engineer, inventor, and amateur shutterbug. When the family moved to a small town in New Jersey, Bourke-White learned to observe nature; it was here that she decided to study snakes when she grew older. At Columbia University she studied with a famous photographer, but to fulfill her childhood dream she transferred to the University of Michigan to study herpetology. In the end, photography won out. After graduating in 1927, she went to Cleveland, Ohio, where she photographed steel mills. When magazine publisher Henry Luce saw her pictures, he recruited her to work for him in New York City.

Bourke-White's first World War II assignment was in North Africa. She traveled with the first WAAC officers overseas in 1942 and accompanied American pilots to North Africa where they bombed German forces. Bourke-White was the first female photojournalist to record such a mission. On another mission she photographed the invasion of Italy. After her air experiences, Bourke-White began to take photos on the ground. She captured Allies advancing through Italy and Germany, recorded the bravery of American soliders, and showed the members of medical mobile units in their life-saving work. In 1945 she was with the American troops who liberated the Nazi death camp at Buchenwald, where Jews and political prisoners were literally worked to death.

One of her most famous photographs came in 1946 when she travled to India. On a worldwide assignment for *Life,* Bourke-White photographed Indian leader Mahatma Gandhi at his spinning wheel. Five years later she developed Parkinson's disease. Margaret Bourke-White died in 1971.

Suggested Activities

Essays Assign the students to make a photo essay about a social problem or some aspect of their lives. They can use pictures cut from magazines or take pictures of their own.

Robert Capa Robert Capa was another famous World War II photojournalist. He took part in the D-Day invasion, but many of his pictures from that event were lost. Find out what happened to them.

Reference

Photographing the World: Margaret Bourke-White by Eleanor H. Ayer (Dillon, 1992).

The Navajo Code Talkers

Despite their poor treatment by the United States throughout history, the Navajo were ready to fight for their country in World War II. A select group of these men were chosen to form the Navajo code talkers. Their work would prove invaluable to the war effort.

On the Pacific front, American intelligence was able to interpret messages using Japan's top secret Purple Code. In turn, Japan was able to decode American messages. This meant that neither side was able to keep a secret. Because Japan employed a larger number of troops, America lost battle after battle. By the spring of 1942, Japan occupied most of the Pacific Ocean. Something had to be done–and quickly.

While military personnel were trying to devise an unbreakable code, a civil engineer for the city of Los Angeles, Philip Johnston, came up with a possible solution. Having been raised among the Navajo, he knew the language fluently and also knew that it was virtually impossible for an adult to master. After taking his idea to the Marines, a 30-man pilot program was initiated. Following the rigors of basic training, the recruits had to learn pages of military terminology. From a list of 211 terms most frequently used in the field, the Navajo wrote code words for each of these terms. An alphabet code was also added. Even intelligence experts could not crack the newly-devised code. Nineteen thousand Marines were dispatched to Guadalcanal in 1942, including the Navajo code talkers. By intercepting messages, U.S. intelligence was able to determine the routes and schedules of Japanese merchant marine ships and destroy them. The new code prevented enemy knowledge of American plans. Once Japan's raw materials supply had been cut off, they could no longer produce military goods or equipment. The Japanese were forced to abandon the island. Thanks to the U.S. code-cracking abilities, the war in the Pacific was drastically shortened.

The code talkers experienced their finest hour in Iwo Jima, a strategic Japanese stronghold. During their first 48 hours on the island, six Navajo radio units worked around the clock and received more than 800 messages without error. Classified until 1968, in 1969 the Navajo war effort finally received the recognition it so rightly deserved. Two years later President Richard Nixon honored the code talkers with a special certificate. Congress declared August 14, 1982 as National Code Talkers Day.

Suggested Activity

Brainstorm Conduct a class brainstorming session of additional questions about the Navajo code talkers. Research answers.

Reference

Navajo Code Talkers by Nathan Aaseng (Walker and Company, 1992).

Japanese Internment

Within weeks after the bombing of Pearl Harbor, Japanese American men were rounded up and jailed like criminals. Their families were forced to obey a curfew and they had a five-mile travel limit. In addition, they were required to turn in their shortwave radios, cameras, binoculars, and firearms to local police.

On February 20, 1942, Executive Order 9066 was carried out and 110,000 persons of Japanese ancestry were ordered to leave their homes. Evacuees were only allowed what they could carry, including linens, clothing, dishes, toys, and utensils. They were taken to assembly centers at nearby fairgrounds and race tracks. These areas were secured with barbed wire fences and sentries were posted in guard towers. One tiny room was assigned to each family. Some of these rooms were nothing more than former horse stalls with linoleum placed directly over manure-covered ground. There was no furniture except for army cots, no running water, and no heat. Communal bathrooms with toilets and showers had to be shared with 300 other people. Lines for meals were long, and the food served was not their usual diet. The Japanese Americans spent the spring and summer of 1942 in these makeshift quarters until they were moved into one of ten different camps in Idaho, California, Wyoming, Arizona, and Arkansas. These "new" camps weren't much better than the ones they had left. Barbed wire surrounded the areas, and sentries stood watch. Rows of black barracks covered with tar paper were their new homes. Rooms were one of three sizes and were assigned one per family, depending on the number of family members. One hanging ceiling light, a closet, and windows decorated each room. Thin walls assured them of no privacy. Evacuees made what furniture they could. Women ordered fabric through mail order catalogs and sewed curtains. People planted outdoor gardens, and students attended camp schools which lacked even basic supplies like books and paper. Japanese Americans were kept in these barracks until 1944.

— Suggested Activities —

Discuss The Constitution provides the rights of liberty and justice for all. How were these rights broken in the case of the Japanese Americans? Find out what restitution was made to those who were held in these camps.

Camp Homes With masking tape make a number of 8' X 10' (3 m X 6 m) rooms on the classroom floor. Assign an equal number of students to each room. Have them do their regular assignments for one day while confined to the "rooms." Discuss the experience in whole group.

The 442nd Regiment After much protest, Japanese Americans were allowed to serve in the war. The 442nd Regiment was the most decorated American unit to serve in World War II. Find out more about this unit and its accomplishments.

Reference

I Am an American by Jerry Stanley (Crown Publishers, Inc., 1994).

Entertainment Overview

Many movies of the forties era featured song and dance routines or large musical numbers. Fred Astaire and Ginger Rogers, Gene Kelly, Donald O'Connor, and Carmen Miranda were some famous standouts from these films. But there were other types of films and entertainment. Some forms are explored below.

Animation In 1940 Walt Disney's *Fantasia* debuted. It combined cartoon characters with classical music and featured an innovative multispeaker system. In 1942 Disney released *Bambi.* There were only 900 spoken words in the film, yet it had taken five years to produce. *Anchors Aweigh* starred Gene Kelly in a dance sequence with cartoon characters Tom and Jerry. Another animation and live character combination occurred in Disney's *Song of the South* in 1946. The song "Zip-A-Dee-Dooh-Dah" is from this film.

Drama Orson Welles wrote, directed, and starred in his 1941 feature film debut, *Citizen Kane.* Loosely based on the life of publisher William Randolph Hearst, it is now regarded as an American classic. *Casablanca,* starring Humphrey Bogart and Ingrid Bergman, won the Oscar for Best Picture in 1943. These films can often be seen on cable TV. Check local listings for viewing times.

Orson Welles

In 1946, *The Best Years of Our Lives* dealt with the readjustment problem of a returning veteran and how it affected his family. Lawrence Olivier directed and starred in the 1944 *Henry V.* At that time it was the most expensive film ever made.

Theater *Oklahoma!* opened on Broadway in 1943. The Rogers and Hammerstein musical broke new ground by incorporating lyrics into the story as though the words were being spoken. The play went on to become the most popular show of the year. Arthur Miller's *Death of a Salesman* opened on Broadway in 1949. The Pulitzer Prize-winning drama tells the story of an aging traveling salesman, Willie Loman, who has never experienced real success. Tennessee Williams scored hits with two plays—*A Streetcar Named Desire* and *The Glass Menagerie.* Both attracted serious audiences.

Disney and the War During World War II, the Disney Studios spent 90% of its time on war-related projects. In addition to producing training films for the army and the navy, Disney characters were painted on Jeeps, trucks, tanks, and aircraft. Mickey Mouse played a special role in the D-Day invasion of Europe. The cartoon character's name was used as the password for the invasion.

Suggested Activities

Innovations Compare the innovations in today's movies with those made in 1940s films.

Musicals Compare the musicals of Roger and Hammerstein to later musicals, such as *Grease* or *Tommy.*

Grace in Action

Musicals were a popular type of movie in the 1940s, and Gene Kelly was one of their most well-known and well-loved stars. His athletic and energetic dance routines often stole the show. In 1952, he won a special Oscar for his 17-minute ballet dance performance in *An American in Paris*. Kelly's special brand of dance and choreography can aptly be described as grace in action.

Gene Kelly

Gene Kelly was the third of five children, three sons and two daughters. His parents were Patrick J. Kelly, a salesman for a gramophone company, and Harriet, a housewife and sometime actress. As a child, Kelly attended dance school and was often teased and beaten up by neighborhood children. After high school, Kelly began attending Pennsylvania State but had to drop out to help out his family financially. He took odd jobs, including pumping gas and digging ditches. After saving enough money he was able to study journalism at the University of Pittsburgh while living at home. During this time he offered dance lessons for fifty cents an hour in the family's basement. He expanded his business after graduation and opened the Gene Kelly Studio of the Dance. The business thrived, spurred on by the success of child star Shirley Temple.

When he was 26 years old, Kelly headed for Broadway, where he quickly won a part. By 1940, he found himself in a starring role and soon was on his way to Hollywood, under contract to MGM Studios. His first movie was *For Me and My Gal* opposite Judy Garland, but he did not achieve star status until his 1944 musical, *Cover Girl*, with Rita Hayworth. The 1952 film, *Singin' in the Rain*, became his most highly regarded work. It featured new star Debbie Reynolds and a memorable dance number through a rainy, city street. *An American in Paris* earned him the highest accolade—an Oscar. After a box office failure (*Brigadoon*) in 1954, Kelly concentrated on choreography and directing. Gene Kelly devoted himself to his children after the death of his second wife. In the years that followed, he accepted only occasional roles. After suffering from a series of strokes, Gene Kelly died on February 2, 1996 at the age of 83.

Suggested Activities

Comparisons Fred Astaire was another popular dancer/actor of the forties who preceeded Kelly on the big screen. Compare the two dancers' styles and personal lives.

Animation In the 1945 film, *Anchors Aweigh,* Gene Kelly danced with Tom and Jerry, animated cartoon characters. Find out the names of other 1940s films in which animation and live action were combined.

Jackie Robinson

Until the 1940s the American and National Baseball Leagues were closed to African American players. They played in separate leagues, called "Negro Leagues," which did not enjoy the same monetary rewards or respect that the all-white leagues did. In 1946 all of that began to change when the Brooklyn Dodgers signed Jackie Robinson to the team.

Jackie Robinson

Jackie Roosevelt Robinson was born in Cairo, Georgia, in 1919. He was only one year old when his father deserted him, his four siblings, and their mother. The family moved to Pasadena, California, where Robinson attended high school, Pasadena Junior College (now Pasadena City College), and UCLA. At UCLA, Robinson was the first student athlete to letter in four different sports: baseball, basketball, football, and track. As talented as he was, he was forced to quit UCLA in his third year to help support his family. During this time, World War II broke out, and Robinson was drafted into the Army.

After returning to civilian life, Robinson signed on to play baseball for the Kansas City Monarchs of the National Negro League. When Branch Rickey, president of the Brooklyn Dodgers, decided to integrate major league baseball, he sent scouts to watch players in the Negro leagues. Jackie Robinson's name appeared on many of the returning reports. In the spring of 1946, Jackie began playing with the Dodgers' top farm team, the Montreal Royals, and by the next year he had joined the Dodgers. It was not an easy transition, as some of his own teammates protested his presence on the team. The Philadelphia Phillies threatened not to play the Dodgers as long as Robinson was on the team. Another team, the St. Louis Cardinals, threatened to strike. Ford Frick, president of the National League, quickly stopped the protests by promising to suspend any team that participated in a strike. In his first year with the Dodgers, Robinson hit .297, scored 125 runs, and led the league in stolen bases. That year the Dodgers won the National League Pennant for the first time since 1941. In 1947 Jackie Robinson became the first African American to play in the World Series and was named Rookie of the Year. Two years later he led his league with a .342 batting average and won the Most Valuable Player Award. In his ten years with the Dodgers, he helped them to six league championships and the 1955 World Series Championship. In 1962, he was elected to the Baseball Hall of Fame.

Suggested Activities

Facts and Figures Tell students to find out what team the Dodgers played in the 1927 World Series and who won.

Comparisons Compare pay, travel, and other conditions in the Negro Leagues with the all-white leagues.

References

Shadow Ball by Ken Burns (Alfred A. Knopf, 1994).

The Forgotten Players by Robert Gardner and Dennis Shortelle (Walker and Company, 1993)

The All-Female Leagues

As more and more men went off to fight the war, American women began to take on new roles. They worked in factories and volunteered for a variety of duties, including driving ambulances. In 1943 another role for women opened up when chewing gum magnate Philip K. Wrigley organized an all-female baseball league. With the major league players gone to war, Wrigley, the owner of the Chicago Cubs, worried about the status of the game. Convinced that women could play baseball and keep the stands filled with fans, Wrigley put his plan into action.

Because there was not enough time to train female athletes from scratch, a combination softball/baseball was developed. Underhand pitches and a 12-inch ball were taken from softball, while rules that allowed leading off and stealing were taken from baseball. Once the rules had been established, Wrigley had special uniforms designed for the players. The uniforms featured a short dress worn with satin panties, and thick, wool knee socks worn with spiked shoes.

Players were required to dress and play like ladies and obey certain rules. For example, when in public, they had to wear skirts and could not smoke or drink. In addition to their regular games, the players had to play in exhibition games for soldiers at military camps, sell war bonds, and teach youngsters how to play. Players were paid $55 to $85 per week and all on-the-road expenses were paid by the team. Scouts recruited women age 15 to 25 and sent them to Wrigley's Chicago ballpark for tryouts. There, they were treated to charm school conducted by the famed Helena Rubenstein. The women were taught the basics of makeup and how to wear their hair. Those who made the final cut were soon on their way to a grueling three-month schedule in which they would play 108 games, half of them away. Because young women in 1943 lived at home until they married, Wrigley had his ballplayers live with host families in the midwestern towns in which they played. Often the players and their families became quite close.

In 1948 the All-American Girls Professional Baseball League began its peak year with ten teams. By the end of that season, more than 910,000 fans paid to see the women play. Four years later, due to decreasing attendace, the teams folded. It had been quite a run and a unique opportunity for women.

Suggested Activity

Status With the class discuss: What is the status of women's baseball today?

References

A Whole New Ball Game by Sue Macy (Henry Holt and Company, 1993).

Belles of the Ballpark by Diana Star Helmer (Millbrook Press, 1993).

Scientists

On this page you will find a sampling of important scientists from the 1940s era. After you read the paragraphs, choose one scientist and complete the activities listed.

Percy Lavon Julian

After years of graduate school and teaching chemistry, Julian traveled to Vienna, Austria, to study for his doctorate. There, he became interested in the medical uses of soybeans. Upon his return to the U.S., he created physostigmine, a drug used to treat glaucoma, and developed a drug used to relieve arthritis pain. His work attracted much attention, and he was hired by the Glidden Paint Company as chief chemist and director of research. In addition to the glaucoma and arthritis drugs, Julian developed "Aero-Foam," which was used during World War II to extinguish gas and oil fires.

Activities a. Construct a chart to compare Julian's accomplishments with those of George Washington Carver.

b. Do research to find out ten more uses that Julian found for soybeans.

Charles Richard Drew

By the 1930s, the scientific community knew that all humans have one of four blood types—A, B, O, or AB. The importance of receiving one's own blood type in the event of a transfusion was also known. There were problems with storing the blood, however, as it spoiled quickly. This problem intrigued African American Charles Drew. During his doctoral studies he learned that blood plasma would keep longer than whole blood. With this valuable information, he was able to develop a method for collecting, processing, and storing plasma. His pioneering work helped save thousands of lives during World War II.

Activities a. Find out what blood type you are.

b. During WW II "colored" blood was kept separate from that obtained from whites. Is there any scientific evidence to support the necessity of such a practice?

Albert Einstein

Albert Einstein was one of the world's greatest physicists. A German Jew, he had moved to the United States in 1932 when Hitler's Nazi Party came into power. Concerned that the Germans might be the first to develop an atomic bomb, Einstein warned President Roosevelt of such a danger. His warning led to the formation of the top secret Manhattan Project. Afterwards, Einstein regretted the fact that an atomic bomb had been produced.

Activities a. Italian Enrico Fermi moved to the U.S. to escape Fascism in his native land. What role did he play in the development of the atomic bomb? What was the Manhattan Project? Who were some of the key players in the project?

b. Einstein formulated the theory of relativity. What did that theory have to do with the building of an atomic bomb?

The Manhattan Project

When the nucleus of an atom is split or broken apart, energy is released. The process begins when a slow-moving neutron is launched to split a uranium atom. Each split uranium atom gives off three more neutrons plus two hydrogen atoms. These new neutrons go on to split other uranium atoms. This happens over and over in what is called a chain reaction.

Throughout the 1920s and 1930s scientists around the world had been finding out more and more about atoms and their behavior. Germans Lise Meitner and Otto Hahn had successfully split the nucleus of a uranium atom. Enrico Fermi expanded on their work in 1942 when he and his team were able to achieve a controlled chain reaction.

By 1939 both German and American physicists were working on practical applications for nuclear fission, specifically a bomb. After scientist Albert Einsten warned President Roosevelt that the Germans were in the process of building an atomic bomb, Roosevelt gave approval for the top secret Manhattan Project. Hundreds of male and female scienctists and technicians were gathered together under the direction of J. Robert Oppenheimer, a theoretical physicist.

Although much of the early work was conducted in New York City, the actual testing site was in New Mexico. On July 16, 1945, three years after the project started, the first test explosion of an atomic bomb took place in New Mexico's Alamogordo Bombing Range. Its awesome force shook the desert floor, and its blinding light illuminated trees and mountains. A mushroom cloud of dust raised high into the sky. The five kilograms of plutonium in the bomb yielded an explosion equivalent to 18,500 tons of dynamite, more than enough to destroy an entire city.

On August 6, 1945, the U.S. Air Force dropped the first atomic bomb over Hiroshima, Japan. Over 200,000 people were killed in the blast. After a second bomb was dropped on Nagasaki three days later, Japan surrendered. Although the true effects of the bomb would not be fully realized for many years, a new Atomic Age had begun.

The scientists who participated in the Manhattan Project knew that what they were working on could kill thousands of people in a single blast, yet they hoped that it would lead to worldwide peace.

Suggested Activities

Code Names "Fat Man" and "Little Boy" were the code names given to the bombs dropped on Hiroshima and Nagasaki. Draw a diagram of each bomb and explain the differences between the two types.

Heavy Water Early nuclear experiments used heavy water (deuterium oxide), an isotope of water. In the forties, heavy water was manufactured in quantity only in Norway. Assign groups of students to research each of the following topics: the nature of heavy water, its role in nuclear reactions, the Allied response to the German occupation of Norway.

What If? German physicists came close to developing an atomic weapon, but Hitler cut back their research, choosing to concentrate efforts on developing rockets, the V-1 and V-2, instead. Discuss the possible outcome of the war if the Germans had developed and used atomic weapons.

Writers of the Forties

A number of important writers emerged throughout the forties. Some used World War II as a backdrop for their novels, while others wrote about their own personal experiences. Read about three of these writers. Choose and complete one activity for each writer.

Richard Wright

Richard Wright's childhood can aptly be described as terrible. He narrowly survived a childhood beating, was abandoned by his father, lived for a time in an orphanage, and, after his mother's stroke, was sent to live with his grandmother. Although the two did not get along and there was never enough to eat, Richard did get to attend school regularly. It was during this time that he determined to become a writer. Not until he moved to New York City, however, did his dreams come true. After the publication of a collection of his stories came the success of *Native Son,* probably his most famous novel. In 1945 his novel *Black Boy* revealed the poverty and racism faced by black children of the time, and its sales surpassed those of his first novel. Wright, died in 1960.

Activities a. Read *Black Boy* (which was reissued in 1996) or *Rite of Passage.* From your reading, how would you characterize life for African Americans during the forties?

   b. For a short time Wright belonged to the Communist Party. Find out how they helped him and why he eventually decided to leave the organization.

James Michener

Born in 1907, James Albert Michener won a Pulitzer prize in 1948 for his collection of stories *Tales of the South Pacific.* The stories describe the life of U.S. servicemen among the people of the Solomon Islands during World War II. The 1949 Oscar and Hammerstein musical comedy *South Pacific,* was based on his book.

Activities a. Michener was a prolific writer. Make a list of his novels.

   b. Locate the Solomon Islands on a map of the Pacific. Find out what famous battle took place there.

Herman Wouk

This American novelist and playwright's most successful book was based on his experiences in the U.S. Navy during World War II. *The Winds of War* (1971) and its sequel, *War and Remembrance* (1978), tell about the effects of World War II on an American naval officer and his family. *The Winds of War* was later made into a television miniseries. Wouk won a Pulitzer Prize in 1952 for his novel *The Caine Mutiny.*

Activities a. Research Wouk's childhood and young adulthood. What life experiences influenced his decision to become a writer?

   b. Read some historical accounts of the bombing of Pearl Harbor. Pretend that you were there and write a first-hand account of the bombing.

The Reys

In the early 1940s, before America entered the war, a number of Europeans immigrated to the United States to escape the Fascist and Nazi governments in their homelands. Many of the immigrants were prominent intellectuals, scientists, and writers. H. A. Rey and his wife, Margaret, were part of this group. The Reys came to America from their native Germany in 1940, and in 1946 they became naturalized citizens of the United States.

Hans Augusto Reyersbach was born on September 16, 1898, in Hamburg, Germany. The son of Alexander and Martha Reyersbach, he legally changed his surname to Rey later on in his life. At the age of two, he was already displaying a talent for drawing. When he could not afford the tuition for art school, Rey attended a German university and did free-lance art work. Later, he accepted a job at a family member's import/export business in Rio de Janeiro, Brazil. It was in Brazil that Hans met Margaret Waldstein, who had also grown up in Hamburg. The pair found that they shared an interest in art and a distaste for the Nazi regime of Germany. They married in 1935 and moved to Paris, where Rey began to write and draw children's books. When Germany invaded France, they were forced to flee the country on bicycles. Soon, they traveled to America with not much more than the clothes on their backs and some manuscripts for children's stories.

As a child, Rey had lived close to a zoo and had developed a fondness for exotic animals, especially monkeys. This probably accounts for his use of animals as the main characters of his books. Curious George was born out of Rey's first book, *Cecily G. and the Nine Monkeys*. George was so appealing that Margaret and Hans continued to collaborate in other adventures for George. Together the couple created a memorable character who is loved by children around the world.

In addition to the *Curious George* books, Margaret wrote a number of other stories, all illustrated by her husband. Hans also authored several books by himself, including two on astronomy.

Suggested Activities

Titles Make a list of all the *Curious George* titles. Which ones have the students read? Conduct a poll to find out which is the class favorite.

New Adventure With the class, brainstorm some adventures Curious George might have had during World War II. Instruct the students to write a story with a new adventure for George.

Background Find out more about Margaret's early years and how she came to meet H. A. Rey in Brazil. Write a short report and present it to the rest of the class.

Art in the Forties

During the late 1940s and early 1950s a new art form, abstract expressionism, emerged, in part as a reaction to the war that was devastating two continents and killing millions. With their world out of whack, American artists responded by producing works of art that no longer suggested recognizable images.

Jackson Pollock

At the forefront of this movement was Jackson Pollock. Called "Jack the Dripper" by *Time* magazine, he threw out his easels, palettes, and paintbrushes and dripped and poured commercial paints onto a huge roll of canvas. Instead of emphasizing perspective and focal points as most paintings did, Pollock's work focused on the creative process.

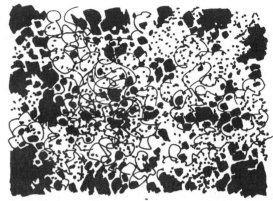

Willem deKooning

Another artist of the abstract expressionism school was Willem DeKooning, also known as the Old Master of Abstract Expressionism. An immigrant from Holland, he worked in a realistic style until 1945, when he developed a style of slashing brushstrokes. Known for his series of paintings titled *Woman,* deKooning's images appear unfinished in their trademark yellow, pink, and buff colors.

Hans Hoffman

This German American painter was a highly influential teacher who advocated a "push-pull" theory on the repulsion and attraction of certain colors. He was one of the first to experiment with pouring paint and freely-splashing pigment. Hoffman is well known for the rectangles of contrasting colors in his paintings.

Suggested Activities

Experience Experience abstract expressionism with the two projects on page 56.

Character Jackson Pollock lived hard and died young. Known for his outlandish behavior, he helped artists see that art comes from within rather than without. Find out more about events in his personal life.

Others Other abstract artists of the period include Arshile Gorky, Franz Kline, and Robert Motherwell. Research and write about the innovations that each contributed to the art world.

Colors Learn the difference between complementary and contrasting colors. Draw some freehand rectangles and paint them in contrasting colors like Hans Hoffman did in his painting titled *The Gate.*

Art Experiences

Students can experience the different styles of artists Jackson Pollock and Willem de Kooning with these two art projects.

Action Painting

Introduction: Display a copy of Pollock's *No.1, 1950 (Lavender Mist)*. Call attention to the black, white, and silver lines. Note the lack of perspective, focal point, or recognizable images.

Materials: black, white, and silver paint; an old sheet or length of white butcher paper taped together; old newspapers; small cans or margarine cups; funnels; craft sticks; etc.

Directions:

- Spread newspaper on the floor to cover the working area completely.
- Place the sheet or paper in the center of the newspaper.
- Dip the can, funnel, or other instrument into one of the paints. Drizzle paint onto the canvas.
- Dip another can into a different color paint and again drizzle the paint onto the canvas.
- Continue until all colors have been used and the artist is satisfied with the design.

Note: Students can create individual murals or small groups can work on one together.

Slash Strokes

Introduction: Display a copy of de Kooning's *Woman, I*. Ask students to share their observations of the artist's style.

Materials: yellow, pink, and buff paints; wide paint brushes; butcher paper

Directions:

- Dip the paintbrush in a color.
- Apply paint to the canvas with wide brush strokes.
- Dip the paintbrush in another color and apply to the canvas with wide strokes.
- Continue in this manner until all three colors have been used to create a figure.

⎯⎯ Suggested Activity ⎯⎯

Museums Jackson Pollock's *No. 1, 1950 (Lavender Mist)* can be seen at the National Gallery in Washington, D.C., while Willem de Kooning's *Woman, I* can be viewed at the Museum of Modern Art in New York City. If possible, visit these museums and view these art works. Find out where some of these artists' other paintings are located or find library books that contain copies of these and other abstract expressionist artists' work.

Norman Rockwell

For 47 years Norman Rockwell painted covers for the *Saturday Evening Post*. His inviting paintings provided an intimate glimpse into the everyday lives of Americans during the first half of the century and have come to be regarded as classic Americana.

Norman Rockwell was born on February 3, 1894, in New York. When he was nine, the family moved to Mamaroneck. To gain acceptance, the resourceful Rockwell drew pictures to entertain his classmates. He left high school to study at the National Academy of Design and earned money by drawing greeting cards. At age 16, he studied at the Art Students League and began illustrating books and magazines. By the time he was 18, Rockwell was the art director for *Boys' Life* magazine.

Rockwell achieved fame after the five illustrations he sold to the editor of *Saturday Evening Post* were used as covers on the magazine. In all, Norman Rockwell provided 318 covers for the *Post* through his 47-year association with them.

Norman Rockwell

When World War I broke out, Rockwell tried to enlist in the Navy, but he was rejected for being underweight. Undeterred, he ate a diet of bananas and donuts until he gained the necessary ten pounds. After acceptance in the service, Rockwell was assigned to the navy yard in Charleston, South Carolina where he painted for the Navy. He also continued to work for the *Saturday Evening Post* and other magazines. After the war, he returned to New York where he built a studio for himself. By that time he was enjoying both fame and fortune from his paintings.

The process used by Norman Rockwell to create a painting was long and detailed. First, he sketched the scene. Next he made individual drawings of each element in the scene. Full-size charcoal drawings were the next step, followed by color sketches. Only then was he ready to begin actual painting.

In the late 1930s Rockwell moved to Arlington, Virginia. Fire destroyed his studio in 1943, along with many of his drawings and paintings. Although he was saddened by the loss, Rockwell began painting more directly from life rather than relying on a model. Although he ceased working for the *Saturday Evening Post* in 1963, he continued to work for other magazines. His latter years were spent traveling to foreign countries. Norman Rockwell died in 1978.

Suggested Activities

Greeting Cards Norman Rockwell drew greeting cards early in his career. Have the students create greeting cards, using the same style of painting that Rockwell used.

Rosie the Riveter Rockwell was responsible for the popular poster of Rosie the Riveter. Find out the names of some of his other famous works.

Of Jazz and Swing

Big bands and swing were still "in" during the 1940s, but other forms of music, jazz and bebop, were also becoming popular. Read about some of the musicians who made the music of forties.

Jazz

It is hard to believe that the multi-talented Duke Ellington had to be forced to practice piano when he was a child. Although in high school he was more interested in art than in music, by age 17 he was regularly sitting in with a group at the Poodle Dog Cafe, where he worked behind the soda fountain. Soon he was playing professionally. In the early 1920s, he formed his own group called the Washingtonians, but they did not meet with real success until they played the Cotton Club in Harlem. Throughout the Great Depression and World War II, Ellington's popularity grew. His most well-known compositions include "Sophisticated Lady" and "The A Train." The group also toured Europe and appeared in several movies. During the fifties, Duke Ellington's popularity waned, but he continued to play, compose, and lead his band until his death in 1974.

Duke Ellington

Activities

- Find out how Ellington got his nickname "Duke."
- Write a one-page report about Ellington's contributions to the world of jazz.

Bebop

The term "bebop" first came into the English language in 1944, when a new style of improvisational jazz music was developed by African American musicians. Charlie Parker, Dizzy Gillespie, and Thelonius Monk were most responsible for creating and popularizing this new type of music. Bebop was characterized by fast tempos, complex melodies, dissonant chords, and eccentric rhythms. It was usually played by small groups and emphasized soloists. Here are a few facts about each of these key players.

Monk

Parker

Gillespie

- **Charlie "Byrd" Parker** taught himself to play the saxophone. At 18 he left home to get work as a musician. He started out playing in swing bands but soon began working on a new kind of music.

- **Dizzy Gillespie** earned the nickname "Dizzy" because he was always clowning around. The youngest of nine children, he showed an early gift for music and studied trombone and trumpet. As a teen he played in local swing bands with Cab Calloway. Like Parker, Dizzy experimented with new ways of playing jazz.

- **Thelonius Monk** began playing piano professionally in his teens. He soon found an after-hours home at a Harlem nightclub. Parker, Gillespie, and other bebop artists could be found there also. Together, they began working out increasingly complex arrangements. Monk's "Round Midnight" is now a jazz standard.

Activities

- Clint Eastwood made a movie about Charlie Parker's life. Look for *Byrd* on video.
- Dizzy Gillespie's trumpet soared upward. Find out how he started that tradition.

Reference

Jazz by Richard Carlin (Facts on File, 1991).

Dance, Music, and Songs

During the Roaring Twenties, a dance called the jitterbug became popular in black nightclubs. It was not until the 1940s, though, that it became the rage as it caught on with the white teenage culture. An athletic dance, it featured fancy footwork and even airborne steps in which the male would swing his female partner over his head and between his legs. Although many adults disapproved of the dance—they felt it was too physical and uninhibited—there was no stopping it. In fact, the jitterbug grew into an international craze when U.S. servicemen introduced the dance in England and Europe.

Frank Sinatra

The typical female jitterbuggers of World War II wore white socks that covered the ankles, saddle shoes, and heavy makeup to look older. Nicknamed "bobbysoxers," they danced in the canteens where soldiers who were on leave went for entertainment. Jitterbuggers danced to any number of popular hits, including Glenn Miller's "Chattanooga Choo Choo" and "In the Mood" and the Andrew Sisters' "Boogie Woogie Bugle Boy."

Every big band had one or more vocalists, and their vocals were also a hit. One singer, Frances Albert Sinatra, became the idol of the bobbysoxers. More commonly known as Frank Sinatra, he started his singing career as a vocalist with the big band of Harry James in 1939. Girls attending his performances screamed and swooned as he sang his ballads. Bing Crosby was another favorite crooner and actor of the era. In the 1942 movie, *Holiday Inn,* he sang "White Christmas," which became one of the most popular songs ever.

Suggested Activities

Dance Watch a dance sequence from a 1940s movie to see how the jitterbug was done or invite a dance instructor to set up a classroom demonstration.

Sinatra Frank Sinatra went on to become a movie star, too. Make a list of some movies in which he appeared. Write a list of forties tunes he made popular. Listen to some of his early music. An excellent resource is *Frank Sinatra: The Best of the Columbia Years.* This four-CD set from Columbia/Legacy covers his singing career from 1943–1952.

Big Band Listen to some Big Band music. Check your local music store or library for tapes, records, or CDs. One title to look for is *Big Band Rensaissance: The Evolution of Jazz Orchestra—the 1940s and Beyond.* The set is from Smithsonian and includes 5 CD's (also available in cassette form).

WW II Songs Make a list of some popular World War II songs. Listen to some typical forties' music. *Command Performance Radio Show Collection* and *We'll Meet Again: The Smithsonian Collection of World War II Love Songs* from the Wireless catalogue (800-669-9999) feature original recordings of the era.

More with Less

In the late 1920s, an unusual inventor was beginning to make a name for himself. Considered eccentric by some, R. Buckminster Fuller developed a philosophical approach to technological innovation. He believed that it was possible to create more with less. In Fuller's view, the role of technology is to provide greater ammenities, using decreased amounts of resources. The first example of this was his 1927 Dymaxion House, featuring automatic vacuum cleaners and a shower that recycled its own water. It was the geodesic dome, though, that brought Fuller the most attention. First built in 1947, the dome was constructed of tetrahedrons, which are solid geometric shapes with four triangular sides.

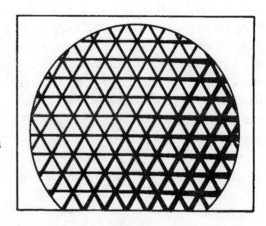

This design was strong, yet light, and equally effective in withstanding Arctic cold and desert heat. Although most of his inventions never enjoyed mass usage, R. Buckminster Fuller certainly gave the world a lot to think about with his innovative ideas and creations.

Suggested Activities

Tetrahedrons Let the students make tetrahedrons, using the pattern below. Have groups of students work together to construct a building with their tetrahedrons.

Dome A challenging construction project is the geodesic dome. Students can make their own with the patterns found in Teacher Created Materials #496 *Focus on Inventors*.

Tetrahedron Pattern

Directions:

Copy the tetrahedron pattern onto construction paper or card stock. Cut out along the solid lines. Fold inward along all dashed lines. Glue or tape the tabs so that they remain inside the pyramid.

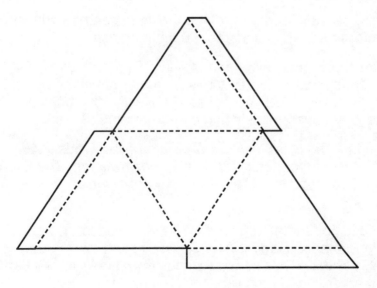

The War Years and Fashions

Take a look at some of the fashions that were popular during the 1940s. Most were born out of necessity and the increasing controls on various materials. Do you see any similarities with the fashions of today?

Zoot Suits

This male fashion rage of the early forties consisted of a suit whose legs bagged below the knees and cuffs which pulled tightly around the ankle. A wide-brimmed hat, suspenders, and chain completed the ensemble.

Bobbysoxers

Young girls typically wore bobby socks, pleated skirts, sweaters, and round collars. Hair was worn tied back wavey or rolled.

Coveralls

Before this era, women did not wear pants, but safety regulations and practical reasons alike led to the coverall. Soon, one-piece coveralls became the accepted work uniform for women.

Hairdos

Women began to wear their hair swept up and pinned in elaborate styles, as seen in the picture at left. Most likely the fashion grew out of the numbers of women working in the factories—safety factors made wearing the hair up a necessity.

Bathing Suits

Bathing suits for women and men in the forties became briefer and were constructed of stretch fabric. Typical suits for women can be seen at the left.

Everyday Dress

Shortages in fabric during the war led to what was known as utility clothing. Shown is a typical early 1940s dress—practical, plain, and comfortable.

Suggested Activities

Bikini The bikini was created in 1946. Find out how it got its name and learn more about its French designer, Lewis Reard.

Dior French designer Christian Dior introduced his "New Look" in 1947. Find pictures of this style and compare it to the utility dress worn during the war and to today's fashions.

Elsewhere . . .

As World War II progressed, a number of events were unfolding worldwide. Below is a list of some of the important happenings during the forties. Instruct the students to find out more about any events that interest them.

1940
- Churchill becomes prime minister of Great Britain.
- Germany invades Denmark and Norway.
- Italy enters the war.
- The Battle of Britain takes place.
- Prehistoric wall paintings of Lascaux caves are discovered in France.

1941
- The German battleship *Bismarck* sinks.
- Churchill and Roosevelt meet to sign the Atlantic Charter.
- Japan bombs Pearl Harbor.

1942
- Rommel captures Tobruk in North Africa.
- Gandhi demands that the British should "quit India."

1943
- Germany surrenders at Stalingrad.
- Mussolini is overthrown; Italy joins the Allies.
- The Aqua Lung is invented by Jacques Cousteau and Emile Gagnan.

1944
- D-Day landing in Normandy on June 6.
- Ho Chi Minh declares Vietnam's independence from France.

1945
- Mussolini is killed by Italian partisans.
- Hitler commits suicide.
- Germany surrenders.
- Wernher von Braun immigrates to the U.S. to continue his work in rocket science.
- The United Nations Charter is signed.
- De Gaulle is elected president of France.
- Japan surrenders; World War II ends.
- Tito becomes head of Yugoslavia.
- The Nuremberg Trials are conducted; Nazi leaders are tried and convicted as war criminals.

1946
- The first session of the UN General Assembly opens in London.

1947
- Burma chooses independence.
- The *Kon-Tiki* sails from Peru to Polynesia.
- The Dead Sea Scrolls are discovered in Wadi Qumran.
- Willard Frank Libby develops the technique of radiocarbon dating.

1948
- On January 30 Gandhi is assassinated by a Hindu fanatic.
- The Jewish state of Israel is proclaimed.
- The World Health Organization is founded.
- The Olympic Games resume and are held in London.
- George de Mestral of Switzerland invents Velcro.
- Mother Teresa sets up hospitals and shelters in Calcutta, India.

1949
- Twelve nations sign a treaty establishing NATO.
- France grants independence to Vietnam.
- The People's Republic of China is established.
- Indonesia declares its independence.
- Nehru becomes Prime Minister of India.
- The Soviet Union tests its first atomic bomb.

Newfoundland

In 1949 Newfoundland and its dependency, Labrador, became the tenth province of the Dominion of Canada. The easternmost point of Canada, Newfoundland is an island in the Atlantic Ocean. Labrador lies on the mainland and stretches in a triangular-shaped strip along the Labrador Sea.

Learn more facts about Newfoundland by circling the correct answer from each pair in the sentences below. Use a book about the province of Newfoundland to help you with the answers.

1. Newfoundland was discovered by **John Cabot/Ferdinand Magellan** in 1497.

2. A small island, it is about the size of **Tennessee/Texas.**

3. People there have their own **Inuit/English** dialect.

4. It is connected to the mainland by airplanes and **radio and television/radar** signals bounced off of space satellites.

5. Newfoundland was **France's/Great Britain's** first overseas colony.

6. **European/Chinese** fleets fished for cod and haddock off its coast.

7. Forests in Newfoundland supplied the Royal Navy with wood to support its ships' **anchors/sails.**

8. In the Atlantic region there was an abundance of underground and undersea **iron ore/coal.**

9. The land in Newfoundland is **rocky/flat** and the winters are cold and windy.

10. The ocean is **cold/moderate** and so clear that one can see all the way to the ocean floor.

11. In the spring, **icebergs/glaciers** float by, some as big as an apartment building.

12. Newfoundland sets its clocks one-half hour ahead of **Atlantic/Pacific** Standard Time.

13. The capital of Newfoundland is **Grand Falls/St. John's.**

14. Today, more than 80% of Newfoundland's population is of **British/Dutch** descent.

15. Newfoundland's population is under **400,000/600,000.**

List some reasons why you would want to live in Newfoundland.

_____

_____

List some reasons why you would not want to live in Newfoundland.

_____

_____

Juan and Evita Perón

During the 1940s, Juan and Evita (or Eva) Perón rose to political power in Argentina. The couple was revered by the masses there for the social and economic reforms which they achieved. Read about these two Argentinian leaders in the chart below. Research and add a sixth statement to each column.

Juan Perón 1895–1974

1. He was born in southern Argentina. After enrolling in military school, he was assigned to teach new cadets. He published books on military history and tactics, engaged regularly in sports, and in 1943 was appointed head of the National Labor Department.

2. After being a widower of some years, Perón met Eva Duarte at a benefit concert to raise money for victims of an Argentinian earthquake.

3. After Perón was elected President of Argentina, he shortened the work week to 40 hours; increased wages; arranged for the construction of new schools, power plants, and hospitals; arranged better retirement pensions, and took over the nation's privately owned railroads, public utilities, and banks.

4. When Perón served as president of Argentina his people sometimes compared him to Simón Bolivar, the liberator of Latin America. Juan and Eva Perón became saints, and statues of them were erected in public places.

5. During his second term, the nation's economic situation turned bad. Making matters worse was Eva Perón's death on July 26, 1952, for she had been his "eyes and ears" throughout his administration.

6. _____

Evita Perón 1919–1952

1. Having spent her childhood in poverty, she decided to quit high school after only two years to pursue a career on stage. Although she lacked a good singing voice, she knew how to make friends. Soon she had minor roles on radio shows and some small parts in movies.

2. An army officer she was dating invited her to a benefit concert. There she met her future husband, Juan Perón.

3. Eva was becoming powerful in her own right. She visited hospitals, factories, and orphanages; arranged for distribution of food and clothing to the poor; established the Eva Perón Foundation which set up clinics and expanded the number of schools and hospitals. Eva purchased a newspaper to report all of her good deeds and also fought for and won the right of Argentinian women to vote.

4. Regarded as equally heroic, Eva Perón was an "Argentine Joan of Arc" to many. She and her husband became more than political leaders. Their pictures were displayed everywhere.

5. Eva Perón died of cancer on July 26, 1952. It was she who had stayed in contact with labor leaders and had personally arranged the day-to-day business of the government.

6. _____

The People's Republic of China

On October 1, 1949, the People's Republic of China was proclaimed by Mao Tse-tung. It had taken the Communists years of fighting to finally gain control. Many changes were instituted, including reforms in how land was owned and worked. Much of the property owned by rich landlords was redistributed to poor peasants. Those who resisted the revolution were reportedly killed. To find out what led up to this new regime in China, review the following timeline.

Mao Tse-tung

1921   The Chinese Communist Party is founded in Shanghai.

1925   Mao Tse-tung (also known as Mao Zedong) sets up peasant unions in the countryside.
The Canton national government came under the control of Chiang Kai-shek.

1927   A provisional national government is formed and recognized by foreign powers. Its president, Chiang Kai-shek, launches a series of campaigns against the Communists. His nationalist party is called the Guomindong.

1934   The Communists have been driven out of their main base.
Mao Tse-tung leads his followers on the Long March, a one-year journey of over 6,000 miles.

1937   Full-scale invasion of China by Japan is underway.

1938   Japan controls the eastern provinces by late 1938.

1945   Japanese troops in China give up. The armies of Chiang Kai-shek, aided by U.S.A. troops, take the surrender of Japan.

1946   Civil war begins in China.

1948   The Communists take Peking (now Beijing) in early 1949.
Chiang Kai-shek's nationalists flee to Formosa (later renamed Taiwan).
Mao becomes head of the new People's Republic.

Suggested Activities

Biography Instruct the students to research and write a short biography of Mao Tse-tung, the man who led the Chinese revolution and founded the new republic.

Cultural Revolution With the class discuss the Cultural Revolution of 1966. Topics to cover: How Mao planned to revitalize Communism, the contents of the "Little Red Book" of the *Thoughts of Chairman Mao.*

Massacre Assign a group of students to find out the events that led to the Tianamen Massacre in April 1989. Have the group report their findings to the rest of the class.

Stronghold of the Pacific

On December 7, 1941, Japan launched a secret attack against the United States at Pearl Harbor Naval Base in Hawaii. Taking advantage of American unpreparedness, the Japanese began aerial attacks on the Philippines that same day. Within a month they had captured American island outposts, Guam and Wake, and within three months had conquered a vast island empire. Singapore, the Philippines, and the Dutch East Indies were among the victims. The last stronghold of defense in the southwest Pacific was Australia.

How long Australia would remain unoccupied was questionable, since it could be supplied only over a long route from Hawaii. The Japanese landings at New Guinea and the Solomon Islands threatened this supply line. Determined to protect this Australian supply line, American and Australian air and naval forces defeated Japan in the five-day battle of the Coral Sea. It wasn't long after this that the Japanese tried to capture Midway Island. Again, they were defeated.

In August 1942 American Marines landed on Guadalcanal in the Solomon Islands and seized the airfield. During the next four months, the island was attacked four times by the Japanese, but the Americans held firm. The following year, the Allied forces launched an offensive in the Pacific. U.S. sea, land, and air forces were aided by forces from Australia and New Zealand in an "island hopping" campaign in which troops moved from island to island, all the while getting closer and closer to Japan. During 1944 the Americans were able to clear the Japanese from New Guinea, the Marshall Islands, and the Marianas. The Philippines fell in late 1944, after the Japanese suffered a crushing defeat in the battle of Leyte. The entire Philippine archipelago had been recovered, and Australia was safe.

Suggested Activities

Enormity The war in the Pacific was an immense operation. To get a sense of just how enormous an undertaking it was, have the students look at a map or globe of the Pacific region around Australia, Japan, and Hawaii. Let them measure distances from one country to another and from one set of islands to another.

Battles Group the students and direct them to make a chart of some of the battles in the Pacific (Leyte, Coral Sea, Guadalcanal, Midway, Iwo Jima). Tell them to include information about when each was fought, which forces were involved, and who won.

Mapping Pairs or groups of students can draw maps of the Pacific region. Have them label all of the lands and islands mentioned in the paragraphs above.

Final Justice

Following World War II, the horrors of the German concentration camps were fully revealed to the world. The Nazi policy of extermination had led to more than six million deaths among Europe's 10 million Jews. In addition, almost six million non-Jewish Europeans, including Poles, Czechs, Russians, Yugoslavs, and Dutch were victims of the evil Nazi regime.

Before the war even ended, the Allies started gathering evidence against leading Nazi officials. Beginning in late 1945, a special international court, the International Military Tribunal, tried major Nazi leaders who had taken part in these mass murders. Although Hitler was already dead and some top officials had fled to Spain and Latin America, 22 of the principal Nazi leaders were captured. For almost a year these leaders were on trial for their crimes against humanity. Evidence shown at the Nuremberg Trials included films of concentration camps as they were being liberated and official documents. This helped to convict twelve who were sentenced to death and seven who were sentenced to life imprisonment. The remaining three were acquitted.

Although the Nuremberg Trials were completed in about one year, trials of hundreds of other war criminals continued for many years in postwar Germany. This group included high-ranking officers, camp guards, minor officials, and doctors who had participated in medical experiments. The Allies, too, continued to pursue a policy of removing former Nazis from all positions of authority in areas such as government, industry, and education.

While some criticized the Nuremberg Trials, others defended them. It is true that the trials were unprecedented because leaders of a defeated nation had never before been punished. But the laws by which the special court acted did exist in various international treaties. It was further hoped that the trials would help preserve peace and lead to new international laws.

In 1948 the UN adopted a convention against further genocide. Overall, the Nuremberg Trials were a final justice for years of suffering, millions of deaths, and countless acts of inhumanity.

Research Topics

Choose a topic from the following list. Research the subject and write a short report to share with the rest of the class.

1. the trial of Adolf Eichmann, a former Nazi official
2. denazification courts of postwar Germany
3. world cases of genocide since World War II
4. Nazi war criminals who escaped and remained at large
5. the Nuremberg Trials—were they fair?

Two Germanys

Intended as a temporary measure, the partition and occupation of Germany which followed World War II led to the establishment of two separate countries, East Germany and West Germany. The reunification of Germany pledged by the Allies finally took place forty-four years later, in 1989. Read about the two Germanys below.

In February of 1945 Churchill, Stalin, and Roosevelt, sometimes called "The Big Three" met at Yalta to coordinate the final military assault on Germany and to plan for the occupation that would follow. They knew that to prevent future wars, Germany must be demilitarized and de-Nazified. Until free democratic elections could be held, the victorious Allies would govern the country. Germany was divided into zones for this occupation. Each Ally, including France, which was not represented at Yalta, would be responsible for a zone.

The partition and occupation were intended as temporary measures, and in February of 1948 Britain, France and the United States agreed to reunite the zones they occupied and establish a constitutional democracy. In May of 1948 these zones became the German Federal Republic, or West Germany, with Bonn as its capital. The new Federal Republic established alliances with the United States and other western countries. Later, in June 1949, the Russian occupied zone became the German Democratic Republic, governed by the Communist party and supported by the Soviet Union.

Although Germany's historic capital, Berlin, was entirely within the Russian occupation zone, the four powers divided it into four zones during the occupation, and it was governed by a committee. When Stalin learned of the reunification of the American, British, and French territories, he ordered a blockade of West Berlin. Beginning on March 31, 1948, the Russians denied the Western Allies land access to the city. Stalin hoped that starvation would force the citizens of the Western occupation zone to accept his government, bringing to an end the joint occupation of the city. The United States and Great Britain responded by initiating the Berlin Airlift, sometimes called "Operation Vittles." Beginning on June 26, 1948, planes delivered up to 2,500 tons of food, fuel, and supplies a day to Berlin. Planes flew around the clock, and during the peak daylight hours, planes landed at the rate of one per minute. The blockade ended in June 1949, but the airlift continued until September 30. In 15 months two million tons of food valued at 224 million dollars had been delivered, and West Berlin remained free. Like Germany itself, Berlin was reunified in 1989.

Suggested Activities

Maps Under the Yalta plans, U. S. and British forces moved into Germany from the West, while Russian troops came from the East. The Western forces stopped at the Elbe River, and the Russians met them there, after securing Berlin. On a map of Germany, have students locate Berlin and the Elbe River. If a pre-1990 map is available, compare the two Germanys to the current European map.

Quotation In the spring of 1945 Stalin told Marshall Tito of Yugoslavia, "This war is unlike all past wars. Whoever occupies a territory imposes his own social system. Everyone imposes his system as far as his army can advance." Discuss this quotation with the class. Ask the students to explain how it does or does not apply to the partition and reunification of Germany. Do they think it was true for Stalin? Did the other Allies hold the same view? Is it true today?

Passages

Births

1940
- soccer great Pele
- professional golfer Jack Nicklaus
- race car driver Mario Andretti

1941
- African American politician Jesse Jackson
- Olympic track star Wilma Rudolph

1942
- boxing legend Muhammed Ali
- singer Aretha Franklin
- singer/actress Barbra Streisand

1943
- tennis great Arthur Ashe

1944
- Pulitzer prize winning author Alice Walker

1945
- violinist Itzhak Perlman

1946
- baseball star Reggie Jackson
- the 42nd president of the U.S., William Jefferson Clinton

1947
- baseball great Johnny Bench
- movie director Steven Spielberg

1948
- Prince Charles, Prince of Wales
- playwright and composer Andrew Lloyd Weber
- operatic tenor José Carreras

Deaths

1940
- F. Scott Fitzgerald, a leading spokesman for the Jazz Age and a symbol of Roaring Twenties life, he wrote *The Great Gatsby.*

1941
- Baseball great Lou Gehrig, known as "Iron Man," he played for the New York Yankees and died of a rare muscle-wasting disease that now bears his name.
- Frederick Banting, discovered insulin
- Ernest Just, biologist who studied the human fertilization process

1942
- Actress Carole Lombard, wife of popular film star Clark Gable, on a return flight from a war bonds rally

1943
- Scientist George Washington Carver, who discovered numerous uses for the peanut
- Stephen Vincent Benét, poet, novelist, and short story writer noted for *The Devil and Daniel Webster.*

1944
- Glenn Miller, big band orchestra leader, died in a plane crash while touring troop bases in World War II.

1945
- American humorist and writer Robert Benchley
- General George S. Patton was killed in an auto accident. During World War II he spearheaded the Allied drive through France and into Germany.

1946
- Artist Joseph Stella, who was the best-known of the futurist painters. He painted pictures of bridges, skyscrapers, and subways.

1947
- Inventor Henry Ford, whose Ford Motor Company had introduced the Model T in 1908.

1948
- Aircraft pioneer Orville Wright who, with his brother Wilbur, flew the first heavier-than-air machine on December 17, 1903, near Kitty Hawk, North Carolina
- Baseball giant Babe Ruth was the first sports superstar, he was a memorable 1920s figure. In 12 different years he led the American League in home runs.

Forties Facts and Figures

1940

Population	140,000,000 (1946)
National Debt	$64.3 billion (1941); $280 billion (1946)
President's Salary	$100,000 in 1949
Airmail Postage	$.08 cents
Movies	*Hamlet* (1940), *Fantasia* (1940), *Citizen Kane* (1941), *The Best Years of Our Lives* (1941), *Lassie Come Home* (1942), *Bambi* (1942), *Casablanca* (1943), *Going My Way* (1944), *The Lost Weekend* (1945), *Song of the South* (1946)
Movie Stars	Humphrey Bogart, Lauren Bacall, Frank Sinatra, Bette Davis, Spencer Tracy, Katharine Hepburn, James Stewart, Judy Garland, Bing Crosby, Dorothy Lamour, Jane Wyman, Jane Russell, Carmen Miranda, Fred Astaire, Gene Kelly, Betty Grable, Rita Hayworth, Mickey Rooney
Songs	"Boogie Woogie Bugle Boy" by the Andrew Sisters, "I'm Dreaming of a White Christmas" by Bing Crosby, "Chattanooga Choo-Choo" (1941), "Zip-A-Dee-Dooh-Dah" (1946), "You Are My Sunshine," "Praise the Lord and Pass the Ammunition," "Sentimental Journey," "Mule Train," "Mona Lisa" sung by Nat King Cole
Books	*Red Cross First Aid Manual*, *Native Son* by Richard Wright, *Curious George* books by H. A. and Margaret Rey, *For Whom the Bell Tolls* by Ernest Hemingway, *The Iceman Cometh* by Eugene O'Neill, *The Naked and the Dead* by Norman Mailer
Radio Programs	*Jack Armstrong, the All-American Boy; Dick Tracy*
Fashions for Men	cropped haircuts, Zoot suits
Fashions for Women	bobbysocks and saddle shoes, short hemlines, long hair, hair piled and pinned on top of head, utility dresses, one-piece coveralls
Comic and Cartoon Characters	Superman, Batman, Captain America
Crazes	blue jeans, the jitterbug, nickel jukeboxes, drive-in movies
Games	the card game Canasta
Toys	jump ropes, rubber balls, metal toys, Slinky, Silly Putty, talking dolls (cost: $5.95)

Famous Firsts

As with every decade, the forties ushered in a number of firsts. Some of these American firsts are listed by year below.

1940
- Penicillin was used to help cure diseases.
- Morton Salt was introduced.
- The first synthetic rubber tires were manufactured.
- Synthetic tooth fillings were developed.
- Tiffany's in New York City was the first fully air-conditioned store.
- The first commercial flights with pressurized cabins were inaugurated.
- The Jeep made its debut on November 11, 1940.
- M&Ms® were manufactured for the U.S. Army.

1941
- The first Superman movie, an animated cartoon, debuted.
- The first disposable aerosol cans were developed by Lyle Goodhue and W. N. Sullivan.

1942
- The first all-star bowling tournament was held.
- The first successful turbo-prop engine was developed.

1943
- The Slinky® was invented but not sold commercially until 1947.

1944
- Harvard University mathematician Howard Aiken built the Mark I computer. The 35-ton machine was capable of finding the product of two 11-digit numbers in just three seconds.

1945
- The first atomic bomb was tested in the New Mexican desert near Alamogordo. The team of scientists was headed by Robert Oppenheimer.
- Grand Rapids, Michigan began fluoridation of its water supply. It had been discovered that small amounts of fluoride could dramatically reduce tooth decay.

1946
- ENIAC (Electronic Numerical Integrator and Computer) was the first eletronic digital computer. Built by Presper Eckert and John W. Mauchly, it filled a 30' x 60' room.
- The first electric blanket was manufactured.

1947
- Elmer's Glue-All was introduced.
- Engineer and inventor Buckminster Fuller built his first geodesic dome. Its unique design encloses the most space, using a given amount of material.

1948
- The first long-playing (LP) phonograph record was introduced by Columbia Records. It held six times as much music as previous records and helped create the modern recording industry.
- Bell Laboratories' physicists invented the transistor. Smaller, cheaper, and faster than a vacuum tube, it revolutionized the field of electronics.
- Edwin Land invented the Polaroid Land® camera. It was the first camera to produce finished prints "instantly" - in this case, 60 seconds. It sold for $89.75.
- Holography was invented by Dennis Gabor. The technique created three-dimensional images.

1949
- Silly Putty® was invented.
- Physicist Harold Lyons built the first atomic clock. Built for the National Bureau of Standards, the clock was accurate to within a few seconds over fifty years.

Writing Prompts and Literature Ideas

Writing Prompts Use these suggestions for journal writing or as daily writing exercises. Some research or discussion may be appropriate before assigning a particular topic.

- Gene Kelly and Fred Astaire were popular dancers and actors in 1940s films. Gene Kelly performed with huge athletic strides while dressed in polo shirts, khaki pants, and white socks. Fred Astaire was known for his nimble and elegant footwork while dressed in a tuxedo and top hat. If you could be either one, which would you choose and why?

- Although both were first ladies, Eleanor Roosevelt and Bess Truman played their roles differently. Eleanor was constantly in the public eye and enthusiastically supported her husband's policies. Bess preferred to remain private and quietly confer with her husband about political issues. If you were first lady, which of these two would you emulate and why?

- You are with Gandhi during one of his fasts. He is becoming weaker and weaker, yet he stands his ground. Most of his time is spent in prayer. How do you feel about his peaceful nonresistance?

- Racial segregation was a fact in the 1940s. Does such segregation exist today?

- James Michener based his writings on his Navy experience in the South Pacific. His book *Tales of the South Pacific* inspired a musical. Richard Wright also wrote during this time of his experiences. His stories told of racial prejudice. *Native Son* is about a victimized African American in Chicago. If you were to write a war novel, what types of experiences would you rather write about, those in combat or those on the home front?

Literature Ideas The following books can be used to supplement and enhance the study of the 1940s.

- *Hiroshima* by Laurence Yep (Scholastic Inc., 1995)
  This novella offers a firsthand account of what it might have been like to have experienced an atomic bomb attack. Based on the compiled stories of many people, the main characters Sachi and Riko are believable children.

- *Sadako and the Thousand Paper Cranes* by Eleanor Coerr (G.P. Putnam's Sons, 1977)
  This is another account of the bomb and its aftermath, leaving a poignant message for peace.

- *The Big Lie: A True Story* by Isabella Leitner (Scholastic Inc., 1992)
  In this moving account, the author tells how her family was uprooted from their home in Kisvarda, Hungary, and taken as prisoners during the time of the Holocaust. How the author manages to survive is a tribute to her spirit and determination.

- *Farewell to Manzanar* by Jeanne Wakatsuki Houston and James D. Houston (Bantam Books, 1973)
  This is the moving, true account of a Japanese American family's internment during World War II, one of the greatest tragedies in American history.

Fifties Overview

- After World War II Korea was divided in two along the 38th parallel. The country was supposed to be reunited after free elections, but the communists, who controlled the North, would not allow the elections to take place. On June 25, 1950, Kim Il Sung directed his North Korean forces to cross into South Korea. President Truman, who was determined to keep communism from expanding into other regions, had the United States lead the United Nations-directed response. Fighting was not easy in Korea and over 33,000 American lives were lost before the war ended in 1953.

- Elsewhere, the Cold War continued, with the United States pledging support to its former Allies. The Soviet Union entered alliances with China and Eastern European countries.

- The nuclear arms race, which began in late 1949 when the Soviets successfully tested an atomic bomb, also continued. The U.S. exploded the first hydrogen bomb, 500 times more powerful than the previous atomic bombs, in 1952. In less than a year the Soviets tested a similar weapon. The threat of these technologies added to the Cold War tension between the U.S. and the Soviets. In America, public and private bomb shelters were built.

- Concerned by the spread of communism in Europe and Asia, some feared it would take over the world and worried about communist subversion in the United States. Senator Joseph McCarthy led the "Red Scare," accusing hundreds of innocent people and ruining their lives. Finally he was condemned by his fellow senators and he quickly lost favor.

- The Supreme Court ruled in 1954 against segregation by race in public schools. In 1955 Rosa Parks's refusal to give up her seat on the bus for a white person sparked the Montgomery bus boycott. The boycott ended a year later with the Supreme Court decision that segregation on buses was unconstitutional. In 1957 in Little Rock, Arkansas, National Guard troops attempted to block the admission of nine black students to a previously all-white school, Central High School. The Guard was removed by an order from the Supreme Court, and 1,000 army paratroopers escorted the students to their high school. The fight for civil rights continued throughout this and the next decades.

- In 1957 the Russians launched the first artificial satellite, *Sputnik I*. American scientists scrambled to compete in the space race.

- Teen idols like James Dean and Marlon Brando were featured in films. Bill Haley's "Rock Around the Clock" heralded a new era in popular music—rock and roll. Buddy Holly, Little Richard, and Jerry Lee Lewis were popular with teens, but Elvis Presley soon eclipsed all of them.

- Television came into more and more homes during the fifties, changing the traditional lifestyle and family structure. People ate TV dinners while perched around the television. New programs depicted ideal family images. Real events could be seen almost as soon as they happened.

- Women were encouraged to stay at home and to take care of their families. Many lived in the suburbs where all the houses were the same.

For Discussion

1. What effect did the space race have on education in U.S. public schools?

2. What were Elvis Presley's contributions to American music?

3. How did television impact the American family?

1950s Legislation

Some important Supreme Court decisions and a number of important pieces of legislation were ratified in the fifties. An outline of some of these measures is provided below.

McCarran Act On September 9, 1950, Congress passed the Internal Security Act sponsored by Senator Patrick McCarran of Nevada. It allowed the government to maintain close control over all communists and their activities in this country. The bill supported Senator Joseph McCarthy's anticommunist campaign.

22nd Amendment This Constitutional Amendment was ratified in 1951 and prohibited the President from serving more than two terms.

Brown v. Board of Education On May 17, 1954, the Supreme Court handed down its decision in Brown v. the Board of Education of Topeka. The law on which the South had maintained its segregated school system was struck down. The court determined that the doctrine of separate but equal was unconstitutional. States were ordered to integrate their schools, but many tried every way they could to block the ruling. In 1957 President Eisenhower ordered a U.S. Army unit to Little Rock to escort black students to Central High School.

Federal Highway Act This 1956 legislation provided billions of dollars to construct a modern interstate highway system. As more and more people began driving to work and the production of cars increased, it was necessary to build an up-to-date network of roads.

Segregation on Buses In December of 1956, the Supreme Court handed down their ruling about segregation on buses. Following Rosa Parks's 1955 arrest, Martin Luther King, Jr., led a boycott of Montgomery buses. For thirteen months they continued the boycott until the Supreme Court ruled that segregation on Alabama buses was unconstitutional.

Civil Rights Act of 1957 The 1957 civil rights bill was passed on August 30 of that year. Although it provided for equal rights for African Americans, it was a weak measure. Senator Strom Thurmond filibustered for 24 hours to hold up its passage. He predicted that the South would strongly resist its provisions.

National Defense Education Act The Russian-launched *Sputnik I* on October 4, 1957, caused some panic in the U.S. Worried that American scientists were falling dangerously behind the Soviet Union in missile technology, Congress funded $887 million dollars to improve science education in both high schools and colleges. This bill was passed on August 23, 1958.

Suggested Activities

Numbered Highways Investigate how U.S. highways are numbered. Provide each group of students with a road atlas of the U.S. See if they can determine any strategy to the numbering of highways. For a more complete explanation of the system, see *The Handy Science Answer Book* published by Visible Ink Press, 1994.

Impact With the class discuss the impact on society today of the above-named legislative acts and Supreme Court decisions.

Land of the Midnight Sun

In 1867 William Seward purchased Alaska for the United States, but the territory did not become a state until January 3, 1959. Below, the map on this page you will find more facts about the 49th state. Notice that some important information is missing. Research the names of the places and label the map at the corresponding numbers.

9.

2.   3.

10.   5.

7.

4.

6.   1.

11.

8.

Alaska is the largest of the 50 states. Two important cities are (1)_____ its capital, and (2)_____ the northernmost point in the United States. From (3)_____ to (4)_____ the Alaska pipeline extends 800 miles north to south. The (5)_____ River runs from east to west, almost through the center of the state's vast expanse. It crosses the (6)_____ mountains which are home to (7)_____ the tallest peak in all of North America. A chain of islands, the (8)_____ Islands, extend west from Alaska toward Russia. In all, Alaska's coastline exceeds that of all the other states combined with the (9)_____ Ocean to the north, (10)_____ Sea to the west, and the (11)_____ Ocean to the south.

Challenge: Write a report about the great state of Alaska. Include these topics: its capital, area, and population; state motto, bird, flower, tree, and song; important physical features; industry and economy; culture; geography of the state; history of the area.

Aloha!

Like Alaska, Hawaii is not connected to the rest of the United States. Instead, it is a group of islands located in the Pacific Ocean southwest of the U.S. mainland. Once an independent kingdom, on August 21, 1959, Hawaii became the fiftieth state. To learn more about the islands that compose Hawaii, label the eight islands pictured below. Then research and write the correct islands for the following clues.

1. _____ Honolulu, the capital city of Hawaii, is located here. It is also home to the Pearl Harbor Memorial. Eighty percent of all Hawaiians live on this island.

2. _____ Years ago Father Damien established a leper colony here. It is called the Friendly Island and contains a dry plateau, as well as rugged mountains and dry canyons.

3. _____ The largest island, it is home to the Kilauea volcano.

4. _____ Of the eight main Hawaiian islands, it was formed first. Mount Waialeale on this island is the rainiest spot in the world. It is called the Garden Island and is almost circular in shape.

5. _____ Often called the Valley Island, many canyons cut through its two volcanic mountains. Haleakala, a massive dormant volcano, can be found here.

6. _____ The smallest of the eight main islands, it has no permanent inhabitants. Until 1993, it was used by the Navy as a bombing range.

7. _____ Known as the Pineapple Island, it is owned by the Dole Company.

8. _____ This island, known as the Forbidden Island, is privately owned and is home to a huge cattle ranch.

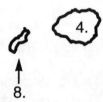

Answers (cover before copying)

1. Oahu 2. Molokai 3. Hawaii 4. Kauai 5. Maui 6. Kahoolawe 7. Lanai 8. Niihau

The Rosenbergs and McCarthy

When Americans learned that the Russians had exploded an atomic bomb in September of 1949, the news sent shock waves throughout the nation. Now that another country had the A-bomb, American security was gravely threatened. Millions of Americans worried about protecting themselves and installed bomb shelters in their backyards. Students in school were regularly drilled on what to do in case of a nuclear attack.

Ethel and Julius Rosenberg

The question next turned to how the Russians had obtained the information to build an atomic bomb. Many Americans believed that Russia did not have the capability of producing such a weapon themselves and assumed that Russia somehow must have learned U.S. secrets. A wave of hysteria was touched off when Dr. Klaus Fuchs, a British physicist, confessed to giving atomic bomb secrets to the Soviet Union. Alger Hiss, a high-ranking official in the State Department, was accused of passing important secrets to communist spies. These cases set the stage for the most sensational spy case of the century. In 1951 Julius and Ethel Rosenberg were charged with treason for plotting to arrange for the transfer of atomic secrets to the Soviet Union during World War II. Ethel's brother, David Greenglass, had been spying for the Soviets, and he named the couple as leaders of his spy ring. Even though the charges were never proven, the Rosenbergs were prosecuted and sentenced to death.

Joseph McCarthy

After the trial the Justice Department began taking drastic measures to protect the U.S. against communist subversion. Loyalty oaths were required for jobs that had nothing to do with national security, and President Truman authorized investigations into the backgrounds of all federal employees. Senator Joseph McCarthy of Wisconsin, a little-known Republican senator, led the Red Scare that was to sweep the country by announcing that he had a list of people working for the State Department who were members of the Communist party. Although he never produced this list of communists, he continued to make even more irresponsible accusations. In the process he destroyed the reputations of many innocent persons, including hundreds of film directors and actors who were blacklisted because of these accusations. Even members of his own staff came under attack. McCarthy met his match, however, when he tackled the U.S. Army. As a result of those hearings, the Senate voted to condemn Senator McCarthy for his abusive actions. His influence quickly declined, but the term "McCarthyism" came to be synonymous with the character assassination that he carried out.

Suggested Activities

Research Have the students research the facts of the Rosenberg trial and find out the evidence against them. Was it enough to convict them, and did the punishment fit the supposed crime?

Witch Hunts With the class discuss some other witch hunts that have been carried out in American history (Salem witch hunts, Red Scare of the 1920s).

Literature Arthur Miller wrote his classic play *The Crucible* in the shadow of McCarthyism. Read the play and discuss its historic, as well as its modern, significance.

A History of the Korean War

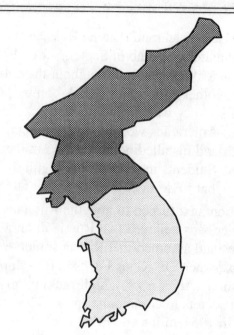

On this page you will find a brief overview of the Korean War. Expand your knowledge of the events preceding and following the war by exploring further any of the research topics at the bottom of the page.

Background Times were prosperous after world War II, yet there was a lingering hint of fear in the air. Many people believed the United States was filled with communists. Indeed, some communist spies were discovered here, the Rosenberg case being the most infamous example. (See page 269 for more about this couple.) There was also the question of the atomic bomb. The U.S. discovered it was no longer alone in this area when Russia tested an atomic bomb soon after the war. China was another threat. Before World War II a civil war had broken out in that country with two groups fighting for control. During World War II they joined forces to fight their common enemy, Japan, but once the war ended they went back to fighting each other, with the communists eventually winning.

War Events At the end of World War II, Korea was divided in two at latitude 38 degrees north (also known as the 38th parallel) with the intention of bringing the two together. Promised free elections were never allowed, and in 1950 Kim Il Sung, the leader of North Korea, sent his powerful army into South Korea. The United Nations responded quickly, imposing military sanctions. The U.S. and 19 other nations committed troops to this "police action." Despite initial heavy losses, the combined UN forces finally began to win. Then the situation changed when General Douglas MacArthur, the commander of UN troops in Korea, disobeyed orders to stay in South Korea. Going beyond the 38th parallel into North Korea brought communist China's well-trained and well-equipped army into the war. When the fighting finally ended in 1953, no one was truly victorious. The 38th parallel dividing line remained intact.

Home Front Back on the home front, the American people worried that communism would take over the United States and dominate the world. Senator Joseph McCarthy spearheaded a communist hunt fueled by these fears throughout the U.S. His television appearances infected the nation with an anti-communist hysteria that ruined numerous lives from politicians to actors and writers. For more on McCarthy read page 269.

Research Topics

Choose one of the following topics to research further. Share your findings with a partner. Explain what the UN and U.S. proved by waging the Korean War.

- Tell how the war might have been different if MacArthur had not invaded North Korea.
- Describe President Truman's policy of containment.
- Detail how the Korean War led to the failure of Democrats to win the 1952 election.

Chronology of the Korean War

Make a transparency of this page for use with the overhead projector. With the class discuss the progression of the Korean War. Have students find the boldfaced locations on a map of Korea. Let the students choose a topic from the chronology to study in depth and have them prepare a short report on their chosen topic.

1950

June 25	**North Korea** invades South Korea.
June 27	UN Security Council asks members to assist **South Korea**.
June 30	Truman orders U.S. ground troops to South Korea.
July 7	General Douglas MacArthur is appointed head of UN command.
Sept. 15	Allied troops stage **Inchon** landing behind enemy lines.
Sept. 26	General MacArthur announces the capture of **Seoul**.
Oct. 7	U.S. troops cross the **38th parallel**.
Oct. 14	**China** moves south into North Korea.
Oct. 19	Allies capture **Pyongyang**.
Oct. 27	Chinese soldiers attack UN troops.
Nov. 26	Allied troops retreat.

1951

Jan. 4	Communist troops occupy Seoul.
Jan. 11	UN proposes a cease-fire agreement.
Jan. 17	Proposal is rejected by Chinese.
Feb. 1	UN declares China to be an aggressor state.
Mar. 14	Allied troops reoccupy Seoul.
Apr. 11	General MacArthur is fired by President Truman and replaced with General Ridgeway.
June 23	Soviets call for a cease-fire.
July 10	Armistice negotiations begin at **Kesong**.
Nov. 26	Demarcation line is established.

1952

May 7	Stalemate occurs in the peace talks over POW issues.
Oct. 8	Peace talks are broken off.

1953

Feb. 22	Proposal is made to exchange sick and wounded.
Apr. 20	Sick and wounded exchanged under Operation Little Switch.
Apr. 26	Armistice talks resume at **Panmunjom**.
July 27	Armistice agreement is signed; the fighting ends.
Aug. 5	Prisoners of war are exchanged under Operation Big Switch.

General Douglas MacArthur

During World War II he was the general in command of American forces in the Pacific, and during the Korean War he was appointed chief of the United Nations Command. General Douglas MacArthur was a controversial figure.

Douglas MacArthur was born on January 26, 1880, in Little Rock, Arkansas. His family had a long tradition of military service, and he was no exception, graduating from both the West Texas Military Academy and the United States Military Academy at West Point. In 1908 he graduated from an engineering school and five years later joined the general staff of the War Department.

His military career began during World War I when he was appointed chief of staff of the 42nd Infantry Division which was sent to France. After distinguishing himself in the war, he returned home to become superintendent of West Point. In 1930 President Hoover appointed him army chief of staff, and two years later he was involved in the unpopular eviction of the Bonus March protestors. Under President Franklin Roosevelt, MacArthur became military adviser to the Philippines and soon was in command of their army. But in 1941 he was forced to retreat when the Japanese invaded the Philippines. "I shall return," he vowed. He was later able to make good on his promise near the end of World War II.

After being appointed supreme commander of the Allied forces, MacArthur was a virtual dictator of Japan throughout the American occupation from 1945–1949. He arranged for food for the Japanese whose cities were in ruins and he rid the government of militarists. In addition, he arranged for free elections and civil liberties for Japanese citizens. When he left his command, Japan had evolved from a wartime military dictatorship to a postwar democracy.

MacArthur's next foray into battle was in 1950 as chief of the United Nations Command the Korean War. After a brilliant counterattack, the communists had been driven back into North Korea, close to the Chinese border. The Chinese, however, sent a huge force of soldiers to drive MacArthur back. From there, neither side made much progress. President Truman wanted to negotiate a peace treaty while MacArthur wanted to expand the war and publicly disagreed with the President. MacArthur was fired from his position. Nevertheless, he returned to the U.S. as a hero. Douglas MacArthur died on April 5, 1964.

Suggested Activities

Debate Have two groups of students debate the question of whether or not President Truman should have fired MacArthur.

Speculation With the class discuss what might have happened if MacArthur had been allowed to take on the Chinese in the Korean War. What would have been some possible outcomes?

Research Research the Inchon landing and find out why it is considered one of the most brilliant plans in warfare history.

Dwight D. Eisenhower

34th President, 1953–1961

Vice President: Richard M. Nixon
Born: October 14, 1890, in Denison, Texas
Died: March 28, 1969
Party: Republican
Parents: David Jacob Eisenhower, Ida Elizabeth Stover
First Lady: Mamie Geneva Doud
Children: Dwight, John
Nickname: Ike
Education: Graduate of West Point Academy

Famous Firsts:

- Eisenhower was the first president to have a putting green installed on the White House lawn.
- His 1956 election marked the first time since 1848 that a president had failed to carry at least one house of Congress for his party.
- He was the first president of all fifty states.
- Eisenhower was the first licensed pilot and the first five-star general elected to the office of president.

Achievements:

- Eisenhower made good on a campaign promise and ended the Korean War.
- In 1953 he appointed Earl Warren, considered to be a moderate, as the new chief justice. Warren led a revolution on the Court when he reversed a 1896 separate-but-equal doctrine.
- He went to Korea to revive the stalled peace talks.

Interesting Facts:

- When he was born, Eisenhower's given name was David Dwight. Later, he switched his first and middle names.
- His mother was a pacifist and cried when he decided to attend West Point.
- Eisenhower ranked 65th in his class of 165 at West Point.
- A professional soldier, he helped General MacArthur break up the Bonus March during the thirties.
- He was the only president to have served in both World Wars.
- During WW II, Eisenhower served as the Supreme Allied commander.
- When Eisenhower was first approached to run for president, he did not have a political party. The Democrats courted him in 1948, but his views were closer to Republican ideas.
- President Eisenhower's favorite sport was golf, and he could often be found on the White House lawn practicing chip shots.
- Eisenhower also enjoyed painting.
- An accomplished cook, vegetable soup and cornmeal pancakes were two of Eisenhower's best dishes.
- Eisenhower was the last president born in the nineteenth century.
- At the time, Eisenhower was the oldest man ever to be president.

(For information about Harry S. Truman, see page 229.)

Bess and Mamie

Bess Truman was more than happy to give up her role as first lady in 1953 and to turn the position over to Mamie Eisenhower. Both were gracious hostesses and both relished their privacy. Yet the two were very different in other respects. Find out more about these first ladies. Read each description below and then circle the correct first lady at the beginning of each phrase. Use history books, biographies, encyclopedias, and other reference materials to help you find the correct answers.

Bess Truman

Mamie Eisenhower

1. **Bess** **Mamie** moved 28 times as husband changed assignments
2. **Bess** **Mamie** husband was a career military man
3. **Bess** **Mamie** the longest-lived first lady in American history
4. **Bess** **Mamie** made few public appearances
5. **Bess** **Mamie** had one daughter, Margaret
6. **Bess** **Mamie** born in Boone, Iowa
7. **Bess** **Mamie** trademark color was pink
8. **Bess** **Mamie** was 60 years old when she became first lady
9. **Bess** **Mamie** liked to watch "As the World Turns" on TV
10. **Bess** **Mamie** husband referred to her as "the Boss" in public
11. **Bess** **Mamie** born in Independence, Missouri
12. **Bess** **Mamie** first met future husband in Sunday School
13. **Bess** **Mamie** loved to entertain and was a popular hostess

14. **Bess** **Mamie** born in November of 1896
15. **Bess** **Mamie** was frugal and practical like her husband
16. **Bess** **Mamie** met her future husband in San Antonio
17. **Bess** **Mamie** adopted no causes as first lady
18. **Bess** **Mamie** died in 1979
19. **Bess** **Mamie** moved to Blair House during White House renovation
20. **Bess** **Mamie** born in 1885
21. **Bess** **Mamie** had a son who died in infancy
22. **Bess** **Mamie** had a daughter who tried to launch a singing career
23. **Bess** **Mamie** distributed buttons as White House souvenirs
24. **Bess** **Mamie** was a late riser, she conducted business from her bed
25. **Bess** **Mamie** had a grandson who married a future president's daughter

Challenge: On the back of this paper, construct a Venn diagram to show the likenesses and differences between these two first ladies. Add two more facts to each category.

Election Facts and Figures

	Election of 1952	Election of 1956
Democrats	Adlai Stevenson, governor of Illinois and grandson of President Grover Cleveland's vice-president, was drafted by his party and agreed to run. Senator John Sparkman of Alabama, a liberal on most issues except civil rights, was chosen as the vice-presidential candidate.	Once again, Adlai Stevenson decided to run despite his failed bid four years earlier. This time, Senator Estes Kefauver from Tennessee became his running mate. Kefauver was known for his fight against government corruption.
Republicans	General Dwight D. Eisenhower, a popular U.S. figure, was the Republican candidate. Although Eisenhower had been approached by both political parties, he chose to run as a Republican. Anti-communist crusader Richard M. Nixon of California was his running mate.	(The Eisenhower-Nixon ticket was left intact.)
Slogans	The Republicans printed "I Like Ike" on buttons, nail files, makeup cases, stockings, and other women's items which were distributed throughout the campaign	
Issues	A strong national defense was at the core of the Republican platform. They felt that Eisenhower symbolized the strength of the military and criticized the Democratic policy of appeasement of communism. In their platform the Democrats called for more civil rights for blacks.	Eisenhower's health worried both Republicans and Democrats. He had suffered a moderate heart attack in 1955 and had intestinal surgery in 1956. However, the Democrats chose not to raise the health issues for fear of offending voters.
Winner	Eisenhower won the election with 33,936,234 popular votes. He earned 442 electoral votes to Stevenson's 89.	Eisenhower-Nixon won with almost 2 million more popular votes than they had received in the previous election. Once again, the House of Representatives and the Senate remained Democratic. This marked the first time since Zachary Taylor's election in 1848 that a president had been unable to carry at least one house of Congress for his party.

The TV Generation

Children born in the late 1940s were the first generation to grow up with television. The full impact of this phenomenon would not be seen for many years. On this page you will read about the beginnings of television.

History During the late 1940s some television programs debuted, but they reached relatively small audiences. In 1948, there were fewer than 17,000 TV sets in the whole United States. By the end of the 1950s Americans owned an estimated 50 million sets.

Criticisms Criticism of the new industry came quickly. Some called the TV an "idiot box" or the "boob tube," claiming that many programs had little value. Educators were concerned about the impact of TV on their students and worried that students might skip their homework to watch shows. The amount of violence and sex depicted in some programs was also worrisome to many.

Lifestyle Changes Almost overnight the lifestyles of millions of Americans changed as people stayed up later to watch shows. Some people stayed inside their homes more, leaving their houses infrequently. With the invention of the TV dinner in 1954, some families even began eating in front of the television set.

Impact One important impact of television was the business of TV commercials which brought in over 1.5 billion dollars in advertising money in the early 1950s. Another way television impacted America was in the coast-to-coast programs which allowed people to view firsthand historical events such as political conventions and presidential inaugurations.

A Scandal Quiz shows were popular during the 50s, but *Twenty-One* created the scandal of the decade. Players answered questions, and if they were correct they could choose to keep going. As the questions grew more and more difficult, the prize money grew larger. One contestant, college instructor Charles Van Doren, amassed $129,000 in prize money. In 1958, however, a Congressional investigation revealed that the show was fraudulent and had given questions to Van Doren and others in advance.

Suggested Activities

Movie View the 1995 movie *Quiz Show* for an indepth look at the quiz show scandal of the fifties.

Response Ask for students' responses to this question: What problems facing television viewers are the same today as they were in the 50s?

Debate Choose two groups to debate this question: Who should be responsible for censoring TV programming, individuals (parents) or the government?

Contrast Contrast the current criticisms of TV viewing with criticisms of TV viewing in the fifties.

Survey Have the students keep a survey of their own or their families' television viewing for one week. Tally and compare the results and discuss them in whole group.

The Billy Graham Crusades

He has been called the greatest evangelist of the 20th century. Since the 1940s he has brought the word of God to people all over the globe. His goals in life were to bring God's message to as many people as possible and to build peace and friendship among all peoples. Meet the man behind these lofty ideals: Reverend Billy Graham.

William Franklin Graham, later called Billy, was born on November 7, 1918, on a farm near Charlotte, North Carolina. As children, he and his brother helped their father with the chores on the farm. Every morning at three o'clock they were up to milk the cows, and after school there were more chores. It is no wonder, then, that Graham had trouble staying awake in class. A poor pupil, he consoled himself with the thought that he did not need to study because he was going to be a farmer. Trouble followed him into high school where he got into fights and skipped classes.

In his senior year, Graham's life changed when he heard evangelist Mordacai Ham speak. Deeply moved by the preacher's words, Graham dropped his wild ways and in the fall entered college. While attending the Florida Bible Institute in Tampa, Graham knew that God was calling him to preach. His thick accent stood in his way, however, so he practiced and practiced until he was taken seriously. In 1939 Graham became a Baptist and a minister.

After graduating from the Bible Institute, Reverend Billy Graham attended Wheaton College in Illinois where he met his future wife, Ruth Bell. Following a two-year courtship, the couple was married. Billy became a pastor and was asked to take over a radio program called *Songs in the Night*. The broadcast was such a hit with listeners that Billy was asked to try something else. The result was a Youth for Christ rally aimed at World War II servicemen. This movement quickly spread to other cities across the U.S. and even into Europe. In 1949 Billy Graham held a crusade in a tent in Los Angeles. Graham's fame grew, and he received invitations to preach all over the world.

During the fifties, Graham conducted crusades all across America, but it was not until 1958 that he returned to his hometown of Charlotte. He had previously refused to hold a crusade in which blacks and whites could not worship together. As he walked out into the crowd opening night, he saw more than 14,000 people, black and white, all waiting to hear his words. Billy Graham continued to bring his spiritual guidance to people well into the 1990s.

Suggested Activities

Discussion With the class discuss the sights and sounds of a crusade held in a tent. Ask students what they might expect to see and hear at one of Graham's crusades.

Presidents Have the students research Graham's relationship with Presidents Eisenhower and Nixon.

A Woman's Place

Say the name Margaret Chase Smith and at least one image comes to mind: a trademark single red rose pinned to her clothing. This former U.S. Representative and Senator left an indelible mark on American politics and proved that a woman's place is in the House . . . and in the Senate.

Margaret Chase was born in Skowhegan, Maine, on December 14, 1897. She grew up with her two sisters and one brother in a white frame house which stood next door to her father's barber shop.

After Chase graduated from high school in 1916, she taught school for a short time in a one-room schoolhouse. Through the years she worked at a variety of jobs until she married Clyde Smith, a local political and business leader, in May of 1930. When Clyde was elected to the U.S. House of Representatives in 1936, Margaret accompanied him to Washington, D.C. In addition to acting as his secretary, she helped write his speeches and conducted research on

Margaret Chase Smith

upcoming legislation. A heart attack kept Smith from running for re-election in 1940, and Margaret agreed to be a temporary candidate until her husband's health improved. Unfortunately, Clyde died after suffering another heart attack. Margaret was then chosen to serve out the remainder of his term.

An enthusiastic worker, Margaret accepted assignments to a variety of committees, always with an eye out for the interests of her home state and women's issues. When a seat in the Senate was being vacated in 1947, Margaret took a risk and went after that Senate seat. Her subsequent win caused quite a stir and gave her the distinction of being the first woman to have served in both the Senate and the House of Representatives.

For the most part, Margaret kept a low profile, but when another senator, Joseph McCarthy, began making unfounded accusations, she stood up to him. In her "Declaration of Conscience" speech she spoke out against McCarthy and warned against the use of the Senate as a forum for character assassination. McCarthy responded by ridiculing Smith and replacing her on an important Senate subcommittee.

After her third term, Senator Smith announced her candidacy for the Republican presidential nomination. Despite her excellent qualifications and a valiant effort, she lost to another Senator, Barry Goldwater of Arizona. Smith continued in the Senate until 1972. On July 6, 1989, she was honored with the Presidential Medal of Freedom, the nation's highest civilian honor.

Suggested Activities

Discussion With the class discuss the differences between Senators and Representatives: their qualifications, duties, and lengths of their terms.

Others Direct students to research and make a list of all the women who currently hold seats in Congress.

Resource An excellent resource for this page is *Women of the U.S. Congress* by Isobel V. Morin (The Oliver Press, Inc., 1994).

An Extraordinary Bus Ride

She has been called the mother of the civil rights movement, but Rosa McCauley Parks does not consider herself to be extraordinary. Born on February 4, 1915, in Tuskegee, Alabama, McCauley had a normal childhood. She grew up on a farm and attended an all-black school in her neighborhood. Her high school education was cut short by her mother's death, but she finished her schooling after her marriage to Raymond Parks. In 1943 she joined the NAACP (National Association for the Advancement of Colored People) and worked with the Voters' League, registering African Americans to vote. Then came the fateful day.

Rosa McCauley Parks

The bus ride on December 1, 1955, began as usual. After completing her job as a seamstress for a Montgomery department store, Parks boarded the bus to go home. As was required, she took a seat in the back of the bus. When all the seats filled up, Parks was asked to vacate hers for a white man who was just getting on the bus. (At that time in Montgomery the law required blacks to sit at the back of the bus and to give up their seats for white people when all other seats were filled.) On this day, however, Parks refused to move. The bus driver stopped the bus and called for policemen who whisked her away to jail. NAACP leader Edgar Daniel Nixon posted her bail and determined that Rosa Parks would be the last African American arrested for such an action.

Along with other black leaders, including Dr. Martin Luther King, Jr., Nixon declared a one-day boycott of all city buses. Leaflets announcing the boycott were distributed throughout the city, and on the appointed day the results were dramatic. Not one African American rode on any buses there. Because it was such a success, the boycott was extended indefinitely.

For their actions blacks were harassed on the street, hundreds of their leaders were arrested, and many lost their jobs. Still, the boycott continued with African Americans turning to alternative methods of transportation, including walking, carpooling, riding bicycles, and even riding mules. The boycott ended when, after 381 days, the U.S. Supreme Court ruled in favor of Rosa Parks and declared Alabama bus segregation laws unconstitutional. It had cost the bus company $750,000 in lost revenues, but the gains in human dignity were *priceless*.

Suggested Activity

Role-Play Group the students and have them write a script for a role-play about Rosa Park's historic bus ride. Let the groups take turns presenting their skits to the rest of the class. For a prepared play, see the book *Take a Walk in Their Shoes* by Glennette Tilley Turner (Puffin Books, 1989).

Making Schools Equal

There was a time in the United States when separate schools for blacks and whites were common, especially in the South, and perfectly legal. The case of Plessy v. Ferguson in 1896 had ruled that schools could be separate as long as they were equal. Unfortunately, the equal part was never realized and conditions in black schools were mostly deplorable. With the case of Brown v. the Board of Education of Topeka in 1953, the tide was finally turned in the right direction. Here is a look at the ruling and the events that led up to the case.

When Oliver Brown went to register his daughter Linda at their neighborhood school, he learned it was for whites only. Topeka, Kansas, where they resided, had city laws which set up separate schools for blacks and whites. Linda would have to walk six blocks through heavy traffic before reaching the bus stop where she would board the school bus for black students. Mr. Brown did not want his daughter subjected to these hazards, particularly when the neighborhood school was a safe seven block walk from their home. The decision was made to fight the Topeka Board of Education in court. Linda Brown was joined by dozens of other students as plaintiffs.

Thurgood Marshall, senior counsel of the NAACP Legal Defense Fund, directed the case. Much of their argument centered on the interpretation of the 14th Amendment. It was the NAACP's stand that the purpose of the Amendment was to put an end to segregation in the area of education. The nine Supreme Court justices heard the arguments, and on May 17, 1954, they announced their decision. In his opinion Chief Justice Earl Warren stated that separate but equal had no place in American education.

Once the decision had been handed down, the justices faced the task of determining how the ruling would be enforced. For a year the debate raged on until the Supreme Court declared that the states had control over how the order would go into effect. Many states dragged their feet and did little about integration until the Civil Rights Act of 1964 was passed.

One district in Little Rock, Arkansas, agreed to begin integration in 1957. The nine black students who tried to enter Central High School were greeted by National Guard troops who prevented them from going into the building. After three weeks, President Eisenhower ordered army paratroopers to escort the nine to school. Other states continued to stall efforts to enroll black students in white schools, and desegregation moved at a slow pace well into the 1960s.

——— Suggested Activities ———

Introduction Introduce this page by reading aloud and discussing *The Story of Ruby Bridges* by Robert Coles (Scholastic, Inc., 1995).

Resource For an in-depth look at this famous case, have the students read *Brown v. Board of Education* by Harvey Fireside and Sarah Betsy Fuller (Enslow Publishers, Inc., 1994).

Man of Many Firsts

The title "Man of Many Firsts" is an appropriate one for Ralph J. Bunche. On the personal side, he was the first member of his family to finish college. The first African American to earn an advanced degree in political science from Harvard University and the first black to win the Nobel peace prize, he proved to be an inspiration and role model for his race. Read on for more about this important politician.

Ralph J. Bunche was born on August 7, 1904, into a poor household which included his parents, aunts, uncle, and grandmother. It was a happy, loving family, and the young Bunche grew up believing in himself. When he was eleven years old, the family moved from Detroit, Michigan, to New Mexico. In school his favorite teacher was Miss Sweet because she taught about the different countries around the world. Bunche was eager to visit these places and to learn more about them.

Ralph J. Bunche

After his parents died, Bunche's grandmother moved the family to Los Angeles, California. The only African American in his class, he earned the highest grades and graduated from his high school with honors. With his outstanding academic record, he was easily admitted to UCLA. In addition to his studies, Bunche played basketball, baseball, and football for UCLA. Although he graduated with honors, a lack of money stood in the way of his dreams of attending Harvard Law School. Fortunately, a women's club in the area raised the money to help him pay for tuition. In 1928 he completed his studies in government and taught at Howard University in Washington, D.C. Two years later he married schoolteacher Ruth Harris. For two years Bunche studied the African people and subsequently earned a Ph.D. in political science.

During World War II Bunche was asked to work for the State Department, and he helped to found the United Nations. His first important negotiating job came during the 1948 war between the Arabs and Israelis. Much to his and the world's relief, a peace treaty was finally signed. In 1950 he was awarded the Nobel peace prize for his efforts in ending the war in the Holy Land. Ralph Bunche was the first African American to win this honor. For 25 years Bunche worked for the UN. Poor health forced him to leave in 1971, and only six months later, on December 7, 1971, he died. The world had lost an invaluable resource.

Suggested Activities

United Nations Define the United Nations and its peace-keeping role. How successful has it been in this respect in recent years?

Holy War Direct the students to find out the causes of the 1948 Holy War. Has a permanent peace been made there?

Peace Prize Ralph Bunche is in fine company with other Nobel prize winners. Tell the students to find out the names of others who won the coveted peace prize during the 1950s.

Discussion With the class discuss some of the adversities that Ralph Bunche faced during his school years and how he overcame them.

Revelations

On January 5, 1931, Alvin Ailey, Jr., was born to Alvin and Lula Elizabeth Ailey. The overcrowded household was already home to Alvin's parents, a grandfather, an aunt and uncle, and eight cousins. When Alvin Ailey was only six months old, his father left. To support her son, Lula Ailey worked at a number of odd jobs. In 1942 she found a high-paying job in an aircraft factory, and she and her son moved to California. It was a good move for young Ailey because he was exposed to concert dance for the first time. Not only did he attend a ballet with his high school class but he later saw performances of the Katherine Dunham Dance Company, an all-black dance troupe. Some years would pass, though, before Ailey would head his own dance troupe.

Alvin Ailey, Jr.

While Ailey attended college at UCLA, he also trained with the Lester Horton Dance Theater in Hollywood. When Horton died suddenly, Ailey took over for awhile as artistic director of the company. A turning point in his career came when he was asked to dance in the Broadway show *House of Flowers*. It featured a number of prominent African American dancers and was a success with its sensuous, energetic dances. Afterwards, Ailey decided to stay in New York City, where he continued to study dance and theater under prominent choreographers and acting teachers. Over the years he won a number of acting roles and some directing assignments.

In 1958 Ailey got his real start on what was to be a 30-year career when he directed and performed at the 92nd Street Y. Because government money was not available to the arts at that time, Ailey and his group constructed their own costumes from old curtains and other found items. Dancers carried their own costumes and props from rehearsal hall to rehearsal hall. It was time to found a permanent company. Glowing reviews of Ailey's dance routines, particularly one called Revelations, helped the group find a permanent residence in 1960.

In 1962 Alvin Ailey's American Dance Theater was chosen by President Kennedy to be part of an international cultural program. The group traveled abroad throughout Asia, Australia, South America, and Europe. Ailey continued to bring his unique dance style to audiences until his death on December 1, 1989.

Suggested Activities

Biography For more information about Alvin Ailey, Jr., read the biography *Alvin Ailey, Jr. A Life in Dance* by Julinda Lewis-Ferguson (Walker and Company, 1994).

Influences Katherine Dunham was influential in Alvin Ailey's career. Find out some facts about her life and write a one-page report.

Rebels and the Movies

Teenagers have a culture all their own. They dress differently than adults, listen to their own music, invent slang words to express themselves, and start new fads. Often, teenagers feel misunderstood by older generations and they rebel against authority figures (parents, teachers, the government). Ever since the 1950s, movies have tried to capture this teen rebellion. On this page you will find summaries to three important youth rebellion movies of the fifties.

The Wild One

This 1954 film is based on a true story and stars Marlon Brando and Lee Marvin. The plot centers around the conflict between the small town of Wrightsville and an outlaw biker gang called the Black Rebels. The bikers quickly disrupt the usual quiet of the town. Johnny, the leader of the gang, is drawn to Kathie, a bar owner's niece, and they become uneasy friends. When Johnny gets into trouble with the law, Kathie testifies on his behalf. He is released and rides out of town alone.

Marlon Brando

Activity Compare this film with the 1969 movie *Easy Rider* starring Jack Nicholson and Peter Fonda. Which is more believable or realistic?

The Blackboard Jungle

A 1955 film, *The Blackboard Jungle* stars Glenn Ford, Vic Morrow, and Sidney Poitier and shows the problems of racism and poverty in schools. The story is really about how these factors affect students and their attitude toward school. Teacher Richard Dadier (Ford) is just out of college. He wants to do something about the students' problems, but they resist and disrespect his efforts. Even the other teachers at the school laugh at Dadier for trying; they have already given up. But Dadier is a fighter, and despite some misunderstandings and physical confrontations with some students, he finally seems to be reaching his class by the end of the film.

Activity In 1967 Sidney Poitier starred as a teacher in working-class London in *To Sir With Love*. What issues were the same in both films? How else are the two films similar?

Rebel Without a Cause

This film was also released in 1955, but it shows that teens from nice homes can also be rebellious. Starring James Dean, Natalie Wood, and Sal Mineo, the story is about suburban teens who are having problems with their parents. James Dean's character has a hard time fitting in. The situation is made even more unbearable with his parents' constant fighting. Other characters have parents who are distant and unavailable for them. The movie is realistically portrayed and displays an acute understanding of teens.

Activity James Dean's performance in *Rebel Without a Cause* helped change the way teenagers were portrayed in films. Learn more about this legend, his other films, and how and when he died.

Reference

Youth Rebellion Movies by Marc Perlman (Lerner Publications Company, 1993).

Burns and Allen

One of the most popular series on television during the 1950s was the comedy program *The George Burns and Gracie Allen Show.* It starred real-life couple George Burns and Gracie Allen and ran from 1950 to 1958 when Allen retired. Although Gracie Allen died six years later, George Burns continued with his show business career almost until his 100th birthday. Read on for some more information about this beloved comedy duo.

George Burns was born Nathan Birnbaum in New York City on January 20, 1896. Gracie Allen was born in San Francisco on July 20, 1906. Together they became one of the finest husband-and-wife comedy acts in American show business. Burns' career started in vaudeville when he was only seven years old. In 1922 Burns was appearing as one half of a male comedy team when a friend introduced him to Gracie Ethel Cecile Rosalie Allen, a 17-year-old secretarial school student. She, too, had show business ties - she was just three when she first performed in her father's act. Burns persuaded Allen to join him in a new comedy act. It would be her job to feed him the straight lines and he would deliver the gags, but it did not stay that way for long. When Allen's character got most of the laughs, Burns quickly rewrote the act and made himself the straight man and Allen the comedian.

When Burns and Allen married in 1926, they had already made it to the Palace Theatre on Broadway, the biggest thing in vaudeville. Radio was becoming the new star machine, and Burns and Allen were just right for the nonvisual medium. For 18 years the couple had a program on the air, one of the most popular shows of its time. In 1950 a new opportunity came in the form of television. *The George Burns and Gracie Allen Show* featured an initial stand-up comedic segment with George Burns and characters who portrayed themselves.

In 1958 Allen announced her retirement; recurring heart problems made it too difficult for her to work. On August 27, 1964, she suffered a fatal heart attack.

The grief-stricken Burns went back to work playing clubs and making movies. At 79, his work in the film *The Sunshine Boys* won him an Academy Award for Best Supporting Actor. His biggest movie role, though, was as the Supreme Being in the film *Oh, God!* and its two sequels. Around this same time he began writing the first of his many books. George Burns died in 1996 at the age of 100. He had explored every medium available from vaudeville to television and had succeeded in all of them.

Suggested Activities

Comparisons Show an episode of *The George Burns and Gracie Allen Show* (available on video from Columbia Tri-Star Home Entertainment) to the students. Compare it to the popular nineties sitcom *Seinfeld.*

Vaudeville Have the students research vaudeville, what it was, where it started, some of its famous performers, and what became of it.

Althea Gibson

In the 1950s Althea Gibson gained worldwide fame for her athletic ability, but part of the fame can be attributed to her becoming the first African American to be admitted to the U.S. Lawn Association Championships at Forest Hills, New York, in August of 1950.

Gibson was born in Sumpter, South Carolina, but was raised in New York City where she played basketball, shuffleboard, and volleyball. Paddle tennis was another of her favorite sports, and she became so good that she won many local competitions. Her athleticism caught the eye of a local coach, Buddy Walker, who bought Gibson her first tennis racket and introduced her to the game of tennis. Harlem, where she lived, did not have many tennis courts, so Gibson had to practice on handball courts. Despite this disadvantage, Gibson became a good player and in 1950, at age 23, became the first African American to play in the U.S. Open. The following year she broke the race barrier again when she became the first African American to play at Wimbledon in England. Following several years of modest success and many disappointments, Gibson was ready to call it quits, but her coach encouraged her to make a foreign tour. She went on to win 18 tournaments. After winning the 1956 Wimbledon championship, she returned home to Harlem and was greeted with a ticker-tape parade. In 1957 Gibson won the women's singles title at the U.S. Open and the following year repeated her Wimbledon and U.S. Open wins.

Althea Gibson overcame the odds and worked hard to achieve her goals and win major titles. She became an inspiration to all women and paved the way for other African Americans to participate in the game. This former tennis queen was inducted into the National Lawn Tennis Hall of Fame in 1972.

Suggested Activities

Others With the class discuss some past and current professional African American tennis players including Arthur Ashe, Zina Garrison, MaliVai Washington, and Chanda Rubin. Learn more about them and how they advanced through the ranks.

Court Visit a nearby tennis court and identify the playing lines. Briefly discuss how the game is played and what the lines signify. You may want to invite the physical education specialist to lecture the class on this topic.

Terms Write some tennis terms on the board and have the groups define each one: *net, love, out, side out, advantage, wide, volley, serve.*

Observe Watch a tennis match with the class. Let them identify various tennis terms, court features, and rules of the game.

Comparisons Compare tennis with racquetball or some other racket sport. Make a Venn diagram to show how the two are alike and different.

Baseball Greats

Four of baseball's greatest hitters of the 1950s are highlighted on this page. Each of these players set and broke amazing records during their careers.

Hank Aaron

Mickey Mantle

Willie Mays

Joe DiMaggio

Hank Aaron

Henry L. "Hank" Aaron, an African American, was born on February 5, 1934, in Mobile, Alabama. At the age of 17 he signed up with a team in a Negro league and in 1954 was drafted by the major league Milwaukee Braves, which moved to Atlanta in 1966. Later in his career he returned to play for the Milwaulkee Brewers. His most memorable baseball moment came when he hit his 715th home run to surpass Babe Ruth's longstanding record. When Aaron retired in 1976 after 23 major league seasons, that home run total had reached 755.

Mickey Mantle

New York Yankee center fielder Mickey Mantle was one of the most-feared power hitters of the 1950s. He led the American League in home runs four times during his eighteen-year career, had ten seasons batting more than .300, four slugging titles, three Most Valuable Player awards, and a lifetime average of .353. He was probably the game's most powerful switch-hitter ever. Mantle was born on October 20, 1931, in Spavinaw, Oklahoma, and died in 1996 after a liver transplant operation.

Willie Mays

Born William Howard Mayes, Jr. on May 6, 1931, in Westfield, Alabama, African American Willie Mays began his professional baseball career with the New York Giants in 1951. Known as the "Say hey kid," this popular batter and centerfielder made the most famous catch in baseball history at the 1954 World Series with his back-to-the plate, over-the-shoulder grab of a 425-foot drive. The Giants moved to San Francisco for the 1958 season. Mayes, always a crowd favorite with New Yorkers, won over the San Francisco fans with his playing ability. Throughout his 22-year career he hit 660 home runs, ending third on the overall home run list just behind Hank Aaron and Babe Ruth.

Joe DiMaggio

Nicknamed "The Yankee Clipper," and "Joltin' Joe," Joe DiMaggio was born on November 25, 1914, in Martinez, California. As a centerfielder for the New York Yankees, he led his team to nine World Series titles. His trademark was his wide stance—the widest of anyone in basebal—which enabled him to earn a lifetime batting average of .325 and a slugging average of .579, making him number six on the all-time list. In 1941 he batted safely in 56 consecutive games. After several injuries, Joe retired in 1952 with 361 career home runs. He went on to marry movie star Marilyn Monroe and became a celebrity television spokesperson.

Suggested Activities

Terms Have students find out the difference between a hitting average and a slugging average. A complete explanation can be found in the book *Sluggers* by George Sullivan (Macmillan Publishing Company, 1991).

Statistics Group the students and have them make charts comparing statistics about the four players listed on this page. For example, chart the number of home runs, runs batted in, and triples.

The Mystery of DNA

If you have ever wondered why you have brown skin or curly hair you have only to look to your biological parents for answers. When you were conceived, cells from the male and female united to form a new organism. Within each of those cells are thin threads called chromosomes which are made up of DNA (deoxyribonucleic acid). Part of these cells are genes. It is the genes which tell your body how to develop. Genes carry coded information about the characteristics of the parents, like the size and shape of the nose, or whether a person is right or left-handed.

Although genes had been identified as early as the 1800s by Austrian monk Gregor Mendel, it was not known what the genes were composed of or how they worked. It was not until 1944 that scientists discovered that the DNA contained in the chromosomes carried the genetic message. During the 1950s a team of scientists, Watson and Crick, was able to build a model of the DNA molecule. Each molecule consists of millions of atoms arranged in a double helix (spiral shape) held together by cross pieces (see diagram). The order in which the atoms are arranged determines the code of genetic information which is then passed on to the next generation.

Today, scientists have developed a technique called *genetic fingerprinting,* which can be used to track criminals and study diseases. Also in the experimental stages is genetic engineering which will offer a method for altering the genes and thus changing the characteristics of an organism.

Suggested Activities

Activity On the lines below make a list of at least 30 physical and personality characteristics that are determined by genes. Be specific, i.e. foot size, shape of a mole, etc., rather than general: looks, personality.

_____   _____   _____

_____   _____   _____

_____   _____   _____

_____   _____   _____

_____   _____   _____

_____   _____   _____

_____   _____   _____

_____   _____   _____

Two Female Physicists

During the 1950s two female scientists carried on important work in the field of physics. Rosalyn Yalow and Chien-Shiung Wu were from very different backgrounds, yet both made great contributions to their respective fields. Here is a brief look at these women.

Rosalyn Yalow, Medical Physicist

Rosalyn Sussman was born on July 19, 1921, in the Bronx, New York, to poor, European immigrants. After graduating from Hunter College, she went on to study physics. In 1943 she married a colleague, Aaron Yalow, and later had two children. After teaching at Hunter College, Rosalyn Yalow was asked to join a team at the VA Hospital to explore how isotopes could be used in medicine. Along with her long-time lab partner, Solomon R. Berson, Yalow showed how radioactive iodine could be used to treat overactive thyroids and thyroid cancer. Together, they developed the RIA (radioimmunoassay) method which can detect small amounts of substances in the blood, including vitamins, poison in corpses, and drugs in human hair. RIA is also useful in the diagnosis of diabetes and some types of cancer. In 1977 Rosalyn Yalow won the Noble Prize for Medicine.

Rosalyn Yalow

Chien-Shiung Wu, Experimental Physicist

Chien Shiung Wu

In 1936 Chien-Shiung Wu left her native China to study physics in the United States. A brilliant student, Wu attended the University of California at Berkeley where she received her Ph.D. and became an expert on nuclear fission. After marrying in 1942, Wu and her husband, also a physicist, moved to New York City where she worked on the Manhattan Project to build the atomic bomb. Following that project, Wu worked with two doctors, Lee and Yang, who were collaborating on a theory to disprove the law of conservation of parity. Although Lee and Yang won the 1957 Nobel Prize for Physics for their work, Wu was not included. However, she received many other honors of her own including the first honorary doctorate awarded to a woman by Princeton University and the National Medal of Science.

━━━━ Suggested Activities ━━━━

Research Direct the students to research five more facts about these two scientists. A good resource is *Extraordinary Women Scientists* by Darlene R. Stille (Students Press Inc., 1995).

Discussion With the class discuss the function of the Manhattan Project and some of the other scientists involved, including the roles of Albert Einstein and Robert Oppenheimer.

Three Sputniks and Explorer I

For years scientists around the world had envisioned artificial satellites that could circle the earth. Their goals were to collect new information about the earth and our solar system and to transmit messages via satellite. Both the USSR and the United States played a key role in the development of these orbiting spacecrafts. Here is a look at the beginning of the satellite in world history.

On October 4, 1957, the Soviet Union launched *Sputnik I*, the world's first artificial satellite. A small metal ball, the aircraft weighed only 184 pounds and contained a radio transmitter that sent out a steady beep-beep to reveal its location. Barely one month later, on November 3, 1957, the Soviets launched a second satellite, *Sputnik II*, which weighed 1,120 pounds, almost six times as much as the original *Sputnik*. *Sputnik II* carried a dog named Laika, which was the first animal in space. The data that was collected on Laika's behavior during the launch and subsequent days in orbit was used to begin plans for a future manned spaceflight.

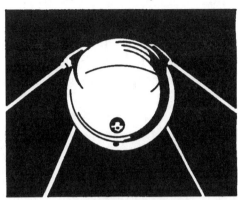

Sputnik I

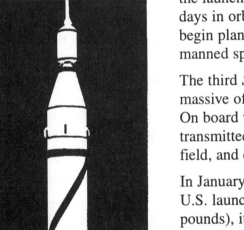

Explorer I

The third *Sputnik* was sent into orbit on May 15, 1958. The most massive of the three spacecrafts, *Sputnik III* weighed 2,926 pounds. On board was a geophysical laboratory which collected and transmitted information about solar radiation, the earth's magnetic field, and charged particles in the earth's atmosphere.

In January of 1958 between the launchings of *Sputniks II* and *III*, the U.S. launched *Explorer I*. Although it was extremely light (11 pounds), its scientific capabilities were greater than any of the *Sputniks*. *Explorer I* was equipped to measure atmospheric temperature, radiation levels, and cosmic ray intensities. One important result of this test was the discovery of the existence of radiation belts called Van Allen belts that surround the earth. With this launch, the U.S. space program was on its way.

Research Topics

This is not the end of the satellite story. Much of our daily information and communication is derived from satellites. Let the students choose a topic from below and write a short report about it.

- The Hubble Space Telescope and its exploration in space
- Antisatellites which are used by the military
- Van Allen belts and their function
- Communications satellites for television, radio, and telephone
- The use of satellites to predict weather conditions
- How satellites are launched and are able to stay up

New Technology for the Fifties

On this page you will find some interesting information about the scientific and technological advances made during the 1950s. As you research the decade, add to this list.

1950

The first kidney transplant surgery is performed.
Electricity is generated for the first time by nuclear fission, in Idaho Falls, Idaho.
The DC 6 passenger plane is developed.

1951

UNIVAC, the first commercial computer, is manufactured.
An underwater television camera is invented by Jacques Cousteau, French oceanographer.
The field ion microscope is invented; it can picture individual atoms.

1952

The first hydrogen fusion bomb (H-bomb) is tested by the U.S. in the Marshall Islands.
The maser is invented by American physicist Charles H. Townes.
Dr. Virginia Apgar introduces the Apgar Score which measures five crucial aspects in a newborn's health.
The Cinerama widescreen process is developed by Fred Waller.
The first 3-D movies are shown in theaters.

1953

On May 18 Jackie Cochran becomes the first woman to break the sound barrier.
The double helix structure of DNA is discovered by the British team of Crick and Watson.

1954

Dr. Jonas Salk develops a vaccine to guard against polio.
The first nuclear submarine, the *Nautilus,* is launched.
RCA markets the first color television.
Robert Moog invents an electronic instrument called a Moog synthesizer.

1955

The first frozen TV dinners are introduced.
The DC 7 passenger plane is developed.
Optical fiber is invented by Dr. Narinder Kapany of England.

1956

The first transatlantic phone cable is installed.
The first nuclear power plant is built.
Dr. Albert Sabin develops an oral polio vaccine.

1957

The Soviet Union launches *Sputnik*, the first artificial satellite.
The Boeing 707 passenger plane is developed.

1958

The first United States' satellite, *Explorer I*, is launched

Engineer Jack Kilby invents the first integrated circuit, or microchip.

Stereophonic recordings come into use.

Van Allen radiation belts around the earth are discovered.
Arthur Shanlow and Charles Townes patent the laser. The name is an acronym for light amplification by stimulated emission of radiation.

1959

The bathyscaphe Trieste descends seven miles into the Marianas Trench.
Anthropologist Mary Leakey discovers skull fragments from early ancestors of modern man in Africa.
The Soviet Union launches *Lunik 2* which makes a hard landing on the moon.

E. B. White

During the 1950s young children enjoyed the stories of such authors as Dr. Seuss, Robert McCloskey (*A Time of Wonder*), and Ludwig Bemelmans (*Madeline* books). Older children read books such as *Amos Fortune, Free Man* by Elizabeth Yates, *Carry On, Mr. Bowditch* by Jean Lee Latham, and *The Witch of Blackbird Pond* by Elizabeth George Speare. In addition to these fine authors, one other writer from the fifties era emerged as a children's favorite for generations to come: E. B. White, author of *Charlotte's Web*. Learn something about White by reading the following paragraphs and filling in the blanks with the correct words from the box below. Share your completed page with a partner.

Elwyn Brooks White, better known as E. B. White, was born on July 11, 1899, in 1._____, New York. The youngest of six children, he had a normal 2._____, yet he often felt lonely. In school he proved to be a good student and won two 3._____ to college. He chose to attend Cornell University where he worked on the *Cornell Daily Sun*, was elected 4._____ of the newspaper in his junior year, and became 5._____ of his fraternity. After graduation, White took a series of editing and 6._____ jobs, and eventually went to work part-time for the *New Yorker*. In 1929 his first two books were 7._____ and he married fellow worker Katherine Angell.

Not until 1939 did E. B. White begin writing his first 8._____ book, *Stuart Little*. It would be six more years, however, before it was published. This novel was followed in 1952 by his well-known work, 9._____. White's third children's book, *Trumpet of the Swans*, was written in 1969.

In between children's stories, White kept busy writing books for 10._____ including a 11._____ for writers, *The Elements of Style*. During his lifetime he was personally honored with the Presidential Medal of 12._____. Numerous 13._____ were also given to him for his writing, the most prestigious of which was the 14._____ Honor Award for *Charlotte's Web*. E. B. White who died of Alzheimer's 15._____ on October 1, 1985, has remained a perennial children's favorite author.

president	Freedom	Mount Vernon	children's	editor in chief
awards	guidebook	*Charlotte's Web*	published	scholarships
childhood	Newbery	writing	disease	adults

The Beat Movement

Although life was good for most people during the fifties, not everyone was content. Some people, particularly American writers and artists, participated in what became known as the Beat Movement. Concentrated mostly in Greenwich Village in New York, San Francisco, and Los Angeles, the Beats were rebellious at heart and had a contempt for conformity. Members of the Beat generation questioned the values of their elders, mainly through their words. They would gather at coffee houses and recite original poems about their social disillusionment. Their literature celebrated freedom and spontaneity and was influenced by jazz, drugs, and Asian religions. At the forefront of this movement was Jack Kerouac who provided the voice for the Beat Generation.

Jack Kerouac

Jean Louis Kerouac, later known simply as Jack Kerouac, was born on March 12, 1922, in Lowell, Massachusetts. After high school he studied briefly at Columbia University and served for a while in the merchant marines. Following those experiences he worked at odd jobs and traveled extensively throughout the United States. It was his travels and his accounts of his adventures that would bring him fame.

Jack wrote of his journeys in a highly personal style, one that employed spontaneous and unconventional prose. In his best-known novel, *On the Road*, he described his life of freedom from conventional middle-class ties and values. Through his characters Kerouac explored the enjoyment of nature and the senses and the freedom from responsibility. Although they have no particular place to go, the characters travel for the adventure and the pleasure of change.

Kerouac's writing contributed to his position as the leading spokesperson of the Beat Generation, and he became the epitome of the Beat lifestyle. Following his success with *On the Road*, Kerouac wrote a series of similarly structured novels. His last book, *Big Sur*, was written in 1962. Jack Kerouac died on October 21, 1969, in St. Petersburg, Florida.

Suggested Activities

Others Allen Ginsberg and Lawrence Ferlinghetti were two other Beat writers of the fifties. Have students find out five facts about each of these authors.

Forerunners Tell students that the Beat movement also advocated peace and civil rights. Discuss with students how their values set the stage for the radical protests of the 1960s.

Compare Compare and contrast the writers of the Beat movement with mainstream fifties writers such as J. D. Salinger, James Baldwin, and James Michener.

Jasper Johns

Abstract Expressionism was an art form that debuted in the late 1940s and continued into the early fifties. Pioneered by such artists as Hans Hoffman and Jackson Pollock, Abstract Expressionist works were noted for their lack of recognizable images. During the 1950s Jasper Johns began to break away from this type of art and forged the way into Pop Art. In his pieces he would take a familiar two-dimensional object as a subject and present it in an uncommon way. Johns's *Three Flags*, for example, stacks three U.S. flags in decreasing sizes. Although the flag is realistically portrayed, the overall picture provides the viewer with a new and different way of looking at the flag.

Jasper Johns was born in the South in the year 1930. He studied art at the University of South Carolina and in the early 1950s worked as a commercial artist in New York City. One of his earliest successes was a window display for the well-known jewelry store, Tiffany's. In the window he arranged actual diamonds among real potatoes and dirt.

Today, Jasper Johns is acknowledged as one of the most famous and esteemed living artists. In addition to painting, Johns also does printmaking and some sculpting. His hallmark is presenting common objects, from flags to numbers to maps, in unusual ways.

Art Project

Create an art project, using Jasper Johns's style by following the directions below.

Materials:

drawing paper or typing paper; rubber stamps of numerals 0–9 and ink pad; colored pencils or crayons

Directions:

Fold a sheet of paper into sixteenths and crease it along the folds. Unfold the paper. Use the stamps to make a different numeral from 0 to 9 in each space. Shade the numerals with black or complementary colors to add depth.

Frank Lloyd Wright

Although Frank Lloyd Wright was born in the nineteenth century, his ideas and architecture were far ahead of their time. His innovative contributions to the American home included these features: cathedral ceilings, built-in furniture and lighting fixtures, carports, and massive fireplaces. In architectural design he offered layouts which flowed seamlessly from room to room and seemed to merge with the outside environment. Perhaps his best example in this area is the Kaufmann House in Bear Run, Pennsylvania. Its lines flow out of the surrounding rock while cantilevered terraces angle out over a running waterfall. Even now Wright's buildings fit right in with current modern lines. One of his most famous designs, the Guggenheim Museum, was considered radical when it was completed in 1959, yet the structure's curves give it a modern, abstract, and almost timeless look.

Not only was Wright's architecture radical, his whole life seemed to be dedicated to outraging the public. From his well-publicized bankruptcies to his scandalous divorces and relationships, he remained newsworthy throughout his 70-year career. A self-assured man, Wright's goal was to be the greatest architect who had yet lived. Indeed, his unique designs are testament to his great genius.

Suggested Activities

Building Blocks Share this bit of information with the students: All Frank Lloyd Wright remembers about elementary school was building with blocks. Ask the students how building with blocks might have helped shape Wright's future architectural career. Then group the students and direct them to build block structures in the style of Frank Lloyd Wright.

Innovations With the class discuss the contributions Frank Lloyd Wright made to the American home. For homework assign the class to find examples of each contribution in their homes or neighborhood or to find pictures in old magazines.

Guest Speaker Invite a local architect to your class to speak about the facets of an architect's life, what high school classes are helpful and necessary, the tools used, and so forth. Help the students prepare possible interview questions ahead of time.

The Roots of Rock 'n' Roll

Students may think that rock 'n' roll was always around, but there was a time when it was not here to stay. Below is a brief history of rock 'n' roll in the U.S.A.

By the midfifties, popular music in the United States was in a rut with bland tunes and monotonous rhythms. Music charts were dominated by white musicians, but increasingly artists were recording softer versions of popular black songs. A breakthrough occurred when "Rock Around the Clock," a single by Bill Haley and the Comets, was used in the film *The Blackboard Jungle*. Haley recognized a growing trend among white teenagers to listen to black music stations. While Haley's idea was correct, his image was not enough to earn him teen-idol status. That honor was left to up-and-coming artist Elvis Presley. With his shy smile and swiveling hips, Elvis captured the hearts and souls of American teens. (For more about Elvis, see page 296.) His music opened doors for other artists, both black and white, to show their talents. Memorable among them are Jerry Lee Lewis, Fats Domino, Little Richard, Chuck Berry, and Buddy Holly.

Fats Domino Fats Domino, a heavy-set musician, played piano and sang; "Blueberry Hill" is probably his most-remembered hit.

Jerry Lee Lewis

Little Richard Little Richard, well-known for "Tutti Frutti" and "Good Golly Miss Molly," was the most outrageous of the pianists. He was noted for his frenetic playing, wild screams, and energetic performances.

Jerry Lee Lewis Jerry Lee Lewis followed in Fats Domino's and Little Richard's footsteps with his piano-pounding ways and electrifying vocals. Both "Whole Lotta Shakin' Goin' On" and "Great Balls of Fire" remain rock 'n' roll classics.

Chuck Berry Chuck Berry, the only non-piano player of the four, was almost twenty-six before he gave his first paid performance. His first hit, "Maybelline," came in 1956, and was followed by rock 'n' roll classics like "Johnny B. Goode" and "Roll Over Beethoven." Berry is noted for his famous shuffle while playing the guitar. Today, Berry still performs and has had one of the longest careers in rock 'n' roll.

Chuck Berry

Buddy Holly Buddy Holly's hits included "That'll Be the Day" and "Peggy Sue." His meteoric rise in the music industry came to an abrupt end in a plane crash on February 3, 1959, near Mason City, Iowa. Also killed in the crash were Ritchie Valens, an up-and-coming singer whose two best-selling songs were "Donna" and "La Bamba," and J. P. Richardson, known as "The Big Bopper," of "Chantilly Lace" fame.

The Roots of Rock 'n' Roll *(cont.)*

Elvis Presley Elvis Presley has been called an idol, an icon, and a legend, but he was indisputably the King of rock 'n' roll. Born on January 8, 1935, in Tupelo, Mississippi, Presley won his first talent contest when he was just eight years old. In 1954 he recorded his first song as a present for his mother. The owner of the recording service had recently started his own record company, Sun, and signed Presley as a new talent. Presley did not have much commercial success with Sun and after a year left for RCA. Thanks in large part to television exposure and appearances on programs such as *The Ed Sullivan Show*, Presley became a huge star all across America. His hip movements and gyrations, however, were cropped from the viewers' sight.

In 1955 Colonel Tom Parker became Presley's manager and signed him to RCA Records at a cost of $40,000. One year later Presley had a number one hit with "Heartbreak Hotel." The same week that it reached number one in the U.S., it also achieved its millionth sale. Eventually, the song also became number one in Great Britain. A string of hits continued with "Hound Dog," "Don't Be Cruel," and "Love Me Tender."

Presley entered the film industry and starred in a number of musicals until he was drafted by the U.S. Army. For two years he served his country, and he was proud to do so. His return to civilian life meant a return to acting, but his singing career was not as hot as it once was. Pop artists of the sixties began to replace his now dated style.

During the seventies, Presley started live tours, and his singing career picked up. Yet his self-destructive lifestyle was catching up with him. On August 16, 1977, Elvis Presley died in Memphis of heart failure caused by prescription drug abuse. He left behind an impressive 94 gold singles and over 40 gold albums. Today, he remains one of the biggest influences on 20th century pop culture and is an enduring idol in the world of rock 'n' roll.

——— Suggested Activity ———

Rating the Songs Have the class listen to some fifties music, including the songs spotlighted above and on page 295. Make copies of the chart below and let the students rate each song.

Song Title: _____

Artist: _____

Score (circle one)

    60   65   70   75   80   85   90   95   100

Reasons (check all that apply):

    I like the words.   I like the beat.

    I like the artist.   It's easy to dance to.

Other _____

_____

New to the Fifties

Among the new inventions of the fifties were 3-D movies, the hula hoop, Frisbees, drive-in movie theaters, and the microchip. In addition are two more familiar brand names: Jif Peanut Butter™ and WD-40™. Below you will find a brief history of these two common household items.

Jif Peanut Butter™

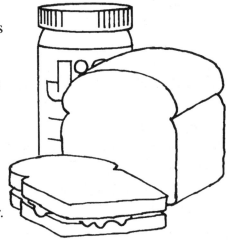

History Peanuts crushed into a paste has been around for centuries - Incas and African tribes ate such a food. In 1890 a doctor made a peanut paste for his geriatric patients with bad teeth. Several brands of peanut butter were on the market by 1914, but after Jif was introduced in 1956, it became the best-selling peanut butter in America. The name Jif is short for "jiffy," the time it takes to make a peanut butter sandwich.

Interesting Facts Jif comes in a number of varieties, including creamy, crunchy, and reduced fat. An opened jar of Jif peanut butter will remain fresh for three months. There are 1,218 peanuts in the typical 28-ounce jar of Jif.

Activity Let students taste test a number of brands of peanut butter. Have them vote on their favorites. Group the students and direct them to make a graph of the results.

WD-40™

History During the early 1950s, the aerospace industry began looking for a product to eliminate moisture from electrical circuitry and to prevent corrosion on airplanes. A satisfactory product was invented by Norman Larsen who was the president and head chemist at the Rocket Chemical Company. His water displacement formula was developed on his fortieth try, thus the name WD-40. When it was discovered that WD-40 worked well to quiet squeaky doors and unstick stuck locks, a number of employees began sneaking the product home. In 1950 the product was made available to the public.

Interesting Facts The WD-40 Company makes more than one million gallons of the lubricant each year. When astronaut John Glenn circled the earth in Frienship VII in 1964, the spacecraft was covered with WD-40 from top to bottom.

Activity Tell students that WD-40 can be found in four out of five American homes. Test the validity of this statistic. For homework, have the students check to see if WD-40 is available in their homes. Tally the number of homes in which the product was present. Compare that figure with the total number of students who participated in the poll. Does the statistic hold up?

Toys of the Fifties

Many of the toys that were invented in the fifties are still around today and in a big way. Take a look at three toys with which you are probably familiar.

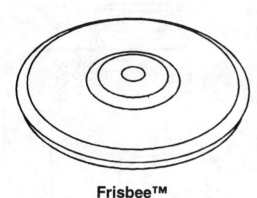

Frisbee™

Frisbee™ The Frisbee story began in the late 1800s with the Frisbie Pie Company in Bridgeport, Connecticut. Their pies, which came in a ten-inch-wide round tin with a raised edge and wide brim, were popular with students at nearby Yale University. At some point, pie-tin catch had become a fad among the young collegians. The fad continued into the 1950s but was changed forever with the introduction of a plastic flying disk called Flyin' Saucer, invented by Walter Frederick Morrison. First marketed as the Pluto Platter, the toy's name was officially changed to Frisbee when Wham-O's president saw Yale students throwing and catching Frisbie pie plates. However, not until the 1960s did sales of the Frisbee take off. Today it remains a popular toy and sport.

Activity Conduct an aluminum pie plate throwing contest. Contrast the throwing ability of pie plates with the plastic Frisbee.

Hula Hoop™ Besides the Frisbee, the Wham-O toy company also manufactured the Hula Hoop. For six months it enjoyed great success as the hula hoop became the fastest-selling toy in history. Just as quickly, however, the craze seemed to die down. Every generation since then has seen a resurgence of the unusual toy. Based on a wooden hoop used by Australian youths, the plastic Hula Hoop was invented by Richard Knerr, a partner in the Wham-O toy manufacturing company.

Activity Invent a new game to play with the hula hoop. Teach a friend how to play the game.

Hula Hoop™

Barbie Doll™ In 1959 the Barbie Doll made her debut. Today, she is the best-selling toy in American history. Her inventor is Ruth Handler, a former secretary and housewife. Ruth noticed that her daughter preferred to play with teenage dolls rather than those designed for her own age group. The problem was that the teenage dolls available at that time were paper cutouts. Ruth designed a more grown-up doll that would wear fashionable clothing and be a little girl's dream of things to come. Barbie, named after Handler's daughter, made her debut at the 1959 New York Toy Show. A huge success, it sold $500 million worth in its first eight years. Ruth Handler went on to become vice-president and then president of Mattel, Inc., the company that manufactures Barbie.

Activity Design a new outfit for a Barbie from a past era.

Dressing for the Fifties

Young people during the fifties were expected to dress much like their elders and according to their gender. Girls, for example, could wear full skirts with petticoats or pencil-slim skirts and sweater sets. Boys typically wore a shirt, tie, and pressed trousers. See more fashions for teens of the fifties on this and the next page.

Typical Clothing for Girls

a man's shirt worn outside
of dungarees (jeans)
penny loafers

Peter Pan collared blouse
fulls skirts and petticoats
(poodle skirts)

pencil-slim skirt

Dressing for the Fifties (cont.)

Typical Clothing for Boys

Hawaiian shirts with
Bermuda shorts

shirt, tie, and pressed
trousers

penny loafers

crewcut

jeans, leather jacket

hair slicked back into a
ducktail

Elsewhere...

This chronology gives a few of the important events around the globe during the 1950s. Have students research further any people and events that interest them.

1950
- British inventor Chris Cockerell invents the hovercraft.
- China and the Soviet Union sign the Sino-Soviet Pact naming the U.S. and Japan as mutual enemies.
- North Korea invades South Korea.
- Russia announces it has an atom bomb.

1951
- The first underwater TV camera is developed by Frenchman Jacques Cousteau.
- The Suez Canal crisis takes place.
- Chinese forces occupy Tibet.
- Juan Peron is re-elected president of Argentina.
- Libya becomes an independent state.
- The first Miss World Contest is staged.

1952
- The Bonn Convention is held; Britain, France, and the U.S. end occupation of West Germany.
- The Mau Mau uprising begins in Kenya, Africa.
- Egypt ousts King Farouk.
- King George VI dies and is succeeded by Queen Elizabeth II.
- Eva Peron dies of cancer in Argentina.
- The first national elections are held in India.

1953
- Sir Edmund Hillary and Tenzing Norgay are the first climbers to reach the top of Mt. Everest.
- Stalin dies.
- Tito becomes president of Yugoslavia.
- Ian Fleming publishes the first of his twelve James Bond novels.
- Crick and Watson develop the first model of the structure of DNA.
- The Queen of England is crowned.

1954
- Roger Bannister of England runs a mile in under four minutes, the first man to do so.
- SEATO (Southeast Asia Treaty Organization) is formed.

1955
- Churchill resigns as prime minister of England.
- South Vietnam becomes a republic.
- Argentine dictator Juan Perón is overthrown.

1956
- The Warsaw Pact is signed by the Soviet Union and the countries it dominates.
- Nasser is elected president of Egypt.
- Khrushchev, the new Soviet prime minister, denounces Stalin.
- Transatlantic cable telephone service is inaugurated.
- The Suez Crisis ends when Britain and France withdraw troops from Egypt.
- Students in Hungary rebel against the Soviet government.

1957
- Laika, a female Samoyed, becomes the first animal in space.
- *Sputnik I* is launched by the USSR, followed by *Sputnik II*.
- The Gold Coast of Africa becomes Ghana.
- Malaya becomes independent.
- The Soviet Union launches an Intercontinental Ballistic Missile (ICBM).

1958
- Charles de Gaulle returns to power as the first president of France's Fifth Republic.
- Egypt and Syria form the United Arab Republic.
- John XXIII becomes the new Pope.
- China crushes the national uprising in Tibet.

1959
- Castro overthrows Batista's government and gains control of Cuba.
- Singapore becomes independent.
- Anthropologist Mary Leakey discovers skull fragments from early ancestors of modern humans in east Africa.
- Mao unites his country.
- The bathyscaphe *Trieste* descends seven miles down to the Mariana Trench in the Pacific Ocean.
- The Soviet Union launches *Lunik 2* which makes a hard landing on the moon.
- The Antarctic Treaty is signed by twelve nations.
- The Dalai Lama flees from Tibet.

Revolution in Cuba

On January 1, 1959, Fidel Castro seized power from president Fulgencio Batista. Initially the United States supported the new Cuban government but was soon forced to reconsider its political position.

This page gives an overview of events in Cuba during Castro's revolutionary days.

Background As a result of the Spanish-American War, Cuba gained its independence from Spain in 1898. Until it became a self-governing republic in May, 1902, it was governed by the American military. During the early 1930s the effective ruler of Cuba was army officer Fulgencio Batista. In 1952 he took over the government directly and two years later was elected president. A number of anti-Batista factions began to emerge, and by 1958 the island was in a state of civil war.

Fidel Castro

Castro Fidel Castro was a lawyer who led a group of well-armed revolutionaries in widespread warfare against the government. The attacks began in 1956 and were based in the mountains of Oriente Province. On January 1, 1959, Castro and his troops marched into the capital of Havana and seized control from the corrupt Batista. Few Cubans opposed the coup.

Conditions Under Batista's cruel dictatorship the rich had become richer but the poor had not fared as well. Although luxury houses, gambling casinos, and Cadillacs were plentiful in Havana, most Cubans were starving and penniless. Jobs were scarce and there were no unemployment benefits or health care.

Initial Response Initially, the United States was supportive of the young Castro, and he was given a fine welcome on his arrival in Washington, D.C., in April 1959. The U.S. was pleased to learn that he would hold free elections in Cuba. Castro was sworn in as prime minister in February. Manuel Urrutiá was the president.

Rethinking In July of 1959 Castro dismissed Urrutiá and made himself president of Cuba. He began to divide and distribute large sugar plantations among Cuban farmers. This worried the U.S. because many of these farms belonged to Americans. For years, the U.S. government had controlled Cuba's economy and imported two-thirds of Cuba's sugar at fixed prices. An even bigger worry was that Fidel Castro seemed to be leaning toward communism.

Sixties In 1960 the Cubans accepted $100 million dollars in credit from the Soviet Union. The U.S. bought fewer sugar imports from Cuba. In 1961, a U.S.-backed revolt against Castro's government failed. (See page 317.)

Suggested Activities

Research Che Guevara was an Argentinian who devoted his life to fighting corrupt regimes. Tell the students to research Che's life and to learn how he helped Fidel Castro gain control of Cuba.

Continuation Ask students about current U.S.–Cuba relations. Discuss any changes since Fidel first came to power there. Direct them to scan the newspapers or the Internet for any new developments.

The Black Pearl

Pelé, born Edson Arantes do Nascimento, was only 17 when he played in his first World Cup of soccer in 1958. Some 60,000 people had jammed into the 50,000-seat arena in hopes that they would see Sweden win its first world title. The Swedish coach thought his team could win if they scored first. Brazil had a tendency to become disorganized when they trailed in a game. What happened at that game, however, stunned everyone—the spectators, coaches, and players. Pelé inspired his teammates with his enthusiastic and energetic pace. It was his magnificent moves on the field, though, that really wowed the crowd. He displayed such control of his body and such athleticism that even the Swedish fans began to chant his name. After their win, the Brazilian team returned home as national heroes and Pelé was nicknamed "The Black Pearl."

Pelé

Pelé was born on October 23, 1940, in a small town in Minas Gerais state. His father, a soccer player, was pleased with his firstborn and predicted that the boy would grow up to become a great soccer player. As a young child Pelé ran and played with the other students in his neighborhood. They had to use grapefruits or socks filled with rags because there was not enough money for a real soccer ball. Bored with school, he quit in the fourth grade and became a cobbler's apprentice. His free time was spent playing soccer. When he was twelve, he was chosen to play on a junior league where he learned the strategies and tactics of professional soccer. By the time he was 14, he was invited to join a professional team. It meant leaving home and moving to Santos near Brazil's largest city, Sao Paulo. Often he would be homesick, but he kept busy attending school between games and practicing with the team. Soon, people began coming out to the games just to watch this remarkable new player. Then, at age 17 he found himself on the Brazilian World Cup team.

Before the team left for Stockholm, Pelé injured his knee. He was fearful that it would not heal correctly and he would be unable to continue his professional career. Though in pain, he put on an unforgettable performance at the World Cup and led his team to victory. He went on to play until he retired from the Santos team in 1974. For three years after that he played for a team in the newly formed North American Soccer League.

Pelé remains a public figure in his native Brazil. He starred in some movies and recorded a hit song. His future plans may include something in the political arena. Whatever his goals, he remains the most popular soccer player in the history of the game.

Suggested Activities

Records Pelé finished his career with 1,216 goals. Is it still an all-time world record?

Defense Have students defend this statement: Soccer is the most popular sport in the world.

Independence in Africa

The 1950s were witness to numerous political changes in Africa as more and more countries gained their independence. Read the dates and countries listed in the chart below and label the map with the names of these countries.

Independence Dates

Year	Countries
1951	Libya
1956	Sudan, Morocco, Tunisia
1957	Ghana
1958	Guinea

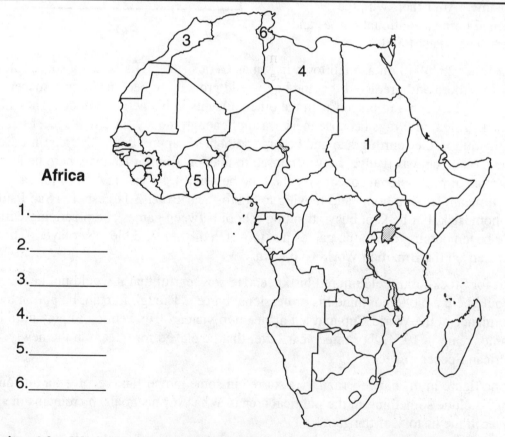

Africa

1._____

2._____

3._____

4._____

5._____

6._____

Activity After World War II, the Kikuyu of Kenya became increasingly dissatisfied with the British rule. In 1952 many of the Kikuyu banded together to form the Mau Mau. Their goal was to drive the Europeans out of their country. Finish this story. Find out how and when the war ended, how long it lasted, and the results.

- -

Answers: Teacher, fold under before copying.

1. Sudan 2. Guinea 3. Morocco 4. Libya 5. Ghana 6. Tunisia

The Leakeys

Mary Douglas Nicol became interested in archaeology through her father, Erskine Nicol. Every autumn the family would travel from England to the continent of Europe. At the age of 11, Mary Nicol became fascinated by the Cro-Magnon cave paintings in France. She went on to study archaelology at the university and participated in several digs. Her special area of interest was stone tools. In 1935 Nichol met Louis Leakey. The son of missionaries, Leakey had studied in England and then returned to Africa, where he was raised. The two became friends, and the following Christmas Eve Louis and Mary were married in London. Shortly afterward the couple left for Africa and settled at Olduvai Gorge in Tanzania, a site Leakey had identified.

The two complemented one another in their work. Louis Leakey was most happy lecturing, traveling, and talking with reporters while Mary Leakey enjoyed the actual excavations. To support their digs, Louis Leakey wrote books, gave lectures, and worked as the head of a museum in Nairobi. The couple had three sons who accompanied them on their archaeological excavations whenever possible.

In 1948 Mary Leakey made an important discovery: the skull of a Proconsul, an early ancestor of the chimpanzee, gorilla, and modern human. Her exacting method of digging had paid off, and today all archaeologists in Africa dig shallow layers rather than deep holes. Altogether, the Leakeys and their assistants found more than 2,000 stone tools and numerous mammal bones. Then in July, 1959, Mary Leakey spotted some teeth sticking up from the rubble. In the next nineteen days, 400 pieces were carefully excavated from the spot. It took another eighteen months to fit all the pieces together. She had uncovered the Zinjanthropus boisei man, nicknamed the Nutcracker Man. A hominid man-ape fossil, it is believed to be 1,750,000 years old.

This discovery of the earliest man brought the Leakeys much publicity and money for research. They were regularly featured in National Geographic magazine and received many awards. Louis Leakey died in 1972, but Mary Leakey continued her search for fossils until she was well into her eighties.

Suggested Activity

More Assign any of the following topics for further research.

- Louis Leakey's sponsorship of Jane Goodall's research on chimpanzees
- Potassium-argon dating, a method of dating artifacts developed in the 50s
- The hoax of the Piltdown man
- Albert Schweitzer's missionary work in Africa
- The importance of the findings at Olduvai Gorge

References

Beakman's Book of Dead Guys and Gals of Science by Luann Colombo (Andrews and McMeel, 1994)

Mary Leakey: In Search of Human Beginnings by Deborah Heiligman (W.H.Freeman and Company, 1995)

Thematic Unit: Archaeology (Teacher Created Materials, #296)

Crisis in the Suez

A crisis occurred at the Suez Canal in 1956 that could have been disastrous if it had not been resolved correctly. On this page are some highlights of the Suez Crisis.

Background After World War II Egypt was in a politically unstable condition. Although it was theoretically an independent nation, it had been dominated by Great Britain for decades. Britain's interest in the country was to protect the Suez Canal and to ensure safe passage to India and the Far East for trade purposes.

Nasser Seizes Control In July of 1952 a group of military officers staged a coup and overthrew Egypt's monarchy, and in 1953 the country became a republic. Colonel Gamal Abdel Nasser, an Arab nationalist, became president of Egypt in 1954. He championed the Arabs' struggle against Israel and drew Egypt into alliance with the Soviet Union and away from the West.

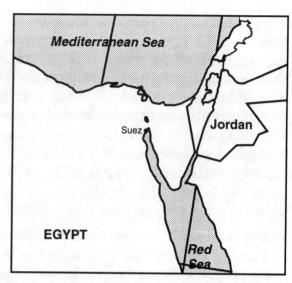

Nationalizing the Canal Historically, the Suez Canal was owned by a corporation dominated by Great Britain and France. In 1954 Britain agreed to gradually withdraw its defense forces, and by June of 1956 British forces were no longer present. On July 26, 1956, Nasser nationalized the canal, with the intention of using canal tolls to pay for the construction of the Aswan High Dam on the Nile River.

Secret Plans Great Britain and France feared that Nasser might close the canal to international traffic. They began secret plans to take control of the canal and oust Nasser, if possible. Israel, who allied itself with the plan, sent brigades into Egypt on October 29, 1956, and defeated the Egyptian forces there. A peacekeeping force was sent by Great Britain and France. Egypt sank 40 ships in the canal, blocking it from use.

Response The plan did not work, however, due to public opposition within Great Britain and France. When the Soviets made threats, the intervention stopped. Through the UN a truce was reached in November, and the British, French, and Israelis withdrew on December 22, 1956, ending the Suez Crisis. A UN salvage team cleared the canal, which reopened in 1957.

Results Nasser became a hero to his people. Great Britain's prime minister, Anthony Eden, resigned.

Suggested Activities

Your opinion What was the U.S. stand on the Suez Crisis? How might the crisis have ended if the U.S. had offered support to Great Britain and France? Write a defense of your argument.

Cartograghy Find a map which includes Great Britain, France, India, and Egypt. Locate the Suez Canal. Trace and measure a route from Great Britain to India through the Suez Canal; trace and measure a route that ships would have to take if the canal were not open to them. Compare the distances.

Presidential Decisions President Eisenhower refused to support the British and French action against Nasser. If you had been president, what actions would you have taken? Explain your reasons.

Speech Writing After the Suez crisis Britain's prime minister, Anthony Eden, resigned. Write a speech he might have given to the British people, explaining his reasons for resignation.

Conquering Mount Everest

The sport of mountaineering began in the late 1700s when Frenchman Michel Paccard climbed Mount Blanc in the Alps. For the next 200 years, climbers continued to explore peaks in the Alps as well as mountains in Africa, the Andes in South America, and the Rockies in North America. Only one mountain seemed out of reach: Mount Everest. Located in the Himalayas between Tibet and Nepal, it is the highest mountain in the world at 29,028 feet (8,848 meters).

One main obstacle had to be overcome before a climb could even be attempted. Permission had to be obtained from Tibet or Nepal to travel through their lands. In 1920 a British team was granted permission to enter Tibet. This fact-finding expedition encountered bad weather and strong winds, and all the climbers were affected by altitude sickness. After returning to England, plans were begun for the next expedition. Through the years other attempts to reach the top of Mount Everest were likewise unsuccessful.

Mount Everest

In 1952 Colonel John Hunt was chosen to lead a 1953 expedition to Mount Everest. He mapped the route, made sure there would be enough supplies, purchased the best equipment, and picked the right team members. Among this group was New Zealander Edmund Hillary and a Sherpa northern Nepalese mountaineer named Norgay Tenzing. Following three weeks of training they began their long, arduous journey. After four days they reached 18,000 feet (5,500 meters) and set up camp. Continuing up the mountain, they established eight more camps. From the ninth camp, Hillary and Tenzing began the final ascent. Once the two mountaineers reached the top of the world, they took photographs, buried small items in the snow, and took some time to enjoy the view. After only 15 minutes, they started the descent to the bottom of the mountain. Back in London, they were given a hero's welcome.

Since 1953 Mount Everest has been climbed many times, some using different routes to get to the top. Not all expeditions have been successful, and many climbers have died in their attempt to reach the summit.

Suggested Activities

Reading Assign the students to read an account of the journey to the top of Mount Everest. One excellent resource is *Hillary and Tenzing Climb Everest* by Bob Davidson (Dillon Press, 1993). Stunning pictures accompany a text which makes the reader feel part of the expedition.

Terms Write some climbing terms on the board and direct the students to define each one. Discuss the terms as they apply to mountain climbing. Some words to include are *altitude sickness, crevasse, acclimatize, avalanche, reconnaissance*, and *traverse*.

Record Book Start a class Mount Everest Record Book. Let students record interesting facts, such as the first European woman to reach the summit, the first person to climb Mount Everest without using oxygen, and the expedition with the worst fatality record.

The ANZUS Treaty

Australia and New Zealand had fought together during World War I, and in World War II they had joined forces with Britain and the United States. In the years following World War II, Australia and the U.S. strengthened the close relationship they had developed during their wartime cooperation. On September 1, 1951, Australia, New Zealand, and the United States signed a mutual defense agreement called the ANZUS Treaty.

The name ANZUS is an acronym formed by the initial letters of the three countries: Australia, New Zealand, and the United States. Below are some other historical acronyms with which you should be familiar. Write the number of the acronym on the line next to the correct description.

Acronym		Description
1. NATO	_____	A. A line of radar installations built across the Arctic
2. OAU	_____	B. Disarmament and arms limitations talks
3. USSR	_____	C. United Nations agency that specializes in child welfare
4. UNESCO	_____	D. Organization that works for civil rights for black Americans
5. DEW	_____	E. Treaty signed by European countries and U.S. to defend against agressions from the Soviet Union
6. UNICEF	_____	F. Before its break-up, it was the largest country in the world
7. SEATO	_____	G. The UN agency that helps develop education in poor countries
8. WHO	_____	H. Thirty African states formed this union in 1963
9. SALT	_____	I. The UN agency that advises countries on health services
10. NAACP	_____	J. A defense treaty signed after the French left Indochina in 1954

On the lines below identify the whole name of each acronym.

1. NATO _____
2. OAU _____
3. USSR _____
4. UNESCO_____
5. DEW _____

6. UNICEF _____
7. SEATO _____
8. WHO_____
9. SALT_____
10. NAACP _____

- -

Answers. Teacher, fold under before duplicating.

A.5 B.9 C.6 D.10 E.1 F.3 G.4 H.2 I.8 J.7

1.North Atlantic Treaty Organization 2.Organization of African Unity 3.Union of Soviet Socialist Republics 4.United Nations Educational, Scientific, and Cultural Organization 5.Distant Early Warning 6.United Nations Children's Fund 7.Southeast Asia Treaty Organization 8.World Health Organization 9.Strategic Arms Limitation Talks 10.National Association for the Advancement of Colored People

Matisse

One of the most important artists of the 20th century is Frenchman Henri Matisse. Born in 1869, he led an art movement called post-Impressionism and was one of the first famous collage artists. Throughout his productive and prolific career, Matisse's style continued to evolve as he experimented with different colors, art forms, and mediums.

When Matisse was growing up, he did not have dreams of becoming a famous artist, but a quirk of fate led him to that new career. While training to become a lawyer, he had to have surgery. During his recuperation, his mother bought him some paints and a how-to book. From then on Matisse was totally devoted to art. His bourgeois father took a dim view of his son's new career path, and as Matisse was leaving for Paris, his father yelled out, "You'll starve!"

After one year at the Academie Julian, Matisse went on to study at the Academie Carriere. Throughout these early years he copied the Impressionistic style of painting and the Japanese style of woodblock prints. As Matisse came in contact with other styles, his work gradually changed.

In 1904 Matisse had his first one-man show which met with little success. By the following year, he was the leader of the Fauvist movement which relied on bright colors and distorted shapes. Critics were shocked by the new forms and called it the work of wild beasts, or *Fauvism* in French. While the actual movement lasted only a few years, its effects on the art world have been felt ever since.

In addition to painting, Matisse opened his own art academy for children in 1908. That same year, he published *Notes of a Painter* in which he expressed his artistic beliefs. Later, he executed murals, created stage designs for a ballet, drew several series of book illustrations, and made sculptures and collages. Those collages were some of the most important pieces of work that he ever produced. Even more impressive is that fact that he created many of them when he was in his eighties and sick in bed. He would instruct his assistants to paint huge pieces of paper with bright colors. Then he would cut out the shapes. As directed, the assistants pinned the shapes onto white paper and then pasted them down.

A master of color, Henri Matisse brought a special joyfulness and a childlike perspective to his art. When Matisse died in 1954, he left a part of himself behind for all future generations to enjoy.

Suggested Activities

Collage Group the students and have them create giant collages. See the instructions in the text above.

Extensions For additional activities on Matisse, see *Teacher Created Materials #494 Focus on Artists*.

Passages

Births

1950
- Olympic swimmer Mark Spitz
- actresses Cybill Sheperd and Holly Hunter
- talk-show host Jay Leno

1951
- actors Kurt Russell, Michael Keaton, Tony Danza, and Mark Harmon
- singers Stevie Wonder and Luther Vandross
- first American woman to orbit the earth, Sally Ride

1952
- actors Robin Williams, Dan Aykroyd, Jeff Goldblum, and David Hasselhoff
- singer Tom Petty

1953
- Amy Tan, author of best-selling novels
- singer Michael Bolton
- actors Alfre Woodard and Pierce Brosnan
- supermodel Christie Brinkley

1954
- radio host Howard Stern
- tennis player Chris Evert
- actors John Travolta and Denzel Washington
- comic Jerry Seinfeld

1955
- Yo Yo Ma, world-famous cellist
- actors Arsenio Hall and Bruce Willis
- singer Billy Idol
- Apple Computer founder Steven Jobs
- lawyer and novelist John Grisham

1956
- Dorothy Hamill, Olympic gold medal winning figure skater
- actor Mel Gibson
- football great Joe Montana
- tennis great Bjorn Borg
- boxing champion Sugar Ray Leonard
- software magnate William H. Gates III

1957
- singers Gloria Estefan and Holly Dunn
- television journalist Katie Couric
- game-show celebrity Vanna White

1958
- actors Annette Bening, Sharon Stone, Alec Baldwin, Kennan Ivory Wayans, and Jimmy Smits

1959
- singers Sade, Madonna, and Randy Travis
- tennis great John McEnroe
- basketball great Magic Earvin Johnson

Deaths

1950
- Charles Richard Drew, scientist who showed how to preserve blood
- Edna St. Vincent Millay, poet
- British author George Orwell

1951
- author Sinclair Lewis
- newspaper magnate William Randolph Hearst

1952
- Shipwreck Kelly, professional stuntman who started flagpole sitting fad
- philosopher John Dewey
- Eva Perón, wife of Argentine leader Juan Perón
- Margaret Wise Brown, children's author

1953
- Jim Thorpe, a great athlete and Olympic winner
- Hank Williams, country western singer
- playwright Eugene O'Neill and writer Dylan Thomas

1954
- French artist Henri Matisse
- Enrico Fermi, Italian-born physicist
- Artist Frida Kahlo

1955
- Albert Einstein, one of the world's greatest geniuses
- James Dean, actor and teen idol
- African American civil rights activist Mary McLeod Bethune
- Matthew Henson, North Pole explorer
- Alexander Fleming, the discoverer of penicillin

1956
- Mildred Babe Didrickson Zaharias, Olympic athlete and sportswoman
- A.A. Milne, children's author

1957
- actor Humphrey Bogart
- Admiral Richard E. Byrd, polar explorer
- artist Diego Rivera
- Gabriela Mistral, Latin America's only winner of a Nobel prize in literature

1958
- actor Tyrone Power

1959
- rock 'n' roll pioneer Buddy Holly and singers Ritchie Valens and the Big Bopper
- opera singer Mario Lanza
- blues singer Billie Holliday

Fifties Facts and Figures

Make a copy of the chart below for each pair of students. Direct them to use the information on this page as a comparison with a chart which they will complete about the current decade. Discuss the similarities and the differences between the fifties and the current decade.

The United States in 1950

Population:	150,697,999
National Debt:	$256 billion
Federal Minimum Wage:	75 cents per hour (raised to $1 per hour in 1955)
Postage:	raised from 3 cents to 4 cents in 1958
Popular Books:	*Profiles in Courage, On the Road, Lord of the Flies, The Lord of the Rings, The Spirit of St.Louis, The Old Man and the Sea, East of Eden, The Catcher in the Rye, The Sea Around Us, Atlas Shrugged, Dr .Zhivago, Hawaii, Goldfinger, Portnoy's Complaint*
Popular Movies:	*Ben Hur, High Noon, The Greatest Show on Earth, Roman Holiday, From Here to Eternity, On the Waterfront, Rear Window, Marty, The Seven Year Itch, Around the World in 80 Days, The Ten Commandments, The King and I, The Man with the Golden Arm, The Bridge on the River Kwai*
Popular Stars:	Brigette Bardot, Grace Kelly, Natalie Wood, Audrey Hepburn, Deborah Kerr, Elizabeth Taylor, Debbie Reynolds, Marilyn Monroe, Charlton Heston, Gary Cooper, John Wayne, Marlon Brando, Yul Brynner, James Dean, Jimmy Stewart, Jack Lemmon, Paul Newman, Sidney Poitier, Glenn Ford, Laurence Olivier, Gene Kelly, William Holden, David Niven
Popular Songs:	"A Bushel and a Peck," "Good Night, Irene," "C'est Si Bon," "Your Cheatin' Heart," "I Saw Mommmy Kissing Santa Claus," "Doggie in the Window," "Mr. Sandman," "The Yellow Rose of Texas," "Davy Crockett," "Sixteen Tons," "Mack the Knife," "Chipmunk Song," "The Flying Purple People Eater," "Catch a Falling Star," "Maria," "Seventy-Six Trombones," "Tom Dooley," "He's Got the Whole World in His Hands," "Rock Around the Clock," "Charlie Brown," "Poison Ivy," "Sixteen Candles"
Popular TV Shows:	*What's My Line?, Father Knows Best, The Ozzie and Harriet Show, Leave It to Beaver, I Love Lucy, Amos 'n' Andy, The Ed Sullivan Show, Milton Berle, The George Burns and Gracie Allen Show, Dragnet, American Bandstand, Gunsmoke, Wagon Train, Roy Rogers, Hopalong Cassidy, The Howdy Doody Show, Captain Kangaroo, Lassie, Kukla, Fran and Ollie, Mickey Mouse Club, Rin Tin Tin, Captain Midnight*
Fashions:	pink shirts for males, chemise dresses for females, poodle skirts, pony-tails and bouffant hairdos; ducktails and crewcuts, jeans, t-shirts, and leather jackets for males
Fads:	hula hoops, 3-D movies, Davy Crockett hats, goldfish swallowing, crowding into sports cars, stuffing people into telephone booths, dancing the cha-cha
Popular Toys:	hula hoops, Frisbees, Barbie dolls, Scrabble®, paint-by-number sets

Buzzwords

New inventions, habits, lifestyles, and occupations cause people to invent new words. The 1950s were no exception. Listed below are some of the words and phrases that came into popular use throughout the decade.

Beat Jack Kerouac coined this word to describe his generation. It means both beatific, or blessed, and defeated. Those who took up the Beat lifestyle believed they were blessed with spiritual powers and misundersood by society.

Beat Generation This name is given to those who rebelled against social conventions, experimented with drugs, spoke their own slang language, and wore clothes different from mainstream America in the 1950s.

Beatniks Individuals who followed the Beat lifestyle were called beatniks.

boycott This term means there is an organized agreement in which a group refuses to have anything to do with another group, company, or organization until certain conditions have been met.

Cold War This refers to a period of tension and hostility between the United States and the USSR that stopped short of war.

cool This is a slang term for good.

crazy This slang term means great.

desegregation This word means to integrate or to abolish racial segregation.

dig In 1950s slang, this meant to like, as in she digs Elvis.

discrimination Prejudice against another person or group, usually because of race or religion, is discrimination.

Edsel After this Ford model debuted in 1957 and failed to sell, the name became synonymous with error or failure.

Indochina This is an area of Southeast Asia that includes the countries of Laos, Cambodia, and Vietnam.

McCarthyism This term means charges made without proof and accompanied by publicity.

orbit The path that a spacecraft or other heavenly body makes as it revolves around another body is its orbit. For example, Sputnik orbited the earth.

Palestine This is the name given by the Arabs to Israel, a country at the eastern end of the Mediterranean.

pad This slang term was used by Beatniks to refer to an apartment.

segregation This term refers to the forced separation of one group from others. For example, some schools, buses, and bathrooms were segregated and marked for colored only or whites only.

Soviet Union This is a shortened version of the Union of Soviet Socialist Republics (USSR), the official name for Russia in the postwar years.

Sputnik This word means fellow traveler in Russian. It was the name of the first unmanned space satellite.

square This slang term was used to refer to someone considered dull or unattractive.

Suggested Activities

Creative Writing Let each student choose one word from the list above and write a creative story explaining how that word came into popular use during the 1950s.

Slang Group the students and instruct them to make a list of the slang terms from the list above. Have them determine if those slang words are still in use today or what words have replaced them.

Writing Prompts and Literature Ideas

Writing Prompts Use these suggestions for journal writing or as daily writing exercises. Some research or discussion may be appropriate before assigning a particular topic.

- Ask the students to write their own Beat poems. Place a stool in front of the room and let students take turns sitting on it while they share their poems.

- Play a video tape of a typical 1950s family sit com such as *Leave It to Beaver* or *Father Knows Best*. After discussing the show, divide the students into small groups. Direct them to write a script for an episode of that program. Remind them to keep in mind the way people talked, what conveniences were in use then, and how students behaved toward their parents and elders.

- In 1957 Dr. Seuss published his first book, *The Cat in the Hat.* Group the students and tell them to read the story. As they do so, have them make a list of all the words used in the text. Direct the groups to write a children's story, using only the words that appear in *The Cat in the Hat.* Let them share their stories with the whole class.

- When company executive Frank McNamara finished a business meeting and realized he had left his cash at home, he persuaded the restaurant owner to wait for payment. To prevent such a recurrence, he worked with a bank to introduce the first multipurpose charge card on February 28, 1950 - the Diners Club. Today, credit cards are used for all kinds of purchases. Write a creative story in which paper money is no longer in existence and people make all their purchases with plastic cards.

- Bette Nesmith Graham was an executive secretary who made plenty of typing errors. To correct her mistakes, she mixed some tempera paint with a few other ingredients and carefully fixed her flubs. So many secretaries were borrowing her invention that she decided to market her Mistake Out, now marketed as Liquid Paper™. Pretend you are Ms. Graham. Write a speech that will convince the exectives at IBM that this will be a worthwhile venture.

Literature Ideas

Literature Ideas The following books can be used to supplement and enhance the study of the 1950s.

- ***The Gold Cadillac*** by Mildred D. Taylor (Dial, 1987)

  A black family is accused and threatened while traveling to the South in their new Cadillac. This story paints an unforgettable picture of growing up black in America during the 1950s.

- ***Youn Hee and Me*** by C. S. Adler (Harcourt Brace & Company, 1995)

  An American family adopts a Korean child. In the process they learn about each other's culture and become a real family. Although it has a contemporary setting, this is a great book to use when studying the Korean War.

- ***. . . If You Lived at the Time of Martin Luther King*** by Ellen Levine (Scholastic, Inc., 1990)

  Your class can learn all about the civil rights movement and the life and times of Martin Luther King, Jr., with this book. It is written in a question-and-answer format and provides answers to some of the most-asked questions about the civil rights era.

Sixties Overview

- In his inaugural address John F. Kennedy challenged Americans, especially young adults, to work for change. Many devoted themselves to the cause of social justice by joining the Peace Corps, while others helped register black voters in Mississippi.

- Legislation in the 1950s had provided for school integration. In the 1960s, attention was focused on eliminating discrimination in all public places and in employment, and on guaranteeing the right to vote. Powerful black leaders emerged and gathered their people to demonstrate against the injustices they had been enduring. They waged their campaign with sit-ins, marches, and other nonviolent means but were often subjected to beatings, bombings, and even shootings.

- The new serious attitudes of young people called for a different style of music. Folk singers with acoustic guitars sang traditional ballads. A new group of young folk artists created new songs about current social problems. These "protest" singers, including Bob Dylan, Joan Baez, and Phil Ochs, often appeared at civil rights and antiwar demonstrations.

- Kennedy's assassination in 1963 shocked and saddened the country.

- The new president, Lyndon Johnson, declared an "unconditional war on poverty" in his first state of the union address and guided the passage of a strong civil rights act and an economic opportunity act.

- Attention focused on the Southeast Asian nation of Vietnam where U.S. troops were helping the South Vietnamese in their civil war against the Communist-held North Vietnam. As the war escalated, students and others began to protest the draft and America's involvement in South East Asia.

- By the middle of the decade, many blacks were discouraged by the slow pace of change through nonviolence. New leaders advocated Black Power, and in major cities, frustration often led to violent confrontations, like the 1965 Watts riots. In 1967 alone there were seventy-five race riots. One of the worst was in Detroit, where forty-three people were killed before peace was restored.

- After the assassination of Martin Luther King, Jr. in 1968, race riots broke out in 124 cities.

- Women demanded equal pay for equal work. No longer content to be suburban housewives, they wanted the same career opportunities and choices afforded to men. Betty Friedan led the women's liberation movement and formed the National Organization of Women.

- Migrant workers united under the leadership of Cesar Chavez and protested the unsafe, low-paying conditions of their labor.

- Lyndon Johnson announced that he would not run in the 1968 presidential election.

- Robert F. Kennedy, brother of the late president Kennedy, decided to seek the Democratic Party nomination. After winning the California primary, he was killed by Sirhan Sirhan.

- The Democratic National Convention was marked by violence between antiwar protestors and police. Jerry Rubin's Youth International Party (Yippies), nominated a pig for president. Ultimately Rubin and seven other radical antiwar leaders were arrested and charged with conspiracy in starting the riots.

- Republican candidate Richard M. Nixon narrowly won the election of 1968. He began his term in office by announcing a plan for Vietnamization of the war and the withdrawal of American forces.

Important Legislation

A number of important pieces of legislation were ratified in the sixties. An outline of some of these measures is provided below.

Peace Corps President Kennedy created the volunteer agency to provide help for developing nations worldwide. For more information about the Peace Corps see page 316.

Twenty-Third Amendment This bill granted residents of the District of Columbia the right to vote in Presidential elections and assigned them three electoral votes.

Test Ban Treaty The United States and the Soviet Union signed a treaty to stop testing nuclear bombs.

Twenty-Fourth Amendment It made poll taxes illegal in federal elections. The taxes had been used throughout the South to keep African Americans from voting. Many were too poor to pay the tax.

Civil Rights Act This act was the most far-reaching civil rights legislation of the twentieth century. It banned discrimination in public places and employment based on race, sex, religion, or national origin.

Economic Opportunity Act Nine hundred forty-seven million dollars in funds was legislated for preschool education and job training.

Medicare This program provided for monetary help for all the elderly to pay their medical bills.

Medicaid Similar to Medicare, it helped those with little or no money to afford a doctor or hospitalization.

Voting Rights Act Under this law the federal government had the power to prevent unfair practices, such as literacy tests and poll taxes, from restricting voter registration.

Twenty-fifth Amendment This measure outlined what will happen in the event of the president's death or disability while in office. It also outlined the order in which various government officials would become president, e.g. President, Vice President, Speaker of the House, etc.

Suggested Activities

Impact Ask the students if they are familiar with any of these legislative measures. Have them find out which are still in effect today and which have been replaced by updated versions.

Amendments At the end of 1969 there were twenty-five amendments to the Constitution. Assign the students to find out how many there are currently. Direct the students to write brief summaries of each new one.

Presidential Succession Read aloud the Twenty-fifth Amendment to the Constitution. Tell the students to make a chart of the presidential succession in the event of the president's death or disability while in office. Have them find out how Ford, and not Spiro Agnew, succeeded to the presidency after Nixon resigned.

The Peace Corps

With the election of John F. Kennedy, a new tide seemed to rise as people eagerly clamored to join the political process. Thousands of Americans wanted to work to help their nation. One proposal was a peace corps. A bill for such a corps had been introduced to Congress in early 1960 but failed. After Kennedy was elected, the organization was officially founded.

What It Is The Peace Corps is a volunteer agency composed of men and women who want to serve as ambassadors of peace. To date, over 100,000 volunteers have served in 91 different countries.

What It Does Peace Corps volunteers perform a variety of skills and services. They teach any number of subjects from reading to beekeeping to sign language, plant trees, help market and sell handicrafts made by villagers, write newsletters, and build ponds to stock with fish.

Qualifications Participants must meet certain qualifications before becoming a Peace Corps volunteer. They must be 18 years of age or older, U.S. citizens, in good health, and willing to serve for two years.

Training Volunteers are trained in the local language, beliefs, and customs of their assigned country. In addition, volunteers must respect the culture and traditions of their host country.

Compensation Peace Corps workers are not given a salary. Instead, volunteers receive a readjustment allowance upon completion of their service. Housing, food, travel, and medical expenses are taken care of by the agency.

Hardships Countries served by the Peace Corps are poor and often lack the most basic facilities and amenities that Americans are accustomed to having and using. Most likely there will be no indoor plumbing, no hot baths, and no television for entertainment. There will no be daily phone conversations with friends and family, as calls (if there are phones available) will be very expensive. In addition, participants have to learn another language, leave most of their possessions behind, and possibly live in huts.

Suggested Activities

Slogan Establish that recruitment ads for the Peace Corps state that the Peace Corps is "the toughest job you will ever love." With the class, discuss what this slogan means.

Preparations For those interested in a possible internship with the Peace Corps, they might want to become exchange students first. Assign the class to write a letter requesting information about the student exchange program at this address: President's International Youth Exchange, Pueblo, CO 81009.

Volunteer To get an idea of what working for the Peace Corps might be like, challenge students to donate their services at a community food bank or volunteer as a Red Cross aide, for example.

1960s Politics and Economics

Listed and described below are some of the most significant political and economic events of the sixties. Further discussions of the topics can be found on the indicated pages.

The Bay of Pigs

In 1959 Fidel Castro led a successful revolution in Cuba and became increasingly friendly with the Soviet Union. Fearing a close Communist neighbor, the Eisenhower administration allowed the CIA to secretly train Cuban exiles. When Eisenhower left office he informed the new president, John Kennedy, of the situation. On April 17, 1961, 1,400 Cubans landed at the Bay of Pigs to lead a revolt against Castro. Their mission failed when promised U.S. air support never arrived.

The Cuban Missile Crisis

In October 1962, a much more serious Soviet Union confrontation occurred. When President Kennedy discovered that the Soviets were building nuclear missile bases in Cuba, he ordered the Navy to surround Cuba. Kennedy then dared the Soviet premier, Nikita Khrushchev, to run the blockade. Disaster was averted when Khrushchev agreed to remove the missiles. In exchange, the U.S. agreed not to invade Cuba.

Vietnam War

When Kennedy took office the U.S. was sending aid to South Vietnam. A decision was made to send military advisers to help train the South Vietnamese, and by 1963 the U.S. was spending one and one half million dollars a day to support the war. After Kennedy's assassination, President Johnson escalated the U.S. operations in Vietnam. See pages 318 to 321 for more about the Vietnam War.

War on Poverty

Despite a thriving economy, not everyone in the U.S. was affluent. While many Americans enjoyed televisions, cars, bikes, and nice houses, there were those who did not even have enough to eat. Determined to do something about the problem, President Johnson saw to it that a civil rights act was passed. In addition, agencies such as Medicare, Medicaid, Operation Headstart, Upward Bound, and Job Corps were instituted.

Civil Rights

Landmark 1950s decisions had paved the way for integration, but the pace was extremely slow. More and more black leaders led marches and demonstrations to obtain the rights which they were being denied. Despite presidential support of civil rights measures, hatred and bigotry continued. Race riots plagued the country. The fight was just beginning. See pages 328 to 330 for more about this topic.

Women's Liberation

During the early sixties women worked quietly in the background to support the civil rights causes and the antiwar protests. They also began to voice their discontent with their roles in society. They began demanding the same freedoms as men—they wanted to be treated as equals. For more about the women's liberation movement see page 331.

Events in Vietnam

The Vietnam War was the costliest and longest war fought in U.S. history. More bomb tonnage was dropped on North Vietnam than on Germany, Italy, and Japan during all of World War II. Over 50,000 American troops died in Vietnam. How did the U.S. become involved in the war and what was the outcome? These and other issues are addressed in the various sections below.

Beginnings During WW II, Japan invaded French Indochina. After the war, the communist Vietminh seized the capital city, Hanoi, and declared the Democratic Republic of Vietnam or North Vietnam. France supported Emperor Bao Dai and helped to establish a new state of Vietnam, or South Vietnam, with a capital at Saigon. The United States recognized the Saigon government. Meanwhile, the French and the Vietminh were at war. In 1954, at the battle of Dien Bien Phu, the French sufffered defeat and withdrew their forces. Under accords drawn at a meeting in Geneva, France and North Vietnam agreed to a truce and future free elections for reunification. Neither side honored the accords, however, and civil war continued. In 1954 the U.S. offered direct economic aid to South Vietnam. The following year U.S. military advisers were sent to train Vietnamese soldiers.

Domino Theory When Kennedy came into office, his predecessor, President Eisenhower, warned him that if the U.S. allowed South Vietnam to fall to the Communists, the next in line would be Laos, Cambodia, Burma, and on into the Subcontinent. This Domino Theory worried Kennedy, and he pledged to help South Vietnam remain independent. U.S. economic and military aid increased. In 1961, 400 army personnel were sent to Saigon to operate two noncombat helicopter units. By 1962 more than 10,000 U.S. military men were in place.

Gulf of Tonkin After President Kennedy was assassinated, President Johnson vowed not to lose Vietnam to communism. On August 2, 1964, it was reported that the USNS Maddox, a U.S. destroyer in the Gulf of Tonkin, had been attacked by North Vietnam. This incident led Congress to pass a resolution allowing the president to use U.S. troops without a formal declaration of war or approval from Congress. The president ordered jets to begin retaliatory bombing of military targets in North Vietnam. In March of 1965, the first ground-force combat units of marines brought the level of U.S. troops to 27,000. By the end of the year there were almost 200,000 American combat forces in Vietnam.

Tet Offensive North Vietnam and its Viet Cong allies launched a huge surprise attack on major cities in the South on January 30, 1968. Because it began during Tet, the Vietnamese New Year, the attack was called the Tet Offensive. The U.S. counterattack was successful, but both sides suffered massive casualties.

Peace Talks Following the Tet Offensive the U.S. halted bombing in Vietnam, and peace talks were initiated in Paris. No agreement could be reached at that time. Early in 1969 President Nixon announced his plan for Vietnamization of the war, and for a gradual withdrawal of U.S. forces. By September of 1969, 55,000 American soldiers had left Vietnam. Secret peace talks between Henry Kissinger of the U.S. and Le Duc Tho of North Vietnam began in Paris in 1970. The talks continued for three years, as did the fighting in Vietnam. Finally, in January of 1973, a cease fire agreement was reached. The U.S. and its allies withdrew from Vietnam in March of that year.

Suggested Activity

Research Have students find out more about the following people and places associated with the Vietnam war.

My Lai Massacre	Haiphong Harbor	POWS
Lt. Calley	Ho Chi Minh Trail	The fall of Saigon
General Wiliam Westmoreland	Laos	Allies of the U.S.
Danang	Cambodia	Allies of North Vietnam

Mapping the Terrain

The terrain and climate of Vietnam was unfamiliar territory to most American soldiers. After all, Vietnam was mostly jungle with thick growths of shrubs and trees. Conditions there were unlike any other ever encountered by the military. Learn more about Vietnam with this mapping activity. Read the story and write the names of the locations on the lines provided.

After the Vietcong defeated combat regiments in May and June of 1965, the government of 1._____collapsed. The United States began pouring in more troops and continued bombing 2.._____.Supported by the Soviet Union and 3._____, guerilla forces multiplied. Reinforcements and munitions were smuggled along the 4._____through 5._____and 6._____into South Vietnam. By mid-1967, there were no signs of the war ending. All U.S. strategy had failed and American combat casualties rose dramatically. On January 31, 1968, the communists launched surprise attacks on every major South Vietnamese village and city. At 7._____, American soldiers found mass graves of people killed by the Vietcong. The Vietcong eventually withdrew from Hue, but fighting for 8._____raged on for 75 days. By the time the offensive had been defeated in March, the U.S. counted 2,000 soldiers dead, the South Vietnamese 4,000, and the North Vietnamese 40,000. Still, the fighting continued.

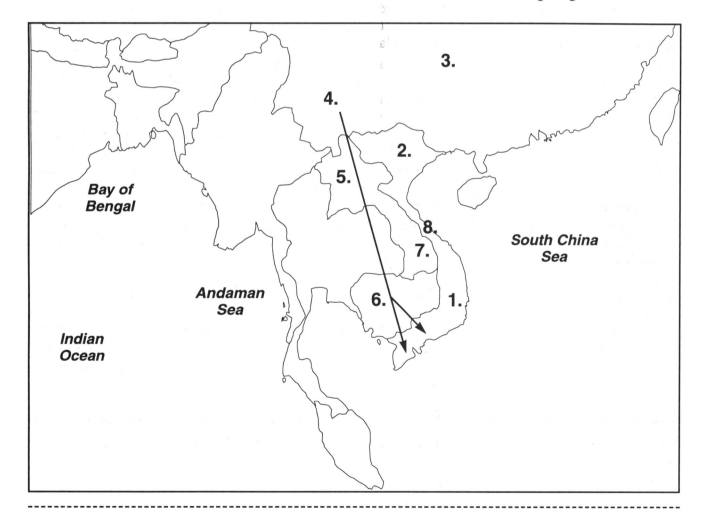

Answers (cover before copying)

1. South Vietnam 2. North Vietnam 3. Communist China 4. Ho Chi Minh Trail 5. Laos 6. Cambodia 7. Hue 8. Khesanh

A Vietnam Interview

Interview an individual who was a teenager or adult during the Vietnam War.

Name_____

Age_____

Occupation _____

1. What do you know about the Vietnam War?_____

   _____

2. What were you doing during the Vietnam War? _____

   _____

3. Did you or anyone else you know serve in Vietnam? _____

   _____

4. If you did not serve in Vietnam, how did you feel about those who did? _____

   _____

5. Did you know anyone who evaded the draft? _____

   _____

6. How did you feel about draft evaders? _____

   _____

7. Did you ever protest against the war in Vietnam? Why or why not? _____

   _____

8. Do you think the U.S. should have become involved in Vietnam?_____

   _____

9. Have your views changed since the war ended? If so, how?_____

   _____

10. If the U.S. became involved in a war today, would you serve in the armed forces? Defend your response._____

   _____

   _____

   _____

"Hell No, We Won't Go"

Read the following paragraphs about the draft. Answer the questions that follow. Use the back of this page, if necessary.

When two batallions of Marines were sent to guard the Danang air base on March 8, 1965, there were already some 20,000 troops in Vietnam. By the end of the year the number had reached 200,000. In order to provide ever-increasing numbers of troops, the army used the draft to force men into military service. Not everyone supported the draft, however. The prospect of dying in a combat zone was very real. Demonstrations and antiwar rallies were held on college campuses across the nation. "Hell no, we won't go," became a national anthem among protestors. Students were required to register for the draft. If they attended school, they automatically received a deferment or postponement of their service. Some young men burned their registration cards, an act that was against the law. An estimated 250,000 avoided registration. Many of them fled to Canada and Europe where they participated in huge demonstrations against U.S. involvement in Vietnam. They remained outside the U.S. until President Carter pardoned them in 1977.

Questions

1. Was the draft fair? Why or why not? Defend your answer. _____

   _____

   _____

   _____

2. The draft did not apply to women. Should women be exempt from the draft?_____

   Explain your answer. _____

   _____

   _____

   _____

3. How were the problems of this draft similar to the draft during the Civil War?

   _____

   _____

   _____

   _____

   _____

John Fitzgerald Kennedy

35th President, 1961–1963

Vice President: Lyndon B. Johnson

Born: May 29, 1917, Brookline, Massachusetts

Died: November 22, 1963

Party: Democratic

Parents: Joseph Patrick Kennedy, Rose Elizabeth Fitzgerald

First Lady: Jacqueline Lee Bouvier

Children: Caroline; John, Jr.; Patrick (who died shortly after birth)

Nickname: JFK

Education: Harvard

Famous Firsts:

- Kennedy was the first president to be born in the twentieth century.
- He was the youngest man ever elected president and was the first Roman Catholic to hold the office.
- He was the first president to appoint a sibling to a cabinet post; his younger brother Robert (Bobby) was his Attorney General.
- Kennedy and Nixon participated in the first televised debates between presidential candidates.

Achievements:

- Kennedy established the Peace Corps in 1961.
- Kennedy served in WW II and was nearly killed when a Japanese destroyer rammed his gunboat, PT-109.
- JFK vowed that the U.S. would land an American on the moon by the end of the decade. To achieve this goal he funded a five-billion-dollar space program. Although Kennedy began plans for a New Frontier, they were accomplished only after his death.
- Included in his plans were stronger civil rights laws, medicare for the elderly, and increased aid for education.

Interesting Facts:

- JFK and each of his eight siblings were given $1 million when they turned 21.
- At 43, Kennedy was the youngest President ever elected, but he was not the youngest President. That distinction is given to Theodore Roosevelt who was 42 when he assumed office after President McKinley was assassinated.
- Kennedy won the 1960 election by a very slim margin—less than 1% of the popular vote—yet he went on to become a very popular president.
- In 1956, Kennedy published *Profiles in Courage*, a look at eight U.S. Senators. The book was awarded the Pulitzer Prize.
- At 29 Kennedy was elected as a Democratic Congressional representative from Massachusetts.

(*For information about Dwight Eisenhower, see page 273.*)

Lyndon Baines Johnson

36th President, 1963–1969

Vice President: Hubert H. Humphrey

Born: August 27, 1908, Stonewall, Texas

Died: January 22, 1973

Party: Democratic

Parents: Sam Ealy Johnson, Jr., Rebekah Baines

First Lady: Claudia (Lady Bird) Alta Taylor

Children: Lynda, Luci

Nickname: LBJ

Education: Southwest Texas State Teachers College

Famous Firsts:

- Johnson was the first Vice-President to witness the assassination of the President whom he succeeded.
- He was the first president to be sworn in by a woman.

Achievements:

- At 46 Johnson became the Senate Majority Leader in 1955.
- During his administration, more civil rights legislation was passed than under any president in U.S. history.
- In his 1964 State of the Union address, Johnson declared a war on poverty.
- His Great Society established Medicare and Medicaid.
- He passed the Civil Rights Act of 1964.
- Johnson established the Head Start and Job Corps programs.
- His Voting Rights Act of 1965 outlawed literacy tests used to keep African Americans from registering to vote.
- Immigration quota laws were changed for the first time since the 1920s.

Interesting Facts:

- Johnson spent one year teaching school before he entered politics.
- LBJ proposed to his wife the day after they first met; the couple married two months later.
- In a surprise move, Johnson announced he would not run for re-election in 1968.

(*For information about Richard Nixon, see page 370.*)

Presidential Quotes

Three presidents were inaugurated during the sixties, and during their terms in office each said words that are still considered important. Read each quote below. On the lines that follow, explain what each one means.

President John Fitzgerald Kennedy

"And so, my fellow Americans, ask not what your country can do for you; ask what you can do for your country. My fellow citizens of the world, ask not what America will do for you, but what together we can do for the freedom of man."–*Inaugural Address, January 20, 1961*

_____

_____

_____

_____

_____

President Lyndon Baines Johnson

"This administration today, here and now, declares unconditional war on poverty in America . . . It will not be a short or easy struggle, no single weapon or strategy will suffice, but we shall not rest until that war is won."–*State of the Union message on January 8, 1964*

_____

_____

_____

_____

_____

President Richard Milhous Nixon

"We have found ourselves rich in goods, but ragged in spirit; reaching with magnificent precision for the moon but falling into raucous discord on earth. We are caught in war, wanting peace. We are torn by divisions, wanting unity."–*First Inaugural Address, January 20, 1969*

_____

_____

_____

_____

_____

Just Like Lincoln

After the 1963 assassination of President Kennedy, some historians began to note some uncanny similarities between his death and that of President Lincoln. For example, both had been shot in the head by an assassin, and at his widow's request, Kennedy's funeral was modeled after Lincoln's.

Let students find out more likenesses between the two with this game. Make a copy of this page for each pair of students. Direct them to cut apart the cards and match the answers to the correct questions. Review the questions and answers in whole group.

1. What do both presidents' last names have in common?	a. They were full of inconsistencies.
2. How well-liked were both presidents?	b. Both inherited a wartime dispute.
3. What is believed about the official reports about the two assassinations?	c. The South–Lyndon from Texas, Andrew from Tennessee.
4. What same last name did the two vice presidents share?	d. Both contain seven letters.
5. What happened to both assassins before they could be brought to trial?	e. Days after the assassinations, both were shot and killed.
6. What role did war play in their administrations?	f. Lincoln and Kennedy were popular with the people but both had enemies.
7. What two things are the same about the names of the presidents' assassins?	g. Both had three names containing a total of 15 letters.
8. From which area of the U.S. did both Johnsons originate?	h. Johnson (Andrew and Lyndon Baines)

A Look Back at Jackie

There has never been a first lady quite like Jacqueline Bouvier Kennedy. She was young, beautiful, and vibrant and added a touch of elegance lacking in the previous older administration. Her hair and clothing styles were simple yet graceful and widely copied by American women. The Jackie look was the fashionable way to dress. When her husband died in office, Jacqueline Kennedy stoically led the country in mourning. She was a special woman, just right for the times.

Jacqueline Lee Bouvier, or Jackie as the world called her, was born on July 28, 1929, in East Hampton on Long Island. Her father was John Vernon Bouvier III, a rich and handsome New York stockbroker; her mother, Janet Lee Bouvier, was a beautiful woman who was also a skilled horsewoman. Jackie Bouvier and her younger sister, Lee, were treated like princesses by their parents and the family's many servants. Even her parents' divorce when she was eight did not diminish her standing in society, and she continued to attend private schools. When she was thirteen, her mother married a rich man, Hugh Auchincloss. Throughout these times Jackie Bouvier kept up with her favorite sport of horseback riding, even boarding her mare, Danseuse, in a nearby stable while attending Miss Porter's School for young women.

In 1946 Jackie Bouvier had her debutante party and was named Queen Deb of the Year by the local press. The social scene failed to impress her, and she entered college that fall. After completing her studies at George Washington University, she got a job at the *Washington Times-Herald* as an inquiring camera girl. Through some friends, she met the most eligible bachelor in Washington, John F. Kennedy. The two were married on September 12, 1953, with 1,700 invited guests from high society and politics.

Jacqueline Bouvier Kennedy quit her job and played the part of perfect political wife. She had three children, Caroline, John F. Kennedy, Jr., and Patrick, who died shortly after birth. When the young family moved into the White House, a transformation seemed to take place. Jackie Kennedy was just 31 and her husband, at 43, was the youngest man ever elected to the presidency. It was, as some called it, Camelot.

During her years as first lady, Jacqueline Kennedy renovated and restored the White House to its historical past and took the entire nation on a televised tour into the White House on February 14, 1962. She supported a number of cultural and artistic endeavors and raised the level of official entertaining by inviting America's best artists to perform at the White House.

Jacqueline Kennedy went on to remarry and then to build a powerful career in the publishing world. She fought to maintain her privacy, both for herself and her children, after the White House Years. For many years, she was among the most admired women in the world and until her death on May 19, 1994, one of the most photographed.

Suggested Activity

Completion Let students research and find out how Jacqueline Kennedy spent the remainder of her years after the White House.

Election Facts and Figures

	Election of 1960	Election of 1964	Election of 1968
Democrats	John F. Kennedy, a senator from Massachusetts, was nominated for president and selected Texas senator Lyndon Baines Johnson as his running mate.	President Lyndon Baines Johnson received the presidential nomination with Minnesota senator Hubert H. Humphrey for vice president.	At a convention marked by protests and violence, Vice President Hubert Humphrey became the presidential candidate with Senator Edmund Muskie of Maine as his running mate.
Republicans	Vice-President Richard M. Nixon ran for president with Henry Cabot Lodge, the U.S. ambassador to the UN, as his vice president.	Barry Goldwater, an extremely conservative senator from Arizona, ran for president with William Miller of New York for vice president.	Former Vice President Richard M. Nixon was paired with Maryland governor Spiro T. Agnew for vice president.
Other			George C. Wallace, former governor of Alabama, broke with the Democrats to form the American Independent Party and ran for president with General Curtis LeMay for vice president.
Issues	Both candidates had similar political ideas. They believed in a strong military that could protect the United States from a Communist attack and supported funding for welfare programs for the poor.	Goldwater's brand of politics scared many Americans. He opposed civil rights legislation, wanted to make Social Security voluntary, and proposed deep cuts in social programs.	Vietnam remained the big issue in this election. Humphrey found it difficult to distance himself from Johnson, to whom he had remained loyal. Nixon talked vaguely about a secret plan to end the war. Wallace campaigned for strict law and order.
Slogans	Kennedy promised to lead Americans to a New Frontier.	Johnson's slogan was "All the way with LBJ;" Goldwater's slogan was "In your heart, you know he's right."	
Results	John F. Kennedy won by a narrow margin—electoral votes, 303 (Kennedy) to 219 (Nixon).	Johnson won by an overwhelming majority—electoral votes, 486 (Johnson) to 52 (Goldwater).	Nixon received less than one percent of the popular vote. The electoral vote was 301 (Nixon) to 191 (Humphrey). Wallace received 45 electoral votes, the strongest third party finish since Theodore Roosevelt in 1912.

The Civil Rights Movement

Civil rights had long been an issue, but not until the sixties did it reach such urgency. Tired of the slow pace of legislative changes, African American leaders emerged and pushed the civil rights movement to the forefront. Listed below are some important 1960s developments in the civil rights cause.

Sit-Ins This nonviolent action was started on February 1, 1960, by a group of four black students who had gone to the Woolworth's store in Greensboro, North Carolina, to buy supplies. When they sat at the lunch counter for coffee, they were told they could not be served. In protest, the group remained seated until the store closed.

Freedom Rides This project protested the segregation of long-distance interstate bus travel. In 1961 a group called CORE (see page 329) announced plans for seven blacks and six whites to begin a Freedom Ride from Washington, D.C., to New Orleans, Louisiana. The bus did not get far before there was trouble. Angry whites beat several riders and set fire to the bus. Nevertheless, several more freedom rides were planned and carried out before the U.S. government initiated very clear rules about integrating bus stations.

March on Washington On August 28, 1963, more than 2,000 buses and thirty special trains had brought a quarter of a million people to Washington, D.C., to protest against discrimination. People of all races and from all over the country traveled to our nation's capital so their voices could be heard. This is where Martin Luther King, Jr., delivered his famous "I Have a Dream . . ." speech.

Mississippi Freedom Summer During the summer of 1964, close to 1,000 students from the North traveled to Mississippi to participate in the Mississippi Summer Project. Bob Moses had planned the event to create a new political party and provide volunteers to register black voters. This angered many whites, and on June 21, three young civil rights workers were killed.

Selma to Montgomery March On March 21, 1965, Dr. Martin Luther King, Jr., began with a group of 4,000 people across the Edmund Pettus Bridge. By the time they reached Montgomery on March 25, they numbered 25,000.

Poor People's Campaign This was Dr. Martin Luther King, Jr.'s, last campaign. In 1968 he had decided to take his cause North to work to eliminate poverty among blacks and whites.

Riots In Los Angeles from August 11–16, 1965, race riots spread throughout the city's Watts area. Sparked by charges of police brutality, National Guardsmen were called in to restore order. During one week in July of 1967, seventy-five race riots erupted in Detroit. Forty-three people died in the conflicts.

Suggested Activities

Changes With the class, discuss what important changes were brought about by the civil rights movement and how the U.S. government helped the cause.

Resource For more information about these issues read . . . *If You Lived at the Time of Martin Luther King, Jr.,* by Ellen Levine (Scholastic, Inc., 1990).

Leading the Cause

Not everyone agreed with Martin Luther King, Jr.'s ideas. Although the civil rights groups and black leaders believed that blacks and whites must be treated equally, their methods were not all the same. Read about some of these groups and leaders of the civil rights cause.

NAACP The oldest civil rights group, the National Association for the Advancement of Colored People, was founded in 1909. Its members believed that the best way to change bad laws was through the court system. Lawyers for the NAACP argued that segregation was wrong and they won several important cases.

CORE The Congress of Racial Equality was founded in Chicago in 1942. Composed of black and white members, they believed in nonviolent direct action and organized the Freedom Rides of 1961.

SNCC Founded in 1960 by students from the sit-ins, the Student Nonviolent Coordinating Committee helped African Americans to register to vote.

SCLC The Southern Christian Leadership Conference was founded by Ralph Abernathy and Martin Luther King, Jr., following the bus boycott in Montgomery, Alabama. See page 330 for more about King's life.

Malcolm X Malcolm X was originally a leader of the Nation of Islam, or Black Muslims. He spoke out against integration and believed that blacks and whites should not live together. After a trip to Mecca in Saudi Arabia, he changed his ideas about hate and violence. Malcolm broke with the Black Muslims to form his own group. In 1964 he was killed by some men in the Muslim group.

Malcolm X

Stokley Carmichael

Medgar Evers As Mississippi field secretary of the NAACP, he coordinated the effort to desegregate public facilities in Jackson, Mississippi. His assassination on June 13, 1963, led President Kennedy to advocate a new, comprehensive civil rights program.

Huey Newton In 1966 Huey Newton and other black activists founded the Black Panther Party, the original purpose of which was to protect African American neighborhoods from police brutality.

Stokely Carmichael When Stokely Carmichael was elected president of the SNCC, he decided to take the organization in a more aggressive direction. He talked about change by any means necessary and black power. In 1966 SNCC expelled all whites from its organization.

Suggested Activities

Nation of Islam Louis Farrakhan became an outspoken leader of the Nation of Islam later in the century. Tell the students to find out his views on civil rights, whites, and integration.

Assassins Medgar Evers' assassins were not brought to trial until some thirty years after the event. Direct the students to find out why it took so long to prosecute his killers.

Update Instruct the students to find out about current changes in the NAACP. Find out who is the current leader and how the organization is affecting social change.

Martin Luther King, Jr.

On April 4, 1968, the world lost one of its greatest heroes of social causes, Martin Luther King, Jr. He was a man who devoted his life to the nonviolent promotion of civil rights, and yet he died a violent death.

King was born in Atlanta, Georgia, on January 15, 1929. His mother was a teacher and his father was a minister. An excellent student, King graduated from high school at the age of 15. He continued his education at Morehouse College and went on to study theology at Crozer Theological Seminar in Chester, Pennsylvania. King later attended Boston University and received his Ph.D. in 1955. While he was in Boston, he met Coretta Scott and they married on June 18, 1953.

For five years during the fifties, King was pastor of Dexter Avenue Baptist Church in Montgomery, Alabama, but he resigned so that he could devote all his time to the civil rights cause. He began to speak out against the discrimination that African Americans were facing. African Americans attended separate and unequal schools, they were forced to sit in the back of buses, and they could not eat at the same lunch counter as whites. It was degrading and unfair, and King was not afraid to speak out about these injustices. After African American Rosa Parks refused to give up her bus seat to a white man, King helped organize the Montgomery bus boycott. King was arrested and jailed, his home was bombed, and threats were made against his life, but he continued his nonviolent protest. As a result, the city changed its segregation laws.

As a student, King had learned about Mohandas Gandhi's technique of nonviolent persuasion for social protest. During a trip to India in 1959, King was able to enhance his knowledge of Gandhi's principles. These were the cornerstone of King's protest.

On August 28, 1963, King led the March on Washington. A quarter of a million people of all races from all over the country traveled to Washington, D.C. to protest discrimination. This demonstration led to the passage of the 1964 Civil Rights Act and the 1965 Voting Rights Act. A charismatic leader and an excellent orator, Martin Luther King, Jr., urged his followers to employ civil disobedience and nonviolent methods of protest. In 1964 he was awarded the Nobel peace prize for his work. It was a fitting tribute to a true hero of the times.

Suggested Activities

Speech Martin Luther King, Jr. was a powerful speaker and is probably best known for his "I Have a Dream . . ." speech. Direct the students to read the complete text of the speech and to write a summary of the important ideas.

Comparisons Compare the lives and works of Medgar Evers and Malcolm X with those of Martin Luther King, Jr. Students can construct a chart or three-way Venn diagram. Alternatively, students can compare King's methods of nonviolence with those of Mohandas Gandhi.

Background Students may be interested to learn what sparked King's dream of equality. Read aloud "Does Friendship Have a Color?" by Valerie Wilson Wesley from the January/February 1996 issue of *Creative Classroom*. Related activities accompany the story.

Women's Liberation

In the years leading up to the 1960s, the role of women in American society was that of the traditional housewife and stay-at-home mother. Several television programs reflected these views. *I Love Lucy*, *Ozzie and Harriet*, and *Leave It to Beaver*, for example, depicted happy households where Mom was content to take care of her family. Writer Betty Friedan questioned this traditionalist view of women, and during the early sixties she investigated women's true feelings. Friedan found that many of them were unhappy and dissatisfied with the limitations of being housewives. As these women began seeking ways to change their lives, the women's liberation movement gathered momentum.

Born Betty Goldstein in Peoria, Illinois, to a wealthy family, she was a bright, outgoing child. After graduating from high school as valedictorian she went on to study psychology at Smith College. There she became editor of the college newspaper.

Betty Friedan

This experience helped her in her job as a labor journalist. However, it did not prepare her for the discrimination she and other women faced in the work force. Her marriage and motherhood only reinforced the limited roles available to women in the sixties. Then she was asked to conduct a poll of her college classmates about their life experiences. Friedan was amazed to find that the 200 women who responded were as dissatisfied with their places in society as she was. Friedan wrote an article about her survey results, but no magazine would publish it. One publisher, however, was interested in a book. After five years of interviews and researching, *The Feminine Mystique* was published in 1963. Enormously popular, the book pointed out that American females received educations that opened their minds yet left them facing closed doors to all but a few career choices. As more and more women were drawn to feminism, Friedan founded a group in 1966 called NOW, the National Organization of Women. NOW worked to achieve equal rights for women and is still an active force in society and politics. Betty Friedan served as its president until 1970 and today continues to promote women's equality.

Suggested Activity

Discussion Conduct a class discussion about women's roles in society today. Do women have equal rights? Are they paid the same as men for equal work? Are the same career opportunities available to women as to men?

The Problem In *The Feminine Mystique*, Betty Friedan called it "the problem that has no name." Ask students to identify and discuss the problem. Does it still exist?

Excerpts Read excerpts from *The Feminine Mystique* aloud to students. Discuss the content with the class.

La Causa

Cesar Chavez knew all too well what life was like for migrant workers, many of whom were Mexican Americans. They lived in tents, often did not have a bathroom to use, and traveled from bean fields to walnut groves with the changing crop seasons. The Chavez family became migrant workers when financial problems forced them to give up their farm near Yuma, Arizona, where Cesar Chavez was born in 1927. Young Chavez frequently went hungry and had very little clothing. By the time of his eighth grade graduation, he had attended 38 different schools. With these background experiences, Chavez was the right candidate for a job with the Community Service Organization. This agency helped poor people deal with a variety of problems, including housing, medical care, and legal aid. Chavez wanted to go beyond these basic services, however. He knew that workers were being taken advantage of by the growers. Pay was far below minimum wage, conditions were unsafe, and children were forced to work long hours.

Cesar Chavez

Chavez believed that a union would help the migrant workers obtain fair wages and safe work and living conditions. In 1962 he started talking to farmers, going from farm to farm, and organized the National Farm Workers Association. The labor union staged a strike against grape growers in 1965. More attention was needed for La Causa to be successful, so Chavez organized a 300-mile march across California. At Chavez's urging, some university students and religious leaders joined the farm workers to help them publicize the cause. When many growers still refused to sign contracts with the union, Chavez called for a boycott. He asked the American people not to buy grapes grown in California. The tactic finally worked. Chavez's union eventually became a part of the United Farm Workers Organizing Committee. In 1970 the name was changed to United Farm Workers of America, but its purpose remained the same. Chavez continued to lead the cause of improving working conditions for farm workers until his death in 1993.

Suggested Activities

Walk in His Shoes Take the students on a one-mile walk. Record the time. Have students figure out how long it would take to walk 300 miles. Ask them to speculate what such a long walk would be like.

Discussion Conduct a class discussion on either of these topics: the effectiveness of labor unions or the effectiveness of boycotts and strikes.

Conscience Cesar Chavez followed his conscience when he led strikes and boycotts against the growers. Some Americans were sympathetic to his cause while others sided with the growers. Ask students whose side they agree with and why.

More Learn more about Cesar Chavez and his cause. See Teacher Created Materials *book #605 Interdisciplinary Unit—Heroes.*

Sidney Poitier

Sidney Poitier is one of the most important African American figures ever to have worked in Hollywood. His groundbreaking roles paved the way for today's group of popular black actors.

Poitier was born in 1924 to a Bahamian couple in Miami, Florida. Most of his childhood was spent in the West Indies, but when he was sixteen years old, he returned to Miami. From there he traveled to New York City and worked at a number of odd jobs, including dishwashing. When an ad in the newspaper called for actors at the American Negro Theatre in Harlem, Poitier applied for a role. After his somewhat wooden audition he was admonished by the director that he was no actor and could not be one. Undeterred, he spent six months training to overcome his strong West Indian accent. He also spent four years in the U.S. Army, and on his return tried out again at the American Negro Theatre. This time he was accepted and was able to join an elite group of African American actors that included Harry Belafonte, Ossie Davis, and Ruby Dee. In 1946 Poitier landed a small role in an all-black Broadway production of *Lysistrata*. He was so nervous that he fumbled some of his lines, and the audience laughed. Critics praised his comic abilities. Poitier continued to work in other American Negro Theatre productions, the most important of which was *A Raisin in the Sun*.

Throughout the fifties Poitier starred in a number of dramatic films including *Blackboard Jungle* and *Cry*. It was the 1958 movie *The Defiant Ones* that made him a star. Poitier's next major role was in the film version of the Broadway hit *A Raisin in the Sun*. Although many critics felt his performance deserved an Oscar nomination, it was his role in the 1963 film *Lilies of the Field* that won him the coveted Best Actor award. In doing so, he became the first African American to win an Academy Award for Best Actor. Later sixties' films saw him as a teacher of a group of poor white students in *To Sir With Love; Guess Who's Coming to Dinner* cast him as the fiance of a wealthy white woman.

During the seventies, Poitier switched from acting to directing. With films such as *Stir Crazy*, he featured a new generation of black actors, including Denise Nicholas and Richard Pryor. Humor was featured in these films while politics took a back seat.

Although not as active in the industry as he once was, Sidney Poitier continues to bring a dignity and compassion to his roles. As one of the first African American actors to portray a hero in a leading part, he left an indelible mark on Hollywood.

Suggested Activities

Since Then Find out if any black actors have won Academy Awards since Poitier.

Research What is the play *Lysistrata* about? Let the students explain it in their own words.

A Hollywood Legend

She was named for two screen legends—Norma Talmadge and Jean Harlow. Norma Jean Baker only lived to be thirty-six years old, yet she left a lasting impression on popular fashion for years to come. As Marilyn Monroe, this actress became a true Hollywood legend.

Born June 1, 1926, Norma Jean's mother, Gladys Baker Mortenson, was a twenty-four year old divorcee. Her biological father was C. Stanley Gifford, a salesman who worked with Gladys at a Hollywood film lab. Gifford refused to marry Mortenson and was never seen by her or his daughter again. While Gladys Mortenson spent time in and out of hospitals for treatment of mental illness, her daughter lived in twelve different foster homes and in an orphanage for awhile. Many of her days were spent in movie theaters where she dreamed of becoming a movie star. When she was just 16, young Mortenson married twenty-one year old merchant marine James Dougherty.

Marilyn Monroe

Discovered by a photographer when she worked in a weapons plant, she became a model. After divorcing her husband, she took her mother's family name and was known as Norma Jean Baker. Her modeling drew the attention of a film studio. Renamed Marilyn Monroe, she had a few small film roles in the late 1940s. It was the 1952 film *Gentlemen Prefer Blondes*, that propelled her to stardom. The next year, she married baseball great Joe DiMaggio, but the union did not last. One year later they were divorced. Weary of the constant pressure of being in the public eye, Monroe began taking sleeping pills at night and often drank alcohol to stay relaxed. By 1955 Monroe was ready for more serious roles. She had grown tired of playing the beautiful dumb blonde. At the Actors Studio in New York she studied acting with the great master, Lee Strasberg. When Monroe returned to Hollywood, she formed her own production company and starred in the hits *Bus Stop* and *The Seven Year Itch*. In 1956 she married American playwright Arthur Miller, but they divorced a few years later. Several more successful films followed. Her last movie, in 1961, *The Misfits*, was especially written for her by her ex-husband Arthur Miller. The following year Marilyn Monroe was found dead in her home, a victim of an overdose of sleeping pills.

Since her death, she has become a pop icon and is immortalized as one of the great movie legends of all time.

Suggested Activities

Warhol Marilyn Monroe was the subject of one of Andy Warhol's famous paintings. Display a copy of this print and have the students write an appropriate title for it.

Modern Monroe Eighties and nineties music pop star Madonna is often compared to Marilyn Monroe. With the class make a Venn diagram of the two entertainers' likenesses and differences.

Fastest Woman in the World

Wilma Rudolph

Wilma Rudolph was a born fighter. The seventeenth of nineteen children, she contracted double pneumonia and scarlet fever early in her life. Fortunately, she survived both. Some years later a bout with polio left one of her legs crippled. Rudolph's determined mother took her to doctors in Nashville, and they provided her with unique water and heat therapy. For many years Rudolph had to wear a leg brace, but with the help and encouragement of her large family, she was able to run and play without a brace before she entered her teen years.

In junior high school she joined a basketball team and also began running track. Her many wins at track meets did not go unnoticed. Ed Temple, a coach from Tennessee State College, was particularly impressed when he watched her compete in 1956. The coach invited Rudolph to compete in a summer college athletic program. She went to Nashville to train, and on the day of the national track meet was victorious in all nine races that she had entered. Coach Temple continued to train Rudolph, but this time it was for the Olympics. As a member of the 1956 U.S. Women's Olympic Relay Team, she won a bronze medal. For four years she continued her training with Coach Temple at Tennessee State University after winning an athletic scholarship. Italy was the site of the 1960 Olympics. Rudolph entered three races and after winning them all became the first American woman to win three medals in track. Her accomplishments won her the Associated Press title Athlete of the Year. She was also known as the fastest woman in the world.

Since then Rudolph worked hard to promote interest in sports among young women. She founded the Wilma Rudolph Foundation to help underprivileged children and served as a consultant on minority affairs at DePauw University in Indiana. Wilma Rudolph died in 1994 at the age of 54.

Suggested Activities

Record Holders Rudolph was proclaimed the fastest woman in the world. Challenge students to find out who currently holds that title. Compare the speed record set by Rudolph with the current recordholder's speed.

Races Have the students run 100-meter and 200-meter races. Make a class graph of their times.

Discussion With the class discuss the traits that helped Rudolph overcome severe adversities and accomplish what no other American female athlete had been able to do before.

Olympics Have the students find out what other track and field events are conducted in the course of the Olympics. An excellent resource for exploring the topic of the Olympics is Teacher Created Materials #064, *Share the Olympic Dream*.

Prince of the Pittsburgh Pirates

Roberto Clemente

In 1961 he was the batting champion of the year. Five years later he was voted Most Valuable Player of the National League. On July 27, 1970, he became only the eleventh player in the history of baseball to achieve 3,000 hits. Who was this baseball superstar? His name was Roberto Clemente, one of the most popular and well-liked players of his time.

Born in San Juan, Puerto Rico, on August 18, 1934, Clemente's family instilled him with solid values. He was taught to share with others, to be honest, and to work hard for what he needed. When the family could not afford to buy real baseballs for Clemente, he and his friends made their own by wrapping string around old golf balls. He could not wait to enter high school because they had real baseball equipment. Small and shy, Clemente emerged as the best athlete ever to graduate from Vizarrondo High School. He was Most Valuable Player on the track team and made the school's baseball all-star team three years in a row.

After high school he joined a winter baseball team in Puerto Rico. Scouts from the major leagues saw him play, and in 1954 Clemente signed a contract with the Pittsburgh Pirates. A quiet, sensitive man, he always gave 100% to his team, even when he was hurting from recurring muscle problems. His lifetime batting average was .317, and he played on twelve National League All-Star teams during his 18-year career. Numerous honors came his way, and the people of Puerto Rico considered him to be a living symbol of the country.

Although baseball was his first love, Clemente found time to help others in need. He took time to visit sick children and donated money to help others. Late in 1972, he organized a relief committee to aid earthquake victims in Managua, Nicaragua. On New Year's Eve, a plane was loaded with supplies; Clemente was also on board. Moments after takeoff from San Juan Airport, there were explosions and the airplane crashed into the ocean. Clemente's body was never recovered.

In 1973 in a special election, Clemente was elected to the National Baseball Hall of Fame. It was a fitting honor for a man who was a role model both on and off the baseball field.

Suggested Activities

World Series In 1960 and in 1971 Roberto Clemente helped the Pirates to World Series victories. Have the students find out who the Pirates played in each series. List some of Clemente's achievements during those games.

Records Before his death in 1972, Clemente learned that he was the eleventh man in major league history to get 3,000 hits. Assign students to research and find the names of any other players who have achieved or surpassed that record.

Nickname Discuss with the class why Roberto Clemente's nickname, Prince of the Pittsburgh Pirates, is an appropriate title.

No Silent Springs

Imagine a silent spring with no chirping birds, bustling insects, or the sounds of nature emerging from the long winter sleep. This chilling scenario is what environmentalist Rachel Carson warned against in her book *Silent Spring*. After a friend alerted Carson, she investigated the aftermath of a bird sanctury that had been sprayed with the pesticide DDT. Besides killing pesky mosquitoes, it also killed many birds and harmless insects. Carson's concerns about what DDT was doing to the environment went unheeded until her book was published in 1962.

Born in 1907 in Pennsylvania, Rachel Carson enjoyed the nature of both the nearby woods and the ocean, a passion she shared with her mother. An avid reader, Carson planned to become a writer, but a college biology class helped her decide to combine the two careers. They were both put to good use in her job at the U.S. Fish and Wildlife Service. In addition to editing all of their publications, Carson wrote articles on the side. After reading one of Carson's articles, an editor at a publishing firm encouraged her to write a book. In 1948 Carson wrote her first bestseller, *The Sea Around Us*. It stayed at the top of the bestseller list for more than a year. After being awarded a fellowship, Carson was financially able to resign from the Fish and Wildlife Service and devote her time to writing. She purchased a summer home on the coast of Maine and studied the ecology of tide pools. The resulting book, *The Edge of the Sea*, examined the interdependence of all living creatures in seaside communities. It was her publication of *Silent Spring*, though, that gathered the most controversy. While some tried to discredit her work, Carson's message came through loudly and clearly. Eventually, the U.S. banned the use of DDT. Sadly, Rachel Carson died in 1964 before the impact of her environmental work had been fully realized.

Suggested Activities

Environmentalists Have the students research some other famous environmentalists and learn what they have done to protect the environment.

Oceanographer Sylvia Earle is an oceaographer who is an outspoken protector of marine life. Compare her causes with those of fellow oceanographer Yves Jacques Cousteau.

DDT Instruct students to find answers to these two questions: What do the letters DDT stand for? What are some other commonly used pecticides and how do they work?

Read Aloud Read aloud some excerpts from *The Sea Around Us* or *Silent Spring*. Discuss the passages with the class.

One Small Step

When President Kennedy was sworn into office in 1961, he vowed to put a man on the moon before the decade was out. Although he did not live long enough to see his dream realized, the nation did witness man's historic voyage to the moon. One of the three astronauts on this momentous mission was Neil Armstrong.

Neil Armstrong

Neil Alden Armstrong was born in 1930 in Wapakoneta, Ohio. During the Korean War he served as a pilot for the U.S. Navy. In 1955 Armstrong graduated from Purdue University and went on to become a civilian test pilot for NASA. At Edwards Air Force Base in Lancaster, California, Armstrong tested the X-15 rocket airplane. When he began astronaut training in 1962, he became the first civilian to join the program. The 1966 Gemini 8 mission was Armstrong's first flight in space. During this flight, he and his partner, David R. Scott, docked their spacecraft with an unmanned spacecraft. After their spacecraft went into a violent roll, the astronauts were able to get the situation under control and safely return to Earth. Three years later, in 1969, Armstrong was chosen to be the commander of the Apollo 11 mission to the moon. Fellow astronaut Edwin E. Aldrin (Buzz) landed and walked on the moon with Armstrong while Michael Collins orbited the moon in the Command module.

As Armstrong made history by becoming the first person to walk on the moon, the world stopped to watch the event on television. On July 20, 1969, Neil Armstrong stepped onto the moon's rocky surface and uttered these famous words, "That's one small step for (a) man, one giant leap for mankind."

After retiring from NASA in 1971, Neil Armstrong became a professor of aerospace engineering at the University of Cincinnati.

Suggested Activities

Exploration Explore the Apollo 11 mission further with the reading and activities on page 339.

Moon Map Pair the students and have them draw and label maps of the moon. Instruct them to include the following landmarks: Sea of Cold, Sea of Rains, Sea of Crises, Sea of Clouds, Sea of Moisture, Sea of Nectar, Sea of Tranquility, and the site of the Apollo 11 landing. A great resource for this activity is *One Giant Leap* by Mary Ann Fraser (Henry Holt and Company, 1993).

Debate Ask for volunteers to debate the issue of space exploration. Instruct them to answer this question and provide defenses for their views: Should the U.S. continue to expand its space program or should it be reduced?

Mission to the Moon

Make a copy of this page for each small group of students. Direct them to read the paragraphs and complete the critical thinking activities that follow the story.

On the morning of July 16, 1969, three astronauts squeezed through the hatch of the spacecraft that was to be their home for the next eight days. As their families anxiously watched on the ground, Neil Armstrong, Buzz Aldrin, and Michael Collins listened to a voice at launch control count off the last ten seconds. Clouds of steam and smoke billowed around the rocket as all engines ignited and lift off was achieved. Only two and a half minutes into the flight, the *Saturn V's* first stage had shut down and fallen into the ocean. Four seconds later, the second stage separated from the *Columbia*, and the astronauts began to experience weightlessness. After the third and final stage fired, the spacecraft orbited around Earth one and a half times before the spacecraft propelled *Apollo 11* toward the moon. A little over four hours into the flight, the astronauts worked to maneuver the Eagle into position. Now they were ready for the job that lay ahead.

On the fifth morning of the mission, the astronauts were awakened by Mission Control. It was landing day, the day for which they had trained. Aldrin and Armstrong moved into *Eagle* while Collins stayed behind in *Columbia*. When Collins released the hatch, the two modules drifted apart. Less than two hours later, *Eagle* began its descent. Skillfully and carefully the two men piloted the craft toward the Sea of Tranquility. Collins, meanwhile, continued to orbit the back side of the moon. As Neil Armstrong stepped cautiously off the ladder onto the moon's surface, the world watched intently and listened to his words: "That's one small step for (a) man, one giant leap for mankind." A dream had become a reality.

—————— Suggested Activity ——————

Knowledge When was the Apollo 11 space mission launched? _____

List five facts from the story. Name the three astronauts on the mission. _____

_____

_____

Comprehension Summarize the Apollo 11 mission in your own words. _____

_____

_____

Application Write about some sights the astronauts would have seen if they had landed on Mars instead of the moon. _____

_____

Analysis Make a list of five things you can conclude about the Apollo 11 mission. _____

_____

Synthesis Rewrite the story from Michael Collins' point of view. _____

Evaluation Defend the value of future space exploration. _____

_____

Modern Cooking

Walk into any convenience store and you are likely to find shelves of prepackaged foods ready for eating. All you have to do is heat up the items in the microwave, and in a matter of seconds the food is piping hot.

It is hard to imagine now, but it was not so long ago that microwave ovens were first introduced into American homes. In 1942 Percy LeBaron of the Raytheon Company in Waltham, Massachusetts, accidentally discovered that microwaves used for signal transmissions would cook food. A chocolate bar in his pocket had melted when it came in contact with the signals.

In 1967 the first compact microwave oven for home use was introduced to the United States by Amana, a subsidiary of Raytheon. Read how the microwave oven works. Label the components with the corresponding number.

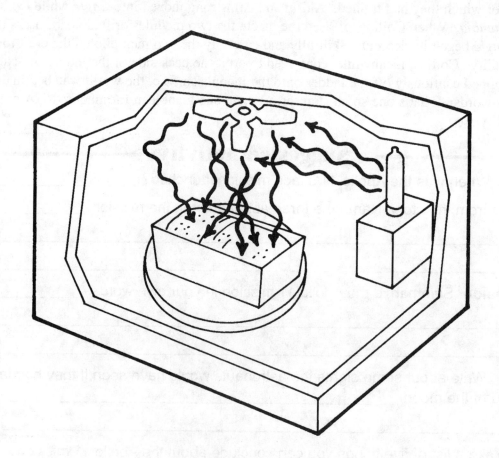

A magnetron (1) produces a beam (2) of microwaves. This microwave beam, which has a high heating power, strikes a spinning fan (3). In turn, the fan reflects the waves onto the food (4) from all directions (5). A turntable (6) moves the food to promote even heating.

Where Are the Wild Things?

All areas of life from politics to fashions were changing radically during the sixties, and the children's book market was no exception. One of the most enduring and often read children's authors and illustrators emerged during this period. His name is Maurice Sendak.

Born on June 10, 1928, Sendak was the youngest of three children born to Philip and Sarah (Schindler) Sendak. As a child, he was sickly after having contracted measles followed by bilateral pneumonia. His reputation as frail made it difficult for him to make friends, and he found that he was not particularly good at sports, not even skating or stoopball. Instead, he stayed home and drew pictures. His peers considered him a sissy. School was no better. Sendak claims he hated it from the first grade on because it stifled his creativity and imagination. However, he did manage to graduate from high school and even attended the Art Students' League for two years.

Maurice Sendak

A number of jobs led to Sendak's future career as a children's book author and illustrator. During high school he worked part time for a comic book syndicate, adapting the newspaper comic strip "Mutt and Jeff" for comic books. One year he and his brother tried to sell their animated wooden toys to F.A.O. Schwartz, the renowned toy store in New York City. Although the store chose not to purchase the toys, they did hire Sendak as a display artist. By 1956 he had written his first book, *Kenny's Window*. It was not his favorite book, but it showed signs of what was to come. After years of writing and illustrating (often illustrating for other authors), Sendak produced one of the most popular yet controversial children's books ever written. The title was *Where the Wild Things Are,* and it features a little boy named Max and a host of unusual looking monsters. Many librarians felt it was too scary for children, but despite this sentiment it was an unprecedented success. In 1964 Sendak was awarded the Caldecott Medal for this book.

Over the years, Maurice Sendak has been the recipient of numerous honors, including the 1970 Hans Christian Andersen Medal for his entire body of work.

Suggested Activities

Reputation Not until he worked with author Ruth Krauss on *A Hole Is to Dig* was Sendak's reputation as an illustrator established. Let the students compare the drawings in Krauss's book with those of *Where the Wild Things Are.*

Controversy Ask students if they think the pictures in *Where the Wild Things Are* are too scary for little children. Instruct them to draw a page for a new version of the book in which the monsters are tame looking.

Princess of Black Poetry

Her given name is Yolanda Cornelia Giovanni, Jr., but the world knows her better as Nikki Giovanni. This African American poet has been labeled the "Princess of Black Poetry" by some critics for her well-attended poetry readings. Recognition for her work first came in the 1960s. Since then she has been the recipient of a number of awards, including a citation for *Ladies Home Journal* Woman of the Year in 1972.

Born on June 7, 1943, in Knoxville, Tennessee, Giovanni grew up in a close-knit family. Her father, Jones, was a probation officer and her mother, Yolanda, was a teacher. When she was very young, the family moved to Ohio, but she maintained a special bond with her grandmother, Louvenia, back in Tennessee. In 1960 Giovanni entered Fisk University in Tennessee. At that time her politics were very conservative. Frequent clashes with the dean of women, though, led to her expulsion. A few years later she returned to Fisk, this time as a serious student and black rights activist. After graduating with honors, she did graduate work at the University of Pennsylvania and Columbia University in New York City.

Nikki Giovanni

Giovanni turned out to be a prolific writer. Between 1968 and 1970 she published three books of poetry. These writings reflected her life experiences during the sixties and depicted her growth as a black woman. Enormously popular, her book *Black Judgement* sold 6,000 copies in three months, more than five times the number of copies sold by the average book of poetry. In 1969 Giovanni began teaching at Rutgers University in New Jersey and also gave birth to her child, Thomas. During the seventies she wrote two books of poetry for children, *Spin a Soft Black Song* and *Ego Tripping and Other Poems for Young Children*. The poems in these collections revolve around the theme of family while voicing racial pride. She also recorded some of her work, bringing her more fame and recognition. These days Nikki Giovanni lectures and tours throughout the U.S. and Europe and continues to be a major force in black consciousness.

Suggested Activities

Define Ask the students to define "ego tripping." Read aloud some poems from her book of the same name. Direct the students to write their own poems which would be appropriate for that book.

Poetry Reading Conduct a class poetry reading. Let students take turns reading a Nikki Giovanni poem of their choice to the rest of the class.

The Peanuts Gang

Almost everyone is familiar with that lovable cartoon character, Snoopy, but not everyone may know the creator of this amusing comic strip. His name is Charles M. Schulz, and he was born on November 26, 1922, in Minneapolis, Minnesota. After attending public high school in St. Paul, Minnesota, Schulz submitted cartoons to most of the major magazines. All he received in turn were rejections and no encouragement. From 1943 to 1945 he served with the Twentieth Armored Division in Europe and achieved the rank of staff sergeant. After World War II, he set about in earnest to find work as an artist. An art correspondence school did hire him to correct basic lessons. Several of his coworkers' names there were used in some of his comic strips. During this job, Schulz continued to mail his own cartoons to major syndicates. One editorial director was very interested in his work and invited him to the New York office. After looking at the samples Schulz had brought along, the company decided to publish his *Peanuts* cartoon strip.

Charles M. Schultz

Schulz's numerous awards include the School Bell award from the National Education Association. A Peabody and an Emmy award went to his 1966 CBS cartoon special, *A Charlie Brown Christmas*. Other teleplays followed with Charlie Brown celebrating various holidays. Titles include *It's the Great Pumpkin, Charlie Brown* and *It's the Easter Beagle, Charlie Brown*.

In addition to creating the *Peanuts* comic strip, writing books, and producing teleplays, Schulz did some illustration work for other authors, including Art Linkletter's *Kids Say the Darnedest Things*. With Charlie Brown's introduction to television in 1965, Peanuts subsidiaries manufactured everything from clothing and toys to lunch boxes and stationery. In 1969 Snoopy made international news when his name became the official name of the Lunar Excursion Module of the Apollo 10 manned flight to the moon.

Peanuts and the gang still enjoy popularity and can be read daily in newspapers across the country.

Suggested Activities

Teleplay Group the students and tell them to write a new play for Charlie Brown and the gang.

Characters Conduct a class poll to find out which characters are their top three favorites. Alternatively, let students rank the characters from best-liked to least-liked.

Cartooning Cut out some *Peanuts* cartoon strips and glue them to a sheet of paper. Block out the dialog in each cartoon strip. Make copies for the class and direct them to write a dialog for each strip. Let the students share their cartoons with partners.

15 Minutes of Fame

The sixties was a period of rebellion and radical change on all fronts, including politics, race, women's rights, and even art and culture. One painter in particular captivated and dominated the art scene with his unique way of looking at the world. The artist was Andy Warhol.

Along with fellow painters Claes Oldenburg and James Rosenquist, Warhol had a background in commercial art. Images in his work were based on neon signs, the mass media, and advertising symbols. Coca Cola bottles, Campbell's soup cans, and Brillo boxes became subjects for his work. This type of art became known as "pop art."

Pop art is characterized by shiny colors and snappy designs which are often blown up to gigantic proportions. Overnight, pop became a marketing phenomenon, as well as an art movement. Its instant success was due in part to the fact that it made people look at the world in a different and pleasing way. Warhol wanted people to re-examine their surroundings, and so he made art out of daily life.

Andy Warhol

Born in 1930, Warhol lived with his mother and twenty-five cats in New York City. He began his career as a shoe illustrator for print ads. In 1960 his acrylic paintings of comic book characters Superman, Batman, and Dick Tracy brought him some recognition. But it was through the soup cans and celebrity posters that he found the most fame. Warhol also made more than sixty films between 1963 and 1968. For the most part, they were about mundane subjects. His silent film *Sleep*, for example, captured six hours of a man sleeping. Although Warhol claimed he wanted anonymity, he was always the center of media attention, and he clamored for the spotlight. With his platinum wig, pale makeup, and dark glasses he became the symbol for pop art in American culture.

Suggested Activities

Quote Andy Warhol once said, "In the future everyone will be famous for fifteen minutes." Ask students to explain what he meant by that statement. Have any of them had their fifteen minutes of fame? How?

Soup Cans Display a picture of Warhol's *100 Cans of Campbell's Soup*. A copy can be found in *The Annotated Mona Lisa: A Crash Course in Art History From Prehistoric to Post-Modern* by Carol Strickland, Ph.D. (Andrews and McMeel, 1992). Direct the class to create its own pop art project. After the class determines a subject, have each student draw a picture of it. Make sure that everyone uses the same sized sheet of drawing paper. With clear tape assemble the completed drawings into a giant art quilt.

Beatlemania

Their first hit, "Love Me Do," reached only number seventeen on British music charts in 1962, but their powerful "beat" and distinctive haircuts helped them stand out from other groups. With the release of "She Loves You" in 1963, the Beatles began a string of major hits. After an appearance on American television in 1964, they enjoyed phenomenal success. At one point, they held the top five spots on U.S. charts—a feat that has yet to be repeated. Quite possibly, the Beatles are the greatest musical group in history.

Just how did four boys from Liverpool make it so big? Their story began in 1957 when John Lennon invited fifteen-year-old Paul McCartney to join his group, the Quarrymen. Guitarist George Harrison had joined the group by August 1961, as well as drummer Pete Best. In 1962 Best was replaced by Ringo Starr. After record store owner Brian Epstein became their manager, they signed with a recording company. It was not long before the Beatles became England's biggest-ever idols. Their live performances were accompanied by unprecedented hordes of screaming fans. After their February 1964 appearance on *The Ed Sullivan Show*, "the Fab Four," as they were sometimes called, became transatlantic chart-toppers. While their first albums had combined pop-soul songs with some of Lennon's and McCartney's original compositions, later albums reflected the whole group's efforts. They even wrote scores for their own films. *Help!* and *A Hard Day's Night* depicted their lives and the hysteria that followed them. In 1966 the Beatles gave up touring to concentrate on studio work. The resulting *Revolver* album has been regarded by many as their finest work, but the most innovative was *Sergeant Pepper's Lonely Hearts Club Band*. Released in 1967, the album was an eclectic mix of styles, combining psychedelia with symphonic sounds. More changes were in the future as the Beatles explored Eastern religion with the Maharishi Mahesh Yogi. After their manager died, they set up their own record company and released "Hey, Jude," their best-selling single. Other albums and a third movie, *Yellow Submarine*, followed, but in 1970 the Beatles broke up their partnership. Ten years later, John Lennon was fatally wounded outside of his New York City apartment building, denying forever a possible, much-rumored reunion.

Suggested Activities

Response Write this quote on the board: "The Beatles were, quite simply, phenomenal. They changed lives, they changed pop music, they changed the world." Ask the students to write a response to this quote.

Investigate Find out more about the three remaining Beatles, Paul, George and Ringo. What paths have their careers followed?

Counterculture's Finest Moment

During the 1960s many young people embraced a lifestyle that was totally different from that of their conservative parents. They questioned everything and refused to conform to society's standards. These baby boomers developed a distinctive style of dress (page 348) and music, as well as their own lingo. "Far out!," "Peace, brother," and "What's happenin'?" were three commonly heard phrases. Some adopted a hippie look and lived in communes while others joined

radical political groups. Each of these groups had one thing in common: they rejected all symbols of authority, especially their parents and the government. They became known as the "counterculture."

For three days in August 1969, Woodstock in upstate New York became the focus of the counterculture revolution. During the idyllic weekend 400,000 people partied peacefully and were part of one huge, loving community. Organizers Michael Lang and Artie Kornfield had spent six months planning the show at the 600 acre farm. Richie Havens, a little known African American folk singer, opened the proceedings which were stopped twice by rain. Musicians, including Janis Joplin; The Grateful Dead; Jimi Hendrix; Jefferson Airplane; Bob Dylan; Crosby, Stills, Nash and Young; Joan Baez; Ravi Shankar; and Santana, entertained the crowd with their own personal styles. From protest to rock to psychedelic, all kinds of music could be enjoyed there. Santana stole the show with "Soul Sacrifice." Jimi Hendrix closed the adventure with an ear-splitting version of "The Star-Spangled Banner." Despite the lack of sanitation and low food and medical supplies, the concert-goers stayed and rocked on to the largest outdoor, overnight festival ever held. Later that same year, the Rolling Stones, unable to attend Woodstock, gave a free concert at Altamont, California. It turned deadly when a man in the crowd pulled a gun and was knifed to death by a Hell's Angel member. The spell of Woodstock was broken; it dealt a serious blow to future outdoor festivals.

Suggested Activities

Drug Scene Drugs were rampant at Woodstock. LSD was used to spike drinks backstage. Audience members smoked pot openly. Have the students find out the short-term and long-term side effects of these drugs. For more information see *Focus on Hallucinogens* by Jeffrey Shulman (Twenty-First Century Books, 1991).

Discuss Ask the students if they think there could ever be another Woodstock. Have them defend their answers.

Reunion Woodstock II was held in 1994 for the twenty-fifth anniversary of the original festival. Research to see who performed, who attended, and how it was similar to or different from the first Woodstock festival.

1960s Inventors and Inventions

A multitude of advances in technology in the 1960s changed the American lifestyle. New devices led to quicker and easier communication, and inexpensive electrical goods became available to ordinary people. Read about some of these devices below. Then read through the activities listed below and choose one to complete.

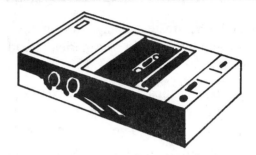

- One of the most important inventions of the era was the computer. At first it was used for data processing and was an extremely bulky machine, sometimes taking up whole rooms.

- In the early 1960s teenagers listened to their favorite tunes on small portable record players with monaural sound. Stereo discs did not become available until the midsixties when powerful hi-fi systems and stereo headphones made their debut.

- Along with stereo systems, cassette tape recorders were first marketed in 1963.

- A number of small electric appliances debuted during the sixties including electric toothbrushes (first manufactured in 1961) and heated hair curlers.

- Fibertip pens were first manufactured in the sixties.

- Improved printing techniques helped posters become a cheap way to decorate a home. Immensely popular, they often depicted images of pop stars and older movie stars.

- In 1962 the first communications satellite Telstar began relaying pictures across the Atlantic, making it possible to report global news instantaneously.

- The first laser was made during the sixties. An acronym for Light Amplification by Stimulated Emission of Radiation, the laser has an intense beam of pure light which is capable of cutting through metal. In 1963 the first hologram, using lasers, was devised. Today, the laser has been perfected so accurately that it is routinely used for many types of surgeries.

Suggested Activities

Comparisons Compare early stereo equipment with the stereo equipment of today. How do they differ in size and in the quality of sound produced?

Records Teenagers in the sixties listened to their favorite songs on $33\frac{1}{3}$ records and long-playing albums. What did these records look like and are they available today? What has now replaced records?

Posters Posters in the sixties typically bore psychedelic images of pop stars such as Bob Dylan, Jimi Hendrix, and Mick Jagger. Have the students draw a psychedelic posters of their favorite pop stars.

Inventors Research and find out about the inventors of any of the advances cited above. For example, Theodore Maiman was the first to develop the laser.

Lasers Although the laser has become an important tool for surgery, it was not originally intended for that use. Do some research to find out some other ways that lasers figure into our daily lives.

Sixties Fashion Trends

Probably the greatest change in fashions came about during the 1960s when new and daring styles were embraced by the youth of America. Read about some of these fashion innovations in the paragraphs below.

Materials Plastics, metals, and even paper were used to create new kinds of clothing. Transparent plastic dresses had to be wiped clean. They would have melted in a hot wash. Disposable paper clothes were meant to be worn only once and then thrown away.

Hemlines Short skirts were not new to the sixties, but the miniskirt was. Introduced in 1965 by English designer Mary Quant, these skirts barely covered the buttocks. Their midthigh lengths made wearing stockings impractical, so Quant introduced tights which were to be worn underneath the minis. Later in the sixties pantyhose were developed and quickly replaced stockings and garter belts.

Boots Leather boots completed the sixties' look. Typically, boots were knee-high with chunky heels.

Pants Two styles of pants dominated the sixties' scene. In the midsixties, hiphuggers were fashionable, but by the end of the decade they had been replaced with bell bottom pants which became wildly popular. Pantsuits for women also became very popular and fashionable.

Makeup The midsixties look consisted of heavy eye makeup, including false eyelashes. Long, straight hair was in. Some women even ironed theirs to straighten it. Teased, bouffant hairdos were also trendy. Later the bob—a short, slanted cut—was introduced by English stylist Vidal Sassoon.

The Unisex Look One of the most enduring trends of the sixties is the unisex look which consisted of denim jeans and a T-shirt. Males and females sported the look.

Twiggy Thin was in, but Twiggy was ultrathin. A famous fashion model, Twiggy was one of London's most famous personalities with her boyish body and large eyes.

Hippies Belief in individual expression led to the hippie look. Favorite styles included caftans, heavy velvet clothes, sheepskin coats, and leather sandals. Beads, vests, and long hair completed the look. Large Afros were worn by some African Americans.

Elsewhere . . .

This chronology gives a few of the important events around the globe during the 1960s. Have students research further any people and events that interest them.

1960

- Nikita Khrushchev becomes premier of the USSR.
- Cyprus and the Congo become independent.
- Mrs. Bandaranaike in Sri Lanka becomes the world's first woman prime minister.

1961

- Communists build the Berlin Wall across the city of Berlin to prevent East German citizens from fleeing to West Germany.
- Soviet Cosmonaut Yuri Gagarin becomes the first man in space.

1962

- Uganda and Tanganyika become independent nations.

1963

- On June 11, Buddhist monk Thich Quang Duyc sets himself on fire to protest South Vietnam's President Ngo Dinh Diem.
- South Vietnam's President Ngo Dinh Diem is assassinated.
- Valentina Tereshkova of the Soviet Union becomes the first woman in space.

1964

- Tanzania and Zambia are founded.
- Malta and Malawi become independent.
- Communist leader Nikita Khrushchev is removed from office in the USSR.
- A group of Palestinian Arabs led by Yasir Arafat forms the PLO (Palestinian Liberation Organization) which carries out terrorist attacks.
- China acquires the atomic bomb.

1965

- War breaks out between India and Pakistan.
- Japan's bullet train opens with average speeds of over 100 mph.
- Soviet Cosmonaut Alexei Leonov makes the first space walk.

1966

- Cultural Revolution is launched in China.
- China's Chairman Mao begins a plan to revitalize communism and attacks all capitalist or western influences.
- The Biafran War rages.
- Guyana becomes independent.
- The Soviet probe Luna 9 lands on the moon and takes photographs and samples of soil.

1967

- The Six Day War begins when Israeli planes attack air bases in Egypt, Syria, and Jordan.
- The King of Greece is exiled after a coup.
- In India, Indira Gandhi becomes the first woman elected to lead a democracy.

1968

- Soviet Union and its allies invade Czechoslovakia forcefully ending the period of openness known as the Prague Spring.
- In Paris, students and workers revolt.
- A massive Tet offensive is mounted in Vietnam.

1969

- Cultural Revolution comes to an end in China.

Cuba in the Sixties

During the 1960s the United States experienced major difficulties with the Caribbean nation of Cuba in two separate but related incidents: the Bay of Pigs invasion and the Cuban Missile Crisis. Read about these events below.

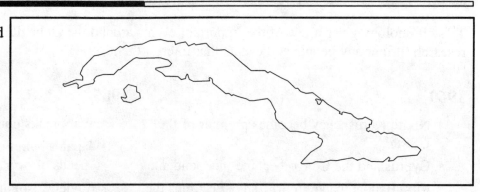

Bay of Pigs, 1961

Fidel Castro seized power in Cuba in 1959 and set up a Communist government. This worried the United States because Castro was so close to their coast. During President Eisenhower's administration, a secret plan was hatched to help oust the dictator. The United States provided training for a group of Cuban exiles but then failed to deliver the necessary support when the plan was actually carried out under President Kennedy. Castro easily defended the Bay of Pigs from the attack. Both the Soviets and the Cubans were angered by this attack while President Kennedy was forced to accept the blame for the failed coup.

Cuban Missile Crisis, 1962

Soviet premier Nikita Khruschev warned the United States that further attacks in Cuba would be considered an act of war. Then U.S. planes discovered Soviet ships unloading weapons in Cuba and saw missile sites being built. The missiles could easily strike major American cities, and they represented a direct threat to the security of the United States.

On October 22, 1962, President Kennedy demanded that Russia withdraw the missiles or else the U.S. would attack Cuba. For one week the tension mounted as American warships established a blockade around Cuba to make sure that no new missiles entered the country. American bombers moved into position in Florida, and U.S. troops prepared for a possible invasion of Cuba. On October 28, Khruschev agreed to remove the missiles if the United States agreed not to invade Cuba. World War III was narrowly averted.

Suggested Activities

Letter Khrushchev wrote President Kennedy a letter with his offer of removing the missiles from Cuba if Kennedy agreed not to invade the island. Write a letter as Khrushchev, explaining the terms of your offer to President Kennedy.

Research Research the role of the Eisenhower administration in planning the Bay of Pigs invasion. Was Kennedy totally to blame for its subsequent failure?

Decision Making With the class review background information about the Cuban missile crisis. Brainstorm a number of options available to the U.S. (invade Cuba, bomb Cuba's missile sites, etc.). Discuss the consequences of each. Let the students vote on an option. Discuss Kennedy's choice. Note: A great resource for this activity is the book *You Are the President* by Nathan Aaseng (The Oliver Press, Inc., 1994).

Canada's Centennial

July 1, which is Canada Day, was a very special birthday in 1967 because Canada celebrated its centennial, or 100 years in existence.

The nation of Canada was born in 1867. At the request of four colonies in North America—Quebec, Ontario, Nova Scotia, and New Brunswick—the British Parliament passed the British North America Act, now known as the Constitution Act, creating a confederation of these four provinces. Since then, six more provinces and two territories have joined the Dominion of Canada.

What do you know about the government of the great country of Canada? Find out some important facts by unscrambling the letter groups at the beginning of each sentence. Write the word correctly on the line provided. Read the completed facts with a partner.

1. **rcamnho**
   Canada recognizes the British_____as its formal head of state.
2. **semtsy**
   Canada's government is modeled largely on the British parliamentary_____.
3. **rafeedl**
   The 1867 Constitution Act provides for separation of_____and provincial or territorial powers.
4. **esefnde**
   The federal government was given control of areas such as_____, customs, and currency.
5. **tudeoican**
   Provinces retained control of matters of local concern, including_____and civil rights.
6. **toaxitna**
   Some areas, such as immigration and_____, were granted joint power.
7. **turneintw**
   Canada's laws and system of government consist of both written and _____codes.
8. **ntiriba**
   These unwritten codes include the parliamentary cabinet system which is patterned after the one used in_____.
9. **vegiliatsel**
   This system links two branches of government, the executive and the_____.
10. **cayjruidi**
    A third branch of the government, the_____, is an appointed body.
11. **ibeanct**
    The monarch, the prime minister, and the_____compose the executive branch.
12. **simtrien**
    Actual executive power in Canada is held by the prime_____and his or her cabinet.

———— Suggested Activity ————

Comparison With the class construct a chart to compare the Canadian system of government with that of the United States. Discuss how the two are alike.

- -

Answers (cover before copying)

1. monarch 2. system 3. federal 4. defense 5. education 6. taxation 7. unwritten 8. Britain 9. legislative 10. judiciary 11. cabinet 12. minister

Reverence for Life

When he was twenty-one years old, Albert Schweitzer determined that he would devote his life to serving humanity. Although he was not exactly sure how he would implement his goal, he planned to continue his studies in theology, philosophy, and music until he was 30. He thought that by then he would have his life's work figured out.

Albert Schweitzer

Albert Schweitzer was born on January 14, 1875, in Kaysersberg, Alsace, a section of Germany that is now a part of France. His father, Louis Schweitzer, was a clergyman and his mother, Adele Schillinger, was the daughther of a pastor. Louis Schweitzer served as his son's music teacher and taught him how to play the piano. When Albert Schweitzer was ten, he left home to begin his secondary education. An average student, he studied philosophy and theology at Strasbourg University. It was there that he found an answer to his life calling. He opened a missionary magazine to an article titled "The Needs of the Congo Mission," and by the time he had finished reading the story, he knew his search was over.

In order to practice medicine in Africa, Schweitzer studied tropical medicine. In 1912 he received his M.D. That same year he married Helene Bresslau, a social worker and nurse. For almost a year the young couple made lists of all the necessary supplies they would take with them and raised money for their venture. When they finally arrived in Lambarene in Gabon, they found conditions far worse than they had envisioned. No doctor had been there for many years, and the only building available for use as a hospital was a converted chicken coop. But the clinic was an overwhelming success. Villagers walked miles to see the doctor for all sorts of diseases ranging from malaria to sleeping sickness to leprosy.

When war broke out between Germany and France in 1914, the Schweitzers were held under house arrest. Because Schweitzer had been born in Germany, the French, who now controlled Gabon, considered him an enemy. During this time, he was not allowed to treat patients. Restless, he wrote his first book, *Philosophy of Civilization*. Not for seven more years would he be able to return to his mission in Africa.

Over the years, a large medical complex was built with donations and money that Schweitzer earned by lecturing and writing books. In 1952 he won the Nobel peace prize and was able to build a village for leprosy patients with the proceeds. After his wife died, Schweitzer remained in Africa until his death on September 4, 1965. He was 90 years old.

Suggested Activities

Biography Read the whole story about Albert Schweitzer. One recommended resource is *Albert Schweitzer* by Harold E. Robles (The Millbrook Press, 1994).

Goals Discuss current areas of greatest need in the world. Group the students and have them develop a plan for helping others. Share the plans in whole group.

The First Heart Transplant

Dr. Christiaan Barnard of South Africa gained international fame when he performed the first heart transplant surgery on December 2, 1967. His patient was Louis Washkansky, a 54-year-old grocer who had life-threatening heart disease. The donor was Denise Duvall, a young woman who suffered fatal injuries in an automobile accident in Cape Town. Because it was the first such operation, little was known about which drugs and how much of them should be used. Mr. Washkansky died of double pneumonia eighteen days after his surgery.

One year later, Dr. Barnard performed another heart transplant. This time he placed the heart of a mixed-race stroke victim into a 58-year-old white dentist. Controversy reigned as apartheid was still in effect in South Africa. The patient, however, fared well, and after seventy-four days in the hospital, was released to go home.

In time, more and more surgeons around the world began to experiment with heart transplants. Dr. Barnard's surgeries were even more successful, and he developed a new type of artificial heart valve. Today, this type of surgery is quite common, but problems of rejection have yet to be overcome.

—— Suggested Activity ——

Below you will find a drawing of a human heart. Write the number of each part listed on the correct line. Use reference sources to help you.

1. left atrium
2. inferior vena cava
3. right atrium
4. left pulmonary veins
5. left ventricle
6. superior vena cava
7. aorta
8. bicuspid valve
9. right pulmonary veins
10. semilunar valve
11. tricuspid valve
12. right ventricle
13. pulmonary artery
14. septum

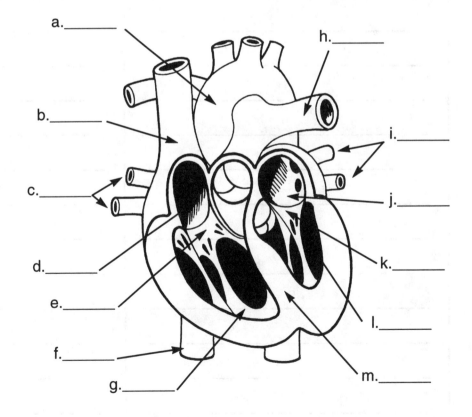

Answers: Teacher, fold under before copying.
a. 7 b. 6 c. 9 d. 3 e. 11 f. 2 g. 12 h. 13 i. 4 j. 1 k. 8 l. 5 m. 14

Tourists on Antarctica

Tourists have been coming to Antarctica since the late 1950s. As a hotel owner, you envision great possibilities for the region and plan to build a hotel and airstrip there. Among the activities people can enjoy are hiking, skiing, camping, mountain climbing, and driving a dogsled team. They can also see and photograph penguins, elephant seals, and other wildlife.

Environmentalists, however, oppose your plans because they say that tourists pose the biggest threat to the environment of the continent. People inadvertently bother penguin rookeries, use rocks for graffiti, and take penguin eggs or rocks as souvenirs.

In the space at the left, write arguments for allowing visitors to enter Antarctica. In the space at the right, write arguments for discontinuing Antarctic visitors.

For	**Against**
_____	_____
_____	_____
_____	_____
_____	_____
_____	_____
_____	_____
_____	_____
_____	_____
_____	_____
_____	_____
_____	_____
_____	_____
_____	_____
_____	_____

Two Female Leaders

Golda Meir and Indira Gandhi were leaders of their respective countries during the 1960s. Compare the two by writing the information from the facts list in the correct sections of the Venn diagram below.

Facts List

- attended Oxford University in London
- born in Kiev, Russia
- retired in 1974
- led her country in war with another nation
- elected prime minister of India in 1967
- assassinated in 1984
- was an activist
- grew up in Milwaukee, Wisconsin
- Israel's first minister of labor
- criticized during her administration
- first woman elected to lead a democracy
- at age 12 organized a branch of the "Monkey Brigade"
- acted as her father's official hostess when he was prime minister member of the Zionists
- became prime minister after the Six Day War in 1969
- worked tirelessly for her country
- served as minister of education and broadcasting
- stepped down from prime minister position in favor of Begin

Gandhi	**Both**	**Meir**

- -

Answers: Teacher, fold under before copying.
Gandhi: attended Oxford . . ., elected prime minister of India . . ., assassinated . . ., first woman elected . . ., at age 12 organized . . ., acted as her father's . . ., served as minister . . . **Both:** led her country in war . . ., was an activist, criticized . . ., worked tirelessly . . .
Meir: born in Kiev . . ., retired in 1974, grew up in Milwaukee. . ., Israel's first . . ., member of the Zionists, became prime minister after . . ., stepped down . . .

Aborigine Rights

In the sixties, Native American civil rights activists in the United States worked to expose the suffering of many Indians. The Native Americans wanted to be involved in the planning and control of the programs that affected them. At the same time on the other side of the globe, another native group, the Aborigines, were receiving similar attention. The Aborigines were an ancient culture in Australia and until the 1960s were not considered Australian citizens. They were not allowed to vote, did not receive full social benefits, and were not even included in their country's census.

Test your knowledge of this ancient civilization by choosing and circling the correct word in each set of parentheses. Use reference resources to help you find correct answers.

1. When white explorers first encountered Aborigines, these Australian natives still lived as they did in the (Stone Age, Bronze Age).

2. Probably the first Aborigines came to Australia 50,000 years ago from (New Zealand, South East Asia).

3. Many Aborigines died from the (food, diseases) introduced by the Europeans.

4. Aborigines obtained their own food by hunting animals and (gathering food, herding cattle).

5. Tribespeople wore ornaments and waistbands but little (makeup, clothing).

6. Aborigines had no permanent (housing, farms) because they were always on the move to find food.

7. To protect themselves, they built huts or found protection under (rocks, the ground).

8. Men hunted large animals with spears, traps, and (boomerangs, Frisbees).

9. Women gathered fruits, vegetables, and small animals such as (arachnids, insects) and lizards.

10. Aboriginal art includes stone engravings, paintings done on bark, and (cave paintings, oil paintings).

Suggested Activities

Today Write a description of the Aborigines in Australia today. Explain the Australian government's policy toward the native group.

Compare Compare and contrast the treatment of the Aborigines by the Australian government with the treatment of the Native Americans by the United States government.

Research Find out more about the roles of men and women in the traditional Aborigine tribe. Compare and contrast theim to the roles of men and women today.

Answers: Teacher, fold under before copying.

1. Stone Age 2. Southeast Asia 3. diseases 4. gathering food 5. clothing 6. housing 7. rocks 8. boomerangs 9. insects 10. cave paintings

The First Woman in Space

In 1961 Yuri Gagarin, a Russian cosmonaut, had become the first man to fly in space, but on June 16, 1963, it was a female's turn for the same feat. On that day, Russia's Valentina V. Tereshkova became the first woman to fly in space. A hero, she gained international attention and was honored with parades and her government's highest honor. Here is her story.

Valentina Tereshkova

Tereshkova was born on March 6, 1937, in a small village near Yaroslavl, a city on the Volga River in the former Soviet Union. From 1939 to 1945, Russia was involved in World War II, and Tereshkova's father was just one of the many casualties. His death left her, her mother, brother, and sister nearly destitute. She was ten before she began school and was seventeen when she became an apprentice at a local tire factory. She continued her studies at night school and soon gained a position at the cotton mill where her mother and sister both worked. In addition, she joined an air sports club and learned how to parachute from planes.

Despite the fact that she had little higher education, Tereshkova wanted more than anything to become a cosmonaut. She wrote to the Soviet space authorities and volunteered for their program. With her parachuting ability and professed love of the cosmonaut program, she was accepted. Training began in 1962, and nine months later she had earned the military rank of junior lieutenant.

Her mission began on June 16, 1963, when she boarded the Vostok 6 capsule at the Baikonur, Kazakhstan, launchpad. During orbit, Tereshkova communicated with a cosmonaut who was orbiting Earth in another spacecraft. Her time aloft was 70 hours and 50 minutes. From four miles above the Earth she ejected and parachuted safely to the ground. Premier Nikita Khrushchev praised her accomplishment, saying that she had proved that women were not the weaker sex. Not until 1982, however, would another female cosmonaut fly in space.

Valentina Tereshkova remained in the cosmonaut program for several years before retiring to enter politics.

Suggested Activities

Cosmonaut In 1982 Svetlana Savitskaya became the second female Russian cosmonaut in space. Direct the students to research (see resources below) and find out more about her accomplishments.

Compare Ask students how spacecrafts return to earth these days. Compare that with the way Savitskaya and her fellow cosmonuats returned during the early days of the space program.

Parachutes Pair the students and have them make parachutes. See Teacher Created Materials #493, *Focus on Scientists,* page 99, for directions. Test the parachutes outdoors.

Resources

U.S. and Soviet Space Programs: A Comparison by David E. Newton (Franklin Watts, 1988)

Women in Space by Carole S. Brigg (Lerner Publications, 1988)

Berlin's Wall

After World War II ended, Germany was divided into four occupied territories controlled by American, British, French, and Soviet military forces. Allied leaders had agreed to reunite the regions at a future date. Soviet leaders, however, broke their agreements and began building an 866-mile fortified border, dividing Germany into east and west. The west part of Germany became a democratic country while the east portion became a Communist state. Allied troops still occupied part of the city of Berlin, however, and it, too, was divided. Its western part became an island of democracy in a Communist country.

In 1961, Soviet leader Nikita Khrushchev demanded that the United States pull out of West Berlin, but President Kennedy refused. With neither side willing to budge, it appeared that war was imminent. The Communists shocked everyone, however, by building a wall between the sections of the city. Barbed wire was installed on top of the wall, and armed guards were ordered to shoot East Germans who tried to flee to West Berlin.

Not until 1989 was the wall torn down when the Communist government of East Germany was overthrown. Nearly 200 people had been killed trying to escape over the wall.

Suggested Activity

Learn about the city of Berlin as it stands today. Use reference materials to help you supply the information requested below.

Population: _____

Size: _____

Ethnic Population: _____

Religion: _____

City Symbol: _____

Two Main Industries: _____

Geography: _____

Highest Point in the City: _____

- -

Answers: Teacher, fold under before copying.

Population: 3,100,000; **Size:** 341 square miles (883 sq. km); **Ethnic Population:** German, some Turks, Yugoslavs, Greeks, Italians; **Predominant Religion:** Protestant; **City Symbol:** the bear; **Two Main Industries:** high-tech electronics/chemicals/pharmaceuticals and machine building; **Geography:** lies on a flat plain; **Highest Point in the City:** TV tower at Alexanderplatz

Passages

Births

1960
- John Fitzgerald Kennedy, Jr.
- Bono, lead vocalist for U2
- supermodels Carol Alt and Kim Alexis

1961
- Heather Locklear, actress
- Dennis Rodman, basketball superstar

1962
- Demi Moore and Tom Cruise, actors
- Jackie Joyner Kersee, track star

1963
- Michael Jordan, basetball great
- Whitney Houston, singer/actress

1964
- Melissa Gilbert, actress
- baseball star Jose Canseco

1965
- Brooke Shields, model/actress

1966
- Mike Tyson, boxing titan
- Janet Jackson, performer

1968
- Molly Ringwald, actress
- Adam Graves, NY Rangers MVP in 1993

Deaths

1960
- Richard Wright, African American novelist

1962
- Marilyn Monroe, actress
- Eleanor Roosevelt, former first lady

1964
- Herbert Hoover, former U.S. President
- General Douglas MacArthur

1965
- Sir Winston Churchill, former leader of England
- Malcolm X, religious leader and political activitist

1966
- Walt Disney, film-maker

1967
- Spencer Tracy, Academy Award winning actor

1968
- Robert F. Kennedy, former Attorney General and presidential hopeful
- Martin Luther King, Jr., civil rights leader and orator

1969
- Dwight D. Eisenhower, former U.S. president
- Judy Garland, singer and actress

Sixties Facts and Figures

The United Stated in 1960

Population:	179,323,175
National Debt:	$289 billion (1961)
Federal Minimum Wage:	raised from $1.25 to $1.40 per hour (1963)
U.S. Postage:	raised from 4 cents to 5 cents (1963)
Popular Books:	*Catch-22* by Joseph Heller; *Portnoy's Complaint* by Philip Roth; *To Kill a Mockingbird* by Harper Lee; *Tropic of Cancer* by Henry Miller; *One Flew Over the Cuckoo's Nest* by Ken Kesey; *Slaughterhouse Five* by Kurt Vonnegut;
Popular Movies:	*The Apartment, West Side Story, Lawrence of Arabia, Tom Jones, My Fair Lady, The Sound of Music, A Man for All Seasons, In the Heat of the Night, Oliver, Midnight Cowboy*
Popular Songs:	"Cathy's Clown," "Spanish Harlem," "Only the Lonely," "Moon River," "I Fall to Pieces," "I Left My Heart in San Francisco," "I Want to Hold Your Hand," "Louie Louie," "Hello Dolly," "Satisfaction," "Stop in the Name of Love," "California Dreamin'," "Respect," "Mrs. Robinson," "Aquarius/Let the Sunshine In"
TV Shows:	*The Super Bowls, Star Trek, Rowan and Martin's Laugh-In, Sesame Street* (premieres on PBS in 1969), *The Smothers Brothers, The Dick Van Dyke Show*
Fashions:	miniskirts, paper throwaway clothes, A-line dresses and skirts, loose fitting shifts, Twiggy, pillbox hats, bouffant hairdos
Fads:	facepainting, wearing flowers in one's hair, the Twist, the Jerk, lava lamps, waterbeds, Day-Glo and black light, posters, flashing a peace sign
Popular Cars:	Volkswagen bug, '64 Ford Mustang, '63 Corvette Sting Ray, Chevy Bel Air, '64 Plymouth Barracuda, '64 Pontiac GTO
Popular Toys:	skateboards, Frisbees, Twister®, Barbie and Ken dolls, G.I. Joe dolls, Troll dolls

Famous Firsts

Every era has its famous firsts, and the sixties is no exception. On this page you will find a number of firsts along with a brief discussion of each. After each one, write about the improvements or advances that have been made in that area today.

Heart Transplant In 1967 the first successful heart transplant operation was performed by Dr. Christiaan Barnard of South Africa. The heart of a 25-year old accident victim was placed in the body of heart-disease patient Louis Washansky, but the procedure was not entirely successful. Washkansky died of pneumonia some weeks later. _____

_____

_____

Giant Bridge The Verrazano-Narrows bridge opened in New York in November of 1964. It stretched 4,260 feet across the entrance to New York City harbor, from Staten Island to Brooklyn. At the time, it was the world's longest suspension bridge. _____

_____

The Minidress Flappers of the Roaring Twenties wore short hemlines which shocked their elders, but they could not compare to the minidresses sported by women in the sixties. Midthigh length skirts became a symbol of the rebellious decade's younger generation. _____

_____

_____

Ocean Depths In 1960 the submersible Trieste descended nearly seven miles to the bottom of the Mariana Trench, the deepest part of the Pacific Ocean. The journey down to the bottom of the ocean floor took five hours. _____

_____

Endangered Species The Department of the Interior issued its first endangered species list on March 1, 1967. Included in the list were seventy-eight birds and animals that were threatened with extinction.

_____

_____

_____

Trekkies On September 8, 1966, the science fiction series *Star Trek* premiered on the NBC television network. Although it only ran for three seasons, it has continued to be popular in reruns and has amassed a huge following of devoted fans (once called "Trekkies" and now called "Trekers"). By the midnineties, the show had spawned several feature films and three other television series.

_____

_____

Writing Prompts and Literature Ideas

Writing Prompts Use these suggestions for journal writing or as daily writing exercises. Some research or discussion may be appropriate before assigning a particular topic.

- During the sixties, Charles Schultz wrote a book titled *Happiness Is a Warm Puppy*. Create your own *Happines Is . . . book*. Write Happiness Is at the top of ten separate sheets of paper. Write a different definition for happiness on each page. Illustrate.

- Jacqueline Kennedy's style inspired the Jackie "look." Describe this look to someone who has never seen a pill box hat or bouffant hairdo.

- During his inaugural ceremonies, President Kennedy invited poet Robert Frost to recite a poem. Find and read a poem written by Frost. Write your own inaugural poem.

- Martin Luther King, Jr., is famous for his "I Have a Dream . . ." speech. Find and read a transcript of the speech. Write a paragraph that begins with I have a dream . . . .

- Pretend to have been chosen to be the first person to walk on the moon's surface during the Apollo 11 mission. Write a speech you will deliver to your fellow Americans as you step into history.

- The Beatles are making their first American appearance on TV. You and your friends are in the audience. Girls scream and the noise is deafening as the group sings. Write a list of ten things you might hear others in the audience saying about the group.

- The Space Race was in full force during the sixties. Although the Soviets were the first to travel successfully in space, it was the Americans who landed first on the moon. Write a story explaining the importance of winning this race.

- Ralph Nader exposed serious safety problems in General Motors cars in his 1966 book Unsafe at Any Speed. Write a chapter for an updated version of his book.

Literature Ideas The following books can be used to supplement and enhance the study of the 1960s.

- *The Story of Ruby Bridges* by Robert Coles (Scholastic, Inc., 1995)
  This is the telling of one particular case in the aftermath of Brown v. the Board of Education of Topeka. Ruby Bridges faces angry protestors daily and is escorted to and from school by federal marshals. With atypical courage and grace for such a young child, Ruby sets an example for all Americans and becomes an unforgettable part of American history.

- *December Stillness* by Mary Downing Hahn (Clarion Books, 1988)
  When her social studies teacher assigns the class to write a paper on a contemporary issue, Kelly chooses the homeless for her topic. She focuses on Mr. Weems, the bearded Vietnam vet who spends most of his time in the town's library. This is a great book for examining the aftermath of the Vietnam War.

- *. . . If You Lived at the Time of Martin Luther King, Jr.* by Ellen Levine (Scholastic, Inc., 1994).
  This question-and-answer format will keep students interested.

- *A Wall of Names* by Judy Donnelly (Random House, 1991)
  This is the story of the funding and building of the Vietnam Memorial.

- *Park's Quest* by Katherine Paterson (Dutton, New York, 1988)
  Park determines to find out about his father who was killed in Vietnam.

Seventies Overview

- The political and social turmoil of the late 1960s continued into the seventies.
- American and South Vietnamese forces entered Cambodia and Laos in 1970 in an attempt to cut North Vietnamese supply lines.
- At Kent State University, students protesting the bombing of Cambodia set fire to an ROTC (Reserve Officers Training Corps) building. Called to stop the riot, National Guardsmen open fire, wounding eight and killing four.
- In a new offensive North Vietnamese soldiers crossed into Quang Tri province, but were stopped by the South Vietnamese. Bombing of North Vietnam by U.S. planes, halted in 1968, resumed in 1972 with railroads and supply lines as principal targets. The harbor at Haiphong was also mined.
- Although peace talks between Henry Kissinger of the United States and Le Duc Tho of North Vietnam began in Paris in 1970, fighting continued until the cease-fire agreement was reached in 1973.
- U.S. troops withdrew from Vietnam in 1973 and from Laos in 1974. In 1975 Saigon fell to the North Vietnamese. The same year, the communist Khmer Rouge came to power in Cambodia, and the Pathet Lao took over the government of Laos.
- In 1971 the publication of the Pentagon Papers, a history of the Vietnam War, added to antiwar sentiments by revealing that the government has not been completely honest.
- A court-martial convicted Lt. William Calley and sentenced him to life in prison for his role in the "My Lai Massacre" of 1968 in which 22 unarmed Vietnamese civilians were killed.
- Early in 1973 the trial of seven men accused of the 1972 break-in and wiretapping of the National Democratic Committee offices in the Watergate building began. Eventually this scandal spread to include members of the president's cabinet and staff and brought the threat of impeachment to President Richard Nixon.
- Spiro Agnew, accused of bribery, conspiracy, and tax evasion, resigned the vice presidency in October 1973. At his trial he pleaded *nolo contendre* and was fined and given probation.
- President Nixon named Gerald Ford, U.S. Representative from Michigan to succeed Agnew. This was the first time the Twenty-fifth Amendment, passed in 1967, was applied.
- In 1974 Richard M. Nixon resigned the presidency. New president Gerald Ford nominated Nelson Rockefeller to fill the office of vice president.
- By 1976 people were quick to embrace Jimmy Carter with his home-spun message of peace and hope as their new president.
- Revelations of misdeeds in government left the activists of the sixties frustrated and disillusioned. They turned their energies inward, embracing fitness, health foods, and transcendental meditation. Some have called the seventies the "me decade."
- Throughout the seventies, the women's movement grew stronger as leaders, including Gloria Steinem and Kate Millet, led the revolution. New opportunities were opened to women and many left the safety of the home to find fulfillment in the workplace.
- In the 1973 landmark Supreme Court decision Roe v. Wade, women were granted abortion rights. A controversial topic, the debate has continued well into the nineties.
- The Arab oil embargo against the Western world had a severe effect on the economy. One effect was a new concern for the environment. Natural foods and fabrics gained popularity, and preventing air pollution and preserving the environment were important growing trends.

For Discussion

How has the women's movement impacted women's lives today?
Does an underlying distrust of the government linger in America today from the Watergate affair?
Is concern for the environment currently a major issue?

Legislation of the 1970s

On this page you will find a list of some of the important legislation of the 1970s. A brief description is given for each one. Research further any topic that interests you.

1970   **EPA** The Environmental Protection Agency was established in July to help the nation control pollution of its air and water.

1971   **Wage and Price Freeze** A Pay Board was established to stop inflationary wage and salary increases. A Price Commission was set up to regulate price and rent increases.

       Twenty-sixth Amendment On June 30 the voting age was lowered from twenty-one to eighteen. See page 365 for more information on this issue.

1972   **ERA** The Equal Rights Amendment called for complete legal equality between the sexes. Passed by both houses of Congress, it did receive enough state support to be ratified.

       Title IX Part of the Education Amendment Acts of 1972, Title IX forbade educational institutions which were receiving federal aid to discriminate on the basis of sex.

1973   **Roe v. Wade** In this still-controversial court case, the Supreme Court ruled that women have the right to obtain an abortion during the first three months of pregnancy. Anti-abortion rights activists continue to oppose and protest the decision on the basis of their belief that abortion is murder.

       The Endangered Species Act This act placed a number of animals threatened with extinction on an endangered species list, thereby providing them with some protection for survival.

1974   **Speed Limits** All states were given until March 2, 1974, to comply with a 55-mph speed limit on U.S. highways or face the withdrawal of federal funding.

1975   **Metric System** A call was made for the voluntary switch to the metric system. Schools began teaching metrics, but adult resistance doomed the movement.

1977   **Panama Canal Treaty** President Carter and Panama's leader Omar Torrijos signed a treaty allowing the Panama Canal to be returned to Panama by the year 2000.

1978   **Bakke Case** In this Supreme Court ruling, it was determined that Allan P. Bakke was the victim of reverse discrimination and that racial quotas had kept the white student out of medical school. The court ruled out quotas but did permit affirmative action, giving extra consideration to minorities.

1978   **Camp David Accord** President Jimmy Carter, Egypt's President Anwar el Sadat, and Israeli Prime Minister Menachem Begin met for twelve days at Camp David to work out their political differences. On September 17, the leaders emerged from their talks to announce their agreement. Egypt became the first Arab nation to recognize Israel's right to exist.

For Discussion

Which pieces of legislation have had a lasting impact on Americans?

What is the most important piece of legislation to come out of the seventies?

The Twenty-sixth Amendment

On June 30, 1971, the Twenty-sixth Amendment to the Constitution was ratified. It lowered the voting age to eighteen. Read the complete text of this amendment below. Then answer the questions that follow. You may have to do some research to find answers.

Section 1. Right to Vote

The right of citizens of the United States, who are eighteen years of age or older, to vote shall not be denied or abridged by the United States or by any State on account of age.

Section 2. Enforcement

The Congress shall have power to enforce this article by appropriate legislation.

1. Write the provisions of this amendment in your own words. _____

_____

2. What events precipitated the passage of the Twenty-sixth Amendment? _____

_____

3. The Fifteenth and Nineteenth Amendments also pertain to voting.

   What are the provisions of the Fifteenth Amendment? _____

   _____

   What year was it ratified? _____

   What are the provisions of the Nineteenth Amendment? _____

   _____

   What year was it ratified? _____

4. Consider all three voting amendments—the Fifteenth, Nineteenth, and Twenty-sixth. _____

   _____

   Who can vote in the United States? _____

   What cannot vote in the United States? _____

5. Presidential elections are held every four years. With that in mind, determine when you will first be eligible to vote.

   year_____

   your age_____

6. Do you think it is important to vote? Explain your answer. _____

_____

_____

History of the Draft

The draft, or conscription for military service, in the United States began in colonial America. Over the course of time, changes were made in the way men were chosen and in the ages of those eligible for service. In the beginning of the 1970s, there was growing opposition to both the draft and the war in Vietnam. More and more frequently, protesters would gather and burn their draft cards in open defiance of the government. Organized violence against a draft system had occurred in 1863, but it did not compare to the actions taken by men in the seventies.

Throughout American history, a number of draft laws were passed to meet specific needs. Both the North and the South had their own conscription acts during the Civil War. In the North, men could avoid service by finding a substitute or paying the government $300. Between the Civil War and World War I, there was no conscription; but after World War I erupted, Congress passed the Selective Service Act. This law provided for eligible men between the ages of eighteen and forty-five to be chosen by a lottery system. Exemptions were allowed, but bounties were eliminated.

The period between World War I and World War II saw a return to the peacetime custom of maintaining a regular army along with National Guard units. When war broke out in 1939, the U.S. began a peacetime draft which was allowed to expire in 1947. Over the next twenty years, a number of draft laws were enacted. All of them required men to register with their local draft boards when they reached eighteen years of age.

In January 1970, Congress instituted a lottery system with men between the ages of nineteen and twenty eligible to be called for a period of one year. Previously, men were eligible for a period of seven years. The following year the draft was extended for two years, but after July 1, 1973, the draft was again left to expire. All young men continued to register with the Selective Service System until March 1975, when the lottery system was discontinued.

Since 1980, men aged nineteen and twenty must register with the Selective Service, but they are not classified or inducted. The purpose of this registration is to compile names for a possible future military draft which would have to be approved by Congress.

In the box below is a sampling of draft classifications that were used during the years of active military conscription. Research and add two more classifications to the list.

1-A: Available for military service

1-A-O: Conscientious Objector; available for noncombat military service only

2-M: Deferred because of study preparing for a medical specialty

3-A: Deferred because of dependency of others

4-A: Has completed military service

4-F: Not qualified for military service

_____

_____

The Iranian Hostage Crisis

What events led to the Iranian hostage crisis? Why did it last so long? How was it finally resolved? These and other questions will be answered in the paragraphs that follow.

For years the United States had supported Iran politically and provided military assistance to help the country stave off Soviet expansion in the Middle East. The U.S. government's main reason for helping Iran was the importance of its rich oil supplies to the U.S. economy. In supporting Iran, the United States also supported its Shah, Mohammad Reza Pahlavi, until he was overthrown in 1979 by Islamic fundamentalists led by the Ayatollah Khomeini. The Shah's leadership had been cruel and authoritarian, and Iranians were resentful of him. After fleeing the country, the Shah went to Mexico where he became ill. He requested and was granted permission by the U.S. government to seek treatment at a New York City hospital. Not many days after that, on November 4, 1979, a mob of Islamic students attacked the U.S. embassy in Teheran and seized the staff. Although the action violated international law, the workers were held as hostages. The student radicals demanded that the Shah be returned to Iran in exchange for the release of the hostages, but President Carter refused. Fifty-two embassy workers were often blindfolded and paraded in front of television cameras while demonstrators chanted "Death to America."

Carter was not willing to submit to terrorism, so he tried diplomatic means to obtain release of the hostages. First, he seized eight billion dollars' worth of Iranian deposits in U.S. banks and then ordered navy warships to the waters off Iran. Neither tactic worked and public pressure continued to grow. In April 1980, over the protests of Secretary of State Cyrus Vance, President Carter gave permission for a rescue attempt. It was a disaster, however. Eight servicemen died when a transport plane collided with a helicopter. Vance resigned his office, and President Carter suffered a serious public image problem. The event also contributed to his stunning loss in the 1980 presidential election.

The hostage crisis was finally resolved on January 19, 1981, when Carter was able to negotiate the release of the hostages. It had been 444 days since they were first held in captivity, and ironically, it was President Carter's last full day in office.

—— Suggested Activities ——

Respond If you were President Carter, what measures would you have taken to obtain the release of the hostages?

Research What became of the hostages after their release? How did their time in captivity affect them?

The Watergate Affair

On this and the next page you will find a step-by-step explanation of the Watergate affair. Make a copy of both pages for each group of students. After reading the text together, have students complete the activities at the bottom of the next page.

1. The setting is two o'clock in the morning on Saturday, June 17, 1972, at the Democratic headquarters in the Watergate building complex. Five suspected burglars are arrested there. The burglars are attempting to adjust the bugs they had previously installed in order to listen in on Democrats as they planned their strategy for the upcoming election. All five men are wearing surgical gloves and armed with walkie-talkies. Their tools, false identification, telephone tapping devices, money, film, and cameras are confiscated by the police.

2. One of those arrested is James W. McCord, security chief for CREEP (Committed to Re-elect the President). The organization is headed by John N. Mitchell, a former U.S. Attorney General in Nixon's cabinet. Mitchell has resigned that post so that he can manage the president's re-election. He denies any wrongdoing or White House involvement.

3. Two reporters for the *Washington Post*, Bob Woodward and Carl Bernstein, are assigned to investigate the allegations. They find out that the break-in has been directed by G. Gordon Liddy, a former FBI agent, and E. Howard Hunt, a former CIA agent.

4. On August 29, 1972, President Nixon declares that no one in his administration is responsible for Watergate. Furthermore, John Dean, an attorney on his staff, has conducted an investigation clearing all White House staff of any wrongdoing.

5. Nixon wins the 1972 presidential election by an overwhelming majority.

6. On January 8, 1973, with Judge John Sirica presiding, the trial of G. Gordon Liddy, E. Howard Hunt, and the five burglars is underway. Sirica is dissatisfied with the questioning and delays sentencing.

The Watergate Affair *(cont.)*

7. On February 7, 1973, the U.S. Senate creates a Senate Select Committee to investigate Watergate more thoroughly. Sam Ervin, a Democratic senator from North Carolina, is chosen to head the committee.

8. In a written statement, McCord reveals that White House officials had conducted a cover-up to hide their involvement and that they had been pressured to plead guilty while not revealing what they knew. With that revelation, the White House cover-up begins to unravel. John Mitchell admits lying and John Dean, President Nixon's attorney, accuses Nixon's closest advisor of participating in Watergate. H. R. Haldeman, President Nixon's chief of staff, and John Ehrlichman, a top presidential advisor, are also implicated. President Nixon continues to maintain his innocence.

9. On May 17, 1973, televised hearings of Watergate begin. It is discovered that secret audiotape recordings have been made of Nixon and his aides as they conferred about Watergate. At first President Nixon refuses to supply the tapes, but he finally releases some of them. One tape contains an eighteen-minute gap that has intentionally been erased. Another tape made on July 23, 1972, clearly proves that Nixon had conspired with his aides to undermine the FBI investigation.

10. The House Judiciary Committee votes to impeach President Nixon, but he resigns on August 8, 1974, before they can take action.

Suggested Activities

Complete these activities on another sheet of paper. Be prepared to discuss your responses with the other groups in the class.

1. Respond in writing to the following statement: Although the Watergate scandal left the country in great turmoil, it proved that the American system of government works.

2. Watergate can be described as Nixon's worst moment and the event for which he is most identified in history. However, he did take some positive actions. What were some highlights of his presidency?

3. Research and find out what became of Dean, Haldeman, Ehrlichman, and Liddy. Write three or four sentences about each one's career following his incarceration.

Richard Milhous Nixon

37th President, 1969–1974

Vice Presidents: Spiro T. Agnew, Gerald R. Ford

Born: January 9, 1913, in Yorba Linda, California

Died: April 22, 1994

Party: Republican

Parents: Francis Anthony Nixon, Hannah Milhous

First Lady: Thelma Patricia (Pat) Catherine Ryan

Children: Patricia, Julie

Nickname: Tricky Dick

Education: Duke University School of Law (ranked third in his class)

Famous Firsts:

- Nixon was the first president to resign from office.

- He was the first president to visit China.

Achievements:

- Nixon worked as a lawyer until 1946 when he won election to Congress.

- During his first year as president, the United States won the space race when *Apollo 11* astronaut Neil Armstrong became the first person to walk on the moon.

- Nixon proposed to end the Vietnam War with *Vietnamization* (replacing American troops with South Vietnamese soldiers). During the Vietnamization process, Nixon ordered an increase in the bombing of North Vietnam. In fact, more bomb tonnage was dropped on North Vietnam in this short period than on Germany, Italy, and Japan combined during all of WW II.

- On June 8, 1969, President Nixon announced that 25,000 U.S. soldiers would leave Vietnam by the end of August and 35,000 more by September 16.

Interesting Facts:

- Nixon was often accused of being paranoid. For example, he ordered his staff to keep a list of enemies, from politicians to businesspersons, athletes, and movie stars.

- Richard Nixon was born in a house built by his father.

- In 1968, Nixon's daughter, Julie, married David Eisenhower, grandson of former President Eisenhower.

Gerald Rudolph Ford

38th President, 1974–1977

Vice President: Nelson A. Rockefeller

Born: July 14, 1913, in Omaha, Nebraska

Party: Republican

Parents: Leslie Lynch, Dorothy King

First Lady: Elizabeth Anne (Betty) Bloomer Warren

Children: Michael, John, Steven, Susan

Nickname: Mr. Nice Guy

Education: University of Michigan (law degree)

Famous Firsts:

- Gerald Ford was the first president who had not been elected president or vice president.

- He was the first vice president to be selected under the Twenty-fifth Amendment to the Constitution which requires the president's choice to be confirmed by both houses of Congress.

- When Ford became president, he chose Nelson A. Rockefeller as vice president, and for the first time in American history neither the president nor the vice president had been elected.

Achievements:

- During World War II, Ford served with the Third Fleet in the South Pacific and earned the rank of lieutenant commander.

- He served 25 years in the House of Representatives and became minority leader in 1965.

- During his administration he introduced a program called Whip Inflation Now (WIN), but it failed to combat the growing recession.

Interesting Facts:

- Despite the fact that he was an excellent athlete (he had been a football star at the University of Michigan), he had a presidential reputation for clumsiness.

- Under his presidency, the nation suffered the worst unemployment and inflation rates since the Depression.

- Ford is one of ten presidents to serve less than one term.

- President Ford legally changed his name from Leslie Lynch King, Jr., after his mother remarried and his stepfather, Gerald Ford, adopted him.

James Earl Carter, Jr.

39th President, 1977–1981

Vice President: Walter F. Mondale

Born: October 1, 1924, in Plains, Georgia

Party: Democrat

Parents: James Carter and Lillian Gordy

First Lady: Eleanor Rosalynn Smith

Children: John, James Earl III, Jeffrey, Amy

Nickname: Hot

Education: U.S. Naval Academy

Famous Firsts:

- He was the first president to be born in a hospital.

- Jimmy Carter was the first president elected from the Deep South since before the Civil War.

Achievements:

- He served in the navy during World War II.

- After his father died, Jimmy Carter resigned from the navy, and he and his wife, Rosalynn, worked in the family's peanut-farming business.

- He was elected to the Senate in 1952.

- In 1966, he ran unsuccessfully for governor of Georgia. In 1970, he was elected governor of the state.

- The Department of Energy and the Department of Education were created under his administration.

- He conducted the Camp David accords in 1978, bringing about peace between Israel and Egypt.

- President Carter pardoned the Vietnam draft evaders.

Interesting Facts:

- Carter was a speed-reader who could read over 2,000 words per minute with 95 percent accuracy.

- When he traveled, President Carter often carried his own luggage.

- Carter left office as one of the most unpopular presidents in history, yet he became one of the nation's most successful and active ex-presidents.

- His best remembered foreign relations event was the Iranian hostage crisis. On his final full day in office, the hostages were released.

- Jimmy Carter and his wife Rosalynn currently serve as regular volunteers for Habitat for Humanity, a program which develops and builds housing for low-income families.

Three First Ladies

During the 1970s there were three First Ladies: Pat Nixon, Betty Ford, and Rosalyn Carter. Each had a distinctive personality and brought a different flare to the White House. Read the short biographies that follow and complete one of the activities at the bottom of the page.

Pat Nixon When Pat Nixon became first lady, she was the mother of two teenage daughters, Tricia and Julie. Continuing in the tradition of Jackie Kennedy, Mrs. Nixon proceeded with the renovation of the White House to make it a museum of American heritage. In addition, she supported the cause of volunteerism and urged Americans to get involved with their communities. Her greatest political success was as a goodwill ambassador on trips to Africa. Pat Nixon died in 1993 and is buried beside her husband in Yorba Linda, California, at the Richard Nixon Library and Birthplace.

Betty Ford Betty Ford is most remembered for her candidness in her personal life. When she spoke publicly about her battle with breast cancer, she raised public awareness of the disease and served as an inspiration to others who faced cancer. As first lady, Betty Ford also supported the Equal Rights Amendment and valued both the traditional role of women and the role of women in the workplace. After leaving the White House, Mrs. Ford publicly described her struggle with addiction to alcohol and pain medication, and she founded the Betty Ford Clinic for substance abuse in Rancho Mirage, California.

Rosalyn Carter When Jimmy Carter was president, his wife Rosalyn served as his most trusted advisor and represented him officially during a trip to Central and South American countries. She sometimes sat in on cabinet meetings where she quietly took notes. These acts aroused much criticism, but there were also those who admired her. Rosalyn's own agenda included supporting mental health reform, actively supporting legislation to reform Social Security, and urging approval of the Equal Rights Amendment. A woman of action, Rosalyn believed firmly in the necessity of women pursuing careers outside the home.

Suggested Activities

History Make a chart of the childhoods and educations of these three first ladies.

Comparison Construct a three-way Venn diagram comparing the accomplishments and roles of these first ladies.

First Ladies Explain how each of these three women changed and impacted the role of First Lady for future First Ladies.

Election Facts and Figures

	Election of 1972	Election of 1976
Democrats	South Dakota Senator George McGovern, a liberal, was the Democratic choice for president. He first selected Thomas Eagleton of Missouri as his vice president but changed to Sargent Shriver when it was announced that Eagleton had received shock treatments for depression.	Jimmy Carter, former governor of Georgia, was a relative unknown in the political arena but his informal style and big, toothy smile helped him win a first ballot victory at the Democratic convention. He talked about restoring people's faith in the government.
Republicans	Richard Nixon and Spiro Agnew easily won their party's renomination. Fewer than 25,000 troops remained in Vietnam, and Nixon campaigned on his record for negotiating peace with the Communists.	Despite a run by former California governor Ronald Reagan, President Ford took the Republican nomination. Nelson Rockefeller would continue as the vice presidential nominee.
Other	Alabama George C. Wallace, who broke with the Democrats in 1968 to run as the American Independent Party candidate, sought the Democratic nomination. He withdrew after he was shot while campaigning in May.	
Slogans		Some of Ford's campaign buttons read, "I'm Voting for Betty's Husband." Another campaign slogan was "Whip Inflation Now" or "WIN."
Issues	McGovern charged that Nixon's administration was the most corrupt in U.S. history. He promised an immediate and complete withdrawal of American troops from Vietnam and was critical of government cuts in spending. He suggested an income tax increase might be necessary in the forthcoming years.	Carter and Ford held two debates. At the second one, which was held in October, Ford mistakenly claimed that Poland was free of Soviet domination. The error hurt him and most likely lost him the race. Carter, in the meantime, promised more jobs, welfare, and tax reform.
Winner	Nixon won by a margin of nearly 20 million votes. He won 49 states, losing only in Massachusetts and the District of Columbia. Nixon's electoral vote total was 520 to McGovern's 17.	It was a very close election with Carter winning by 2 percent of the popular votes. This election was notable for its low voter turnout. Carter garnered 297 electoral votes to Ford's 240.

Earth Day

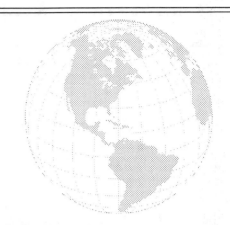

The first Earth Day was celebrated on April 22, 1970. Environmentalists conducted demonstrations and rallies across the nation to call attention to the growing problem of pollution. Today, the movement is still growing strong, and there is a bigger commitment than ever to protect the environment and to keep it clean.

On this page are a number of activities you can do to keep the spirit of Earth Day alive all year long. Complete at least two activities from the list below.

Suggested Activities

Learn Keep yourself informed about current environmental issues by reading articles in newspapers and magazines. Share what you have learned with members of your class and family.

Recycle I Think twice before throwing away paper that has only been used on one side. Save it and use it for scrap paper for math calculations, rough drafts, or even for doodling. When both sides have been used, deposit the paper into a recycling bin.

Recycle II Most items can be used a number of ways. Plastic margarine cups are a good example. Clean and save them for food storage, mixing paints, and storing small items such as paper clips. What other uses can you think of? Save other types of plastic, paper, and glass containers and think of new uses for them.

Save Water Be aware of how much water you waste and consume. Take shorter showers rather than baths. Turn the water off while you are brushing your teeth. Remind others in your household to follow the same guidelines.

Conserve To conserve electric lights, dust them regularly. Turn out the lights in a room when you or no one else is using them. In addition to conserving, you will also help your folks save money on the electric bill.

Save the Rain Forest Rain forests play a vital role in the biosphere. In addition to affecting worldwide weather, these forests absorb harmful carbon dioxide and help supply the Earth with oxygen. The rainforests are also our most important source of raw materials for creating new medicines. Help save the rainforests by writing to the Rainforest Action Network, 300 Broadway, Suite 28, San Francisco, CA, 94133. Ask them what you can do to help.

Avoid Styrofoam Styrofoam, or polystyrene foam, is a non-biodegradable material which means that it will never deteriorate—not even if it sits out in the sun or is buried in dirt for five hundred years. As much as possible, avoid using foam cups and plates. Remind your family to purchase eggs packed in paper cartons rather than foam containers.

Read There are plenty of good books out there to help you find ways to preserve and protect the environment. Take a look at *50 Simple Things Kids Can Do to Save the Earth* by The Earthworks Group (Andrews and McMeel, 1990) or ask your librarian to recommend some other titles.

The Oil Crisis

Read the paragraphs about the events which led to the Arab oil embargo and its effects on the U.S. economy. On a separate sheet of paper, answer the questions that follow.

The creation of the state of Israel on May 14, 1948, angered Arab nations because this new state was composed of land claimed by both Arabs and Jews. Over the years that followed, Arabs and Israelis launched several attacks and counterattacks against one another. On October 6, 1973, the Jewish holiday of Yom Kippur, the Arab states attempted once again to destroy Israel. A massive United States-backed airlift of supplies aided Israeli defenders and incensed the Arabs. In an unparalleled show of unity, the Arab states retaliated by using their vast oil resources as an economic weapon. On October 17, 1973, they declared an embargo on all oil shipments to Europe and North America.

Almost immediately, the affected countries were impacted by the strict measure. In the United States, a number of energy-saving measures were instituted. Some gas stations began closing on Sundays, speed limits were lowered, and rationing systems were installed. Buyers began to look more closely at foreign-made cars which were smaller and consumed less gas than their American counterparts. Petroleum-based products doubled in price, and research of alternate energy sources was stepped up.

The U.S. and other countries quickly realized that they could no longer depend on the Middle East for an inexhaustible supply of cheap oil. Although the Arabs lifted the oil embargo on March 18, 1974, oil prices remained high, nearly double what they had been just a year prior.

Suggested Activities

Knowledge Identify three energy-saving measures which were instituted as a result of the Arab oil embargo.

Comprehension In your own words, describe the events that led up to the Arab oil embargo against the Western world.

Application Predict how Americans reacted to news of the oil embargo and what inconveniences bothered them the most.

Analysis Draw conclusions about the impact that the oil embargo had on the auto industry and identify what changes were made in U.S. automobiles as a result of the embargo.

Synthesis Propose your own ideas for energy saving measures that could be employed in case of another oil embargo.

Evaluation Assess the impact of the oil embargo on our present economy, or determine which of the energy saving measures instituted in 1973 have left positive, long-term effects on the economy.

Feminists of the Seventies

The women's movement was probably the greatest social change of the seventies decade. At the helm of this movement was Gloria Steinem, the leading feminist and proponent of women's rights during the era. Ms. Steinem was not alone in her fight, however. Some other leading figures of women's liberation included Betty Friedan (see page 331), Bella Abzug, and Shirley Chisholm. Below, you can read about each of these women and her role in the feminist cause.

Gloria Steinem Despite an impoverished and insecure childhood, Gloria Steinem was able to attend Smith College from which she graduated magna cum laude. Instead of studying the traditional literature and art, Steinem majored in government. After graduation she went to India on a two-year scholarship. When she returned to the Uinted States, she worked in journalism. In 1972, Ms.Steinem and thirteen other women published the first issue of *Ms. Magazine*. Her articles

Gloria Steinem

and personal appearances helped build feminism into a national movement.

Bella Abzug Bella Savitzky Abzug was born on July 24, 1920, into a loving family, but tragedy struck early in her life when her father died suddenly. Barely thirteen, she felt the loss deeply. At school she earned a reputation as a political activist, and it was no surprise when she decided to pursue a law degree. Even her marriage to Martin Abzug did not deter her. After graduating from Columbia University, Bella Abzug joined a law office specializing in labor union cases. Over the years she took up a number of social causes and in 1970 decided to make a bid for a seat in Congress. After an aggressive campaign, she won a seat in the House of Representatives. She worked for the passage of the Equal Rights Amendment and with Shirley Chisholm sponsored a bill for federal support of day-care centers for the children of working mothers. Considered a radical by some, Ms. Abzug maintained that she was merely an idealist who was fighting for the ordinary man and woman.

Shirley Chisholm After she earned a master's degree in education from Columbia University, Shirley Chisholm worked in New York City's day-care system. Angered by the inequalities that African American women and children faced, she entered politics in 1964 in an effort to get government support for them. She became the first black woman elected to the U.S. Congress. For fourteen years Ms. Chisholm served as a U.S. Representative. She supported the Equal Rights Amendment and helped found the National Women's Political Caucus.

Resources

Focus on Women (Teacher Created Materials, #495)

Herstory: Women Who Changed the World, edited by Ruth Ashby and Deborah Gore Ohrn (Viking, 1995)

Is There a Woman in the House . . . or the Senate? by Bryna J.Fireside (Albert Whitman & Company, 1994)

Marian Wright Edelman

Growing up in the Wright household meant doing chores, getting good grades in school, and helping others in the community. These were lessons that Marian Wright learned well and brought with her when she took up a the social cause of children's rights.

Wright grew up with her siblings in a segregated neighborhood. Her father, Arthur, worked hard to make their community a better place to live. When black children were not allowed to play in the white park, for example, he built a playground behind his church. Although Arthur Wright died when his daughter was only fourteen, she never forgot his concern for others.

After graduating from high school in 1956, Wright attended Spelman College, the first college for black women in the nation. The civil rights movement was just beginning, and she wanted to be part of it. While working for the NAACP in Atlanta, she decided to become an attorney. In 1963 Wright graduated from Yale Law School, and after passing the bar, she began to defend many civil rights cases. She also began devoting time to the Head Start programs in Mississippi. After marrying Peter Edelman in 1968, she wrote a report about the government's failure to help poor children get a good education. It made headlines but failed to bring about any action. Her next step was to organize a group that included church groups, women's organizations, and the National Education Association. Together they would propose bills that would provide help for children. In 1973 the group was expanded into the Children's Defense Fund (CDF) which would look out for the needs of all children in the United States, but particularly poor children. Today, Marian Wright Edelman continues to be active in the CDF. She has received numerous honors for her tireless work on behalf of American children.

Suggested Activities

Children's Defense Fund The CDF is a nonprofit organization dedicated to the betterment of all children. Funded by individual donations and corporations, the CDF actively sponsors research, publicity, public education, legislation, and advocacy programs on children's issues. Since its inception in 1974 the organization has been responsible for the passage of the Education for All Handicapped Children Act of 1974, the growth of the Head Start program, and the first comprehensive child care and family support legislation which was passed in 1990. Research and find out what roles Edward M. Kennedy and Hillary Rodham Clinton had in the CDF.

Resources

Marian Wright Edelman by Joann J. Burch (The Millbrook Press, 1994)

Herstory: Women Who Changed the World edited by Ruth Ashby and Deborah Gore Ohrn (Viking, 1995)

The Occupation of Wounded Knee

For many years Native Americans were ashamed of their heritage and faced discrimination and persecution. The civil rights movement of the 1960s inspired some of their leaders to fight for their rights. Here is their story.

The civil rights movement began in the United States during the 1950s, but it did not reach its peak until the sixties. By then, Americans of all ages, races, nationalities, and sexes were lobbying for equal rights. Ignored in all the protests and demonstrations, however, were the Native Americans. For years, this group had been discriminated against. Many still lived on Indian reservations where conditions were poor. They had other justifiable grievances, including limited opportunities and the lack of basic rights.

In 1968 the American Indian Movement was established, and Congress passed the Indian Civil Rights Act. This law guaranteed Indians the rights and privileges outlined in the Bill of Rights and recognized the legality of tribal law. It was a step in the right direction, but the Native Americans wanted more. Activists from several tribes banded together to present their grievances. When they were rebuffed, the group seized an abandoned federal prison on Alcatraz Island near San Francisco. For a year and a half they occupied the prison amidst a swirl of publicity. Their next seige was at Wounded Knee, South Dakota, the site of the 1890 massacre of the Sioux by the Seventh Cavalry. On February 28, 1973, members of the American Indian Movement, led by Dennis Banks and Russell Means, took over a trading post there.

Overall, these planned takeovers made non-Indians aware of the plight and grievances of Native Americans. As a result, some Native Americans began to take more pride in their heritage. But the most lasting effect was in the court actions which granted rights that had been in dispute for many years. For example, in 1971 the Aleuts and other native Alaskans won forty million acres of land as well as nearly one billion dollars in settlements from the government. Despite similar awards, several tribes still suffer from high unemployment and alcoholism rates.

Suggested Activities

Wealth In the 1980s and 1990s, gambling casinos cropped up on Indian reservations across the country. Have the students find out what this meant to the welfare of the Native Americans, and why it has raised controversy.

Discuss Ask students why they think Native American rights had been overlooked for so long.

Wounded Knee Wounded Knee, South Dakota, was the site of a previous Sioux massacre. Have students research events that led to that massacre.

Novel Idea Find some books or articles about the 1890 Wounded Knee incident written from the Native American's point of view. Compare their version to what is printed in your school's history textbooks.

Adam Clayton Powell, Jr.

U.S. representative, minister, and civil rights leader are all titles that aptly describe Adam Clayton Powell, Jr. President Lyndon Johnson once called him one of the most powerful men in America. He was the first African American congressman to come from the East, serving as representative from the Harlem district in New York from 1945 to 1970. Powell also chaired the influential House Committee on Education and Labor and was instrumental in the establishment of the National Endowment for the Humanities.

Born in New Haven, Connecticut, in 1908, Powell was the son of Adam Clayton Powell, Sr., a minister and an author. Young Powell grew up in New York City and attended Colgate University in upstate New York. Following his education there, he attended Columbia University in 1932 and earned an M.A. degree. In addition to his studies, Powell assisted his father who was the minister of the Abyssinian Baptist Church in Harlem. During this time he decided to become a minister like his father. After attending Shaw University in Raleigh, North Carolina, for his doctor of divinity degree, Powell took over for his father at the Abyssinian church.

Like his father, Adam Powell, Jr., became an advocate for African American rights. He helped organize a buying power movement which was a way to force white-owned businesses that depended on black customers to hire more black employees. Through picket lines, boycotts, and mass protests, some 10,000 new jobs were brought to Harlem. In 1941 he was elected to the New York City Council, and the following year he started publishing a weekly newspaper, *The People's Voice*.

This show of leadership and political activity helped Powell to his first term as a U.S. representative in 1945. During the Kennedy and Johnson administrations, Powell was instrumental in obtaining federal aid for colleges and universities and legislated bills to fund teacher education and more libraries.

In the sixties Powell encountered some legal difficulties when he was accused of misusing public funds. As a result he was expelled from the House of Representatives, but the following month he was re-elected by the voters who disagreed with the expulsion. Powell served in Congress for a few more years until he was defeated in 1970. Only two short years after retiring, Powell died of cancer.

Suggested Activities

Expelled Another senator, Christopher Dodds, was also accused of misuse of funds, but he was allowed to keep his seat in Congress. Find out why Powell was expelled for the same alleged misuse.

Boycotts Discuss boycotts with the class and how they were effective in Powell's buying power movement.

Resource Learn more about Powell's political life in the book *Adam Clayton Powell* by James S. Haskins (Africa World Press, Inc., 1992).

Hale House

Clara Hale was a widow with three children in 1932. She needed to work but wanted to be able to stay at home with her youngsters. A home day-care center proved to be the answer. In 1968 Hale retired, but about a year later embarked on a new career when her daughter brought home a drug-addicted baby. Within a few short years, Hale House was founded to provide care for these infants.

Clara Hale

Clara McBride Hale was born in Philadelphia, Pennsylvania, in 1905. After her father died, her mother supported the family by cooking and renting out rooms in their home. Clara McBride attended school regularly and after graduating from high school married Thomas Hale. The young couple moved to Harlem in New York City where Thomas Hale had a floor waxing business. Clara Hale worked nights cleaning theaters to help supplement their income. When her husband died in 1932, she was left with three young children to support. At first she continued her night job but added housecleaning jobs during the day. To be able to stay home with her children, Clara Hale began a day-care center and also took in foster children.

In 1968, one year after Clara McBride Hale retired, her daughter, Lorraine Hale, noticed a heroin addict who was falling asleep in the park with her infant falling out of her arms. Lorraine, who held a doctorate degree in child development, gave the young woman an address—her mother's—where the woman could get help. The following day, the woman showed up to surrender her baby while she got treatment for herself. Word spread quickly on the streets, and soon Clara Hale was caring for twenty-two drug-addicted babies.

At first, the venture was financed by Hale's three children who worked overtime to raise money to support it, but by the early seventies the city began to provide some funding. The Hales used the money to purchase and renovate a five-story home in Harlem. Hale House, as it was called, officially opened in 1975.

The only facility in the United States to treat the tiny victims of mothers who abused drugs, Hale House employed a social worker, a teacher, and a part time staff of doctors and nurses. After the babies went through withdrawal and their mothers were healthy, they would be reunited. Hale's success rate was a phenomenal 97 percent, and less than one baby per year had to be put up for adoption.

When President Ronald Reagan cited Clara Hale's work in his 1985 State of the Union address before Congress, Hale House received national recognition and private funding. Today, the program has been expanded to help infants and mothers with AIDS. Lorraine Hale has continued her mother's work since Clara Hale's death in 1992.

Suggested Activity

Government Aid Discuss with the class the role that the government should play in assisting programs such as Hale House. Ask students if they would be willing to work overtime to help support this cause.

Mikhail Baryshnikov

When he was young, Mikhail Baryshnikov worried about his height because he was always the shortest boy in class. Eventually he learned to let go of his worries, and today he is regarded as one of the foremost ballet performers in the world.

Baryshnikov was destined to become a ballet dancer when he was born on January 27, 1948, in Riga, Latvia. His father was a military topographer in the Russian army and his mother was a seamstress who loved ballet. It was she who encouraged Baryshnikov and enrolled him in ballet school. Although he was considered old for a beginning student (he was twelve years of age), he showed a great feeling for music. His body type was not ideal for ballet because he was not tall and slender, but he proved to be a talented student and was later admitted to the Vaganova Ballet School in Leningrad. There he studied under the famous ballet teacher Alexander Pushkin who treated Baryshnikov like a son. For the following three years he studied and practiced ballet for hours every day.

Upon graduation in 1966 Baryshnikov joined the Kirov Ballet Company. As a soloist for the dance troop, he gained international attention and won numerous awards. In 1968 a ballet was written especially for him by a famous Russian choreographer, as were all his later ballets. The Soviet government would not allow Baryshnikov to perform the work of other choreographers. While he was performing in Canada in 1974, Baryshnikov defected from the Soviet Union. He asked for political asylum in Canada, explaining that he had chosen to leave Russia for his artistic growth.

Later, he joined the American Ballet Theater in New York where he worked with another Soviet dancer, Natalia Makarova, who had also defected from Russia in the 1970s. Baryshnikov often collaborated with American choreographers, including the famous Twyla Tharp. In 1980 Baryshnikov became the ballet theater's artistic director. In addition to dancing and choreographing, he launched a career in motion pictures and appeared in two films, *The Turning Point* (1976) and *White Nights* (1985).

Suggested Activities

Ballet Research and make a list of some of the basic ballet positions. Draw a picture to show how each step is executed. Try some of the positions yourself.

Roles Ask students what the difference is between the role of a male ballet dancer and that of the female dancer.

Bravura Mikhail Baryshnikov employed a style of dancing known as *bravura*. Assign the students to find out what is meant by this style and to learn about other styles of ballet.

Actor, Writer, and Director

As a child he was a loner who spent little time with his sister and classmates. In his adult life he continued to be a loner both in his personal and stage personas. Who is this person? None other than comedian, writer, actor, director, and producer Woody Allen.

Allen was born Allen Stewart Konigsberg in 1935 to Orthodox Jewish parents. His father, Martin, held a a variety of short-lived jobs while his mother, Nettie, worked as an accountant in a flower shop. Allen disliked school despite the fact that he was considered bright. Only one subject seemed to interest him, and that was English composition. Allen avoided after-school activities and spent much time reading by himself. As a teenager he wrote and sent quips to newspaper gossip columnist Earl Wilson and earned money for one liners he wrote for a press agent. After graduating from Midwood High School in Brooklyn, he briefly attended New York University and City College of New York. Low grades and poor attendance caused him to be expelled.

Woody Allen

Allen found work as a writer for Sid Caesar's popular television weekly, *Your Show of Shows*, and then moved on to work for *The Garry Moore Show*. Despite an excellent salary, Allen decided to leave the writing business to someone else and became a stand-up comedian. In his act, Allen portrayed himself as a hapless nerd who did not have any girlfriends. A breakthrough came when he was appearing in a New York nightclub. A film producer saw his act and offered him a job writing a screenplay for a movie. Although the film was a success, Allen did not like having so little say on how the project turned out. In the late 1960s, he wrote a screenplay for the first of many movies in which he would also star and direct. From *Take the Money and Run* (1969) to *Sleeper* (1973) to *Love and Death* (1975), Allen's audiences loved his sense of humor.

Another movie, *Annie Hall* (1977), made movie history when it swept the Oscar awards and won best picture, best director, best actress, and best original screenplay. A very funny look at male-female relationships, the movie starred Allen and Diane Keaton. Keaton's performance also introduced a whole new way for women to dress. The Annie Hall look, which featured tweed jackets worn over high collared shirts, a long scarf, and long skirts or baggy trousers, was soon adapted by women everywhere. Other films followed, but none has matched the success of *Annie Hall*, although many have been popular and award-winning. Allen continues to live in New York City and can sometimes be seen playing clarinet with Dixieland bands at small pubs.

Suggested Activities

Plays Group the students and assign them to write, direct, and act in a short play or skit about the problems of boy-girl relationships. Let the groups take turns presenting their plays.

One-Liners Woody Allen began his career by writing one-line jokes. Have the students write new one-liners or share their favorite one-line jokes with the rest of the class.

Chris Evert

Called the Ice Maiden by some, her outwardly calm demeanor belied the fierce and competitive spirit underneath. Nothing seemed to distract her, and she impressed everyone with her accurate groundstrokes and unusual two-handed backhand. The athlete is, of course, Chris Evert.

Chris Evert was born on December 21, 1954, in Fort Lauderdale, Florida. The second of five children, she learned to play tennis from her father, Jimmy Evert, a one-time national junior tennis champion himself. Mr. Evert was also the manager and a teaching professional at the Holiday Park Tennis Center. The whole family spent time there and learned to play the game. At first, young Evert had problems holding the racket firmly with one hand, particularly on the backhand stroke, so the six-year-old took to using both hands. Most players considered the two-handed backhand unorthodox, but after Chris Evert began playing and winning tournaments, the two-hander became widely copied.

By the time she began entering junior tournaments, she was practicing several hours a day. That left her no time to attend parties or sleepovers with friends. She continued to do well in school and even graduated with honors from high school. By the time Evert was fourteen, she had already begun playing against top women players, and at age fifteen she beat Australian Margaret Court, a high-ranking woman player. When Evert joined the tennis circuit the following year and arrived at the U.S. Open, she had already won forty-six consecutive singles contests.

At age eighteen, Chris Evert turned professional. One of the biggest money winners in tennis at the time, she was the first woman to earn more than one million dollars. Another milestone was reached in 1974 when she won thirty-five consecutive titles by midyear. She was also engaged to the top men's player, Jimmy Connors, but that union was broken off a few months later.

During her career, Chris Evert earned numerous tennis titles and awards, including being named the 1976 *Sports Illustrated* Sportswoman of the Year. She continued her number-one ranking until the rise of Martina Navratilova. The two alternately shared the number one spot until Evert retired.

In 1989 Evert left competitive tennis. Since then she has provided color commentary for televised tennis events. On a personal note, she is the mother of three sons. Although she enjoyed her tennis years, she claims that family is more important to her now.

Suggested Activities

Women's Role Tell students to find out what role Billie Jean King played in promoting women's tennis.

Rivals Chris and Martina Navratilova were fierce rivals on court. Find out more about Navratilova. Compare her style of play to Evert's.

Baseliner Chris Evert was a baseline player. What does that mean? What is the difference between a baseliner and a serve-and-volley player?

Innovations of the 70s

The Seventies was a very productive decade in the field of science and technology. On this page you will find an overview of some of the most important innovations of the decade.

1970

- The first inexpensive (under $10) pocket calculators, developed by Clive Sinclair, are retailed in the United States.

1971

- The CAT (computerized axial tomography) scan, a tool for imaging the brain, is invented.
- The first commercial microprocessor is built. This invention makes it possible to build smaller, cheaper, and more efficient computers.
- Sociobiology is founded after Harvard biologist Edward O. Wilson studies the behavior of ants and other insects that live in groups.
- Lasers come into wide use to cut through metal, perform eye surgery, and create holograms.
- The first digital watches are manufactured.

1972

- The United States. bans the used of the pesticide DDT when it is found harmful to plants, animals, and humans.
- *Pong*, the world's first commercial video game, is demonstrated.

1973

- Skylab is launched by the U.S. (page 386).

1974

- The Heimlich maneuver is developed by Cincinnati surgeon Henry Jay Heimlich to help save choking victims.
- UPCs (universal price codes) appear on food packages scanners at checkout counters. They help speed up the process.

1975

- The world's first miniature television is produced.

1976

- The Concorde is the first civilian jet to break the sound barrier.
- On July 20, *Viking I* lands on Mars.
- CB's (citizen band radios) are the rage, and everyone from truckers to retirees uses them to communicate with one another.
- Scientists report that gases from spray cans can damage the ozone layer.

1977

- London to New York passenger service on the Concorde begins.
- MRI (magnetic resonance imaging) is first used in the medical industry.
- *Voyager* is launched.
- The first personal computer (Apple II) is manufactured.

1978

- The world's first-test tube baby, Louise Joy Brown, is born in Great Britain.
- The Sony Walkman is introduced. It is the world's first personal stereo cassette player.

Suggested Activity

Importance Choose the most significant development from the list above. Explain your choice and how it has impacted your life today.

Skylab

On May 14, 1973, the United States launched Skylab, its first space station. Over the next nine months, three different flight crews were sent to live inside the orbiting spacecraft. Read on for more information about this historic space experiment.

Description Skylab was a space station in which people could work and live for extended periods of time. The main section of the craft contained a workshop where the crew lived. Inside the workshop were storage areas for food and water and crew quarters which contained individual sleeping compartments, toilets, a collapsible shower stall, exercise equipment, and a work area for experiments.

Equipment On the outside of Skylab were eight telescopes to study the sun, a shield to protect it from meteoroids, and six winglike solar-cells to convert the sun's energy into electricity. Finally, a multiple docking adapter allowed rockets to connect to Skylab. Astronauts would then enter the craft through an air-lock module.

Crews Three different crews of three men each lived and worked on Skylab during a nine-month period. Each crew consisted of a commander, a science pilot (an expert on science experiments), and the pilot (an expert on space flight). The first crew spent 28 days in space, the second crew 59 days, and the third crew 84 days.

What Was Learned Over 160,000 pictures of the sun were taken during the three Skylab missions. Solar flares or eruptions were captured on film. Other photos showed much about the earth's surface, including oil and mineral deposits and signs of air and water pollution. In addition, the crews recorded data about their own ability to adapt to a zero gravity environment and observed the behavior of minnows, spiders, and other small creatures in space.

End of Skylab After the third Skylab crew returned safely to Earth, Skylab continued to orbit the earth for five more years. On July 12, 1979, it fell to Earth with some pieces landing in Australia and others plunging into the ocean.

Suggested Activity

Research Assign student pairs or groups to research further any of the following questions:

How did the astronauts reach Skylab?

What kinds of problems were encountered during the whole project?

What were the purposes of Skylab and were they achieved?

How did the astronauts do everyday things like taking a shower and going to the bathroom?

What effect does the lack of exercise in space have on the body?

Pluto's Moon

While taking photographs at the Lowell Observatory in Arizona, astronomer Clyde Tombaugh discovered a new planet. The date was February 13, 1930. Since then, regular observations of the planet continued. Nothing new was discovered until 1978 when astronomer James W. Christy noticed a bulge on a photograph that he had taken of Pluto. As he scanned earlier photos of the planet, Christy noticed that the same bulge appeared in different spots. This exciting discovery was Pluto's moon, Charon.

Today, scientists know much more about Pluto and Charon than they did in the late seventies. Some amazing facts can be found below. Certain information is missing, though, and you will have to replace it. Complete the math problems in the box below and write the answers on the corresponding lines. Read the facts after all the blanks have been filled in.

1. $6,400 \div 800$	4. $17,860 \div 47$	7. $132.94 \div 46$
2. $35,719 - 23,319$	5. $10,148 - 6,552$	8. $1,710 \div 95$
3. 29.8×25	6. $99.830 + 147.850$	

1. Earth is 80 times more massive than the moon, but Pluto is only_____times more massive than Charon.

2. Pluto and Charon are separated by only_____miles (19,950 km). That is just $\frac{1}{20th}$ of the distance between the Earth and the moon.

3. The diameter of Charon is_____miles (1200 km), which is nearly one-half the diameter of Pluto.

4. Pluto and Charon are extremely cold with temperatures of_____degrees below zero Fahrenheit (230 degrees Celsius).

5. Pluto's average distance from the sun is_____million miles (5,896 million kilometers).

6. It takes Pluto_____Earth years to make one orbit around the sun.

7. Pluto's average orbital speed is_____miles (4.74 km) per second.

8. While Earth rotates once every 24 hours, Pluto rotates once every 6 days, 9 hours,_____minutes.

——————— Suggested Activity ———————

Learn More Interested in learning more about this distant planet of Pluto? Choose one of the following activities to complete.

- Make a chart comparing facts about the Earth and its moon with Pluto and its moon, Charon.

- Find out why this statement is true: Pluto and Charon make up the closest thing we know of to a double planet.

- How were the names Pluto and Charon chosen? What do the names represent?

Space Explorations

The United States launched a number of spacecraft during the seventies. Below you will find a brief introduction to each of these missions. After completing some research, add two or three more factual sentences to each description.

Apollo 13 You may already know about this flight from the 1990s movie of the same name. In 1970 this ill-fated mission was scheduled to land on the moon. Instead, an oxygen tank exploded, draining the air from the capsule. The astronauts were forced to move into the lunar module.

_____

_____

Mariner 9 In 1971, when *Mariner 9* orbited Mars, it became the first man-made object to orbit another planet.

_____

_____

Apollo 16 **and** *17* Both of these missions made trips to the moon.

_____

_____

Skylab Launched for a variety of experiments in space, *Skylab* was visited by three different crews during 1973 and 1974. The craft contained living quarters for the crew and was outfitted with solar equipment.

_____

_____

Mariner 10 This satellite transmitted detailed pictures of both Venus and Mercury back to Earth.

_____

_____

Viking I In 1976 this space probe landed on Mars. It sent back information about conditions on the planet, and it also searched for signs of life.

_____

_____

Voyager I On August 20, 1977, NASA launched the first of two *Voyager* spacecraft. *Voyager I* arrived at Jupiter in 1979 and discovered thin rings around the planet.

_____

_____

Voyager II Launched two weeks after *Voyager I*, it carried a twelve-inch gold phonograph record containing greetings in dozens of Earth's languages.

_____

70s Inventions

On this page you can read about some inventors and the new ideas they formulated in the seventies. Research and write a one-page report about the invention that interests you most. Explain why you chose it and what lasting benefits it has brought to mankind.

Microprocessor In 1971 three Intel Corporation engineers built the first commercial microprocessor. This tiny, integrated circuit, or microchip, contained a computer processor which was the basis for the computer revolution of the 80s and 90s.

Food Processor Built in the same year as the microprocessor, the food processor was a new and versatile kitchen tool. It was invented by Frenchman Pierre Verdon and could be used to mix, chop, or slice food.

Home Video Game In 1972 Ralph Baer invented the world's first home video game. This simulated table tennis game was called Odyssey and was played with a special console that was hooked up to a regular television screen. Two knobs on the console controlled the up and down movements of the paddles. Later that year, Atari released the first coin-operated video game called *Pong*. Developed by computer pioneer Nolan Bushnell, the game was an electronic version of ping-pong. In the late Seventies some video games began to use vector graphics, and a whole series of *Pac Man* games became popular.

CAT Scanner X-rays had traditionally been used to view dense parts of the body, particularly the bones, but it provided poor pictures of the soft tissue in the brain. In 1972 British researcher Godfrey Hounsfield developed the CAT (computerized axial tomography) scanner to get a better look inside the brain. The scanner took thousands of X-ray pictures before spending hours analyzing them. Images were then displayed on a screen so doctors could see the brain from a number of different angles.

MRI Scanner Five years after the CAT scanner was invented in 1972, the MRI scanner was developed. MRI, or magnetic resonance imaging, allowed doctors to look inside a person's body without using harmful X-rays. In 1984 the Food and Drug Administration gave final approval for the sale and use of the MRI scanner.

Personal Computer The Altair 8800 was the first commercial personal computer, but it came in kit form and lacked a keyboard and screen. Two California college dropouts, Steven Jobs and Stephen Wozniak, created and marketed the first truly useful personal computer in 1976 and called it the Apple.

Skylab In 1973 the United States launched an unmanned space station in orbit. During the next nine months three different crews visited the craft. For additional information about *Skylab* see page 386.

Do a Little Dance

Discotheques, nightclubs that featured recorded music for dancing, became popular in the seventies. Teach students a basic disco dance. Make a transparency of the patterns and directions on this page for use on the overhead projector. Read them together and then demonstrate the steps to the class. Let students practice the steps without music. Then play a disco tune and do a little dance!

Boys

6. Step forward to your basic position and start the sequence over.

5. Bring the right foot next to the left foot and step together.

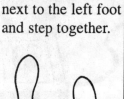

4. Now move your left foot in a diagonal movement in front of you.

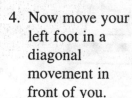

3. As soon as your right foot is planted, touch your left foot next to it.

2. Touch your right foot next to your left and begin to move your right foot to the right on a diagonal.

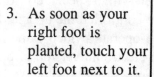

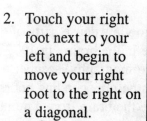

1. Bring your left foot towards your left on a diagonal.

Basic Position: Both feet side by side, shoulder width apart

(Start Here)

Girls

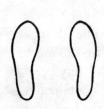

6. Step forward to your basic position and start the sequence over.

5. Bring the left foot next to the right foot and step together.

4. Now move your right foot in a diagonal movement in front of you.

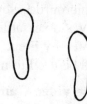

3. As soon as your left foot is planted, touch your right foot next to it.

2. Touch your left foot next to your right and begin to move your left foot to the left on a diagonal.

1. Bring your right foot towards your right on a diagonal.

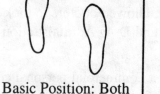

Basic Position: Both feet side by side, shoulder width apart

(Start Here)

Resource

Disco Dancing by Joetta Cherry and Gwynne Tomlan (Grosset and Dunlap, 1979)

Roots

1977 saw the birth of a new phenomenon: the television mini-series. Written by Alex Haley, this first mini-series, *Roots*, was the story of Haley's family, from its origins in Africa through the time of slavery to emancipation. More than three-fourths of the viewing population watched the televised eight-part series. In addition to being the first of its kind, *Roots* also was significant because of its realistic portrayal of African Americans. Most movie and television parts before that time portrayed blacks in a negative, stereotypical fashion.

Alex Haley

Alex Palmer Haley was born on August 11 1921, in Ithaca, New York. His father, Simon Alexander Haley, was a professor and his mother, Bertha George Palmer Haley, was a teacher. Haley followed in their footsteps and attended Elizabeth City Teachers College for two years. After changing his mind about his choice of career, he joined the U.S. Coast Guard, in which he served for twenty years.

When Haley left the Coast Guard in 1959 to become a freelance writer, he had been married to Nannie Branch for eighteen years. Writing proved to be less than lucrative, and his already unstable financial situation put a strain on their relationship. By 1964, the marriage was over. That same year, Haley married Juliette Collins, but they divorced also.

Undeterred, Haley kept on writing and produced numerous articles but only two books. In 1965, he helped Malcolm X write his autobiography titled *The Autobiography of Malcolm X*. Eleven years later, Haley's book *Roots: The Saga of an American Family* gained him international fame. When the tale was produced as a television series, Haley acted as a consultant on the project. He also consulted on the television sequel, *Roots: The Next Generation*. Following the success of this program, he spent much of his time promoting and speaking about the novel. Although some critics wondered about the accuracy of his book, he was quick to point out that the events have a basis in actual history. Dialogue and characters' thoughts, however, were his creation.

Some time later, Haley was able to devote time to writing *My Search for Roots*, in which he detailed the research involved in writing the original manuscript, but he never produced another novel. *Roots* had taken twelve years to research and write. In addition to being a best-seller, *Roots* earned Haley a Pulitzer prize and the NAACP's Spingarn Medal in 1977. Alex Haley died in 1992.

Suggested Activities

Video *Roots* may be available at your local video rental store or through your school district's media center. Show selections to the class and discuss the portrayal of African Americans at that time in history.

Mini Roots Assign the students to write a mini-version of *Roots* about their own family heritage.

Judy Blume

Beginning with the introduction of the book *Are You There God? It's Me, Margaret* in 1970, Judy Blume became a leading children's author. Her first book, *The One in the Middle Is the Green Kangaroo*, published in 1969, had already earned her respect in the children's literary world. Sometimes her work has caused concern or controversy, but Judy Blume still remains one of the most popular authors for children.

Judy Sussman Blume was born on February 12, 1938, in Elizabeth, New Jersey. Her father, Rudolph Sussman, was a dentist and her mother was Esther Rosenfeld Sussman. As a child Judy Sussman was an A student and did exactly as she was told, even though on the inside she wished she could rebel. She loved to read Nancy Drew mysteries, biographies, and horse stories but also longed to read about characters who shared problems that she and other young people were facing. She attended New York University and the year before she graduated, in 1960, she married John W. Blume, an attorney. The couple had one daughter, Randy Lee, and a son, Laurence Andrew, but the marriage ended in divorce in 1975. Blume married George Cooper, a writer, in 1987.

Since her first published book in 1969, Judy Blume has amassed awards from all over the U.S., but her writing is not without controversy. Blume's direct, humorous style is part of her appeal, along with her ability to discuss openly and realistically subjects that are of concern to her readers. Sometimes her choice of themes and explicit treatment of mature issues has brought her writing controversy. Some adults do not approve of Blume's use of frank language, and as a result some of her books have faced censorship by parents and librarians. Readers, on the other hand, are pleased to find an adult who seems to understand them and their real-life problems. Their fan letters relay this message over and over, and some even ask for the author's advice.

In addition to writing several juvenile fiction books, Judy Blume has authored young adult and adult books. *Wifey*, her first adult book, was published in 1978. That same year, an adaptation of her book *Forever* was made for television. Blume also contributed to the project *Free to Be You and Me* for the Ms. Foundation in 1974.

In recent years, Judy Blume founded KIDS Find and remains on the council of advisors for the National Coalition of Censorship.

Suggested Activities

Censorship Write the word *censorship* on the board. Discuss its meaning with the class. Ask the students whether they think adults have the right to censor what young people read. Debate whether Judy Blume's, or any author's, books should be censored.

Reading Assign students to read a Judy Blume book or read one to the class. Have the students identify the problems facing the main character. Discuss the problems and how they are resolved. Ask students if these problems believable or if they have experienced similar situations in their lives.

Christo

The seventies were filled with innovative art forms. One such form came from a conceptual artist known as Christo. He added a new dimension to the art world when he began to specialize in wrapping familiar objects such as flowers, magazines, and boxes. From these he progressed to monuments and eventually went on to envelop whole physical land areas such as in the Running Fence project (below). Because of their size, these creations are known as earthworks.

Christo, whose full name is Christo Javacheff, was born and raised in Bulgaria in 1935, but he later became an American citizen. From 1952 to 1955 he attended the Academy of Art in Bulgaria and spent weekends in the country with groups of students whose job was to beautify the scenery. The students also showed farmers how to display their tractors to best advantage and encouraged them to cover haystacks with tarps. Possibly this early experience influenced Christo's later work as a wrap artist.

Christo begins his large projects with sketches. He then does the actual construction work. He films and photographs the work before unwrapping the entire project. By selling these films and photos, Christo raises money for his next project. Through his work, Christo seeks to lead people to see familiar scenes in a new way and to show the susceptibility of society to packaging. Despite the transitory nature of his work, Christo remains one of the most popular artists in the world.

Christo's *Running Fence* project was begun in 1972 and was finally completed September 10, 1976. The fence extended east and west near Freeway 101, north of San Francisco, on the private properties of fifty-nine ranchers. Carefully planned, it ran through two counties, crossing fourteen towns and allowing passage for cars and cattle. Eighteen feet (5.4 m) high and 24.5 miles (38.4 km) long, Running Fence consisted of 165,000 yards of heavy, white nylon fabric hung from a steel cable and strung between 2,050 steel poles. Two weeks after the sculpture's completion, it was removed. All of its materials were then given to the ranchers.

Suggested Activities

Wrap With the students, brainstorm a list of materials they could use for wrapping other items such as newspapers, plastic bags, aluminum foil, and so forth. Direct the students to use any material of their choice to wrap a common classroom object (book, clock, chair, etc.). Display all wrapped objects for one or two days before removing the wrapping materials.

Research Instruct the students to research other artistic innovations and popular expressions of the seventies. Two possibilities are graffiti art and album cover art. Students can find out about the history of the art styles as well as bring in examples.

The Many Faces of Rock

Rock music continued to evolve and change in the seventies, and a number of new musical forms were popular. Read about some of the prominent musical styles and musicians of the Seventies. Research further any individual or group that especially interests you.

Glam Rock Rock artists donned makeup and outrageous clothing such as foil-like suits, glitter, and stacked heels. David Bowie is perhaps the best known in this category. He even adopted different characters, the most famous of which is Ziggy Stardust. Queen and Elton John were also prominent glam rockers.

Punk Punk music began in New York City and was exported to Britain by a clothing store manager. Cut up jeans and T-shirts, harsh makeup, safety-pin jewelry, and spiked and dyed hair completed the look. Blonde was a noteable punk group.

Disco A shortened form of *discotheque*, a French term for a night club that features dancing, this dance music craze had been growing in New York City for some time as a social outlet. It did not become mainstream until the 1978 movie *Saturday Night Fever* brought it to national attention. The Bee Gees sang many of the hits from the movie track, but singer Donna Summer was the undisputed queen of disco.

Reggae A combination of rock, rhythm and blues, and Jamaican music, reggae is distinctive with its lilting, off-beat style. Popularized by Bob Marley, the reggae style was successfully adapted by other successful groups such as The Clash and The Police.

Rock Opera In 1975, the rock opera album *Tommy* by The Who was made into a film. Elton John and Tina Turner starred as did two members of the band, Roger Daltrey and Keith Moon. Another popular rock opera of the seventies was *Jesus Christ Superstar*.

The following is a list of some other favorite seventies artists and their songs.

Simon and Garfunkel sang "Bridge Over Troubled Water" which became the first big hit of 1970.

Marvin Gaye's 1971 album *What's Going On?* was a social commentary on Vietnam, pollution, and the world in which we live.

Janis Joplin's single "Me and Bobby McGee" became a posthumous hit in 1971.

Carole King had a laid-back, soft-rock approach. Her album *Tapestry* sold thirteen million copies.

Stevie Wonder continued to touch upon social matters with his *Innervisions* album.

Pink Floyd focused on the dark side of life with its *Dark Side of the Moon* album.

Bruce Springsteen was the authentic blue-collar rock hero with his *Born to Run* album.

Peter Frampton came alive with songs like "Do You Feel Like We Do?" and "Show Me the Way."

Fleetwood Mac had the top album (*Rumours*) in the United States and Britain in 1977.

Electric Light Orchestra (ELO) was a space-age smash with its *Out of the Blue* album.

Blondie took a disco approach with *Heart of Glass*.

Linda Ronstadt

She started out as a rock and roll musician but won her first Grammy for singing a country tune. In the years to follow she experimented with standards, musicals, and folk music from her Mexican heritage. Linda Ronstadt's faithful fans never know quite what to expect from her.

Linda Ronstadt was born on July 15, 1946, in Tucson, Arizona. She was the third child in a family of two boys and two girls. Her father, Gilbert, an accomplished musician, ran his father's business. Her mother, Ruthmary Copeman, was a member of a prominent Michigan family, who first met her husband while she was attending an Arizona college.

As a child Linda Ronstadt was introduced to Mexican folk music by her father. She also loved to listen to music on the radio, especially the country tunes of Hank Williams. In her early teens, she and her sister and older brother formed a singing group. They played small gigs in and around Tucson. After high school Ronstadt left for Los Angeles to become a professional singer on her own. The Stone Poneys was her first group, but after a series of minor successes they broke up. However, Ronstadt's voice had not gone unnoticed. A problem of ever-changing backup bands hindered her work, as did her dependence on producers to shape her sound, but when Ronstadt found Peter Asher she finally felt comfortable musically and was able to obtain the elusive commercial and critical success that she longed for. Her 1974 album *Heart Like a Wheel* put her on the charts. Out of this platinum album came her first Grammy for Best Female Country Vocal for her rendition of the Hank Williams' tune "I Can't Help It." A 1976 album, *Hasten Down the Wind*, earned her a second Grammy. The following year Ronstadt changed musical direction again when she took the advice of the Rolling Stones' singer Mick Jagger to try harder rock. The result was her version of the Stones' "Tumbling Dice" on the platinum winning album *Simple Dreams*.

In the years that followed, Ronstadt departed from rock and roll by performing in the Gilbert and Sullivan musical *Pirates of Penzance*. During the 1980s she revamped her style even more and performed standard pop and jazz tunes with Nelson Riddle's big band and recorded a country album with Dolly Parton and Emmylou Harris. Most recently, Linda Ronstadt has returned to the folk music she learned during her childhood.

Suggested Activities

Listening Compare Linda Ronstadt's version of a song with that of the original artist. Explore the differences she contributes to the new versions.

Currently Ronstadt won a Grammy for Best Performance by a Mexican American. Learn more about the album that earned her this award.

Making Life Easier

Throughout the 1970s, a number of new items made their way to the supermarket shelves. Today these things are common to most households. Read each description below. Mark an X next to each item described that you or someone in your home uses today.

Maybelline™ Nail Color Maybelline cosmetics had been around since 1917, when it first introduced mascara, eye shadow, and eye pencils. In 1973 the company branched out into lip and nail products, including nail polish. Today Maybelline is the second largest cosmetic company in the United States.

Bounce™ This fabric softener was different because it came in sheets that were placed into the dryer along with a load of clothes. Invented in 1972, Bounce fabric softener sheets are now available in a variety of fragrances.

L'eggs™ With the 1970 introduction of these pantyhose, two marketing firsts were established: they were packaged in plastic eggs and they could be found in supermarkets and convenience stores. These days, the eggs have been replaced by cardboard containers, but L'eggs remain the best selling pantyhose in America.

Tidy Cat™ Ed Lowe had already been selling Kitty Litter to pet stores when he persuaded grocery stores to stock his product. He changed the name to Tidy Cat, and today it is the best selling cat-box filler in the United States.

Mr. Coffee Filters™ Inventor Vince Marotta was in search of a better way to make coffee when he observed restaurants using a white cloth in their percolators. Marotta used a paper filter in his coffeemaker and today more than ten billion Mr. Coffee filters are sold each year.

Ziploc Storage Bags™ The Dow Chemical Company manufactured a number of new consumer products during the 50s and 60s, including Saran Wrap, Handi-Wrap, and Dow Oven Cleaner. Ziploc Storage Bags debuted in 1970 and are unique because of their watertight, zipper-like seal.

Clairol Herbal Essence™ Commercial shampoos had been around since the 1880s, but in 1971 Clairol invented a shampoo with herbal fragrance. The product was designed to target the back-to-nature movement embraced by many young people in the early 70s.

Choose one of the products described above. In the space below, write at least five different uses for that product other than its intended use.

_____

_____

_____

_____

_____

The 70s Wardrobe: Fashions for Women

A wide variety of clothing styles evolved during the Seventies. At the beginning of the decade, jeans and the unisex look were popular, but the 1978 movie *Annie Hall* spawned a new look, as did the disco craze. Even the back-to-earth movement influenced fashions with the peasant look.

On this and the next page you can see some of the most popular styles during this time period.

Farrah Fawcett bangs
hot pants
platform shoes

Annie Hall
Granny dresses and boots

The 70s Wardrobe: Fashions for Men 1970s

Men's fashions were also influenced by the jogging craze, punk music, and a growing interest in black cultural identity.

rooster cuts
dyed hair, slashed T-shirts and jeans

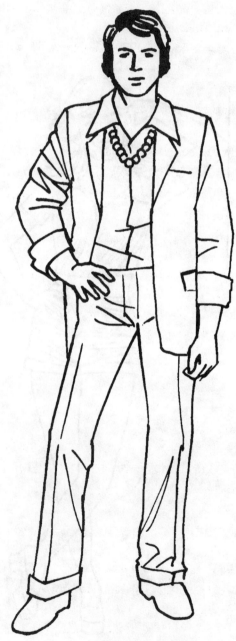

gold chains
open neck shirt
bellbottoms
neat, clean cuts with long sideburns

Elsewhere . . .

1970

- Charles DeGaulle dies.
- Salvador Allende, a Marxist, is elected president of Chile.
- Cyclones and floods kill 500,000 in East Pakistan.
- Thirty thousand die in Peru due to earthquakes, floods, and landslides.
- Five planes are hijacked by Black September Palestinian guerillas.
- The United States invades Cambodia.
- Civil war erupts in Jordan.

1971

- SALT agreement is reached at Moscow Summit.
- People's Republic of China enters the UN.
- War breaks out between India and Pakistan.
- The nation of Bangladesh is created.
- In Switzerland, women are granted the right to vote.
- Fighting in Indochina spreads to Laos and Cambodia.
- Three Russian cosmonauts die when their *Soyuz 11* capsule develops a leak on re-entry into the Earth's atmosphere.

1972

- The Berlin Wall is opened to allow family visits.
- Israeli athletes are murdered at the Munich Olympics.
- The U.S.S.R. agrees to purchase $750 million worth of U.S. surplus grain.
- Ceylon becomes a republic and changes its name to Sri Lanka.
- Philippine leader Ferdinand Marcos declares martial law.
- Okinawa is returned to Japan.
- Bangladesh is established as a sovereign state.
- The U.S.S.R. wins fifty gold medals at the Summer Olympics in Munich.
- A forty-seven day coal strike cripples Great Britain.

1973

- Vietnam declares a cease-fire.
- A military coup occurs in Chile.
- The Yom Kippur Arab-Israeli War takes place.
- Arabs raise oil prices and impose an oil embargo on the United States.
- Mid-East peace talks open in Geneva.
- The Bahamas are granted their independence from British rule.
- Spanish premier Luis Carrero Blanco is assassinated.

1974

- Grenada, a former British colony, declares its independence.
- Ethiopian emperor Haile Selassie is deposed.
- India explodes its first atomic bomb.
- Civil war breaks out in Cyprus.
- Russian writer Alexander Solzhenitsyn goes into exile.
- Golda Meir steps down.
- Yitzhak Rabin is named to head the Israeli cabinet.
- British Prime Minister Edward Heath resigns and is succeeded by Harold Wilson.
- U.S. Secretary of State Henry Kissinger negotiates a cease-fire on the Golan Heights.
- In Argentina, Juan Peron dies and is succeeded by his wife, Maria Estela.
- Two Arab countries lift the oil embargo against the U.S.

1975

- Papua, New Guinea and Surinam gain their independence.
- Communists take over Cambodia and South Vietnam.
- Egypt reopens the Suez Canal.
- Saigon falls in Vietnam.
- Mozambique and Angola become independent.
- Ethiopian emperor Haile Selassie dies.
- The International Women's Year is proclaimed.
- The Helsinki Agreement is signed.
- King Faisal of Saudi Arabia is assassinated by a nephew who is punished by beheading.
- A Japanese woman becomes the first female to climb Mt. Everest.

Elsewhere . . . *(cont.)*

1976

- Rioting takes place in Soweto, Africa.
- Civil war breaks out in Angola.
- Former Chairman of China, Mao Tse-tung, dies.
- The Concorde makes it first trans-Atlantic flight.
- The president of Argentina is overthrown.
- The Summer Olympics are held in Montreal, Canada; the Winter Olympics are held in Innsbruck, Austria.
- Great Britain introduces high-speed trains.
- North and South Vietnam are united.
- In Nicaragua civil war breaks out.

1977

- Steve Biko, black trade union leader, dies in police custody in South Africa.
- Egypt's leader Anwar Sadat makes an historic trip to Israel on November 19.
- Indira Gandhi resigns as prime minister of India.
- Israeli Prime Minister Yitzhak Rabin resigns and is succeeded by Menaham Begin.
- The Pakistan army overthrows the government and General Zia comes to power.
- French is adopted as the official language of Quebec.
- Great Britain celebrates the Silver Jubilee of Queen Elizabeth II.
- In Pakistan, General Zia comes to power.
- London to New York passenger service on the Concorde begins.

1978

- In England, the first test-tube baby is born.
- More than 900 Americans commit suicide in Jim Jones' People's Temple in Guyana, South America.
- Violence sweeps Nicaragua as Sandanista guerillas attempt to overthrow the government.
- A military junta seizes power in Afghanistan.

- The Nobel Peace Prize is awarded to Israeli Premier Menachem Begin and Egyptian President Anwar Sadat.
- Earthquakes hit Greece, Japan, Mexico, Iran, and central Europe.
- Former Italian prime minister Aldo Moro is murdered.
- John Paul II becomes the first Polish pope.
- A massive oil spill occurs along the coast of France when the tanker *Amoco Cadiz* wrecks.

1979

- Maria Pintassilgo becomes Portugal's first female prime minister.
- The Shah of Iran abdicates.
- Ayatollah Khomeini returns from exile.
- Iran becomes the Islamic Republic.
- Hostages are seized as students occupy the American embassy in Tehran.
- The Vietnamese depose the Pol Pot regime in Cambodia.
- Russia invades Afghanistan.
- The Camp David Accord leads to an Egypt-Israel peace treaty.
- Idi Amin, president of Uganda, is overthrown.
- Mother Teresa wins the Nobel Peace Prize.
- The SALT 2 arms treaty is signed but withdrawn after Soviet troops invade Afghanistan.
- Rhodesian peace talks lead to promise of an independent Zimbabwe.
- Margaret Thatcher becomes prime minister in Britain.
- War is fought between China and Vietnam.
- The United States and China establish diplomatic relations.
- General Anastasio Somoza of Nicaragua is overthrown.

Olympic Highlights

Some of the most notable Olympic games ever were held during the 1970s. Records were set, perfect scores were earned, and terrorist activity marred one summer Olympics. Research the Olympics of the seventies decade and fill in the blanks with the names of the correct athletes.

1972 Summer Olympics, Munich, West Germany

1. A twenty-two year old American swimmer,_____, won an unpredecented seven gold medals.
2. For the first time since 1908, the marathon was won by an American,_____.
3. Soviet_____introduced a more acrobatic style to gymastics.
4. Australia's_____won five medals here and broke the oldest record in the books during the 100-meter.
5. _____of Kenya won two gold and two silver medals in his races at the 1968 and 1972 Olympics.
6. American swimmer_____was stripped of his gold medal after it was learned he took a drug for his asthma condition before competing.

1972 Winter Olympics, Sapporo, Japan

7. _____, an American figure skater, skated gracefully to win the women's gold medal.
8. Austrian skier_____was disqualified from the games because of alleged violations of the amateur code.

1976 Summer Olympics, Montreal, Canada

9. Fourteen-year-old Romanian_____became the first gymnast to earn a perfect ten.
10. American_____won the gold in the grueling decathalon event.
11. A protege of former Olympian Dr. Sammy Lee,_____won a silver medal in platform diving.
12. Cuban_____won an unprecedented double in the 400- and 800-meter events.
13. American boxers struck gold, including Michael Spinks, Leon Spinks, and light welterweight_____.

1976 Winter Olympics, Innsbruck, Austria

14. _____, a speedskater from Detroit, won a gold, a silver, and a bronze medal.
15. Austrian skier_____came from behind to win the gold medal in the downhill.
16. Russian pairs skaters Aleksandr Zaitsev and_____captured the hearts of many as well as the gold medal.

Pierre Trudeau

Canadian Prime Minister Pierre Trudeau has the distinction of serving longer than any other contemporary leader in the modern Western world. From 1968 to 1984 he guided his country through some of its most tumultuous times. He was quite popular with the Canadian people.

Pierre Trudeau was born on October 18, 1919, in Montreal, Canada. His father was a lawyer who also owned a chain of service stations. When the elder Trudeau died in 1935, he left his family a five-million dollar fortune. Young Trudeau graduated from the University of Montreal Law School in 1943 and continued with his education at Harvard University in the United States, the University of Paris, and the London School of Economics. For a while, Trudeau traveled through Eastern Europe to China during its 1949 revolution. He also visited Vietnam and Cambodia while they were fighting the French. These actions earned him the reputation of being a radical and prevented him, at first, from obtaining a teaching position at the University of Montreal. Later in 1961, Trudeau did earn a teaching post there but left in 1965 to join the Liberal party. That same year he was elected to the House of Commons and successfully argued against the French-speaking separatists who were lobbying for the secession of Quebec. He was appointed minister of justice and attorney general of Canada in 1967. During his brief term, he worked to expand social welfare programs and liberalize laws pertaining to areas such as divorce and gambling. Following Prime Minister Lester Pearson's retirement in 1968, Trudeau was selected as his replacement.

Trudeau's main cause was a just society in which he reorganized various governmental departments and introduced laws to guarantee the rights of the French-speaking minority, as well as native Canadians. His administration also helped pass the Official Languages Act which recognized English and French as Canada's two official languages.

One of his policies was not so popular, however. The American government was displeased when he avoided entering into military alliances and sought, instead, to keep Canada neutral in international affairs. The 1970s provided Trudeau with his biggest challenge when the country suffered increasing unemployment inflation and labor unrest. Throughout the decade, his Liberal party began to lose support. When French-speaking separatists in Quebec began to employ terrorist tactics, Trudeau was forced to declare a national emergency. In 1984, Trudeau resigned and was succeeded by Liberal John Turner.

This charismatic leader returned to practicing law after he left office.

Suggested Activity

Debate Conduct a class debate on the topic of Quebec and whether or not the province should be allowed to be an independent country.

The Amazon Rain Forest

In 1971, construction began in Brazil for a major trans-Amazon highway to open up remote areas of the rain forest for settlement and development. Huge areas of the Amazon rain forest were cut down and burned to make way for about one million new settlers. Because the large cities were so overcrowded and most people were unable to find work there, the government offered lucrative incentives to families who moved to the Amazon. Each family would be given a 240-acre piece of land, housing, and a small salary for a few months. Plans were made to build schools, health facilities, and other services. Thousands made the move but had to give up after only a few months because life in the rain forest was so difficult. The project was deemed a failure.

Not only was the project a failure, but it led to the destruction of a great deal of the Amazon rain forest. The result of this devastation was that much of the rain forest habitat was lost forever and the soil eroded and turned into poor agricultural land. This is indeed a tragedy because the rain forest is so important to the ecology of not only the Amazon but of the world.

Listed below are some ways in which the rain forest is important to mankind. Choose and circle the best response in each parentheses.

1. The rain forest provides (protection/habitats) for many species of plants and animals.
2. When their habitats are destroyed these organisms no longer have a (function/home), and the whole species comes in danger of dying off.
3. More than (200,000/500) different Indian tribes live in the Amazon rain forest.
4. Their (existence/instinct), however, is threatened by the destruction of the land which is their home.
5. Everything that they need—clothing, food, shelter, medicine—can be provided by (resources/animals) found in the rain forest.
6. Western civilization is dependent on the Amazon rain forest for its source of new (medicines/wood).
7. As more and more land is destroyed, many medicinal plants will become (extinct/expensive).
8. Another concern for the Amazon environment is (global warming/fossil fuels).
9. Fossil fuels produce (carbon dioxide/carbon monoxide emissions).
10. Trees are necessary to take in this carbon dioxide and release (oxygen/hydrogen) which is so important to human and animal life.
11. In addition, huge areas of trees like those in the rain forest are important to the (rainfall/water cycle).
12. All of the (grassland/tropical climate) depends on the success of the water cycle.

Answers: Teacher, fold under before copying.

1. habitats 2. home 3. 500 4. existence 5. resources 6. medicines 7. extinct 8. global warming 9. carbon dioxide 10. oxygen 11. watedcycle 12. tropical

Vietnam Reunified

In 1973 the United States and North Vietnam reached a cease-fire agreement, and the last American combat personnel were withdrawn. But the peace was short-lived, elections were not held, and by 1974 the war between North and South Vietnam resumed. On April 18, 1975, Secretary of State Henry Kissinger, sensing the end of the war, ordered the evacuation of all remaining Americans from South Vietnam. *Operation Frequent Wind* evacuated close to 7,000 people, including fourteen hundred Americans. On April 30, 1975, North Vietnamese troops arrived in Saigon, and South Vietnam quickly surrendered. As North Vietnamese tanks made their way to the United States' headquarters there, a few hundred remaining Marines and civilians gathered on the building's rooftop. Helicopters plucked them up and airlifted them to waiting warships. It was a chaotic scene as thousands of South Vietnamese men, women, and children, many of whom had been allies of the Uinted States, filled the street around the headquarters. They fought and pleaded with officials to be taken away by helicopter, but there was not enough room for them.

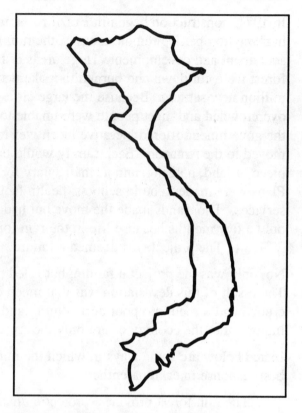

When General Duong Van Minh announced the surrender of South Vietnam and the reunification of Vietnam, it had been twenty years since the Geneva Accords which called for an end to foreign rule and free elections for reunification. Many Americans wondered what had been accomplished by the long years of U.S. support and involvement.

Suggested Activities

Chronology Make a chronology of important events in the war in Vietnam during the 1970s.

Evaluate Write a list of lessons the United States might have learned from its involvement in the Vietnam conflict.

Unofficial War Explain how the United States could carry on such a large war operation in Vietnam despite the fact that no war was officially declared by Congress.

Chart Construct a chart of the Viet Cong and the Army of the Republic of Vietnam. Compare their leaders, losses, and countries which backed them.

Current Relations Explore current U.S. relations with Vietnam whether time has healed the wounds between the two countries.

Memorial On November 11, 1982, the Vietnam Veterans Memorial was unveiled in Washington, D.C., to commemorate the 58,000 American lives lost in Vietnam between 1959 and 1975. Find a picture of the memorial and draw your own design for a suitable memorial.

Islamic Revolution

By 1978, opposition to the Shah of Iran, Mohammed Reza Pahlavi, had reached monumental proportions. He was attacked for his excessive personal lifestyle and was condemned for the corruption in his government. Rapid industrial growth had been offset by a decline in agriculture; thirty-five percent of the country's food had to be imported. In addition, the Islamic clergy was unhappy with the reforms and restraints on their powers.

Western influences were considered an insult to Islam. Many Iranians blamed the increasing inflation rate on the United States support of the Shah. Amid mass demonstrations and civil unrest, the Shah was forced to flee the country in 1978.

Ayatollah Khomeini returned from exile to lead the Islamic Revolution and easily took over power in Iran in February 1979. One of his first acts was to proclaim the country an Islamic Republic. He vowed to rid the nation of all Western influences and instituted a strict code of Islamic behavior. Severe punishment awaited anyone who broke these laws. A difficult period followed as unemployment rose and ethnic unrest erupted with the Kurds in northwestern Iran. A severe drop in the production of oil caused a panic among the industrialized countries. Anti-Western feeling continued to increase in the following months.

While the Western world was dealing with the women's movement and increasing its recognition of women's roles in society, the Islamic movement did just the opposite. Under Khomeini's rule, women had to wear traditional garb and keep their hair, and at certain times their faces, covered. Women were not allowed to own the clothes they wore, nor did they have rights over their children. There was little or no protection against a violent husband. In fact, a husband who killed his wife could go free unless the wife's family could pay a large price for his death sentence. A man could marry many wives, and he could order his wife out of the house or divorce her without even telling her.

On the lines below, explore one of these topics:

1　Explain why you think such fundamentalism would or would not work in Western countries.

2. Tell how you think the women's movement would be greeted by men and women in Islamic countries.

_____

_____

_____

_____

_____

The Sydney Opera House

Construction on the Sydney Opera House began in 1958, and by 1973 it was completed. Read about this magnificent structure, one of the architectural wonders of the world. Then complete the exercise that follows.

One of the most famous and unusual buildings in Australia is the Sydney Opera House. Designed by Danish architect Jorn Utzon, it is set in the largest natural harbor in the world. This impressive concrete and glass structure has a roof designed to look like sails on a ship and a body that resembles a ship's body. Inside there is a full-size concert hall, an opera theatre, a smaller theatre, an auditorium, and a film-screening theatre. Classical operas, plays, ballets, and concerts are performed there. Several companies are headquartered there, including the Australian Ballet, the Sydney Symphony Orchestra, and the Australian Opera Company.

Problems with the building's sails caused construction costs to soar from an estimated seven million dollars to 102 million. It was a difficult task and required workers to climb up the slippery roof by using ropes. Afterwards, the laborers worked by sitting in small chairs with safety belts around their waists.

Small individual tiles were cemented to large tile lids which in turn were bolted to the shell structure. In all, more than one million small tiles covering 4,000 lids were attached to the building with 10,000 bronze bolts. Glass covers the inside of the sails, and there are more than 2,000 double-thick glass windowpanes.

In September of 1973, the Sydney Opera House was completed, and in a grand ceremony was opened by Queen Elizabeth of England.

Read each statement below. Circle I if the information can be inferred from the paragraphs. Circle O if the statement expresses an opinion. Be prepared to defend your answers.

1.   I   O   The Sydney Opera House is a beautiful structure.

2.   I   O   It took many years to build the Sydney Opera House.

3.   I   O   Work on the roof was tedious and difficult.

4.   I   O   Utzon's design for the building was a good one.

5.   I   O   The building is soundproof.

6.   I   O   Construction costs were high.

7.   I   O   A variety of events can be conducted at the Opera House.

8.   I   O   Movies can be seen at the Opera House.

Answers: Teacher, fold under before copying. These are suggested answers. Accept any answers which the students can successfully defend.

1.O 2.I 3.I 4.O 5.O 6.I 7.I 8.I

Irish Peace Activists

In 1977 the Nobel Peace Prize was awarded to two women, Mairead Corrigan and Betty Williams, for their role in reconciling Northern Ireland's two warring sides. Drawn together by a tragic accident, the two women joined forces to begin a peace movement. Below is a look at their lives and how two ordinary citizens won worldwide acclaim.

Mairead Corrigan   Betty Willams

Mairead Corrigan Mairead Corrigan was born in 1944 to working-class parents in a Catholic section of West Belfast, Northern Ireland. The second child in a family of five girls and two boys, she attended Catholic school until she was fourteen years old. Then she joined the Legion of Mary, a Catholic organization devoted to helping others and continued as a volunteer with the society into her adult years. Corrigan strongly opposed the strife that was occurring between the Catholics and the Protestants in Northern Ireland. Roman Catholics there wanted to be free of British rule while the Protestants sided with Great Britain. In 1976, she came face to face with the violence when her sister and her sister's three children were hit by a runaway IRA car. All three children were killed and Corrigan, along with her brother-in-law, appeared on television to condemn the IRA's actions.

Betty Williams Born in a Catholic section of Belfast in 1942, Betty Williams had a mother who was Catholic and a father who was Protestant. Tolerance was advocated in their household: there was no room for bigotry. At thirteen, she took on the responsibility of raising her younger sister after their mother suffered a debilitating stroke. Later, Williams became a secretary. On August 10, 1976, she witnessed the accident that killed Mairead Corrigan's three nieces. Determined to do something to facilitate a peaceful solution to the two sides' differences, Betty Williams drafted a petition and went from door to door collecting 6,000 signatures. After presenting the petition on television, she and Mairead Corrigan joined forces.

That fall, the two women led tens of thousands of Belfast women on peace marches. Corrigan and Williams were harassed, beaten, and threatened, but still they did not give up. They even traveled to foreign countries, including Australia, Canada, and the United States to spread the word about their peace movement. Violence in Northern Ireland decreased by 54 percent during this period, and in 1977 Corrigan and Williams became the first women to win the Nobel Peace Prize since 1944.

▬▬▬▬▬▬ Suggested Activity ▬▬▬▬▬▬

Discussion Discuss the following questions with the class:

What is the current status between Catholics and Protestants in Northern Ireland?

What is the IRA and when was it founded?

Why have Protestants and Catholics been fighting in Northern Ireland for the past seventy years?

Passages

Births

1970
- Ricky Shroeder and River Phoenix, actors
- Andre Agassi, tennis superstar

1973
- Tempest Bledsoe, actress

1975
- Drew Barrymore, actress and granddaughter of John Barrymore

1976
- Jennifer Capriati, tennis star

Deaths

1970
- Gypsy Rose Lee, entertainer and stripper
- Charles De Gaulle, France's leader
- Erle Stanley Gardner, creator of Perry Mason

1971
- Jim Morrison of the Doors
- Louis Armstrong, African American jazz musician
- Audie Murphy, World War I hero
- Coco Chanel, French fashion designer

1972
- Harry S. Truman, former U.S. president
- Mahalia Jackson, African American gospel singer
- J. Edgar Hoover, FBI director since 1924
- Jackie Robinson, first African American to play major league baseball
- Roberto Clemente, baseball great

1973
- Lyndon B. Johnson, former U.S. president
- Pearl S. Buck, author of books about China
- Pablo Picasso, French painter
- Pablo Casals, Spanish cellist
- David Ben-Gurion, Israeli founder and former premier
- Betty Grable, actress and WW II pin-up girl

1974
- Charles Lindbergh, aviation pioneer
- Jack Benny, American actor and comedian
- Samuel Goldwyn, pioneer Hollywood producer

1975
- Chiang Kai-shek, president of Nationalist China
- Emperor Haile Selassie of Ethiopia
- Josephine Baker, African American singer and dancer

1976
- Agatha Christie, mystery novelist
- Guy Lombardo, big band leader
- Howard Hughes and J. Paul Getty, both American billionaires
- Mao Tse-tung, leader of People's Republic of China
- Alexander Calder, American sculptor

1977
- Elvis Presley, the king of rock and roll
- Groucho Marx, actor and comedian
- Maria Callas, Greek American operatic singer
- Erroll Garner, jazz pianist
- James Jones, American novelist

1978
- Hubert Humphrey, former U.S. vice president
- Margaret Mead, American anthropologist
- Golda Meir, former Prime Minister of Israel
- Norman Rockwell, illustrator and painter of Americana

1979
- Nelson Rockefeller, former U.S. vice president
- Emmett Kelly, famous American clown
- Jack Haley, the Tin Man in *The Wizard of Oz*
- Lester Flatt, country singer

Seventies Facts and Figures

The United States in 1970

Population:	203,235,298
National Debt:	$450 billion
Federal Minimum Wage:	rose from $2.10 per hour to $2.30 per hour in 1976; in 1979 it rose from $2.65 per hour to $2.90 per hour
U.S. Postage:	raised from 10 cents to 13 cents in 1975
Movies:	*French Connection, The Godfather* and *The Godfather Part II, The Sting, One Flew Over the Cuckoo's Nest, Rocky, Network, Annie Hall, The Deer Hunter, Butch Cassidy and the Sundance Kid, True Grit, Catch 22, Taxi Driver, All the President's Men, Star Wars, Saturday Night Fever, Grease, Animal House, MASH, Blazing Saddles, Jaws, American Graffiti, Sleeper, Shaft, Patton, The Bad News Bears, Love Story*
Movie Stars:	Barbara Streisand, Jane Fonda, Robert Redford, Elliot Gould, George C. Scott, Glenda Jackson, Liza Minelli, Gene Hackman, Marlon Brando, Woody Allen, Jack Lemmon, Faye Dunaway, Al Pacino, Sylvester Stallone, Louise Fletcher, Jack Nicholson, James Caan, Lily Tomlin, Alan Arkin, George Burns, Talia Shire, Jason Robards, Robert de Niro, Richard Roundtree, John Travolta, Olivia Newton John, Liv Ullman, Jodi Foster, Carrie Fisher, Vanessa Redgrave, Marsha Mason, Richard Dreyfuss, John Belushi, Cicely Tyson, Meryl Streep, John Voight, Dustin Hoffman
Songs:	"Bridge Over Troubled Water," "Let It Be," "Signed Sealed Delivered," "American Woman," "Joy to the World," "My Sweet Lord," "Me and Bobbie McGee," "The First Time Ever I Saw Your Face," "Lean on Me," "Crocodile Rock," "Superstition," "The Way We Were," "Annie's Song," "Sundown," "Fame," "One of These Nights," "Fifty Ways to Leave Your Lover," "You Light Up My Life," "Margaritaville," "Hotel California," "You Don't Bring Me Flowers," "Staying Alive," "I Will Survive," "We Are Family," "Raindrops Keep Falling on My Head"
Books:	*Winds of War* by Herman Wouk, *Breakfast of Champions* by Kurt Vonnegut, *Roots* by Alex Haley, *Chesapeake* by James Michener, *The Thorn Birds* by Colleen McCullough, *The Bell Jar* by Sylvia Plath, *Trinity* by Leon Uris, *Watership Down* by Richard Adams, *Jaws* by Peter Benchley, *Sophie's Choice* by William Styron
TV Programs:	*All in the Family, The Mary Tyler Moore Show, Happy Days, Saturday Night Live, The Partridge Family, The Jeffersons, The Dukes of Hazard, MASH, The Muppet Show, The Brady Bunch, Charlie's Angels, Columbo*
Fashions:	granny dresses, corduroy jeans, leather chokers and bracelets, flared pants or bellbottoms, army fatigues, Annie Hall look, designer label jeans, preppy and Ivy League styles, kaftans, Indian shirts and gauze smocks, puka shell necklaces
Fads:	home video games played on the television screen, streaking, disco music and dancing, mood rings, pet rocks, jogging, transcendental meditation, yoga

Buzzwords

New inventions, habits, lifestyles, and occupations cause people to invent new words, but sometimes events can spawn new vocabulary, too. Listed below are some of the words and phrases that came into popular use during the Seventies.

Affirmative Action This term refers to the policy of giving extra consideration to minorities when hiring new employees.

CB This is an abbreviation for citizen band radio, which truckers used to communicate with one another. They developed their own shorthand terms, which they used when talking.

CREEP This is an acronym for the Committee to Reelect the President. Some members of this committee broke into the Democratic headquarters in the Watergate building to find out election secrets.

Cult This term refers to a religion or religious sect whose members often blindly follow the dictates of one powerful leader.

Detente A political term, detente means a relaxation of strained relations. During the 1970s the U.S.S.R. and the U.S. reached detente in their political relationship.

Embargo This term means to impose a restriction on trade. In 1973 the Arabs issued an oil embargo against the Western world.

ERA This abbreviation stands for the Equal Rights Amendment. Designed to give equal rights to women, it never gained the necessary state support to be ratified.

Feminism This is the women's movement which worked to win full and equal rights and respect for women in society.

Get my head together This expression meant that a person was trying to sort out his or her feelings and attempting to find fulfillment with his or her life.

Glam Rock Rock artists put glamour into rock with elaborate costumes and makeup. David Bowie's character Ziggy Stardust was the epitome of glam rock.

Graffiti A name given to pictures and words spray-painted or scribbled on walls, advertising posters, freeways, etc.

Microprocessors These are intergrated circuits on a single chip which contain the central processing unit of a computer.

Oil Crisis This worldwide economic crisis was brought on when Arab oil-producing nations drastically cut production and sharply raised the prices of oil. What followed was a shortage of oil, loss of production, and high inflation and unemployment rates.

SALT This acronym stands for Strategic Arms Limitation Talks. These discussions between the United States and the U.S.S.R. helped to limit nuclear arms.

Sociobiology This term means the study of animal societies.

Watergate Scandal After some of Nixon's aids were apprehended breaking into Democratic headquarters in the Watergate building, the whole scandal was named after the building.

Writing Prompts and Literature Ideas

Writing Prompts Use these suggestions for journal writing or as daily writing exercises. Some research or discussion may be appropriate before assigning a particular topic.

- If you had been alive during the 1970s, who is the one person you would have liked to have met? Pretend you are a reporter whose job it is to interview this person. Write the questions and answers to this interview.

- Choose any two individuals who were prominent in the seventies. Write a creative story about a time when the two might have met. Include a conversation the two might have had.

- You are an artist or a fashion designer and very much admire the styles of the seventies. Critique the fashions and write a review for a national art or fashion magazine.

- Pick a figure from the seventies who contributed something to world peace. Write a story about how and why this individual might have decided to work for the cause of world peace.

- Write a letter to an individual from the seventies whom you admire. Explain to him her how you think he or she made the world a better place.

- Pet rocks were a popular fad in the seventies. They came packaged in their own carryall with a set of tongue in cheek directions for their care. They were priced at just five dollars each. Go outside to find a suitable rock. Create a container for the rock, name your pet, and write directions for the care and feeding of the rock.

- How-to books were popular in the seventies. Determine a topic that interests you and write a how-to report.

- Brainstorm a list of things you can do to clean up and protect the environment at home or at school on a daily basis.

- Citizen band radios were popular during the seventies, especially among truckers. They invented their own vocabulary or lingo to communicate with one another. Make your own CB vocabulary dictionary.

Literature Ideas The following books can be used to supplement and enhance the study of the 1970s.

- *Drylongso* by Virginia Hamilton (Harcourt Brace Jovanovich, 1992)
  The setting of this tale is the small town of Osfield in the western part of Mississippi during 1975. It was a period of drought much like the one that hit the mid-West during the Great Depression. One day a young boy, Drylongso, emerges out of the wall of dust surrounding the town. He stays for a while and helps one family by finding water.

- *Julie of the Wolves* by Jean Craighead George (Harper & Row, 1972)
  Miyax, an Eskimo girl, lives in Alaska with her father from whom she learns her people's traditions and customs. Her life is difficult for her, and when she is just thirteen, it becomes even worse when she is forced into an arranged marriage. After her husband assaults her, she sets out for San Francisco, but all does not go well as she finds herself lost in the vast tundra and out of food. How she manages to survive is a story of courage and self-discovery that will keep students engrossed until the conclusion of this exciting novel.

Eighties Overview

- President Jimmy Carter leaves the presidency. On his last day in office, American hostages in Iran are finally released after more than a year in captivity. The release dovetails with the inauguration of President Ronald Reagan.

- Pope John Paul II is shot, but he recovers and gains the admiration of the world by forgiving his attacker. President Ronald Reagan is also shot, and he, too, recovers. A third victim, Indira Gandhi, Prime Minister of India, is shot and killed by her body guards.

- Rock musician, John Lennon, is shot and killed in front of his New York apartment. Millions of fans grieve his loss.

- Britain and Argentina go to war over the Falkland Islands. The United States invades Panama and Grenada and bombs Libyan terrorist bases. Israel forces the PLO from Lebanon. Iran and Iraq go to war. Russia continues its invasion of Afghanistan for nearly a decade.

- A new strategic defense initiative called "Star Wars" gains momentum. The world superpowers agree to reduce nuclear missiles.

- Famine in Ethiopia kills millions. Many make great efforts to relieve the famine, most notably rock musician Bob Geldof and his concert called Live Aid, which earns millions for relief.

- Mikhail Gorbachev comes to power in Russia, bringing about a push toward democracy.

- A nuclear power reactor explodes in Chernobyl, Russia, killing and wounding thousands. The effects of the blast are far-reaching.

- Chinese students in Tiananmen Square protest the government in China. Many are killed by government soldiers who squelch the uprising.

- The Soviet Union begins to unravel, and numerous Soviet bloc countries overthrow communism. The Berlin Wall comes down, and East and West Germany are unified.

- The world's stock markets crash. Insider trading scandals rock the financial world.

- Congress holds hearings over the Iran-Contra affair, uncovering a secret arms deal with American antagonist Iran. Marine Lieutenant Colonel Oliver North admits secretly funneling money to the Contras, an army of Nicaraguan rebels.

- Sandra Day O'Connor becomes the first female American Supreme Court Justice. Sally Ride becomes the first American woman in space. Elizabeth Dole becomes the first woman to head the U.S. Department of Transportation. Geraldine Ferraro becomes the first female candidate on a major party ticket for the office of vice president.

- Technology revolutionizes the American home with personal computers, VCRs, compact disc players, and more.

- Terrorism around the world is on the rise with a number of highjackings, bombings, and hostage situations, most for political reasons.

- A battle against apartheid continues in South Africa and around the world.

- Corazón Aquino is elected Philippine president, replacing President Ferdinand Marcos who is implicated in the murder of Aquino's husband, a former presidential hopeful.

- Human Immunodeficiency Virus (HIV), a retrovirus, is discovered to be the cause of Acquired Immune Deficiency Syndrome (AIDS). The first permanent artificial heart is placed in a patient.

Soviet Invasion of Afghanistan

In December of 1979, the Soviet Union began sending thousands of troops to Afghanistan. This military intervention was in support of the Marxist Afghan government, which was threatened by growing unrest among the people of Afghanistan.

In reaction to the Soviet invasion, opposition to the government became a national resistance movement. The *mujahideen* (Islamic warriors) were poorly equipped but relentless in their defense and attacks. Using guerilla tactics, they persisted for several years. The Soviets and Kabul government retaliated by bombing villages at will, but the mujahideen—although outnumbered and out-powered—could not be stopped.

Nations around the world ardently criticized Soviet actions. President Carter of the United States stopped delivery of seventeen million metric tons of grain that was to be transported to Russia. Considering the Soviet actions a "serious threat to peace," Carter imposed a limited trade embargo and cut back the availability of American waters for Soviets to fish. In addition, all cultural and economic trades were cancelled. Finally, Carter pressured the U.S. Olympic Committee to withdraw from the Summer Games to be held in Moscow in 1980.

The Russians called Carter "wicked and malicious." They declared that they were not, in fact, invading Afghanistan, but rather they were supporting the Kabul government there. Carter believed, however, that the Soviet presence in Afghanistan would pose a serious threat to Iran and Pakistan. Throughout the occupation, the United States did not let up on its protests.

A United Nations resolution in 1986 called for a negotiated settlement of the war. In 1987, an international Islamic conference asked the Soviet Union to withdraw from Afghanistan, and the Kabul government announced plans for a cease-fire. The resistance forces rejected the cease-fire. Later that year a nationwide gathering of tribal leaders approved a new constitution and elected Sayid Mohammed Najibullah president.

Finally, in April of 1988, accords were reached which established a timetable for Soviet withdrawal. The accords were signed by Afghanistan, Russia, Pakistan, and the United States, but not by the politically divided mujahideen. The mujahideen continued to fight, attacking Russian troops as they left the country. The United States and the Soviet Union agreed in 1991 to stop giving military aid to the warring factions. In April of 1992 the resistance finally succeeded in overthrowing the Kabul government. Factions of the mujahideen agreed to a transitional government; however, fighting continued among the factions themselves as they each competed for power in the new government.

Suggested Activities

Cartography Draw maps of Afghanistan, Russia, Pakistan, and Iran, showing their relationships to one another.

For Thought Have the students consider and discuss why the U.S. was so opposed to the invasion since the Soviets were working with the Afghanistan government.

New Administration Research to find out how the Reagan administration felt about the Soviet occupation of Afghanistan. Did Reagan agree with Carter? What was his administration's relationship to the Soviet Union?

Hostages in Iran

Revolutionaries in Iran would come to have great significance to the lives of fifty-two Americans.

In the late 1970s, Iranian revolutionaries who opposed Shah Mohammed Reza Pahlavi banded together under Ayatollah Ruhollah Khomeini, a Muslim religious leader. Mass demonstrations, strikes, and riots broke out against the shah, and finally, in January of 1979, the shah left the country. Khomeini, who had been in exile in France, returned to Iran and established an Islamic republic.

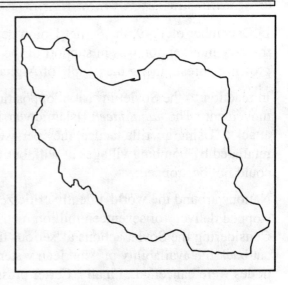

The shah was allowed to enter the United States in November of 1979 for medical treatment. The new Iranian government demanded that he and the money he took with him be returned to Iran. However, President Jimmy Carter refused their demands.

Anti-American sentiment was high in the new government even before Carter's refusal. Because the United States had supported the shah, hatred of Americans was intense. In retaliation, a mob of five hundred students invaded and seized the American Embassy in Teheran, Iran, on November 20, 1979, taking 66 hostages.

President Carter demanded their release. The terrorists refused, and Carter immediately froze all Iranian assets in the United States. The students declared that the hostages would be released only when the shah and the money were returned, and the United States apologized for its role in supporting the shah. They then paraded the bound and blindfolded hostages before television cameras, chanting, "Death to America, death to Carter, death to the shah." They burned effigies of Carter and Uncle Sam, and they spat on, trampled, and burned the U.S. flag.

Mediators were sent to negotiate for the release of the hostages, but there was very little success. Thirteen hostages, primarily women and blacks, were released, leaving fifty-three hostages.

In April of 1980, the United States attempted a rescue mission. However, equipment broke down, the mission was aborted, and during the withdrawal a helicopter collided with a plane. Eight American servicemen were killed. The rescue mission was a drastic failure, and the Iranians cheered in the streets, declaring that they "had inflicted defeat and flight upon Americans."

In June of 1980, the shah died in Cairo; however, the terrorists refused to release the hostages. Days and months dragged on. Americans were shocked and grieved at the prolonged act of terrorism. Everywhere, people wore yellow ribbons and tied them to their cars as a show of support for the hostages and the acknowledgment that they would never rest until the prisoners were returned.

In November of 1980, President Carter lost the presidential election by a considerable margin. One factor leading to his defeat was his failure to optain release of the hostages. Ironically, the hostages were finally released on the day of Ronald Reagan's inauguration. The date was January 20, 1981, and the hostages had spent a total of 444 days in captivity.

Suggested Activity

Up to Date Learn about Iranian-American relations since 1981. How have they changed? What are the current conditions?

Star Wars

The 1980s saw Star Wars come to prominence, but Luke Skywalker was nowhere to be found. The term was used to describe a defense system proposed by President Ronald Reagan in 1983, six years after the movie of the same name was released. Reagan's Star Wars, the Strategic Defense Initiative (SDI), called for an antiballistic missile defense system using a system of ground-and space-based weapons technologies that could stop a first strike (initial nuclear attack) from the Soviet Union. The goal was to intercept and destroy incoming missiles high above the earth. Reagan said that he believed the new system would end the threat of a surprise nuclear attack. Others feared that the system could be used offensively.

Over the next few years, Reagan and General Secretary Mikhail Gorbachev of the Soviet Union participated in a series of summit meetings to negotiate a number of topics. In 1985, the summit opened with Gorbachev's call for an end to Star Wars and Reagan's adamant refusal. The two could come to no agreement on the issue.

In 1987, Reagan and Gorbachev did make some headway in the direction of nuclear disarmament. Following a serious breakdown in their talks, the two were able to come together again to sign the Intermediate Range Nuclear Forces Treaty, the first comprehensive nuclear arms control treaty. It called for the destruction of 1,500 Soviet and 350 American warheads. The destruction of these arms would result in a reduction of American-Soviet warheads by approximately four percent. The two nations also agreed to a series of checks on one another to verify that the treaty was being honored.

Negotiations for arms limitations continued under President George Bush. In 1991 the first Strategic Arms Reduction Treaty, START I, which called for a 25 percent reduction in warheads, was signed by Bush and Gorbachev. The dissolution of the Soviet Union in 1991 slowed START I's implementation, requiring separate treaties with former members of the USSR. START II, signed in January of 1993, provides for elimination of almost three-fourths of the nuclear warheads held by the signers over a nine-year period.

In 1993, President Bill Clinton formally ended SDI. In its place, the Ballistic Missile Defense Organization (BMDO), a land-based antimissile system, was established.

Suggested Activities

Science Find out about nuclear weapons, how they work, and their potential for damage.

Debate As a class, debate the efficacy of nuclear weapons. Some believe they are necessary for protection and as a deterrent. Others believe that their lethal power makes them inhumane and unacceptable.

Cold War The term Cold War first came into being in the 1940s. Find out about the history of the word.

SALT and START Research to learn more about the Strategic Arms Limitation Talks (SALT) of the 1970s and the Strategic Arms Reduction Treaties (START I and II) of 1991 and 1993.

Iran-Contra Scandal

The American people were shocked in the mid-eighties to learn of a secret arms deal with Iran, a Middle Eastern country and United States antagonist. United States policy expressly forbade the trading of arms for the release of hostages; however, the American people learned that the administration under Ronald Reagan secretly sold missiles and missile components to Iran. United States hostages held by Lebanese terrorists were released as a result of the sale. Moreover, profits from the illegal sale of arms were used to provide aid to the Contras, a band of rebels in Nicaragua. The Reagan administration supported the Contra efforts against the Sandinistas, but Congress stopped financial support in 1983. Illegal support continued, however, through the sale of the missiles.

Oliver North

At the forefront of the support to the Contras was a Marine Lieutenant Colonel named Oliver North, a member of the U.S. National Security Council. Oliver North told Congress, in a televised hearing in 1987, that he did, indeed, deliver financial aid to the Contras, but North also said that he acted only at the command of his superiors and that he always believed President Reagan was fully aware of his actions.

The public became torn over the issue of Oliver North. Some believed that the government was using him as a scapegoat to keep blame from themselves. Others saw him as a hero, doing the work he was trained to do in good faith. Others in the government were implicated, and two were forced to resign. The National Security Council Chief Vice Admiral John Poindexter resigned his post as did Donald Regan, White House Chief of Staff. Throughout it all, Ronald Reagan adamantly denied any knowledge of the missile sale and exchange or the aid to the Contras. For the most part, he was believed by the American people; however, Reagan's reputation in office was never quite the same.

Oliver North was convicted in a federal court on three charges in the Iran-Contra affair. Poindexter was convicted of conspiracy and of lying to Congress during the investigation; however, his conviction was overturned in appeals court. In 1992, President George Bush pardoned several others who had been involved, including Caspar W. Weinberger, Reagan's Secretary of Defense.

Suggested Activities

Research and Compare Find out about other scandals such as Watergate in the Nixon administration and Whitewater under President Clinton. Report to the class on what you find as well as how it affected the American public.

Nicaragua and Iran Learn about the nations of Nicaragua and Iran since the mid-eighties. What became of the Contra rebels and the Sandinista government?

After the Hearings Research to find what happened to Oliver North after the congressional hearings.

Discussion Hold a class discussion about the issues involved in the Iran-Contra hearings, such as the exchange of weapons for hostages and government aid to foreign rebel forces.

Insider Trading

A star of Wall Street, the financial wizard Michael Milken took a huge fall in 1989. Throughout most of the eighties, he had been a celebrity of sorts, earning $550 million a year and more than a billion dollars by the time he was forty years old. Yet, in 1989, he was facing a $600 million fine and ten years in jail.

The 1980s were a time of economic struggle for millions, but for some Wall Street wizards like Michael Milken, they were a financial paradise. Milken was a Wall Street bond trader who knew how to play the market effectively. He was a junk-bond king, and his economic prowess saw him at the inception of the cable industry, the cellular industry, Ted Turner's broadcasting empire, and more. His bonds even made it possible for MCI's David to compete with AT&T's Goliath. It seemed there was nothing this young wizard could not foresee, and certainly there was no way of stopping him from turning his vision to gold.

What a crash it was when, in 1989, Milken was charged with 98 counts of racketeering and securities fraud. At first, Milken maintained his innocence; however, he eventually cut a deal with the federal government. He pled guilty to some charges in exchange for others being dropped. His sentence was ten years in prison and $600 million in fines.

Michael Milken

In the eighties, Milken had been a symbol of success, the American dream at its best. Countless young people followed in his lead, briefcase in hand, using their ambition and drive to climb the ladder of success. Milken's fall was quite a wake-up call, and it and other events seemed to turn the tide of the "Greedy Eighties." The following decade saw a societal shift toward family values instead of the single life of the young urban professional (YUPpie as they came to be called) fighting for a piece of the pie. Milken's fall had far-reaching effects, for himself and society as a whole.

Suggested Activities

Research Research to learn about the life of Michael Milken since his conviction. He has been in the news on a consistent, although sporadic, basis.

Wall Street See page 123 to learn more about how the stock market works. Follow the activities there.

Economic Split In the eighties, the world of the yuppie could be mirrored against millions of Americans living in poverty, many homeless and starving. Research to find out more about the conditions of the people who were not living the American dream. Discuss the relationship between the very rich and the very poor. Also discuss capitalism and its effects.

The Berlin Wall

On November 9, 1989, the wall came tumbling down. Here is its history.

Following World War II, Germany was divided, creating Soviet East Germany and West Germany. Berlin, located inside of East Germany, was also divided into East and West zones. In the late 1940s and the 1950s, crossing from East Berlin to West Berlin in Germany became a popular way to escape Soviet communism. Thousands fled Soviet control in this way, and in 1961, more than one thousand East Germans were escaping each day. In order to stop the flight which drained the trained workforce of East Germany, East German police began to construct a wall on August 13, 1961. The wall was made of concrete topped with barbed wire. East Germans continued to escape after the wall was built, but nearly two hundred died in the attempt. Border guards shot them at sight.

The wall became a symbol of the Iron Curtain, the military, political, and ideological barrier that existed between the Soviet bloc and western Europe during the Cold War.

West Berlin itself was constantly under threat of having its supplies cut off. In 1971 Britain, France, and the Soviet Union reached an agreement that provided for free movement between West Berlin and West Germany. As the seventies and eighties progressed, relations between East and West Berlin began to improve.

In 1989 communist governments were failing, and crowds of people were leaving East Germany through Hungary, Poland, and Czechoslovakia. People throughout East Germany were demanding freedom. In November of that year, the East German government succumbed, agreeing to free movement by its citizens. Consequently, the wall that had stood for nearly thirty years was opened. Thousands of people crossed the border within the first few hours of freedom. Citizens began to dismantle the wall any way they could, using picks and shovels and whatever tools were available. People climbed the wall and danced on top, and tourists came from around the world to see the wall come down. Many took home small pieces of it as a reminder of the importance of freedom.

By the end of 1989, communism in East Germany was hanging by a thread. Leaders came and went, and in 1990, communism was voted out. In October of 1990, East and West Germany became a single nation with Berlin as the capital. A few sections of the Berlin wall are still standing and have become outdoor art galleries.

Suggested Activities

Airlift In the late forties, West Berlin was cut off from its supply lines. Research to learn how long the seige lasted and what was done to support the people of Berlin.

JFK John Kennedy was president when the wall was erected. During his visit to West Berlin in 1963, he spoke in German. Find out what he said and explain what it meant to the people of Berlin.

Cartography Draw maps of Germany before and after the unification.

Read Read firsthand accounts of people who witnessed the tearing down of the wall. Newspapers around the world carried the story for weeks.

Write Write a story as though you are an East Berliner present on the day the wall is opened.

Jesse Jackson

Born in Greenville, South Carolina, on October 8, 1941, Jesse Louis Burns took the name Jackson after his mother, who had delivered him while an unmarried teenager, married Jesse's stepfather, Charles Jackson. The Jackson family was poor, but young Jesse always felt their love and support.

While growing up in the South, Jackson was very aware of the disparity between black and white and the conditions in which they lived. All around him were signs that said "Whites Only." While good school were nearby, Jackson had to walk five miles to an all-black school.

Jesse Jackson

The University of Illinois offered Jackson a football scholarship, and he accepted. However, he felt thwarted in his efforts to take an active role on campus, so he left Illinois to attend North Carolina Agricultural and Technical College, an all-black school. There he became a leader in the fight for civil rights. It was also there that he decided to take his faith in God and natural gift for public speaking and become a minister. After graduating from college, he enrolled at the Chicago Theological Seminary.

While joining in a civil rights march in Selma, Alabama, in 1965, Jackson met the leader, Martin Luther King, Jr. He decided to leave the seminary college to work under King, heading Operation Breadbasket in Chicago. He organized boycotts against white-owned businesses that did not hire blacks although they were in black neighborhoods. Jackson followed this work with the development of PUSH (People United to Serve Humanity). He also spent a great deal of time visiting young people in school, encouraging them and warning them against the use of drugs and teen pregnancy.

By the time the 1980s arrived, Jackson had a strong following and was a respected social leader and public speaker. In 1984, he decided to make a run for the presidency of the United States. He ran under the heading of the Rainbow Coalition, hoping that his platforms would appeal to people of all colors. He received 3.3 million votes in his bid for the Democratic nomination. Jackson ran again in 1988. He more than doubled his vote from the previous election, and in March of 1988, he took the Michigan primary. This was the first time in the history of the United States that a black person won a presidential primary election.

Jackson did not win the nomination or the presidency in either election, but he did break new ground by gaining the votes of people of all colors. He holds a distinguished place in the politics of the eighties.

Suggested Activities

Civil Rights Jesse Jackson is one of many civil rights leaders of the twentieth century. Write a report on one such leader and present your findings to the class.

Since Then Jackson has continued to be active in politics and social change. Read to find out more about his life since the 1988 election.

Ronald Wilson Reagan

40th President, 1981–1989

Vice President: George Bush

Born: February 6, 1911, in Tampico, Illinois

Party: Republican

Parents: John Edward Reagan, Nelle Wilson

First Lady: Nancy Davis

Children: Maureen, Michael, Patricia, and Ronald

Education: Eureka College

Nickname: Dutch (given by his father)

Famous Firsts:

- Ronald Reagan was the first former film star to become president. He appeared in more than fifty feature films and several television shows.
- Reagan was the oldest man elected president. He was 69 at the time.
- He was the first to appoint a woman, Sandra Day O'Connor, to the Supreme Court. The post of secretary of transportation also went to a woman for the first time, Elizabeth H. Dole.
- During Reagan's administration, the federal budget deficit reached a record level.
- In 1994, he became the first former president to publicly announce a personal battle with Alzheimer's disease.

Achievements:

- Reagan was a two-time California governor. He was also a longtime president of the Screen Actors Guild.
- In 1985 Reagan and Soviet General Secretary Mikhail Gorbachev agreed to unprecedented cultural, educational, and scientific exchanges between their nations.
- In 1987 Reagan signed a treaty with Gorbachev, reducing nuclear arms.
- The government under Reagan helped arrange for the removal of PLO units from Lebanon.
- He opened the Ronald Reagan Presidential Library in Simi Valley, California. It holds documents and other items related to his presidency.

Interesting Facts:

- American hostages held in Iran for more than a year were finally released on the day of Reagan's inauguration. They were on a plane out of Iran just minutes after he was inaugurated.
- In 1980, not only did Reagan win the election but the Republicans took the majority in the Senate for the first time since 1952.
- There was an attempted assassination on Reagan in 1981. He was shot in the chest, but he fully recovered. In 1985 Reagan experienced another life-threatening battle, this time with colon cancer. He recovered rapidly again.
- His first job was as a lifeguard. He used money from that job and a partial scholarship to put himself through college. After college, he worked as a sports announcer.
- Reagan was initially a Democrat. In 1962, he became a Republican.
- Both of Reagan's presidential election victories were landslides.

George Herbert Walker Bush

41st President, 1989–1993

Vice President: J. Danforth (Dan) Quayle

Born: June 12, 1924, in Milton, Massachusetts

Party: Republican

Parents: Prescott Sheldon Bush, Dorothy Walker

First Lady: Barbara Pierce

Children: George, Robin, John, Neil, Marvin, Dorothy

Education: Yale University

Nickname: Poppy

Famous Firsts:

- The largest oil spill ever to take place in U.S. waters occurred when the *Exxon Valdez* struck a reef near an Alaskan port. Nearly eleven million gallons of crude oil spilled into the ocean.
- Bush and Russian leader Mikhail Gorbachev signed the first treaty to call for reduction in the existing long-range nuclear weapons (START I).
- He was the first future president to request, in writing, the resignation of a current president, Richard M. Nixon.

Achievements:

- Bush was a war hero who received the Distinguished Flying Cross for his heroism in World War II when his plane was shot down.
- Bush was a successful independent oilman in Texas before entering politics.
- From 1976–1977, Bush was the head of the Central Intelligence Agency (CIA).
- Bush sent troops to Somalia to help end the mass starvation there.
- Bush made significant strides with Russian relations. During his time in office, the Strategic Arms Reduction Treaties (START I and START II) were signed.

Interesting Facts:

- Bush was acting president for eight hours while President Ronald Reagan was in surgery for cancer.
- His father was a senator from Connecticut for several years.
- Barbara Bush's father was the publisher of *McCall's* and *Redbook* magazines.
- Bush was captain of the baseball team during his senior year at Yale.
- In college, Bush was elected to the Phi Beta Kappa honor society.
- As vice president to Ronald Reagan, Bush enjoyed a more active role than past vice presidents.
- Bush suffered from Graves' disease, a disorder of the thyroid gland that gave him an irregular heartbeat.

Election Facts and Figures

	Election of 1980	Election of 1984	Election of 1988
Democrats	President Jimmy Carter and Vice President Walter F. Mondale ran once more.	Former Vice President Walter Mondale took as his running mate Representative Geraldine A. Ferraro of New York, the first woman ever nominated to the presidential ticket of a major party.	Governor Michael S. Dukakis of Massachusetts was nominated with long-time Senator Lloyd Bentsen of Texas as his running mate.
Republicans	Ronald Wilson Reagan, former actor and California governor, ran with running-mate George Bush.	President Reagan and Vice President Bush were easily nominated again by their party.	Vice President George Herbert Walker Bush was nominated for the candidacy. Senator Dan Quayle of Indiana was nominated as his running mate.
Other	Representative John Anderson of Illinois broke with the Republican Party to run as an independent.		
Issues	The primary issues were inflation, unemployment, and taxes. Seriously dampening Carter's chances was the hostage situation in Iran. Reagan urged his "supply-side theory of economics," an emphasis on tax reduction to stimulate business activity.	Economic growth, U.S.–Soviet relations, and inflation were the primary issues.	Bush attacked Dukakis' lack of experience in foreign affairs and track record with leniency in some criminal cases. Dukakis questioned Bush's avowed lack of knowledge in the Iran-Contra affair, and he pointed out the many social service programs that had been cut or terminated under the Reagan-Bush administration.
Winner	Prior to the election, analysts thought the race would be close, primarily due to Iran. However, Reagan took 489 electoral votes to Carter's 49. President Carter carried only six states and the District of Columbia. The popular vote was about 44 million to 35 million. An Independent candidate, John Anderson of Illinois, earned about 5.5 million popular votes. At age 69, Reagan became the oldest president elected.	In a sweeping landslide, Reagan took 525 electoral votes to Mondale's 13. The popular vote was about 54.5 million for Reagan and 37.5 million for Mondale.	Bush won the election handily with 436 electoral votes to Dukakis' 111. The popular vote was closer with approximately 49 million going to the Republicans and 42 million to the Democrats. Interestingly, vice presidential nominee Bentsen earned one electoral vote of his own.

Chernobyl and the Exxon-Valdez

In each decade there are sure to be a variety of natural disasters such as earthquakes and hurricanes that strike areas around the world. These disasters often claim many lives and destroy millions of dollars in property. In the eighties, two disasters with far–reaching consequences were caused not by forces of nature but by human error.

The worst nuclear accident ever known occurred on April 26, 1986, near Kiev, Ukraine, which was at the time part of the Soviet Union. One of four reactors at the Chernobyl nuclear power plant went out of control. Due to improper supervision, the water cooling system turned off. This led to an uncontrolled reaction which caused a steam explosion. As a result, the roof was blown off the building, releasing massive amounts of radioactive material into the atmosphere. The radiation easily spread from the eastern Soviet Union to northern and central Europe, causing much concern throughout the area and, in fact, the world. Normal radiation counts jumped to 1,000 times their norm. Farm crops and grazing lands were contaminated as far away as Poland, Scotland, and Great Britain.

According to the Soviets, thirty-one people died immediately of burns and radiation sickness, and more than 300 were injured seriously. However, these numbers are debated elsewhere, and many people believe that they are, in reality, much higher. Medical experts generally believe that there will prove to be an increase in cancer experienced by those closest to the accident. More than 100,000 Soviet citizens were evacuated from the areas surrounding the reactor site.

Three years after the Chernobyl accident, the world's attention shifted to Prince William Sound in southeastern Alaska. An American petroleum company, the largest in the world, the Exxon Corporation, was transporting oil from the Trans-Alaska Pipeline on March 24 of 1989. Its tanker, the *Exxon Valdez*, ran aground and began leaking oil. The leakage continued for two days, spilling nearly eleven million gallons (42 million liters) of crude oil into the water. This was the largest oil spill in North American history. Thousands of marine animals and birds were killed, and 1,100 miles (1,770 km) of Alaska's shoreline were contaminated. Cleanup of the spill cost Exxon approximately two billion dollars. Criminal charges were filed against the company by the United States government in 1990, and in 1991 a plea bargain was accepted. Exxon agreed to pay $1,025,000,000 in penalties and the company pleaded guilty to four misdemeanor charges.

Suggested Activities

Discussion Have the class discuss the following: Is nuclear power worth the risk to life and the environment?

Science Learn about nuclear power and how it is manufactured. Also learn about the uses of crude oil.

Environment What was involved in the cleanup of Prince Edward Sound? What about Chernobyl? Read to find the continuing costs to the environment since the time of both accidents as well as what people are doing (and have done) to better the situations.

Mount Saint Helens

When Mount Saint Helens erupted on May 18, 1980, the blast was about 500 times more powerful than an atomic bomb and was heard 135 miles (217 kilometers) away.

The peak is located 95 miles (153 kilometers) south of Seattle, Washington, in the Cascade Mountains. When it erupted, 57 people died, and the combination of heat, hot mud, ash, rock, and residual fires caused the deaths of countless birds and animals as well as the destruction of a hundred thousand acres of forest. More than 1,000 feet (300 meters) was blown from the top of the mountain, resulting in hundreds of millions of dollars in damages.

The eruption of Mount Saint Helens was the first to take place in the United States, outside Alaska and Hawaii, since 1917, when California's Lassen Peak erupted. Mount Saint Helens itself had been inactive from 1857 until that fateful day in 1980.

When the mountain erupted, the heat caused a great deal of snow to melt, and flooding and mud slides added to the countless other tragedies of the volcanic activity. The most pervasive effect was the layer of ash that spread over an extensive area, destroying crops and polluting the air. People as far away as Oregon and Idaho were affected. Many people wore surgical masks when they were outdoors to filter the ash and to protect their lungs. Many car engines and a variety of machines were ruined by the ash as well.

In a few months the ash had settled, and solidified lava capped the mountain. Over the next six years, many minor eruptions occurred, but they did not do extensive damage. Mount Saint Helens is expected to continue to erupt during the coming years.

Suggested Activities

Geology Learn about the three types of volcanoes: cinder cones, shield volcanoes, and composite volcanoes. What are their similarities and differences? Create charts and drawings to show your findings.

Claims to Fame A number of volcanoes have become famous over the years. Identify as many of the following as possible, telling about their famous eruptions and what type of volcano each is: Aconcagua, Cotopaxi, El Chichón, Krakatau, Lassen Peak, Mauna Loa, Mont Pelée, Mount Etna, Mount Pinatubo, Mount Tambora, Nevado del Ruiz, Paricutin, Stromboli, Surtsey, Thira (formerly Santorin), and Vesuvius.

AIDS

First identified by doctors in 1980 and 1981, acquired immune deficiency syndrome (AIDS) became a major issue of the eighties. Since 1981, AIDS has been found in more than 150 countries around the world. The World Health Organization estimates that there may be more than twenty million HIV and AIDS cases by the turn of the century.

In the early eighties, doctors began to see an increase in rare forms of cancer, pneumonia, and serious infections among previously healthy young men. Previously these infections and diseases occurred mainly in transplant patients receiving treatment to suppress their immune systems. The doctors soon found evidence that the syndrome spread through direct blood contact or an exchange of bodily fluids. In 1983 and 1984, scientists in France and the United States isolated a retrovirus from AIDS patients and identified it as the cause of AIDS. They named the virus human immunodeficiency virus, or HIV. French researchers then isolated another virus, HIV-2, which occurs mainly in Africa.

HIV attaches itself to certain white blood cells that are essential in the normal functioning of the immune system. The virus then inserts its genes in these cells where it replicates itself and progressively destroys the immune system. HIV can be present in a person for two to twelve years before any symptoms occur and can be transmitted to another person even if there are no symptoms. Scientists do not know exactly how or where HIV infections began. Similar viruses exist in some African monkeys and other animal populations, but these viruses do not affect humans. Researchers have shown that people died of AIDS as early as the sixties and seventies.

To date there is no known cure for or vaccine against HIV infection. Education and research have been the focus of the battle against AIDS since the early eighties. In 1987, a drug known as AZT became the first antiviral drug approved in the United States for HIV and AIDS infection. New drug therapies focus on preventing replication of HIV within the cells of people infected with HIV. Widespread educational campaigns teach people preventive measures and encourage testing for the virus.

Throughout the eighties, AIDS patients and their families suffered from ostracism and violence caused by the mistaken belief that AIDS could be "caught" by touching an infected person or sitting near him or her. In 1987, a family in Florida received bomb threats when their three sons, all infected with AIDS through blood transfusions tried to attend the local school. Others, like teenage victim Ryan White, led a campaign of education to heighten public awareness and to spread accurate information about AIDS.

In the nineties, research and public education continued, as did the controversy about the ways in which HIV is spread and the preventive measures sometimes suggested. Meanwhile, scientists remain hopeful for a cure.

Suggested Activity

Science Learn more about HIV and AIDS, focussing on the physiology of retroviruses.

Status Report Research to learn the latest developments in the battle against this epidemic.

Environmentalism

Throughout the decade, environmentalism was an issue at the forefront of political debate, social action, and public awareness. Concerns first expressed in the sixties and seventies gained new audiences. People became interested in the quality of air and water, the survival of the rain forest, the depletion of the ozone layer, and other issues. Curbing pollution, recycling, and stopping waste were prominent themes.

Suggested Activity

Environmental Bingo Complete three in a row on the bingo card below or make your own card and fill it in. In order to mark a space, the task must be completed.

Environmental Bingo

Find a water leak at home, school, or in a local business. Report it.	Snip each section of a six-pack ring before you discard it.	Clean out your closet or cupboard and with your parent's permission, donate things you do not want to a needy organization.
Next time you find a bug in your home or classroom, do not kill it. Help it get back outside safely.	Create your own ecology project such as a newsletter, fund-raising event, play, or letter-writing campaign to help others become environmentally aware.	Use a recycling box at home for paper, taking it to a recycling center when the box is full.
Construct an art project from recycled material.	Turn off the water while you brush your teeth, turning it on only for rinsing.	For a week, use only cloth towels and napkins.

"First Ladies"

Many women came to political prominence in the eighties. Three noteworthy women are Sandra Day O'Connor, Geraldine Ferraro, and Wilma Mankiller.

Sandra Day O'Connor was born in 1930 in El Paso, Texas, and she received a Stanford University law degree in 1952. In 1965, she became attorney general for Arizona, and in 1969 she was appointed to complete a term in the state senate. She was elected to the Arizona senate in the following year and again in 1972, and she was senate majority leader in 1973. O'Connor became a judge of a county trial court in 1974, and in 1979, she was appointed by the Arizona governor to the state court of appeals, which is the second highest court in the state.

O'Connor came to national prominence when United States Supreme Court Justice Potter Stewart retired in 1981. President Ronald Reagan, in one of the earliest acts of his presidency, named her to fill the vacancy. She accepted and was approved by Congress in a vote of 99–0.

Sandra Day O'Conner

Associate Justice O'Connor's record of conservative perspectives as a judge made her an ideal candidate for the conservative president's appointment. However, the thing that drew most public attention to her was the fact that she was the first woman ever to be named to the United States Supreme Court. Many women at the time hoped that she would be an active proponent for women's rights; however, her activities did not vary from what she had traditionally done.

Geraldine Ferraro

Geraldine Ferraro also had a strong political career when she gained national attention for her role in national politics. She became the first woman to be nominated for vice president on a major party ticket. In the 1984 election, she was the running-mate of Democratic presidential nominee and former Vice President Walter Mondale.

Ferraro, the daughter of Italian immigrants, was a lawyer and former assistant district attorney in Queens County, New York. She first won election to the United States House of Representatives in 1978. She continued in that office until 1984, when she received the Democratic vice presidential nomination. She was chosen by the party not only for her political abilities but also for the express purpose of breaking traditions and political obstructions. The hope was to defeat popular President Reagan. A Mondale aide is quoted as saying, "She's a woman, she's ethnic, she's Catholic . . . we have broken the barrier."

"First Ladies" *(cont.)*

Although the Mondale-Ferraro ticket made a respectable showing in the months prior to the election, they lost the final election in one of the most drastic landslides in history, with Mondale-Ferraro taking only one electoral vote. However, regardless of the major loss, the two will always be remembered for breaking new political ground.

Wilma Pearl Mankiller was born into poverty in the hills of Oklahoma in 1945. While attending college, she met a group of Native American Activists; Mankiller them realized that her mission was to serve her people. In 1985, she became the first woman to serve as the principal chief of the age-old Cherokee Nation. Her activities in that position have brought the Nation long overdue recognition in the United States and greater political weight than ever before.

Willma Mankiller

The history of the Cherokee people takes many turns, but many people remember the Cherokee in connection with the tragic Trail of Tears, the time in 1838 when 13,000 Cherokee were forcibly evacuated from their land in the southeast woodlands to Indian Territory, 1,000 miles (1,610 kilometers) away. The people were allowed to take nothing with them, and they were made to travel by foot. It is estimated that 4,000 died during the journey. Approximately 300 people hid in the Great Smoky Mountains of their homeland. Since that time, members of the Nation have been trying to rebuild it. Mankiller has made great leaps in doing just that.

Wilma Mankiller has worked diligently to preserve the history, traditions, and customs of the Cherokee Nation, as well as to carve the people a strong and important place in the United States. Under her leadership, the people have regained much of tradition and pride that was lost to them over the years.

For her efforts, Wilma Mankiller was inducted into the Oklahoma Women's Hall of Fame in 1986. In 1993, she was named as one of the United States' outstanding women. Mankiller announced in 1995 that she would not seek re-election.

Suggested Activities

Politics Learn more about the political views of Sandra Day O'Connor, Geraldine Ferraro, and Wilma Mankiller. In your opinion, would any of the women make a good candidate for the United States presidency?

Madam President Some women have run for president, but not on a major party ticket. Find out about one of the women who has run as well as her political career.

Read Wilma Mankiller's autobiography is called *Mankiller: A Chief and Her People* (St. Martin's Press, 1993). It is an excellent resource, telling not only about her life but about the history of the Cherokee Nation.

Discussion Hold a class discussion on the topic of leadership and the sexes. Ask the students to discuss if and how a person's sex affects his or her ability to lead.

Supreme Court Learn about the Supreme Court of the United States and how it operates. Pay close attention to the decisions made since O'Connor's appointment.

The Cos

On Thursday nights in the 1980s, millions of Americans turned on the television to *The Cosby Show*, one of the most popular shows of all time. For much of the 1980s, *The Cosby Show* was rated number one in the Nielsen rating system, demonstrating that people of all ages, races, and socio-economic backgrounds loved to watch "The Cos."

Billy Cosby

William Henry Cosby, Jr., was born in Philadelphia, Pennsylvania, in 1937. He began his career in entertainment as a stand-up comedian on the nightclub circuit while he was a student at Temple University. He began to record his comedy as well, making over twenty albums and reaching audiences around the world. People not only laughed at but were charmed by the *family warmth* and gentle, good-natured humor that pervaded his routines.

In 1965, Cosby became the first black actor to co-star in a prime-time dramatic series on television. The show, *I Spy*, ran until 1968. Cosby received three consecutive Emmys for his work. Cosby had become a star. He followed the show with a number of movie roles, including *Hickey and Boggs* in 1972 and *Uptown Saturday Night* in 1974. Nineteen seventy-two was also the year of Cosby's television debut as Fat Albert, the lead character in the Cosby-produced and hosted cartoon series, *Fat Albert and the Cosby Kids*. Fat Albert was a character Cosby had created for his comedy routines. Fat Albert became so popular with children that even Cosby's son, Ennis, is remembered as having been overjoyed to learn that his father was, in fact, Fat Albert. The character had another purpose, as well, serving as the basis for the doctoral dissertation in education that Cosby earned from the University of Massachusetts in 1977.

In 1984 Cosby's new situation comedy, *The Cosby Show*, debuted. It was an instant success, running until 1992 and continuing ever since in rerun syndication. The show was loosely based on Cosby's own experiences as the father of five children, one boy and four girls. The fame of the show made Cosby a star of the highest order, and he was frequently counted as one of the wealthiest entertainers in the world.

Cosby also authored several books in the eighties, including *Fatherhood* in 1986, *Time Flies* in 1987, and *Love and Marriage* in 1989. His books are filled with the easily recognizable Cosby humor.

Other television series followed *The Cosby Show*, but none matched the phenomenal success of the show from the eighties. Early in 1997 Cosby's only son was killed by a gunman on a Los Angeles freeway. Within weeks of this personal tragedy Cosby was on television and on the road, continuing to do what he does best, making people laugh.

Suggested Activities

Read, Watch, and Listen Share excerpts from some of Cosby's books with the class. Also, watch a video tape of *The Cosby Show* and listen to one of his recordings. Most of Cosby's work is acceptable for people of all ages. Use your own discretion.

Writing In small groups, write original scripts for episodes of *The Cosby Show*.

Music Television (MTV)

The first music videos were used mainly to promote new groups and new songs. In the late 1970s, European record companies began showing well produced music videos in nightclubs and on television. The result was increased sales. This persuaded American record producers to attempt something similar. In 1981 Warner Amex Satellite Entertainment Company (WASEC) launched Music Television (MTV) as a 24-hour music video channel.

It was patterned after existing radio formats, with an announcer called a VJ (video jockey) to present the segments and give other vital information in much the same way a disc jockey (DJ) did on the radio. Each rock music video would feature a three-(minute) to four-minute performance by the recording artist.

MTV began its broadcast with a video entitled "Video Killed the Radio Star" and, indeed, video did transform the entire music industry. MTV brought rock videos into the mainstream and made the visual just as important as the audio for all rock music to come. In fact, some would argue that the visual became even more important. Music videos have beome an art form, constantly seeking to achieve new video styles through the use of special effects. These styles have had an influence on television shows, commercials and feature films. It is commonly asserted that some major rock stars of the eighties, like Madonna and Michael Jackson, skyrocketed to success because of their video presence.

The initial cost for MTV was twenty million dollars. In the first eighteen months, the channel had earned seven million dollars in ad revenues, and by mid-1983 it had 125 advertisers. Ad revenue reached a million a week by 1984, with an audience of approximately twenty million made up primarily of 12 to 34 year olds.

MTV developed exclusive rights to new videos with four record companies by mid-1984. At that time, it branched out into a second channel, VH-1, intending to reach an older audience by focussing on other forms of pop music, like soft rock. Competing video shows turned up on most major networks, but none achieved the success of MTV.

By the end of the eighties, MTV had changed its format considerably, introducing a variety of regular programs, such as news and game shows, in addition to music videos. It also included a variety of music styles, focussing on rap and other forms that became popular over the years. Sometimes controversial for the sex and violence displayed in some rock videos, MTV has nonetheless grown into a power house in the cable industry as well as in the music industry.

Suggested Activities

View and Discuss At your own discretion, view some music videos. Choose carefully and be sure to get the approval of your school administrators and students' parents. There are videos that are acceptable and are, in fact, worthy of discussion in social as well as artistic terms.

Research Study to find out the specific effects that MTV has had on the cable television and music industries. The effects, particularly to music, have been enormous.

Olympic Stars

The Olympic Games in the eighties were marked by controversy and triumph.

At the 1980 Winter Olympics in Lake Placid, New York, where the impossible—or so many people thought—happened. The United States hockey team won the Olympic gold medal. Comprised of twenty college students, the U.S. team first defeated the team from the Soviet Union, a group of players that most experts believed to be the greatest in the world. Not only did they beat the Soviets, they went on to beat the team from Finland to become the gold medal winners. No U.S. hockey team had ever won the gold. In fact, the U.S. team was usually not even considered a contender. These were mere amateurs against the best professionals. It was an awesome victory.

Not to be outdone, Eric Heiden, a twenty-one-year-old speed skater, took home gold medals in all of the men's speed skating events. He became the first athlete to win five gold medals in one Winter Olympics.

The Summer Olympics of the same year were to be held in Moscow, but the events were overshadowed by events in Afghanistan. In response to the Soviet invasion of Afghanistan, President Jimmy Carter imposed an embargo against the U.S.S.R. The Soviets refused to remove their troops, and Carter pressured the U.S. Olympic Committee to boycott the Games. Athletes from the United States and more than forty other nations did not participate. The Games were dominated by the Soviets and its allies.

The Soviets took their turn and boycotted the 1984 Summer Olympics in Los Angeles, California. The reason they gave was that the Games in L.A. were too commercial and that security would be too weak to protect their athletes. The Soviet-bloc nations joined in the boycott. Despite the absence of the Soviets and about six other nations, the Games were competitive and exciting. Track sensation, Carl Lewis and gymnast Mary Lou Retton were the stars of the Games. Lewis took four gold medals, and Retton became the first American woman to win the gold in the women's all-around gymnastics category. She also took home four other gold medals.

No one boycotted the Summer Olympics of 1988 in Seoul, South Korea, and politics had almost no part in them. However, they were marred to some extent by the presence of illegal drugs. Track star Ben Johnson of Canada amazed the world with his record 100-meter dash, but six days later the gold medal was taken from him because of his use of anabolic steroids, drugs that increase physical stamina and performance. Ten other athletes were also disqualified during the Games for use of steroids.

Two other athletes came to international attention during the 1988 Summer Games, Florence Griffith-Joyner and Jackie Joyner-Kersee.

Suggested Activity

Research Learn more about any of the athletes named above and what has become of them since the time of the Olympics.

The Greatest

Wayne Getzky

Few athletes make it to the professional leagues, and even fewer became famous in their sport. It is a rare athlete, indeed, who gains not only international fame but is considered by some to be the greatest athlete of all time. One of these rare few is Wayne Gretzky.

Born in Brantford, Ontario, Canada, in 1961, Gretzky became a professional hockey player in 1978 at the age of seventeen. At the time, he played with the Indianapolis Racers of the World Hockey Association (WHA). He was traded to the Edmonton Oilers, also of the WHA, later in 1978. At the end of the season, the WHA disbanded and the Oilers became a part of the National Hockey League (NHL).

In 1980, Gretzky became the youngest player ever to win the Hart Memorial Trophy for the most valuable player in the NHL. He was twenty years old. He went on to win the award each year for the next seven seasons, and he won it again in 1989. Gretzky led the Oilers to four Stanley cup championships.

Gretzky holds a total of 50 records for his playing, more records than nearly any athlete in any sport. In his third year as a professional he set records for goals, assists, and total points, becoming the first player to score 200 points in one season. In 1986 Gretzky had a record 163 assists and broke his own record with 215 season points. In 1989 he broke Gordie Howe's 1,850 career scoring record, and in 1994 his career goal record surpassed Howe's record of 801 goals.

In 1988, Gretzky was traded to the Los Angeles Kings, a move that many criticized because the Oilers were a championship team and the Kings a losing one. The move proved to be excellent for the Kings franchise and, in Gretzky's opinion, challenging and fulfilling for himself. The Kings played to sellout crowds, unknown for the little-noticed team prior to Gretzky's arrival. Suddenly, they became a Los Angeles pastime. The attention they brought to the sport with the direct assistance of Gretzky may have paved the way for a new team in the area, the Anaheim Mighty Ducks.

Gretzky completed his run with the Kings in the 1995–1996 season, and he played out the season with the St. Louis Blues. Then, as a free agent, he signed with the championship New York Rangers, beginning with the 1996–1997 season and rounding out a phenomenal career that has lasted nearly two decades. It is no wonder that people call him "The Greatest."

Suggested Activities

Reading Read excerpts from Gretzky's book entitled *Gretzky: An Autobiography*, co-written with Rick Reilly (HarperCollins, 1990).

Physical Education Learn the basics of street hockey and play the game. You can simply wear tennis shoes instead of skates.

Canada In Canada, hockey is the national sport in much the same way that baseball is in the United States. Learn more about Canada's relationship to hockey and what the trade to an American team might have meant to Gretzky.

The Heart of the Matter

The human heart took on some different forms during the 1980s. Here are two of them.

A retired dentist from Seattle, Washington, became the first human recipient of a permanent artificial heart in the winter of 1982. Barney Clark's own heart was failing rapidly, so a surgical team headed by Dr. William C. DeVries at the University of Utah Medical Center replaced Clark's damaged heart with the Jarvik-7, an artificial heart created by inventor Robert Jarvik.

The Jarvik-7 is a mechanical heart that is powered by an air compressor that remains outside of the body. Two plastic hoses connect the compressor to the heart. The heart was first tested on animals and approved by the United States Food and Drug Administration (FDA) for human use.

Clark lived for 112 days after the surgery, recovering enough to walk and move about, but eventually his other organs failed and he died in March of 1983. Doctors attempted the surgery once more in 1984, this time with 54-year-old William J. Schroeder. Schroeder experienced a number of strokes after receiving the heart, and although he was able to leave the hospital and continued to live for 620 days, he died as well.

Many doctors became concerned over the dangers associated with the Jarvik-7, particularly the possibility of stroke. In 1990, the FDA withdrew its approval for the artificial heart.

An artificial heart had been used many years earlier but only as a temporary replacement. It was placed in the chest of a human patient for sixty hours in 1969 in order to keep the patient's blood circulating until a suitable human heart became available for transplanting.

In 1984, another kind of heart transplant was attempted, this time from animal to human. Doctors at Loma Linda University Medical Center in California transplanted the heart of a baboon into a baby born with a fatal heart defect. The baby lived for three weeks. The transplant also registered a great deal of controversy in the medical community, particularly since it was so experimental.

Suggested Activities

Science Learn about the functioning of a heart. Draw diagrams of a normal, healthy heart. Also research diseases of the heart.

Research Find out about the medical advances made in the 1990s concerning the human heart. What has been accomplished? What questions or concerns have been raised?

Discussion Allow the students to discuss the controversies of using animals for medical research and of scientific experimentation on human beings. These topics are likely to generate strong opinions, and it is usually best for the teacher to remain neutral.

Women in Space

The 1980s brought groundbreaking changes for women in many areas but perhaps none as great as those made in space. Three notable women changed the face of the space program forever.

Sally Ride

In 1983, Dr. Sally Ride became the first American woman to travel into space. She was born in Los Angeles, California, in 1951, and she graduated from Stanford University with a degree in English and another in astrophysics. She continued her study of astrophysics, earning both master's and doctoral degrees in the field. In 1978, she was chosen to be a part of NASA's astronaut training program, and in 1983, she made her famous flight aboard the space shuttle *Challenger* as the mission specialist. After her flight in 1983, she became a national hero.

Dr. Judith A. Resnick, an engineer and astronaut, was the second American woman in space. She made her first shuttle flight aboard the shuttle *Discovery* in September of 1984. Her second shuttle flight was as a mission specialist on the ill-fated tenth voyage of the *Challenger*. Resnick was born in 1949 in Akron, Ohio. She received her degree in engineering from Carnegie Tech University and earned a Ph.D. in electrical engineering from the University of Maryland in 1977. She was an accomplished classical pianist.

Christa McAuliffe

Another famous space traveller in connection with the *Challenger* was Christa McAuliffe. She was the first teacher ever selected to fly in space. Born Sharon Christa Corrigan in 1948, McAuliffe graduated from Framingham State College in 1970 and from Bowie State College in 1978 with a master's degree. She was a social studies teacher at Concord High School in Concord, New Hampshire, when she was selected by NASA from 11,000 applicants to be the first teacher in space.

McAuliffe began a diary at the time she was chosen in order to record her experiences for posterity. She planned to write about the journey while she was experiencing it; however, on January 28, 1986, after less than 80 seconds in flight, the *Challenger* exploded in air, killing all seven crew members. (See page 436.) Since the explosion, McAuliffe's fame has continued to spread, scholarships have been established in her honor, and schools and libraries around the nation have been named for her.

Suggested Activities

Read Read *Sally Ride, Astronaut: An American First* by June Behrens (Children Press, 1984) and *The Story of the Challenger Disaster* by Zachary Kent (Childrens Press, 1986).

Other Notable Women Other women worth mentioning in terms of the space program include Dr. Mae C. Jemison, Dr. Kathryn Sullivan, and Lt. Col. Eileen Collins. Research to learn about each of them and their contributions to the space program.

Famous Firsts As a class, brainstorm for the names of women throughout history who have accomplished "famous firsts." A number of such women are named throughout the many pages of this book.

Discuss President Ronald Regan first suggested sending a teacher into space. Ask the students to discuss why they think he made this suggestion and why NASA agreed. Also ask them if they would like to be selected for space flight and why or why not.

Space Shuttles

In the sixties, scientists learned how expensive space travel could be. The expendable booster rockets used to launch satellites for commercial and government use were expensive. A reusable spacecraft, together with launch facilities, mission control, and a system of tracking and data control satellites, would create a new Space Transportation System (STS).

These new spacecraft had to be designed for safety, performance, endurance, and longetivity. There are three components to the shuttle: the orbiter, the external tank, and the solid fuel rocket boosters. The orbiter, which looks like a delta wing fighter, has a wing span of 78 feet (23.79 m) and is 122 feet (37.2 m) long. In its launch phase, it is a stage of a rocket, in orbit it is a spacecraft, and in reentry it is a hypersonic glider. The orbiter contains living space for the astronauts, a large cargo bay, and the engine compartment. The design allows for more crew members than previous spacecrafts and enables the astronauts to bring home large quantities of weighty cargo. There is plenty of room for a variety of work, such as satellite repair, experimentation, the construction of space stations, and deployment of satellites. In theory each orbiter could make one hundred voyages, although the engines would only last through about fifty-five launches. The first orbiter, *Enterprise*, was ready in 1977. It was used solely for drop tests from a Boeing 747 Jumbo Jet, which tested its ability to land after space travel.

An external tank holds cylinders of liquid hydrogen and oxygen to fuel the orbiter's three main engines. Two solid fuel rocket boosters are used to help propel the orbiter to the upper atmosphere. Each one produces 2.65 million pounds (1.20 kg) of thrust.

On April 12, 1981, the first operational shuttle, *Columbia*, piloted by astronauts John W. Young and Robert L. Crippen, went into orbit. They circled the Earth thirty-six times over a period of more than two days. During this flight, the astronauts deployed scientific equipment and ran a variety of tests checking out the abilities of the shuttle.

The sixth shuttle flight in April of 1983 was the first for the orbiter *Challenger*. When *Discovery* was launched in 1984, the crew included Charles Walker of the McDonnell Douglas Corporation, the first person from industry assigned to a shuttle mission. In 1985, U.S. senator Jake Garn flew on the shuttle and took part in medical experiments. The fourth orbiter, *Atlantis*, made its debut for the twenty-first shuttle flight in October of 1985.

Challenger successfully completed nine flights, but on its tenth, the twenty-fifth shuttle mission, in January of 1986, it exploded less than two minutes after take-off. (See page 436.) The space shuttle program was halted until the problem could be completely remedied.

The program resumed with shuttle mission twenty-six, completed October 3, 1988 by *Discovery*.

Suggested Activities

Space Flight Learn about other space vehicles of the 1980s, such as *Voyager*. How were they constructed? What did they do? How were they different from those that came before? Also find out about plans for the future of space flight and space exploration.

Read There are many excellent resources about the space shuttle program. Two of them are *Space Shuttle* by N.S. Barrett (Franklin Watts, 1985) and *I Want to Fly the Shuttle* by David Baker (Rourke Enterprises, 1988). Read them as well as others to learn more.

Building Construct models of the space shuttle.

Astronaut Learn about Guion Bluford, the first African American to fly into space. He was the mission specialist on the third flight of the *Challenger*.

Disaster in the Air

"Oh, I have slipped the surly bonds of earth, . . . Put out my hand, and touched the face of God." When President Ronald Reagan quoted Canadian World War II pilot, John Gillespie Magee, Jr., who was killed in action at the age of nineteen, he referred not to Magee but to the seven members of the space shuttle *Challenger's* flight crew who died in a tragic explosion just over a minute after lift-off on January 28, 1986. Thousands of onlookers, including family and friends of the crew, watched the shuttle blow apart nine miles (14.5 kilometers) in the sky, and millions more saw the scene on their television screens as it was replayed throughout the next several days and weeks. The American space program had known tragedy but nothing on this order. Moreover, it seemed that people had come to take space flight, already in existence for more than two decades, almost for granted. The explosion of the craft brought waves of shock and disbelief.

The tenth flight of the *Challenger* was particularly noteworthy since its crew included the first teacher ever selected to fly into space. Chosen from among 11,000 applicants, Christa McAuliffe was a high school social studies teacher from Concord, New Hampshire, who was selected to be the ambassador to educators and schoolchildren from around the nation. Many students watched the lift-off on televisions in their schools. Around the nation, the spirits of the children fell as the reality of what had happened sunk in. Teachers and students at McAuliffe's own school were sent home just an hour after the tragedy occurred.

Lifting off at 11:38 A.M., the shuttle no longer existed by 11:40. A gas leak from a faulty seal in a solid-fuel booster rocket caused the explosion. Recordings of voices from the crew cockpit confirm that the crew knew there was a problem, but only briefly. The pilot said, "Uh-oh," just before the explosion.

In addition to McAuliffe, the crew included Commander Michael J. Smith, Commander Francis "Dick" Scobee, Dr. Judith A. Resnik, Dr. Ronald E. McNair, Lieutenant Colonel Ellison S. Onizuka, and Gregory B. Jarvis. Jarvis was an engineer from the Hughes Aircraft Company, and like McAuliffe, this was his first shuttle flight.

The immediate cause of the fiery explosion was a defect in one of the solid-fuel booster rockets, but in the months that followed, reports also showed that pressure on NASA to launch the shuttles was partly responsible for the tragedy. Some engineers had recommended that the flight be delayed, but these recommendations were overlooked in order to get the shuttle into space. After the accident, the space shuttle program was completely shut down until all such problems and potential hazards could be remedied. On September 29, 1988, two and a half years after the *Challenger* explosion, the space shuttle *Discovery* was launched without incident. The nation breathed a collective sigh of relief.

——— Suggested Activity ———

Read Read more about the explosion of the *Challenger* and what it meant to the space program. One good resource is listed on page 434.

The Technological Home and Office

The average American home of the eighties differed quite a bit from the same home in the seventies, and technology was the reason. Suddenly it seemed there were new technologies to handle a variety of tasks. Answering machines took phone messages, video-cassette recorders (VCR's) taped television shows when people were not home to watch them, cable television broadened the spectrum of television viewing options, compact discs (CDs) enhanced sound for the listener of recorded music, and personal computers rapidly became an exciting new source of entertainment and productivity.

VCRs Perhaps most significant and influential in the technologic advances of the decade were the VCR and the personal computer. VCRs brought about a revolution in the entertainment industry. Previously, people's choice of films was limited to what could be seen in theaters or the occasional few that were screened on network television. Children of the middle decades can recall special television events when popular movies such as *The Wizard of Oz* were broadcast annually. With the advent of VCR's, people could buy or rent video tapes of movies and watch them whenever they chose. They could also record any movie or show from television to watch at their leisure. Some even began watching a show on one channel while taping one on another. With the dawn of the VCR came a new line of stores that sold and rented videos. This became one of the fastest growing industries of the 1980s.

Initially developed in the late fifties and early sixties, VCR technology grew from the need of television studios for a reliable method of recording programs for viewing in different time zones, or for repeat usage. These early systems were far too complex and expensive for home use, however. In 1975 Sony Corporation introduced its Betamax based on the system used by stations and networks. Matsushita Electric Industrial Corporation quickly released a competing system called Video Home System, or VHS. When the VHS system was adopted by the leading American television manufacturer, popularity of the Betamax waned. The VCR industry boomed throughout the eighties.

PCs The personal computer also took off in popularity throughout the decade. Although in 1979 only 325,000 Americans had personal computers in their homes, by 1984 the number of owners had climbed to fifteen million.

The first home computers were used primarily for entertainment with such games as Space Invaders and Pac Man. Advances in microchip technology and the availability of affordable peripherals like modems and user friendly software led to growing awareness of the computer's usefulness, particularly to students. By 1985, students had become the largest users of personal computers.

While the price of both VCRs and personal computers has dropped over time, VCRs are usually more affordable for the average family, while personal computers, still relatively expensive, are often out of reach. However, most schools have computers so that students are exposed to them before entering into the business world where they are a staple.

Suggested Activities

Viewing Watch *The Desk Set*, a classic Hepburn-Tracy movie that comically demonstrates the advent of computers—at that time huge, monstrous things—in the business world.

Survey Have the students conduct surveys concerning the number of VCRs and personal computers in homes in their neighborhoods (or, perhaps, extended families). Graph the results.

Challenge Test the students' basic understanding of the operation of VCRs and personal computers. Conduct challenges where students test themselves against one another.

Technology Learn about the technological operations of the VCR and the personal computer.

Live Aid

In the early eighties, famine struck the nation of
Ethiopia, killing countless people through starvation
and malnutrition. People around the world gave their
sympathy, but not everyone rallied to help the
people's plight. One who did was Irish rock star Bob
Geldof. Geldof was perhaps most noted for his
performance in the rock film called *The Wall*, as
performed by the classic group Pink Floyd.

Geldof became aware of the famine through the news
media, just as most other people did. However, he
felt driven to make a difference.

Bob Geldorf

In 1984, Bob Geldof organized the recording of a
collaborative song for release during the Christmas
season. It was entitled "Do They Know It's
Christmas?" The song tells of the trouble in Africa,
asking the people of the world to look beyond their
own small spheres to see the starving people in
Ethiopia for whom Christmas and other joys would
mean nothing when compared to their life-threatening circumstances. Music superstars from several
nations joined together in collaboration on the record, and it became one of the most successful records
of the year.

However, this success was not enough for Geldof. He took the momentum of the song and organized
two of the largest rock concerts ever and called them *Live Aid*. On July 7, 1985, the two concerts were
broadcast around the world, and statistics show that one-third of the world's population watched the
concerts live. One concert took place in Philadelphia's JFK Stadium and the other in London's
Wembley Stadium. Performers for the concerts included such music stars as The Who, Madonna, Paul
McCartney, U2, Led Zeppelin, Bob Dylan, and Dire Straits. Throughout the shows, the performers
asked listeners to donate money for Ethiopian famine relief. In all, approximately $53 million was
raised.

Live Aid became a catalyst for other such efforts, including *Farm Aid* which continues to perform
annually to help American farmers keep their farms.

Suggested Activities

Listening Listen to a recording of "Do They Know It's Christmas?" Have the students listen
with their eyes closed. Afterwards, without talking, have them write their responses to the
song.

Making a Difference As a class, brainstorm for ways in which you might make a difference
in relieving world hunger. Together, choose one of your ideas to do. Be sure to follow
through with the idea to completion. It will benefit the students tremendously to see how they
can make a difference.

John Lennon

John Winston Lennon was born in October 9, 1940, in Liverpool, England. As a child Lennon preferred drawing and writing to studying. Because of his artistic talent, he was accepted as a student at the Liverpool Art College, where he pursued commercial art. At the age of sixteen he organized his first band, called the Quarrymen, to play popular music. Their music that was heavily influenced by early stars of rock and roll like Little Richard, Jerry Lee Lewis, and Chuck Berry. In 1957 Lennon met Paul McCartney, who soon joined the group. Later, George Harrison and Ringo Starr (Richard Starkey) joined the group, and the name was changed to the Beatles.

In 1960 Lennon dropped out of art school to devote time to his music He and Paul McCartney were the creative forces behind the singles such as "I Want to Hold Your Hand," "Please, Please Me," and "Love Me Do" that brought worldwide success and fame to the group. Over the years their music matured, and they developed rich instrumentations. Their lyrics often and social reflected the turbulence and social issues of the times. Such albums as *Sergeant Pepper's Lonely Hearts Club Band* and *Revolution* are considered classics in modern rock. No group in the history of popular music reached the phenomenal success and fan appeal that the Beatles did in the sixties. In 1965, Queen Elizabeth II made Lennon and the other Beatles Members of the Order of the British Empire (MBE), a prestigious honor.

In 1968 John Lennon divorced his wife, Cynthia Powell. The following year he married Yoko Ono, a Japanese artist he met at an art show in 1966. Ono introduced herself to him simply by handing him a card that read "Breath." After their marriage, Lennon changed his middle name from Winston to Ono.

The Beatles last live preformance was in 1969, and in 1970 the band disbanded over creative differences. Even before the breakup of the group, Lennon was performing both as a solo artist and with Ono. Over the next decade he continued to write and record his music, sometimes with a group called The Plastic Ono Band.

Lennon was a pacifist and a proponent of social causes. His songs "Give Peace a Chance" and "Imagine" became anthems of the movement calling for peace in the world during and after the Vietnam War. Lennon and Ono once staged a sit-in in the bed in their New York apartment, calling for peace while thousands outside their building gathered and sang "Give Peace a Chance."

While returning from a recording session with his wife on December 8, 1980, John Lennon was shot and killed by a twenty-five-year-old amateur guitarist named Mark David Chapman in front of the Dakota, the New York apartment complex where Lennon and Ono lived with their young son. Later that day, hundreds of fans gathered outside the apartment, singing "All You Need Is Love," another of Lennon's songs. Millions of people were shocked and grieved over the violent and untimely end of the musician who had spoken so eloquently for peace and love.

Sales of the *Double Fantasy* album by Lennon and Ono, released earlier in the year, skyrocketed after Lennon's death.

In the nineties, the three remaining Beatles did reunite to record new material, incorporating recordings Lennon had made prior to his death.

Suggested Activity

Listen and Write Play a few of Lennon's songs for the class, particularly his anthems of peace and love. Have the students write their own anthems.

Whitney Houston

The youngest of three children, Whitney Houston was born in Newark, New Jersey, on August 9, 1963. At the age of eleven, she gave her first musical performance in front of an audience. It seemed just moments from then that she was a superstar.

Born to John and Cissy Houston, Whitney learned early how to perform. She was born with an extraordinary voice, but her mother, a professional singer, taught her how to use it. She first performed for her church, the New Hope Baptist Church, where her mother was choir director. Houston began touring with her mother after that, performing backup vocals. While on stage, she drew the attention of talent scouts who began offering her concert bookings. She also received many modeling offers, and in her teens she appeared in a variety of magazines such as *Seventeen*, *Cosmopolitan*, and *Glamour*. Houston was appeared in small roles in some television situation comedies such as *Gimme a Break* and *Silver Spoons*.

In 1983, the president of Arista Records, Clive Davis, signed Houston to a recording contract. He was the man behind such talent as Barry Manilow, Billy Joel, and Janis Joplin, all extremely successful recording artists. Davis believed so deeply in Houston's talent that the contract he gave to her included a clause stating that if he ever left Arista Records, she could go with him.

Houston's first album was painstakingly planned out, and the top producers and writers in the business were selected. It was two years in the making, but when Whitney Houston debuted on February 14, 1985, it quickly became the number one album on the music charts, producing hit after hit. Followed in 1987 by *Whitney*, Houston's success grew in leaps and bounds. The second album debuted at number one, the first album by a female artist to do so. Her song "I Wanna Dance With Somebody" went to the top of eight different charts.

Houston's beauty served to improve her career, arriving as she did with the great new medium of the eighties, the music video. Her videos received almost constant airtime, as did her songs on the radio.

With each of the first two albums, Houston received the highest honors in the music field, Grammy awards and American Music Awards. She became known for her thanks to God during her acceptance speeches. Houston has always maintained that her talent is God-given, and her job is merely to use it.

Houston's success brought inevitable movie contracts and additional albums, each hugely successful. Throughout the eighties, she became one of the biggest superstars in the music industry, and her success continued unabated into the nineties.

Suggested Activities

Listen Listen to some of Houston's music. A good selection from her early years is called "Greatest Love," a song about believing in oneself. The video of the song includes Houston's mother, as well.

Family Houston came from a supportive, musical family. Both her mother and her cousin, Dionne Warwick, lead successful musical careers and helped her develop her own. Have the students write about a talent shared in their families and what sort of business their family might be able to do together if they chose.

Michael Jackson

Born to a musical family in Gary, Indiana, in 1958, Michael Joseph Jackson came to be arguably the biggest pop music star of all time. His music career began at the age of five when he and his four brothers started performing under their father's management as the Jackson Five. Jackson became the group's lead singer and dancer, delighting fans with his intricate footwork and mature vocals. In the 1970s, the Jackson Five became the main characters in a Saturday morning cartoon series for children. In 1976, they changed their name to the Jacksons. By the late seventies, Michael Jackson had left the group.

Michael Jackson recorded his first solo album in 1972, *Got to Be There*. He established himself as a solo artist in 1979 with *Off the Wall*, a highly successful album. But it was the release of *Thriller*, the largest selling album of all time, in 1982 that propelled him to superstardom and unparalleled success. The album sold about forty million copies internationally and produced a number of chart-topping single hits, including the title song, "Beat It," and "Billie Jean." The album also introduced a new type of music video, longer than the standard three-to four-minute version. Jackson's video for the title song was a minimovie thirteen minutes long. It included dialogue, prolonged dance segments, and special effects. Many other Jackson videos followed this lead, breaking new and innovative ground in the music video industry.

After *Thriller*, Jackson became a household name. Concerts around the world sold out instantly. People clambered to see the dancing and singing sensation, known for his amazing dance moves and his single, spangled glove. When he gave a rare performance during a televised tribute to Motown during the mid-eighties, millions of people tuned in just to see him. After the performance, dance legend Fred Astaire complimented Jackson on his exceptional dancing skills.

Jackson later said that Astaire's compliment was one of the most meaningful he had ever received, because dance had always been important to him. Jackson began developing his unique style at an early age by watching entertainers like James Brown and studying their movements. Although he found it frustrating when televised programs concentrated on singers' faces instead of feet, Jackson was able to mimic their styles and incorporate them into a style all his own.

Over the decade, the artist became known for other things as well, particularly the many plastic surgeries he underwent to alter and mold his features. Pictures of the man today are drastically different from the artist of the early eighties.

During the eighties, Jackson became the most popular and wealthiest entertainer in the world. In 1988, he published his autobiography, entitled *Moonwalk*. In 1994, he married the daughter of legendary rock musician, Elvis Presley. Lisa Marie Presley and Jackson soon divorced. Jackson's second wife, Debbie, a former nurse he had met during his surgical procedures, gave birth to his first child, a son, early in 1997.

Suggested Activities

When I Grow Up Michael Jackson was a performer almost from the time he was born. Have the students write about their dreams if they could do anything they wished to do.

Moonwalk Jackson became famous for a dance move called the Moonwalk. Learn to do the dance.

Maya Lin

The artist and architect Maya Lin was born in Athens, Ohio, on October 5, 1959. Her parents were immigrants from China who both served on the faculty of Ohio University. Lin spent a great deal of time there while she was growing up. She herself attended Yale University.

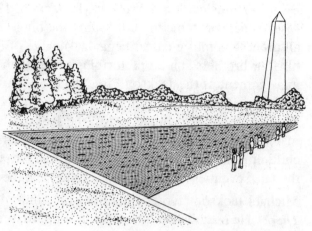

The Vietnam Veterans Memorial Fund, a nonprofit organization begun by a group of Vietnam veterans, wanted to build a memorial at the nation's capital to veterans of the Vietnam War. In the fall of 1980 they announced a competition to design the new memorial. They asked for entries that would pay tribute to the veterans in a meaningful way, and they wanted the names of all American Vietnam War soldiers who were killed or missing placed on the memorial in some way. All entries were to be sent on two-by-four foot (60 cm x 120 cm) panels. By the deadline on March 31, 1981, the organization had received a total of 1,421 entries.

When all of the entries were set up for display, they stretched for more than a mile (1.6 kilometers). The names on the entries were replaced with numbers, and the judging began. The judges were prominent architects and landscape designers, and they did their judging over the course of one week.

Entry number 1,026 was not done in the same style as most of the others. It was submitted by Maya Lin, who was a twenty-one year old undergraduate art student at the time. She had only recently decided to be an architect, and her work was somewhat smudged and lacked the professional quality of many of the others. However, the judges said that they were haunted by her design. The panel of judges narrowed the enormous field of entries to thirty-nine and then to eighteen finalists. Finally, in early May of 1981, a winner was chosen. It was entry number 1,026.

Maya Lin became an instant celebrity. Not only did she gain fame through the use of her design in an enduring national memorial, but she was paid $20,000 which she used to further her education. Lin's design was very simple. Two walls of black marble delved into the earth, meeting at their highest points. Together, they comprised two sides of a triangle. The walls descended into the earth rather than being placed above it. On the face of the walls were carved the nearly 58,000 names. Public opinion was very positive about her design at first, but as publicity spread, some began to protest. Several wanted a traditional looking memorial, such as a statue, while others were troubled that an individual of Asian descent had designed a memorial for a war fought in Southeast Asia. The memorial was placed in the Constitution Gardens of the Mall on Capitol Hill, between the Lincoln and Washington Memorials.

Today, Maya Lin's tribute to the Vietnam War veteran has become one of the most famous landmarks in the United States, usually referred to simply as The Wall. Lin herself went on to receive her master's degree in architecture from Yale University and an honorary doctor of fine arts degree from Yale as well. In 1988, she received the Presidential Design Award for her design of the Vietnam Veterans Memorial.

■ Suggested Activities ■

Memorials Learn about the other memorials in Washington, D.C., what they look like, how they came to be, and what they represent.

Architect Have each student choose a topic that he or she believes should be memorialized. Let each design a memorial in tribute.

Uncle Shelby

Not everyone knows his name, but many adults and children know his work. The man is Shel Silverstein, and he was one of the most successful writers of the eighties.

Shelby Silverstein was born in Chicago, Illinois, in 1932. In the 1950s, he served with the United States armed forces in Korea and Japan. In 1956, he became a writer and cartoonist for *Playboy* magazine. His first book, *Now Here's My Plan: A Book of Futilities*, was published in 1960. More books followed quickly: *Uncle Shelby's ABZ Book: A Primer for Tender Minds* in 1961, *A Playboy's Teevee Jeebies* in 1963, and *Uncle Shelby's Story of Lafcadio, the Lion Who Shot Back*, a book for children, in 1963. Huge success came with his 1964 publication, *The Giving Tree*, although it nearly was not published and started slowly when it was. Silverstein's publisher thought that it had limited appeal and was too sad for children and too simple for adults. Initial sales were mild, but once churches and other groups started sharing it for its allegoric message, the book caught on and began to skyrocket.

Many other books followed, including *Where the Sidewalk Ends* in 1974, *The Missing Piece* in 1976, and *A Light in the Attic* in 1981. Each of these books proved hugely successful with all audiences, both children and adults. *Where the Sidewalk Ends* sold a million hardback copies by 1980, 250,000 of them in that year alone. *A Light in the Attic*, published as a children's book, became a breakthrough publication when it reached the top of the adult nonfiction charts in 1981. In 1985, Silverstein's *Attic* had reached an extraordinary 112 weeks on the *New York Times* bestseller list.

Silverstein is also a playwright, composer and lyricist. His songs include "The Unicorn Song" and "The Boa Constrictor Song." They have been recorded by Johnny Cash, Dr. Hook, the Irish Rovers, and Jerry Lee Lewis. He received an Academy Award nomination for music he composed for the film *Postcards From the Edge*. Renowned actor Richard Dreyfuss starred in his one-act play, *The Lady and the Tiger*.

Although Silverstein once gave a number of interviews, over the past two decades he has withdrawn from public communications. He wishes to communicate through his writings. As Silverstein says, "I'll keep on communicating, but only my way."

Suggested Activities

Read Select a variety of poems from Silverstein's poetry collection or read one of his books for children to the class. Let the students talk about what they read and hear.

Writing Have the students write poems or stories in the style of Shel Silverstein.

Illustrating Silverstein developed his own style to illustrate his stories. Let the students select a Silverstein poem or humorous song to illustrate in their own styles.

Meryl Streep

One of the most celebrated actresses of the eighties was Meryl Streep. Her performances in movies beginning in the seventies brought her to the public's attention, and an Academy Award in 1979 brought even greater notoriety. Throughout the eighties, she was largely considered to be among the greatest living actresses.

Mary Louise Streep was born in Summit, New Jersey, in 1949. She began voice lessons when she was twelve, which led to starrring roles in several high school musicals. Streep became a student of acting at Vassar College where she received her bachelor's degree and continued her studies as part of the Vermont Repertory Company. Later she received her master of fine arts as the Yale School of Drama, and she received an honorary degree from Dartmouth in 1981. Streep made her stage debut in New York City in 1975 with the New York Shakespeare Festival. She won critical acclaim for her performances in a variety of key roles, including *The Taming of the Shrew*. Streep's movie debut in *Julia* in 1977 drew the attention of critics and audiences alike. Her first major role was in *The Deer Hunter* in 1978, and she was nominated for an Acadmey Award. She won an Emmy Award in 1978 for her role in television's *Holocaust*. This was followed by *Manhattan*, *The Seduction of Joe Tynan*, and *Kramer vs. Kramer* in 1979. Her role in *Kramer* earned her the 1979 Academy Award for Best Supporting Actress. In 1982, she won an Academy Award as Best Actress for her memorable performance in *Sophie's Choice*.

In *Sophie's Choice*, Streep demonstrated her ability to imitate believably a wide range of dialects and accents. In the film she spoke both English with a Polish accent and Polish. She has managed Italian, American midwestern, and other accents, all with seeming ease. The actress is also noted for the variety of characters she can play. There is no one "Meryl Streep" type character. She plays them all.

Throughout the years, Streep has been nominated for and won a variety of acting awards, including the Emmy, Oscar, Golden Globe, National Society of Film Critics award, Los Angeles Film Critics award, New York Film Critics award, Obie award, and Cannes Film Festival award. Her honors and acclaim thus far indicate that she will be remembered as one of the best actresses ever known on stage and screen.

Suggested Activities

Listen and Record Play a recording of Streep's 1985 narration of *The Velveteen Rabbit*. Allow the students to make recordings of their favorite children's books, using Streep's model as an example.

Acting Let the students work in groups to prepare one-act skits for the class. The class can vote on the skit they think was best presented.

Barbara Walters

Barbara Walters was a broadcast journalist long before the eighties, and by 1976, she was the first female co-anchor on a television news show and the highest paid reporter in the world with a million-dollar-a-year salary. Her renowned interview specials also began in 1976, so her name and face were well established by 1980. That is exactly why she is included here: Barbara Walters was a staple of television throughout the decade.

Born Barbara Jill Walters in 1929, she moved up the ladder of broadcast journalism like no woman had before her. For her, pursuit of her career was relentless. She covered Kennedy's assassination and funeral, Fidel Castro considered her his favorite journalist, Ted Kennedy granted her an exclusive interview after the tragedy at Chappaquiddick, and Middle Eastern leaders Anwar el-Sadat and Menachem Begin provided her with an unheard of joint interview.

Walters spent years working her way through the rank and file of network journalism. In the sixties she was asked to host *Today* on NBC. It was a golden opportunity, and she held the position for fifteen years. She then became the first woman to co-anchor a nightly news show, also on NBC. In 1976 she moved to ABC, joining Harry Reasoner as co-anchor of the network's nightly news. Reasoner, however, did not want to share his anchor spot with Walters. She moved to another ABC show, *20/20*, a weekly news magazine, which she has co-anchored with Hugh Downs for more than two decades.

For all of her work and accomplishments, Barbara Walters is probably best known for her series featuring interviews with famous and infamous people. The programs began in the late seventies and are aired as specials by the network. On each, she interviews three famous people, usually from the fields of politics, entertainment, or sports. Some of her interviews have become classic in terms of television history. People still jokingly ask Walter's famous question first asked of actress Katherine Hepburn: "If you were a tree, what kind would you be?" (Hepburn answered "An oak.")

Although it seems that Walter's professional star was always on the rise, her personal life was often troubled, sad, and lonely. She experienced a sad, although pampered, childhood, marred by the death in her family of an older brother and her parents' great sadness over the retardation in her older sister. Walters herself said that she had trouble accepting and coping with her sister's handicap. The losses from Walter's childhood crept over into her adulthood. She divorced three times and experienced prolonged estrangements and conflict with her only child, a daughter.

Suggested Activities

Interview View a variety of Walter's interviews if you have access to them. Let the class study the way she conducts her interviews. Have them discuss what they see and then assign the students to conduct their own interviews of one another. Have them carefully plan their questions and practice their techniques. If successful, it would be worthwhile to let them interview individuals brought into the classroom, for example local workers and career people.

Video As a class, write a news program and videotape it like a nightly news show. If desired, small groups of students can prepare individual broadcasts.

Terrorism

It seemed throughout the 1980s that acts of terrorism around the world were an almost constant occurrence. Travelers and citizens around the globe reacted in fear and trepidation. Here are a few of the significant terrorist situations.

TWA Flight 847 On June 14, 1985, *TWA Flight 847*, bound for Rome, Italy, from Athens, Greece, was hijacked just after takeoff by two armed men. There were 153 passengers on board. The gunmen, members of the Islamic Jihad (holy war) forced the plane to fly to Beirut, Lebanon, and to land there. In Beirut, the hijackers demanded that Israel release 766 prisoners, primarily Shiite Muslims. Members of the Shiite militia joined the hijackers on the plane, and together they had the plane fly back and forth between Beirut and Algiers four times. Between each flight, some hostages were freed and one, an American, was killed. The remaining thirty-nine American male passengers were held captive in Beirut. At first, the United States and Israel held strong against the terrorist tactics, but on June 24, Israel released 31 prisoners, although they said that the release was unconnected with the hostage situation. On June 30, the remaining hostages were freed.

Achille Lauro On October 7, 1985, an Italian cruise ship called the *Achille Lauro* sailed off the coast of Egypt. Four gunmen seized the ship which held 400 passengers. The men were members of the Palestine Liberation Front (PLF), a guerilla faction of the Palestine Liberation Organization (PLO). They threatened to blow up the ship unless Israel agreed to release fifty PLO prisoners. To demonstrate that they meant what they said, the terrorists killed one passenger, Leon Klinghoffer, a 69-year-old Jewish American man who was confined to a wheelchair. His body was thrown overboard. On October 9, Egypt's president Hosti Mubarak and PLF leader Mohammed Abbas persuaded the terrorists to give up. The United States demanded that they be charged and punished. Instead, Mubarak released the terrorists to Abbas, and the group boarded a commercial Egyptian flight bound for Tunisia. On the next day, U.S. jets intercepted the Egyptian plane and forced it to land in Sicily, where the terrorists were turned over to the Italian government.

Pan Am Flight 103 On December 21, 1988, *Pan Am Flight 103* exploded in midair over Lockerbie, Scotland. All 259 passengers and crew members were killed. Eleven people on the ground were also killed, and two rows of houses were destroyed. Investigators looked for a cause for the crash of the plane, which simply disappeared from radar screens while flying from London to New York. British investigators discovered that the plane had been blown apart by a bomb hidden in a suitcase stored in the luggage compartment of the plane. Terrorists had planted the bomb, and evidence eventually led to two Libyans. However, they were protected by their government, which would not release them for trial.

Suggested Activities

Research Find out more about the Islamic Jihad and PLO. Learn why terrorist actions are sometimes a part of their activities.

History Learn about the role of terrorism throughout history, from ancient times to the present.

Indira Gandhi

Indira Gandhi was the first female prime minister in India, elected in 1966. Born to an influential family in Allahabad, India, she held the office of prime minister from 1966 to 1977 and again from 1980 until her assassination in 1984.

Born November 19, 1917, Indira Priyadarshini Nehru was the daughter and only child of Jawaharlal Nehru. From childhood the country's politics played a great part in her life. Her grandfather was a leader in India's fight for independence from Britain, and her father was India's first prime minister from 1947 to 1964. She graduated from Visva-Bharati University in Bengal and studied at Oxford University in England. In 1942 she married a lawyer, Feroze Gandhi (no relation to the Indian freedom leader, Mohandas Gandhi). Shortly after their marriage, the couple spent thirteen months in prison for their part in India's Independence Party, which sought freedom from Britain. Feroze Gandhi died in 1960.

When India became independent and Gandhi's father took office as prime minister, she served as his official hostess and as one of his advisors. She also accompanied him on trips. In 1955 Gandhi was elected to the executive body of the Indian National Congress party and in 1959 became its president.

After her father's death in 1964, Gandhi became India's minister of information and broadcasting under prime minister Lal Bahadur Shastri. When Shastri died in 1966, Indira Gandhi succeeded him. The following year she was elected to the office of prime minister by the Congress party. In 1971 she led her party to a landslide victory.

In June of 1975, a court found Gandhi guilty of illegal campaign practices during the 1971 election. Many called for her resignation. Gandhi responded by declaring a state of emergency two weeks after the ruling, arresting many of her opponents and censoring the press. In 1977 she called for a new election, which she hoped would demonstrate popular support for her regime. The Congress party suffered a sweeping defeat, and she was voted out of office. However, she made a comeback in the elections held in January of 1980 and formed a new majority government.

In 1984 Gandhi moved to suppress Sikh insurgents. The capture of the Golden Temple in Amritsar, the headquarters of the Sikh religious faction, outraged many of the groups, members. October 31, 1984, two Sikh members of her security guard shot her at very close range, killing her.

Suggested Activities

Assassination Many world leaders of the twentieth century were assassinated. Learn who they were and why they were assassinated. Also find out about failed assassination attempts.

Politics Politics in India in the twentieth century have changed dramatically, largely due to the freedom the nation gained from Britain in the 1940s. Find out about India's political history over the last century.

Mikhail Gorbachev

Mikhail Sergei Gorbachev was born in Privolnoye, Russia, on March 2, 1931, to peasant farmers. In 1952, while attending the university in Moscow, he joined the Communist Party. After receiving a law degree in 1955, Gorbachev pursued a career with the Communist Party. He worked his way up, becoming the head of the regional Communist Party Committee in 1970. He went to Moscow in 1978, and finally, in 1980, he became a full member of the Communist Party's chief policymaking division, called the *Politburo*.

At this time, the general secretary of the Communist Party was the ranking Soviet leader and the most powerful political figure. When Yuri Andropov became secretary general in 1982, he placed Gorbachev at the helm of the nation's economic policy. Andropov died in 1984 and was replaced by Konstantin U. Chernenko. When Chernenko died in 1985, Gorbachev became the general secretary (head) of the Communist Party. In 1988 he assumed the title of chairman of the Presidium of the Supreme Soviet, or president of the U.S.S.R., a post that was largely ceremonial but which under his leadership gained in significance.

The youngest Soviet leader since Stalin, Gorbachev differed from previous Soviet leaders in other ways as well. Most Soviet leaders had not been college educated, and unlike his predecessors, who usually stayed within Soviet borders, he traveled the world.

Gorbachev is best remembered for the work he did from 1985 through 1991 as the last leader of the Soviet Union. He initiated *perestroika* (reform), a program of economic and political reform, and encouraged *glasnost* (openness) in political and cultural affairs. In 1990, Gorbachev won the Nobel peace prize for his painstaking work toward world peace and the strides he made in Soviet relations with nations around the world.

Many other nations looked on with approval at the changes Gorbachev brought to the Soviet Union, but those changes were instrumental in bringing the end of the U.S.S.R. in 1991. (See page 486.)

Gorbachev worked diligently to keep the Soviet Union together while bringing about his reforms. In 1991 he resigned as Communist party general secretary, appointed reformers to head the military and KGB, and permitted Estonia, Latvia, and Lithuania to become independent republics. On December 8, 1991, the U.S.S.R. voted itself out of existence, and on December 25 of the same year, Gorbachev resigned as president.

Gorbachev continued to work in politics after his resignation, primarily with the Foundation for Social, Economic, and Political Research, sometimes called the Gorbachev Foundation, in Moscow.

Suggested Activities

Communism Research to find out what communism is, how it started, and where it exists in the world today.

History Learn about the formation of the Soviet Union as well as its destruction. Also learn about the significant players in the beginning and in the end.

Tiananmen Square Massacre

Following the death of former Communist Party Secretary General of China Hu Yaobang in April of 1989, students began peaceful memorial demonstrations in several cities. They considered Hu a hero because he had favored liberalization and modernization. Prodemocracy demonstrations continued and grew as participants ignored the government's demand that they end their actions.

In May of 1989, Soviet president Mikhail Gorbachev traveled to China to discuss improving relations between the Soviets and China. Approximately two million people, primarily Chinese students, gathered in the streets to support Gorbachev and his policy of *glasnost* (openness) in the Soviet Union. Several thousand more students gathered in Tiananmen Square in Beijing, staging a hunger strike to protest their government and as a call for democracy. The Chinese government, embarrassed by the actions of the young people, kept Gorbachev away from the square.

Martial law was declared on May 20; however, other protestors around the nation began to rally as well. Chinese troops were sent to stop the protestors, but the people blocked their passage. Some even lay down in the streets. In the end, however, the protestors proved no match for the government troops. At first many protestors were arrested, including some who built a model of America's Statue of Liberty in the capital city's square. Then the troops moved to stop the protests completely. Tanks began to roll, driving over everyone and everything that stood in their way. Thousands of guns were fired, and many people were killed in one of the most brutal massacres in history. It was reported by the protest leaders that approximately two to five thousand people were killed by the troops, although the exact number may never be known. International television cameras and journalists captured much of the violence. Later, the government banned the foreign press and conducted widespread arrests, summary trials, and executions. The government refused to make public the names of those who died.

Deng Xiaoping called the protesters thugs and hoodlums. He went on Chinese television to declare that their insurgency against the government had been squelched and that their threat to the national welfare was ended.

Many nations protested the actions of the government. Chinese relations with some Western nations, including the United States, took a turn for the worse. Making matters worse, the Chinese government officially stated that the massacre at Tiananmen Square had never happened. Even in the face of witnesses and cameras, they declared this to be true. The government had tried to rewrite history; however, modern communication made this impossible.

Suggested Activities

Politics Learn about the politics of China today as well as feelings of any dissenting groups.

Protests In the United States in the sixties and seventies, a number of student groups held protests for a variety of reasons. They met with different kinds of opposition and different results. Learn about some of them and the effects of their protests.

Cartography Draw maps of modern China, including its capital city of Beijing.

Polish Solidarity

Government in Poland changed dramatically in the 1980s. That was due in large part to a group called Solidarity and to a man named Lech Walesa.

Walesa was a shipyard worker in Poland in 1980. At that time, workers decided to strike to protest poor working conditions and low wages. Workers first staged a strike at a shipyard in Gdansk. The strike spread and soon workers from other yards and factories were striking. In all, half a million workers took part in the strikes. The striking workers called for the release of political prisoners, improved labor laws, and the right to free speech. They continued their strike for two months, and it finally proved successful. Lech Walesa emerged as the leader of the strikes and of Solidarity.

Lech Walesa

The government gave in to the striking workers and allowed them to form a trade union. This was the first time that a communist nation supported the development of a union.

Workers in various places around Poland continued to hold strikes and to make other demands, When the government changed hands in 1981, the new leader, General Wojciech Jaruzelski, wanted to put an end to the workers' protests. Jaruzelski increased the military's power, banned public meetings and demonstrations, and outlawed Solidarity. Lech Walesa and other workers were arrested.

On May 1, 1982, Labor Day in many nations around the world, thousands of workers marched through Warsaw, protesting the government's military rule and calling for the support of Solidarity. Their protests served to heighten government control. The Polish government cancelled major sporting events and banned the use of private automobiles.

The actions of Jaruzelski had international effects. Some nations such as the Soviet Union supported him; others like the United States spoke out in protest. President Ronald Reagan revoked the "most-favored nation" status that Poland enjoyed with the United States. This status had kept export charges from Poland to the United States at a low. The revocation hurt Poland economically.

Once again, the government was forced to relent. Walesa and others were released from prison, and in 1983, Walesa received the Nobel peace prize for his efforts to bring reform and peace to Poland.

Tensions and protests continued throughout the following years. In 1988, strikes became rampant throughout Poland. The government was forced to meet with Solidarity leaders, including Walesa, to discuss negotiations. In 1989, the government officially recognized Solidarity as a legal union. The union then became a political party, and many of its leaders were elected to the Polish National Assembly. Lech Walesa himself was elected as president in 1990. Solidarity had succeeded in overthrowing the communist government.

Suggested Activities

Politics Learn about the politics and government of Poland today as well as prior to the communist takeover.

Cartography Draw maps of Poland, including the capital of Warsaw.

Charles and Diana

The royal romance that opened the decade grew to be a royal failure by the next, but in the beginning there was pageantry and fairy tale dreams come true.

The story began with His Royal Highness The Prince Charles Philip Arthur George, Prince of Wales, Duke of Cornwall, Earl of Chester, Duke of Rothesay, Earl of Carrick, Baron Renfrew, Lord of the Isles, Prince and Great Steward of Scotland— also known as Prince Charles. He asked Lady Diana Spencer, a British aristocrat, to be his bride. In all likelihood, she would one day become the queen of England just as Charles, as heir apparent, would be king. Nineteen-year-old Lady Diana accepted the proposal. In the following months, the media began to follow Lady Diana wherever she went. Soon, her popularity eclipsed that of the prince. Reporters found out everything about her life and history, and she was followed everywhere. Not only was she of interest as the future princess and, perhaps, queen, but she was beautiful, charming, and engagingly shy with the camera. The public adored her.

On July 29, 1981, the couple were married. It is estimated that 700 million people around the world watched the ceremony which was aired on international television. During it, they saw pomp and pageantry for which England is legendary. It seemed truly the stuff of which fairy tales are made.

The couple quickly had two children, Prince William Arthur Philip Louis (next in line to his father for the throne) in 1982 and Prince Henry Charles Albert David in 1984. However, as time wore on, the media began to report that the couple's marriage was strained. News of their troubles and tensions began to appear in the papers almost daily. Although the palace denied the reports or refused to comment, the media coverage continued. Finally, amid great controversy, the couple separated in December of 1992 and later divorced. The controversy and scandal caused by the failed marriage, as well as reasons for the failure, have caused a great deal of discussion concerning the future of the British monarchy. When Charles and Diana were married, it was widely rumored that Charles' mother, Queen Elizabeth, would abdicate the throne and allow her son to become king. However, a decade later, many began to suspect that Charles never would be king. The divorce settlement itself guaranteed that Diana never would be queen.

Suggested Activities

Monarchy Trace the line of the British monarchy, learning about some of the prominent and influential British monarchs over time. Also learn about the other existing monarchies of the world.

Fairy Tales Another great romance in the twentieth century history of the British monarchy is the story of King Edward and Wallis Simpson. Learn about the couple and what happened to them. (See page 204.)

Today Find out about Charles and Diana today as well as the state of the monarchy.

Pope John Paul II

Pope John Paul II, leader of the Roman Catholic Church, became one of the most influential leaders of the 1980s. He was also brought into the forefront due to a nearly successful assassination attempt on his life.

He was born Karol Jozef Wojtyla Wadowice, Poland, in 1920. During World War II he worked in a stone quarry and a chemical factory while preparing for the priesthood at an underground seminary. After he was ordained a priest in 1946, he taught philosophy and ethics while serving as a chaplain for university students. He was appointed auxiliary bishop of Krakow in 1958, archbishop of Krakow in 1964, and he became a cardinal in 1967. In 1978 he was elected pope, the first non-Italian pope since Adrian VI of Holland in 1523.

In May of 1981, a Turkish terrorist named Mehmet Ali Agca shot Pope John Paul II as he entered Saint Peter's Square. The pope was severely wounded but recovered fully. He earned the admiration of many around the world when he went to his imprisoned attacker and forgave him for his actions. A second attempt was made on the pope's life during a 1982 visit to Portugal, but he was not injured. Since then the pope has taken great care in his audiences. Normally he goes among the crowd in an especially designed vehicle with a large dome of bulletproof glass, affectionately called "the pope-mobile."

John Paul has published poetry and, under the name Andrzej Jawien, a play called *The Jeweler's Apprentice*. In addition, he has written several books on ethics and theology. Since becoming pope, he has published more than twelve encyclicals (letters) which address a variety of moral and theological issues.

John Paul's views are not always greeted supportively. He tends to be conservative, sticking closely to traditional church views. At the same time, many in the Catholic church differ with him on various topics, particularly the right of priests to marry and the right of women to become priests. John Paul adamantly opposes both. Yet, he is a great proponent for world peace and international relations. His avowed goal is the unification of people. Many believe that due to his engaging and charismatic personality, he will go a long way in achieving his goal.

Throughout the eighties and nineties, John Paul traveled to Asia, Africa, and the Americas, visiting more than sixty nations and working to unite people around the world. He is credited with influencing the restoration of democracy and religious freedom in the countries of Eastern Europe, especially in Poland, his native land. In the nineties he visited the Baltic republics, formerly members of the USSR. His meetings with world leaders from many nations were generally well received and successful.

Suggested Activities

Discussion Ask the students to discuss ways in which the people of the world might be brought closer together.

History Learn about the history of the Roman Catholic Church as well as of the papacy.

The Iron Lady

Great Britain's government had a woman at the helm throughout the entire decade of the 1980s. Her name was Margaret Thatcher, but her country knew her as the Iron Lady.

Margaret Hilda Roberts was born in Grantham, Lincolnshire, England, in 1925. She attended Oxford University where she earned a degree in chemistry. In 1951 she married a businessman named Denis Thatcher, who was supportive of her education and political ambitions. She became a tax attorney in 1953.

Thatcher's political career began in 1959 when she was elected to Britain's House of Commons as a member of the Conservative Party. From 1970 to 1974, she served as secretary of state for education and science. The Conservative Party was defeated by the Labor Party in 1974. In 1975, Thatcher was elected to lead the Conservative Party, the first woman ever to hold that position.

In the last half of the seventies, times became difficult in Great Britain. The economy declined and there were numerous labor disputes. A labor strike kept oil from being delivered to homes, schools, and businesses during an especially cold winter. Thatcher attacked the Labor Party government and called on citizens to enter a vote of no confidence. In the election of 1979 they did so, electing Thatcher and her party. Margaret Thatcher became the first female prime minister of Great Britain.

Thatcher was a hard-line politician who stuck fiercely to her principles and beliefs. This is why she became known as the Iron Lady. She advocated a free-enterprise economy, tight monetary policies to control inflation, lower taxes, lower government spending, privatization of nationalized industries (including health care, public housing, and schools), and restrictions on trade unions. Her policies, especially her emphasis on private enterprise, became known as "Thatcherism."

In 1982, Argentine forces occupied the Falkland Islands, which both Great Britain and Argentina claimed. Thatcher and her government sent a task force that defeated the Argentines. The success of the Falkland Islands policy aided in Thatcher's reelection in 1983.

In the years that followed, she met frequently with U.S. presidents Ronald Reagan and George Bush, strengthening Britain's Western alliance. She also called on Mikhail Gorbachev and established a working relationship. Thatcher was recognized as a world leader.

She was elected for a third term in 1987, the first British prime minister to win three consecutive elections in more than 150 years. Support for Thatcher diminished toward the close of the decade. By 1990, she had lost the support of the Conservative Party, so she resigned as her party's leader and as prime minister. However, she remained as a member of the Parliament until 1992, and she became a member of the House of Lords.

Suggested Activities

Cartography Draw maps of Great Britain.

History Learn about the political structure of Great Britain over time. What role does the monarchy play? How are Britain's leaders selected? Answer these as well as other pertinent questions.

Definition Margaret Thatcher was an ardent Conservative. Have the class define conservative and determine what it means politically.

Anwar el-Sadat

In 1918, Anwar el-Sadat was born in Egypt near the Nile River Delta. After his graduation from the Egyptian Military Academy in 1938, he joined with Gamal Abdel Nasser and other militants to overthrow British rule in Egypt. He served time in prison for his revolutionary activities, but in 1952 he and the others were successful in overthrowing King Faruk. Sadat quickly rose through the ranks of Egypt's government after that, serving as vice president from 1954 to 1967 and again from 1969 to 1970 under the presidency of Nasser.

When Nasser died, Sadat became president and remained the leader until his death. Sadat continued the work of Nasser, calling for the return of the Sinai Peninsula and Gaza Strip from Israelis, who had held the land since 1967. Disputes over Gaza and conflict between the two nations date to ancient times.

Sadat became world renowned for his peacemaking efforts with Israel. In 1977 Sadat met with Israel's leader, Menachem Begin, and offered recognition of Israel on certain conditions. In 1978 American President Jimmy Carter arranged meetings with the two leaders at Camp David to end the Arab-Israeli conflict. They reached an agreement that included a peace treaty between the two nations and the withdrawal of Israel from the Sinai. It also called for self-government for the Gaza Strip. The treaty was officially signed in 1979, and Israel completely left the Sinai in 1982. Sadat and Begin shared the Nobel peace prize in 1978 for their work.

Although nations around the world applauded the work of Sadat, many in his own country were angry. Other Arab leaders felt that he had acted independently, and they were unhappy with his work. On October 6, 1981, Anwar el-Sadat was assassinated in the city of Cairo by a group of religious militants from his own country. Their reason for the assassination was opposition to Sadat's policies.

Suggested Activities

Leaders Learn about Menachem Begin and his contributions to Israel. Also learn about Jimmy Carter's role in the negotiations and what his motives were.

Cartography Draw maps of Egypt and Israel, pinpointing the sources of conflict between the two nations in the late seventies.

Today Research to find out about the relationship between Egypt and Israel today. What strides have been taken, both forward and backward?

Middle East Throughout the eighties, there was a great deal of conflict in many areas of the Middle East. Other topics and places to research and to learn about include Iraq and Iran, the *USS Stark*, Lebanese Civil War, Shiites, and the Palestine Liberation Organization (PLO).

Marathon of Hope

Cancer is a disease that causes aberrations in normal body cells and tumorous growths. One young Canadian, Terry Fox, fought valiantly in 1980 to end the suffering caused by cancer.

Terrence Stanley Fox was born in Winnipeg, Manitoba, Canada, in 1958 and grew up in British Columbia. In 1977, while still a teenager, Fox was diagnosed with bone cancer. Due to this illness, his doctors thought it best to amputate his right leg above the knee. From that time forward, Fox used an artificial leg, learning to walk and even to run.

While receiving treatment for cancer, Fox developed empathy for the suffering he saw around him in the hospitals and treatment centers. He knew firsthand that cancer was a painful disease. He felt inspired to make a difference, so he began to run.

Fox trained for more than a year, conditioning himself as a marathon runner. Then, in April 1980, at St. John's, Newfoundland, Fox began what he called the Marathon of Hope. In this marathon, Fox intended to run across the entire width of Canada, raising money for cancer research while he ran. He called his run a marathon because he intended to run a marathon length, 26 miles (42 kilometers), each day.

In all, Fox ran for a total of 143 days, each day averaging his desired distance. He ran through all sorts of weather conditions, including hail, snow, and grueling heat. His total distance was 3,339 miles (5,374 kilometers); however, this distance was short of his desired goal. On September 1, 1980, Fox was forced to stop near Thunder Bay, Ontario. His cancer had spread to his lungs. He was hospitalized for treatment and died ten months later without returning to his marathon. However, during the time he did run, he earned twenty-five million dollars for cancer research.

Before his death, Fox was awarded Canada's highest honor for civilians, the Order of Canada. Since the time of his death, marathons have been run annually in Fox's memory. These annual runs also raise money for cancer research.

In 1985, another cancer amputee, Steve Fonyo, ran the entire distance that Terry Fox had intended to run. Nineteen-year-old Fonyo ran a total of 4,924 miles (7,920 kilometers) across the nation of Canada. The run took him a total of fourteen months.

Suggested Activities

Research Find out about the disease of cancer and the advances that have been made in its treatment since 1980.

Special Athletes There are a number of athletes who play and compete with physical and mental challenges. Learn about one or some of these athletes and the odds they overcame to play their sport.

Marathons The marathon originated in ancient Greece. Learn about its history.

Cartography Draw a map of Canada, marking the distance across the nation at quarterly intervals. Draw a line showing Terry Fox's path from Newfoundland to Thunder Bay, Ontario.

Corazón Aquino

From 1965 until 1986, the Philippines were led by President Ferdinand Marcos. A World War II hero, Marcos was a popular leader until he established martial law in the early seventies and gave himself even more power. Under his leadership, the country grew increasingly impoverished. In 1981 Marcos lifted martial law and returned law-making rights to the National Assembly. He even released some political prisoners. The president was elected for another six years.

At this time, another leader, Benigno Aquino, was gaining in popularity. Aquino was a leading member of the opposition party when martial law was declared in 1972. He was imprisoned from 1972 until 1980, when he was allowed to move his family to the United States. In August of 1983 he returned to the Philippines to work in the legislative election. In spite of high security, he was killed by an unknown gunman when he disembarked from his plane in Manila.

Marcos denied having anything to do with the assassination, and the gunman could not be linked to any political faction. However, the people did not believe Marcos, and many began to riot and protest. They called for Marcos' resignation.

Corazón Aquino returned to the Philippines for her husband's funeral and stayed to work in the legislative election campaign. The opposition party won one third of the seats in 1984. When Marcos called for a presidential election in 1986, Corazón Aquino became the opposition candidate. The people rallied behind her. Marcos declared himself the winner of the February 7 election and staged his inauguration on February 25. Popular demonstrations and an army revolt led to the inauguration of Aquino on the same day. Faced with charges of murder and election fraud, Marcos and his wife fled the country by helicopter, seeking asylum in the United States. Aquino formed a provisional government, and many nations around the world recognized her as the new leader. She was the first female leader of the Philippine nation.

The situation in the Philippines did not improve dramatically with the removal of Marcos, but the people did rally behind Aquino. She implemented a new constitution and held a legislative election in 1987. Poverty and a poor economy were still of great concern. Communist insurgents carried on with political assassinations and guerilla activity. In 1989 rebels in the Philippine military attempted to take over the government. However, The United States, under the leadership of President George Bush, stepped in to aid Aquino and the Philippine government. The rebels were quickly overthrown.

By the close of the decade, Aquino was still in power, but her troubles were not over. Turmoil in the Philippines continued, although many believed that the government under her leadership was far superior to that of the previous two decades. Slowly, the economy did begin to grow, but Aquino chose to leave office in 1992, declining to run for another term.

Suggested Activities

Women Aquino is one of several women who came to or experienced political prominence throughout the world in the eighties. Find out about another such woman and write her story.

Cartography Draw a map of the Philippines.

Colors Aquino consistently wore yellow throughout the election and the beginning of her presidency. Find out the reason for her color choice.

Passages

Births

1980

- Chelsea Clinton, only child of American President Bill Clinton
- MaCauley Culkin, American actor

1981

- Jonathan Taylor Thomas, American actor

1982

- Prince William Arthur Philip Louis, heir apparent to the British throne
- Dominique Moceanu, U.S. Olympic gymnast
- LeAnn Rimes, American country music singer

1984

- "Baby Fae," infant born with defective heart; receives transplant of heart from baboon

- Henry Charles Albert David, British prince
- Jeffrey Maier, boy who caught fly ball in 1996 World Series, earning home run for the Yankees

1985

- Alexandra Nechita, professional artist (sold $2 million by age eleven)

1987

- South African triplets, carried and delivered by their mother's mother
- Yugoslavian boy, the five billionth inhabitant of the world (according to the U.N. Secretary General)

1989

- Jessica Dubroff, died in 1996 while attempting to be the youngest pilot ever to cross the U.S.

Deaths

1980

- Mae West, American actress
- Jean-Paul Sartre, French philosopher and author
- Henry Miller, American author
- Marshall McLuhan, Canadian media author
- Tex Avery, American film animator
- Jimmy Durante, American comedian
- Sir Alfred Hitchcock, English-born, American movie director
- John Lennon, English musician
- Jean Piaget, Swiss psychologist
- Colonel Harland Sanders, American restaurateur
- Jesse Owens, American athlete

1981

- Christy Brown, Irish novelist and artist
- Hoagy Carmichael, American songwriter
- Bill Haley, American rock star
- Joe Louis, American boxing champion
- Anwar el-Sadat, Egyptian president
- Natalie Wood, American actress
- Bob Marley, Jamaican musician

1982

- John Cheever, American writer
- Ayn Rand, American novelist
- Satchel Paige, American baseball player
- Menachem Begin, Israel's prime minister
- Henry Fonda and John Belushi, American actors
- Grace Kelly, princess of Monaco and former American actress

1983

- Benigno Aquino, Philippine presidential hopeful
- Umberto, last King of Italy
- Tennessee Williams, American playwright
- Buckminster Fuller, American philosopher and architect
- Karen Carpenter, American singer
- Ira Gershwin, American lyricist
- Muddy Waters, American blues musician

1984

- Truman Capote, American writer
- Ansel Adams, American photographer
- Marvin Gaye, American singer
- Ethel Merman, American singer
- Ray Kroc, founder of McDonald's

1985

- Orson Welles, American filmmaker
- Laura Ashley, English designer
- Yul Brynner, American actor
- Marc Chagall, French artist
- Rock Hudson, American actor
- Dian Fossey, American zoologist
- Ricky Nelson, American singer

1986

- Olaf Palme, Swedish prime minister
- James Cagney and Cary Grant, American actors
- Georgia O'Keefe, American artist
- Benny Goodman, American bandleader

1987

- Andy Warhol, American artist
- James Baldwin, American novelist
- Fred Astaire and Danny Kaye, American actors and dancers
- Jackie Gleason, American comedian and actor
- Maria von Trapp, Austrian singer and author
- Andres Segovia, Spanish classical guitarist

1988

- Sean MacBride, Irish politician and Nobel peace prize winner
- Robert Heinlein, American writer of science fiction
- Roy Orbison, American singer

1989

- Hirohito, Emperor of Japan
- Samuel Beckett, Irish playwright
- Sir Laurence Olivier, English actor
- Lucille Ball and Bette Davis, American actresses
- Salvador Dali, Spanish artist
- Irving Berlin, American songwriter
- Sugar Ray Robinson, American boxer
- Nicolae Ceausescu, Romania's president

Famous Firsts

In the 1980s, the United States saw the first

. . . live debates in the Senate broadcast over television.

. . . IBM personal computer.

. . . compact disc.

. . . woman graduate from West Point Academy.

. . . woman (Mary Decker) to run the mile in less than 4.5 minutes.

. . . "mouse" and "pulldown menu" for personal computers.

. . . solar-cell power plant.

. . . long-distance solar-powered airplane flight.

. . . solar-powered flight across the English Channel.

. . . nonstop flight around the world with no refueling.

. . . genetically engineered commercial product (insulin produced by bacteria).

. . . space shuttle flight.

. . . permanent artificial heart to be placed in a human patient.

. . . spacecraft to leave the solar system.

. . . artificially created chromosome.

. . . genes from an ancient species to be cloned.

. . . astronauts to fly in space without being tethered to a spaceship.

. . . photos of a planetary system around another "sun," Beta Pictoris.

. . . vaccine for humans made by genetic engineering.

. . . billionaire of the microcomputer industry (Bill Gates).

. . . scientifically produced vertebrate (a mouse) to receive a patent.

. . . B-2 "Stealth" bomber.

. . . DNA tests used as evidence in some criminal cases.

. . . lasers used to clear blocked arteries.

. . . holographic image on a credit card.

. . . blue corn chips.

. . . woman Supreme Court associate justice.

. . . American woman in space.

. . . black astronaut in space.

. . . private citizen in space.

. . . director of national drug control policy (William J. Bennett).

. . . movie to earn more than $700 million (*E.T.—The Extra-Terrestrial*).

. . . broadcast of MTV.

. . . inline skates.

Buzzwords

New inventions, habits, lifestyles, and occupations cause people to invent new words. The ninth decade of the new century was no exception. Listed below are some of the words and phrases that came into popular use throughout the decade.

AIDS This is an acronym for acquired immune deficiency syndrome, a condition caused by a virus that affects the immune system.

break dancing This form of dance incorporates rippling movements of the body, unusual twisting of the limbs, and spinning on the back and head.

compact disc Music and other audios are recorded on a laser disc, replacing vinyl records.

cross-training This is the process of preparing oneself physically for different athletic skills or abilities at the same time.

fax This shortened form of facsimile refers to an electronic reproduction of documents on paper, sent via the phone system.

focus group This term refers to a group of individuals gathered by an organization in order to share their insights and opinions on a given topic or topics.

glasnost This word means openness in Russian and is used to describe a political and social trend.

home shopping Items available for purchase are presented on television. The shopper orders by telephone.

Iron Lady This nickname was given to British Prime Minister Margaret Thatcher, denoting her stalwart type of leadership.

junk bond This is a type of corporate bond (certificate of debt guaranteeing payment plus interest) having a high yield and a high risk.

linear thinking This phrase describes a thought process that moves from point to point in a singular fashion, without deviance.

moonwalk This dance step, in which the dancer appears to move forward while actually moving backward, was popularized by performer Michael Jackson.

music video This is a brief movie visually depicting the content or sense of a corresponding song.

PC This is abbreviation originally referred to an IBM personal computer.

quality time This term refers to time spent with one's children that is characterized by positive interaction.

Solidarity This was the name given to the Polish labor organization.

space shuttle This is the name given to a reusable space developed by NASA.

spin doctor This term refers to an individual in charge of tailoring actual events regarding an individual, group, or organization to present a favorable image of the person, etc., to the public.

thirty-something This term refers to someone in the age group of thirty to thirty-nine and was popularized by a television drama of the same name.

Valley girl This phrase is used to describe a particular style of speech and attitude characteristic of the 1980s associated with the San Fernando Valley, California.

VCR This is the acronym for video-cassette recorder, a machine attached to a television that plays or records movies and shows.

VJ This is a short form of video jockey, an announcer and host of music video broadcasts in the same style as disc jockeys of a radio station.

wannabee This describes an individual who appears to "want to be" like another individual or group.

Yuppie This term stands for "young urban professional," individuals whose lives revolve around professional careers and socio-economic advancement.

Writing Prompts and Literature Ideas

Writing Prompts Use these suggestions for journal writing or as daily writing exercises. Some research or discussion may be appropriate before assigning a particular topic.

- Imagine you are a fan at one of the two Live Aid concerts. Describe what you see and how you feel.

- You are standing atop the Berlin Wall on the day it is finally opened. Describe the experience.

- You are part of the crowd watching the space shuttle *Challenger* takeoff for its tenth mission. Suddenly, it explodes in midair. Describe the scene as though it is happening now.

- Write a speech that might have been given by one of the major world leaders of the eighties.

- Write the storyboard for a music video to go along with one of your favorite songs.

- Write your ideas for putting an end to terrorism.

- Name a leader from the eighties whom you admire. Describe him or her and the reasons for your admiration.

- Imagine you are a child from 1888 who has been magically transported into a home in 1988. Write a story about what happens and what you experience.

Literature Ideas The following books can be used to supplement and enhance the study of the 1980s. They were either published in the decade or depict a segment of life from the time.

- ***The Indian in the Cupboard*** by Lynn Reid Banks (1980)
  One of the most popular books of the eighties, *The Indian in the Cupboard* tells the fantasy story of a boy and a magical cupboard that brings toys to life.

- ***The Day They Came to Arrest the Book*** by Nat Hentoff (1982)
  This story of censorship takes place in a high school circa 1980.

- ***A Ring of Endless Light*** by Madeleine L'Engle (1980)
  One of many books for young adults from the eighties that deals with mystical and even spiritual themes, this is a story of a girl's communion with dolphins.

- ***Strider*** by Beverly Clearly (1991)
  This poignant and popular story tells of a boy living a life common to many children in the eighties, being raised by single parents.

- ***Journey*** by Patricia MacLachlan (1991)
  Many of MacLachlan's books take place in this period of time. This story is regionally midwestern. It is the moving tale of a young boy's journey for his identity. He finds it through the loving help of his grandfather.

- ***A Light in the Attic*** by Shel Silverstein (1981)
  Silverstein's whimsical, funny, and sometimes touching poetry is enjoyed by people of all ages. Share several of his poems from this collection with your class.

- ***1984*** by George Orwell (1949)
  Although this book is difficult to understand and should only be attempted by mature students, it is worth noting as an interesting look into the future by an author of the 1940s. Use discretion.

1990 and Beyond Overview

- The decade opened with the fall of the Union of Soviet Socialist Republics (U.S.S.R.), followed by restructuring and civil wars throughout the area. Mikhail Gorbachev, the Soviet leader who had been instrumental in bringing about the change, fell out of power and a new era, under the leadership of Boris Yeltsin and others, began.

- War tore apart the nation of Bosnia-Hercegovina, once a part of Yugoslavia, in the aftermath of the Soviet demise.

- Women were on the rise in the United States. The nineties saw the first female attorney general, Janet Reno. Madeline Albright became the first female secretary of state. The position of first lady, the wife of the president, also saw an increased sphere of power and influence in Hillary Rodham Clinton.

- Citizens throughout the United States grieved over the bombing of the Alfred P. Murrah Federal Building in Oklahoma City, Oklahoma, in which 168 people were killed.

- Nelson Mandela, the former political prisoner, became the president of South Africa. Apartheid, the law of racial inequity and separation, ended.

- Hundreds of thousand of black men "marched" to Capitol Hill in Washington, D.C., in a show of solidarity and commitment to racial and family values. Promoters, calling for one million men to join in the march, named the event the *Million Man March.*

- Sports superstars of phenomenal prowess came to the forefront, including the young Tiger Woods who revolutionized the world of golf and brought its appeal to millions of Americans. Also noteworthy were the women's gymnastics, swimming, volleyball, softball, and basketball teams of the United States in the 1996 Summer Olympics. Their record-breaking firsts—and gymnast Kerri Strug's act of heroism—have become legendary.

- The Microsoft Company grew to be one of the most powerful in the world under the creative leadership of its founder, Bill Gates, and the revolutionizing Windows program.

- Technology was at the forefront of industry, education, and home life. Everywhere around the world, people were "surfing the net," computing through CD-ROM, exploring virtual reality, and talking on the go via their cellular phones.

- Amid the Israeli-Palestinian peace talks, an assassin killed prime minister Yitzhak Rabin, the Israeli leader at the forefront of peace negotiations. In 1994, Rabin shared the Nobel peace prize with fellow Israeli Shimon Peres and Palestine Liberation Organization leader Yasir Arafat.

- Bill Clinton became the president of the decade with comfortable wins in the 1992 and 1996 elections. However, third-party candidacy was on the rise, largely through the leadership of Reform Party candidate Ross Perot.

- Little green men from Mars were not such an unlikely thing: evidence of life was found on the fourth planet.

- Rap music filled the airwaves while gang-related violence filled the streets. Several of the world's most successful rap stars were gunned down in gang activity, including Tupac Shakur and the Notorious B.I.G. Both were part of the rap movement known as gangsta rap.

Operation Desert Storm

The Persian Gulf War, or Operation Desert Storm, was waged in early 1991 between Iraq and a coalition of thirty-nine nations organized by the Unites States and the United Nations. Leading the coalition were the U.S., France, Great Britain, Egypt, Syria, and Saudi Arabia.

Iraq began the war by invading the tiny nation of Kuwait on August 2, 1990. Prior to this, the two nations had tried unsuccessfully to settle disputes. Iraq wanted Kuwait because of its long coastline and harbor as well as the wealth to be had through its petroleum. The interests of the coalition revolved around protecting the petroleum supply upon which they were dependent.

After the invasion, Iraq quickly gained control of Kuwait. The Iraqis then set up troops along Kuwait's border with Saudi Arabia, spurring fears that it intended to attack the Saudis. Since Saudi Arabia was also a prominent supplier of petroleum, the nations of the world grew increasingly alarmed. The coalition united to send protective troops to Saudi Arabia.

In late November 1990, the United Nations Security Council agreed to use "all necessary means" to dispel Iraq from Kuwait after January 15, 1991. The coalition spent several months attempting to pressure Iraq into leaving Kuwait but to no avail. Finally, on January 17, 1991, the coalition began to bomb the Iraqi military and major industries. Iraq answered by directing Scud missiles at heavily populated areas of Israel and Saudi Arabia. It hoped to draw Israel into the war due to the longstanding disputes between the nations, but Israel did not enter. The Scud missiles were crude by Western standards, but they killed thousands of civilians.

Military casualties and mass desertions reduced the number of Iraqi troops to approximately 183,000 by late February. At four in the morning on February 24, the coalition began a massive ground attack into southern Iraq and Kuwait. The attack included military operations at various locations, which proved to be too much for the limited Iraqi troops to handle. By February 28, the Iraqis were defeated. However, in making their retreat from Kuwait, they set fire to oil wells, destroying much of Kuwait's resource and causing severe air pollution throughout the area. They also dumped oil into the Persian Gulf.

Although members of the coalition suffered fewer than 400 deaths, perhaps close to 100,000 Iraqi troops died, although the figure is not clear. Also, thousands of Iraqi and Kuwaiti civilians were killed, and the devastation to the area was enormous.

A formal cease-fire was accepted by Iraq on April 6, 1991. The U.N. Security Council declared an official end to the war on April 11. As a result of the cease-fire agreement, Iraq agreed to pay war damages to Kuwait, to destroy all chemical and biological weapons, and to destroy all materials and facilities it had for producing nuclear weapons. Although no nuclear weapons were used in the war, the Iraqi government was attempting to construct them.

Suggested Activities

History Trace the rule of Saddam Hussein in Iraq, how it started and where things stand today.

Peace Accords Operation Desert Storm spurred United States interest in renewing its previous diplomatic efforts to bring peace to the Middle East. Read about the efforts on page 487.

Cartography Draw a map of the Persian Gulf area, including Iraq, Saudi Arabia, Kuwait, Iran, and Israel.

Petroleum Find out about the world's uses for petroleum and the extent of its supply.

Oklahoma Bombing

The deadliest and most costly terrorist act ever to take place in the United States occurred on April 19, 1995, at the Alfred P. Murrah Federal Building in Oklahoma City, Oklahoma. The day started normally as employees reported to their government offices and federal agencies to begin their day's work. Parents who worked in the building dropped off their children at the day-care center on the ground floor. Citizens were in line at the federal offices, waiting patiently for their turns. All was normal. Yet everything changed drastically in just minutes.

On the morning of April 19, a truck containing a highly explosive bomb was parked in front of the Murrah building. When the bomb exploded, it ripped away the entire front section of the building, collapsing story upon story. Some people died in the explosion, and others were crushed. Even some rescuers died while trying to save the victims. The explosion blew out windows, cracked walls in neighboring buildings, and was felt for miles around.

Reporters rushed to the scene, and immediately the tragedy was on the national airwaves. A number of people near enough to help rushed to the building to determine how they might be of service. Civilian volunteers joined the local fire and police departments to take survivors to safety. In the days that followed, rescue teams from other communities and agencies arrived and began to sift through the rubble to find other survivors.

After all the searching was complete and it was clear there were no more bodies, the Murrah building was razed. It was determined that a total of 168 people died in the bombing, including nineteen children, most of whom were being cared for at the day-care center. Some of their parents died with them, and some survived.

Initially many people believed the Oklahoma City bombing was the act of international terrorists. However, federal officials quickly determined that the terrorists were, in fact, American citizens. Investigators focused on Timothy J. McVeigh and Terry L. Nichols, both natural-born citizens of the United States who had expressed strong opposition to the federal government. In just days the two were arrested and charged with the bombing. They were also charged with constructing the bomb. Later, a third party, Michael Fortier, was charged with aiding McVeigh and Nichols. Fortier pleaded guilty with the possibility of testifying against McVeigh and Nichols. The trial of the three began in 1997.

If any light could be found in the darkness of this tragedy, it is this: the people of Oklahoma City and the nation rallied together in the aftermath of the bombing to rebuild and renew the area and to support the survivors, the injured, and the families of the dead in any ways possible. Medical expenses were paid by anonymous donors. As has been shown countless times in history, the human spirit triumphs over adversity.

Suggested Activity

What Happened Next? Research magazines and newspapers to find out about Oklahoma City today and the events and outcome of the court case.

General Colin Powell

Colin Luther Powell, the first black to serve as chairman of the Joint Chiefs of Staff (JCS), was born in New York City's Harlem district on April 5, 1937, the son of Jamaican immigrants. When Luther Theopolis Powell and Maud Ariel McKoy married and moved to Harlem, the area was a thriving and prosperous one, rich with the culture of the Harlem Renaissance (page 131). Yet just a few years later, the Great Depression changed all that, and by the time Colin was born, Harlem was in serious decline. The family moved to the Bronx. Although that area declined as well and poverty surrounded them, the family persevered, instilling in their children respect for education, hard work, and the equality of all people.

Powell was only an average student while in elementary school, not applying himself in any effective way. His poor performance made it impossible for him to attend the Bronx High School of Science, one of the best in the nation, where he had hoped to go. Powell got more serious about his work then, and he became a leader at Morris High School, although his grades were still average. He graduated from high school, an achievement neither of his parents had accomplished, and then went on to the City College of New York for his undergraduate degree. He showed the same lack of enthusiasm for school that he had in the past, but just when his interest was at its lowest, he became aware of the Army Reserve Officers Training Corps (ROTC) on campus. Powell enrolled in the ROTC program in 1954.

In 1958, Powell graduated and was commissioned a second lieutenant in the army. Although he only expected to serve a couple of years, he found he enjoyed the army life, and he never left. From 1968 to 1969 he served in the army's 23rd Division in Vietnam. Continuing to move up the military ladder, he then served as commander to ground forces in South Korea, West Germany, and the United States. Powell was promoted to commanding general of the Fifth Corps in Frankfurt, Germany, in 1986, and the next year President Ronald Reagan appointed him as assistant to the president for national security affairs.

In the summer of 1989, Powell was promoted to the rank of four-star general. On October 3, 1989, he was sworn in as the chairman of the JCS, the highest military advisory group in the U.S. During the swearing-in ceremony, Powell's wife of twenty-seven years, Alma, held the Bible. Powell served as chairman from 1989 until his retirement in 1993. During that time, he oversaw the deployment of U.S. troops into Panama to combat General Noriega, and he served as General H. Norman Schwarzkopf's link to the president and the Congress during Operation Desert Storm. Schwarzkopf was the military leader of the operation. Both Schwarzkopf and Powell came out of the war as national heroes.

Since Powell's retirement, it has been rumored that he would one day become a candidate for the U.S. presidency. Thus far, he has declined to run, although the hopes of his many supporters remain high for the future.

Suggested Activities

ROTC Learn more about the ROTC and the kind of training it provides for young people.

Panama The U.S. invasion of Panama took place in 1990. Find out what happened and why.

Military General Powell was a four-star general. Research to find out how one becomes a gineral and what the stars mean.

Attorney General Janet Reno

Janet Reno, the first female attorney general of the United States, was born in Miami, Florida, on July 21, 1938. Her parents, Henry and Jane, were newspaper reporters who worked in the city. In 1946, they moved to the Florida Everglades. Henry Reno continued to drive into town, but his wife wrote at home and built the family house. Janet, her sister, and two brothers helped in whatever ways they could, but their mother dug the foundation, laid the brick, and put in the plumbing. Mr. Reno helped at night with any heavy labor.

The family did not have a television, so they enjoyed an active, outdoors life. As a child, Reno loved hiking, canoeing, riding horses, and camping. Reno did well in school, and in high school she was a national debating champion. At Cornell University, she studied chemistry. In 1960, she entered Harvard Law School and became one of only sixteen women in a class of 500 students to graduate. However, because she was a woman, she found it difficult to get a job as a lawyer. It took four years, but she finally was offered a job as a junior partner in the Lewis and Reno law firm.

In 1971 Reno received her first political appointment, staff director of the judiciary committee in the Florida House of Representatives. While there, she helped to reorganize the court system. In 1972 she ran for the Florida state legislature, but she lost. She worked on the Florida senate's Criminal Justice Committee and helped to reorganize the criminal code in 1973. Also in 1973, Florida State Attorney Richard Gerstein hired Reno to organize a juvenile department for youths who had been arrested. Many others had tried and failed, but Reno did what was asked in just two months. When Gerstein retired in 1978, there were still a few months left in his term. He suggested that the governor appoint Reno. He did, and she became the first female state attorney of Florida. While serving in this position, Reno worked hard to fight crime at as young an age as possible. She campaigned for better care, education, and parenting of children and supported programs to provide housing, jobs, and drug counseling to keep people out of jail. Reno's tactics proved successful, and she earned the respect of her state, so much so that she was elected to the position four times, the last time unopposed.

When Bill Clinton was elected president he asked Reno to be the new attorney general, the highest law officer in the land. On March 12, 1993, Janet Reno was sworn is as the first female attorney general the United States had ever known.

Since that time, Reno has worked to reduce crime in the nation. She has her critics, but generally she is well respected and has the reputation of being tough but fair.

Suggested Activities

Research Find out about your state legal system as opposed to the federal one. Also, learn about the criminal code, what it is and how it works.

Read An excellent book about Janet Reno, ideal for students, is entitled *Janet Reno: First Woman Attorney General* by Charnan Simon (Childrens Press, 1994).

Writing Have the students write about an important person in their lives who has shown exceptional perseverance and determination, much as Jane and Janet Reno have.

William Jefferson Clinton

42nd President, 1993–

Vice President: Albert Gore, Jr.

Born: August 19, 1946, in Hope, Arkansas

Party: Democrat

Parents: William Jefferson Blythe III, Virginia Cassidy (stepfather Roger Clinton)

First Lady: Hillary Rodham

Children: Chelsea

Education: Yale Law School

Nickname: Bill; Bubba

Famous Firsts:

- Clinton was the first president to have been a Rhodes scholar, studying at Oxford University in England for two years.
- He was the first president from the Baby Boom generation.
- He was the first to name a woman to the position of U.S. attorney general.

Achievements:

- When he was elected governor of Arkansas at age thirty-two, Clinton was the youngest governor in the nation. He served as Arkansas governor from 1979–1980 and again from 1983–1992.
- He worked as a Red Cross volunteer during the riots in Washington, D.C., following the assassination of Martin Luther King, Jr. (page 330).
- In 1976 he was elected attorney general for Arkansas.
- As president, Clinton appointed more women and minorities to his cabinet than had any previous president.
- During his presidency, the unemployment rate and the national deficit both declined. These were major issues in the eighties and nineties.
- He succeeded in raising the legal minimum wage, altering welfare laws, and passing an anticrime law that included the restriction of certain assault weapons.
- Under his leadership, former President Jimmy Carter succeeded in returning power to Haitian President Jean-Bertrand Aristide from military rule.
- The North American Free Trade Agreement (NAFTA) was approved in late 1993. NAFTA is meant to diminish trade barriers among the United States, Mexico, and Canada.

Interesting Facts:

- Clinton's biological father died in a car accident three months before Clinton was born. Clinton took his stepfather's last name when he was fifteen.
- He decided to make a career of politics after meeting President John F. Kennedy. Clinton was seventeen at the time.
- He is an accomplished tenor saxophone player.
- On at least one occasion, Clinton stood up to his alcoholic stepfather to protect his mother from abuse.
- He worked through his troubles with his stepfather before the elder man's death in 1967.
- Throughout college, Clinton took jobs in politics to help pay for his education.

Election Facts and Figures

Note to Teacher: Prior to 2000, have the students make predictions in the chart. During and after the election, have them fill in the accurate information.

	Election of 1992	Election of 1996	Election of 2000
Democrats	Governor Bill Clinton of Arkansas ran with Senator Al Gore of Tennessee as his running mate.	President Clinton and Vice President Gore were renominated by their party without opposition.	
Republicans	President Bush ran for a second term, again with Vice President Dan Quayle.	Senator Robert (Bob) Dole of Kansas and Congressman Jack Kemp of New York received the nomination from the Republican Party.	
Other	Ross Perot ran for president as the Indepent Reform Party candidate. Admiral James Stockwell, a former POW in Vietnam, was his running mate.	Ross Perot ran for a second time as the Reform Party candidate with economist Pat Choate as vice presidential candidate.	
Slogans	Clinton urged "It's Time for a Change" and claimed he was a "new kind of Democrat."		
Issues	Domestic issues as opposed to foreign affairs (the focus of the last administrations) were a topic of much discussion. These included unemployment, the budget deficit, the banking scandal, and the socio-economic gap between rich and poor.	Trouble during the Clinton Administration was a topic of much debate, including the Whitewater Development Corporation scandal and the failure of Clinton's reform for the national health care system. Also discussed were gun control, the economy, and taxation. Clinton stressed the improvements made during his first term.	
Winner	The president lost the election with a count of 168 electoral votes to Clinton's 370. The popular vote was closer with Clinton just under 45 million and Bush just over 39 million. Perot, took nearly 20 million popular votes but earned no electoral votes. It is possible that his candidacy cost Bush the election.	Clinton took the election with 379 electoral votes and 45.5 million popular votes. Dole received 159 electoral and nearly 38 million popular. Perot received no electoral and just under 8 million popular. His effect on the election was not as severe as in 1992.	

Ross Perot

Many people have run as independent or minor-party candidates in the U.S. presidential elections, and some, most notably the Rev. Jesse Jackson in the eighties, have strongly influenced the outcomes. However, it is quite possible that no independent candidate in the history of the United States affected an election quite so significantly as did Ross Perot in 1992.

Born Henry Ray Perot in Texarkana, Texas, in 1930, Perot legally changed his name in 1942 to Henry Ross Perot. He was a 1953 graduate of the U.S. Naval Academy and served in the navy from 1953 until 1957. In 1962, he founded Electronic Data Systems (EDS), a computer services company which designed, installed, and operated computer systems on a contract basis. The company was highly successful. General Motors (GM) purchased EDS in 1984, and Perot joined their board of directors. He left GM in 1986 and founded another computer services company, Perot Systems, in 1988.

Perot was a patriot and in 1969 he attempted to deliver food, medicine, mail, and clothing to American POWs in Vietnam. In 1979 Perot organized a private commando rescue of two EDS employees and other prisoners jailed in Iran following that country's revolution.

In the early 1990s, Perot declared he would enter the race as an independent if his name was placed on the ballot of all fifty states by November 1992. In July 1992 he retracted his offer, claiming that he could not win enough votes to be elected. However, his supporters did get his name on all fifty ballots, and in October Perot officially announced his candidacy.

Perot, the self-made billionaire businessman, promised to run the nation as he did his businesses. He spent much of his campaign discussing the nation's budget deficit, using business graphs and charts to show the public how inefficient the United States accounting had been. Because he had been so successful in business, many people felt strongly that he could do what he promised—balance the enormous federal budget and eradicate the deficit. People were also intrigued by the fact that Perot was a political "outsider," meaning he was probably unconnected to interest groups.

The deficit was of great concern to people in the early nineties, and Perot made it even more so by constantly bringing the issue to the forefront. It became one of the major—if not the most significant—issues of the 1992 election.

In the end, Perot took no electoral votes, but he did earn nineteen percent of the popular vote. The incumbent, President George Bush, earned thirty-eight percent of the popular vote, and the Democratic candidate, Bill Clinton, took forty-three percent. Had Perot declined to run, it is likely that Bush would have won the election since experts generally agree that the damage Perot did was to Bush's bid for the presidency.

Suggested Activities

Research Make a list of other third party candidates in the twentieth century. Find out about their political careers and how they affected the presidential races in which they ran.

Business It is often said that business and politics are closely tied. Some people refer to this as a "revolving door." Find out about the connection and what is meant by the phrase "revolving door."

Hillary Rodham Clinton

Born Hillary Diane Rodham in Chicago, in 1947, she became one of the most active and prominent first ladies in the history of the United States. A 1969 graduate of Wellesley College, she was the first former student ever asked to give the commencement address at the college. While attending Yale University Law School, she met Bill Clinton, a fellow law student. The two developed a friendship and began to date.

After working as a staff attorney for the Children's Defense Fund (see page 378) and the special U.S. House panel investigating the impeachment of President Richard Nixon, she moved to Arkansas. In 1974, she and Bill Clinton both joined the faculty of the University of Arkansas Law School. They married in 1975. When the Clintons moved to Little Rock, Arkansas, in 1977, she joined the Rose Law Firm. Her specialty was patent infringement and intellectual property. The same year she also founded Arkansas Advocates for Families and Children.

Hillary Clinton played a strong role in her husband's election to governor in 1980, serving as a campaign advisor. During his terms of office she was instrumental in creating some of his major programs, especially education reforms. A daughter, Chelsea, was born to the Clintons in 1980.

Hillary Clinton continued her work with the Rose Law Firm until 1992, when Bill Clinton was elected president. She had promised repeatedly during the presidential campaign "If you elect Bill, you get me," and she was an important part of his advisory team. In October 1993, President Clinton offered to Congress a plan for reforming the nation's health care system. The plan had been developed by committee under the leadership of his wife. Although the plan was debated at length, it failed to pass Congress. However, in August of 1996 two important provisions of the plan were included in the Kennedy-Kassebaum bill, which was passed by Congress and approved by the president. The provisions were that workers could change their jobs without losing medical insurance coverage and that workers cannot be refused for medical insurance coverage due to a preexisting illness.

In response to criticism that her role in the presidency was too significant, Mrs. Clinton took a more subdued role during the 1996 campaign and pursued her work for children, education, and other interests. In 1996 Hillary Rodham Clinton published a book, *It Takes a Village to Raise a Child: And Other Lessons Children Teach Us*, in which she encourages community participation in the care of all children. She also received a Grammy Award for the audiotape of her book.

Suggested Activities

Read Read Clinton's book, *It Takes a Village: and Other Lessons Children Teach Us.* Discuss its contents.

Discussion Have the class discuss the role of first lady and what her responsibilities and influence should be. For interest, ask them to consider if the president were a woman and her husband had the role usually played by first lady. Would the position differ in their eyes? What would his title be?

First Ladies Research the lives of other prominent first ladies of the twentieth century, such as Eleanor Roosevelt and Rosalyn Carter.

Million Man March

On October 16, 1995, hundreds of thousands of black men arrived in Washington, D.C., to take part in the Million Man March. The men traveled by airplane, bus, car, and train to arrive at their destination.

The purpose of the Million Man March was to focus on the responsibilities of black males for themselves, their families, and their communities. Organizers urged the mentoring of young people, voting in local, state, and national elections, and taking personal responsibility for one's own children. Many of the men who took part in the "march" said that the importance of the event was the feeling that pervaded it and the union of men joined for a common, positive cause. In the black community, the march was generally hailed as a significant, triumphant experience.

However, controversy surrounded the march as well. Its primary organizers were Louis Farrakhan, the leader of the Nation of Islam, and Rev. Benjamin Chavis, former head of the National Association for the Advancement of Colored People (NAACP). Farrakhan had long been a controversial figure. While supporting and honoring blacks, he has often been accused of prejudice against whites and Jews. To his credit, under Farrakhan's leadership the Nation of Islam has helped to curb illegal drug traffic in housing projects and to arrange peace pacts between street gangs in major U.S. cities. As for Chavis, he was once a respected leader who left the NAACP under allegations of financial mismanagement, further complicated when it was revealed that the march left organizers nearly $70,000 in debt.

Nonetheless, the general feeling among the march's supporters was that the message of the march was the important thing, not the messengers. Many people took enormous pride in being a part of it and in having their husbands, fathers, and sons attend. The event seemed to offer a strong feeling of hope for the future.

Since the march, positive changes have taken place. A report from the Joint Center of Political and Economic Studies shows that although the number of voters overall was much lower in 1996 than in 1992, 1.7 million more African Americans voted in the 1996 national elections than in the elections held in 1992. Experts tend to agree that the increase was largely due to the efforts of the Million Man March. In addition, mentoring programs in which adult black males agreed to support and interact with fatherless black children, providing them with a necessary male role model, took off in cities around the nation,

In 1996 on the anniversary of the march, a World's Day of Atonement was organized by Farrakhan in New York City's Dag Hammarskjöld Plaza. Also in that year, acclaimed director Spike Lee released *Get on the Bus*, a movie about a bus full of black men leaving Los Angeles and heading for the march in Washington, D.C. While the movie provides interesting insights into the event, it should only be viewed by mature audiences.

Suggested Activities

Causes As a class, determine some causes for which you would like to join with thousands of others to take a stand.

Discussion The Million Man March was in part a protest and in part a celebration. Discuss how it was both those things.

Farrakhan Louis Farrakhan is a controversial figure. Learn more about his life and beliefs. As a class, discuss what you find.

Women and Children Some women and children also participated in the march, but the primary focus was on men. Discuss as a class what some possible reasons for this might be. Should future events be expanded to include women and children?

Holocaust Memorial Museum

In 1980, the United States Congress established the U.S. Holocaust Memorial Council to oversee construction of a museum to honor and remember the victims of the twentieth century holocaust in Europe. In 1993, the Holocaust Memorial Museum in Washington, D.C., was completed and opened to the public. It has since become one of the most frequently visited sites in the nation's capital.

Although the holocaust took place in Europe, it holds great significance for the United States. Many who fled the Nazis immigrated to the U.S. in order to find sanctuary in a democratic nation. American ideals of freedom of religion and of expression and the right to protest were in direct opposition to Nazi thought, so the U.S. had a vested interest in promoting democracy over the Nazi ideology. In the forties, these were part of the motivation for the U.S. and the other Allies to fight the Nazis and to liberate the prisoners of the concentration camps. In the nineties, they were the reasons why the nation felt compelled to build a museum. People wish to remember so that the holocaust's horrors will not be repeated.

The museum's exhibits are arranged in a progressive fashion, beginning with the rise of Naziism in the thirties and ending with the liberation of the concentration camps in 1945. The more than one thousand exhibits include photographs, films, eyewitness testimonies, and artifacts such as gas canisters used in the camps and a train car that was used to transport the Jews to their prisons. The building also contains a library and research facilities dedicated to the holocaust.

The museum was funded by private donations. Hollywood director Steven Spielberg (see page 484) was a significant contributor. He also devoted a great deal of time to recording the stories of every survivor of the holocaust whom he could locate, and he continues to do this work. In 1993, Spielberg released what he considers to be his most significant film, *Schindler's List*. It is a powerful and poignant drama set during the European holocaust.

(For more on the holocaust, see page 228.)

Suggested Activities

Report Have the students report on the holocaust and prepare visual presentations. Put these on display in the school for your own holocaust museum.

Holocausts The holocaust in Europe is not the only one in history. Research to find out about other mass killings motivated by race, religion, and politics. Compare them to this holocaust.

Discussion How can the world put an end to holocausts? Have the class discuss the issue. This is also a good topic for individual writing.

Superman

In the 1970s, Christopher Reeve came to the public's attention as (Superman, the Man of Steel,) in a series of popular movies. However, his celebrity at that time did not come close to the fame he gained in the nineties, not through popular success but through tragedy and triumph.

Reeve pursued a successful acting career throughout the eighties and into the nineties. Noted for his winning smile, good looks, and strong physique, he was the perfect actor to play the role of Superman. It seemed that many more such roles would be part of his future.

Reeve was also an avid horseman. On May 27, 1995, while riding in Virginia, Reeve was thrown from his horse. He landed on his head and crushed the upper two vertebrae in his spine. He was immediately paralyzed, unable to walk, control his body, or feed himself.

Although he requires around-the-clock assistance, a specialized wheelchair, and a house altered to meet his special needs, since the accident, Reeve has demonstrated tremendous courage and a positive outlook. He became the chairman for the American Paralysis Association and has done a great deal to build public awareness in and raise funds for spinal injury research. A benefit concert he sponsored in early 1997 raised thousands of dollars for the Christopher Reeve Foundation, a new organization created to support such research.

Reeve directed a movie, *In the Gloaming,* released to cable in 1997, and he plans to direct more. The actor/director is also coauthoring a book about his life, scheduled for publication in 1998. Reeve has continued to enjoy life, accepting what has happened. He also says that he treasures the lessons the accident has taught him, such as spending time with old friends and appreciating love as "more important than any activity."

In 1996, Reeve was interviewed by acclaimed television journalist, Barbara Walters (page 445). The interview was one of the most watched in Walters' long history, and it received rave reviews and public support. People were moved by the grace, dignity, and courage with which Christopher Reeve has chosen to live his life. They were also touched by the commitment shared by Reeve and his wife, Dana. After the interview, Barbara Walters said that he touched her like no other individual had.

Suggested Activities

Physiology Learn about the physiology of the spinal cord and how it functions. Also learn about injuries to the spine and how they can affect the body.

Discussion Have a class "what-if" discussion. Ask the students to imagine that they did not have the use of some part of their bodies—such as their arms, eyes, hands, etc. Have them discuss how life might be different and what they could do about it.

Write You can write to the Christopher Reeve Foundation at P.O. Box 277, F.D.R. Station, New York, NY 10150-0277. The students can write to show support or to ask for information about the foundation. They can write to other such foundations as well.

Unlikely Heroes

Oseola McCarty

The newspapers in the nineties were filled with accounts of average citizens doing extraordinary things, becoming heroes in the public's eye. Here are three of their stories.

Oseola McCarty She worked for seventy-five years. She never had a college degree and never, in fact, went beyond the sixth grade. Instead, Oseola McCarty had a natural work ethic and a strong desire to help others. She saved as much as she could from the ten dollars she earned for washing each bundle of laundry, her occupation, and in 1995 she did a remarkable thing.

McCarty began her laundry service in her backyard around the time of World War II, and when she finally retired, she was 88 years old. In those years, she somehow managed to save more than $150,000. However, she did not choose to use it for herself. Instead, she began a scholarship fund for African American students at the University of Southern Mississippi, located in her hometown of Hattiesburg.

Since her generous donation, McCarty has received an honorary degree from Harvard University, has met the president of the United States, and has been seen on television shows and magazine covers around the nation. In 1996, she published her story, *Oseola McCarty's Simple Wisdom for Rich Living* (Longstreet Press).

Carolyn McCarthy

Carolyn McCarthy While traveling on a New York commuter train in 1993, Carolyn McCarthy's husband was killed and her son injured by a crazed gunman, Colin Ferguson. Deeply grieved, McCarthy, a registered nurse, began a campaign with other victims of the crime to ban assault weapons, the type used in the train violence. The ban passed, but later McCarthy's congressional representative, Dan Frisa, voted to repeal it. McCarthy was infuriated. She told her friends, "I'm so mad, I could run against Dan Frisa," and that is exactly what she did. In 1996, with no previous political experience, she was elected to the United States House of Representatives by the citizens of New York. McCarthy felt confident that her lack of experience would not be an obstacle. In fact, she considered her role in Congress to be similar to her role as a nurse. She stated that in both occupations, an individual is hired to be there for others, representing their wishes and minimizing her own.

Binti-Jua Binti-Jua was not an American citizen. In fact, she was not a citizen of any nation. Rather, she was a resident at an Illinois zoo. Binti-Jua was a gorilla. In 1996 a three-year-old boy was visiting the zoo with his family. Although reports are not clear, somehow the boy fell into the gorilla pit. To the amazement of the eyewitnesses there—and, in fact, to people around the world, thanks to the home movies made by another tourist—Binti-Jua, the gorilla, gingerly picked up the boy and carried him to the safety of the zookeepers. Almost certain tragedy was replaced by the love of a mother—mother gorilla, that is. After the incident, the child, unconscious throughout the ordeal, fully recovered, and Binti-Jua returned to raising her own child, Koola.

Suggested Activities

Local Heroes Have the students each report on a local hero. Put their reports together in a book for other students and parents to read.

Writing Write a short story about one of the three heroes on this page.

Olympic Heroes

The Olympic Games of the 1990s brought forward a number of sports heroes with amazing, record-breaking stories. Here are some of them.

Michael Johnson A flash of light in the 1996 Olympics, Michael Johnson and his golden Nikes set two world records, making him the fastest human in world history. First, Johnson won the 400-meter race at the record time of 43.49 seconds, and then he won the 200-meter race at 19.32, again a record. Never before had an athlete won gold in both events, and never before had an athlete run so fast. When asked about his accomplishment, Johnson said "Never in my wildest dreams did I think I could run so fast." The expression on Johnson's face at the moment he knew of his record time will remain in the minds of many spectators for years to come.

Dan Jansen Favored to win in his speed-skating events in the 1988 Games, Dan received news that his older sister, Jane, had died of leukemia just nine hours before he was to skate. To honor his sister, Jansen skated anyway, but he fell during the race. At the next race two days later, he fell again. In the 1992 Olympic Games the result was the same. When he qualified for the 1996 Olympics, Jansen knew that after the games he would retire. In his first event, the 500-meter race, he slipped twice and came in eighth. Four days later, up for the last time in his Olympic career, Jansen pulled out the miracle everyone hoped for. Not only did he win the 1,000-meter race, but he set a world record. When Jansen stepped onto the podium to receive his medal and the national anthem played, he looked to the sky and saluted his sister. Before he skated his victory lap, Jansen moved to the side of the arena where his wife, Robin, handed him their infant daughter, Jane. Baby Jane and her father took the lap together.

U.S. Women's Swim Team Amy Van Dyken, Angel Martino, Catherine Fox, and Jenny Thompson, the women of the United States swim team, awed the world with their gold-medal performances in four events, earning them nearly twenty percent of the gold medals received by U.S. women in the 1996 games. Van Dyken further earned the admiration of the crowd by dedicating her medals to all the "nerds" who are "picked on" and cast aside. Van Dyken said she had been one of that class, and she hoped she could inspire others by her achievements.

U.S. Women's Gymnastic Team The teenagers of the U.S. Women's gymnastic team became perhaps the most memorable heroes of the 1996 Olympics, by earning America's first team gold medal in a sport dominated by Russia and Eastern bloc nations. To the front of the pack came tiny Kerri Strug. On her first vault in the final match, she fell, twisting her ankle. Strug attempted another vault, in spite of the incredible pain. Her second vault was beautiful, and she landed on both legs to earn the score that gave her team the gold. However, within a moment she was hunched on the ground, and the world saw what she had been facing. The crowd went wild when Strug's coach, Bela Karolyi, carried the diminutive teen to the podium to receive her gold medal with her teammates. For many, she embodied the Olympic spirit.

Suggested Activities

Report Find out about other Olympic heroes over time and put together a class book about their achievements.

Olympics Hold a class Olympics, creating your own events and making your own awards. Events can be traditional—like running—or creative—like a shoelace-tying race.

Women The 1996 summer games were exceptional for American women. Research to find out more about their accomplishments.

Tiger Woods

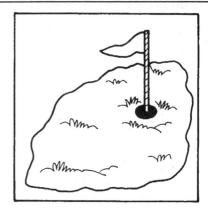

Tiger Woods is the man the world knows as the most extraordinary golfer of all time. In 1997 the twenty-one year old became the youngest winner of professional golf's Masters tournament. Along the way, Woods set new records with his 12-stroke finish and his 18 under par 72-hole score. He was also the first black man to win the tournament.

He was born Eldrick Woods on December 30, 1975, in Cypress, California, the only son of Earl and Kultida Woods. His father nicknamed him Tiger in honor of Nguyen Phong, an army officer he fought with in Vietnam. Born with a mixture of races running through his blood, he is an American with Thai, African, Chinese, Cherokee, and European ancestry. Although he experienced racism when he was growing up, his family always taught him to use anger generated from the experiences in creative ways, making something positive of it.

Woods has always maintained a close relationship with both his parents, but particularly with his father. In fact, Earl asserts that the purpose of his life was to raise and teach Tiger, whom he calls a "Chosen One." Earl believes it is his son's destiny to lead, transform, and bring together people from around the world in much the same way great social and religious leaders of the past have done, such as Buddha and Gandhi. From his mother, a practicing Buddhist, Woods learned serenity and mental control. Always an exceptional child, Woods could stand at six months of age, and at eleven months he could swing a sawed-off club, driving the ball to a target net. At the age of two he made an appearance on the Mike Douglas Show, and at five he was featured on *That's Incredible!*, a program that showcased daring and exceptional accomplishments. Indeed, his accomplishments were exceptional. When he was four, he would spend a day at the golf course, challenging and betting with adult golfers. The disbelievers went home poorer, and the preschooler went home with his pockets full.

In 1996 having won three straight U.S. Amateur titles, and the NCAA championship, Tiger Woods turned professional at the age of twenty and was named the Sportsman of the Year by *Sports Illustrated*. As a professional, he immediately won two PGA tour events, scoring in the sixties in twenty-one of his first twenty-seven rounds and tripling the size of the crowds in attendance. He became the first PGA Tour player to average more than 300 yards after thirty rounds of golf, an exceptional show of skill and endurance. Golf legend Jack Nicklaus says that Woods has "the most fundamentally sound" swing he has ever seen.

Of his role today, Woods declares, "I like the idea of being a role model. It's an honor. People took the time to help me as a kid, and they impacted my life. I want to do the same for kids." In the future, Woods' plans may include a Tiger Woods Foundation, funding scholarships and setting up clinics and coaching for inner-city children. He has signed endorsement deals with Nike and Titleist for forty million and twenty million dollars respectively over five years. These contracts are significantly higher than any athlete's in history.

Suggested Activities

Golf Learn about the game of golf and how it is scored. If possible, learn the proper swing and stroke during your physical education time.

Race Woods is bringing about some racial changes in the game of golf. As his Nike commercial says, there are some golf courses in the United States on which he is not allowed to play. Discuss this as a class.

Air Jordan

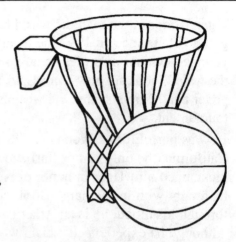

He got his nickname because it seemed as though he could fly straight into the air. His name is Michael Jordan, and his flight is just part of his exceptional talent. It is said that he is the best basketball player who ever lived.

Born to James and Deloris Jordan on February 17, 1963, in Wilmington, North Carolina, Jordan spent a great deal of time playing backyard basketball with his brother Larry, but he did not always win. In fact, when he was a sophomore in high school, he did not make the school basketball team. Since he loved the sport, Jordan became determined to excel. He began to rise early each day to practice, taking his parents' advice on the importance of effort over talent.

When it came time for Jordan to attend college, he chose his mother's favorite, the University of North Carolina. In his freshman year, he helped the team win the NCAA championship for the first time in twenty-five years, scoring the game-winning basket. While still an amateur, Jordan was chosen for the U.S. Olympic basketball team in 1984, and they won the gold. That same year, he was up for the National Basketball Association (NBA) draft. Surprisingly, the extraordinary player was not selected until third. He was chosen by the fortunate Chicago Bulls.

In his first game with the Bulls, Jordan scored sixteen points, and the rest is legend. Scores of forty and fifty points for Jordan alone became commonplace. With his help, the Bulls made the NBA playoffs for the first time in many years. In his first year, Jordan was selected for the NBA All-Star game and won the Rookie of the Year Award. He made shots others could not make or had not tried. Sometimes he even changed in midair and made a different shot than originally planned. He seemed to jump higher and to stay in the air longer than any other player. Jordan worked constantly to be an excellent all-around player, always putting his best efforts into his game. He led the Bulls to three NBA championships in a row.

In 1992, the United States allowed professional basketball players to play in the Olympics, and Jordan became part of the "Dream Team," the best the U.S. had to offer. There was no competition. Jordan and his team practically had the gold won before they stepped onto the court. The following year, Jordan felt he had accomplished all he could as a basketball player, and so he retired from the sport at the age of thirty. He then pursued his love of baseball and signed with the Chicago White Sox minor league team for one season. Although he had not played baseball for fifteen years, Jordan held his own and even scored three home runs.

In 1995 Jordan decided to return to the Bulls and the game he loves. In just his fifth game back, he scored fifty-five points. Ever since, the Bulls have been virtually unstoppable. Many experts wonder if other basketball teams are even in the same league as the Chicago Bulls.

Suggested Activities

Basketball As a class, play a game of basketball during physical education time.

Read An excellent book about Michael Jordan written for children is called *Michael Jordan* by Nick Edwards (Scholastic, 1995).

Professionals and Amateurs Learn about the differences between professional and amateur status and what each is entitled to do.

Billionaire Bill

When William Henry Gates was a boy, he was immensely interested in the relatively new technology of the modern computer. This interest, coupled with exceptional intelligence, foresight, and perseverance, have made Bill Gates and his company, Microsoft, two of the biggest names of the nineties.

Gates was born in Seattle, Washington, in 1955. At age fifteen, he and his friend, Paul Allen, began their first computer software company. Five years later, the two young men began to design programs for personal computers, new to the marketplace, and in 1975 they founded Microsoft.

In 1980, the International Business Machines (IBM) Corporation selected Microsoft to design the operating system for its first personal computer. An operating system is the organizational program that provides the instructions for a computer's operation. IBM PC's grew to become the standard in the industry, but they returned the software rights to Microsoft. Many would say that this was one of the worst business decisions in history. It is this technology that later skyrocketed the Microsoft Corporation into the microcomputing stratosphere.

The program provided by Gates for IBM was called the Microsoft Disk Operating System (MS-DOS). Millions of copies of the system were sold for use in IBM PC's and those that were IBM-compatible (able to run with IBM software). Businesses around the world used Gates' technology, and MS-DOS could be found in offices, schools, and homes in nearly every nation.

Gates became the sole owner of Microsoft when his partner opted to retire. Under his leadership, Microsoft has grown into one of the most powerful businesses in the world. It seems that everything the company touches turns to gold. In 1985, Microsoft introduced Windows, a graphical interface which made access to programs easier. Windows became the system of the future, computer owners added it to their MS-DOS computers, and Gates capitalized once again on the very same markets. New programs were written to take advantage of the new technology,

Windows allows the computer user to manage the system by pointing an arrow and clicking on an icon (picture) or word rather than typing in instructions. It also allows the user to open a variety of "windows" simultaneously, speeding up task switching. Millions of copies of Windows were sold.

In 1995, Gates once again revolutionized the industry, this time with Windows 95, an updated and improved technology based on the previous Windows program. Computer users around the world replaced their technology with the new Windows. Gates and Microsoft benefitted from the same market yet again.

Although in the late eighties Gates became the first billionaire of the software industry, he is noted for his general lack of interest in wealth. He and his wife have stated that when they die, they will leave their money to charities rather than to their children. They believe it is important for their children to earn their livings on their own.

Currently, Gates and his wife are using their enormous wealth to build a state-of-the-art home in Seattle. Fully computerized, the home includes everything the imagination can conjure. Even the art on the walls will be ever-changing since it will consist of computerized projections.

Suggested Activity

Computers Trace the history of computers. Allow the students hands-on experience with MS-DOS, Windows, or Windows 95.

The Techno World

Technology in the nineties, just as in the eighties, grew by leaps and bounds. The use of cellular phones and personal pagers became widespread. Not many people, it seemed, were beyond instantaneous reach, and if a person could not be reached by phone, one could always contact him by e-mail.

Here is some detailed information about one of the major technological phenomena of the nineties for those who are a bit less techno-centered.

Internet The term means "interconnected network of networks." It is a wide-reaching system of computers that links businesses and individuals around the globe. Many thousands of individual networks are joined together via the Internet, and the information that can be gained from it comes across in written words, pictures, and sounds.

The history of the Internet can be traced to the sixties. The United States Department of Defense developed a computer linking system for government and military purposes, primarily for security reasons. Shortly thereafter, universities developed a similar network. When the two networks combined, the Internet was formed. Today, anyone with a modem, computer, and Internet software can access the Internet.

The Internet has become one of the most widely used sources of information on any topic imaginable. Internet users can learn about a topic, join in discussions with others, play games, listen to audios, and watch videos. Information may be read "on line" or downloaded to a file or to a printer. The Internet is also used to relay messages from one computer to another. This process is called electronic mail, abbreviated to e-mail.

Modems are used to access the Internet. The modem is connected to the phone line, linking it to the computer. Internet information travels by telephone lines. With the increase in Internet traffic, traditional copper phone lines are being replaced by fiber-optic cables which can transport much more information.

Experts project that the Internet will eventually become a part of the information superhighway, linking computers, telephone companies, cable television companies, financial institutions, and more. Technology for this system is still being developed.

Suggested Activity

Surf the Net In order to use the Internet, you will need the following:

Hardware You will need access to a 386 or faster personal computer or 68030 Mac or Power Mac with at least eight megabytes of random access memory, a 250-megabyte or larger hard drive, and a modem with a speed of at least 14,400 bits per second

Software Web Browser programs, which permit access to audios, videos and web pages, require a Windows platform. Internet service providers generally supply the software necessary to use their systems, including: e-mail software, Telnet software, Newsreader software, World Wide Web browser, File-Transfer-Protocol (FTP) client software, TCP/IP software, and Gopher client software. As an alternative, software packages like the *Microsoft Internet Explorer Starter Kit* are readily available.

Note to the Teacher : You may wish to install a filtering program which limits access to objectionable material before students begin to "surf." *SurfWatch* from Spyglass is included in some software packages and may be available from your Internet Service Provider (ISP). More information on this program is available at 888-677-9452, or online at http://www.surfwatch.com/index.html.

Woman in Space

Beginning on March 22, 1996, astronaut Shannon Lucid started an adventure that would put her in the record books. Together with two Russian cosmonauts, Yuri Onufrienko and Yuri Usachev, Lucid lived on the Russian space station, Mir, until September of that year. The length of time she spent in the space station established an American record for time spent in space.

Shannon Lucid

Lucid's home for those long months was located 250 miles (403 kilometers) from her Earth home in Houston, Texas. While in her home away from home, she spent her days conducting scientific experiments in biology, photosynthesis, weightlessness, and more, as well as exercising to maintain good muscle tone. The weightlessness of the space station can cause a person's muscles to become weak through lack of use, so it was crucial for Lucid and her companions to exercise on a regular basis. The three also shared meals together, alternating Russian and American food. Many people feel that this type of joint effort between the Russians and the Americans would not have been possible even ten years previous, due to the Cold War.

Lucid was born in 1943. She always maintained an interest in science and finally opted to become a bio-chemist. She began working for NASA in the seventies and was an accomplished member of NASA's team of astronauts before she made her historic journey to Mir. In addition, she went through extensive training in Russia.

Lucid's predecessor on Mir, astronaut Norman Thagard, warned NASA of the "cultural isolation" one could experience at the Russian space station, so Lucid came prepared. She took reading materials to help her, and NASA allowed her daily contact with her family via e-mail as well as weekly phone calls and videoconferencing, which combines phone conversations with video images.

When discussing her experiences during her long stay in space, Lucid said that it was important for her to stay in touch with her family as well as to allow herself the time and opportunity to daydream. She laughingly shared that while watching the earth from such a distance, she became aware of the many places to which she would like to travel. Lucid thought her family would not be so pleased with the "travel bug" she picked up on her half-year journey away from home.

Suggested Activities

Women Learn about other female astronauts. Some names to study include Sally Ride, Mae Jemison, Judith Resnick, Eileen Collins, and Christa McAuliffe.

Russia The Russian space program has been moving forward neck-and-neck with the American program. Research to find out about the two and then create a Venn diagram comparing and contrasting them.

Long-Distance Calls When Shannon Lucid spoke with her family from space, some specialized phone equipment was required. Learn about the communications system used by today's astronauts.

Life on Mars

In 1984, a meteorite was found in Allan Hills on the continent of Antarctica and brought to NASA in the United States. It was named ALH84001, a coded abbreviation for "Allan Hills, 1984, first meteorite found that year." Scientists determined that it had landed on Earth approximately 13,000 years ago. The meteorite weighed 4.2 pounds and did not appear to have any significance. Several years after it was found, scientists began to look closer, and soon they found evidence which convinced them that the rock had come

from Mars. Gas trapped in small pockets in the rock matched the atmospheric composition found by *Viking* landers on Mars in 1976. The gas did not match Earth's atmosphere.

The scientists then used radioactive dating and other measuring techniques to determine the age of the rock. They learned that it had been blasted from the surface of Mars sixteen million years in the past by the impact of a comet or asteroid. After traveling through space, the meteorite landed in Antarctica. Researchers now knew they had the twelfth known Martian meteorite found on Earth.

Even more startling information came from NASA in August, 1986. Scientists there reported that, while looking into the rock with an electron microscope, they had found fossil-like structures dating back 3.6 million years. Although they were minuscule, some of these structures resembled fossils of bacteria on Earth, while others looked like slugs, and one even resembled a segmented worm. Further studies revealed PAHs (polycyclic aromatic hydrocarbons). PAHs form on Earth when microbes decompose.

The information led many to believe that life existed in Mars 3.6 billion years ago, a time when life existed on Earth in the form of microbes. This conclusion was further supported by the findings of some British scientists who discovered similar evidence of life in a Martian meteorite dating back 600,000 years. If life did, in fact, exist on Mars as recently as 600,000 years ago, then many experts suggest it may still exist today, although perhaps in some minuscule, undeveloped way. While some scientists suggest that the evidence of the meteorites is also strong evidence for the existence of life on many other planets throughout the universe, other researchers are more skeptical. They suggest that the evidence on the meteorites is due to contaminants that invaded the rocks during their many years lying on Earth.

In November 1996, NASA sent the *Mars Global Surveyor* to the fourth planet. It is scheduled to arrive in September 1997, and to begin an orbit of the planet, observing it from above. In December 1997, another launch will leave Earth and head directly and quickly to Mars, arriving on July 4, 1997. This launch, *Pathfinder*, will land on Mars, deploying a rover that will probe the planet's surface.

——— Suggested Activities ———

Writing Have the students write science fiction stories about life on Mars, incorporating actual scientific information.

Mars Learn about the fourth planet, its composition, atmosphere, temperature, geology, and more. Put together a class report.

Hip-Hop

Rap music, also known as hip-hop, did not begin in the nineties, but it certainly became the music of the nineties. In 1989, MTV (page 430) began a music segment entitled "Yo! MTV Raps." This segment was meant to broaden its audience, so it turned to the ever-increasing interest in rap music.

Rap, like most forms of popular modern music, began in the black community. It consists of rhyming verses on topical issues recited over live or recorded background music and is characterized by a heavy, regular beat, and a steady, dense, rhyme pattern. Originally, it told of life on the streets and teenage experiences. In the nineties, it took a more pronounced turn into a movement known as gangsta rap. This type of hip hop comes directly from street gangs and often includes lyrics promoting gang activity and violence against law enforcement officers.

When rap originated, it was a folk art performed by and for neighborhood people. Rappers challenged themselves to create syncopated rhymes, while a D.J. provided a background by mixing and alternating bits of previously recorded music. To add interest, the D.J. would also "scratch," moving the needle back and forth across the record to produce interesting tones. Soon, other parts of the community took notice, and eventually record producers were hooked by the "catchiness" of the beat. As rap developed, electronic synthesizers, drum machines, and electronic sampling of recorded materials were added.

Rap music generated a popular style of dance, known as hip-hop. This dance is highly aerobic and energetic, combining pronounced movements and jumps with quick, active footwork. Performers such as M.C. Hammer and Salt and Peppa have made hip-hop dance extremely popular.

The music also came with a style. Baggy pants, hooded sweatshirts, reversed baseball caps, big gold jewelry, and expensive, high-top tennis shoes are all a part of the hip-hop look. In the nineties, it was not unusual to see teenagers, boys and girls alike, dressed in this manner. Although most wore the clothes because of popular fashion, hip hop cannot escape its gang affiliation, and some wear the clothes as part of a gang look. This correlation has troubled some parts of society.

When hip-hop first came to the awareness of the general public in the eighties, several white performers came to the forefront, including the Beastie Boys and Vanilla Ice. However, their fame did not last long. They were easily usurped by strong black performers who have consistently remained at the top of the hip-hop charts. The lyrics of such musicians range from the humorous to the inspirational to the violent.

The hip-hop sound is engaging due to its rhyme and rhythm, but its connection to gang violence is a cause of public concern. As the nineties progress, the two seem more and more entwined.

Suggested Activities

Listen Find some rap music with neutral or inspirational lyrics. Those of the Fresh Prince are usually humorous. Coolio also released an inspirational rap in 1995 entitled "Gangsta's Paradise." It tells of the inevitable troubles of the gang lifestyle and became the theme song for the hit movie and television show of the mid-nineties, *Dangerous Minds*.

Write After listening to some rap music, have the students write their own raps. If desired, provide them with guidelines for the lyrics. This is an excellent opportunity to teach poetic rhyme and meter.

The King of Late Night

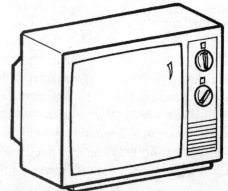

In 1992, the king of late-night television, Johnny Carson, abdicated his throne. From 1962 until his retirement in 1992, Carson was a nightly fixture in homes around the nation.

Carson was born in 1925 in Corning, Iowa, to Homer and Ruth Carson. The family moved to Norfolk, Nebraska, where Carson was raised. He began his show business career at the age of twelve, performing magic tricks for his family, and at fourteen earned his first money (three dollars) as an entertainer at the local Rotary Club.

In high school, Carson wrote a humor column for the school paper and appeared in a variety of school productions. After serving in the navy in World War II, he returned to Nebraska to attend college, where he wrote a thesis entitled *Comedy Writing*.

Carson's first professional job was as a comedy writer and interviewer at radio station WOW in Omaha, Nebraska. He later became an announcer at WOW's television station. In 1951, he moved to Los Angeles, where he became an announcer for KNXT, a local television station. KNXT soon offered him a half-hour comedy show on Sunday afternoons. The show, which ran for thirty weeks, always began with the announcement, "KNXT cautiously present's *Carson's Comedy Cellar*." Established comedians such as Red Skelton were attracted to Carson's humor.

When Carson's show came to an end, Skelton offered him a job as a comedy writer for the *Red Skelton Show*. Carson's big break came in 1954 when Skelton was injured just before the live performance. The producer asked Carson to fill in with the material he had written. Carson was so successful that the executives of the network, CBS, offered him his own national show. *The Johnny Carson Show* ran for thirty-nine weeks but was cancelled in 1956. Carson moved to New York and did guest shots on television. In 1957 the producers of an ABC quiz show, *Who Do You Trust?*, offered him the job of host. He accepted, and the show ran for five years.

In the ensuing years, Carson sometimes filled in as guest host for Jack Paar on the *Tonight Show*, a successful NBC program. Paar left the show in 1962, and the popular guest host was asked to be the full-time replacement. The rest is television history. When people think of the *Tonight Show*, they think of Carson, the man who hosted it for three decades.

Carson's *Tonight Show* included an opening monologue in which he would joke about recent news events and a variety of other topics. His humor was usually good-natured and not controversial. Often, Carson would include comedy skits in his show. The bulk of the show was filled with conversation with various guests, usually from the entertainment field. He shied away from serious guests and topics, keeping the program light and humorous. For thirty years, Carson's show was extremely popular.

The show moved from New York to Burbank, California, in 1972. Carson retired to his Malibu, California, home after leaving the show. Always a private person, he has remained out of the limelight since his departure. Comedian Jay Leno became the replacement host upon Carson's retirement.

Suggested Activity

The Afternoon Show As a class, prepare an entertainment show in the style of Carson's *Tonight Show*. Write the monologue, skits, and guest dialogues. Prepare the set and, if possible, tape your production.

The Queen of Talk

Oprah Wintrey

Oprah Gail Winfrey was born on January 29, 1954, in Kosciusko, Mississippi, to a single mother. Her mother intended to name her Orpah after a woman in the Bible, but the name was misspelled on the birth certificate, and her mother decided to keep it. For the first six years of her life, she was raised on the farm by her grandmother, who taught Winfrey to read by the age of three. She also helped her granddaughter develop a love for their church. Winfrey's favorite thing to do when young was to speak publicly, especially reciting poems she had memorized. When asked what she wanted to do when she grew up, Winfrey said she wanted to be paid to talk.

Winfrey moved several times as a child, living with her mother in Milwaukee, Wisconsin, and her father and his wife in Nashville, Tennessee. In Wisconsin, Winfrey became angry and rebellious, lying and sometimes stealing from her mother. At the age of nine, she was abused by a teenage cousin but was too afraid and ashamed to tell anyone. Today, she is an advocate for abused women and children.

At fourteen Winfrey returned to Nashville to live with her father, and she credits her father's love and discipline for saving her life. In Nashville, she continued her public speaking and her excellence in her school work. She was offered a job by the local radio station, WVOL, and in her senior year, she won a full college scholarship in a speech contest,

Winfrey enrolled at Tennessee State University and did well in her studies. As a teenager, she became Miss Black Tennessee. She also became a television anchorwoman at the age of nineteen. Two months before graduating from college, she accepted a job as a reporter at a Baltimore, Maryland, television station. Winfrey never felt comfortable remaining neutral in her work, and at the age of twenty-two, she was fired. Her boss offered her another job as co-host of a morning show, *People Are Talking*. She was an immediate success and stayed with the show for seven years.

Winfrey had always wanted to live in Chicago, so she sent tapes of her work to the producers of *A.M. Chicago*, who liked her work and hired her in 1984. The show's name was changed to *The Oprah Winfrey Show* in 1985, and it was syndicated (made available for broadcast nationally) in 1986. Suddenly, Winfrey had millions of viewers. Her astronomical success was due in part to the journalistic integrity of her shows and their positive messages.

By the 1990s, she had become one of the richest people in the entertainment industry. Many consider her the most powerful woman in television. In addition to her Emmy winning show, her company, Harpo Productions, produces movies and television projects. She is one of three women in television/film history to own and produce her own show. The other two were Mary Pickford (page 97) and Lucille Ball.

Winfrey is also an accomplished actress and received an Academy Award nomination for her role in 1985's *The Color Purple*.

Through the Vernon Winfrey Scholarship Fund, named for her father, she offers ten scholarships a year at Tennessee State University. Winfrey also devotes a great deal of time and money to children's projects, promoting their education and welfare. She is noted for her generous heart and genuine care for people.

Suggested Activity

Public Speaking Hold a class speech contest. Have the students memorize their work and practice their diction, expression, and eye contact.

The Dynamic Duo

Two of the biggest names in Hollywood in the 1990s are Steven Spielberg and George Lucas. Many consider them to be the producers/directors of the generation. They are also great friends.

Spielberg, born in 1946 in Cincinnati, Ohio, screened his first short films for friends when he was twelve. At the age of sixteen, his first feature played in the local movie theater, and at twenty, a short student film, *Amblin'*, drew the attention of Universal Studios, which signed him to a television contract. Many people still remember his suspenseful television movie of 1971 entitled *Duel*, starring popular actor Dennis Weaver. Spielberg truly came to the public's notice in the late seventies with such Hollywood box-office hits as *Jaws* and *Close Encounters of the Third Kind*. Projects since then have covered a wide range of subjects, from *E.T.-the Extra-terrestrial* to *The Color Purple*. In addition to his production company, Amblin' Entertainment, Spielberg has joined Jeffrey Katzenberg and David Geffen to form Dreamworks SKG, a multimedia production company.

George Lucas was born in 1944 in Modesto, California. A film he made as a student project at USC, *THX-1138,* caught the attention of the industry, and his successful *American Graffiti* paved the way for the *Star Wars* trilogy. *Star Wars* originally achieved huge success in 1977, winning seven of the eleven Academy Awards for which it was nominated. Lucas followed the film with two other sensations, *The Empire Strikes Back* and *Return of the Jedi*. These films were landmarks in the development of special effects, and drew in audiences like no movies of the past had ever done. In 1997 all three were re-released in special editions which included additional footage and enhanced special effects, again to great success. Three new episodes of the *Star Wars* saga are planned for release in the 1990s. Today, Lucas is considered one of the foremost authorities on specialized sound and images. Industrial Light and Magic, a division of his Lucas Digital Limited, has provided amazing effects for countless films, including *Forrest Gump* and *Jurrasic Park*. A second division, Skywalker Sound, is devoted to presenting the best sound possible.

In the eighties, Spielberg and Lucas teamed for the popular *Indiana Jones* series, starring the Star Wars actor, Harrison Ford. The movies were produced by Lucas and directed by Spielberg. For both moviemakers, the films celebrated their love for the action adventures of their childhoods.

The catalog of films the two have made top the list of box office sensations. Their work is also critically acclaimed. Spielberg's *Schindler's List*, a moving story set during the holocaust, earned him the Academy Award.

Suggested Activities

Movies In as much as possible, write, produce, and direct movies. Determine what equipment is available to you and the students and let them use their creativity in much the same way that Spielberg and Lucas do, although on a much smaller budget!

Viewing Watch any of the *Star Wars* movies. All of the films are excellent studies in the traditional literary structure of good v. evil. They are acceptable for most audiences.

Catalog Brainstorm a list of films by Spielberg and/or Lucas. Include films by others that have used Lucas Digital Limited technology.

The Bosnian War

Bosnia-Hercegovina, often called Bosnia, is a country in the Balkan peninsula in southeastern Europe. Bosnia has always been a potentially volatile place due to the cultural and religious differences of its primary cultures: Muslims, Serbs, and Croats.

To understand the outbreak of war in the nineties, it is important to understand some of Bosnia's history. In 1908 it was annexed by Austria-Hungary. In 1918, it became a part of Serbia. Following World War II, in 1946, Bosnia-Hercegovina became one of the six member republics of Yugoslavia, a Communist controlled country. During the 1980s, relationships between the cultures of Bosnia became strained, particularly between Serbs and non-Serbs.

In 1990 the Communist Party relinquished its hold over the republics. Bosnia held free elections for the first time in 1990, and non-Communists won. In February and March 1992, Bosnia voted on independence. A majority of Muslims and Croats voted for independence, but a majority of Serbs were against it. However, both the European Community and the United States recognized Bosnia as an independent nation. In April 1992 Serbia and Montenegro united to form a new Yugoslavia, but they did not receive international recognition. At this juncture, the Bosnian Serbs started a civil war to establish their own republic. The self-proclaimed Yugoslavia supported the Bosnian Serbs with weapons and troops. Croatians declared their own independent community. Soon the Croats and Bosnian Muslims were fighting in western Hercegovina, and Bosnian Serbs fought both Muslims and Croats. Within two months, two-thirds of the nation had been taken over by the Serbs, who used "ethnic cleansing" to remove all non-Serbs from their territory.

The United Nations stepped forward in May, placing a trade and oil embargo against Yugoslavia. In June, UN peacekeeping forces arrived in Bosnia.

By October 1992, reports were coming through of human rights abuses to prisoners held in detention camps. Serbs were torturing and killing Muslims and Croats while they were prisoners. War continued throughout 1993. In February 1994, the Bosnian Croats and Bosnian Muslims signed a cease-fire agreement, and in March they united to form a joint government. Yugoslavia directed the Serbs to accept a peace plan in July, but the Serbs continued to fight. Nations of the North Atlantic Treaty Organization (NATO) announced that they would bomb Bosnian Serbs if they did not cease fire in Sarajevo and UN-protected locations. The Serbs responded by shelling Sarajevo, and NATO countered by bombing the Serb military. When Bosnia, Croatia, and Serbia agreed to a peace pact in September, NATO ceased bombing. Peace negotiations continued through November, and in December 1995, the plan was finally signed. According to the plan, Bosnia would be divided in two, one a Muslim-Croat federation and the other Bosnian Serb. The first would receive fifty-one percent of the country and the latter would receive forty-nine percent. Sixty-thousand NATO troops remained to oversee the results of the peace pact. In September 1996, the first elections were held.

Suggested Activity

Cartography Draw a map of Bosnia as it stands today. Mark the section belonging to the Muslim-Croats as well as the section that is Bosnian Serb.

The Fall of the U.S.S.R.

The decline and fall of the Union of Soviet Socialist Republics (U.S.S.R.) took place over many years. See pages 74 and 142 for the beginning of the Soviet story. The events listed below follow the last six years of the nation.

1985   Mikhail Gorbachev became the Communist Party head, the first of a new generation of leaders. All the old guard leaders had died out.

Gorbachev introduced new policies of openness (*glasnost*) and economic reform (*perestroika*). Books by opponents to communism became available in stores.

1989   The first contested elections in Soviet history were held for the newly formed Congress of People's Deputies. Many top officials lost their positions.

Soviet control over Eastern Europe ended.

There was popular support for reform throughout the eastern region. Many government officials were unseated.

1990   In March, the new office of president of the U.S.S.R. was created, and Gorbachev was chosen. The office replaced the Communist Party head as the most powerful position. Gorbachev also remained as party head.

The Soviet government allowed non-Communist political parties for the first time.

Lithuania declared independence. Estonia and Latvia called for gradual separation from the U.S.S.R. By the end of 1990, all fifteen republics had declared their independence.

1991   To prevent further collapse, Gorbachev negotiated a treaty giving the republics a large amount of independence. Ten nations agreed, and five were scheduled to sign on August 20.

A coup attempt on August 19 preceded the signing. The coup leaders imprisoned Gorbachev and his family. Boris N. Yeltsin, the president of the Russian republic, opposed the coup and helped to end it. On August 21, Gorbachev was released. Yeltsin's prestige increased.

Gorbachev resigned from the Communist Party.

The Soviet parliament suspended all Communist Party activities.

In December, the Commonwealth of Independent States was formed.

Gorbachev resigned as president, and the Soviet Union ceased to exist.

Suggested Activities

History Follow through to determine what has happened in the former Soviet nations since 1991. Also follow the further career of Boris Yeltsin.

Culture Throughout Communist rule, Russian culture and that of other nations was suppressed. Choose one former Soviet nation and research to find out about its cultural heritage.

Palestinian-Israeli Peace Accord

Palestine has been the center of conflict for thousands of years. In the 1990s, historic peace accords were finally reached, pulling battling nations closer together than ever before, but the conflicts were not completely over. Following is a time line of events in the long history.

1918   Palestine, under the rule of the Ottoman Empire for four hundred years, becomes a part of the British Empire after World War I. Arab and Jewish residents continue to fight for control.

1949   In the aftermath of war between Jews and Arabs (1948–1949), Palestine is divided among Israel, Jordan, and Egypt.

1956   The Suez-Sinai War between Israel and Egypt over the Gaza Strip is ended by a UN resolution.

1964   The Palestine Liberation Organization (PLO) is founded. It is the political group that represents the Arab people of Palestine, many of them displaced. The PLO pledges to liberate Palestine.

1967   War breaks out again. A United Nation (UN) cease-fire ends the so-called Six Day War in 1967, but Israel has already gained control of the Gaza Strip and the West Bank as well as Egypt's Sinai Peninsula and Syria's Golan Heights.

1973   Egypt and Syria wage war on Israel. Most of the fighting ends in a month.

1974   The UN recognizes the PLO as the representative of the Palestinian Arabs. The PLO does not recognize Israel's right to exist.

1978   Egypt and Israel sign the Camp David Accord to settle their conflicts. The nations' leaders win Nobel peace prizes. President Jimmy Carter is influential in bringing them together.

1982   Israel withdraws from the Sinai Peninsula in Egypt.

1987   Arabs stage protests throughout the nation, and general violence ensues. Israeli troops kill many protesters.

1993 and 1995 Israel and the PLO sign agreements. These call for the withdrawal of Israeli troops from the Gaza Strip and most of the West Bank by early 1996. Palestinians take control immediately as the Israelis withdraw.

1994   In October, Israel and Jordan sign a treaty, formally ending the war that has taken place since 1948.

Yasir Arafat (PLO leader), Shimon Peres (Israeli foreign minister), and Yitzhak Rabin (Israeli prime minister) share the Nobel peace prize for 1994.

1995   Prime Minister Yitzhak Rabin is assassinated (page 488). Peres becomes prime minister.

1996   Palestinians elect a president and a legislature.

Benjamin Netanyahu defeats Peres in the first elections in which Israelis vote directly for the prime minister.

Suggested Activities

Religion Trace Palestine's religious significance. Write a report explaining the importance of religion in the Palestinian conflicts.

Cartography Draw a map of all involved nations, highlighting the Gaza Strip, the West Bank, the Sinai Peninsula, and Golan Heights.

Yitzhak Rabin

Prime Minister Yitzhak Rabin of Israel played a significant role in the peace movement among Israel, Egypt, and the PLO in the nineties, but shortly after winning the 1994 Nobel peace prize with his fellow negotiators, Rabin was assassinated.

Born in Jerusalem in 1922, Rabin was the first Israeli prime minister to actually have been born in Israel. All previous prime ministers had been born in Europe. Rabin's political career leading up to this memorable first was a long and influential one.

In 1941 a teenaged Rabin joined the Jewish underground army in Palestine, called the Palmach. He served as deputy commander in 1948 during the war fought between Israel and the Arabs. Several years later, from 1964 to 1967, he headed the defense forces of all Israel. It was his strategy that won Israel the Arab lands in the Gaza Strip and the West Bank.

In 1968 to 1973, Rabin served as ambassador for Israel to the United States, and in 1973, he was elected to Israel's parliament. A member of the Labor Party, he became party head and subsequently prime minister in 1974 and served as such until 1977. From 1984 to 1990, his military experience served him well as minister of defense. Once again in 1990, Rabin became Labor Party head and prime minister, appointing himself as minister of defense.

It was during his second term as prime minister that Rabin truly made a name for himself in history by signing an agreement with the Palestine Liberation Organization (PLO) that would lead to Israel's withdrawal from the Gaza Strip and the West Bank, the locations he had been instrumental in capturing. He also agreed with the PLO to work out all remaining conflicts. For these efforts, as well as the formal end of the war with Jordan that had begun in 1948, Rabin was awarded the 1994 Nobel peace prize. He shared the award with Israel's foreign minister Shimon Peres and PLO leader Yasir Arafat.

Many people around the world celebrated the efforts of Rabin, but some closest to home did not agree with him. One right-wing university student from Israel decided to take matters into his own hands. On November 4, 1995, he killed the prime minister in Tel Aviv, Israel.

Following Rabin's death, Peres became prime minister. In an election of 1996, that position went to Benjamin Netanyahu who continued to talk with Yasir Arafat and to follow through on the peace agreements.

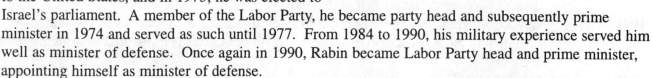

Suggested Activities

Israel Today Research to find out the state of Israel today. Has the nation followed through with all their promises from the 1994 peace accords? Have more conflicts broken out, or is the nation relatively peaceful?

Prime Minister Trace the history of prime ministers in Israel. Why were they formerly of foreign birth? Who is the current prime minister?

End of Apartheid

Background In 1910, former British colonies and two Boer (Dutch) republics formed the Union of South Africa and received dominion status from England. Although whites composed less than 20% of the population, they held all the power, and ruled the country. *Apartheid*, or racial separation, was a common practice in South Africa, but it did not become the law until 1948. When the National Party came to power in 1948, it set up a system called apartheid. The word *apartheid* is from the Afrikaan language of South Africa's Dutch settlers and literally means "apartness." This system kept advantages for white people while limiting those for nonwhites. The policy provided for separate development and eventual independence of the African homelands. The homelands consisted of overpopulated regions with few resources, reserved for 74% of the total population. Independence meant that black Africans had no voting rights in South Africa.

Nelson Mandela

Apartheid Policies Daniel F. Malan of the National Party became Prime Minister of South Africa in 1948. His government defined apartheid policies and divided the population into four groups: whites, people of mixed race, blacks, and those of Asian origin. Public places had separate sections for whites and nonwhites. White students attended separate all-white schools, and railways reserved some first–class coaches for whites only. A later bill required all applicants of color to prove their qualifications in order to vote. More restrictive measures were eventually passed.

ANC The African National Congress (ANC) began in 1912 as a nonviolent civil rights organization. Its purpose was to change the social conditions in South Africa through peaceful protest, dialogue, and education. When more blacks entered the urban work force and apartheid became government policy, membership in the ANC increased, and it became more militant. Strikes, demonstrations and, in some cases, attacks on whites followed. For their part in the uprisings, many ANC activists were imprisoned or executed. One prominent ANC leader, Nelson Mandela, served almost 30 years behind bars for his "crimes."

Second Half of the Century As more African countries joined the British Commonwealth, they pressured Great Britain to force South Africa to abolish apartheid. South Africa refused, however, and left the Commonwealth in 1961 to become an independent republic. Faced with economic sanctions from abroad and violence at home, reform finally began in 1985. Restrictions on the ANC and other political groups were lifted in 1990, and the basic laws of apartheid were repealed in 1991. In 1992 a referendum by white voters approved the end of white minority rule in South Africa, finally ending apartheid. Nelson Mandela became the first black elected as president of South Africa in 1994.

Suggested Activities

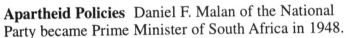

Today Research current racial policies in South Africa and prepare a short report.

Mandela Find out about the life of Nelson Mandela and his role in the South African government today.

Passages

Births

Deaths

Births (At the time of publication, individuals born after 1989 have not yet made their mark. You may have students add the names of family and friends, or add notables as they emerge.)

_____

_____

_____

_____

_____

_____

_____

_____

_____

_____

1990
- Sammy Davis, Jr., American entertainer
- Sarah Vaughan, American singer
- Jim Henson, American puppeteer and creator of the Muppets
- Lawrence Durrell, English author
- Michael Landon, American television actor

1991
- Rajiv Gandhi, son of former Indian prime minister, Indira Gandhi
- Miles Davis, American jazz trumpeter
- Redd Foxx, American comedian
- Rufino Tamayo, Mexican artist
- Isaac Bashevis Singer, Yiddish writer
- Robert Motherwell, American artist

1993
- Audrey Hepburn, American film actress
- Vincent Foster, White House aide
- Pat Nixon, former First Lady

1994
- Richard Nixon, former United States president
- Kurt Cobain, American "grunge" rock musician

1995
- Yitzhak Rabin, Israeli prime minister

1996
- Barbara Jordan, American congresswoman and activist
- Mary Leakey, archeologist
- Ella Fitzgerald, American singer
- Juliet Prowse, American dancer
- Tupac Shakur, American rap musician
- Margaux Hemingway, American actress and model

Famous Firsts

In the 1990s, the United States saw the first

. . . female secretary of state.

. . . female attorney general.

. . . black woman named chief of a major city police department.

. . . eleven-year-old, two-million-dollar prodigy in art.

. . . time all fifty states honored Martin Luther King, Jr. Day.

. . . black American to win the Nobel Prize for Literature.

. . . time more people watched the women's NCAA basketball championship than watched the men's.

. . . movie to become the top grosser of all time in its second release.

. . . eighteen-year-old starting professional basketball player.

. . . American women's Olympic gymnastic team to win the gold medal.

. . . women boxers.

. . . black secretary of commerce.

. . . Stealth bomber (unseen by the public prior to the nineties).

. . . evidence of life on Mars.

. . . Democratic president to be take office since 1964.

. . . coffee cola.

. . . Rhodes scholar president.

. . . terrorist bombing on U.S. soil by U.S. citizens.

. . . female cadets to enter the Citadel.

. . . Republican dominated Congress.

. . . Pultizer prize awarded for jazz.

. . . black to win the PGA Masters tournament.

. . . woman to pilot the space shuttle.

. . . Web T.V. providing Internet access through a television set.

. . . feature-length animated film generated completely by computers.

Other interesting events at home and elsewhere include . . .

. . . the complete cloning of a goat and monkey, recreating perfects mammals.

. . . Scarlett the cat rescuing her kittens, one by one, from a burning building.

. . . former Beatle, Paul McCartney, becoming a knight.

. . . a presidential library opening in California at Yorba Linda, the site of Richard Nixon's birth.

. . . a group of researchers entering the Biosphere, a metal and glass greenhouse enclosure, in order to study the ecology of closed systems for two years.

. . . the return of Disney animation to critical and popular acclaim.

. . . the marriage of America's "most eligible bachelor," John Kennedy, Jr.

. . . the divorce of the royal couple Prince Charles and Princess Diana.

. . . the capture of the Unabomber.

Buzzwords

New inventions, habits, lifestyles, and occupations cause people to invent new words. The last decade of the new century was no exception. Listed below are some of the words and phrases that came into popular use throughout the decade. (**Note:** Many of the computer terms were in existence before the nineties, but they were not popularly known until then.)

Bulletin boards These are services usually set up by an on-line organization in order to provide or exchange information; computer uses on the Internet form discussion groups here.

CD-ROM This acronym stands for compact disc read-only memory. It is a disc which holds up to 600 megabytes of information.

Cyberspace This is a slang term for the Internet.

Desktop publishing This is the process of creating printed documents that look professionally produced.

Dinks This is an acronym for double income no kids or a married couple who both work and have no children.

DNA testing This refers to the genetic testing of an individual's DNA. It can be used in criminal cases to help free or convict the accused.

E-mail This is a popular abreviation for electronic mail, messages sent and received through the Internet.

Gangsta rap This form of rap or hip-hop music focusses on gang violence themes.

Generation X This term refers to the generation born in the late sixties and early seventies.

Hip hop This type of music is characterized by a heavy, regular beat and a steady, dense, rhyme pattern.

Infomercial This term defines extended television advertising which provides lengthy information about the product. It is a combination of information and commercial.

Information superhighway This refers to a computer network still under development which will link computers with a variety of businesses.

Internet This is defined as an "interconnected network of networks" and is an extensive network of computers linked by cable telephone lines.

Morph An abbreviation for metamorphosis, this term means the ability to change form.

POG These game playing disks were originally bottle caps.

Shock jock This refers to a radio disc jockey who uses the time on air to shock the listeners.

Surf the net This term means to browse through the Internet.

Virtual reality This refers to a computer simulated environment which appears to be real.

World Wide Web This is the feature of the Internet that provides graphics, video, and audio to enhance document information.

Writing Prompts and Literature Ideas

Writing Prompts Use these suggestions for journal writing or as daily writing exercises. Some research or discussion may be appropriate before assigning a particular topic.

- You are at the 1996 Olympic games when the women's gymnastic team wins the gold medal. Describe the crowd response.
- Write a letter to one of the world leaders of the nineties, living or dead.
- What will the next century bring? Free-write your ideas.
- You are a part of the Million Man March. Write a diary account of your experiences.
- You are in the Russian space station, replacing Shannon Lucid. Describe your typical day.
- While visiting South Africa, you have an opportunity to meet Nelson Mandela. Write your conversation.
- Write a rap song.
- Bill Gates is a master computer programmer. On paper, write a plan for your own computer system design.
- Many nations in the nineties experienced internal or international wars. What advice could you give them for maintaining peace?
- Which prominent figure from the nineties do you most admire, and why?
- If you could achieve the prominence Tiger Woods has in the sport of your choice, what would it be and what would you do? Provide details.
- Imagine you are at the Republican or Democratic national convention in 1992 or 1996. Describe what you see and hear.
- You want to run for president in the nineties. Describe your platform.
- Women have begun to box in the Olympic games. What do you think?
- Write a story as though you are a tiny being trapped inside the Internet.

Literature Ideas The following books can be used to supplement and enhance the study of the 1990s.

- *Maniac Magee* by Jerry Spinelli (HarperCollins, 1990)
  This Newbery-winning novel is the story of an adolescent boy whose life becomes legendary to the people around him due to his athletic achievements and other feats that amaze his peers. Magee is also without a home. His story is humorous and touching.

- *It Takes a Village: and Other Lessons Children Teach Us* by Hillary Rodham Clinton (Simon and Schuster, 1996)
  The first lady's book deals with issues concerning children and their welfare and development. Other topics include parenting and family relationships. The students are likely to enjoy excerpts from her book and can then write essays of their own in the same style.

- *Star Trek: Federation* by Judith and Garfield Reeves-Stevens (Simon and Schuster, 1994)
  This detailed and involving story, based on the television programs of the same name, provides an interesting account of life on Earth and space from about the present to a few centuries in the future. If discussing possible changes in the world to come, this book or another science fiction account may add a great deal to your discussion.

Research Report

An ideal way for the students to use the knowledge and insights they have gained through a study of the twentieth century is to prepare individual research reports. Directions for completing the report are written below the dotted line. They can be duplicated and handed to the students along with the forms on pages 495–500.

Note: While you can allow each student to choose an individual, you can also narrow the field by assigning each student a decade or year from which to choose. If you prefer, you can have the students draw names or assign them names directly.

Research Report

Directions:

1. **Selection** Choose a person of significance who was an important figure in the twentieth century. Confirm your choice with your teacher.

2. **Investigation** Research the life and significance of the individual. You must use at least five sources. Note your sources on the form provided.

3. **Location** Color the places on the world map that are of significance to the life and work of the individual on whom you are reporting. Also write the names of those places on the map to identify them. Provide a map key, if necessary.

4. **Interview** Write responses to the questions asked on the interview form. Answer them as though you are the individual you are researching. Make the answers thorough ones so that they say something important or interesting about the individual. Add additional questions and answers if you wish.

5. **Personal Information** Use reference materials to complete the personal information sheet provided. Leave no blank spaces unless the information has been confirmed not to exist. Write the sources of your information on the back of the form, listing the titles, authors, publisher, year of publication, and page number, as well as date and reference number if your source is a periodical.

6. **Time Line** Using the form provided, make a time line of important world or national events that happened within your subject's lifetime.

7. **Comparison** Complete the Venn diagram, comparing yourself and your time to the individual of your choice and his or her time.

8. **Recipe** Find a recipe that would have been popular at the time and place where your subject had most significance. Write the recipe on the recipe card provided, including a picture of the food, if possible. Note: Extra credit can be earned by making the recipe and bringing it into the class.

9. **Photo or Illustration** Include a full-page photograph or illustration of your subject. If desired, you may draw the picture yourself, using actual photos as your reference.

10. **Binding** Bind all pages of your report together. Place them in a handmade or manufactured cover. Be sure that all pages are securely fashioned. Your name and your subject's name should appear on the cover.

11. **Due Date** Your project is due in class in its completed form on _____.

World Map

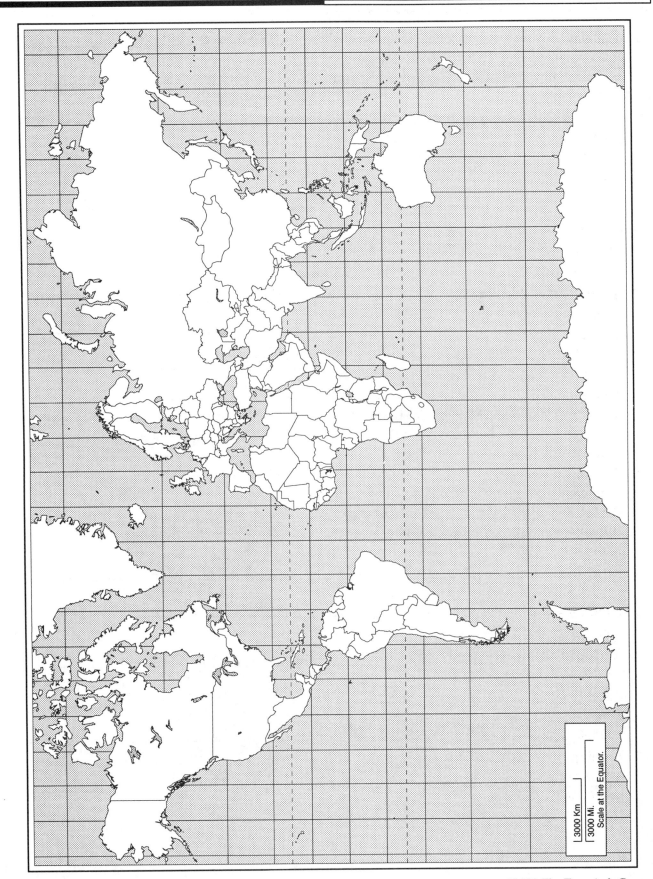

Interview Form

1. Who were your most important influences when you were young?_____

_____

_____

2. What are your interests? _____

_____

_____

3. What are your future goals? _____

_____

_____

4. Do you believe that you deserve the notoriety you have achieved? _____

_____

_____

5. What do you think of your accomplishments? _____

_____

_____

6. Whom do you most admire? _____

_____

_____

7. What do you think are the most significant events of your time?_____

_____

_____

496

Personal Information Sheet

Birth date: _____

Name at birth: _____

Place of birth: _____

Nation of residence: _____

Parents' names: _____

Childhood family: _____

_____

Adult family: _____

_____

Education: _____

Career: _____

_____

Achievements: _____

_____

_____

_____

Interesting facts: _____

_____

_____

_____

Reasons for significance to the twentieth century: _____

_____

_____

_____

_____ Time in History
(subject's name)

Year	Person/Event

Venn Diagram Comparison

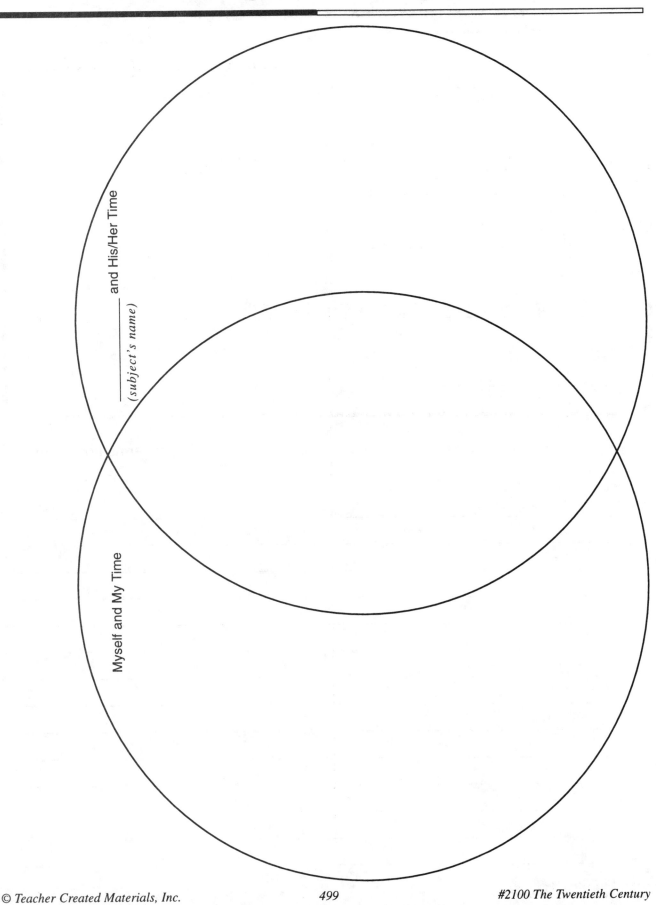

and His/Her Time

(subject's name)

Myself and My Time

Recipe Card and Bibliographic Sources

_____
(recipe name)

Ingredients: _____ _____

_____ _____

_____ _____

_____ _____

Preparation: _____

_____

_____

_____

List your reference sources here in bibliographic form. Use additional paper as necessary.

1._____

_____

_____

2._____

_____

_____

3._____

_____

_____

4._____

_____

_____

5._____

_____

Culminating Activities

The Twenty-First Century

Hypothesize what advances, changes, and/or additions will be made in the twenty-first century for one topic listed on this page. Support your hypothesis with sound reasoning. An "hypothesis" is a guess or prediction that is made using common sense. Support shows the logic you have used to reach your hypothesis. Use the form at the bottom of this page on which to write your ideas.

- land vehicle transportation
- air transportation
- space transportation
- space exploration
- cures for diseases
- artificial limbs and organs for human beings
- elementary education
- high school education
- college education
- movie industry
- personal computers
- compact discs

- photography and video
- amusement parks
- surgery
- communications
- gang violence
- travel/vacationing
- sports
- personal care and hygiene
- housing
- energy and power
- household utilities
- world peace
- pets

- food/sustenance
- pollution and the environment
- international boundaries/national holdings
- agriculture
- household items
- weather/climate
- television
- medicine
- clothing
- new businesses
- currently existing businesses

Note to the Teacher: You may wish to add additional topics. A good way to do so would be to brainstorm with the class.

Topic:

Hypothesis: _____

_____

_____

_____

_____

_____

Reasoning: _____

_____

_____

_____

_____

Overview Presentation

As a class, prepare a presentation that shows an overview of the century. The format of the presentation can be decided upon as a class. Ideas include the following:

- play
- book
- video/film
- slide show
- readers theater

The presentation should feature some or all of the following topics within the century:

- presidents
- world leaders
- social leaders
- technological advances
- wars
- major political events
- sports
- music
- clothing
- toys/games
- literature
- film
- fads
- popular language

In order to prepare the presentation, allow individual students or small groups to work on various aspects of it, periodically reporting to the whole group on what has been accomplished.

You may wish to prepare this presentation for a parent and/or school audience. What an excellent way to demonstrate what has been learned!

Note to the teacher: Advanced classes can prepare different presentations in small groups.

Song of the Century

Throughout history, ballads have been written to chronicle the stories of people and events. Now is your opportunity to become a balladeer. You will write a song that tells the story of the twentieth century, including at least 50 of the major people and events. Your song can use the melody of another song you know, or you can create the melody yourself.

On the back of this paper, list the names and events you would like to include. Then begin to write a first draft of your song lyrics. (For some people, it helps to choose the melody first. Others like to create the melody after the lyrics.) You will need to revise your lyrics, honing them to be the best you can write. Share your draft with a friend or two and allow him or her to give you feedback on your song. Finally, revise it for your final version. Be prepared to share it with the class.

Notes to the Teacher: You may wish to have this project done in small groups if it seems too great a task for individuals. Also, some students may feel awkward about sharing their songs before the class. Use your discretion. Perhaps you might have them sing the song for you privately or make taped recordings. Listening to "We Didn't Start the Fire" by Billy Joel may help to inspire the students.

Character Diary

Create a character born in 1900. Imagine every aspect of this individual until he or she seems real to you. Complete the information sheet on the next page, filling in details about the character you have created.

You will need to imagine the entire life of the individual, as though he or she lived from 1900 until the present time. Follow the pattern below to create a time line, filling in major events in your character's life as well as corresponding events in the world at the time.

Next, make duplicates of the diary sheet on the last page. On the diary pages, write excerpts from your character's diary, spanning the course of his or her entire life. There should be at least one paragraph entry for each year of the century.* Paragraphs must refer specifically to the time—culturally, socially, politically, economically, etc., so that a reader can see the progression of time in the world beyond the individual events of the character's life. Staple the diary together, including the time line, and bind it in a cover, including your name and your character's name on the front.

*Note to the Teacher: Alter the length, as desired.

Year	Character's Life	Real World
1900s		
1910s		
1920s		

Character Information Sheet

Name: _____

Birth date: _____

Birthplace: _____

Parents: _____

Brothers and Sisters: _____

Education: _____

_____

Career: _____

_____

_____

_____

Marriage and Family: _____

_____

_____

_____

Hobbies: _____

_____

_____

_____

Friends: _____

_____

_____

_____

Diary Page

_____
(date)

Dear Diary,

_____

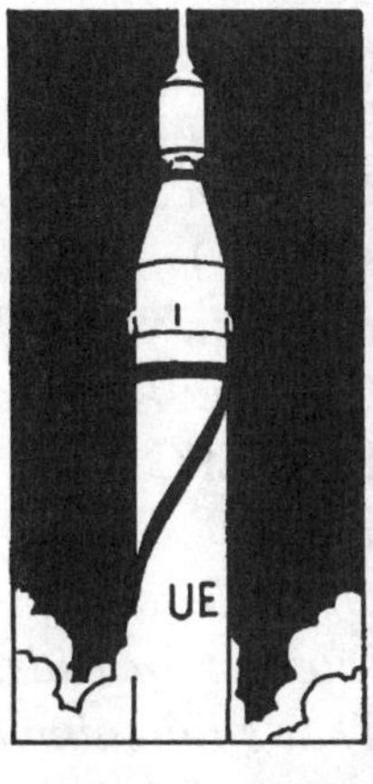

_____

_____

_____

_____

_____

_____

_____

_____

_____

_____

_____

UE

Software in the Classroom

More and more software is finding its way into the classroom. Many of the multimedia packages allow students to access photos, speeches, film clips, maps, and newspapers of various eras in history. Although a program may not be written specifically for the topic you are studying, existing software may be adapted for your purposes. To get the maximum usage from these programs and to learn how to keep up with technology, try some of the suggestions below.

Software

American History CD. Multi-Educator

The Chronicle. Sunburst Communications

Chronicle of the 20th Century. DK Multimedia

Compton's Encyclopedia of American History. McGraw Hill

Compton's Interactive Encyclopedia. Compton's New Media, Inc.

The Cruncher. Microsoft Works

Encarta (various editions). Microsoft House

Ideas That Changed the World. Ice Publishing

Our Time: Multimedia Encyclopedia of the 20th Century (Vicarious Point of View Series 2.0). Scholastic

Presidents: *A Picture History of Our Nation*. National Geographic

Time Almanac. Compact Publishing, available through Broderbund, 800-922-9204

TimeLiner. Tom Snyder Productions, 800-342-0236

Time Traveler CD! Orange Cherry

Vital Links. Educational Resources (includes videodisc and audio cassette)

Where in America's Past Is Carmen Sandiego? Broderbund

Using the Programs

After the initial excitement of a new computer program wears off, you can still motivate students by letting them use the programs in different ways.

1. Print out a copy of a time line for each group of students. Assign each group to a different topic, like entertainment, politics, etc. Direct the groups to research their topics and to add text and pictures to their time lines.

2. Let each pair of students choose a specific photo from the time period you are studying. Have them research the event and write a news story to go with the picture.

3. Not enough computers? Hook your computer up to a television screen for large-group activities or pair the students and let them take turns typing. Keep a kitchen timer handy. For more ideas, see *Managing Technology in the Classroom* from Teacher Created Materials or the booklet *101+ Ways to Use a Computer in the Classroom* (Oxbow Creek Technology Committee, Oxbow Creek School, 6050 109th Ave. N., Champlin, MN 55316).

Keeping Current

To keep current with ever-expanding lists of available software programs, you may have to turn to a number of sources, including the ones below:

Magazines: *Instructor* and *Learning* (technology review columns and feature articles)

Children's Software Revue, 520 North Adams Street, Ypsilanti, Michigan 48197-2482. (Write for a free sample.)

PC Family and *PC Kids* (available at newsstands).

On Line: A database of more than 900 reviews can be accessed through America Online; go to HOMEPC in the newsstand.

Books:

Great Teaching and the One-Computer Classroom (Tom Snyder Productions, 800-342-0236).

Internet for Kids! by Ted Pederson and Francis Moss (Price Stern Sloan, Inc., 1995).

That's Edutainment! by Eric Brown (Osborne/McGraw, 1994).

Bibliography

Adams, Simon. *Visual Timeline of the 20th Century*. DK Publishing, 1996

Altman, Susan. *Extraordinary Black Americans: from Colonial to Contemporary Times*. Children's Press, 1989

American Heritage Illustrated History of the United States (series). Silver Burdett Press, Inc., 1989

Ashby, Ruth and Deborah Gore Ohrn, ed. *Herstory: Women Who Changed the World*. Viking, 1995

Blassingame, Wyatt. *The Look-It-Up Book of Presidents*. Random House, revised ed., 1993

Brenner, Barbara. T*he United Nations 50th Anniversary Book*. Atheneum Books for Young Readers, 1995

Chronicle of the 20th Century. Chronicle Publishing, 1987

Davis, Kenneth C. *Don't Know Much About History*. Crown Publishers, Inc., 1990

Dodds, John W. *Everyday Life in Twentieth Century America*. G.P. Putnam's Sons, 1965

Fashions of a Decade (series). Facts on File, 1992

Garraty, John A., ed. *Young Reader's Companion to American History*. Houghton Mifflin, 1994

Grun, Bernard. T*he Timetables of History*. Simon and Schuster, 1991

Hopkinson, Christina. *The Twentieth Century*. Usborne Publishing Ltd., 1993

Igus, Toyomi. *Book of Black Heroes: Great Women in the Struggle*. Just Us Books, Inc., 1991

Japanese American Journey: *The Story of a People*. The Japanese American Curriculum Project, Inc., 1985

Karl, Jean. *America Alive: A History*. Philomel Books, 1994

Krull, Kathleen. *Lives of the Writers*. Harcourt Brace & Jovanovich, Co., 1994

Murphy, Paul C. Since 1776: *A Year-by-Year Timeline of American History*. Price Stern Sloan, 1988

Napoli, Tony, ed. *Our Century* (series). Gareth Stevens Publishing, 1993

Rappaport, Doreen. *American Women: Their Lives in Their Words*. HarperTrophy, 1990

Reynoldson, Fiona. *Women and War*. Thomson Learning, 1993.

Rubel, David. *Encyclopedia of the Presidents and Their Times*. Scholastic, Inc., 1994

Rubel, David. *The United States in the 20th Century*. Scholastic, Inc., 1995

Seuling, Barbara. *The Last Cow on the White House Lawn and Other Little-Known Facts About the Presidency*. Doubleday & Co., 1978

Smith, Carter, ed. *Presidents of a World Power*. The Millbrook Press, 1993

Timelines (series). Macmillan Publishing House, 1989

Twist, Clint. *Take Ten Years* (series). Steck-Vaughn Company, 1994

Weitzman, David. *My Backyard History Book*. Little, Brown and Company, 1975

Teacher Created Materials

>#018 *Masterpiece of the Month*
>
>#064 *Share the Olympic Dream*
>
>#232 *Thematic Unit: Inventions*
>
>#281 *Thematic Unit: Flight*
>
>#480 *American History Simulations*
>
>#493 *Focus on Scientists*
>
>#494 *Focus on Artists*
>
>#496 *Focus on Inventors*
>
>#605 *Heroes*

Index

Index *(cont.)*

Answer Key

Page 33
1. i
2. e
3. a
4. j
5. h
6. b
7. g
8. c
9. d
10. f

Page 36
A. catcher
B. batter
C. pitcher
D. first base
E. second base
F. third base
G. shortstop
H. right fielder
I. center fielder
J. left fielder
K. umpire

Page 92
1. machine gun
2. 120-mm gun
3. ammunition
4. frontal armor
5. continuous track
6. engine and transmission
7. driver
8. gunner
9. commander
10. loader

Page 123
1. market in which stocks go down in value
2. person who sells stocks
3. a percentage of profits from a company paid to stockbrokers
4. place where stocks are bought and sold
5. Securities and Exchange Commission, the government agency that regulates stocks and bonds
6. market in which stocks rise in value
7. period of wild selling
8. a share or part in a company
9. buying stock with some money down and borrowing the rest
10. the business of buying stocks and bonds

Page 125

1. 29 ½
2. 53 ¾
3. Bank of America
4. 2,974,000
5. $1.09
6. 9 ¾

Page 145
All items should be circled except milk, cheese, butter, eggs, steak, and yogurt.

Page 157
1. T
2. T
3. F
4. F
5. F
6. F
7. T
8. T
9. T
10. T
11. F
12. T

Page 175
1. 1,440,000
2. 250,000
3. $28
4. .0017 cents
5. 36 million
6. 14.29%
7. 40.8 million
8. 171,000

Page 192
m = 7
f = 14
y = 4
c = 3
d = 13
r = 5
n = 12
h = 6
v = 1
b = 15
s = 2
l = 10
p = 8
w = 9
t = 11

Page 202
1. quintet
2. quintuple
3. quint
4. quintuplicate
5. quiquennial
6. quintuplets
7. quintessence
8. quintillion
9. quintus
10. quintal

Page 203
1. sails
2. pink
3. dumps
4. blessings
5. pond
6. bucks
7. public
8. forwards
9. shoulders
10. game
11. Weigh
12. handsome

Page 204
1. Josephine
2. Lois Lane
3. Antony
4. Priscilla
5. Maid Marian
6. Blondie
7. Juliet
8. Beauty
9. Juan
10. Eve
11. John Lennon
12. Olive Oyl
13. Petunia
14. Abé lard
15. Gracie Allen
16. Minnie
17. Elizabeth Barrett Browning
18. Ulysses
19. Prince Charming
20. Cupid

Page 205
1. string quartet
2. flute
3. oboe
4. bass clarinet
5. drums
6. horns
7. bassoon

Page 207
A large section of North America was owned by France in the beginning of the 19th century. In 1802 their emperor, Napoleon, sent an army to America to stop a rebellion in the Caribbean. It was not long before the troops were devastated by yellow fever. Only 4,000 of the 33,000 men sent to America escaped the epidemic.

Answer Key (cont.)

Page 208
1. supporters, year, mile
2. Long March
3. Women, children
4. Baggage, horses
5. eight, survived
6. followers, communist
7. plotted, China

Page 230
a.	5	i.	14
b.	13	j.	9
c.	1	k.	2
d.	8	l.	7
e.	15	m.	12
f.	6	n.	11
g.	3	o.	4
h.	10		

Page 232
1.	1940	5.	1948
2.	1944	6.	1940
3.	1940	7.	1940
4.	1948	8.	1948

Page 255
1.	John Cabot	8.	coal
2.	Tennessee	9.	rocky
3.	English	10.	cold
4.	radio and television	11.	icebergs
5.	Great Britain's	12.	Atlantic
6.	European	13.	St. John's
7.	Sails	14.	British
		15.	600,000

Page 267
1.	Juneau	7.	Mt. McKinley
2.	Point Barrow	8.	Aleutian
3.	Prudhoe	9.	Arctic
4	Valdez	10.	Bering
5.	Yukon	11.	Pacific
6.	Alaska Range		

Page 268
1.	Oahu	5.	Maui
2.	Molokai	6.	Kahoolawe
3.	Hawaii	7.	Lanai
4.	Kauai	8.	Niihau

Page 274
1.	Mamie	14.	Mamie
2.	Mamie	15.	Bess
3.	Bess	16.	Mamie
4.	Both	17.	Both
5.	Bess	18.	Mamie
6.	Mamie	19.	Bess
7.	Mamie	20.	Bess
8.	Bess	21.	Mamie
9.	Mamie	22.	Bess
10.	Bess	23.	Bess
11.	Bess	24.	Mamie
12.	Bess	25.	Mamie
13.	Mamie		

Page 291
1. Mount Vernon
2. childhood
3. scholarships
4. editor-in-chief
5. president
6. writing
7. published
8. children's
9. Charlotte's Web
10. adult
11. guidebook
12. Freedom
13. awards
14. Newbery
15. disease

Page 319
1. South Vietnam
2. North Vietnam
3. China
4. Ho Chi Minh Trail
5. Laos
6. Cambodia
7. Hue
8. Khesanh

Page 325
1.	d	6.	b
2.	f	7.	g
3.	a	8.	c
4.	h		
5.	e		

Page 340

Page 353
a.	7	h.	13
b.	6	i.	4
c.	9	j.	1
d.	3	k.	8
e.	11	l.	5
f.	2	m.	14
g.	12		

Page 387
1.	8	5.	3,596
2.	12,400	6.	247.68
3.	745	7.	2.89
4.	380	8.	18

Page 401
1. Mark Spitz
2. Frank Shorter
3. Olga Korbut
4. Shane Gould
5. Kip Keino
6. Rick DeMont
7. Peggy Fleming
8. Karl Schranz
9. Nadia Comaneci
10. Bruce Jenner
11. Greg Louganis
12. Alberto Juantorena
13. Sugar Ray Leonard
14. Sheila Young
15. Franz Klammer
16. Irina Rodnina